COMPARISON OF TWO OR MORE POPULATIONS	ANALYSIS OF THE RELATIONSHIP BETWEEN TWO VARIABLES	ANALYSIS OF THE RELATIONSHIP AMONG TWO OR MORE VARIABLES
Analysis of variance Chapter 13 Kruskal–Wallis test Section 18.4	Simple linear regression and correlation Chapter 15	Multiple regression Chapter 16
χ^2-test of a contingency table Section 14.3	χ^2-test of a contingency table Section 14.3	
Kruskal–Wallis test Section 18.4		

ESSENTIALS OF BUSINESS STATISTICS

A SYSTEMATIC APPROACH

Gerald Keller
Wilfrid Laurier University

Brian Warrack
Wilfrid Laurier University

Wadsworth Publishing Company
Belmont, California
A Division of Wadsworth, Inc.

DEDICATION *To the memory of my father, Hyman Keller*
G. K.

To the memory of my mother, Marnie Warrack
B. W.

Acquisition Editor: Kristine M. Clerkin
Editorial Assistant: Nancy Spellman
Production Editor: Carol Dondrea, Bookman Productions
Print Buyer: Randy Hurst
Designer: Vargas/Williams/Design
Copy Editor: Steven Gray
Technical Illustrator: Alexander Teshin Associates
Compositor: Polyglot Compositors
Cover: Vargas/Williams/Design
Signing Representative: Peter Jackson
Cover Illustration: Pauline Phung

Printed in the United States of America
2 3 4 5 6 7 8 9 10—95 94 93 92 91

Library of Congress Cataloging-in-Publication Data

Keller, Gerald.
    Essentials of business statistics : a systematic approach / by
Gerald Keller and Brian Warrack.
        p.   cm.
    Includes index.
    ISBN 0-534-14676-7
    1. Commercial statistics.   I. Warrack, Brian.   II. Title.
HF1017.K396   1991
519.5′02465—dc20   90-41062
                                                                           CIP

BRIEF CONTENTS

DETAILED CONTENTS

PREFACE

It's been three years since our first book *Statistics for Management and Economics; A Systematic Approach* was published. During the writing of that book and in the ensuing years, we received comments and suggestions from statistics professors across the United States and Canada. It is evident that our approach to teaching statistics has received wide acceptance. But at the same time there is clearly a need for another kind of business statistics text.

A substantial number of business statistics instructors want a book that covers a core of statistical techniques but does not present all of the methods provided by the larger books. Most professors who teach 20 to 30 methods do not want to use a book that provides 50 or more techniques. They feel that a large book needlessly intimidates students. As one reviewer facetiously commented, "Students are afraid of books that weigh more than they do." Moreover, larger books tend to be written for the mathematically more sophisticated student. Professors who teach less mathematically inclined students prefer a friendlier, less formal approach.

One of the criticisms of shorter books is that they tend to be cookbooks that delete any discussion of concepts and principles. They also tend to provide unrealistic examples and exercises. In our discussions we found that all professors want to motivate their students by showing them real-life practical applications of statistics.

Our objective in writing this book was to provide a shorter book that covered the essential techniques and contained many of the features of our larger book. In the final analysis, we wanted to create a book that professors and students would find interesting and that would motivate students and convince them that statistics can be as useful as any other course in their program. We attempt to fulfill our goal in several ways.

ESSENTIAL CORE OF TOPICS

If you examine the table of contents, you will see that we have covered most or all topics that are considered essential. We have excluded subjects that are not vital to the development of a statistically aware business student. For example, calculation of the probability of a type II error, inference about variance, and inference about a matched pairs or blocked experiment have been omitted. Our presentation of probability (Chapter 4) focuses on concepts and procedures that are critical to the understanding of how probability is used in statistical inference; we avoid a wide-ranging discussion of probability.

FLEXIBLE COVERAGE

Even though we have limited our presentation to essential subjects, we recognize that some instructors would prefer to delete certain of these or to discuss them in a different way. We have written the book to facilitate flexibility. For example, we introduce estimation and hypothesis testing in separate chapters. Instructors then have the option of not teaching one of them or of teaching them in a different order.

SYSTEMATIC APPROACH

The systematic approach, introduced in our first statistics book, teaches students how to recognize which statistical technique to use. We believe that this skill is the most important one to develop, and yet it is the one students have the greatest difficulties in mastering. When each technique is introduced, we show how statisticians identify when that method is to be used. When we demonstrate examples, we begin the solution by reviewing how we know that the method to be used is the correct one to apply. One of the major benefits of our approach is that it allows professors to de-emphasize mathematical manipulation. Consequently, students can spend more time setting up the procedure properly and interpreting the statistical results and less time grinding out the arithmetic.

CASES

There are 26 cases scattered throughout the book. These have been adapted from actual studies published in journals and magazines. Students are expected to analyze the cases and draw conclusions in the same way the original authors did. These cases are neither summaries of what some statistician did to solve a problem nor glorified exercises; they give students the opportunity to see for themselves how statistical problem solving works.

COMPUTER OUTPUT AND INSTRUCTIONS

For most of the worked examples, we provide Minitab software output. This exposes students to how statistics is actually applied in the real world. We also provide Minitab instructions in the appendixes of many chapters. In addition, we have made available a student version of Microstat II—a commercial statistics software package. This comes with a manual keyed to the textbook.

REVIEW CHAPTERS

There are two review chapters to help students practice identifying the correct techniques. Chapter 12 appears midway through our discussion of statistical inference, and Chapter 19 reviews all the statistical methods covered. Each provides exercises and cases that require the use of several different statistical procedures and thus provide practice in the technique identification skills that are required on statistics exams and ultimately in any real-life application of statistics.

EXERCISES

There are approximately 750 exercises of varying levels of difficulty in this book. At the end of most sections, we supply exercises under the heading *Learning the Techniques*, which help students learn the arithmetic involved in a specific procedure. *Applying the Techniques* exercises then stress when and why the technique is used and how the results assist in the decision-making process. *Supplementary Exercises* appear at the end of each chapter. Because they cover all the topics presented in that chapter, they give students practice in identifying which of the techniques encountered in that chapter should be employed. They also tend to be more realistic (and for this reason are considered somewhat more difficult) than the other two types of exercises.

We're optimistic that our approach will be successful in helping students understand how, when, and why statistics is used. We hope that the realistic examples, exercises, and cases we present will make the subject more interesting and will convince students that statistics can play a vital role in managerial decision making.

This text is suitable for a one- or two-semester course in a business program. Although various sections can be omitted, we strongly urge instructors to attempt to complete most of the statistical inference part of the book. Like a house under construction, the structure of the systematic approach is stronger when most of the various components are in place. Nonetheless, the book has been designed so that it is relatively easy to omit chapters.

To assist professors, we provide an *Instructor's Resource Book,* which includes the following:

1. Suggestions about how to teach statistics using the systematic approach.
2. Transparency masters keyed to the teaching suggestions.
3. Teaching notes for each case, detailing goals of the case, assignment questions, analysis and solution, and teaching strategy.
4. Test bank containing about 450 problems and answers.
5. A guide to setting up exams that can be marked by computer (with possible part marks) and calculation-free exams.

A *Solutions Manual* that furnishes detailed solutions for all of the textbook's exercises is also available. These solutions were produced by the authors and independently double-checked by teaching assistants.

For students, we have written a *Study Guide* that contains overviews of each chapter in the text, examples illustrating specific techniques, and exercises and their solutions. The guide attempts to anticipate specific student problems and answer what we believe are the most commonly asked questions.

This book was developed from several courses that we've taught in business and economics programs in a total of six universities over a combined 35 years of teaching. We are most grateful to our students, whose helpful suggestions, comments, and criticisms have benefited this text and to Wilfrid Laurier University for their financial assistance. We also acknowledge the excellent work of our word processor, Elsie Grogan.

Finally, we would like to thank the following reviewers: Rich Behr, Broome Community College; Harry C. Benham, University of Oklahoma; Steven E. Eriksen, Babson College; Jacqueline F. Hoell, Virginia Polytechnic and State University; William P. Lovell, Cayuga Community College; Mary Maples, Oklahoma City Community College; Tom Noser, Western Kentucky University; Khalid Pathan, Lewis University; Harrison Reinken, Phoenix College; Susan Simmons, Sam Houston State University; Charles E. Tychsen, North Virginia Community College.

WHAT IS STATISTICS?

INTRODUCTION TO STATISTICS

To some people, statistics means summarized numerical data such as unemployment figures or the number of runs, hits, and errors in a baseball game. To others, it means an unpleasant course on the way to a business or economics degree. Neither description is adequate. In presenting our subject as a method of obtaining information from data to help managers make decisions, we will show that statistics comprises various techniques with a wide range of applications to practical problems. Managers today have access to more data than ever, through the ever-increasing use of computers, and they risk confusion unless they can effectively screen the data for useful information.

Examples from different areas of business and economics will provide illustrations of the many applications of statistical methods. Statistical techniques will be applied to problems in production (such as quality control), finance (investment analysis and forecasting), marketing (analysis of market surveys), and accounting (statistical auditing).

Statistics is a body of principles and methods concerned with extracting useful information from a set of data—frequently, but not necessarily, numerical data. It can be subdivided into two basic areas: descriptive statistics and inferential statistics. **Descriptive statistics** deals with methods of organizing, summarizing, and presenting data in a convenient form. For example, a fast-food franchiser may wish to compare the weekly sales levels over the past year at two particular outlets. Descriptive statistical methods could be used to summarize the actual sales levels (perhaps broken down by food item) in terms of a few numerical measures, such as the average weekly sales level and the degree of variation from this average that weekly sales may undergo. Tables and charts could be used to enhance the presentation of the information so that a manager could quickly focus on essential differences in the sales data from the two outlets.

There is much more to statistics, however, than these descriptive methods. Decision makers are frequently forced to make decisions based on a set of data that represents only a small subset (sample) of the total set of relevant data (population). **Inferential statistics** is a body of methods for drawing conclusions (that is, making inferences) about characteristics of a population based on information available in a sample taken from the population. The following example illustrates the basic concepts involved in inferential statistics.

A cable television company is contemplating extending its selection of pay TV offerings to include a business channel, whose programming is devoted to stock market quotations, news reports, and commentaries from the world of business. After some careful financial analysis, the company has determined that the proposed new channel would break even if at least 10% of all households subscribing to the company's basic service also signed up for the new channel. This collection of all households of interest is called the **population.** To obtain additional information before reaching a decision on whether or not to proceed with the new business channel, the cable company has decided to conduct a survey of 500 of the households subscribing to its basic service. These 500 households are referred to as a **sample** of households, selected from the entire population. Each household in the sample is asked if it would subscribe to the proposed channel if this were offered at some specified price. Suppose that 60 of the households in the sample reply positively. While the positive response by 60 out of 500 households (12%) is encouraging, it does not assure the cable company that the proposed new channel will be profitable.

If the cable company concludes, based on the sample information, that at least 10% of *all* households in the population would subscribe to the proposed channel, the company is relying on inferential statistics. The company is drawing a conclusion, or making a **statistical inference,** about the entire population of households on the basis of information provided by only a sample taken from the population. All that the available data tell us is that 12% of this particular sample of households would subscribe; the inference that at least 10% of *all* households would subscribe to the new channel may or may not be correct. It may be that, by chance, the company selected a particularly agreeable sample and that, in fact, no more than 5% of the entire population would subscribe.

Whenever an inference is made about an entire population on the basis of evidence provided by a sample taken from the population, there is a chance of drawing an incorrect conclusion. Fortunately, other statistical methods allow us to determine how **reliable** the statistical inference is. They enable us to establish the **degree of confidence** we can place in the inference, assuming that the sample has been properly chosen. These methods would enable the cable company to determine, for example, the likelihood that less than 10% of the population of households would subscribe, given that 12% of the households sampled said they would subscribe. If this likelihood is deemed to be small enough, the cable company will probably proceed with its new venture.

SECTION 1.2

THREE KEY STATISTICAL CONCEPTS

The foregoing example introduced three key considerations involved in the solution to any statistical problem: the population, the sample, and the statistical inference. We will now elaborate more fully on each of these.

POPULATION

A **population** is the set of all items of interest in a statistical problem. It is frequently very large and may, in fact, be infinitely large. Unlike its meaning in everyday usage, the word *population* in statistics does not necessarily refer to a group of people. It may, for example, refer to the population of diameters of ball bearings produced at a large plant.

In another case, it may refer to the population of owners of cars, where the measurement of interest is the make of car. Although, technically speaking, a population consists of a set of observations or measurements, we will not attempt to make the fine distinction between the observations per se and the objects about which the observations are made. Thus, for practical purposes, the population in our preceding example may be taken either as the set of all households subscribing to the basic cable service or as the set of all responses given by these households.

A descriptive measure of a population is called a **parameter.** The parameter of interest in the pay TV example was the proportion of all households that would subscribe to the new business channel. As another example, consider the population consisting of all ball bearings produced at a particular factory on a specified day. Two possible parameters of this population would be the *average* of the ball bearing diameters, and the *proportion* of diameters in the population that exceed a specified size.

SAMPLE

A **sample** is a subset of data drawn from the population. For example, if we observe the diameters of 100 ball bearings in the population just described, that set of observations would represent a sample drawn from the population. Notice that the sample is only a part of the whole population, which consists of thousands of ball bearings. Other examples of samples include the total sales by a department store on each of 30 particular days last year, the annual dividends paid last year by 50 companies listed on the New York Stock Exchange, and the annual incomes of 100 doctors in Albuquerque. Once again, each of these samples is only a part of the entire population from which it is drawn.

A descriptive measure of a sample is called a **statistic.** In the previously mentioned sample of 100 ball bearings, the proportion of these 100 whose diameters exceed a specified size would constitute a sample statistic that could be used to estimate the corresponding population parameter. Unlike a parameter, which is a constant at any given time, a statistic is a variable whose value varies from sample to sample. The variability of sample statistics is what we investigate in this book.

STATISTICAL INFERENCE

Statistical inference—the process of making an estimate, forecast, or decision about a population based on the sample information—is the primary purpose of statistics. Because populations are very large, it is impractical and expensive to investigate or survey every member of a population. (Such a survey is called a **census.**) It is far cheaper and easier to take a sample from the population of interest and to draw conclusions about the population based on information provided by the sample.

For instance, the Nielsen ratings provide television network executives with estimates of the number of television viewers who are tuned into each network. Despite the fact that the number of potential viewers is more than 200 million in the United States and 20 million in Canada, the inference is based on a sample of only 2,000 viewers. Likewise, on the basis of a sample of about 1,500 voters, political pollsters predict how the entire population of voters will cast their ballots; and quality-control supervisors estimate the proportion of defective units being produced in a production process from a sample of several hundred units.

Because a statistical inference is usually based on a relatively small subset of a large population, statistical methods can't usually decide or estimate with certainty. Since decisions involving large amounts of money often hinge on statistical inferences (millions of dollars of advertising revenue ride on the Nielsen ratings, for example), the reliability of the inferences is very important. As a result, each statistical technique includes a measure of reliability of the inference. For example, if a political pollster predicts that a candidate would receive 40% of the vote if the election were held today, the measure of reliability might be that the true proportion (determined on election day) will be within 3% of the estimate on 95% of the occasions when such a prediction is made.

You will find, as we progress through this text, that the choice of the appropriate technique to use depends on the population involved and the type of information you want. In turn, the measure of reliability depends on the technique you select.

SECTION 1.3

PRACTICAL APPLICATIONS

Throughout the text, you will find cases that describe actual situations from the business world in which statistical procedures have been used to help make decisions. For each case, you will be required to choose and apply the appropriate statistical technique to the given data in order to reach a useful and valid conclusion. Following are summaries of a few of these cases, without the data, to illustrate additional applications of inferential statistics. You'll have to wait until you work through these cases yourself to determine the proper conclusion and results.

CASE 1.1*

When consumers shop outside their local trading area, the phenomenon is called *outshopping*. Small communities are much affected by outshopping: the prosperity of the area declines if outshopping becomes too prevalent. If local retailers can figure out what factors cause outshopping, they may be able to curtail it. In a study to explore this phenomenon, three researchers (Samli, Riecken, and Yavas) examined a small locality where everyone outshopped to some extent.

The study involved a survey of a sample of 113 residents, some of whom outshopped frequently and some of whom did not. The survey solicited information concerning the residents' demographic characteristics, the number of outshopping trips they made each year, and the types of products they purchased. After using

---

* Adapted from A. C. Samli, A. Riecken, and G. Yavas, "Intermarket Shopping Behavior and the Small Community: Problems and Prospects of a Widespread Phenomenon," *Journal of the Academy of Marketing Science* 11(1, 2) (1983): 1–14.

descriptive statistical methods to summarize the data collected from the survey, the researchers used techniques from inferential statistics to determine whether differences existed between frequent outshoppers and infrequent outshoppers with respect to such demographic characteristics as age and income. Statistical tests were also conducted to determine which (if any) types of products (groceries, jewelry, furniture, and so on) were more likely to be purchased out of town than in town. The results of such tests could assist local retailers in determining where they should concentrate their efforts in attempting to curtail outshopping.

CASE 1.2*

Investors frequently entrust their funds to an "active" investment manager, who seeks to invest the funds in a portfolio of stocks that will earn a rate of return higher than the market average, as measured (for example) by the Dow Jones Industrial Average. Because investors often select investment managers on the basis of their past performance, an important question is whether or not past performance is a reliable indicator of future performance. This question was addressed by Dunn and Theisen,* who collected annual returns for 201 institutional portfolios covering the period from 1979 through 1982.

The stock portfolios were then ranked—first according to how well they performed over the period 1979 through 1981, and second according to how well they performed in 1982. It would be too much to expect the two rankings to coincide; however, statistical techniques can be used to determine if the disparity that does appear between the two rankings is too great for an investor to reasonably conclude that portfolio managers who perform well in one period will continue to perform well over the next period. Based on a statistical investigation of the portfolio performance rankings for several pairs of consecutive periods, the study drew conclusions regarding the ability and consistency of active portfolio managers.

CASE 1.3†

Bonanza International is one of the top 15 fast-food franchisers in the United States. Like McDonald's, Burger King, and most others, Bonanza uses a menu board to inform customers about its products. One of Bonanza's bright young executives believes that not all positions on the board are equal. That is, he feels that the position of the menu item on the board influences sales. If this opinion proves to be true, Bonanza should place its high-profit items in the positions that produce the highest sales. After watching the eye movements of several people, the executive noticed that customers first look at the upper right-hand corner, then across the top row toward the

---

* Patricia C. Dunn and Rolf D. Theisen, "How Consistently Do Active Managers Win?" *Journal of Portfolio Management* 9(1983): 47–50.

† Adapted from M. G. Sobol and T. E. Barry, "Item Positioning for Profits: Menu Boards at Bonanza International," *Interfaces* (February 1980): 55–60.

FIGURE 1.1   DIRECTION OF EYE MOVEMENT ACROSS MENU BOARD

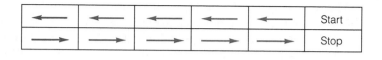

upper left-hand corner, then down to the lower left-hand corner, and finally across the bottom toward the right (see Figure 1.1).

This analysis suggested that items placed in the upper right-hand corner are likely to produce higher sales than items placed in the lower left-hand corner. In order to test this hypothesis, 10 Bonanza stores with similar characteristics were chosen as sites for the test, and two moderately popular items were selected as variables. During weeks 1 and 3 (of a four-week study), item A was placed in the upper right-hand corner and item B was placed in the lower left-hand corner. In weeks 2 and 4, these positions were reversed. The number of sales of each item was recorded for each week and for each store. Statistical procedures were then applied to this sample of data to determine whether the young executive was correct in thinking that menu position influences sales.

CASE 1.4*

A successful television advertisement must attract and hold the attention of the viewer. Among the many techniques used for this purpose, one of the most popular is to use ads with sexual content. At the same time, however, some viewers may be offended by such advertisements. In an investigation of the effectiveness of advertisements with sexual content, two groups of university students were selected. The 53 students in Group A were shown 10 ads with sexual content, while the 60 students in Group B were shown 10 similar ads without sexual content. Immediately after viewing each ad, the students in both groups were asked to rate the ad (on a scale of 1 to 5) on its power to attract and hold attention.

A second phase of the investigation attempted to measure the effect of an advertisement's sexual content on the viewer's ability to recall the product advertised. Two days after viewing the advertisements, each student was asked to name the specific brands mentioned in the ads. The responses from both phases of the study were then summarized and used as a basis for making statistical inferences regarding the effectiveness of sexual content in advertisements in attracting attention, holding attention, and increasing product recall. As always, the statistical inferences were made on the assumption that the responses of the sample of students fairly represented the responses of the entire population of viewers.

---

* Adapted from L. T. Patterson and J. K. Ross, "A Study of Sex in Advertising," *Developments in Marketing Science* 7 (1984): 244–48.

■■■■■■ **CASE 1.5**

The National Patent Development Corporation (NPD) has recently acquired a new product that can be used to replace the dentist's drill. The product, called Caridex, is a solution that dissolves decayed matter in cavities, without drilling. NPD would like to forecast its first-year profits from sales of the solution and the solution's dispensing unit, which is approximately the size of a large radio.

NPD has learned that some 100,000 dentists in the United States treat cavities. (An additional 35,000 do work that does not involve cavities.) The dispensing unit costs NPD $200, and the company intends to sell the unit for $800. The solution costs $0.50 per cavity and will be sold to dentists for $2.50 per cavity. Fixed annual costs are expected to be $4 million.

To complete the collection of information necessary to forecast profits, NPD might undertake a survey of several hundred doctors. Armed with relevant survey results—such as the proportion of dentists in the sample who would purchase the dispensing unit, and the average number of cavities filled each week by these dentists— NPD could use statistical procedures to make inferences about its expected share of the entire market. NPD could then combine these results with its other information to estimate its expected profit in the first year of operation.

SECTION 1.4 **STATISTICS AND THE COMPUTER**

In many practical applications of statistics, the statistician must deal with large amounts of data. For example, in Case 1.1 the data would include (among other variables) the ages and incomes of the 113 people who were surveyed. As part of the statistical analysis, the statistician would have to perform various calculations using the data; and although the calculations do not require any esoteric mathematical skills, the sheer number of computations involved makes this aspect of the statistical method time-consuming and tedious. Fortunately, numerous commercially prepared computer programs are available to perform some or all of the arithmetic work involved.

An introduction to one of the most commonly used packages of computer programs—Minitab—can be found in Appendix 1.A (see page 10). Instructions for using it in specific applications appear in appendixes to the relevant chapters.

If you have access to this computer package, we advise you to become acquainted with it, for several reasons. Using a computer will save you a great deal of time and frustration (particularly if, like most human beings, you are prone to making arithmetic errors). It will also allow you to concentrate on the more important aspects of statistical analysis: recognizing which technique to use, and understanding the computations. In addition, since the computer is almost always used in real-life statistical applications, learning how to use it effectively will help you apply appropriate statistical techniques to problems in actual business and economic settings. Even if you do not anticipate being employed in a job that requires you to perform statistical calculations, you will very likely have to read and interpret computer output at some point. Therefore, at the very least, you should become familiar with the format of the output.

The approach we prefer to take is to minimize the time spent on manual computations and to focus instead on selecting the appropriate technique to deal with a problem and on interpreting the output after the computer has performed the necessary computations. To this end, many of the examples in this book have been solved using a computer package. Whenever possible, immediately following these examples, we provide the output that was generated by the computer package Minitab.

IMPORTANT TERMS

Statistics	Sample
Descriptive statistics	Parameter
Inferential statistics	Statistic
Population	

EXERCISES

UNDERSTANDING THE CONCEPTS

1.1 In your own words, define and give an example of each of the following statistical terms:

a. population

b. sample

c. parameter

d. statistic

e. statistical inference

1.2 Briefly describe the difference between descriptive statistics and inferential statistics.

1.3 In each of the five real cases outlined in this chapter, more than one statistical inference is required. For each of Cases 1.1, 1.3, and 1.5, describe one of these statistical inferences. Your answer should briefly describe the population and its parameter, the sample and its statistic, and the type of inference that is required.

INTRODUCTION TO STATISTICAL APPLICATION PACKAGES

This textbook will describe how to use approximately 40 different statistical techniques. All of the exercises and examples that require these methods can be performed with the assistance of an inexpensive pocket calculator, since they have relatively small databases. In real-life applications of statistics, however, the sample sizes are quite large, and solving a problem often requires the application of several techniques. The amount of calculation involved in solving the problem can be formidable. As a result, in practice the computer is almost always employed for statistical problem solving. Fortunately, statisticians do not have to create their own programs for this use. Previously prepared programs—often referred to as **"canned" computer programs** or, in modern terminology, **statistical application packages**—are quite readily available.

In this book we will provide instructions for using one of the most popular statistical application packages: Minitab. Minitab is quite popular with students because it is extremely user-friendly and because the commands it operates on are quite short.

Instructions for Minitab are provided in appendixes of chapters for which the system performs the statistical techniques there described. For example, Appendix 3.A gives instructions for commanding the computer to produce various descriptive statistics that are presented in Chapter 3; ways of inputting, editing, and printing data are also discussed in this appendix. Other chapters that have appendixes containing computer instructions are Chapters 8, 9, 10, 11, 12, 13, 14, 15, and 16.

GRAPHICAL DESCRIPTIVE METHODS

INTRODUCTION

In Chapter 1, we pointed out that statistics is divided into two basic areas: descriptive statistics and inferential statistics. The purpose of this chapter, together with Chapter 3, is to present the principal methods that fall under the heading of descriptive statistics.

Managers frequently have access to large masses of potentially useful data. But before the data can be used to support a decision, they must be organized and summarized. Consider, for example, a video store manager who has just received a detailed record of the thousands of purchases made at his store during the past year. In its present form, the data set is simply too voluminous to give the manager a clear picture of the store's operations. But by using descriptive statistical methods, the manager can determine the average weekly sales levels, the peak periods of activity, the relative success of various products, and so on.

Descriptive statistics, then, involves arranging, summarizing, and presenting a set of data in such a way that the meaningful essentials of the data can be extracted and grasped easily. Its methods make use of graphical techniques and numerical descriptive measures (such as averages) to summarize and present the data in a meaningful way. *Graphical descriptive methods* are the topic of this chapter, while numerical descriptive measures will be discussed in Chapter 3. Although descriptive statistical methods are relatively straightforward (and far less space in this book is devoted to these methods than to inferential statistics), their importance should not be underestimated. Most students of business and economics will encounter numerous opportunities to make valuable use of descriptive statistics when preparing reports and presentations in the workplace.

Recall, from Chapter 1, that a **population** is the entire set of observations or measurements under study, whereas a **sample** is a set of observations selected from the population and is therefore only a part of the entire population. The descriptive methods to be presented in this chapter and in Chapter 3 apply equally well to data consisting of an entire population and to data consisting of a sample drawn from a population.

TYPES OF DATA

The term **data** refers to the actual observations that result from an investigation or survey.* They may be either quantitative (numerical) or qualitative (categorical). Examples of quantitative data include the wages earned by a company's employees, the daily closing prices of gold bullion over the last year, and the number of beers

---

* Notice that the word *data*, like the word *observations*, is a plural noun.

consumed weekly by students on a particular campus. In each of these examples of quantitative data, the observations are real numbers.

> **Quantitative Data**
>
> **Quantitative data** are numerical observations.

If 75 managers are surveyed and asked to state their age and their annual income, the numerical responses they give are quantitative data. If the managers are also asked to indicate their marital status (single, married, divorced, or widowed), their responses are nonnumerical; but each response can still be classified as falling into one of four categories. Observations that can be sorted into categories on the basis of qualitative attributes such as marital status, sex, occupation, or type of dwelling inhabited constitute qualitative data.

> **Qualitative Data**
>
> **Qualitative data** are categorical observations.

With qualitative data, all we can do is count the number of observations in each category and then calculate the proportion or percentage of all observations that fall into each category.

EXERCISES

2.1 For each of the following examples of data, determine whether the data are quantitative or qualitative.

a. The starting salaries of graduates from an MBA program.

b. The months in which a firm's employees take their vacation.

c. The final letter grades received by students in a statistics course.

d. The number of miles driven annually by employees in company cars.

2.2 Information concerning a magazine's readership is of interest both to the publisher and to the magazine's advertisers. A survey of 20 subscribers to a magazine included the following questions. For each question, determine whether the possible responses are quantitative or qualitative.

a. What is your age?

b. What is your sex?

c. What is your marital status?

d. Is your annual income less than $20,000, between $20,000 and $40,000, or over $40,000?

e. How many other magazines do you subscribe to?

2.3 For each of the following examples of data, determine whether the data are quantitative or qualitative.

a. The month of highest sales for each firm in sample.

b. The department in which each of a sample of university professors teaches.

c. The weekly closing price of gold throughout a year.

d. The size of soft drink (large, medium, or small) ordered by each of a sample of customers in a restaurant.

e. The number of barrels of crude oil imported monthly by the United States.

FREQUENCY DISTRIBUTIONS

In this section, we consider methods that are useful for summarizing *quantitative data*. Often the first step taken toward making sense out of a mass of quantitative data is to form what is known as a *frequency distribution*. This is a simple, effective method of organizing and presenting numerical data so that one can get an overall picture of where measurements are concentrated and how spread out they are.

Consider a Dallas firm that is interested in the duration of long-distance telephone calls placed by its employees. For many large companies, such as national accounting firms, the cost of these calls runs into the hundreds of thousands of dollars per month, so controlling the cost is important. Suppose that, three months ago, our Dallas firm instituted a program to encourage employees to reduce the cost of long-distance calls. Employees were urged to reduce the number of calls of longer duration by minimizing the amounts of small talk and file searching during a call. At the same time, the firm sought to reduce the number of calls of very short duration. For example, several calls of short duration were placed daily to the Houston office to check individual customers' credit. Cost savings would result if fewer such calls were placed, with more than one credit check requested per call, since the long-distance charge per minute falls dramatically after the first few minutes.

Suppose that you were given the job of collecting and summarizing some relevant data on the firm's calls and that you have recorded the times of a sample of 30 long-distance calls placed in a given week, as shown in Table 2.1.*

Your next task is to extract some meaningful information from the data. You might begin by noting the smallest and largest measurements. In this case, the shortest call was 2.3 minutes and the longest was 19.5 minutes. The remaining times all fall between 2.3 and 19.5 minutes. Aside from the two extreme values, we are usually less interested in particular observations than in how these are distributed between the smallest and largest observations. That is, we wish to determine the proportion of observations that lie in various intervals between the two extreme observations. For example, do about 75% of long-distance calls last more than 14 minutes, with only a small proportion lasting less than 5 minutes? Or do most calls last about 10 minutes, give or take a few minutes, with only a small proportion falling within a few minutes of either extreme?

This information is easily obtained by forming what is called a **frequency distribution**—an arrangement or table that groups data into nonoverlapping intervals called **classes** and records the number of observations in each class. An example of a frequency distribution for the data in Table 2.1 is given in Table 2.2. (The column of tallies is not part of the frequency distribution; rather, it represents an interim step toward obtaining the frequencies.)

As Table 2.2 illustrates, a set of data presented in the form of a frequency distribution is more manageable than the original set of raw data, although some of the detailed information is lost. For example, the information in the frequency distribution does not allow us to say anything about the actual values within each class.

---

* While 30 is a convenient sample size for instructional purposes, the value of the concepts we'll be covering would be easier to appreciate if we used a sample size of 300 or 3,000 instead.

TABLE 2.1   *DURATION OF LONG-DISTANCE CALLS (in minutes)*

11.8	3.6	16.6	13.5	4.8	8.3
8.9	9.1	7.7	2.3	12.1	6.1
10.2	8.0	11.4	6.8	9.6	19.5
15.3	12.3	8.5	15.9	18.7	11.7
6.2	11.2	10.4	7.2	5.5	14.5

TABLE 2.2   *FREQUENCY DISTRIBUTION OF TELEPHONE CALL DURATIONS*

Class Limits	Tally	Frequency
2 up to 5*	|||	3
5 up to 8	⌗		6
8 up to 11	⌗ |||	8
11 up to 14	⌗ ||	7
14 up to 17	||||	4
17 up to 20	||	2
TOTAL		30

* Class contains all measurements from 2 up to but not including 5.

When constructing a frequency distribution, we must first decide upon the appropriate number and size of classes to use. The choices of these, as well as of the appropriate class limits, are intertwined. It is usually best to experiment with a few different choices in order to find the frequency distribution that you feel provides the greatest clarity. Despite the arbitrary nature of choosing classes, a few guidelines can be given. First, the classes must be nonoverlapping and must contain all observations. That is, each observation must fall into exactly one class. Second, the number of classes used normally varies between 5 and 20, with smaller numbers of classes being used for smaller data sets. The number of classes must not be too large, or else you will be faced with having many classes that each contain only a few measurements. When too much detail is provided, it becomes difficult to detect the major clusterings of observations that help reveal the shape of the distribution. An example of this is shown in Table 2.3(a). On the other hand, if the number of classes is too small, too much detail is lost, as is shown in Table 2.3(b). The proper number of classes to use is ultimately a subjective decision.

TABLE 2.3   FREQUENCY DISTRIBUTIONS WITH DIFFERENT NUMBERS OF CLASSES

(a) Twelve Classes		(b) Three Classes		(c) Five Classes	
Class	Frequency	Class	Frequency	Class	Frequency
2 to 3.5	1	2 to 8	9	2 to 5.5	4
3.5 to 5	2	8 to 14	15	5.5 to 9	9
5 to 6.5	3	14 to 20	6	9 to 12.5	10
6.5 to 8	3			12.5 to 16	4
8 to 9.5	5			16 to 19.5	3
9.5 to 11	3				
11 to 12.5	6				
12.5 to 14	1				
14 to 15.5	2				
15.5 to 17	2				
17 to 18.5	0				
18.5 to 20	2				
TOTAL	30		30		30

Third, once the number of classes to be used has been chosen, the approximate size or width of each class is given by the following equation:

$$\text{Approximate class width} = \frac{\text{Largest value} - \text{Smallest value}}{\text{Number of classes}}$$

It is usually best to give all classes the same width, to facilitate interpretation of the frequency distribution. Finally, the actual class intervals, defined by the class limits, are specified. Whenever possible, the values of the class limits (which depend on the class width) should be chosen with ease of recognition in mind. For example, the class defined by "2 up to 5" is a better choice than the class defined by "2.2 up to 5.2."

With the preceding considerations in mind, let's look at how the frequency distribution was constructed for the data in Table 2.1. Having already noted that the largest and smallest measurements are 19.5 and 2.3, respectively, we know that the range of values for our data is $19.5 - 2.3 = 17.2$. We must now decide upon the number of classes to use to subdivide the entire range of values. If five classes are used, the width of each class will be about $17.2 \div 5 = 3.4$, while six classes will result in a class width of about $17.2 \div 6 = 2.9$. For ease of reading, it is suggested that these approximate class widths be rounded to 3.5 and 3.0, respectively. Employing five classes, each with a width of 3.5, we obtain the frequency distribution shown in Table 2.3(c). However, using six classes, each with a width of 3, results in a frequency distribution (see Table 2.2) that we feel offers somewhat better insight into the pattern of telephone call durations. The lower limit of the first class has been set at 2 so that the smallest measurement will fall into that class. The remainder of the class limits are obtained by successively adding 3.

Care must be taken in defining the class limits to ensure that each measurement falls into exactly one class. The first class, defined by "2 up to 5," contains all measurements from 2 up to but not including 5. Alternatively, we could have used "2–5" to denote the first class, with the understanding that measurements equal to the upper limit value are not included in that class. A third way of identifying this class would be to use "2–4.99"; here, because the upper-limit values used have more significant digits than the measurements themselves, no ambiguity can arise in determining the class to which any measurement belongs. Ultimately, the choices concerning the number, size, and description of the classes are subjective and are determined by what the analyst feels will result in the most readable table that accurately depicts the data.

Having decided upon the classes, we next count and record the number or **frequency** of measurements belonging to each class. The frequency distribution is then complete, as shown in Table 2.2. The column of tally marks, of course, is created only to facilitate counting the measurements; it is omitted when a frequency distribution is put in its final form.

HISTOGRAMS

The information in a frequency distribution is often grasped more easily—and the presentation is made more visually appealing—if the distribution is graphed. One very common graphical presentation is the **histogram,** which is constructed by marking off the class limits along the horizontal axis and erecting over each class interval a rectangle whose height equals the frequency of that class. The histogram corresponding to the frequency distribution in Table 2.2 is shown in Figure 2.1. Casual inspection of the histogram quickly reveals the general pattern or distribution of values: the distribution is reasonably symmetrical, with the majority of calls lasting between 5 and

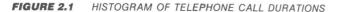

FIGURE 2.1   *HISTOGRAM OF TELEPHONE CALL DURATIONS*

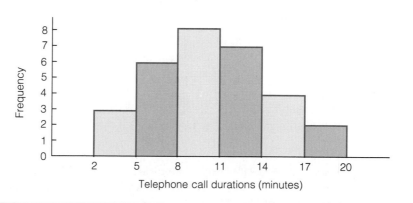

14 minutes. As the Dallas firm had hoped, the proportion of calls having either a very short or a very long duration is now relatively small.

COMPUTER OUTPUT FOR TELEPHONE CALL DURATIONS*

Minitab

```
Histogram of Durations        N = 30

    Midpoint              Count
      3.50                3***
      6.50                6******
      9.50                8********
     12.50                7*******
     15.50                4****
     18.50                2**
```

Notice that Minitab produces a histogram lying on its side.

Instead of showing the absolute frequency of measurements in each class, it is often preferable to show the proportion (or percentage[†]) of measurements falling into the various classes. To do this, the class frequency is replaced by the **class relative frequency.**

$$\text{Class relative frequency} = \frac{\text{Class frequency}}{\text{Total number of measurements}}.$$

We can then talk about a **relative frequency distribution** (see Table 2.4) and a **relative frequency histogram** (see Figure 2.2). Notice that, in Figure 2.2, the area of any rectangle

TABLE 2.4   *RELATIVE FREQUENCY DISTRIBUTION OF TELEPHONE CALL DURATIONS*

Class Limits	Relative Frequency
2 up to 5	3/30 = .100
5 up to 8	6/30 = .200
8 up to 11	8/30 = .267
11 up to 14	7/30 = .233
14 up to 17	4/30 = .133
17 up to 20	2/30 = .067
TOTAL	30/30 = 1.000

* Appendix 3.A provides the Minitab instructions that produced this output.

† Over the course of this book, we express relative frequencies (and later, probabilities) variously as decimals, fractions, and percentages.

FIGURE 2.2   RELATIVE FREQUENCY HISTOGRAM OF TELEPHONE CALL DURATIONS

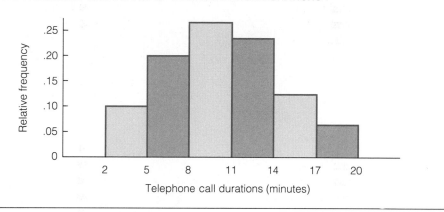

is proportional to the relative frequency, or proportion, of measurements falling into that class. These relative frequencies are useful when you are dealing with a sample of data, since they provide insights into the corresponding relative frequencies for the population from which the sample was taken. Furthermore, relative frequencies should be used when you are comparing histograms or other graphical descriptions of two or more data sets. Relative frequencies permit a meaningful comparison of data sets even when the total numbers of measurements in the data sets differ.

As was previously mentioned, it is generally best to use equal class widths whenever possible. In some cases, however, *unequal class widths* are called for, to avoid having to represent several classes with very low relative frequencies. For example, suppose that, instead of having 6.7% of the telephone call durations falling between 17 and 20 minutes, we have 6.7% of the durations sparsely scattered between 17 and 29 minutes. This new situation might be best represented by the relative frequency histogram shown in Figure 2.3, where the uppermost four classes have been combined.

FIGURE 2.3   RELATIVE FREQUENCY HISTOGRAM WITH UNEQUAL CLASS WIDTHS

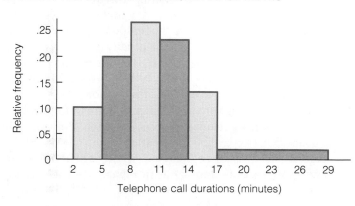

TABLE 2.5   *PERCENTAGE DISTRIBUTION OF AMERICAN FAMILY INCOME FOR 1987*

Class Limits ($1,000s)	Percentage
Under 5	4.4
5 up to 10	7.3
10 up to 15	9.1
15 up to 20	9.5
20 up to 25	9.2
25 up to 35	17.5
35 up to 50	20.2
50 and over	22.9

SOURCE: *Statistical Abstract of the United States: 1989.*

It is important, however, that the height of the corresponding rectangle be adjusted (from .067 to .067/4) so that the area of the rectangle remains proportional to the relative frequency of all measurements falling between 17 and 29 minutes.

The measurements in the preceding example all fall within a fairly compact range. In some cases, however, measurements may be sparsely scattered over a large range of values at either end of the distribution. If this situation arises, it may be necessary to use an **open-ended class** to account for the measurements, as shown in the relative frequency distribution in Table 2.5. Because incomes ranging from $50,000 to millions of dollars are scattered fairly sparsely over a wide range of values, we use a single class with no specified upper limit to capture these incomes.

FREQUENCY POLYGONS

Another common way of presenting a frequency distribution graphically is the **frequency polygon** (see Figure 2.4). A frequency polygon is obtained by plotting the frequency of each class above the midpoint of that class and then joining the points with straight lines. The polygon is usually closed by considering one additional class (with zero frequency) at each end of the distribution and then extending a straight line to the midpoint of each of these classes. Frequency polygons are useful for obtaining a general idea of the shape of the distribution.

As with histograms, we can plot relative frequencies rather than frequencies, thereby obtaining a **relative frequency polygon.** Polygon *A* in Figure 2.5 is the relative frequency counterpart of the frequency polygon in Figure 2.4. Relative frequency polygons allow visual comparison of two distributions, by superimposing one frequency polygon over another as in Figure 2.5. The second frequency polygon (*B*) in Figure 2.5 might represent, for example, the distribution of telephone call durations

FIGURE 2.4   FREQUENCY POLYGON OF TELEPHONE CALL DURATIONS

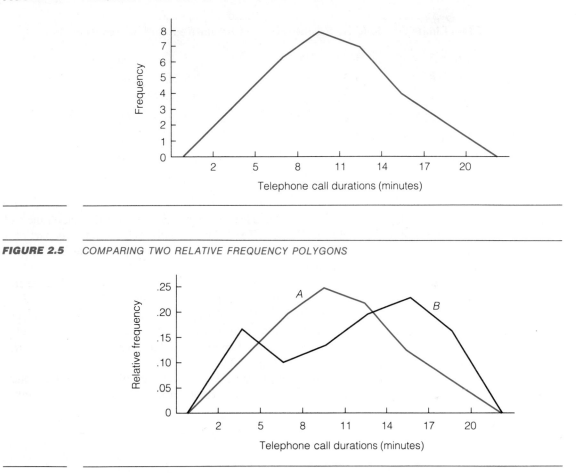

FIGURE 2.5   COMPARING TWO RELATIVE FREQUENCY POLYGONS

before the Dallas firm instituted the cost-cutting program. The difference in the shapes of the two distributions is readily apparent from the graphs.

Given a set of measurements that have been grouped into classes, we've seen that the relative frequency distribution identifies the proportion of measurements falling into each class. In some instances, however, our needs may be served better by working with a cumulative relative frequency distribution. The **cumulative relative frequency** of a particular class is the proportion of measurements that are less than the upper limit of that class. The cumulative relative frequency of a class is therefore obtained by adding the relative frequency of that class to the relative frequencies of all prior classes.*

---

* We assume here that the classes have been ordered, from smallest to largest, according to the magnitude of the measurements they contain.

TABLE 2.6 *CUMULATIVE RELATIVE FREQUENCY DISTRIBUTION OF TELEPHONE CALL DURATIONS*

Class Limits	Relative Frequency	Cumulative Relative Frequency
2 up to 5	3/30 = .100	3/30 = .100
5 up to 8	6/30 = .200	9/30 = .300
8 up to 11	8/30 = .267	17/30 = .567
11 up to 14	7/30 = .233	24/30 = .800
14 up to 17	4/30 = .133	28/30 = .933
17 up to 20	2/30 = .067	30/30 = 1.000

Table 2.6 displays the cumulative relative frequency distribution for the telephone call durations. The second column shown in Table 2.6 normally isn't included as part of a cumulative distribution. We include it here only to help illustrate how the cumulative relative frequencies are obtained.

From the cumulative relative frequency distribution shown in Table 2.6, we can state, for example, that 30% of the telephone calls lasted less than 8 minutes. And since 80% of the calls were shorter than 14 minutes, we know that 20% of the calls were longer than 14 minutes. This type of information can also be read from the graph of a cumulative relative frequency distribution, which is called an **ogive.** The ogive for the telephone call durations is shown in Figure 2.6.

Notice how the construction of an ogive differs from that of a relative frequency polygon. The cumulative relative frequency of each class is plotted above the *upper*

FIGURE 2.6 *OGIVE OF TELEPHONE CALL DURATIONS*

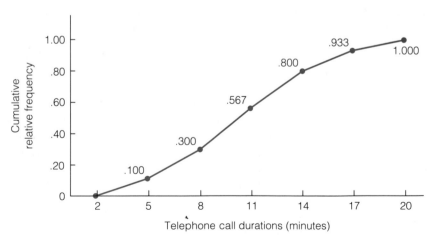

limit of the corresponding class, and the points representing the cumulative relative frequencies are then joined by straight lines. The ogive is closed at the lower end by extending a straight line to the lower limit of the first class. Once an ogive like the one shown in Figure 2.6 has been constructed, the approximate proportion of measurements that are less than any given value on the horizontal axis can be read from the graph. Thus, for example, we can estimate from Figure 2.6 that the proportion of calls shorter than 12 minutes is approximately .65.

STEM AND LEAF DISPLAYS

A statistician named John Tukey introduced a method of organizing quantitative data called the **stem and leaf display.** This display, which may be viewed as an alternative to the histogram, is most useful in preliminary analysis. In particular, it provides a useful first step in constructing a frequency distribution and histogram. The histogram remains the best display to use in formal presentations.

Suppose that we wish to organize the data shown in Table 2.7 into a more usable form. These data represent the annual incomes, in thousands of dollars, of a sample of 30 factory workers.

A stem and leaf display for these data is shown in Table 2.8. The first step in developing the display is to decide how to split each observation (income) into two parts: a stem and a leaf. In this example, we have defined the **stem** as the digits to the left of the decimal and the **leaf** as the digit to the right of the decimal. The first two incomes in Table 2.7 are therefore split into stems and leaves as follows:

Income	Stem	Leaf
19.1	19	1
20.0	20	0

The remaining observations are split into their stem and leaf components in a similar manner.

TABLE 2.7   *SAMPLE OF 30 ANNUAL INCOMES (in $1,000s)*

19.1	19.8	18.0	19.2	19.5	17.3
20.0	20.3	19.6	18.5	18.1	19.7
18.4	17.6	21.2	19.7	22.2	19.1
21.1	19.3	20.8	21.2	21.0	18.7
19.9	18.7	22.1	17.2	18.4	21.4

TABLE 2.8   *STEM AND LEAF DISPLAY FOR 30 ANNUAL INCOMES (in $1,000s)*

Stem	Leaf
17	623
18	4705147
19	1983627571
20	038
21	12204
22	12

Having determined what constitutes the stem and the leaf of an observation, we next list the stems in a column from smallest to largest, as shown in Table 2.8. Once this has been done, we consider each observation in turn and place its leaf in the same row as its stem, to the right of the vertical line. The resulting stem and leaf display (as in Table 2.8) presents the original 30 observations in a more organized fashion. The first line in Table 2.8, describing stem 17, has three leaves: 6, 2, and 3. The three observations represented in the first row are therefore 17.6, 17.2, and 17.3. Similarly, seven observations are represented in the second row. Whether to arrange the leaves in each row from smallest to largest (as is done in the next example) or to keep them in order of occurrence is largely a matter of personal preference. The advantage of having the leaves arranged in order of magnitude is that, for example, you can then determine more easily the number of observations less than $19,500. The disadvantage is that it's more troublesome to do the arranging.

From the stem and leaf display in Table 2.8, we can quickly determine that the incomes range from $17,200 to $22,200, that most incomes fall between $18,000 and $20,000, and that the shape of the income distribution is not symmetrical. A stem and leaf display is similar to a histogram turned on its side, but the display holds the advantage of retaining the original observations. Moreover, because the stems are listed in order of size, the middle observation(s) can be determined fairly easily. In this example, the two middle incomes are $19,500 and $19,600; splitting the difference, we can assert that half the incomes are below $19,550 and half are above it. On the other hand, a histogram can readily accommodate a large number of observations, can display relative frequencies, and can be adapted more easily to changes in the classes used.

The appropriate definitions of the stem and the leaf depend, in part, on the range of the observations. Suppose that the incomes in the preceding example had ranged from $17,200 to $55,500; in such a case, it would be reasonable to define the stem as the first digit and the leaf as the remaining two digits. The income 19.1 ($19,100) would then have stem 1 and leaf 9.1, and there would be five stems or classes in all. Since each leaf would consist of more than a single digit, the leaves in any row should be separated by commas for clarity.

Besides serving an end in itself, a stem and leaf display can form the first step in constructing a frequency distribution and histogram. Table 2.9 shows the stem and

TABLE 2.9   STEM AND LEAF DISPLAY FOR TELEPHONE CALL DURATIONS

Stem	Leaf
2	3
3	6
4	8
5	5
6	128
7	7
8	0359
9	16
10	24
11	2478
12	13
13	5
14	5
15	39
16	6
17	
18	7
19	5

leaf display for the original data on telephone call durations given in Table 2.1 (see page 15), where the stem is defined as the digits to the left of the decimal and the leaf as the digits to the right of the decimal. This display can be created fairly quickly, but you may feel that it is insufficiently compact for your needs. Even so, it will be helpful when you undertake to choose the classes to use in grouping the data into a frequency distribution.

SAMPLE OR POPULATION?

Before proceeding, we should note that the descriptive methods in this chapter apply equally well to samples and to populations of data. If you are interested only in the durations of telephone calls for some particular week, and if all of the calls for that week are accounted for in the data set given in Table 2.1, then those 30 observations can be considered a population, and your task is simply to summarize the durations of those 30 calls. On the other hand, if your primary interest is to obtain information concerning the distribution of the population of durations of all long-distance calls placed by employees at any time, the 30 durations represented in Table 2.1 may be treated as a sample, and you will want to make sure that the sample has been properly selected so that it may be used as a basis for statistical inference about the population.

 EXERCISES

2.4 The grades on a statistics exam are as follows:

75	66	77	66	64	73	91	65	59	86
61	86	61	58	70	77	80	58	94	78
62	79	83	54	52	45	82	48	67	55

a. Construct a stem and leaf display for these data.

b. Construct a frequency distribution for these data, using six class intervals.

c. Construct a relative frequency histogram for these data.

2.5 Refer to Exercise 2.4.

a. Construct a cumulative relative frequency distribution for the grades.

b. What proportion of the grades are less than 70? Greater than 70?

2.6 The real-estate board in a wealthy suburb wishes to investigate the distribution of prices of homes sold during the past year. The following sample of prices (in $1,000s) was collected:

274	429	229	435	260
222	292	419	242	202
235	215	390	359	409
375	209	265	440	365
319	338	414	249	279

a. Construct a stem and leaf display for these prices.

b. Construct a frequency distribution for the prices, using five class intervals and the value 200 as the lower limit of the first class.

c. Construct a relative frequency histogram for the prices.

2.7 Refer to Exercise 2.6.

a. Construct an ogive for the house prices.

b. What proportion of the prices are less than $300,000? Greater than $300,000?

2.8 Table 2.8 shows a stem and leaf display for the annual incomes listed in Table 2.7.

a. Use the stem and leaf display to construct a frequency distribution.

b. Draw a histogram for the incomes.

c. Draw a frequency polygon for the incomes.

2.9 The percentage distribution of American family incomes for 1987 is shown in Table 2.5.

a. Use this table to construct a cumulative relative frequency distribution.

b. Graph the cumulative relative frequency distribution.

c. What percentage of family incomes were less than $200,000 in 1987?

d. Use the graph in part (b) to estimate the income below which the incomes of 50% of American families fell.

2.10 The president of a local consumer advocacy group is concerned about reports that similar generic drugs are being sold at widely differing prices at local drug stores. Upon surveying 30 stores, she collected the following set of prices at which one drug was being sold:

6.49	7.15	6.09	5.99	8.65	9.49
5.25	10.75	9.89	7.20	7.69	7.19
8.34	7.15	10.29	8.35	10.99	7.90
7.75	7.60	9.20	7.69	7.35	8.09
8.75	6.29	7.99	6.89	5.61	6.25

a. Construct a stem and leaf display for these data.

b. Construct a frequency distribution for these data. Use six class intervals, with $5.00 as the lower boundary of the first class.

c. Construct a relative frequency histogram for these data.

d. The consumer advocate discovers that all of the drug stores buy the product from the same wholesaler at $4.50. Given that the president considers a markup of more than 100% to be unfair to the consumer, what fraction of the stores sampled will not meet with her approval?

2.11   A guard sitting beside the main door to a large office building decided to count the number of people entering the building during a 30-minute period. Using a system by which, for example, all times in the minute beginning with 7:45 sharp were recorded as 7:45, he obtained the following data:

Time	No	Time	No	Time	No
7:45	1	7:50	7	7:55	15
7:46	4	7:51	10	7:56	21
7:47	2	7:52	8	7:57	9
7:48	0	7:53	4	7:58	12
7:49	4	7:54	9	7:59	6

Time	No	Time	No	Time	No
8:00	4	8:05	0	8:10	1
8:01	10	8:06	0	8:11	0
8:02	2	8:07	4	8:12	0
8:03	0	8:08	0	8:13	1
8:04	3	8:09	1	8:14	0

a. Construct a relative frequency distribution for the arrival times, using six classes.

b. Construct a cumulative relative frequency distribution for the arrival times.

c. Assume that everyone working in the building is supposed to start work at 8:00 sharp. What fraction of the employees sampled were late? (Those arriving at 8:00 are considered late.)

d. What assumption must you make if you want to use these sample data to estimate the fraction of employees who arrive late on any given day?

2.12   A compilation of the number of sales calls made during the past week by a sample of 20 salesmen for a large computer firm produced the following data:

10	10	13	12	8	8	8	8	14	4
7	9	12	6	10	9	11	15	9	8

a. How might you improve upon the data presentation?

b. The sales manager feels that any salesman worth his salt can make at least eight calls per week. Estimate the fraction of salesmen in the firm who are not worth their salt.

SECTION 2.4

PIE CHARTS AND BAR CHARTS

Several types of commonly used graphical presentations are available besides histograms and frequency polygons. The graphical presentations considered in this section are used primarily for *qualitative data.* The increasing availability of desktop computers with color graphics enables managers to quickly summon a bar chart showing sales in various regions, a pie chart displaying major causes of accidents within their firm, or a line chart depicting the trend in productivity over time. Although the number of types of graphical presentations is large, only a few of the more popular ones will be discussed here.

If the raw data to be summarized are quantitative and come from a single population, as was the case with the telephone data in Table 2.1, the descriptive methods presented in the previous section (frequency distributions, histograms, stem and leaf displays, and so on) are useful and appropriate. These methods basically group the raw data into categories, which we call *classes,* and record the number of measurements that fall into each category. The categories are defined in a rather arbitrary manner, with the objective of conveying some idea of how the data are distributed. We next consider a situation in which the raw data can be naturally categorized in a more meaningful and less arbitrary manner.

PIE CHARTS

The student placement office at a small Ontario university conducted a survey of last year's graduates from the business school to determine the general areas in which the graduates found jobs. The placement office intended to use the data to help it decide where to concentrate its efforts in attracting companies to the campus to conduct job interviews. The data collected are given in Table 2.10.

The data in this example—namely, the five employment areas—are qualitative. The student placement office would likely find the percentages more useful than the absolute numbers of graduates in each category, particularly if the results are to be compared with those of other years or other schools. For one thing, percentages permit a more meaningful comparison of graduating classes of different sizes.

A more visually appealing presentation of the employment data may be obtained by using a pie chart. A **pie chart** is simply a circle subdivided into a number of slices that represent the various categories. It should be drawn so that the size of each slice is proportional to the percentage corresponding to that category, as shown in Figure 2.7. Since the entire circle corresponds to 360°, every 1% of the observations should correspond to $(.01)(360) = 3.6°$. The angle between the lines demarcating the accounting sector in Figure 2.7 is therefore $30(3.6) = 108°$.

Pie charts are effective whenever the objective is to display the components of a whole entity in a manner that indicates their relative sizes. Because of their eye-catching appearance, they are used extensively by newspapers and magazines—especially to show the breakdown of a budget. Similarly, a treasurer may use a pie chart to show the breakdown of a firm's revenues by department, or a marketing analyst may use one to display the market shares of various brands of beer. The raw data in all of these examples are qualitative, and the categories are defined in a natural way rather than arbitrarily.

Pie charts can also be used to compare two breakdowns. Figure 2.8 shows the sources of revenue for the conglomerate Gulf & Western Industries before and after it sold off a large portion of its operations.

TABLE 2.10 AREAS OF EMPLOYMENT FOR BUSINESS GRADUATES

Area	Number of Graduates	Percentage of Graduates
Accounting	75	30
Marketing	62	25
Finance	50	20
General Management	38	15
Other	25	10
TOTAL	250	100%

FIGURE 2.7   PIE CHART OF EMPLOYMENT AREAS

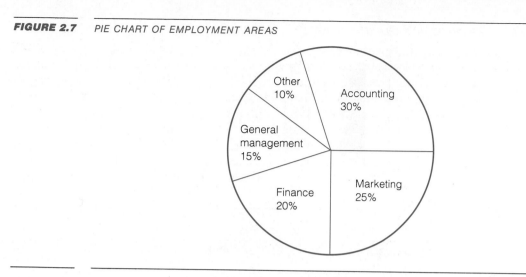

FIGURE 2.8   PIE CHARTS OF GULF + WESTERN'S SOURCES OF REVENUE

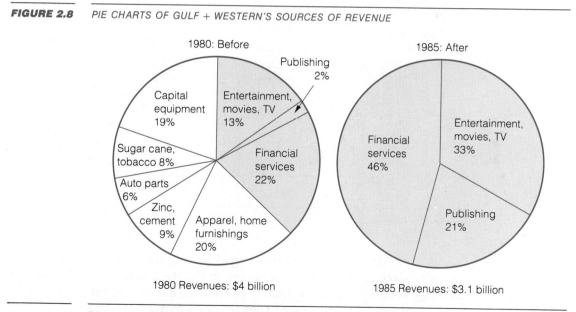

SOURCE: *New York Times,* 23 February 1986, p. 8F.

BAR CHARTS

A bar chart provides an alternative pictorial representation of *qualitative data,* such as the employment data in Table 2.10. A **bar chart** represents the frequency (or relative frequency) of each of the categories as a bar rising vertically from the horizontal axis; the height of each bar is proportional to the frequency (or relative frequency) of the

FIGURE 2.9   *BAR CHART OF EMPLOYMENT AREAS*

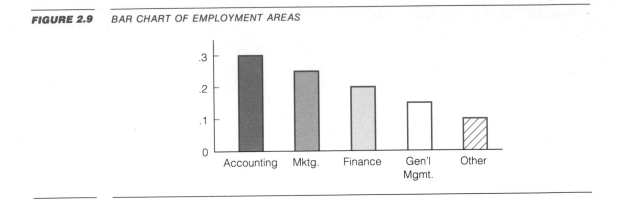

FIGURE 2.10   *BAR CHART SHOWING TOTAL VALUE OF MERGERS AND ACQUISITIONS*

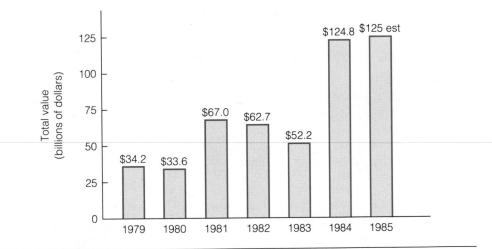

SOURCE: *New York Times,* 29 December 1985, p. 1F.

corresponding category. Since the bars correspond to categories or points, rather than to class intervals (as the rectangles of a histogram do), the widths assigned to the bars are arbitrary, although all must be equal. (The distorted impression that can be created by using unequal bar widths will be addressed in Section 2.5.) To improve clarity, a space is usually left between bars. Figure 2.9 displays a bar chart for the employment data in Table 2.10.

Another bar chart is illustrated in Figure 2.10, showing the total value of all mergers and acquisitions of American firms from 1979 to 1985. The number of billions of dollars corresponding to each category (year) is indicated on the bars—a laudable practice that removes any uncertainty as to the exact heights of the bars.

Rather than using a separate bar for each category, we could use a **component bar chart.** In this case, all categories are represented within a single bar. The bar is

FIGURE 2.11   *COMPONENT BAR CHARTS SHOWING BREAKDOWNS OF GASOLINE PRICE*

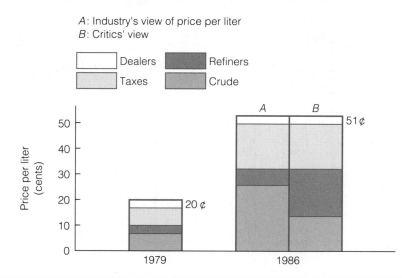

A: Industry's view of price per liter
B: Critics' view

SOURCE: *Globe and Mail,* 21 February 1986, p. 1.

partitioned into components, with the height of each component proportional to the frequency (or relative frequency) of the category that it represents. Component bar charts offer a good alternative to using two pie charts, when a comparison of two breakdowns is desired. Component bar charts usually enable the reader to detect the magnitude of the changes in the category sizes more easily than do pie charts. For example, Figure 2.11 shows breakdowns of the price of a liter of gasoline in Toronto.

BAR CHART OR PIE CHART?

Since either a bar chart or a pie chart can be used to represent qualitative data graphically, which representation should be used? The answer is that it all depends on what you want to emphasize. For example, consider the data in Table 2.11, which gives a breakdown of fourth quarter car sales by manufacturer for 1988 and 1989.

TABLE 2.11   *FOURTH QUARTER CAR SALES*

Manufacturer	1988	1989
General Motors	87,092	72,750
Ford	50,670	45,551
Chrysler	35,035	28,260
Overseas	64,289	66,303

SOURCE: *Toronto Star,* 5 January 1990, p. Cl.

FIGURE 2.12 BAR CHART EMPHASIZING CHANGE BY MANUFACTURER

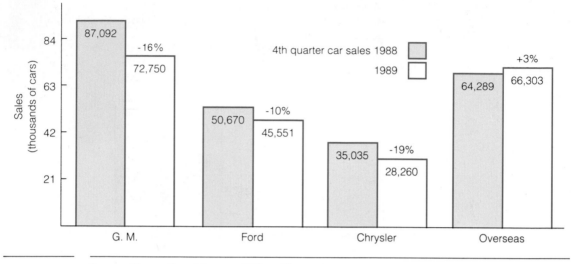

SOURCE: *Toronto Star*, 5 January 1990, p. C1.

FIGURE 2.13 BAR CHARTS EMPHASIZING CHANGE BY YEAR

4th Quarter Car Sales

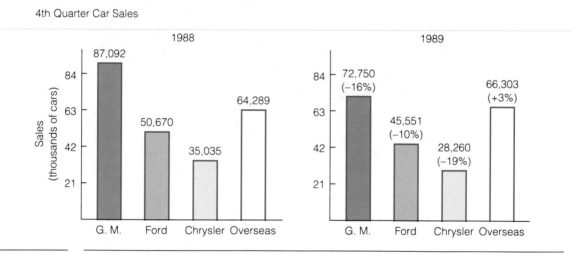

If we want to emphasize the drop in sales by the domestic manufacturers, we can group the sales by manufacturer to produce the bar chart shown in Figure 2.12. If instead we want to focus on the overall sales profiles for the years 1988 and 1989, we can group the sales by year to produce the bar charts shown in Figure 2.13. Finally, we can highlight the manufacturers' changing market shares by constructing a pair of pie charts, as shown in Figure 2.14.

FIGURE 2.14   *PIE CHARTS EMPHASIZING CHANGE BY MARKET SHARE*

4th Quarter Market Shares (Cars)

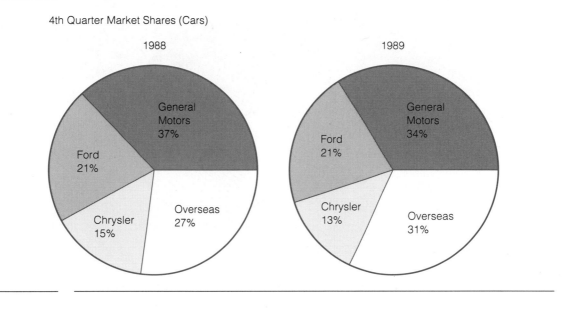

FIGURE 2.15   *BAR CHART OF NETWORKS' SHARES OF 18- TO 34-YEAR-OLD MARKET*

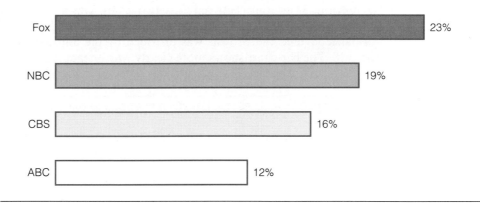

SOURCE: *The Wall Street Journal,* 25 May 1989, p. B1.

Although market shares are usually displayed graphically with a pie chart, professional chartists sometimes opt for the bar chart, as did *The Wall Street Journal* when it published the bar chart shown in Figure 2.15. This figure shows the share of the 18- to 34-year-old market enjoyed by each of the major television networks between 7 and 9 P.M. during May 1989. Figure 2.16 displays the conventional pie chart of the networks' market shares. But Figure 2.15, which omits the very sizable "Other"

FIGURE 2.16   *PIE CHART OF NETWORKS' SHARES OF 18- TO 34-YEAR-OLD MARKET*

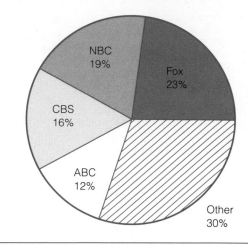

category, is preferable if the objective is to emphasize Fox's leadership over the big networks.

As a final example, we turn to an imaginative use of a bar chart that appeared in a 1989 issue of *Newsweek*. Prior to the December 1989 NFL playoff game between the Cleveland Browns and the Houston Oilers, it was noted that the Browns had won 25 of the previous 39 meetings between these two teams. This information is captured by the pie chart in Figure 2.17. But even greater support for the contention that past performance favored the Browns was provided by the unusual bar chart shown in Figure 2.18. The bar chart shows more clearly which team has been dominant in re-

FIGURE 2.17   *PIE CHART OF BROWNS-OILERS RIVALRY OVER PREVIOUS 39 GAMES (25–14)*

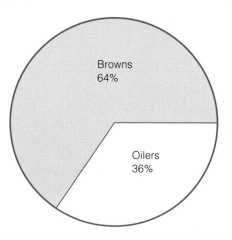

FIGURE 2.18 *BAR CHART OF BROWNS-OILERS RIVALRY OVER PREVIOUS 39 GAMES (25–14)*

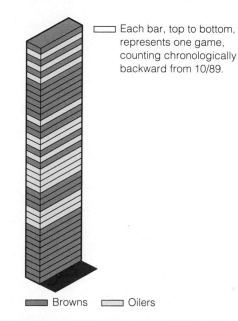

Each bar, top to bottom, represents one game, counting chronologically backward from 10/89.

Browns Oilers

SOURCE: *Newsweek*, 25 December 1989, p. 4.

cent years: the Browns. The sum of the shaded areas of the bar chart, expressed as a percentage of the total area of the bar chart, is still 64%—the same percentage represented by the shaded area of the pie chart in Figure 2.17. Once again we see that the type of chart selected for use depends on the particular information the user wants to emphasize.

LINE CHARTS

The last graphical technique to be considered here is the line chart. A **line chart** is obtained by plotting the frequency of a category above the point on the horizontal axis representing that category, and then joining the points with straight lines. Since a line chart is normally used when the categories are points in time, it is known alternatively as a *time-series chart*. Suppose that we wish to graph the total value of all mergers and acquisitions of firms in the United States from 1979 to 1985. A bar chart for these data is given in Figure 2.10, but if the objective of the graph is to focus on the trend in the value over the years—rather than on the relative sizes of the total amounts in different years—then a line chart is appropriate, as shown in Figure 2.19.

Line charts have the added advantage of clearly depicting the trend in the components of the total over time. When mergers and acquisitions are opposed by the management of the firm being taken over, they are referred to as *hostile*. Assuming that the breakdown of all takeovers into hostile and nonhostile types was known, the breakdown could be plotted in the same style shown in Figure 2.19.

FIGURE 2.19 *LINE CHART SHOWING TREND IN TOTAL VALUE OF TAKEOVERS*

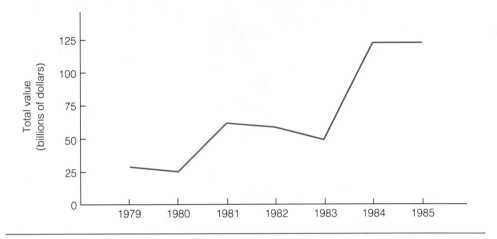

Pie charts, bar charts, and line charts are used extensively in reports compiled by businesses, governments, and the media. Variations on these and other pictorial representations of data abound, and their possibilities are limited only by their creators' imaginations. The objective of all such charts is to present a summary of the data clearly and in a form that allows the reader to grasp the relevant comparisons or trends quickly.

EXERCISES

2.13 A variety store's monthly sales (in thousands of dollars) for the last year were as follows:

Month	Sales	Month	Sales
January	65	July	88
February	61	August	93
March	70	September	91
April	74	October	78
May	72	November	68
June	80	December	84

a. Construct a relative frequency bar chart for these data.

b. Construct a line chart depicting these data.

2.14 The United States is Canada's most important trading partner, as is evidenced by the following table showing the percentage distribution of exports from and imports to Canada in 1985.

a. Use a graphical technique to depict the information given in the table.

b. Explain why you selected the particular technique you used in part (a).

Region	Exports (1985)	Imports (1985)
United States	78%	69%
Asia/Pacific	9%	13%
Western Europe	8%	13%
Latin America	3%	4%
Other	2%	1%

SOURCE: *Financial Post,* 6 April 1987, p. 34.

2.15   Inco Limited is the (noncommunist) world's major producer of nickel, which is used in the production of such alloy products as stainless steel. The annual demand for nickel in the noncommunist world and the amount supplied by Inco are shown in the accompanying table. Use a component bar chart to display the data.

Year	Word Demand (Millions of lb)	Inco Deliveries (Millions of lb)
1980	1,150	345
1981	1,095	342
1982	985	251
1983	1,145	314
1984	1,260	356

SOURCE: Inco Limited, *Annual Report*, 1984, p. 5.

2.16   The cover story for the February 6, 1989, edition of *Time* magazine was entitled "The Other Arms Race." It reported the purchase by United States citizens of more and deadlier guns. To dramatize the extent of the problem, the magazine used a bar chart to compare the number of people killed by handguns in different countries. Reconstruct the bar chart from the data in the accompanying table.

PEOPLE KILLED BY HANDGUNS IN 1985

Country	(Population)	Number
Canada	(25 million)	5
Britain	(57 million)	8
Japan	(121 million)	46
U.S.	(239 million)	8,092

SOURCE: *Time*, 6 February 1989, p. 18.

2.17   Americans today are waiting longer before getting married for the first time. A major contributing factor to this trend is the sharp increase in the percentage of women who now wish to become established in a career before taking on family responsibilities.

a. Use a graphical technique to compare the 1970 and 1987 percentages of people who have never married, broken down by age.

b. Explain why you selected the particular technique you used in part (a).

PERCENTAGE WHO HAVE NEVER MARRIED

Age	Men		Women	
	1970	1987	1970	1987
20–24	55%	78%	36%	61%
25–29	19%	42%	11%	29%

SOURCE: *Wall Street Journal*, 14 October 1987, p. 33.

2.18   Nestlé S.A., the international food giant, had worldwide sales in 1987 of $23 billion. The percentage distribution of sales according to geographic region is shown in the accompanying table.

a. Show how this information can be conveyed to shareholders, using a graphical technique.

b. Explain why you selected the particular technique you used in part (a).

1987 SALES FOR NESTLÉ

Region	Sales
Europe	43%
North America	29%
Asia	13%
Latin America and Caribbean	10%
Africa	3%
Australia, New Zealand, and Pacific Islands	2%

SOURCE: *New York Times*, 1 January 1989, p. F1.

2.19   Unlike the banking system in the United States, which consists of thousands of regional banks of varying sizes, the Canadian banking system is dominated by a handful of national banks that have branches throughout the country. Use both a bar chart and a pie chart to depict the information in the following table of bank deposits.

Bank	Millions of Dollars*	Market Share (%)*
1. The Royal Bank	81,787.6	22.3
2. Bank of Montreal	67,347.7	18.9
3. Bank of Commerce	64,242.7	17.5
4. Bank of Nova Scotia	53,533.0	14.6
5. Toronto-Dominion Bank	42,535.3	11.6
6. National Bank	18,051.8	4.9
7. Foreign Bank Subsidiaries	21,479.4	5.9
8. Others	17,337.9	4.3
TOTAL MARKET	366,315.4	100.0

* As of April 1985.
SOURCE: *Financial Times of Canada,* 23 September 1985.

SECTION 2.5 DECEPTION WITH GRAPHS

The use of graphs and charts is pervasive in newspapers, magazines, business and economic reports, and seminars. This is in large part due to the increasing availability of computers and software that allow the storage, retrieval, manipulation, and summary of large masses of raw data. It is therefore more important than ever to be able to evaluate critically the information presented by means of graphical techniques. In the final analysis, graphical techniques merely create a visual impression, and it is easy to create a distorted one. Although the heading for this section mentions deception, it is quite possible for an inexperienced person to create distorted impressions with graphs inadvertently. In any event, you should be aware of possible methods of distortion. This section illustrates a few of them.

The first thing to watch for is a graph without a scale on one axis. The time-series graph of a firm's sales in Figure 2.20 might represent a growth rate of 100% or of 1% over the five years depicted, depending on the vertical scale. It is best simply to ignore such graphs.

FIGURE 2.20 *GRAPH WITHOUT A VERTICAL SCALE*

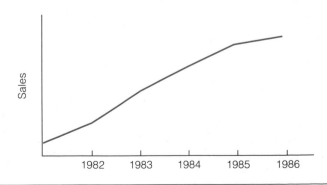

FIGURE 2.21   DIFFERENT CAPTIONS FOR THE SAME GRAPH

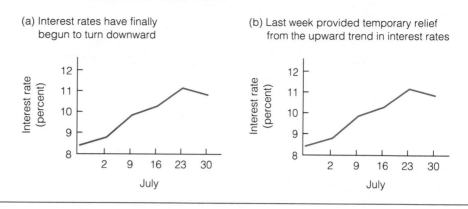

A second trap to avoid is to be influenced by the caption appearing on a graph. Your impression of the trend in interest rates may be different, depending on whether you read a newspaper carrying caption (a) or caption (b) in Figure 2.21.

Perspective is often distorted if only absolute changes in value, rather than percentage changes, are reported. A $1 drop in the price of your $2 stock is relatively more distressing than a $1 drop in the price of your $100 stock. On January 9, 1986, newspapers throughout North America displayed graphs similar to the one shown in Figure 2.22 and reported that the stock market, as measured by the Dow Jones Industrial Average (DJIA), suffered its worst one-day loss ever, on the previous day. The loss was 39 points, exceeding even the loss of Black Tuesday—October 28, 1929. While the loss was indeed a large one, many news reports failed to mention that the 1986 level of the DJIA was much higher than the 1929 level. A better perspective on the situation could be had by noticing that the loss on January 8, 1986, represented a 2.5% decline, while the decline in 1929 was 12.8%. As a point of interest, we note that the

FIGURE 2.22   HISTORIC DROP IN THE DJIA, 1986

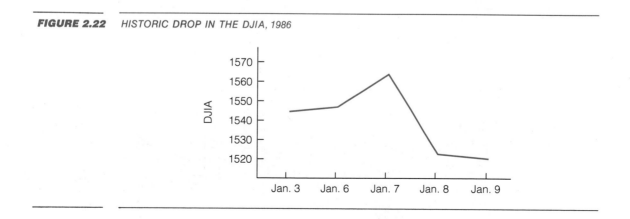

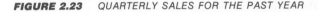

FIGURE 2.23 QUARTERLY SALES FOR THE PAST YEAR

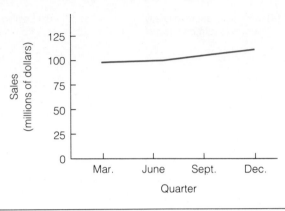

stock market was 12% higher within two months of this historic drop, and 40% higher one year later. The worst one-day loss ever, 22%, occurred October 19, 1987.

We now turn to some rather subtle methods of creating distorted impressions with graphs. Consider the graph in Figure 2.23, which depicts the growth in a firm's quarterly sales over the past year, from $100 million to $110 million. This 10% growth in quarterly sales can be made to appear more dramatic by *stretching the vertical axis*— a technique that involves changing the scale on the vertical axis so that a given dollar amount is represented by a greater height than before. As a result, the rise in sales appears to be greater, since the slope of the graph is visually (but not numerically) steeper. The expanded scale is usually accommodated by employing a break in the vertical axis (see Figure 2.24(a)) or by truncating the vertical axis (see Figure 2.24(b)) so that the vertical scale begins at a point greater than zero. The effect of making slopes appear steeper can also be created by shrinking the horizontal axis, in which case points on the horizontal axis are moved closer together.

FIGURE 2.24 STRETCHING THE VERTICAL AXIS

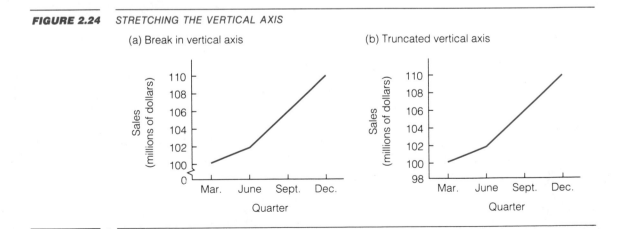

FIGURE 2.25   *QUARTERLY PROFITS OVER TWO YEARS*

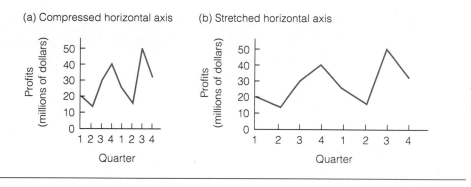

Just the opposite effect is obtained by *stretching the horizontal axis*—that is, spreading out the points on the horizontal axis to increase the distance between them so that slopes and trends will appear to be less steep. The graph of a firm's profits presented in Figure 2.25(a) shows considerable swings, both upward and downward, in the profits from one quarter to the next. However, the firm could convey the impression of reasonable stability in profits from quarter to quarter by stretching the horizontal axis, as shown in Figure 2.25(b).

Similar illusions can be created with bar charts, by stretching or shrinking the vertical or horizontal axis. Another popular method of creating distorted impressions with bar charts is to construct the bars so that their widths are proportional to their heights. The bar chart in Figure 2.26(a) correctly depicts the average weekly amount spent on food by Canadian families during three particular years. This chart correctly uses bars of equal width so that both the height and the area of each bar are proportional to the expenditures they represent. The growth in food expenditures is exaggerated in Figure 2.26(b), in which the widths of the bars increase with their heights. A quick glance at this bar chart may leave the viewer with the mistaken

FIGURE 2.26   *AVERAGE WEEKLY FOOD EXPENDITURES BY CANADIAN FAMILIES*

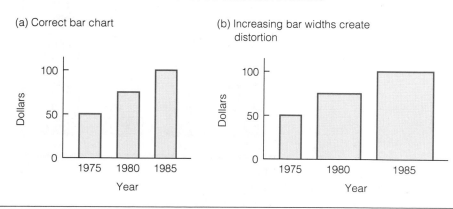

FIGURE 2.27 INCORRECT PICTOGRAM

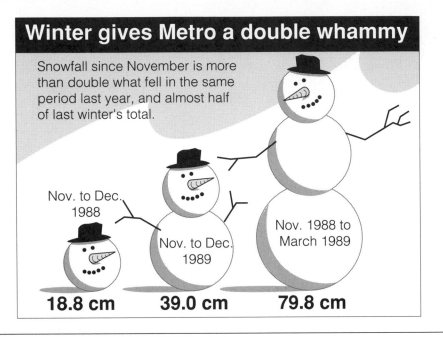

Winter gives Metro a double whammy

Snowfall since November is more than double what fell in the same period last year, and almost half of last winter's total.

Nov. to Dec. 1988

Nov. to Dec. 1989

Nov. 1988 to March 1989

18.8 cm   **39.0 cm**   **79.8 cm**

SOURCE: Reprint with permission—The Toronto Star Syndicate.

FIGURE 2.28 CORRECT PICTOGRAM

Shareholders Get More for Their Money

Return on Heinz shareholders' equity, in percent.

14.6%   18.0%   21.0%   24.6%

'78   '81   '84   '87

SOURCE: *New York Times,* 8 May 1988, p. F1.

impression that food expenditures increased fourfold over the decade, since the 1985 bar is four times the size of the 1975 bar.

Size distortions should be watched for particularly in **pictograms,** which replace the bars with pictures of objects (such as bags of money, people, or animals) to enhance the visual appeal. Figure 2.27 displays the misuse of a pictogram, since the snowman grows in width as well as in height. The proper use of a pictogram is shown in Figure 2.28, which effectively uses pictures of the H.J. Heinz Company's most recognizable product.

The preceding examples of creating a distorted impression using graphs are not exhaustive, but they include some of the more popular methods. They should also serve to make the point that graphical techniques are used to create a visual impression, and the impression you obtain may be a distorted one unless you examine the graph with care. You are less likely to be misled if you focus your attention on the numerical values that the graph represents. Begin by carefully noting the scales on both axes; graphs with unmarked axes should be ignored completely.

SECTION 2.6

SUMMARY

Descriptive statistics is concerned with methods of summarizing and presenting the essential information contained in a set of data, whether the set be a population or a sample taken from a population. This chapter focused on graphical methods of summarizing and presenting data. According to a Wharton Business School study, top managers reach a consensus 25% faster when responding to a presentation in which graphics are used.

A collection of quantitative data can be usefully summarized by grouping the measurements to form a frequency distribution. Constructing a stem and leaf display is often helpful during preliminary analysis of the data. Either a histogram or a frequency polygon can then be used to convey the shape of the distribution of the measurement data graphically. On the other hand, if the set of data is qualitative, the relative frequencies of the categories can be graphically displayed by means of pie charts or bar charts. The type of chart to use in a particular situation depends on the particular information the user wants to emphasize.

IMPORTANT TERMS

Graphical descriptive methods
Quantitative (numerical) data
Qualitative (categorical) data
Frequency distribution
Classes
Class width
Class frequency
Histogram
Relative frequency distribution

Relative frequency polygon
Cumulative relative frequency distribution
Ogive
Stem and leaf display
Pie chart
Bar chart
Line (or time series) chart
Stretching the vertical (or horizontal) axis
Pictogram

██████████   **SUPPLEMENTARY EXERCISES**

2.20   The number of items rejected daily by a manufacturer because of defects was recorded for the last 25 days. The results are as follows:

21	8	17	22	19
18	19	14	17	11
6	21	25	19	9
12	16	16	10	29
24	6	21	20	25

a. Construct a frequency distribution for these data. Use five class intervals, with the lower boundary of the first class being 5 items.

b. Construct a relative frequency histogram for these data.

c. What is the relationship between the areas under the histogram you have constructed and the relative frequencies of observations?

2.21   A large investment firm on Wall Street wants to review the distribution of the ages of its stockbrokers. The firm feels that this information will be useful in developing plans relating to recruitment and retirement options. The ages of a sample of 25 brokers are as follows:

50	64	32	55	41
44	24	46	58	47
36	52	54	44	66
47	59	51	61	57
49	28	42	38	45

Construct a stem and leaf display for the ages.

2.22   Refer to Exercise 2.21. Construct a frequency distribution for the data, using five class intervals and the value 20 as the lower limit of the first class.

2.23   Refer to Exercise 2.21.

a. Construct a relative frequency histogram for the data, using five class intervals and the value 20 as the lower limit of the first class.

b. Construct an ogive for the data.

c. What proportion of the total area under the histogram constructed in part (a) falls between 20 and 40?

2.24   A financial analyst is preparing to give a talk on stock market activity in North America. Following is one of the tables she intends to show to her audience.

a. Use a graphical technique to depict the information given in the table.

b. In what way is your graphical display superior to the tabular presentation?

1988 TRADING ACTIVITY ON NORTH AMERICAN STOCK EXCHANGES

Rank	Exchange	Value (in $ billions)
1	New York	1,643.2
2	Midwest	101.7
3	Toronto	68.1
4	American	55.7
5	Pacific	49.0
6	Philadelphia	32.4
7	Boston	25.4
8	Montreal	15.1
9	Cincinnati	8.5
10	Vancouver	3.3
Total		2,002.4

Source: *Globe and Mail*, 4 April 1989, p. B10.

2.25   According to the *Statistical Abstract of the United States: 1989*, the percentage of households with video cassette recorders has increased over the years, as shown in the accompanying table.

a. Use a graphical technique to depict the information given in the table.

b. Explain why you selected the particular technique you used in part (a).

Year	Households with VCRs (in %)
1980	1.1%
1982	3.1
1983	5.5
1984	10.6
1985	20.8

Year	Households with VCRs (in %)
1986	36.0
1987	48.7
1988	58.1

2.26 As a result of a prolonged economic boom, Toronto is undergoing several changes that are referred to by some observers as the "Manhattanization" of Toronto. One serious problem is the lack of affordable housing for young people.

a. Use a graphical technique to depict the information in the accompanying table.

b. Explain why you selected the particular technique you used in part (a).

1988 MEDIAN HOUSE PRICES IN METRO TORONTO

Month	Price	Month	Price
January	$174,000	July	$198,842
February	179,250	August	204,729
March	187,000	September	208,135
April	198,207	October	215,807
May	203,044	November	215,475
June	200,115	December	219,464

SOURCE: *Toronto Star,* 11 January 1989, p. A29.

CASE 2.1* PACIFIC SALMON CATCHES

A national publication has presented a detailed study about commercial salmon fishing in the United States, Canada, Japan, and the U.S.S.R. These four nations account for the bulk of the total annual Pacific Rim catch of salmon, which can be worth as much as $5 billion. The total size of the salmon catch in 1987 for each of these countries is shown in the following table, together with a breakdown of their catches by species.

Develop an interesting and informative graphical descriptive method to exhibit the data. Your graphical presentation should emphasize the relative sizes of the total catches for the four countries, as well as the relative importance (according to size) of the species caught for each country.

1987 SALMON CATCHES (IN METRIC TONS)

Species	United States	Canada	Japan	U.S.S.R.
Sockeye	102,165	14,650	945	11,521
Pink	75,914	26,045	17,000	96,390
Chum	40,440	10,490	145,440	23,810
Coho	18,450	8,320	3,300	4,224
Chinook	18,444	5,607	—	2,304
Cherry	—	—	3,310	—
Total	255,413	65,112	169,995	138,249

* Adapted from Jere Van Dyk, "Long Journey of the Pacific Salmon," *National Geographic* 178 (July 1990): 3–37.

C H A P T E R **3**

NUMERICAL DESCRIPTIVE MEASURES

INTRODUCTION

In this chapter we continue to look at how to summarize a large set of raw data so that the meaningful essentials can be extracted from it. Thus far, we have looked at how to group the data set into a more manageable form and how to construct various graphical representations of it. Faced with a set of measurements like the telephone data in Table 2.1, we began by finding the smallest and largest values, and then we formed a frequency distribution and histogram. These revealed the approximate shape of the distribution and indicated where the measurements were concentrated.

Although a frequency distribution is certainly useful in providing a general idea about how the data are distributed between the two extreme values, it is usually desirable to summarize the data even further by computing a few numerical descriptive measures. Numerical descriptive measures provide precise, objectively determined values that can easily be manipulated, interpreted, and compared with one another. In short, they permit a more careful analysis of the data than do the general impressions conveyed by tabular and graphical summaries. This is especially important when the data represent a sample from which inferences must be made concerning the entire population.

MEASURES OF CENTRAL LOCATION

In computing numerical descriptive measures of the data, interest usually focuses on two measures: a measure of the central or average value of the data, and a measure of the degree to which the observations are spread out about this average value. Measures of central location (averages) are discussed in this section, and measures of dispersion are discussed in Section 3.3. Of the various types of measures of central location, we will consider only three: the arithmetic mean, the median, and the mode.

ARITHMETIC MEAN

By far the most popular and useful measure of central location is the **arithmetic mean,** which we will simply refer to as the *mean*. Widely known in everyday usage as the *average,* the mean of a set of measurements is defined as

$$\text{Mean} = \frac{\text{Sum of the measurements}}{\text{Number of measurements}}.$$

Before expressing this algebraically, we should introduce some notation.* If we are dealing with a population of measurements, the total number of measurements is denoted by N, and the mean is represented by μ (the lower-case Greek letter mu). If the set of measurements is a sample, the total number of measurements is denoted by n, and the sample mean is represented by $\bar{x}$ (referred to as **x-bar**). (If the measurements under consideration are represented by another letter, such as y, the sample mean is denoted by $\bar{y}$.) Since the measurements in a sample are a subset of the measurements in the parent population, $n \leq N$ if the parent population consists of N measurements. In actual practice, you won't normally have access to all of the measurements in a population, so you will most often calculate the sample mean. As we'll see in Chapter 8, the sample mean $\bar{x}$ is used to make inferences about μ (the mean of the population from which the sample was taken). In particular, the value of $\bar{x}$ is frequently used as an estimate of μ.

Sample Mean

The **mean of a sample** of n measurements $x_1, x_2, \ldots, x_n$ is defined as

$$\bar{x} = \frac{\sum_{i=1}^{n} x_i}{n}.$$

EXAMPLE 3.1

The mean of the sample of six measurements, 7, 3, 9, -2, 4, and 6, is given by

$$\bar{x} = \frac{\sum_{i=1}^{n} x_i}{n} = \frac{7 + 3 + 9 - 2 + 4 + 6}{6} = 4.5.$$

The formula for calculating the mean of a population is the same as the formula for calculating the mean of a sample, differing only in the notation of the variables.

Population Mean

The **mean of a population** of N measurements $x_1, x_2, \ldots, x_N$ is defined as

$$\mu = \frac{\sum_{i=1}^{N} x_i}{N}$$

---

* Students unfamiliar with summation notation should read Appendix 3.C for further background.

EXAMPLE 3.2

Suppose that the telephone call durations in Table 2.1 (see page 15) represent a population of measurements. Then the population mean is

$$\mu = \frac{\sum_{i=1}^{N} x_i}{N} = \frac{11.8 + 3.6 + \cdots + 14.5}{30} = 10.26.$$

Referring to the histogram of telephone call durations back in Figure 2.1 (page 17), we see that the value 10.26 is located at approximately the center of the distribution.

EXAMPLE 3.3

When many of the measurements in a sample (or population) have the same value, the measurements are often summarized in a frequency table. Suppose that the numbers of children in a sample of 16 employees' families were recorded as follows:

Number of children	0	1	2	3
Number of employees	3	4	7	2

Notice that we are dealing with a total of $n = 16$ measurements here—one for each employee. To find the sample mean $\bar{x}$ of the number of children per employee, we divide the total number of children by the total number of employees. That is,

$$\bar{x} = \frac{\sum_{i=1}^{16} x_i}{n} = \frac{0 + 0 + 0 + 1 + \cdots + 2 + 3 + 3}{16}$$

$$= \frac{3(0) + 4(1) + 7(2) + 2(3)}{16}$$

$$= \frac{24}{16} = 1.5.$$

Notice that we could find $\bar{x}$ by skipping directly to the next to last line in this computation, where each distinct value of the measurement (number of children) is multiplied by the frequency with which it occurs, and then divided by the total number of measurements.

The sum of deviations of individual measurements from the mean is zero, or

$$\sum_{i=1}^{n} (x_i - \bar{x}) = 0.$$

This property has an interesting physical interpretation. Imagine that the individual measurements are marked off along a weightless bar and that a 1-lb weight is placed at each such mark, as depicted in the accompanying diagram (based on measurements from Example 3.1). The bar will be in perfect balance if a support is placed at the mean; therefore, the arithmetic mean may be interpreted as the center of gravity or the balance point.

The mean is a popular measure because it is simple to compute and interpret and because it lends itself to mathematical manipulation. More importantly for decision makers, it is generally the best measure of central location for purposes of statistical inference. *Its one serious drawback is that it is unduly influenced by extreme observations.* For example, if the sample of six measurements in Example 3.1 is enlarged to include a seventh measurement that has a value of 22, the mean of the resulting sample of seven measurements is $49/7 = 7$. Adding a single relatively large value to the original sample of measurements substantially increases the value of the mean. This is one reason why we sometimes resort to another measure of central location, the median.

THE MEDIAN

Median

The **median** of a set of measurements is the value that falls in the middle when the measurements are arranged in order of magnitude.

When an even number of measurements is involved, any number between the two middle values would satisfy the preceding definition of *median*. In such a case, however, it is conventional to take the midpoint between the two middle values as the median.

Calculating the Median

Given n measurements arranged in order of magnitude,

$$\text{Median} = \begin{cases} \text{Middle value, if } n \text{ is odd} \\ \text{Mean of the two middle values, if } n \text{ is even.} \end{cases}$$

In the examples that follow, we have arbitrarily chosen to arrange the measurements in ascending order (from smallest to largest) as a preliminary step in locating the median. Arranging them in descending order would, of course, yield identical results. The median has intuitive appeal as a measure of central location: at most, half of the measurements fall below the median; and at most, half fall above. Because of the distorting effect of extreme observations on the mean, the median is often the preferred measure in such situations as salary negotiations.

EXAMPLE 3.4

The annual salaries (in $1,000s) of the seven employees of a small government department are as follows:

$$28, 60, 26, 32, 30, 26, 29$$

To find the median salary, first arrange the salaries in ascending order: 26, 26, 28, 29, 30, 32, 60. The median salary is therefore $29,000, which is clearly more representative of a typical salary than is the mean value ($33,000).

EXAMPLE 3.5

Suppose that we wish to find the median of the following values:

$$28, 60, 26, 32, 30, 26, 29, 31$$

Arranging the values in ascending order, we have 26, 26, 28, 29, 30, 31, 32, 60. For an even number of measurements, the convention is to locate the median at the midpoint between the two middle values. Therefore, the median in this case is 29.5—the midpoint between 29 and 30.

MODE

A third measure of central location is the mode, which indicates the most frequently occurring value in a series. The mode doesn't necessarily lie in the middle of the set of measurements, although it often does; its claim to be a measure of central location is based on the fact that it indicates the location of greatest clustering or concentration of values (just as a population center describes a location of concentrated population).

> **Mode**
>
> The **mode** of a set of measurements is the value that occurs most frequently.

EXAMPLE 3.6

The manager of a men's store observes that the ten pairs of trousers sold yesterday had the following waist sizes (in inches):

$$31, 34, 36, 33, 28, 34, 30, 34, 32, 40$$

The mode of these waist sizes is 34 inches, and this fact is undoubtedly of more interest to the manager than are the facts that the mean waist size is 33.2 inches and the median waist size is 33.5 inches.

The mode is useful when the level of demand for an item is of interest—perhaps for the purpose of making purchasing or production decisions—and the item is produced in various standard sizes. But when the number of possible data values is quite large, the mode ceases to be useful as a measure of central location. Sometimes no single value occurs more than once, making all of the measurements modes and providing no useful information. This, in fact, is the situation with the telephone data in Table 2.1. In such a case, it is more useful to group the data into classes and refer to the class with the largest frequency as the *modal class*. A distribution is then said to be *unimodal* if there is only one such class, and *bimodal* if there are two such classes. While the *midpoint of the modal class* is sometimes referred to as the mode, it does not identify the measurement that occurs most frequently (as the true mode does) but the measurement about which there is the greatest clustering of values; thus, it corresponds graphically to the highest point on the frequency polygon.

If the data are qualitative, such as the employment areas in Table 2.10 (page 28), it is senseless to use the mean or the median; the mode must be used. The modal value (or employment area) in that example is accounting, since that category contains the most students. On the other hand, if the measurement data are quantitative, all three measures of central tendency are meaningful. Because the mean is the best measure of central location for the purpose of statistical inference, it will be used extensively from Chapter 8 onward. But for descriptive purposes, it is usually best to report the values of all three measures, since each conveys somewhat different information. Moreover, the relative positions of the mean and the median provide some information about the shape of the distribution of the measurements.

The relationship among the three measures of central location can be observed from the smoothed relative frequency polygons in Figure 3.1.* If the distribution is symmetrical and unimodal, the three measures coincide, as shown in Figure 3.1(a). If a distribution is not symmetrical, it is said to be **skewed.** The distribution in Figure 3.1(b) is *skewed to the right,* or **positively skewed,** since it has a long tail extending off to the right (indicating the presence of a small proportion of relatively large extreme values) but only a short tail extending to the left. Distributions of incomes commonly exhibit such positive skewness. As mentioned earlier, these extreme values pull the mean to the right more than the median. A mean value greater than the median therefore provides some evidence of positive skewness.

The distribution in Figure 3.1(c) is *skewed to the left*, or **negatively skewed,** since it has a long tail to the left but a short tail to the right. Once again, the extreme values affect the mean more than they do the median, so the mean value is pulled more noticeably in the direction of the skewness. A mean value less than the median is an indication of negative skewness.

---

* Relative frequency polygons tend to look more and more like smooth curves as their underlying data sets get larger.

FIGURE 3.1   *RELATIONSHIPS AMONG MEAN, MEDIAN, AND MODE*

(a) Symmetric distribution

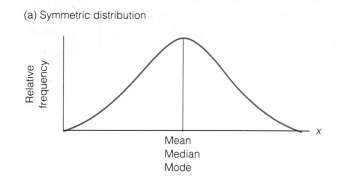

(b) Distribution skewed to the right (positively skewed)

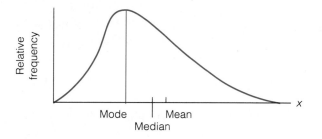

(c) Distribution skewed to the left (negatively skewed)

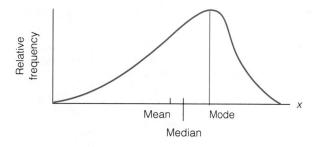

   **EXERCISES**

LEARNING THE TECHNIQUES

3.1 The number of days for which each of 15 office workers was absent during a one-month period is as follows:

0, 1, 1, 3, 0, 0, 2, 5, 0, 1, 1, 2, 0, 1, 1

Compute the mean, the median, and the mode of the number of days absent.

3.2 The following data represent the number of product defects found during each 8-hour shift of each day for a week:

	M	T	W	Th	F
Shift 1:	24	17	35	15	19
Shift 2:	21	13	15	20	18

Find the mean number of defects found per shift.

3.3 What are the characteristics of a set of data for which the mean, median, and mode are identical?

3.4 Given a set of qualitative (categorical) data, what measure of central location is always appropriate?

APPLYING THE TECHNIQUES

Self-Correcting Exercise (See Appendix 3.B for the solution.)

3.5 The ages of the employees of a fast-food outlet are as follows:

$$19, 19, 65, 20, 21, 18, 20$$

a. Compute the mean, the median, and the mode of the ages.

b. How would these three measures of central location be affected if the oldest employee retires?

3.6 When a certain professor left one university to teach at another, a student was heard to remark, "That move will surely raise the average IQ at both universities." Explain the meaning of the remark.

3.7 The cash compensation (excluding such benefits as stock options) received in 1986 by the highest-paid executives of Canadian companies whose shares are listed on U.S. stock exchanges is shown in the accompanying table. (Other Canadian companies needn't disclose executive compensation, since disclosure laws in Canada are less strict than those in the United States.)

Executive	Company	Compensation (in $1,000s)
Frank Stronach	Magna International	$2,215

Executive	Company	Compensation (in $1,000s)
E. M. Bronfman	Seagram	1,888
P. E. Beekman	Seagram	1,477
E. G. Fitzgerald	Northern Telecom	1,059
A. J. de Grandpré	Bell Canada Enterprises	977
Manfred Gingl	Magna International	956
G. H. Drabinsky	Cineplex Odeon	947
M. I. Gottlieb	Cineplex Odeon	924
C. R. Bronfman	Seagram	899
J. R. McAlpine	Magna International	856
M. R. Hottinger	Magna International	856
J. V. R. Cyr	Bell Canada Enterprises	803

SOURCE: *Financial Post*, 13 April 1987, p. 16.

a. Find the mean compensation and the median compensation of the executives.

b. Comment on the skewness of the distribution of the executives' compensations.

c. Repeat part (a), ignoring the highest compensation. Is the mean or the median more affected by dropping the highest compensation?

3.8 Twenty families were asked how many cars they owned. Their responses are summarized in the following table.

Number of Cars	Number of Families
0	3
1	10
2	4
3	2
4	1

Determine the mean, the median, and the mode of the number of cars owned per family.

3.9 Some observers claim that, while smaller companies are the most important source of new jobs for Americans, large companies are best able to compete in international markets. Shown in the accompanying table are the 20 largest American companies, ranked according to their market value in 1986.

Company	Market Value (in $1 billions)
1. IBM	$91.7
2. Exxon	40.1
3. General Electric	34.7
4. General Motors	26.5
5. AT&T	24.3
6. DuPont	17.4
7. Sears Roebuck	16.7
8. Bell South	15.7
9. Amoco	15.6
10. Ford	15.1
11. American Express	14.6
12. Philip Morris	14.2
13. Eastman Kodak	13.5
14. Coca Cola	13.3
15. Chevron	12.9
16. Procter & Gamble	12.4
17. Bell Atlantic	12.3
18. Mobil	12.1
19. 3M	12.0
20. Nynex	11.9

Source: *Business Week,* 18 April 1986, p. 50.

a. Compute the mean market value of the 20 largest companies.

b. Find the median market value.

c. Repeat parts (a) and (b) after eliminating IBM from the data set. How are the mean and the median affected by this change?

3.10 Canada's third most important crop is rapeseed (canola), almost half of which is grown in the province of Alberta. The accompanying table gives the number of acres planted in rapeseed and the average yield per acre, broken down by agricultural reporting area (ARA), for 1974 and 1984.

ALBERTA RAPESEED PRODUCTION

ARA	Yields (bushels/acre)	Area (thousands of acres)
1974		
1–3	18.2	177.3
4–6	17.1	476.3
7	14.8	496.4
1984		
1	16.3	18.0
2	18.4	246.1
3	11.4	216.0
4	21.8	1,070.8
5	26.2	351.4
6	22.9	229.4
7	15.4	768.3

Source: Alberta Agriculture (Statistics Branch), *Agricultural Statistics,* December 1978 and January 1985.

a. Find the number of bushels of rapeseed grown in ARA 1 in 1984.

b. Find the average rapeseed yield (bushels per acre) for the entire province in 1974 and in 1984.

c. If you were asked to compare the 1974 and 1984 rapeseed yields for each ARA, you would be unable to do so, since the only data available for 1974 are somewhat aggregated. The only comparisons that can be made, aside from those involving ARA 7, require that you compute the average 1984 yields for the combined areas 1–3 and 4–6. What values do you obtain for these two average yields?

3.11 Sporting competitions that use judges' scores to determine a competitor's performance often drop the lowest and highest scores before computing the mean score, in order to diminish the effect of extreme values on the mean. Suppose that competitors *A* and *B* receive the following scores:

  A: 6.0, 7.0, 7.25, 7.25, 7.5, 7.5, 7.5
  B: 7.0, 7.0, 7.0, 7.25, 7.5, 7.5, 8.5

a. Compare the performances of competitors *A* and *B* based on the mean of their scores, both before and after dropping the two extreme scores.

b. Repeat part (a), using the median instead of the mean.

MEASURES OF DISPERSION

We are now able to compute three measures of central location. But these measures fail to tell the whole story about a distribution of measurements. For example, if you were told only that the average maximum temperature is 83.2°F in Honolulu and 79.4°F in Las Vegas, you might ask why Honolulu attracts significantly more sun-seekers in the winter months than does Las Vegas. A contributing factor may be that Honolulu's climate is much more temperate year-round. Honolulu's monthly average maximum temperatures vary only from 79°F to 87°F, while those of Las Vegas vary from 56°F to 104°F. Clearly, the average maximum temperature of 83.2°F for Honolulu is far closer to the maximum monthly temperatures likely to be encountered than is Las Vegas' average maximum temperature to its maximum monthly temperatures.

Once we know the average value of a set of measurements, our next question should be: how typical is the average value of all measurements in the data set? Or in other words, how spread out are the measurements about their average value? Are the measurements highly variable and widely dispersed about the average value, as depicted by the smoothed relative frequency polygon in Figure 3.2(a), or do they exhibit low variability and cluster about the average value, as in Figure 3.2(b)?

The importance of looking beyond the average value is borne out by the fact that many individuals make use of the concept of variability in everyday decision making, whether or not they compute a numerical measure of the dispersion. Consider the case of Tuffy Rocknee, a college football coach, agonizing over which player to assign punting duties to in Saturday's big game. Tuffy has decided to base his decision on the

FIGURE 3.2   *SMOOTHED RELATIVE FREQUENCY POLYGONS*

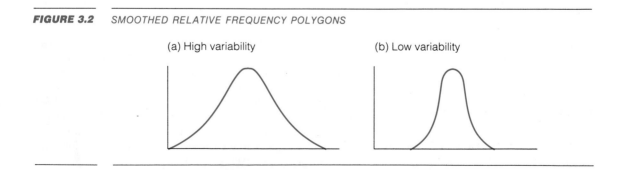

(a) High variability   (b) Low variability

results of ten practice kicks by each player. The recorded yardages are as follows:

> *A*:   41, 55, 30, 38, 50, 42, 39, 25, 28, 52
>
> *B*:   39, 42, 38, 42, 44, 40, 41, 38, 36, 40

The mean number of yards punted by each player is 40 (as you should verify); but if Tuffy is looking for consistency, he will select player *B*. Without actually computing a measure of dispersion (and probably not caring to know how to), Tuffy will choose the player whose punts exhibit the lowest variability.

The concept of variability is of fundamental importance in statistical inference. It is therefore important that we, unlike Tuffy, be able to measure the degree of variability in a set of measurements.

RANGE

The first and simplest measure of dispersion is the range, which we already encountered when forming frequency distributions.

> **Range**
>
> The **range** of a set of measurements is the numerical difference between the largest and smallest measurements.

The usefulness of the range stems from the ease with which it can be computed and interpreted. The first observation we made concerning the telephone data in Table 2.1 was that the shortest and longest telephone calls were 2.3 and 19.5 minutes, respectively, which established that the range was $19.5 - 2.3 = 17.2$ minutes. We later computed the mean duration of the telephone calls as 10.26 minutes.

A major shortcoming of the range is that it provides us with no information on the dispersion of the values falling between the smallest and largest measurements. These intermediate values might all be clustered very closely about the mean value of 10.26, or they might be dispersed fairly evenly across the range between the two extreme values, or they might be clumped in two groups near each extreme (resulting in a barbell-shaped distribution). Information concerning the location—and hence the dispersion—of these intermediate values can be conveyed by means of percentiles.

PERCENTILES

> **Percentile**
>
> The *p*th **percentile** of a set of measurements is the value for which *at most* $p\%$ of the measurements are less than that value and *at most* $(100 - p)\%$ of the measurements are greater than that value.

The pth percentile is defined in much the same manner as is the median, which divides a series of measurements in such a way that at most 50% of the measurements are smaller than the median and at most 50% of the measurements are greater. In fact, the median is simply the 50th percentile. And just as we have a special name for the percentile that divides the ordered set of measurements in half, we have special names for percentiles that divide the ordered set of measurements into quarters and into tenths: **quartiles** and **deciles.*** The following list identifies some of the more commonly used percentiles, together with notation for the quartiles:

$$
\begin{aligned}
&\text{First (lower) decile} &&= \text{10th percentile} \\
Q_1 = &\text{First (lower) quartile} &&= \text{25th percentile} \\
Q_2 = &\text{Second (middle) quartile} &&= \text{Median (50th percentile)} \\
Q_3 = &\text{Third (upper) quartile} &&= \text{75th percentile} \\
&\text{Ninth (upper) decile} &&= \text{90th percentile}
\end{aligned}
$$

EXAMPLE 3.7

To find the quartiles for the set of measurements

7, 18, 12, 17, 29, 18, 4, 27, 30, 2, 4, 10, 21, 5, 8

we must first arrange the measurements in ascending order:

2, 4, 4, 5, 7, 8, 10, 12, 17, 18, 18, 21, 27, 29, 30.

↑	↑	↑
lower quartile	median	upper quartile

The lower quartile is the value for which at most $.25 \times 15 = 3.75$ of the measurements are smaller and at most $.75 \times 15 = 11.25$ of the measurements are larger. The only measurement satisfying these criteria is 5, so 5 is the first quartile. The median is 12—the middle value. The upper quartile is the value for which at most $.75 \times 15 = 11.25$ of the measurements are smaller and at most $.25 \times 15 = 3.75$ of the measurements are larger. The only measurement satisfying these criteria is 21, so 21 is the third quartile.

Occasionally you will find that the percentile you are seeking falls between two of the measurements in the data set. When this happens, to avoid becoming unnecessarily pedantic, simply choose the midpoint between the two measurements involved. This will usually provide an adequate approximation of the required percentile. To illus-

---

* Quartiles are dividers—values that divide the entire range of measurements into four equal quarters. In practice, however, the word *quartile* is sometimes used to refer to one of these quarters. A measurement "in the first quartile" is in the bottom 25% of the measurements, whereas a measurement "in the upper quartile" is among the top 25%.

trate this convention, suppose that we wish to find the 20th percentile of the measurements in Example 3.7. The 20th percentile would be the value for which at most 3 of the measurements are smaller and at most 12 of the measurements are larger. Since any number between the measurements 4 and 5 (inclusive) satisfies this criterion, we choose 4.5—the midpoint between 4 and 5—as the 20th percentile.

Percentiles per se are measures of location, and they are widely used as measures of relative position because they are so easy to interpret. For example, they are frequently used to indicate the relative scores of applicants on admission tests. Percentiles are also a popular means of conveying the relative performances of pension fund investment portfolios over the most recent year. To provide a good indication of the dispersion of a set of measurements, however, a number of percentiles must be computed.* In contrast, variance, the next measure of dispersion to be considered in this chapter, can summarize the variability of the measurements in a single number.

VARIANCE

Variance is one of the two most widely accepted measures of the variability of a set of data (the other is standard deviation). Closely related to one another, variance and standard deviation take into account all of the data in a set and (as we will see in Chapter 8) are of fundamental importance in statistical inference.

Consider two very small populations, each consisting of five measurements:

A: 8, 9, 10, 11, 12

B: 4, 7, 10, 13, 16.

The mean of both population A and population B is 10, as you can easily verify. The population values are plotted along the horizontal x-axis in Figure 3.3. Visual inspection of these graphs indicates that the measurements in population B are more widely dispersed than those in A. We are searching for a measure of dispersion that confirms this notion and takes into account each measurement in the population.

Consider the five measurements in population A. To obtain a measure of their dispersion, we might begin by calculating the deviation of each value from the mean:

$$(8 - 10), (9 - 10), (10 - 10), (11 - 10), (12 - 10).$$

The four nonzero deviations are represented by the double-pointed arrows above the x-axis in Figure 3.3. It might at first seem reasonable to take the average of these deviations as a measure of dispersion, but the average of deviations from the mean is always zero. This difficulty can be overcome, however, by taking the average of the *squared* deviations as the required measure of dispersion. This measure of the dispersion, or variability, of a population of measurements is called the **variance;** it is denoted by σ^2, where σ is the lower-case Greek letter *sigma*.

---

* The number of percentiles that must be computed can be limited to two if the manager is content to report only the *interquartile range*—the difference between the third and first quartiles. While knowing this range is helpful, since it defines where the middle 50% of measurements fall, it (like the range) is based on two measurements only.

FIGURE 3.3 DEVIATIONS OF MEASUREMENTS FROM THE MEAN

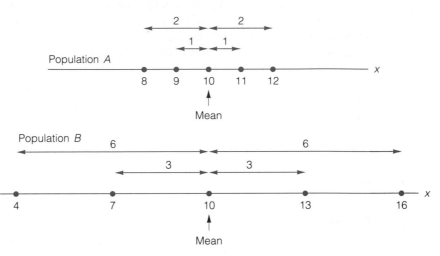

Letting σ_A^2 denote the variance of population A, we obtain

$$\sigma_A^2 = \frac{(8 - 10)^2 + (9 - 10)^2 + (10 - 10)^2 + (11 - 10)^2 + (12 - 10)^2}{5}$$

$$= \frac{(-2)^2 + (-1)^2 + 0^2 + 1^2 + 2^2}{5} = \frac{10}{5} = 2.$$

Proceeding in an analogous manner for population B, we obtain

$$\sigma_B^2 = \frac{(4 - 10)^2 + (7 - 10)^2 + (10 - 10)^2 + (13 - 10)^2 + (16 - 10)^2}{5} = 18.$$

The variance of B therefore exceeds the variance of A, consistent with our initial visual impression that the values in population B are more dispersed than those in population A.

Variance of a Population

The **variance of a population** of N measurements $x_1, x_2, \ldots, x_N$ having mean μ is defined as

$$\sigma^2 = \frac{\sum_{i=1}^{N}(x_i - \mu)^2}{N}$$

We suggest that, rather than blindly memorizing this formula, you think of the variance as being the *mean squared deviation*—the mean of the squared deviations of the measurements from their mean μ. This should help you both to remember and to interpret the formula for the variance.

Now suppose that you are working with a sample, rather than with a population. If you are given a sample of n measurements, your interest in computing the variance of the sample (denoted by s^2) lies in obtaining a good estimate of the population variance (σ^2). While it would seem reasonable to define the sample variance s^2 as the average of the squared deviations of the sample measurements from their mean $\bar{x}$, doing so tends to underestimate the population variance σ^2. This problem can be rectified, however, by defining the sample variance s^2 as the sum of the squared deviations divided by $n - 1$, rather than by n.

Variance of a Sample

The **variance of a sample** of n measurements $x_1, x_2, \ldots, x_n$ having mean $\bar{x}$ is defined as

$$s^2 = \frac{\sum_{i=1}^{n}(x_i - \bar{x})^2}{n - 1}$$

Computing the variance of a large sample can be made less tedious by using a shortcut formula derivable through simple algebraic manipulation of the formula just presented. The sample mean is usually calculated before the sample variance, in which case the value of the second summation in the shortcut formula is already known.

Shortcut Formula

The shortcut formula for the sample variance is

$$s^2 = \frac{1}{n - 1}\left[\sum_{i=1}^{n} x_i^2 - \frac{\left(\sum_{i=1}^{n} x_i\right)^2}{n}\right]$$

EXAMPLE 3.8

Find the mean and the variance of the following sample of measurements:

3.4, 2.5, 4.1, 1.2, 2.8, 3.7.

Solution. The mean of this sample of six measurements is

$$\bar{x} = \frac{\sum_{i=1}^{6} x_i}{6} = \frac{3.4 + 2.5 + 4.1 + 1.2 + 2.8 + 3.7}{6}$$

$$= \frac{17.7}{6} = 2.95.$$

To find the sample variance by means of the shortcut formula, we first compute

$$\sum_{i=1}^{6} x_i^2 = (3.4)^2 + (2.5)^2 + (4.1)^2 + (1.2)^2 + (2.8)^2 + (3.7)^2 = 57.59.$$

From the computation of the mean, we already know that

$$\sum_{i=1}^{6} x_i = 17.7.$$

Therefore,

$$s^2 = \frac{1}{5}\left[\sum_{i=1}^{6} x_i^2 - \frac{(\sum_{i=1}^{6} x_i)^2}{6}\right] = \frac{1}{5}\left[57.59 - \frac{(17.7)^2}{6}\right] = 1.075.$$

Alternatively, we could compute s^2 directly, using the definition of sample variance:

$$s^2 = \frac{(3.4 - 2.95)^2 + (2.5 - 2.95)^2 + (4.1 - 2.95)^2 + (1.2 - 2.95)^2 + (2.8 - 2.95)^2 + (3.7 - 2.95)^2}{5}$$

$$= 1.075.$$

One important application of variance arises in finance, where variance is the most popular numerical measure of risk. For example, we might be concerned with the variance of a firm's sales, profits, or return on investment. In all cases, the underlying assumption is that a larger variance corresponds to a higher level of risk. The next example illustrates this important application of variance.

EXAMPLE 3.9

Mutual funds are becoming an increasingly popular investment alternative among small investors. To help investors decide on the particular fund to invest in, the *Financial Times of Canada* regularly reports the average annual rate of return achieved by each of more than 100 mutual funds over the past 10 years.* The publication also indicates each fund's level of risk, by classifying the historical variability of each fund's rate of return as high, intermediate, or low.

If the annual (percentage) rates of return over the past 10 years for two mutual funds are as follows, which fund would you classify as having the higher level of risk?

Fund *A*:   8.3, −6.2, 20.9, −2.7, 33.6, 42.9, 24.4, 5.2, 3.1, 30.5
Fund *B*:   12.1, −2.8, 6.4, 12.2, 27.8, 25.3, 18.2, 10.7, −1.3, 11.4

---

* The annual rate of return of a mutual fund is given by $(P_1 - P_0)/P_0$, where P_0 and P_1 are the prices of the fund's shares at the beginning and end of the year, respectively. This definition assumes that no dividends are paid by the fund during the year.

Solution. For each fund, we must find the variance of the sample of rates of return. To avoid having to compute several squared deviations of returns from their mean, we'll use the shortcut formula for calculating a sample variance. For Fund A we have

$$\sum_{i=1}^{10} x_i = 8.3 - 6.2 + \cdots + 30.5 = 160.0$$

$$\sum_{i=1}^{10} x_i^2 = (8.3)^2 + (-6.2)^2 + \cdots + (30.5)^2 = 5{,}083.06.$$

The variance for Fund A is therefore

$$s_A^2 = \frac{1}{9}\left[\sum_{i=1}^{10} x_i^2 - \frac{(\sum_{i=1}^{10} x_i)^2}{10}\right] = \frac{1}{9}\left[5{,}083.06 - \frac{(160.0)^2}{10}\right] = 280.34 \ (\%)^2.$$

For Fund B we have

$$\sum_{i=1}^{10} x_i = 12.1 - 2.8 + \cdots + 11.4 = 120.0$$

$$\sum_{i=1}^{10} x_i^2 = (12.1)^2 + (-2.8)^2 + \cdots + (11.4)^2 = 2{,}334.36.$$

The variance for Fund B is therefore

$$s_B^2 = \frac{1}{9}\left[\sum_{i=1}^{10} x_i^2 - \frac{(\sum_{i=1}^{10} x_i)^2}{10}\right] = \frac{1}{9}\left[2{,}334.36 - \frac{(120.0)^2}{10}\right] = 99.38 \ (\%)^2.$$

Notice that, since the calculation of s^2 involves squaring the original measurements, the sample variance is expressed in $(\%)^2$, which is the square of the unit (percent) used to express the original measurements of rate of return.

From the sample data, we conclude that Fund A has the higher level of risk as measured by variance, since the variance of its rates of return exceeds that of Fund B's rates of return. Notice that Fund A has also enjoyed a higher average rate of return over the past 10 years. Specifically, the mean rates of return for Funds A and B were

$$\bar{x}_A = \frac{160.0}{10} = 16\%$$

and

$$\bar{x}_B = \frac{120.0}{10} = 12\%$$

This is in keeping with our intuitive notion that an investment that involves a higher level of risk should produce a higher average rate of return.*

---

* Students of finance will realize that, strictly speaking, the mutual funds must be well-diversified for this statement to hold when variance is used as the measure of risk.

STANDARD DEVIATION

Because calculating variance involves squaring the original measurements, the unit attached to a variance is the square of the unit attached to the original measurements. For example, if our original measurements are expressed in minutes, the variance is expressed in minutes squared. While variance is a useful measure of the relative variability of two sets of measurements, statisticians often want a measure of variability that is expressed in the same units as the original measurements, just as the mean is. Such a measure can be obtained simply by taking the square root of the variance.

> **Standard Deviation**
>
> The standard deviation of a set of measurements is the positive square root of the variance of the measurements.
>
> Sample standard deviation: $\qquad s = \sqrt{s^2}$
>
> Population standard deviation: $\quad \sigma = \sqrt{\sigma^2}$

For instance, the standard deviations of the samples of rates of return for Funds A and B in Example 3.9 are

$$s_A = \sqrt{s_A^2} = \sqrt{280.34} = 16.74\%$$

and

$$s_B = \sqrt{s_B^2} = \sqrt{99.38} = 9.97\%.$$

As you can see, the measurements in sample A are more variable than those in sample B, whether we use variance or standard deviation as our measure of variability. But standard deviation is the more useful measure of variability in situations where the measure is to be used in conjunction with the mean to make a statement about a single population, as we shall see in the next section.

COEFFICIENT OF VARIATION

The **coefficient of variation,** denoted by CV, of a data set is the set's standard deviation divided by its mean. Thus, we have

$$CV = \frac{s}{\bar{x}}$$

or

$$CV = \frac{\sigma}{\mu},$$

depending on whether the data set represents a sample or a population. Rather than comparing two variances, we can often obtain a more accurate assessment of the relative variability of two data sets by comparing their coefficients of variation, which adjust for differences in the magnitudes of the means of the data sets.

For instance, the coefficients of variation of the sample rates of return for Funds A and B in Example 3.9 are

$$CV_A = \frac{s_A}{\bar{x}_A} = \frac{16.74}{16} = 1.05$$

and

$$CV_B = \frac{s_B}{\bar{x}_B} = \frac{9.97}{12} = .83.$$

In this particular case, comparing coefficients of variation and comparing standard deviations lead to the same conclusion: the measurements in sample A are more variable.

The coefficient of variation is sometimes multiplied by 100 and reported as a percentage, which effectively expresses the standard deviation as a percentage of the mean. Thus, for the Fund A returns in Example 3.9, the coefficient of variation is 105%.

COMPUTER OUTPUT FOR EXAMPLE 3.9 (FUND A)*

Minitab

	N	MEAN	MEDIAN	TRMEAN	STDEV	SEMEAN
C1	10	16.00	14.60	15.41	16.74	5.29

	MIN	MAX	Q1	Q3
C1	-6.20	42.90	1.65	31.27

The output includes the following statistics:

N   (the sample size)

MEAN

MEDIAN

TRMEAN   (the mean of the observations, after the largest and smallest 5% are trimmed or omitted)

STDEV   (the sample standard deviation)

---

* Appendix 3.A provides the Minitab instructions that produced this output.

SEMEAN   (the standard error of the mean, which equals STDEV/$\sqrt{N}$; this statistic is discussed in Chapter 8)

MIN   (minimum observation)

MAX   (maximum observation)

Q1   (first or lower quartile)

Q3   (third or upper quartile)

EXERCISES

LEARNING THE TECHNIQUES

3.12 Compute the range, variance, and standard deviation for the following sample of data:

5, 7, 12, 14, 15, 15, 17, 20, 21, 24.

3.13 Calculate $\bar{x}$, s^2, and s for the following sample of data:

3, −2, −4, 1, 0, −1, 2.

3.14 Calculate $\bar{x}$, s^2, and s for each of the following samples of data:

a. 14, 7, 8, 11, 5

b. −3, −2, −1, 0, 1, 2, 3

c. 4, 4, 8, 8

d. 5, 5, 5, 5

3.15 Treating each of the four sets of data in Exercise 3.14 as populations, calculate μ, σ^2, and σ for each of the four populations.

3.16 What are the special names for the 25th, 50th, and 75th percentiles?

3.17 The number of hours a student spent studying over the past seven days was recorded as follows:

2, 5, 6, 1, 4, 0, 3.

Compute the range, $\bar{x}$, s, and s^2 for these data. Express each answer in appropriate units.

3.18 Given a set of quantitative data, what is the most popular measure of central location? What is the best measure of variability? Explain both answers.

3.19 In Exercise 2.4, you were asked to depict graphically the distribution of the following sample of grades:

75	79	58	73	82	94
61	77	54	77	65	67
62	61	64	45	58	86
66	83	70	91	48	78
86	66	52	80	59	55

a. Find the mean and the median of this set of grades.

b. Using the frequency distribution in Exercise 2.4, determine the mode as the midpoint of the modal class.

c. Locate the mean, the median, and the mode on the relative frequency histogram constructed in Exercise 2.4.

d. Use the shortcut formula to find the variance of this sample of grades.

APPLYING THE TECHNIQUES

Self-Correcting Exercise (See Appendix 3.B for the solution.)

3.20 The 15 stocks in your portfolio had the following percentage changes in value over the past year:

3	0	6	−5	−2
5	−18	20	14	18
−10	10	50	−20	14

a. Compute μ, σ^2, and σ for this population of data. Express each answer in appropriate units.

b. Compute the range, median, 20th percentile, and 60th percentile for these data.

3.21 The owner of a hardware store that sells electrical wire by the meter is considering selling the wire in precut lengths in order to cut down on labor costs. A sample of lengths (in meters) of wire sold over the course of one day produced the following data:

$$3, 7, 4, 2.5, 3, 20, 5, 5, 15, 3.5, 3$$

a. Find the mean, the median, and the mode of the lengths of wire sold on the given day.

b. For each of the three measures of central location, indicate its weakness in providing useful information to the store owner.

c. Find the upper and lower quartiles of the lengths of wire sold.

d. How might the store owner decide upon the appropriate precut lengths to sell?

3.22   Consider once again the two mutual funds, A and B, in Example 3.9. For convenience, their annual percentage rates of return over the past 10 years are repeated here. Suppose that, 10 years ago, you formed a portfolio by investing equal amounts of money in each of the two funds. The rate of return you would have earned on the portfolio over the first year would then have been $0.5(8.3) + 0.5(12.1) = 10.2\%$.

Fund A: 8.3, −6.2, 20.9, −2.7, 33.6,
42.9, 24.4, 5.2, 3.1, 30.5

Fund B: 12.1, −2.8, 6.4, 12.2, 27.8,
25.3, 18.2, 10.7, −1.3, 11.4

a. Compute the rate of return earned on the portfolio for each of the 10 years.

b. Find the mean return on the portfolio over the past 10 years.

c. Find the standard deviation of the portfolio returns over the past 10 years.

d. Rank the three possible investments (Fund A, Fund B, and the portfolio) according to their average returns and according to their riskiness (as measured by standard deviation) over the past 10 years.

3.23   The annual total rates of return on Canadian common stocks and long-term government bonds, for each of 25 years, are shown in Table E3.23. To understand the meaning of these returns, consider the 15.56% return that was realized on common stocks in 1963. This means that $100 invested in common stocks at the beginning of 1963 would have yielded a profit of $15.56 over the year, leaving you with a total of $115.56 at year's end.

a. Find the mean, the median, the range, and the standard deviation of this sample of common-stock returns.

b. Find the upper and lower quartiles of the common-stock returns.

c. Repeat parts (a) and (b) for the bond returns.

d. Which type of investment (common stocks or bonds) appears to have the higher level of risk? The higher average return?

TABLE E3.23

ANNUAL TOTAL RATES OF RETURN (in %)

Years	Common Stocks					Long-term Government Bonds				
1960−64	1.66	32.54	−7.25	15.56	25.30	7.10	9.78	3.05	4.60	6.59
1965−69	6.54	−7.10	18.00	22.36	−0.96	0.96	1.55	−2.20	−0.52	−2.31
1970−74	−3.60	8.07	27.31	−0.42	−26.61	−21.98	11.55	1.11	1.71	−1.69
1975−79	19.70	10.94	9.93	29.22	44.38	2.82	19.02	5.97	1.29	−2.62
1980−84	29.93	−10.29	5.51	34.84	−2.44	2.06	−3.02	42.98	9.60	15.09

SOURCE: *Report on Canadian Economic Statistics: 1924–1984* (Canadian Institute of Actuaries, May 1985), pp. 22, 32.

e. Compute the mean stock return for each of the five 5-year periods.

f. Compute the mean and the standard deviation of the five mean returns in part (e). Compare these values with the mean and the standard deviation calculated in part (a), and explain any differences observed.

3.24   Individual firms in the toy industry find that their annual growth rates in sales tend to fluctuate substantially from year to year, because of changing fads. In comparison, the growth rate in total industry sales remains relatively stable.

a. Determine whether this statement is supported by the data in the accompanying table, by comparing the variances of the growth rates in sales for Mattel, Tonka, and the entire toy industry.

b. Answer part (a) of this exercise by comparing coefficients of variation, rather than variances.

PERCENTAGE GROWTH RATES IN SALES

	1980	1981	1982	1983	1984
Mattel	13.7	23.9	18.3	−52.8	39.1
Tonka	−21.7	4.1	−22.9	8.3	58.3
Industry	8.4	14.0	28.9	−19.9	50.0

INTERPRETING STANDARD DEVIATION

By now you probably understand how variance and standard deviation can be used as relative measures of dispersion. Given the standard deviation of a single set of measurements, however, you would likely have difficulty interpreting that value intuitively. The standard deviation would be more useful if it could be used to make a statement about the percentage of measurements that fall into various intervals of values. For example, suppose that you are told that the average daily maximum temperature in Honolulu is 82°F, with a standard deviation of 1.5 Fahrenheit degrees. You would probably find it helpful to be able to say something about the percentage of days on which the maximum temperature falls within a specified range—between 79°F and 85°F, for example.

A good estimate of this percentage is available if the distribution of the data is mound-shaped (or bell-shaped). An example of a mound-shaped distribution is shown in Figure 3.4, which reproduces the relative frequency histogram of the telephone call durations. (A smoothed outline of the histogram would resemble a mound.)

A rule of thumb called the *Empirical Rule* has evolved from empirical studies that have produced samples possessing mound-shaped distributions. For a sample of measurements with a mound-shaped distribution, the Empirical Rule gives the approximate percentage of the measurements that fall within 1, 2, or 3 standard deviations of the mean.

Empirical Rule

If a sample of measurements has a mound-shaped distribution, the interval

$(\bar{x} - s, \bar{x} + s)$ contains roughly 68% of the measurements;

$(\bar{x} - 2s, \bar{x} + 2s)$ contains roughly 95% of the measurements;

$(\bar{x} - 3s, \bar{x} + 3s)$ contains virtually all of the measurements.

FIGURE 3.4   *MOUND-SHAPED HISTOGRAM*

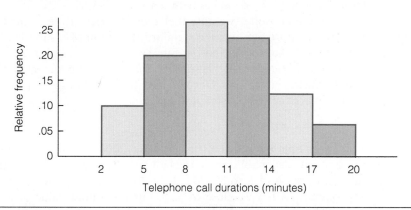

Telephone call durations (minutes)

EXAMPLE 3.10

The data in the sample of telephone call durations in Table 2.1 have a mean of $x =$ 10.26 and a standard deviation of $s = 4.29$. Moreover, the durations have an approximately mound-shaped distribution (see Figure 3.4). Consequently, according to the Empirical Rule, approximately 68% of the durations lie in the interval

$$(\bar{x} - s, \bar{x} + s) = (10.26 - 4.29, 10.26 + 4.29)$$
$$= (5.97, 14.55)$$

You can check this result by counting the actual contents of the specified interval. In fact, this interval contains 70% (21 out of 30) of the durations—a percentage very close to the Empirical Rule's approximation.

Similarly, the Empirical Rule states that approximately 95% of the durations lie in the interval

$$(\bar{x} - 2s, \bar{x} + 2s) = (10.26 - 2[4.29], 10.26 + 2[4.29])$$
$$= (1.68, 18.84)$$

In fact, all but the largest of the 30 durations fall within this interval; that is, the interval actually contains 96.7% of the telephone call durations—a percentage that comes very close to the Empirical Rule's approximation.

Example 3.10 may also be used to anticipate an idea that will be expanded upon in Chapter 5, when we deal with a particular mound-shaped distribution called the *normal distribution*. We noted in Section 2.3 that the area of any rectangle erected as part of a histogram is proportional to the percentage of the measurements that fall into the class it describes. As we've just observed, the Empirical Rule states that about 95% of the telephone call durations fall between 1.68 and 18.84 minutes. Therefore, approximately 95% of the area under the mound-shaped histogram in Figure 3.4 lies between 1.68 and 18.84. More generally, approximately 95% of the area under *any* mound-shaped histogram lies between $\bar{x} - 2s$ and $\bar{x} + 2s$.

As a final point, we note that the Empirical Rule forms the basis for a crude method of approximating the standard deviation of a sample of measurements that has a mound-shaped distribution. Since most of the sample measurements (about 95%) fall within 2 standard deviations of the mean, the range of the measurements is approximately equal to 4s. Once we have found the range of the measurements, we can approximate the sample standard deviation by

$$s \cong \text{Range}/4$$

This **range approximation of** *s* is useful as a quick check to ensure that our computed value of *s* is reasonable, or "in the ballpark." For example, the range of the telephone call durations is 17.2, so $17.2/4 = 4.3$ is an approximation of *s*. In this case, the range approximation is very close to 4.29, our computed value of *s*. Such accuracy isn't generally to be expected. More will be said about this approximation in Chapter 8.

EXERCISES

LEARNING THE TECHNIQUES

3.25 The mean and the standard deviation of the grades of 500 students who took an economics exam were 69 and 7, respectively.

a. What are the numerical values of the endpoints of the intervals $(\bar{x} - s, \bar{x} + s)$, $(\bar{x} - 2s, \bar{x} + 2s)$, and $(\bar{x} - 3s, \bar{x} + 3s)$?

b. If the grades have a mound-shaped distribution, approximately how many students received a grade in each of the three intervals specified in part (a)?

3.26 The mean and standard deviation of the wages of 1,000 factory workers are $25,600 and $2,200, respectively. If the wages have a mound-shaped distribution, how many workers receive wages of between $23,400 and $27,800? Between $21,200 and $30,000? Between $19,000 and $32,200?

APPLYING THE TECHNIQUES

3.27 The following 20 values represent the number of seconds required to complete one spot-weld by a sample of 20 automated welders on a company's production line:

    2.1, 2.7, 2.6, 2.8, 2.3, 2.5, 2.6, 2.4, 2.6, 2.7,
    2.4, 2.6, 2.8, 2.5, 2.6, 2.4, 2.9, 2.4, 2.7, 2.3.

a. Calculate the variance and the standard deviation for this sample of 20 measurements.

b. Use the range approximation of *s* to check your calculations in part (a). What assumption must you make in order to use this approximation?

Self-Correcting Exercise (See Appendix 3.B for the solution.)

3.28 A bookstore has determined that weekly sales of *Newsweek* have an approximately mound-shaped distribution, with a mean of 85 and a standard deviation of 6.

a. For what percentages of the time can we expect weekly sales to fall in the intervals $\bar{x} \pm s$ and $\bar{x} \pm 3s$?

b. For what percentage of the time can we expect weekly sales to have a value that is more than 2 standard deviations from the mean?

c. If the bookstore stocks 97 copies of *Newsweek* each week, for what percentage of weeks will there be too few copies to meet the demand? (HINT: A mound-shaped distribution is symmetrical.)

3.29 Last year, the rates of return on the common stocks in a large portfolio had an approximately mound-shaped distribution, with a mean of 20% and a standard deviation of 10%.

a. What proportion of the stocks had a return of between 10% and 30%? Between 10% and 50%?

b. What proportion of the stocks had a return that was either less than 10% or more than 30%?

c. What proportion of the stocks had a positive return? (HINT: A mound-shaped distribution is symmetrical.)

3.30 Refer to Exercise 3.23, which deals with stock and bond returns.

a. Compute the standard deviation of both the common-stock returns and the bond returns.

b. Use the range approximation of s to check your answers to part (a).

3.31 In Exercise 2.6, you were asked to depict graphically the distribution of the following sample of house prices (in $1,000s):

274	429	229	435	260
222	292	419	242	202
235	215	390	359	409
375	209	265	440	365
319	338	414	249	279

a. Calculate the variance and the standard deviation of this sample of prices.

b. Compare the range approximation of s to the true value of s. Explain why you would or would not expect the approximation to be a good one for this sample.

SECTION 3.5 APPROXIMATING DESCRIPTIVE MEASURES FOR GROUPED DATA

The two most important descriptive measures are the mean and the variance (or alternatively, the standard deviation). This section looks briefly at how to approximate these two measures for data that have been grouped into a frequency distribution.

You will find that the approximations given here are useful in two types of situations. The first is when you are confronted with a large set of ungrouped data. Although you could calculate the mean and the variance precisely in such cases with the aid of a computer, you may decide that approximations of these measures suffice to meet your needs. If so, you may find it faster and cheaper to group the data into a frequency distribution and then to use the methods described here. The second situation, which arises frequently in practice, occurs when you rely on secondary data sources such as government publications. Data collected by others is usually presented in the form of a frequency distribution, and you do not have access to the ungrouped data. In this case, you have no choice but to approximate the descriptive measures.

Consider a sample of n measurements that have been grouped into k classes. If f_i denotes the frequency of class i (for $i = 1, 2, \ldots, k$), then $n = f_1 + f_2 + \cdots + f_k$. A good approximation of the sample mean $\bar{x}$ can be obtained by making the assumption that the midpoint m_i of each class closely approximates the mean of the measurements in class i. This assumption is reasonable whenever the measurements in a class are dispersed fairly symmetrically about the midpoint. The sum of the measurements in class i is then approximately equal to $f_i m_i$.

The approximation of the sample variance is obtained by approximating the shortcut formula for the sample variance of ungrouped data, which was given in Section 3.3. The approximation of the sample variance actually requires a stronger assumption than the assumption of symmetry mentioned earlier: each measurement in a class is assumed to be equal to the midpoint of that class. The more accurate this assumption is, the better the approximation of the sample variance will be. If the grouped data represent a *population* of n measurements, the formula for approximating σ^2 is $(n-1)/n$ times the formula used to approximate s^2.

Approximate Mean and Variance for Grouped Data

$$\bar{x} \cong \frac{\sum_{i=1}^{k} f_i m_i}{n}$$

$$s^2 \cong \frac{1}{n-1}\left[\sum_{i=1}^{k} f_i m_i^2 - \frac{\left(\sum_{i=1}^{k} f_i m_i\right)^2}{n}\right]$$

EXAMPLE 3.11

The frequency distribution for the telephone call durations, introduced in Section 2.3, is reproduced in Table 3.1. Three additional columns have been included in the table to record the information required by the formulas for approximating the mean and the variance of the durations from these grouped data. We are now treating the 30 telephone call durations as a sample; and the sample mean and variance are approximated as follows:

$$\bar{x} \cong \frac{\sum_{i=1}^{6} f_i m_i}{30} = \frac{312.0}{30} = 10.4$$

$$s^2 \cong \frac{1}{29}\left[\sum_{i=1}^{6} f_i m_i^2 - \frac{\left(\sum_{i=1}^{6} f_i m_i\right)^2}{30}\right] = \frac{1}{29}\left[3751.5 - \frac{(312)^2}{30}\right] = 17.47.$$

TABLE 3.1   EXTENDED FREQUENCY DISTRIBUTION OF TELEPHONE CALL DURATIONS

Class i	Class Limits	Frequency f_i	Midpoint m_i	$f_i m_i$	$f_i m_i^2$
1	2 up to 5	3	3.5	10.5	36.75
2	5 up to 8	6	6.5	39.0	253.50
3	8 up to 11	8	9.5	76.0	722.00
4	11 up to 14	7	12.5	87.5	1,093.75
5	14 up to !7	4	15.5	62.0	961.00
6	17 up to 20	2	18.5	37.0	684.50
TOTAL		$n = 30$		312.0	3,751.50

These approximations match the true values of $\bar{x} = 10.26$ and $s^2 = 18.40$ reasonably well.

![EXERCISES]

EXERCISES

Self-Correcting Exercise (See Appendix 3.B for the solution.)

3.32 a. Approximate the mean and the variance of the sample of data presented in the accompanying frequency distribution.

Class	Frequency
0 up to 16	50
16 up to 32	160
32 up to 48	110
48 up to 64	80

b. Use the range approximation of s to check your approximation of the variance in part (a).

3.33 a. Approximate the mean and the variance of the sample data presented in the accompanying frequency distribution.

Class	Frequency
−20 up to −10	8
−10 up to 0	21
0 up to 10	43
10 up to 20	48
20 up to 30	25
30 up to 40	15

b. Use the range approximation of s to check your approximation of the variance in part (a).

3.34 a. Approximate the mean and the variance of the sample of data presented in the accompanying frequency distribution.

Class	Frequency
0 up to 10	90
10 up to 20	50
20 up to 30	40
30 up to 40	120

b. Use the range approximation of s to check your approximation of the variance in part (a). Comment on the degree to which these two approximations differ from each other.

3.35 The gross hourly earnings of a group of workers randomly selected from the payroll list of a large industrial concern were organized into the following frequency distribution:

Hourly Earnings	Number of Workers
$8 up to $10	11
$10 up to $12	17
$12 up to $14	32
$14 up to $16	27
$16 up to $18	13

a. Approximate the mean and the standard deviation of hourly earnings for this sample of workers.

b. Your answers to part (a) are only approximations of the true values of $\bar{x}$ and s for this group's earnings. Explain why this is so.

3.36 A national car-rental agency recently bought 1,000 identical new compact cars from a major car manufacturer. After the customary 1,000-mile break-in period, it selected 100 cars at random and obtained the following mileage data on them:

Gasoline Mileage (miles per gallon)	Number of Cars
24 and under 28	9
28 and under 32	13
32 and under 36	24
36 and under 40	38
40 and under 44	16

Approximate the average gasoline consumption and the standard deviation of consumption for this sample.

3.37 The ages of Americans who were classified as having work disabilities in 1988 are summarized in the following frequency distribution:

Ages	Number of Americans (in 1,000s)
16 up to 25	1,177
25 up to 35	2,292
35 up to 45	2,508
45 up to 55	2,522
55 up to 65	4,854

SOURCE: *Statistical Abstract of the United States: 1988.*

Approximate the mean and the standard deviation of the ages of the *population* of Americans with work disabilities. (Notice that the width of the first class differs from that of the others.)

SECTION
3.6

SUMMARY

This chapter extended our discussion of descriptive statistics, which deals with methods of summarizing and presenting the essential information contained in a set of data, whether the set be a population or a sample taken from a population. After constructing a frequency distribution to obtain a general idea about the distribution of a data set, we can use numerical measures to describe the central location and the dispersion of the data. Three popular measures of central location, or averages, are the mean, the median, and the mode. Taken by themselves, these measures provide an inadequate description of the data because they say nothing about the extent to which the data are dispersed about their central value. Information regarding the dispersion, or variability, of the data is conveyed by such numerical measures as range, percentiles, variance, standard deviation, and coefficient of variation.

For the special case in which a sample of measurements has a mound-shaped distribution, the Empirical Rule provides a good approximation of the percentages of measurements that fall within 1, 2, or 3 standard deviations of the mean. Beginning in Chapter 8, you will learn how these two important descriptive measures (mean and standard deviation), computed for a sample of measurements, can be combined to support inferences about the mean and the standard deviation of the population from which the sample was taken.

IMPORTANT TERMS

Measures of central location
Mean
Median
Mode
Unimodal

Bimodal
Skewed
Measures of dispersion
Range
Percentiles
Quartiles

Interquartile range
Variance
Standard deviation
Coefficient of variation
Empirical Rule

SUMMARY OF FORMULAS

$$\bar{x} = \frac{\sum_{i=1}^{n} x_i}{n}$$

$$\mu = \frac{\sum_{i=1}^{N} x_i}{N}$$

$$\sigma^2 = \frac{\sum_{i=1}^{N} (x_i - \mu)^2}{N}$$

$$s^2 = \frac{\sum_{i=1}^{n} (x_i - \bar{x})^2}{n - 1}$$

$$s^2 = \frac{1}{n-1} \left[\sum_{i=1}^{n} x_i^2 - \frac{(\sum_{i=1}^{n} x_i)^2}{n} \right]$$

$$CV = \frac{s}{\bar{x}}$$

$$s \cong \text{Range}/4$$

$$\bar{x} \cong \frac{\sum_{i=1}^{k} f_i m_i}{n}$$

$$s^2 \cong \frac{1}{n-1} \left[\sum_{i=1}^{k} f_i m_i^2 - \frac{(\sum_{i=1}^{k} f_i m_i)^2}{n} \right]$$

SUPPLEMENTARY EXERCISES

3.38 Determine the mean, the median, and the standard deviation of the following sample of data:

43	46	44	55	59	48
44	50	40	54	52	42

3.39 Consider the following population of measurements:

11	−1	5	2	8	7
12	4	−6	−10	1	5

a. Find the mean, the median, and the standard deviation of this population of measurements.

b. Find the upper and lower quartiles of these measurements.

3.40 Find the median, the mode, $\bar{x}$, s^2, and s for the data in Exercise 2.20. Do not approximate these values, but use the shortcut formula for s^2.

3.41 Refer to Exercises 2.20 and 3.40.

a. What proportion of items fall into the interval $\bar{x} \pm 2s$?

b. Does it appear that the population from which this sample was taken has a mound-shaped distribution?

c. Compare the actual proportions of items falling into the intervals $(\bar{x} - s, \bar{x} + s)$ and $(\bar{x} - 2s, \bar{x} + 2s)$ with the proportions suggested by the Empirical Rule.

3.42 The American airline industry has changed considerably since its deregulation in 1979. Numerous mergers and bankruptcies of airlines have occurred, and most major airports are now dominated by one of the eight major carriers. The accompanying table shows, for a sample of seven airports, the market share of the dominant carrier in 1979 and in 1987.

Airport	Dominant Carrier	Market Share of Dominant Carrier	
		1987	1979
Cincinnati	Delta	68%	37%
Detroit	Northwest	65	20
Houston	Continental	72	17
Minneapolis	Northwest	82	40
Pittsburgh	U.S. Air	83	48
St. Louis	TWA	82	43
Salt Lake City	Western	71	42

SOURCE: *New York Times,* 20 November 1988, p. 1F.

a. On the basis of inspection only (without performing any calculations), which year would you guess had the higher mean market share of the dominant carrier? The higher standard deviation?

b. Check your answers to part (a) by computing the mean and the standard deviation of the market shares for 1979 and for 1987.

3.43   In Exercise 2.21, the ages of a sample of 25 brokers were recorded as follows:

50	64	32	55	41
44	24	46	58	47
36	52	54	44	66
47	59	51	61	57
49	28	42	38	45

a. Construct a stem and leaf display for the ages. (If you did Exercise 2.21, you've already constructed this display.)

b. Find the median age.

c. Find the lower quartile of the ages.

d. Find the upper quartile of the ages.

e. Find the 80th percentile of the ages.

f. Does this firm have reason to be concerned about the distribution of ages of its brokers?

3.44   Refer to Exercise 3.43.

a. Compute the mean of the sample of data.

b. Compute the variance of the sample of data.

c. Compute the standard deviation of the sample of data.

3.45   Refer to Exercise 3.43.

a. Compute the range of the data.

b. Compute the range approximation to the standard deviation of the data.

3.46   Refer to Exercise 3.43.

a. Construct a frequency distribution for the data, using five class intervals and the value 20 as the lower limit of the first class. (If you did Exercise 2.21, you've already constructed this frequency distribution.)

b. Approximate the mean and the variance of the ages, based on the frequency distribution constructed in part (a).

3.47   The price-earnings ratio of a stock is of interest to investment analysts because it provides information about both the risk and the growth opportunities of the stock. The price-earnings ratios for 30 bank stocks (as of August 30, 1985) are given in the accompanying table.

a. Compute the mean and the standard deviation of the sample of 30 price-earnings ratios.

b. Construct a relative frequency histogram for the price-earnings ratios.

c. Determine the median price-earnings ratio, and locate the mean and the median on your histogram.

d. Use your relative frequency distribution to estimate the mean and the standard deviation of the 30 price-earnings ratios, and compare your estimates with the values obtained in part (a).

6.3	9.6	10.6	8.0	8.6	9.2
6.1	4.8	9.9	8.0	6.4	9.7
7.7	5.3	7.6	6.9	8.4	8.1
6.9	6.2	9.4	8.6	11.0	8.9
8.4	7.9	9.0	8.1	10.0	7.0

SOURCE: Value Line, *Selection & Opinion,* 30 August 1985.

3.48   The price-earnings ratios (as of August 30, 1985) of the stocks of 25 firms engaged in food processing or wholesaling are shown in the accompanying table.

a. Compute the mean and the standard deviation of the sample of 25 price-earnings ratios.

b. Construct a relative frequency histogram for the price-earnings ratios.

c. Determine the median price-earnings ratio, and locate the mean and the median on your histogram.

d. Use your relative frequency distribution to estimate the mean and the standard deviation of the 25 price-earnings ratios, and compare your estimates with the values obtained in part (a).

11.4	11.6	12.5	13.4	12.4
14.0	13.0	10.8	9.5	15.2
17.0	12.1	10.3	12.8	15.4
15.5	10.3	15.2	12.3	12.7
13.4	12.8	11.5	12.5	11.3

SOURCE: Value Line, *Selection & Opinion,*
30 August 1985.

3.49 The yield of a common stock is obtained by dividing its annual dividend by its price. The yields for the next 12 months (following August 30, 1985) were estimated for 30 bank stocks. They are expressed as percentages in the accompanying table.

a. Compute the mean and the standard deviation of the sample of 30 yields.

b. Construct a relative frequency histogram for the yields.

c. Find the median of the 30 stock yields, and locate the mean and the median on your histogram.

4.0	2.9	4.3	3.1	3.5	3.4
5.2	6.8	4.5	3.3	4.9	3.4
4.3	6.4	3.0	4.7	4.4	4.1
5.0	4.9	3.6	3.7	1.9	3.1
4.0	4.0	3.7	4.4	6.3	4.4

SOURCE: Value Line, *Selection & Opinion,* 30 August 1985.

3.50 The yields for the next 12 months (following August 30, 1985) were estimated for the common stocks of 25 firms engaged in food processing or wholesaling. They are given as percentages in the accompanying table.

a. Compute the mean and the standard deviation of the 25 yields.

b. Construct a relative frequency histogram for the yields.

c. Find the median of the 25 stock yields, and locate the mean and ·the median on your histogram.

d. Refer to Exercise 3.49. Determine whether the yields of bank stocks or of food processing stocks are more concentrated about their mean value, by inspecting their respective histograms.

e. Answer part (d) by comparing their respective standard devations.

0	3.2	2.6	0.2	1.5
2.6	3.3	0	0	2.0
1.4	3.3	4.1	3.9	1.1
2.6	2.7	1.6	2.8	1.8
3.2	2.8	1.0	2.2	3.2

SOURCE: Value Line, *Selection & Opinion,* 30 August 1985.

MINITAB INSTRUCTIONS

INTRODUCTION

Minitab is most often accessed on a mainframe computer terminal equipped with a screen or printer. Instructions are input from a keyboard. When you complete a line of instruction, you simply press the RETURN key. Before doing so, however, you should make sure that the line is correctly typed. Any errors you discover at this point can easily be corrected by backspacing and retyping; but once the carriage return is pushed, the error may be more difficult to correct. A second way to use Minitab is through a microcomputer. The instructions here should be valid for either; they assume that you are in interactive mode on a mainframe computer or that you are using a microcomputer.

LOGGING

To log on, you will likely need an account number, an identification number, and a password. These should be provided to you by your computer center. Once you have logged on, in order to access the Minitab package, you generally have to type the word MINITAB. Once again, your computer center will provide you with guidance.

At this point, we assume that you are in the Minitab system. When the computer is ready to accept a command from you, it will prompt you with MTB⟩.

DATA INPUT

In order for the Minitab program to perform the statistical computations, data must first be input. The following command can be used:

READ C1

where C1 represents *column 1*. After typing this line, press the RETURN or ENTER key on your keyboard. Then type in (and enter) the data, one number per line. The computer will prompt you after each entered line with

DATA⟩

When all of the data have been input, type

END

For example, suppose that you have the following five observations: 12, 15, 18, 16, and 9. These data would be input as follows, where the underlined terms are the computer prompts:

```
MTB⟩   READ C1
DATA⟩ 12
DATA⟩ 15
DATA⟩  8
DATA⟩ 16
DATA⟩  9
DATA⟩ END
```

In all further illustrations of the instructions we will not show the computer prompts.
     If two or more groups of data are to be read you could type

```
READ C1 C2
```

or

```
READ C1 C2 C3
```

or

```
READ C1-C3
```

Another way of inputting data is by using the SET command. This command allows you to type numbers consecutively on one or more lines. For example:

```
SET C1
12    15    8    16    9
END
SET C2
17    25    13   15    32
26    20    5    3
END
```

CORRECTIONS

Suppose that after inputting the data you discover an error. The following three instructions allow you to correct errors:

1. To replace an erroneous entry, use the L E T instruction. For example,

   ```
   LET C1(2) = 5
   ```

   changes the second value in column 1 to 5.
2. To delete rows 2 to 5 from column 1, type

   ```
   DELETE 2:5 C1
   ```

3. To insert a new row of data between rows 3 and 4, type

   ```
   INSERT BETWEEN ROWS 3 AND 4 OF C1, C2
           7      15
   END
   ```

OUTPUT

To check to see if the data have been input correctly, type

```
PRINT C1
```

or

```
PRINT C1 C2 C3
```

or

```
PRINT C1-C3
```

SAVING DATA

If you intend to use the same set of data at another time, you can save and retrieve it. In order to save a data set type:

```
SAVE  '[name of data set]'
```

Once the data set has been saved, at any time you can retrieve it with the following command:

```
RETRIEVE  '[name of data set]'
```

You can use any file name you like. However, rules governing S A V E and R E T R I E V E may vary among computer centers. If you have difficulty with these two commands, seek advice from your computer center.

If your database is quite large, we suggest that you periodically save your data to avoid problems associated with accidental erasure of columns.

OTHER COMMANDS

To create new variables from existing ones, use the L E T command. For example:

```
LET C3 = C1 + C2
```

creates a variable that is the sum of the first two and stores the values of this variable in column 3. Some useful arithmetic operations, identified by their Minitab symbols, are

+   add
–   subtract
*   multiply
/   divide
**   exponentiate (raise to a power)

In some situations it is useful to name the variables. To do so, type

NAME C1 = 'name of variable 1', C2 = 'name of variable 2'

Commands such as PRINT and DELETE can subsequently use the variable name instead of the column number. For example, after you have entered the command

NAME C1 = 'INCOME', C2 = 'AGE'

the command

PRINT C1 C2

is equivalent to the command

PRINT INCOME AGE

To erase columns, type

ERASE C1

or

ERASE C1 C2 C3

or

ERASE C1-C3

When you have completed your work in Minitab, type

STOP

This command returns you to the computer operating system, from which you can sign off.

At any time you may receive help by typing

HELP '[command]'

in order to get help concerning that command. For example:

HELP READ

will produce a brief explanation of READ.

HELP HELP

will give you a summary of other help that you can get from Minitab.

CHAPTER 2 INSTRUCTIONS

The instructions that follow will allow you to perform some of the techniques described in Chapter 2.

To create a histogram when the data are stored in column 1, type

```
HISTOGRAM C1 K1 K2
```

where K1 is the first midpoint and K2 is the interval size. For example, to create a histogram of the data in Table 2.1 of Chapter 2, use the following commands:

```
SET C1
11.8 8.9 10.2 15.3 6.2 3.6 9.1 8.0 12.3 11.2 16.6 7.7 11.4 8.5 10.4
13.5 2.3 6.8 15.9 7.2 4.8 12.1 9.6 18.7 5.5 8.3 6.1 19.5 11.7 14.5
END
HISTOGRAM C1 3.5 3
```

These commands would produce the following output:

```
Histogram of C1    N = 30
Midpoint       Count
    3.50       3***
    6.50       6******
    9.50       8********
   12.50       7*******
   15.50       4****
   18.50       2**
```

CHAPTER 3 INSTRUCTIONS

The command

```
DESCRIBE C1
```

causes Minitab to print a number of useful statistics. For example, we produce the descriptive statistics for Fund *A* in Example 3.9 as follows:

```
SET C1
8.3 -6.2 20.9 -2.7 33.6 42.9 24.4 5.2 3.1 30.5
END
DESCRIBE C1
```

The resulting output is

	N	MEAN	MEDIAN	TRMEAN	STDEV	SEMEAN
C1	10	16.00	14.60	15.41	16.74	5.29

	MIN	MAX	Q1	Q3
	-6.20	42.90	1.65	31.27

    If you want to know the number of times each value of the variable occurs, use the TABLE command. For example, the following commands

```
SET C1
1 2 2 2 3 1 3 3 1 2 2 1
END
TABLE C1
```

produce the output

```
ROWS: C1
          COUNT
  1         4
  2         5
  3         3
 ALL       12
```

    If there were two variables, the TABLE command would produce a cross-classification table (which counts the number of times each combination occurs), list the totals for each variable, and print them in the margins of the table. For instance, suppose that the following data are input:

```
READ C1 C2
1 2
1 1
1 1
1 2
1 1
1 1
1 1
1 2
1 1
2 2
2 2
2 1
2 2
END
```

In this situation, the command

```
TABLE C1 C2
```

would create the following output:

```
ROWS:   C1        COLUMNS:   C2
                1          2        ALL
  1             6          3          9
  2             1          3          4
 ALL            7          6         13
CELL CONTENTS -
                            COUNT
```

Other output can be generated by using several possible subcommands. In order to use a subcommand, you must end the preceding commands in semicolons, and you must end the last subcommand in a period. The following subcommands can be used with the TABLE command:

TOTPERCENTS (outputs the percent instead of the actual count)

ROWPERCENTS (prints the row percentage)

COLPERCENTS (outputs the column percentage)

For example, the commands

```
TABLE C1 C2;
ROWPERCENTS;
COLPERCENTS.
```

would print both the row and column percentages.

COMPUTER EXERCISES

3.51 Consider the following sample of measurements:

183	193	172	178	164
175	187	189	168	190
181	170	155	196	174
185	161	181	192	176
198	179	185	172	167

a. Construct a histogram for the data, using 150 as the lower limit of the first class and 10 as the class width.

b. Find the mean and the standard deviation of the measurements.

3.52 Consider the following sample of measurements:

306	265	230	278	334
275	210	215	274	270
223	280	289	250	229
315	340	384	472	267
258	276	208	276	254
331	241	350	261 ·	282
298	225	302	365	310
313	325	348	295	404

a. Construct a histogram for these measurements, using 200 as the lower limit of the first class and 50 as the class width.

b. Find the mean and the standard deviation of the measurements.

SOLUTIONS TO SELF-CORRECTING EXERCISES

3.5 a. The mean age is

$$\mu = \frac{\sum_{i=1}^{7} x_i}{7}$$

$$= \frac{19 + 19 + 65 + 20 + 21 + 18 + 20}{7}$$

$$= \frac{182}{7} = 26.$$

To find the median, first arrange the ages in ascending order:

$$18, 19, 19, 20, 20, 21, 65.$$

The median is the middle age, which is 20. There are two modes: 19 and 20; these are the ages that occur most frequently.

b. Suppose that the highest age, 65, is removed from the data set. The new mean age is

$$\mu = \frac{\sum_{i=1}^{6} x_i}{6}$$

$$= \frac{19 + 19 + 20 + 21 + 18 + 20}{6}$$

$$= 19.5.$$

The ages, arranged in ascending order, are now

$$18, 19, 19, 20, 20, 21.$$

The median is now 19.5, which represents the mean of the two middle ages. There are still two modes: 19 and 20. Notice that the mean has decreased substantially, the median has decreased only slightly, and the modes haven't changed at all.

3.20 a.

$$\mu = \frac{\sum_{i=1}^{15} x_i}{15} = \frac{3 + 5 + \cdots + 18 + 14}{15}$$

$$= 5.67\%$$

$$\sigma^2 = \frac{\sum_{i=1}^{15} (x_i - \mu)^2}{15}$$

$$= \frac{(2 - 5.67)^2 + (5 - 5.67)^2 + \cdots + (18 - 5.67)^2 + (14 - 5.67)^2}{15}$$

$$= 277.16(\%)^2$$

$$\sigma = \sqrt{277/16} = 16.65\%.$$

b. Range = Largest value − Smallest value
$$= 50 - (-20)$$
$$= 70\%.$$

Arranging the 15 measurements in ascending order, we obtain

$$-20, -18, -10, -5, -2, 0, 3, 5,$$
$$6, 10, 14, 14, 18, 20, 50.$$

The median is the middle value, which is 5%.

The 20th percentile is the value for which at most $.2 \times 15 = 3$ measurements are smaller and at most $.8 \times 15 = 12$ measurements are larger. Since these conditions are satisfied by both -10 and -5, we take the 20th percentile to be their mean: -7.5%.

The 60th percentile is the value for which at most $.6 \times 15 = 9$ measurements are smaller and at most $.4 \times 15 = 6$ measurements are larger. Since these conditions are satisfied by both 6 and 10, we take the 60th percentile to be their mean: 8%.

3.28   a. Weekly sales will fall, 68% of the time, in the interval

$$\bar{x} \pm s = 85 \pm 6 = (79, 91).$$

Weekly sales will fall, virtually all of the time, in the interval

$$\bar{x} \pm 3s = 85 \pm 3(6) = (67, 103).$$

b. Weekly sales will have a value more than 2 standard deviations from the mean $(100 - 95) = 5\%$ of the time.

c. The number 97 is 2 standard deviations greater than the mean: $97 = 85 + 2(6)$. Since a mound-shaped distribution is symmetrical, demand will exceed 97 copies $(5/2) = 2.5\%$ of the time.

3.32   a.

Class	f_i	m_i	$f_i m_i$	$f_i m_i^2$
0 up to 16	50	8	400	3,200
16 up to 32	160	24	3,840	92,160
32 up to 48	110	40	4,400	176,000
48 up to 64	80	56	4,480	250,880
TOTAL	400		13,120	522,240

$$\bar{x} \cong \frac{\sum_{i=1}^{4} f_i m_i}{400} = \frac{13,120}{400} = 32.8$$

$$s^2 \cong \frac{1}{n-1}\left[\sum_{i=1}^{4} f_i m_i^2 - \frac{\left(\sum_{i=1}^{4} f_i m_i\right)^2}{n}\right]$$

$$= \frac{1}{399}\left[522,240 - \frac{(13,120)^2}{400}\right] = 230.34.$$

b. $s \cong \dfrac{\text{Range}}{4} \cong \dfrac{64-0}{4} = 16$

$$s^2 \cong 16^2 = 256.$$

The range approximation of s indicates that the value computed for s^2 in part (a) is at least in the ballpark.

SUMMATION NOTATION

This appendix offers an introduction to the use of summation notation. Because summation notation is used extensively throughout statistics, you should review this appendix even if you've had previous exposure to summation notation. Our coverage of the topic begins with an introduction to the necessary terminology and notation, follows with some examples, and concludes with four rules that are useful in applying summation notation.

Consider n numbers $x_1, x_2, \ldots, x_n$. A concise way of representing their sum is

$$\sum_{i=1}^{n} x_i.$$

That is,

$$\sum_{i=1}^{n} x_i = x_1 + x_2 + \cdots + x_n.$$

REMARKS

1. The symbol $\sum$ is the capital Greek letter sigma, and means "the sum of."
2. The letter i is called the *index of summation*. The letter chosen to represent the index of summation is arbitrary.
3. The expression $\sum_{i=1}^{n} x_i$ is read "the sum of the terms x_i, where i assumes the values from 1 to n inclusive."
4. The numbers 1 and n are called the *lower* and the *upper limits of summation,* respectively.

Summation notation is best illustrated by means of examples.

▨▨▨▨▨▨▨▨ **EXAMPLES**

1. Suppose that $x_1 = 5$, $x_2 = 6$, $x_3 = 8$, and $x_4 = 10$. Then:

(i) $\displaystyle\sum_{i=1}^{4} x_i = x_1 + x_2 + x_3 + x_4 = 5 + 6 + 8 + 10 = 29$.

(ii) $\displaystyle\sum_{i=3}^{4} x_i = x_3 + x_4 = 8 + 10 = 18$

(iii) $\displaystyle\sum_{i=1}^{2} x_i(x_i - 1) = x_1(x_1 - 1) + x_2(x_2 - 1)$

$$= 5(5 - 1) + 6(6 - 1)$$
$$= 50.$$

(iv) $\displaystyle\sum_{i=1}^{3} f(x_i) = f(x_1) + f(x_2) + f(x_3)$

$$= f(5) + f(6) + f(8).$$

2. Suppose that $x_1 = 2$, $x_2 = 3$, $x_3 = 4$, $y_1 = 8$, $y_2 = 9$, and $y_3 = 13$. Then:

(i) $\displaystyle\sum_{i=1}^{3} x_i y_i = x_1 y_1 + x_2 y_2 + x_3 y_3$

$$= 2(8) + 3(9) + 4(13)$$
$$= 95.$$

(ii) $\displaystyle\sum_{i=2}^{3} x_i y_i^2 = x_2 y_2^2 + x_3 y_3^2$

$$= 3(9^2) + 4(13^2)$$
$$= 919.$$

(iii) $\displaystyle\sum_{i=1}^{2} (x_i - y_i) = (x_1 - y_1) + (x_2 - y_2)$

$$= (2 - 8) + (3 - 9)$$
$$= -12.$$

REMARK

It is not necessary that the index of summation be a subscript.

▨▨▨▨▨▨▨▨ **EXAMPLES**

1. $\displaystyle\sum_{x=0}^{4} x = 0 + 1 + 2 + 3 + 4 = 10$.

2. $\displaystyle\sum_{x=1}^{3} (x^2 - x) = (1^2 - 1) + (2^2 - 2) + (3^2 - 3) = 8$.

3. $\displaystyle\sum_{x=1}^{2} 5x = 5(1) + 5(2) = 15.$

4. $\displaystyle\sum_{x=0}^{3} f(x) = f(0) + f(1) + f(2) + f(3).$

5. $\displaystyle\sum_{x=1}^{2} f(x, y) = f(1, y) + f(2, y).$

6. $\displaystyle\sum_{y=3}^{5} f(x, y^2) = f(x, 3^2) + f(x, 4^2) + f(x, 5^2).$

RULES OF SUMMATION NOTATION

1. If c is a constant, then

$$\sum_{i=1}^{n} cx_i = c \sum_{i=1}^{n} x_i.$$

2. If c is a constant, then

$$\sum_{x=1}^{n} c = nc.$$

3. If a and b are constants, then

$$\sum_{i=1}^{n} (ax_i + by_i) = a \sum_{i=1}^{n} x_i + b \sum_{i=1}^{n} y_i.$$

4. If c is a constant, then

$$\sum_{i=1}^{n} (x_i + c) = \sum_{i=1}^{n} x_i + nc.$$

REMARK

Notice that

$$\sum_{i=1}^{n} x_i^2 \neq \left(\sum_{i=1}^{n} x_i \right)^2.$$

To verify this, observe that

$$\sum_{i=1}^{n} x_i^2 = x_1^2 + x_2^2 + \cdots + x_n^2$$

while

$$\left(\sum_{i=1}^{n} x_i \right)^2 = (x_1 + x_2 + \cdots + x_n)^2.$$

███████   ***EXERCISES***

1. Evaluate $\sum_{i=1}^{5} (i^2 + 2i)$.

2. Evaluate $\sum_{x=0}^{2} (x^3 + 2x)$.

3. Using the following set of measurements, evaluate

a. $\sum_{i=1}^{13} x_i$

b. $\sum_{i=1}^{13} (2x_i + 5)$

c. $\sum_{i=1}^{6} (x_i - 5)^2$

i	1	2	3	4	5	6	7	8	9	10	11	12	13
x_i	3	12	10	−6	0	11	2	−9	−5	8	−7	4	−5

C H A P T E R *4*

PROBABILITY

INTRODUCTION

Probability theory is an integral part of all statistics, and in particular it is essential to the theory of statistical inference. Statistical inference provides the decision maker—perhaps a businessperson or an economist—with a body of methods that aid in decision making under uncertainty. The uncertainty arises because, in real-life situations, we rarely have perfect information regarding various inputs to a decision. Whether our uncertainty relates to the future demand for our product, the future level of interest rates, the possibility of a labor strike, or the proportion of defective widgets in the next production run, probability theory can be used to measure the degree of uncertainty involved. Probability theory allows us to go beyond ignoring uncertainty or considering it in a haphazard fashion, by giving us a foundation for dealing with uncertainty in a consistent, rational manner.

ASSIGNING PROBABILITIES TO EVENTS

RANDOM EXPERIMENT

A logical development of probability begins with considering a random experiment, since this process generates the uncertain outcomes to which we will assign probabilities. Random experiments are of interest because they provide the raw data for statistical analysis.

> **Random Experiment**
>
> A **random experiment** is a process or course of action that results in one of a number of possible outcomes. The outcome that occurs cannot be predicted with certainty.

Following is a list of some random experiments together with their possible outcomes:

1. Experiment: Flip a coin.
   Outcomes: shows heads, shows tails

2. Experiment: Roll a die.
   Outcomes: 1, 2, 3, 4, 5, 6

3. Experiment: Roll a die.
   Outcomes: even number, odd number

4. Experiment: Observe the unit sales of a product for one day.
   Outcomes: 0, 1, 2, 3, . . .

5. Experiment: Solicit a consumer's preference between product A and product B.
   Outcomes: prefer A, prefer B, indifferent

6. Experiment: Observe change in IBM share price over one week.
   Outcomes: increase, decrease, no change

An important feature of a random experiment is that the actual outcome cannot be determined in advance. That is, the outcome of a random experiment may change if the experiment is repeated. The best we can do is talk about the probability that a particular outcome will occur.

To determine, in advance of an experiment, the probabilities that various outcomes will occur, we first have to know what outcomes are possible. The first step in finding the probabilities, then, is to list the possible outcomes, as we did for the foregoing six examples of random experiments. For any such listing to suit our needs, of course, the listed outcomes must be **exhaustive;** that is, each trial of the random experiment must result in some outcome on the list. Furthermore, the listed outcomes must be **mutually exclusive;** that is, no two outcomes on the list can both occur on any one trial of the experiment. Such a listing of the possible outcomes is called a **sample space,** denoted S.

> **Sample Space**
>
> A **sample space** of a random experiment is a list of all possible outcomes of the experiment. The outcomes listed must be mutually exclusive and exhaustive.

Stated another way, the set of possible outcomes constituting a sample space must be defined in such a way that each trial of the experiment results in exactly one outcome in the sample space. For each of the foregoing six examples of random experiments, the accompanying list of possible outcomes is a sample space for that experiment.

The individual outcomes in a sample space are called **simple events.** In assigning probabilities, you should *define simple events in such a way that they cannot be broken down, or decomposed, into two or more constituent outcomes.* For example, in the foregoing die-tossing experiment, the outcome "an even number is observed" should not be used as a simple event in a sample space, since it can be further decomposed into three outcomes: 2, 4, and 6. An outcome such as "an even number is observed," which comprises a collection of simple events, is called an **event.**

> **Event**
>
> An **event** is any collection of one or more simple events.

Events are denoted by capital letters and may be defined either in words or by listing their component simple events. For example, the event "an even number is observed" may be described alternatively as $A = \{2, 4, 6\}$, where $\{\ \}$ is read "the set consisting of." It is conventional, when using letters to list the simple events that form a sample space, to use E_i to denote the ith simple event in the list.

Ultimately, we want to find the probability that an event A will occur, which is denoted $P(A)$. You undoubtedly have some idea of what is meant by the word *probability,* but now let's look more closely at its meaning.

THREE INTERPRETATIONS OF PROBABILITY

Beginning students of this subject are usually disconcerted when they learn that *probability* has no precise definition. Any attempt to define it leads you around a circular series of statements consisting of such synonymous terms as *likelihood, chance,* and *odds.* There are, however, three distinct interpretations of probability that offer three approaches to determining the probability that a particular outcome will occur.

The **classical approach** attempts to deduce the probability of an outcome logically from the symmetric nature of the experiment. If a perfectly balanced coin is flipped, for example, it is logical to expect that the outcome heads and the outcome tails are equally likely. Hence we assert that the probability of observing an occurrence of heads is 1/2. More generally, if an experiment has n possible outcomes, each of which is equally likely, the probability of any particular outcome's occurring is $1/n$. The classical approach can often be used effectively in games of chance. Our development of probability frequently uses examples from this area to illustrate a point, since these examples are easy to relate to. More practical situations, however, do not lend themselves to the classical, deductive approach. A businessperson will usually use either the relative frequency approach or the subjective approach.

The **relative frequency approach** expresses an outcome's probability as its long-run relative frequency of occurrence. Suppose that a random experiment is repeated n times, where n is a large number. If x represents the number of times a particular outcome occurred in those n trials, the proportion x/n provides an estimate of the probability that that particular outcome will occur. For example, if 600 out of the last 1,000 customers entering our store have made a purchase, the probability that any given customer entering our store will make a purchase is approximately .6. The larger n is, the better will be the estimate of the desired probability, which may be thought of as the limiting value of x/n as n becomes infinitely large. Using the relative frequency approach, then, means determining empirically the probability that a particular outcome will occur.

In many practical situations, the experimental outcomes are not equally likely, and there is no history of repetitions of the experiment. This might be the case, for example, if you wished to estimate the probability of striking oil at a new offshore drilling site, or the likelihood of your firm's sales' reaching $1 million this year. In such situations, we resort to the **subjective approach,** under which the probability assigned to an outcome simply reflects the degree to which we believe that the outcome will occur. The probability assigned to a particular outcome thus reflects a personal evaluation of the situation and may be based simply on intuition.

In many cases, however, a businessperson's intuition or subjective evaluation has probably been influenced by outcomes in similar situations, so the relative frequency approach often plays a role in the formation of the subjective probabilities. Consider, for example, a producer about to launch a new Broadway musical. The producer's subjective estimate of the probability that the show will return a profit to investors will be based on several factors, such as the reputation of the musical's principals, the quality of other Broadway shows currently running, and the state of the economy; but the producer will also be mindful of the fact that only about 25% of all Broadway musicals are profitable—a fact based on the relative frequency approach.

ASSIGNING PROBABILITIES

Having reviewed much of the necessary terminology, we now turn to the matter of assigning probabilities to outcomes and events. To each simple event E_i in a sample space, we wish to attach a number $P(E_i)$—called the *probability* of E_i—representing the likelihood that that particular outcome will occur. Whichever of the three ways of assigning probabilities (classical, relative frequency, or subjective) is used, the probabilities assigned to simple events must satisfy the two conditions specified in the accompanying box. Keep in mind, too, that the simple events E_i that form a sample space must be mutually exclusive and exhaustive.

Requirement of Probabilities

Given a sample space $S = \{E_1, E_2, \ldots, E_n\}$, the probabilities assigned to the simple events E_i must satisfy **two basic requirements:**

(i) $0 \leq P(E_i) \leq 1$ for each i.

(ii) $\sum_{i=1}^{n} P(E_i) = 1$.

Suppose for a moment that probabilities have been assigned to all of the simple events. We still need a method for finding the probabilities of an event that is not a simple one. Recall that an event A is just a collection of simple events; therefore, its probability can be determined in the manner shown in the following box.

Probability of an Event

The probability of an event A is equal to the sum of the probabilities assigned to the simple events contained in A.

It follows from the two basic requirements that the probability of an event that is certain to occur is 1, since such an event must contain all of the simple events in the sample space and since the sum of all simple event probabilities must be 1. On the other hand, the probability of an event that cannot possibly occur is 0.

The two basic requirements tell us nothing about how to assign probabilities; they simply state conditions that must be met by probabilities once they have been assigned. In practice, a business manager or economist will usually resort to either the relative frequency approach or the subjective approach in assigning probabilities to events. For example, a promoter choosing a week during which to hold a two-day, outdoor rock concert might consult meteorological records. If a particular week has been rain-free for 35 of the past 50 years, then $35/50 = .7$ would be a relative frequency estimate of the probability of that week's being rain-free this year. In many decision-making situations, however, a history of comparable circumstances is not available, and a businessperson must rely on an educated guess (that is, on the subjective approach). Such is the case with a bank manager who must estimate the probability of loan default by a country whose repayment ability has been impaired by declining oil prices.

Nevertheless, the examples that follow illustrate the assignment of probabilities to events under the classical approach. Not only will this be helpful in situations that do call for the classical approach, it will help clarify basic principles underlying the formulation of a sample space and the assignment of probabilities under any approach.

Before taking up these examples, however, let's look at how to combine events to form new ones. In arithmetic, new numbers can be created from existing ones by means of operations such as addition and multiplication. Similarly, in probability, new events can be created from events already defined by means of operations called *union, intersection,* and *complementation.*

Union

The **union** of any two events A and B, denoted $A \cup B$, is the event consisting of all simple events in A or in B or in both.

Thus, the event $A \cup B$ occurs if A occurs, if B occurs, or if both occur. The key word here is *or.*

Intersection

The **intersection** of any two events A and B, denoted $A \cap B$, is the event consisting of all simple events in both A and B.

Thus, the event $A \cap B$ occurs only if both event A and event B occur together. The key word here is *and.* The event $A \cap B$ is sometimes called the **joint event.**

> **Complement**
>
> The **complement** of any event A, denoted $\bar{A}$, is the set of all simple events in the sample space S that do not belong to A.

Thus, $\bar{A}$ denotes the event "A does not occur."

We'll frequently refer to the probability of occurrence of the union, intersection, or complement of events. The notation for these probabilities is as follows:

$$P(A \cup B) = P(A \text{ **or** } B \text{ **or** both occur})$$
$$P(A \cap B) = P(A \text{ **and** } B \text{ both occur})$$
$$P(\bar{A}) = P(A \text{ does not occur})$$

EXAMPLE 4.1

The number of spots turning up when a six-sided die is tossed is observed. Consider the following events:

    A: The number observed is 3, 4, or 5.

    B: The number observed is at least 4.

    C: The number 2 turns up.

  a. Define a sample space for this random experiment, and assign probabilities to the simple events.

  b. Find $P(A)$.

  c. Find $P(A \cup B)$.

  d. Find $P(A \cap B)$.

  e. Find $P(\bar{A})$.

  f. Are events B and C mutually exclusive?

FIGURE 4.1
VENN DIAGRAM FOR EXAMPLE 4.1

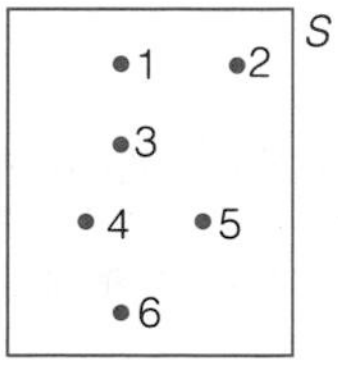

Solution

  a. A sample space is $S = \{1, 2, 3, 4, 5, 6\}$. Since each of the six simple events is equally likely to occur,

$$P(1) = P(2) = P(3) = P(4) = P(5) = P(6) = 1/6.$$

A useful geometrical representation of this sample space, called a **Venn diagram,** is presented in Figure 4.1. In a Venn diagram, the entire sample space S is represented by a rectangle; points inside the rectangle represent the individual outcomes, or simple events, in S. For this reason, the simple events constituting a sample space are sometimes referred to as **sample points.**

  b. The event $A = \{3, 4, 5\}$ is represented in a Venn diagram by a closed region containing the simple events that belong to A, as shown in Figure 4.2. Since the

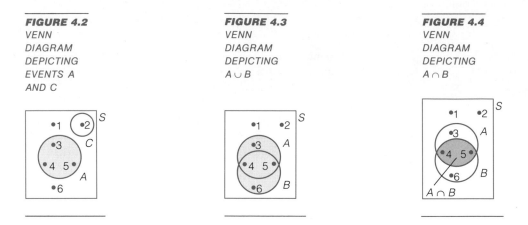

FIGURE 4.2
VENN
DIAGRAM
DEPICTING
EVENTS A
AND C

FIGURE 4.3
VENN
DIAGRAM
DEPICTING
$A \cup B$

FIGURE 4.4
VENN
DIAGRAM
DEPICTING
$A \cap B$

probability of an event A is equal to the sum of the probabilities assigned to the simple events contained in A,

$$P(A) = P(3) + P(4) + P(5)$$
$$= \frac{1}{6} + \frac{1}{6} + \frac{1}{6} = \frac{3}{6}.$$

c. Since $A = \{3, 4, 5\}$ and $B = \{4, 5, 6\}$, either A or B occurs if the number observed is 3, 4, 5, or 6. That is, $A \cup B = \{3, 4, 5, 6\}$, which is depicted by the shaded area in Figure 4.3. Therefore,

$$P(A \cup B) = P(3) + P(4) + P(5) + P(6) = \frac{4}{6}.$$

d. Both A and B occur if the number observed is 4 or 5, so $A \cap B = \{4, 5\}$. Therefore,

$$P(A \cap B) = P(4) + P(5) = \frac{2}{6}.$$

The event $A \cap B$ is depicted by the shaded area in Figure 4.4.

e. The complement of event A is $\bar{A} = \{1, 2, 6\}$. Therefore,

$$P(\bar{A}) = P(1) + P(2) + P(6) = \frac{3}{6}.$$

The three simple events in $\bar{A}$ are represented in Figure 4.2 by the points lying outside the region describing event A.

f. Two events B and C are mutually exclusive if the occurrence of one precludes the occurence of the other—that is, if $B \cap C$ contains no simple events. The events B and C defined in this example are mutually exclusive because they cannot both occur. If the number observed is 2, it is not 4 or more.

> **EXAMPLE 4.2**

An investor who has $3,000 invested in each of four stocks must sell two to help finance his daughter's education. Since he feels that all four stocks are of comparable quality and have the same likelihood of appreciating in price over the coming year, he simply chooses at random the two stocks to be retained and sells the other two. Suppose that, one year later, two of the original four stocks have increased in value and two have decreased.

    a. Find the probability that both of the retained stocks have increased in value.

    b. Find the probability that at least one of the retained stocks has increased in value.

Solution.   Let I_1 and I_2 represent the two stocks that increased in value, and let D_1 and D_2 represent the two stocks that decreased in value. Since the random experiment consists of choosing two stocks from these four, a sample space for the experiment is

$$S = \{I_1I_2, I_1D_1, I_1D_2, I_2D_1, I_2D_2, D_1D_2\},$$

where each simple event represents a possible pair of retained stocks. Each pair of stocks had the same chance of being selected, so the probability that any particular one of the six pairs of stocks was retained is 1/6.

    a. Let A be the event in which both of the retained stocks increased in value. Then $A = \{I_1I_2\}$ and $P(A) = 1/6$.

    b. Let B be the event in which at least one of the retained stocks increased in value. Then the event B consists of all simple events for which either I_1 or I_2 is retained. That is, $B = \{I_1I_2, I_1D_1, I_1D_2, I_2D_1, I_2D_2\}$. Since the probability of an event is the sum of the probabilities of the simple events contained in that event, $P(B) = 5/6$.

> **EXAMPLE 4.3**

Keep Kool Inc. manufactures window air conditioners in both a deluxe model and a standard model. An auditor engaged in a compliance audit of the firm is validating the sales account for April. She has collected 200 invoices for the month, some of which were sent to wholesalers and the remainder to retailers. Of the 140 retail invoices, 28 are for the standard model. Of the wholesale invoices, 24 are for the standard model. If the auditor selects one invoice at random, find the following probabilities:

    a. The invoice selected is for the deluxe model.

    b. The invoice selected is a wholesale invoice for the deluxe model.

    c. The invoice selected is either a wholesale invoice or an invoice for the standard model.

Solution.   The sample space S here consists of the 200 invoices. Whenever the simple events can be classified according to two relevant characteristics—in this case,

TABLE 4.1   CLASSIFICATION OF INVOICES

	Wholesale W	Retail $\bar{W}$	Total
Deluxe D	36	112	148
Standard $\bar{D}$	(24)	(28)	52
TOTAL	60	(140)	(200)

according to model sold and type of purchaser—it is worthwhile to display the pertinent information in a cross-classification table, such as Table 4.1. The numbers given in this example have been circled in Table 4.1; you should check to confirm that you can fill in the remaining numbers yourself from the given information.

The events of interest are as follows:

W: Wholesale invoice is selected.

$\bar{W}$:   Retail invoice is selected.

D: Invoice for deluxe model is selected.

$\bar{D}$:   Invoice for standard model is selected.

a. Since each invoice has the same chance of being selected, the probability that any particular invoice will be selected is 1/200. Since there are 148 invoices for the deluxe model, event D contains 148 simple events. Summing the probabilities of the simple events in D, we find that the probability that the invoice selected was for the deluxe model is

$$P(D) = \frac{148}{200} = .74.$$

b. Since there are 36 wholesale invoices for the deluxe model, the event $D \cap W$ contains 36 simple events. Hence, the probability that the invoice selected was a wholesale invoice for the deluxe model is

$$P(D \cap W) = \frac{36}{200} = .18.$$

c. The number of invoices that are either wholesale invoices or invoices for the standard model is $36 + 24 + 28 = 88$. Thus, the event $W \cup \bar{D}$ contains 88 simple events. Summing the probabilities of the simple events in $W \cup \bar{D}$, we obtain

$$P(W \cup \bar{D}) = \frac{88}{200} = .44.$$

EXERCISES

LEARNING THE TECHNIQUES

4.1 Explain what is meant by the statement: "The simple events that constitute a sample space are mutually exclusive and exhaustive."

4.2 Express in your own words what is meant by each of the following terms:

a. Random experiment

b. Sample space

c. Simple event

d. Event

4.3 Specify a sample space S for each of the following random experiments, by listing the simple events in S.

a. The results of three flips of a coin are observed.

b. The time required to complete an assembly is recorded to the nearest minute.

c. The marital status of a loan applicant is solicited.

d. Two six-sided dice are tossed, and the sum of the spots turning up is noted.

e. The number of customers served by a restaurant on a particular day is recorded.

f. After 20 shoppers are asked if they are satisfied with parking accessibility, the number of positive responses is recorded.

4.4 A contractor has submitted a bid on each of three separate contracts. Consider the random experiment that consists of observing which of the contracts are won and which are lost.

a. Letting W denote a contract that is won and $\bar{W}$ a contract that is lost, list the simple events in the sample space S.

b. List the simple events in the event "all three contracts are won or all three contracts are lost."

c. Describe in words the event defined by $A = \{W\bar{W}\bar{W}, \bar{W}W\bar{W}, \bar{W}\bar{W}W\}$.

d. Describe in words the event defined by $B = \{WWW, WW\bar{W}, W\bar{W}W, \bar{W}WW\}$.

4.5 A manager must decide which two out of four applicants (Anne, Bill, Cynthia, and David) should receive job offers.

a. What is the random experiment?

b. List the simple events in S.

c. List the simple events in the following events:

   L: Cynthia receives an offer.

   M: Bill doesn't receive an offer.

   N: At least one woman receives an offer.

4.6 The number of spots turning up when a six-sided die is tossed is observed. A sample space for this experiment is $S = \{1, 2, 3, 4, 5, 6\}$. Answer each of the following questions, and use a Venn diagram to depict the situation graphically.

a. What is the union of $A = \{2, 3\}$ and $B = \{2, 6\}$?

b. What is the intersection of $A = \{2, 3, 4, 5\}$ and $B = \{3, 5, 6\}$?

c. What is the complement of $A = \{2, 3, 4, 5\}$?

d. Is either $A = \{3\}$ or $B = \{1, 2\}$ a simple event?

e. Are $A = \{3\}$ and $B = \{1, 2\}$ mutually exclusive events? Explain.

4.7 A sample space for the experiment consisting of flipping a coin twice is $S = \{HH, HT, TH, TT\}$. Consider the following events:

$A = \{HT, TH\}$

$B = \{HH, HT, TH\}$

$C = \{TT\}$.

a. Describe each of the events A, B, and C in words.

b. List the simple events in $A \cup B$, and use a Venn diagram to depict the union graphically.

c. List the simple events in $A \cap B$, and depict the intersection graphically.

d. List the simple event in $\bar{A}$, and depict the complement graphically.

e. Is A, B, or C a simple event?

f. Is there a pair of mutually exclusive events among A, B, and C? Explain.

4.8 During a recent promotion, a bank offered mortgages with terms of one, two, and three years at a reduced interest rate. Customers could also choose between open and closed mortgages. From the file of approved mortgage applications, the manager selects one application and notes both the term of the mortgage and whether it is open or closed. A sample space for this experiment is $\{O1, O2, O3, C1, C2, C3\}$, where, for example, $O2$ represents selection of an open, two-year mortgage. Consider the following events:

$A = \{O1, O2, O3\}$

$B = \{O2, C2\}$

a. Describe each of the events A and B in words.

b. List the simple events in $A \cup B$, and use a Venn diagram to depict the union graphically.

c. List the simple events in $A \cap B$, and depict the intersection graphically.

d. List the simple events in $\bar{B}$, and depict the complement graphically.

e. Are A and B mutually exclusive events? Explain.

4.9   Consider the sample space
$S = \{E_1, E_2, E_3, E_4\}$.

a. Find $P(E_1 \cup E_2 \cup E_3 \cup E_4)$.

b. Find $P(E_4)$, if $P(E_1) = P(E_2) = .1$ and $P(E_3) = .5$.

c. Find $P(E_4)$, if $P(E_1) = P(E_2) = P(E_3) = .2$.

4.10   Consider a sample space $S = \{E_1, E_2, E_3, E_4\}$, where $P(E_1) = .25$, $P(E_2) = .40$, $P(E_3) = .15$, and $P(E_4) = .20$. Calculate the following probabilities by summing the probabilities of the appropriate simple events:

a. $P(E_1 \cup E_2)$

b. $P(\bar{E}_2)$

c. $P(\bar{E}_3)$

d. $P(E_3 \cap E_4)$

4.11   The number of spots turning up when a six-sided die is tossed is observed. List the simple events in each of the following events, and then find the probability of each event occurring.

S: An event in the sample space is observed.
A: A 6 is observed.
B: The number observed is less than 4.
C: An odd number is observed.
D: An even number greater than 2 is observed.

4.12   The result of flipping two fair coins is observed.

a. Define the sample space.

b. Assign probabilities to the simple events.

c. Find the probability of observing one heads and one tails.

d. Find the probability of observing at least one heads.

APPLYING THE TECHNIQUES

4.13   In Exercise 4.5, we considered a manager who was deciding which two of four applicants (Anne, Bill, Cynthia, and David) should receive job offers. Suppose that the manager, having deemed the applicants to be equally qualified, chooses at random the two who will receive job offers.

a. Assign probabilities to the simple events in the sample space.

b. Find the probability that Cynthia will receive an offer.

c. Find the probability that one man and one woman will receive an offer.

d. Find the probability that at least one woman will receive an offer.

Self-Correcting Exercise (See Appendix 4.A for the solution.)

4.14   A store that sells personal computers and related supplies is concerned that it may be over-stocking surge suppressors. The store has tabulated the number of surge suppressors sold weekly for each of the last 80 weeks. The results are summarized in the following table:

Number of Suppressors Sold	Number of Weeks
0	36
1	28
2	12
3	2
4	2

The store intends to use the tabulated data as a basis for forecasting surge suppressor sales in any given week.

a. Define the random experiment of interest to the store.

b. List the simple events in the sample space.

c. Assign probabilities to the simple events.

d. What approach have you used in determining the probabilities in part (c)?

e. Find the probability of selling at least three surge suppressors in any given week.

4.15 The trustee of a company's pension plan has solicited the employee's feelings toward a proposed revision in the plan. A breakdown of the responses is shown in the accompanying table. Suppose that an employee is selected at random, with the relevant events defined as follows:

B: The employee selected is a blue-collar worker.

W: The employee selected is a white-collar worker.

M: The employee selected is a manager.

F: The employee selected favors the revision.

Decision	Blue-collar Workers	White-collar Workers	Managers
For	67	32	11
Against	63	18	9

a. Define a sample space for this experiment.

b. List the simple events belonging to the event F.

c. Find $P(B)$, $P(W)$, $P(M)$, $P(F)$, and $P(\bar{F})$.

d. Find the probability that the employee selected is not a manager.

4.16 Refer to Exercise 4.15. Express each of the following events in words, and find its probability:

a. $B \cup W$

b. $F \cup M$

c. $\bar{F} \cap W$

d. $F \cap \bar{M}$

4.17 Referring to Exercise 4.8, suppose that 300 mortgage applications were approved and that the numbers of mortgages of each type were as shown in the following table. The manager selects one mortgage application at random, and the relevant events are defined as follows:

L: The application selected is for a one-year mortgage.

M: The application selected is for a two-year mortgage.

N: The application selected is for a three-year mortgage.

C: The application selected is for a closed mortgage.

Type of Mortgage	Term of Mortgage (years)		
	1	2	3
Open	32	36	60
Closed	80	48	44

a. Find $P(L)$, $P(M)$, $P(N)$, $P(C)$, and $P(\bar{C})$.

b. Find the probability that the term of the mortgage selected is longer than one year.

4.18 Refer to Exercise 4.17. Express each of the following events in words, and find its probability.

a. $L \cup M$

b. $L \cup C$

c. $M \cap \bar{C}$

d. $\bar{N} \cap C$

4.19 Although the international debt situation no longer captures front-page headlines on a regular basis as it did during the crisis of 1981, the situation continues to pose a serious threat to the banking system. The 1984 debt of various high-debt countries, expressed as a percentage of their gross national product (GNP), is shown in the accompanying table. Suppose that one of these countries is selected at random and its debt percentage is observed. Each country has the same chance of being selected.

Country	1984 Debt as Percentage of GNP
Argentina	65%
Bolivia	138
Brazil	53
Chile	116
Costa Rica	124
Israel	95
Mexico	60
Morocco	94
Turkey	46
Uruguay	67
Venezuela	75

SOURCE: *Finance & Development* (March 1989): 36.

a. Define the random experiment.

b. List the simple events in the sample space.

c. Assign probabilities to the simple events.

d. What approach have you used in determining the probabilities in part (c)?

e. What is the probability that the debt of the country selected is greater than its GNP?

CONDITIONAL PROBABILITY

When finding the probability of an event, we can sometimes make use of partial knowledge about the outcome of the experiment. For example, suppose that we are interested in the probability that the share price of IBM increased today. If we hear on the radio that the Dow Jones Industrial Average rose 20 points today (and no individual stock prices are given), we can expect that occurrence to have a bearing on the probability that the price of an IBM share has gone up. In light of the new information, we may wish to find the *conditional probability* that the price of IBM increased, given that the DJIA rose 20 points.

For an illustration of the notion of conditional probability, consider once again Example 4.3, involving the audit of Keep Kool Inc. Suppose that we are told that the invoice selected by the auditor is a wholesale invoice (W). We may then determine the probability that this invoice is for the deluxe model (D), making use of our knowledge that it is a wholesale invoice. In other words, we are seeking the **conditional probability** that D will occur, given that W has occurred: this is written $P(D \mid W)$. (The vertical stroke $\mid$ is read "given that"; it is followed by the event that has occurred.) In attempting to find this conditional probability, we first note that knowing the information that a wholesale invoice was selected restricts our inquiry to the first column of Table 4.1. That is, the new information has reduced the size of the sample space to 60 possible simple events. Of these 60 simple events in the **reduced sample space,** 36 belong to event D. Hence the desired conditional probability is

$$P(D \mid W) = \frac{36}{60} = .6,$$

which differs from the (**unconditional**) probability $P(D) = .74$.

We now present a slightly different but equivalent way of calculating $P(D \mid W)$. The information displayed in Table 4.1 can be expressed alternatively as probabilities, by dividing the number in each category by the total of 200, as shown in Table 4.2.

TABLE 4.2   *PROBABILITIES FOR INVOICE CLASSIFICATIONS*

Model	Wholesale W	Retail $\bar{W}$	Total
Deluxe D	.18	.56	.74
Standard $\bar{D}$	.12	.14	.26
TOTAL	.30	.70	1.00

The four probabilities in the interior of Table 4.2 are referred to as **joint probabilities,** since they express the likelihood of the occurrence of joint events. For example, .18 is the probability that the joint event $(D \cap W)$ will occur. The four probabilities .30, .70, .74, and .26, which appear at the margin of the table, are called **marginal probabilities.** They are, respectively, the marginal probabilities that $W, \bar{W}, D,$ and $\bar{D}$ will occur. Marginal probabilities are simply unconditional probabilities.

Computing the conditional probability $P(D \,|\, W)$ as the ratio of two probabilities now follows from our previous calculation of $P(D \,|\, W)$:

$$P(D \,|\, W) = \frac{36}{60} = \frac{36/200}{60/200}$$

$$= \frac{.18}{.30} = \frac{P(D \cap W)}{P(W)}.$$

Similarly, we can compute the conditional probability that the invoice selected is to a wholesaler, given that it is for a deluxe model:

$$P(W \,|\, D) = \frac{P(D \cap W)}{P(D)} = \frac{.18}{.74}.$$

Having worked through the calculation of a particular conditional probability, we now present the general formula for a conditional probability.

Conditional Probability

Let A and B be two events such that $P(B) > 0$. The **conditional probability** that A occurs, given that B has occurred, is

$$P(A \,|\, B) = \frac{P(A \cap B)}{P(B)}.$$

In the preceding example, we saw that $P(D) = .74$ and $P(D \,|\, W) = .6$, so $P(D) \neq P(D \,|\, W)$. That is, the fact that event W occurred changes the probability that D will occur. Such events D and W are called **dependent** events. On the other hand, if the occurrence of one event does not change the probability of occurrence of the other event, the two events are said to be **independent.**

Independent and Dependent Events

Two events A and B are said to be **independent** if

$P(A\,|\,B) = P(A)$

or

$P(B\,|\,A) = P(B).$

Otherwise, the events are **dependent.**

If one equality in the preceding definition holds, so does the other. The concept of independence is illustrated in the following example.

EXAMPLE 4.4

A group of female managers working for an insurance company has lodged a complaint with the personnel department. While the women agree that the company has increased the number of female managers, they assert that women tend to remain in lower-level management positions when promotions are handed out. They have supported their argument by noting that, over the past 3 years, only 8 of the 54 promotions awarded went to women. The personnel department has responded by claiming that these numbers are misleading on two counts: first, there are far fewer female managers than male managers; second, many of the female managers have been hired during the past year, and employees are virtually never promoted during their first year at the managerial level. The personnel department has compiled the data shown in Table 4.3, in which managers who have been employed for at least one year are classified according to gender and to promotion record. The department claims that the decision to promote a manager (or not) is independent of the manager's gender. Would you agree?

Solution.   The events of interest are as follows:

M: A manager is male.

$\bar{M}$:   A manager is female.

TABLE 4.3   CLASSIFICATION OF MANAGERS

Manager	Promoted	Not Promoted	Total
Male	46	184	230
Female	8	32	40
TOTAL	54	216	270

A: A manager is promoted.

$\bar{A}$:   A manager is not promoted.

In order to show that the decision about whether or not to promote a manager is independent of the manager's gender, we must verify that

$$P(A \mid M) = P(A).$$

If this equality holds, the probability that a man is promoted is no different from the probability that any manager is promoted. Given no information other than the data in Table 4.3, the probability that a manager is promoted is

$$P(A) = \frac{54}{270} = .20.$$

If we now consider only male managers, we restrict our attention to the first row of Table 4.3. Given that a manager is a male, the probability that he is promoted is

$$P(A \mid M) = \frac{46}{230} = .20.$$

Note the distinction between this conditional probability and the joint probability that a manager is both male and promoted, which is $(P(A \cap M) = 46/270 = .17$. In any case, we have verified that $P(A) = P(A \mid M)$, so the events A and M are independent. From the data in Table 4.3, we must conclude that there is no discrimination in awarding promotions.

As indicated in the definition of independent events, an alternative way of showing that A and M are independent events is to verify that $P(M \mid A) = P(M)$. The probability that a manager is male is $P(M) = 230/270 = 46/54$, which equals $P(M \mid A)$, the probability that a manager who is promoted is male. Thus, we again conclude that events A and M are independent.

Before concluding this section, we draw your attention to a common misconception. Students often think that independent events and mutually exclusive events are the same thing. They are not. For example, events A and M in the preceding example are independent events, but they are not mutually exclusive, since the event $A \cap M$ contains 46 simple events. In fact, it can be shown that *any two independent events A and B that occur with nonzero probabilities cannot be mutually exclusive.* For if A and B were mutually exclusive, we would have $P(A \cap B) = 0$ and $P(A \mid B) = 0$; but since A occurs with nonzero probability, $P(A) \neq P(A \mid B)$, so A and B cannot be independent events.

EXERCISES

LEARNING THE TECHNIQUES

4.20   Consider a sample space $S = \{E_1, E_2, E_3, E_4\}$, where $P(E_1) = .1$, $P(E_2) = .2$, $P(E_3) = .3$, and $P(E_4) = .4$. Define the events:

$A = \{E_1, E_2, E_3\}$

$B = \{E_2, E_3, E_4\}$

$C = \{E_3, E_4\}$.

Calculate the following probabilities:

a. $P(A|B)$ c. $P(A|C)$ e. $P(B|C)$

b. $P(B|A)$ d. $P(C|A)$ f. $P(C|B)$

4.21 Consider a sample space $S = \{E_1, E_2, E_3, E_4\}$, where $P\{E_1\} = .1$, $P(E_2) = .2$, $P(E_3) = .3$, and $P(E_4) = .4$. Define the events:

$A = \{E_1, E_2, E_3\}$

$B = \{E_2, E_3, E_4\}$

$C = \{E_3, E_4\}$.

Calculate the following probabilities:

a. $P(A|B)$

b. $P(B|A)$

c. $P(A|C)$

d. $P(C|A)$

4.22 Consider a sample space $S = \{E_1, E_2, E_3, E_4\}$, where $P(E_1) = P(E_4) = .3$ and $P(E_2) = P(E_3) = .2$. Define the events:

$A = \{E_1, E_2\}$

$B = \{E_2, E_3\}$

$C = \{E_3, E_4\}$.

Which of the following pairs of events are independent? Explain.

a. A and B

b. B and C

c. A and C

4.23 Consider a sample space $S = \{E_1, E_2, E_3, E_4\}$, where $P(E_1) = P(E_4) = .4$ and $P(E_2) = P(E_3) = .1$. Define the events:

$A = \{E_3, E_4\}$

$B = \{E_2, E_3\}$

$C = \{E_1, E_3\}$

Which of the following pairs of events are independent? Explain.

a. A and B

b. B and C

c. A and C

Self-Correcting Exercise (See Appendix 4.A for the solution.)

4.24 An ordinary deck of playing cards has 13 cards of each suit. Suppose that a card is selected at random from the deck.

a. What is the probability that the card selected is an ace?

b. Given that the card selected is a spade, what is the probability that the card is an ace?

c. Are "an ace is selected" and "a spade is selected" independent events?

4.25 Suppose that A and B are two mutually exclusive events. Do A and B represent independent events? Explain.

APPLYING THE TECHNIQUES

4.26 Of a company's employees, 30% are women and 6% are married women. Suppose that an employee is selected at random. If the employee selected is a woman, what is the probability that she is married?

4.27 A firm classifies its customers' accounts in two ways: according to the balance outstanding, and according to whether or not the account is overdue. The accompanying table gives the proportion of accounts falling into various categories. One account is selected at random.

Account Balance	Overdue	Not Overdue
Under $100	.08	.42
$100–$500	.08	.22
Over $500	.04	.16

a. If the account selected is overdue, what is the probability that its balance is under $100?

b. If the balance of the account selected is over $500, what is the probability that it is overdue?

c. If the balance of the account selected is $500 or less, what is the probability that it is overdue?

4.28 A department store manager wishes to investigate whether the method of payment chosen by customers is related to the size of their purchases. The manager has cross-classified a sample of 250 customer purchases, as shown in the following table. One of these 250 customers is selected at random.

Size of Purchase	Method of Payment	
	Cash	Credit Card
Under $20	51	31
$20 or more	65	103

a. What is the probability that the customer selected paid by credit card?

b. What is the probability that the customer selected made a purchase of under $20?

c. Are the events "payment by cash" and "purchase of under $20" mutually exclusive? Explain.

d. Are the events "payment by cash" and "purchase of under $20" independent? Explain.

4.29 A personnel manager has cross-classified the 400 employees of a firm according to their record of absenteeism last year and according to whether or not they were smokers, as shown in the accompanying table. One of these employees is selected at random.

Number of Days Absent	Smoker	Nonsmoker
Less than 10	34	260
10 or more	78	28

a. What is the probability that the employee selected was a nonsmoker?

b. What is the probability that the employee selected was absent for 10 or more days?

c. Are the events "nonsmoker" and "absent less than 10 days" mutually exclusive? Explain.

d. Determine whether an employee's being absent for 10 or more days last year was independent of the employee's being a smoker.

4.30 Refer to Exercise 4.14. Find the probability that the store sells exactly two surge suppressors in a week, given that is sells at least one that week.

4.31 Refer to Exercise 4.15.

a. Determine whether F and M are independent or dependent events. Explain.

b. Repeat part (a) for events F and B.

4.32 Insurance companies rely heavily on probability theory when computing the premiums to be charged for various life insurance and annuity products. Probabilities are often computed on the basis of life tables like the accompanying one, which tabulates the average number of American males per 100,000 who will die during various age intervals. For example, out of 100,000 male babies born alive, 1,527 will die before their first birthday and 29,721 will live to the age of 80. Answer the following questions based on this life table.

a. What is the probability that a newborn male will reach the age of 50? The age of 70?

b. What is the probability that an American male will reach the age of 70, given that he has just turned 50?

c. What is the probability that an American male will reach the age of 70, given that he has just turned 60?

NUMBER OF DEATHS AT VARIOUS AGES OUT OF 100,000 AMERICAN MALES BORN ALIVE

Age Interval*	Number of Deaths
0–1	1,527
1–10	495
10–20	927
20–30	1,901
30–40	2,105
40–50	4,502
50–60	10,330
60–70	19,954
70–80	28,538
80 and over	29,721
TOTAL	100,000

* Interval contains all ages from lower limit up to (but not including) upper limit.

SOURCE: *Life Tables, Vital Statistics of the United States* (1978), U.S. Department of Health and Human Services.

PROBABILITY RULES AND TREES

Once some of the simpler probabilities of experimental outcomes and events have been determined, we may use various rules of probability to compute the probabilities of more complex, related events. Consider, for example, an aerospace company that has submitted bids on two separate federal defense contracts, A and B. Suppose that the company has estimated $P(A)$ and $P(B)$, the probabilities of winning each of the contracts, as well as $P(A\,|\,B)$, the probability of winning contract A given that it wins contract B. Using the rules of probability, the company can then readily calculate various related probabilities such as $P(\bar{A})$, the probability of failing to win contract A; $P(A \cap B)$, the probability of winning both contracts; and $P(A \cup B)$, the probability of winning at least one of the two contracts.

COMPLEMENT RULE

The first rule of probability follows easily from the basic requirement that the sum of the probabilities assigned to the simple events in a sample space must be one. Given any event A and its complement $\bar{A}$, each simple event must belong to either A or $\bar{A}$. We therefore must have

$$P(A) + P(\bar{A}) = 1.$$

The complement rule is obtained by subtracting $P(\bar{A})$ from each side of the equality.

> **Complement Rule**
>
> $$P(A) = 1 - P(\bar{A})$$
>
> for any event A.

Despite the simplicity of this rule, it can be very useful. The task of finding the probability that an event will not occur and then subtracting this probability from 1 is often easier than the task of directly computing the probability that it will occur.

EXAMPLE 4.5

Suppose that we intend to flip a coin until heads comes up for the first time; and suppose further that we wish to determine the probability that at least two flips will be required. A possible sample space for this experiment is $S = \{1, 2, 3, 4, \ldots\}$, where each integer indicates a possible number of flips required. If A represents the event that at least two flips are required, then $A = \{2, 3, 4, \ldots\}$. A direct approach to finding $P(A)$ would entail calculating and summing the probabilities $P(2)$, $P(3)$, $P(4)$, ... A simpler approach, however, is to recognize that the probability that event A will not occur is the probability that heads will come up the first flip:

$$P(\bar{A}) = P(1) = 1/2.$$

Therefore, the probability that at least two flips will be required until heads first appears is

$$P(A) = 1 - P(\bar{A}) = 1/2.$$

ADDITION RULE

The second rule of probability enables us to find the probability of the union of two events from the probabilities of other events.

> **Addition Rule**
>
> $$P(A \cup B) = P(A) + P(B) - P(A \cap B)$$
>
> where A and B are any two events.

If A and B are mutually exclusive, we have $P(A \cap B) = 0$, and the addition rule simplifies to $P(A \cup B) = P(A) + P(B)$.

FIGURE 4.5
ENTIRE
SHADED
AREA IS
$A \cup B$

> **Addition Rule for Mutually Exclusive Events**
>
> $$P(A \cup B) = P(A) + P(B)$$
>
> for any two mutually exclusive events A and B.

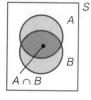

In general, however, we must subtract the joint probability $P(A \cap B)$, in order to avoid double-counting a simple event that belongs to both A and B. This is apparent from the Venn diagram in Figure 4.5, in which $A \cup B$ is represented by the entire shaded area. When finding the probability $P(A \cup B)$ by summing $P(A)$ and $P(B)$, we must subtract $P(A \cap B)$ to avoid double-counting the probability of event $A \cap B$, which belongs to both A and B.

MULTIPLICATION RULE

The third rule of probability, which is used to find the probability of a joint event, is simply a rearrangement of the definition of conditional probability. Since

$$P(A \mid B) = \frac{P(A \cap B)}{P(B)}$$

and

$$P(B \mid A) = \frac{P(A \cap B)}{P(A)},$$

we obtain the following rule for computing the joint probability $P(A \cap B)$.

Multiplication Rule

$$P(A \cap B) = P(A) \cdot P(B \mid A)$$
$$= P(B) \cdot P(A \mid B)$$

for any two events A and B.

Notice that the two expressions for using the multiplication rule to find a joint probability are equivalent. Which expression to use in a particular situation depends on the information given.

For the special case in which A and B are independent events, we have $P(B \mid A) = P(B)$, so we can simply write $P(A \cap B) = P(A) \cdot P(B)$.

Multiplication Rule for Independent Events

$$P(A \cap B) = P(A) \cdot P(B)$$

for any two independent events A and B.

EXAMPLE 4.6

A computer software supplier has developed a new record-keeping package for use by hospitals. The company feels that the probability that the new package will show a profit in its first year is .6, unless a competitor introduces a product of comparable quality this year, in which case the probability of a first-year profit drops to .3. The supplier suggests that there is a 50–50 chance that a comparable product will be introduced this year. Define the following events:

A: A competitor introduces a comparable product.

B: The record-keeping package is profitable in its first year.

a. What is the probability that both A and B will occur?

b. What is the probability that either A or B will occur?

Solution. Summarizing the given information, we know that

$$P(A) = .5$$
$$P(B) = .6$$
$$P(B \mid A) = .3.$$

a. Applying the multiplication rule, we conclude that the probability that a competitor will introduce a comparable product and that the first year will be profitable is

$$P(A \cap B) = P(A) \cdot P(B \mid A)$$
$$= (.5)(.3) = .15.$$

b. Notice that $P(A \cup B)$ can be determined only after $P(A \cap B)$ has been calculated. The probability that either a competitor will introduce a comparable product or the record-keeping package will be profitable in its first year is

$$P(A \cup B) = P(A) + P(B) - P(A \cap B)$$
$$= .5 + .6 - .15 = .95.$$

PROBABILITY TREES

Another way of calculating probabilities is to use a probability tree, in which the various possible events of an experiment are represented by lines or branches of the tree. When you want to construct a sample space for an experiment, a probability tree is a useful device for ensuring that you have identified all simple events and for assigning the associated probabilities.

The mechanics of using a probability tree can be illustrated by reference to the random experiment consisting of flipping a coin twice. A sample space for this experiment is

$$S = \{HH, HT, TH, TT\}.$$

where the first letter of each pair denotes the result of the first flip. An alternative representation of S, differing only in the notation used, is

$$S = \{H_1 \cap H_2, H_1 \cap T_2, T_1 \cap H_2, T_1 \cap T_2\}.$$

where the events are defined as follows:

H_1: Heads is observed on the first flip.
H_2: Heads is observed on the second flip.
T_1: Tails is observed on the first flip.
T_2: Tails is observed on the second flip.

A probability tree for this experiment is shown in Figure 4.6.

FIGURE 4.6 *PROBABILITY TREE FOR COIN EXAMPLE*

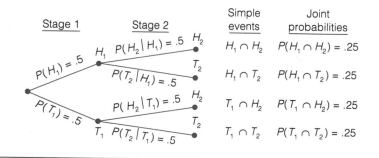

Whenever you can break the process of observing the result of an experiment down into stages, with a different aspect of the result observed at each stage, you can represent the various possible sequences of observations with a probability tree. In the coin example, stage 1 observes the outcome of the first flip, while stage 2 observes the outcome of the second flip. The heavy dots in Figure 4.6 are called **nodes,** and the branches emerging from a particular node represent the alternative outcomes that may occur at that point. The probability attached to each branch is the conditional probability that that branch outcome will occur, given that the outcomes represented by preceding branches have all occurred. For example, the probability attached to the top branch at stage 2 is $P(H_2 | H_1) = .5$—the probability of obtaining a result of heads on the second flip, given that a result of heads was obtained on the first flip. Since the branches emerging from any particular node represent all possible outcomes that may occur at that point, the sum of the probabilities on those branches must equal 1.

The initial (unlabeled) node is called the **origin.** Any path through the tree from the origin to a terminal node corresponds to one possible simple event, the probability of which is the product of the probabilities attached to the branches forming that path. For example, if we follow along the top two branches of the tree, we observe the simple event $H_1 \cap H_2$, which (according to the multiplication rule) has the probability

$$P(H_1 \cap H_2) = P(H_1) \cdot P(H_2 | H_1) = (.5) \cdot (.5) = .25.$$

You may be wondering why we went to all the trouble of using a probability tree to determine that each of the four possible simple events occur with a probability of 1/4, since this may have been obvious to you from the beginning. The main point of this example was to introduce the mechanics of probability trees; the next two examples illustrate the advantages of using probability trees. In Example 4.7, the probability tree helps sort out the given information and clarify what has to be calculated to reach a solution. The benefits of using a probability tree to identify the possible simple events and their associated probabilities should become even more apparent in Example 4.8. If you remain unconvinced, try solving Example 4.8 without the aid of a probability tree.

EXAMPLE 4.7

The proprietor of a men's clothing store has recorded the buying behavior of customers over a long period of time. He has established that the probability that a customer will buy a shirt is about .4. A customer buys a tie 50% of the time when a shirt is purchased, but only 10% of the time when a shirt is not purchased. Find the probability that a customer buys the following:

a. A shirt and a tie

b. A tie

c. A shirt or a tie

d. A tie but not a shirt

Solution.   The random experiment consists of observing, for each customer, whether a shirt or a tie is purchased. The two basic events of interest are therefore:

   R: A customer buys a shirt.

   T: A customer buys a tie.

Summarizing the given information, we have $P(R) = .4$, $P(T \mid R) = .5$, and $P(T \mid \bar{R}) = .1$. Before constructing a probability tree, we should search the given probabilities for an unconditional probability. In this example, we are given the unconditional probability that event R will occur, so event R is considered at the first stage and event T at the second. We can now construct the probability tree for this experiment, as shown in Figure 4.7.

   Collecting the simple events at the end of the tree, we find that a sample space for the experiment is

$$S = \{R \cap T, R \cap \bar{T}, \bar{R} \cap T, \bar{R} \cap \bar{T}\}.$$

Calculating the required probabilities is now quite simple, amounting to little more than reading off the joint (simple event) probabilities from the tree.

a. The probability that a customer buys a shirt and a tie is

   $$P(R \cap T) = .20.$$

b. The probability that a customer buys a tie is

   $$P(T) = P\{R \cap T, \bar{R} \cap T\}$$
   $$= P(R \cap T) + P(\bar{R} \cap T)$$
   $$= .20 + .06 = .26.$$

c. The probability that a customer buys a shirt or a tie is

   $$P(R \cup T) = P\{R \cap T, R \cap \bar{T}, \bar{R} \cap T\}$$
   $$= P(R \cap T) + P(R \cap \bar{T}) + P(\bar{R} \cap T)$$
   $$= .20 + .20 + .06 = .46.$$

FIGURE 4.7   PROBABILITY TREE FOR SHIRTS AND TIES

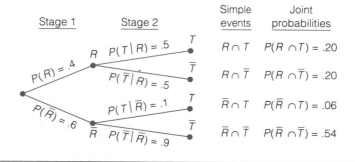

d. The probability that a customer buys a tie but not a shirt is
$$P(\bar{R} \cap T) = .06.$$

EXAMPLE 4.8

Suppose that you have one nickel, two dimes, and one quarter in a box. If you select two coins from the box without looking, what is the probability of your selecting a dime and a quarter?

Solution.   An organized procedure for solving this problem entails first constructing a relevant sample space, and then assigning probabilities to the simple events. As we have already seen, the sample space associated with a random experiment is not unique. One possibility in this case is

$S' = \{$nickel and dime, nickel and quarter, two dimes, dime and quarter$\}$,

where, for example, "nickel and dime" represents the selection of a nickel and a dime, with no consideration given to the order of selection. With this sample space, however, you might be tempted to assign (incorrectly) a probability of 1/4 to each simple event. How can you be sure that the probabilities you assign are correct?

Using a probability tree is an effective method of simplifying the assignment of probabilities. A probability tree essentially presupposes that there is an order in which the observations of outcomes occur, each stage corresponding to one observation. For this example, the process of observing which two coins are selected can be broken down into two stages, as shown in Figure 4.8. (Rather than resorting to subscripts, as we did in the previous example, we have chosen to denote each simple event by a pair of letters, where the first letter of each pair indicates the first coin selected.)

FIGURE 4.8   PROBABILITY TREE FOR SELECTING TWO COINS FROM FOUR

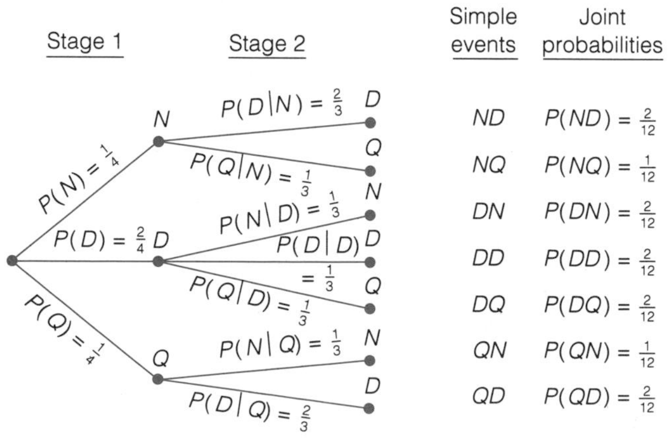

Once the branches are drawn, assigning the corresponding branch probabilities becomes relatively easy. For example, consider the top branch of the second stage. If the first coin selected is a nickel, two dimes and a quarter remain in the box. Thus $P(D \mid N) = 2/3$. We next identify the seven simple events corresponding to the seven terminal nodes, and obtain the sample space

$$S = \{ND, NQ, DN, DD, DQ, QN, QD\}.$$

Finally, we obtain the probability of a simple event by taking the product of the probabilities attached to the branches leading to that simple event. This is simply an application of the multiplication rule. For example,

$$P(ND) = P(N) \cdot P(D \mid N) = (1/4)(2/3) = 2/12.$$

Having constructed the probability tree, we can next determine the probability of selecting a dime and a quarter. Let the event E be the selection of a dime and a quarter; then $E = \{DQ, QD\}$, so

$$P(E) = P(DQ) + P(QD) = 2/12 + 2/12 = 1/3.$$

Before leaving this question, notice that we can now go back and easily assign probabilities to the outcomes in the first sample space, S', that was suggested:

P(nickel and dime) $= 4/12$

P(nickel and quarter) $= 2/12$

P(2 dimes) $= 2/12$

P(dime and quarter) $= 4/12$

EXERCISES

LEARNING THE TECHNIQUES

4.33 If $P(A) = .6$, $P(B) = .5$, and $P(A \cup B) = .9$, find $P(A \cap B)$ and $P(A \mid B)$.

4.34 If $P(A) = .2$, $P(B) = .4$, and $P(A \cup B) = .5$, find $P(A \cap B)$ and $P(B \mid A)$.

4.35 Given that $P(A) = .3$, $P(B) = .6$, and $P(B \mid A) = .4$, find the following probabilities:

a. $P(A \cap B)$

b. $P(A \cup B)$

c. $P(A \mid B)$

4.36 Given that $P(A) = .4$, $P(B) = .5$, and $P(B \mid A) = .8$, find the following probabilities:

a. $P(A \cap B)$

b. $P(A \cup B)$

c. $P(A \mid B)$

4.37 Let A and B be two mutually exclusive events for which $P(A) = .25$ and $P(B) = .6$. Find the following probabilities:

a. $P(A \cap B)$

b. $P(A \cup B)$

c. $P(A \mid B)$

4.38 Let A and B be two independent events for which $P(A) = .25$ and $P(B) = .6$. Find the following probabilities:

a. $P(A \mid B)$ c. $P(A \cap B)$

b. $P(B \mid A)$ d. $P(A \cup B)$

4.39 Let A and B be two mutually exclusive events for which $P(A) = .15$ and $P(B) = .4$. Find the following probabilities:

a. $P(A \cap B)$

b. $P(A \cup B)$

c. $P(B \mid A)$

4.40 Let A and B be two independent events for which $P(A) = .15$ and $P(B) = .4$. Find the following probabilities:

a. $P(A \mid B)$

b. $P(B \mid A)$

c. $P(A \cap B)$

d. $P(A \cup B)$

4.41 Let $P(A) = .6$, $P(B \mid A) = .1$, and $P(B \mid \bar{A}) = .3$.

a. Sketch a properly labeled probability tree to depict this situation.

b. Use the probability tree to find $P(A \cap \bar{B})$ and $P(\bar{B})$.

4.42 Let $P(\bar{A}) = .7$, $P(\bar{B} \mid A) = .8$, and $P(B \mid \bar{A}) = .4$.

a. Sketch a properly labeled probability tree to depict this situation.

b. Use the probability tree to find $P(A \cap B)$ and $P(\bar{B})$.

4.43 Let $P(A) = .3$, $P(B \mid A) = .4$, and $P(B \mid \bar{A}) = .8$.

a. Sketch a properly labeled probability tree to depict this situation.

b. Use the probability tree to find $P(A \cup B)$ and $P(\bar{A} \cap B)$.

4.44 Let $P(\bar{A}) = .4$, $P(\bar{B} \mid A) = .3$, and $P(B \mid \bar{A}) = .6$.

a. Sketch a properly labeled probability tree to depict this situation.

b. Use the probability tree to find $P(A \cup B)$ and $P(\bar{A} \cap B)$.

4.45 A fair coin is flipped three times. Use a probability tree to find the probability of observing:

a. No heads

b. Exactly one heads

c. Exactly two heads

d. At least one tails

APPLYING THE TECHNIQUES

Self-Correcting Exercise (see Appendix 4.A for the solution.)

4.46 An aerospace company has submitted bids on two separate federal government defense contracts, A and B. The company feels that it has a 50% chance of winning contract A and a 40% chance of winning contract B. Furthermore, it believes that winning contract A is independent of winning contract B.

a. What is the probability that the company will win both contracts?

b. What is the probability that the company will win at least one of the two contracts?

4.47 Suppose that the aerospace company in Exercise 4.46 feels that it has a 60% chance of winning contract A and a 30% chance of winning contract B. Given that it wins contract B, the company believes it has an 80% chance of winning contract A.

a. What is the probability that the company will win both contracts?

b. What is the probability that the company will win at least one of the two contracts?

c. If the company wins contract B, what is the probability that it will not win contract A?

4.48 A sporting goods store estimates that 20% of the students at a nearby university ski downhill and 15% ski cross-country. Of those who ski downhill, 40% also ski cross-country.

a. What percentage of these students ski both downhill and cross-country?

b. What percentage of the student do not ski at all?

4.49 A union's executive conducted a survey of its members to determine what the members felt were the important issues to be discussed during upcoming negotiations with management. Results showed that 74% felt that job security was an important issue, while 65% felt that pension benefits were an important issue. Of those who felt that pension benefits were an important issue, 60% also felt that job security was an important issue.

a. What percentage of the members felt that both job security and pension benefits were important?

b. What percentage of the members felt that at least one of these two issues was important?

4.50 Young Presidents' Organization is an international group whose membership is restricted, among other things, to those who have become president or chairman and CEO of a relatively large company before the age of 40. Members must leave the organization upon reaching 50. *Canadian Business* (September 1985) reported that three-quarters of the members are 40 years old or older and 67 percent are under 45. One member of the organization is chosen at random. Define the events:

A: The member chosen is at least 40 years old.
B: The member chosen is under the age of 45.

Express in words, and compute, the following probabilities:

a. $P(\bar{A})$ d. $P(A \cap B)$

b. $P(\bar{B})$ e. $P(A \mid B)$

c. $P(A \cup B)$ f. $P(B \mid A)$

4.51 A certain city has one morning newspaper and one evening newspaper. It is estimated that 20% of the city's households subscribe to the morning paper and 60% subscribe to the evening paper. Of those who subscribe to the morning paper, 80% also subscribe to the evening paper. What proportion of households:

a. Subscribe to both papers?

b. Subscribe to at most one of the papers?

c. Subscribe to neither paper?

4.52 Individuals wishing to pursue a career in investment analysis are often encouraged to obtain the professional designation of Chartered Financial Analyst (CFA). A candidate must pass three exams to obtain this designation and can take only one exam in a given year. The results of the exams held in 1989, reported by the Institute of Chartered Financial Analysis in *The CFA Study Guide (1990)*, are summarized in the accompanying table. One candidate is selected at random from those who took a CFA exam in 1989.

Exam	Number of Candidates Writing	Percentage Who Passed
I	4,149	54%
II	2,484	64%
III	1,431	79%

a. What is the probability that the selected candidate passed?

b. What is the probability that the selected candidate took Exam I and passed?

c. If the selected candidate passed, what is the probability that the candidate took Exam III?

Self-Correcting Exercise (See Appendix 4.A for the solution.)

4.53 An assembler has been supplied with ten electronic components, of which three are defective. If two components are selected at random, what is the probability that neither component is defective?

4.54 Approximately three out of every four Americans who filed a 1986 tax return received a refund. If three individuals are chosen at random from among those who filed a 1986 tax return, find the probabilities of the following events:

a. All three received a refund.

b. None of the three received a refund.

c. Exactly one received a refund.

4.55 A door-to-door saleswoman sells rug shampoo in three tube sizes: small, large, and giant. The probability of finding a person at home is .6. If the saleswoman does find someone at home, the probabilities are .5 that she will make no sale, .2 that she will sell a small tube, .2 that she will sell a large tube, and .1 that she will sell a giant tube. The probability of selling more than one tube of shampoo at a house is 0.

a. Find the probability that, in one call, she will not sell any shampoo.

b. Find the probability that, in one call, she will sell either a large tube or a giant tube.

4.56 To determine who pays for coffee, three students each toss a coin and the odd person pays.

If all coins show heads or all show tails, the students toss again. What is the probability that a decision will be reached in five or fewer tosses?

4.57 Of 20,000 small businesses surveyed, "about 82% said they employed women in some capacity." Of those that employed women, 19.5% employed no female supervisors, 50% employed only one female supervisor, and the remainder employed more than one female supervisor (*Globe and Mail,* October 1985).

a. How many of the businesses surveyed employed no women?

b. What proportion of businesses surveyed employed exactly one female supervisor?

c. What proportion of businesses surveyed employed no female supervisors?

d. Given that a firm employed women, what is the probability that it employed at least one female supervisor?

4.58 All printed circuit boards (PCBs) that are manufactured at a certain plant are inspected for flaws. Experience has shown that 50% of the PCBs produced are flawed in some way. Of the flawed PCBs, 60% are repairable, while the remainder are seriously flawed and must be discarded. A newly manufactured PCB is selected before undergoing inspection. What is the probability that it will not have to be discarded?

4.59 In a forest plantation, it is important that trees grow very straight so that they can be used to produce lumber. A forest products firm estimates that 20% of all trees planted will die before maturity. Of the trees that survive, 90% will grow straight enough to be used to produce lumber. If a newly planted tree is selected at random, what is the probability that it will not be used to produce lumber?

4.60 A manufacturer of biodegradable plastic bags has determined that different lighting conditions lead to different lengths of time required for complete degradation to occur. In a lab study, using several different lighting conditions, it was found that 85% of the bags degraded within 10 days of light exposure. Of the bags that had not degraded after 10 days, 20% also had not degraded after 20 days. If a bag is exposed to a lighting condition chosen at random, what is the probability that the bag will degrade within 20 days?

SUMMARY

Gamblers, businesspeople, and economists frequently find themselves in decision-making situations involving uncertain events. Probability is the basic tool they use to make rational judgements in such situations. The first step in assigning probabilities to uncertain events is to form a sample space—a listing of all the simple events that can result from a random experiment. A probability (number between 0 and 1) is then assigned to each simple event, measuring the likelihood of occurrence of that outcome. The use of a probability tree often facilitates both the formation of a sample space and the assignment of probabilities to its simple events. Probabilities may then be computed for more complex events in accordance with rules of probability dealing with the complement, union, and intersection of events. The notion of conditional probability allows us to express the altered probability that an event will occur when some partial knowledge of the experimental outcome is available.

IMPORTANT TERMS

Random experiment	Event	Conditional probability
Exhaustive	Probability of an event	Independent events
Mutually exclusive	Union of events	Probability tree
Sample space	Intersection of events	
Simple event	Complement of an event	

███████████   **SUMMARY OF FORMULAS**

$$P(A \mid B) = \frac{P(A \cap B)}{P(B)}$$

$$P(A) = 1 - P(\bar{A})$$

$$P(A \cup B) = P(A) + P(B) - P(A \cap B)$$

$$P(A \cap B) = P(A) \cdot P(B \mid A)$$

$$= P(B) \cdot P(A \mid B)$$

███████████   **SUPPLEMENTARY EXERCISES**

4.61 There are three approaches to determining the probability that an outcome will occur: classical, relative frequency, and subjective. Which is appropriate in determining the probability of each of the following events?

a. It will rain tomorrow.

b. A coin toss will result in heads.

c. A Michelin tire will last more than 40,000 miles.

d. When a single card is selected from a well-shuffled deck, it will be a diamond.

e. An automobile will past quality-control inspection.

f. A firm's sales will grow by at least 10% next year.

4.62 The result of three flips of a fair coin is observed. Consider the following events:

A: At least two heads are observed.
B: Exactly one tail is observed.
C: Exactly two tails are observed.

a. Define an appropriate sample space S for this experiment.

b. Assign probabilities to the simple events in S.

c. Find $P(A)$, by summing the probabilities of the simple events in A.

d. Find $P(B)$.

e. Find $P(B \cap C)$.

f. Find $P(A \cap B)$.

g. Find $P(B \mid A)$.

h. Is there a pair of independent events among A, B, and C?

i. Is there a pair of mutually exclusive events among A, B, and C?

4.63 Two six-sided dice are rolled, and the number of spots turning up on each is observed. Find the probability of each of the following:

a. Three spots show on one die, and five spots show on the other.

b. Exactly one die has two spots showing.

c. The sum of the spots showing is 7.

d. The sum of the spots showing is 8.

e. The sum of the spots showing is an even number.

f. The sum of the spots showing is 8, given that the sum is an even number.

4.64 Referring to Exercise 4.63, define the following events:

A: The sum of the spots showing is 2, 3, or 12.
B: The sum of the spots showing is an even number.

Are A and B independent events? Explain.

4.65 Exactly 100 employees of a firm have each purchased one ticket in a lottery, with the drawing to be held at the firm's annual party. Of the 80 men who purchased a ticket, 25 are single. Only 4 of the women who purchased a ticket are single.

a. Find the probability that the lottery winner is married.

b. Find the probability that the lottery winner is a married woman.

c. If the winner is a man, what is the probability that he is married?

4.66 A customer service supervisor regularly conducts a survey of customer satisfaction as part of a management control system. The results of his latest survey show that 5% of those surveyed are not satisfied with the service they receive. While only 30% of those surveyed are in arrears, 80% of the dissatisfied customers are in arrears. If the report on one customer surveyed is selected at random, find the probability that this customer is as follows:

a. In arrears and dissatisfied

b. Either in arrears or dissatisfied, or both

4.67 As input into his pricing policy, the owner of an appliance store is interested in the relationship between the price at which an item is sold (regular or sale price) and the customer's decision about whether or not to purchase an extended warranty. The owner has constructed the accompanying table of probabilities, based on a study of 2,000 sales invoices. Suppose that one sales invoice is selected at random, with the relevent events being defined as follows:

A: Item is purchased at regular price.
B: Item is purchased at sale price.
C: Extended warranty is purchased.
D: Extended warranty is not purchased.

Price	Extended Warranty	
	Purchased	Not Purchased
Regular Price	.21	.57
Sale Price	.14	.08

Express each of the following probabilities in words, and find its value:

a. $P(A)$ f. $P(D\,|\,B)$

b. $P(\bar{A})$ g. $P(B\,|\,D)$

c. $P(C)$ h. $P(C\,|\,D)$

d. $P(C\,|\,A)$ i. $P(A \cup B)$

e. $P(C\,|\,B)$ j. $P(A \cap D)$

4.68 A *Forbes* survey of students attending leading American MBA schools determined that 96% expect a starting salary in excess of $25,000, while 92% expect their starting salary to be under $50,000 (*Forbes,* 3 June 1985). What is the probability that one of these students, selected at random, expects a starting salary between $25,000 and $50,000?

4.69 The director of an insurance company's computing center estimates that the company's computer has a 20% chance of "catching" a computer virus. However, she feels that there is only a 6% chance of the computer's "catching" a virus that will completely disable its operating system. If the company's computer should "catch" a virus, what is the probability that the operating system will be completely disabled?

4.70 It is known that 3% of the tickets in a certain scratch-and-win game are winners, in the sense that the purchaser of such a ticket will receive a prize. If three tickets are purchased at random, what is the probability of each of the following?

a. All three tickets are winners.

b. Exactly one of the tickets is a winner.

c. At least one of the tickets is a winner.

4.71 A financial analyst estimates that a certain mutual fund has a 60% chance of rising in value by more than 15% over the coming year. She also predicts that the stock market in general, as measured by the S&P 500 Index, has only a 20% chance of rising more than 15%. But if the Index does so, she feels that the mutual fund has a 95% chance of rising by more than 15%.

a. Find the probability that both the S&P 500 Index and the mutual fund will rise in value by more than 15%.

b. Find the probability that either the Index or the mutual fund, or both, will rise by more than 15%.

4.72 Because the likelihood of an event's occurring is sometimes expressed in terms of betting odds rather than as a probability, it is useful to be able to convert odds into probabilities, and vice versa. If the odds of an event's occurring are a to b, then the probability that the event will occur is $a/(a + b)$. The probability that the event will not occur is therefore $b/(a + b)$. Find the probability that an event A will occur, if the odds that A will occur are as follows:

a. 4 to 1   b. 3 to 2   c. 3 to 5

4.73 A novelty shop sells coins that come up heads two-thirds of the time. The result of flipping two of these coins is observed.

a. Define a sample space for this experiment.

b. Assign probabilities to the simple events.

c. Find the probability of observing exactly one head.

4.74 A modern version of Russian roulette was invented the other day on a small southern Ontario campus by three students (Able, Baker, and Carter):

Line up six identical cars, two of which have had the master brake cylinder secretly removed by participating sweethearts, near the edge of a cliff. Each player then randomly selects one car and one by one (in alphabetical order) they drive at high speed toward the edge of the cliff. At the cliff, they slam on the brakes in time to stop. The first player over the cliff loses the game and the game stops.

Before they will agree to play the game, however, they want to understand the odds better, so they have posed the following two questions:

a. What is each player's probability of losing?

b. What is the probability that there will be no loser?

If it were your job to advise them, how would you answer each of these probing questions?

4.75 Consider a roulette wheel that is divided into 36 equal segments, numbered from 1 to 36. The wheel has stopped at an even number on each of the last 16 spins. On the next spin of the wheel, would you bet on an even number or an odd number? Explain your answer.

4.76 Bill and Irma are planning to take a two-week vacation in Hawaii, but they can't decide whether to spend one week on each of the islands of Maui and Oahu, two weeks on Maui, or two weeks on Oahu. Agreeing to leave the decision to chance, Bill places two Maui brochures in one envelope, two Oahu brochures in a second envelope, and a brochure from each of the two islands in a third envelope. Irma is to select one envelope, and they will spend two weeks on Maui if it contains two Maui brochures, and so on. After selecting one envelope at random, Irma removes one brochure from the envelope and notes that it is a Maui brochure. What is the probability that the other brochure in the envelope is a Maui brochure? (HINT: Proceed with caution!)

■■■■■■■ **CASE 4.1   LET'S MAKE A DEAL**

A number of years ago there was a popular television game show called "Let's Make a Deal." The host, Monty Hall, would randomly select contestants from the audience and as the title suggests he would make deals for prizes. Contestants would be given relatively modest prizes and then would be offered the opportunity to risk that prize to win better ones.

Suppose that you are a contestant on this show. Monty has just given you a free trip worth $500 to a locale that is of little interest to you. He now offers you a trade: give up the trip in exchange for a gamble. On the stage there are three curtains, A, B and C. Behind one of them is a brand new car worth $20,000. Behind the other two curtains the stage is empty. You decide to gamble and you select Curtain A. In an attempt to make things more interesting Monty then exposes an empty stage by opening Curtain C (he knows that there is nothing behind Curtain C). He then offers you the free trip again if you now quit or if you like, propose another deal. What do you do?

CASE 4.2*   *GAINS FROM MARKET TIMING*

Many investment managers employ a strategy called *market timing,* which involves forecasting the direction of the overall stock market and adjusting one's investment holdings accordingly. A study conducted by Sharpe[†] provides insight into how accurate a manager's forecasts must be in order to make a market-timing strategy worthwhile.

Sharpe considers the case of a manager who, at the beginning of each year, either invests all funds in stocks for the entire year (if a good year is forecast) or places all funds in cash equivalents for the entire year (if a bad year is forecast). A good year is defined as one in which the rate of return on stocks (as represented by the Standard and Poor's Composite Index) is higher than the rate of return on cash equivalents (as represented by U.S. Treasury bills). A bad year is one that is not good. The average annual returns for the period from 1934 to 1972 on stocks and on cash equivalents, both for good years and for bad years, are shown in the accompanying table. Two-thirds of the years from 1934 to 1972 were good years.

a. Suppose that a manager decides to remain fully invested in the stock market at all times rather than employing market timing. What annual rate of return can this manager expect?

b. Suppose that a market timer accurately predicts a good year 80% of the time and accurately predicts a bad year 80% of the time. What is the probability that this manager will predict a good year? What annual rate of return can this manager expect?

c. What is the expected rate of return for a manager who has perfect foresight?

d. Consider a market timer who has no predictive ability whatsoever, but who recognizes that a good year will occur two-thirds of the time. Following Sharpe's description, imagine this manager "throwing a die every year, then predicting a good year if numbers 1 through 4 turn up, and a bad year if number 5 or 6 turns up." What is the probability that this manager will make a correct prediction in any given year? What annual rate of return can this manager expect?

| | **Average Annual Returns** | |
Type of Year	Stocks	Cash Equivalents
Good year	22.99%	2.27%
Bad year	−7.70%	2.68%

---

* Your instructor may wish to postpone this case until expected value has been covered, in Chapter 5.

† William F. Sharpe, "Likely Gains from Market Timing," *Financial Analysts' Journal* 31 (1975): 60–69.

SOLUTIONS TO SELF-CORRECTING EXERCISES

4.14 a. The random experiment consists of observing the number of surge suppressors sold in any given week.

b. $S = \{0, 1, 2, 3, 4\}$

c. $P\{0\} = 36/80$, $P\{1\} = 28/80$, $P\{2\} = 12/80$, $P\{3\} = P\{4\} = 2/80$

d. The relative frequency approach was used.

e. $P\{3, 4\} = P\{3\} + P\{4\} = 2/80 + 2/80 = 4/80 = .05$

4.24 Define the events:

A: An ace is selected.
B: A spade is selected.

a. Since 4 of the 52 cards in the deck are aces,

$$P(A) = \frac{4}{52} = \frac{1}{13}.$$

b. Since there are 13 spades and 1 ace of spades in the deck,

$$P(A\,|\,B) = \frac{P(A \cap B)}{P(B)} = \frac{1/52}{13/52} = \frac{1}{13}.$$

c. Yes, since $P(A) = P(A\,|\,B)$.

4.46 Define the events:

A: The company wins contract A.
B: The company wins contract B.

Since A and B are independent,

$$P(A\,|\,B) = P(A) = .5$$
$$P(B\,|\,A) = P(B) = .4.$$

a. $P(A \cap B) = P(A) \cdot P(B\,|\,A)$
$\qquad\qquad\quad = (.5)(.4)$
$\qquad\qquad\quad = .2$

b. $P(A \cup B) = P(A) + P(B) - P(A \cap B)$
$\qquad\qquad\quad = .5 + .4 - .2$
$\qquad\qquad\quad = .7$

4.53 Refer to Figure 4.A.1 on page 126. Define the events:

D_1: First component selected is defective.
D_2: Second component selected is defective.

The probability that neither component is defective is 42/90, or .47.

FIGURE 4.A.1 PROBABILITY TREE FOR EXERCISE 4.53

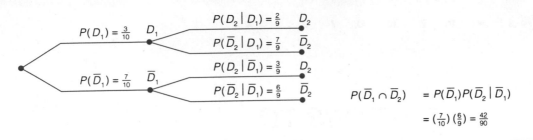

C H A P T E R **5**

PROBABILITY DISTRIBUTIONS

INTRODUCTION

This chapter extends our development of probability by introducing the concept of a random variable, which allows us to summarize the results of an experiment in terms of numerical-valued outcomes. For example, if the experiment consists of selecting five items from a production run and observing how many are defective, the appropriate random variable would be defined as "the number of defective items." This random variable enables us to focus solely on the number of defectives observed, rather than having to concern ourselves with exactly which of the items selected are defective, the nature of the defects, and other such nonessential details.

After introducing random variables, we consider probability distributions, which summarize the probabilities of observing the various numerical observations. Two descriptive measures of a random variable and its probability distribution—expected value and variance—are covered next. The remainder of the chapter looks in detail at three specific, commonly used probability distributions: the binomial, Poisson and normal distributions.

RANDOM VARIABLES AND PROBABILITY DISTRIBUTIONS

In most random experiments, we're interested only in a certain aspect of the experimental outcome. The instrument we use to focus our attention on this particular aspect of an outcome (and to assign a numerical value to the outcome accordingly) is called a **random variable**. Consider once again the experiment described in Example 4.7, which involved the selection of two coins from a box of four coins: a nickel, two dimes, and a quarter. Recall that the sample space for this experiment is $S = \{ND, NQ, DN, DD, DQ, QN, QD\}$. Our primary interest in this experiment might be in the total sum of money selected, in the number of dimes selected, or in whether the quarter was selected. Each of these aspects of the outcome corresponds to a different random variable. Suppose, for example, that we're interested in the total sum of money selected. If X denotes the total sum of money observed, the value that X takes on will vary randomly from trial to trial of the experiment, and hence X is called a random variable. In fact, X is a function that assigns a numerical value to each simple event in the sample space S, with the possible values of X being 15, 20, 30, and 35, as shown in Figure 5.1.

A formal definition of *random variable* might therefore read as follows.

FIGURE 5.1   *RANDOM VARIABLE X ASSIGNING VALUES TO SIMPLE EVENTS*

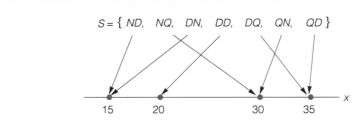

Random Variable

A **random variable** is a function that assigns a numerical value to each simple event in a sample space.

Less formally, we might simply state that *a random variable is a variable whose numerical value is determined by the outcome of a random experiment.* Throughout this chapter, we will stress the distinction between a random variable and the values it can assume, by following the convention of using capital letters such as X or Y to denote a random variable and using lowercase letters such as x or y to denote one of its values. Although many people feel that this distinction in notation is unnecessary, we believe that it is useful to maintain while you are becoming familiar with the notion of a random variable. This notational distinction is dropped in subsequent chapters, however, since the interpretation of x will usually be clear from the context in which it is used.

A random variable summarizes the results of an experiment in such a way that the numerical-valued outcomes represent the events of interest to us. If our interest in the preceding experiment centers on the number of dimes selected from among the four coins, we could define a new random variable Y to be "the number of dimes selected." The possible values of this random variable Y would be 0, 1, and 2. There are two main types of random variables, distinguished from one another by the number of possible values that they can assume.

Discrete and Continuous Random Variables

A random variable is **discrete** if it can assume only a countable number of possible values. If a random variable can assume an uncountable number of values, it is said to be **continuous**.

A **discrete random variable** has a finite or countably infinite number of possible values. In most practical situations, a discrete random variable counts the number of times a particular attribute is observed. Examples of discrete random variables include the number of defective items in a production batch, the number of telephone calls received in a given hour, and the number of customers served by a tavern on a given day. Thus, if X denotes the number of customers served by a tavern on a particular day, then X can take any one of the values $x = 0, 1, 2, \ldots$.

A **continuous random variable** is one that has an uncountably infinite number of possible values; that is, it can take on any value in one or more intervals of values. Continuous random variables typically record the value of a measurement such as time, weight, or length. For example, if X represents the time taken by a student to write a 60-minute exam, then X can take any one of infinitely many possible values: $0 \leq x \leq 60$. For the time being, however, we will restrict our attention to discrete random variables.

Having considered the values of a random variable, we now turn to the probabilities with which those values are assumed. Once we know the possible values of a random variable and the probabilities with which those values are assumed, we have what is called the **probability distribution** of the random variable, our main object of interest.

> **Discrete Probability Distribution**
>
> A table, formula, or graph that lists all of the possible values that a discrete random variable can take on, together with their associated probabilities, is called a **discrete probability distribution.**

The probability associated with a particular value of a random variable is determined in a manner that you can probably anticipate. Let x be a value of a random variable X. Then the probability that X assumes the value x, denoted either by $P(X = x)$ or by $p(x)$, is the sum of the probabilities associated with the simple events for which X assumes the value x.

TABLE 5.1   *VALUES OF X CORRESPONDING TO SIMPLE EVENTS*

Simple Event	x	Probability
ND	15	2/12
NQ	30	1/12
DN	15	2/12
DD	20	2/12
DQ	35	2/12
QN	30	1/12
QD	35	2/12

Let's apply this rule to the experiment involving the selection of two coins from a box of four coins (Example 4.7). If the random variable X represents the total sum of money selected, X can assume any one of the values 15, 20, 30, or 35. Probabilities can be assigned to the values of X with the help of Table 5.1, which records each simple event together with its probability and corresponding value of x. (Recall that the simple event probabilities shown in Table 5.1 were calculated in Example 4.7, with the help of a probability tree.) For example, X takes the value 15 if either the simple event ND or the simple event DN occurs, so

$$P(X = 15) = P(ND) + P(DN)$$
$$= 2/12 + 2/12 = 4/12.$$

The distinct values of X and their associated probabilities are summarized in Table 5.2, which gives the probability distribution of X. The probability distribution of X can be presented in the tabular form shown in Table 5.2, in the graphical form of Figure 5.2, or by using the following formula:

$$p(x) = \begin{cases} 2/12 & \text{if } x = 20 \text{ or } 30 \\ 4/12 & \text{if } x = 15 \text{ or } 35. \end{cases}$$

TABLE 5.2   PROBABILITY DISTRIBUTION OF X

X	$p(x)$
15	4/12
20	2/12
30	2/12
35	4/12

FIGURE 5.2   GRAPHICAL PRESENTATION OF PROBABILITY DISTRIBUTION

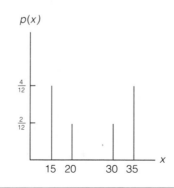

In an example like this one, where the formula is rather cumbersome, the tabular representation of the probability distribution of X is most convenient. But whichever representation is used, a discrete probability distribution must satisfy two properties, which follow from the basic requirements for probabilities that were outlined in Chapter 4.

Requirements of Discrete Probability Distribution

If a random variable X can take values $x_1, x_2, \ldots, x_n$, then

1. $0 \leq p(x_i) \leq 1$ for $i = 1, 2, \ldots, n$.

2. $\sum_{i=1}^{n} p(x_i) = 1$.

Once a probability distribution has been defined for a random variable X, we may talk about the probability that X takes a value in some range of values. The probability that X takes a value between a and b inclusive, denoted by $P(a \leq X \leq b)$, is obtained by summing the probabilities $p(x)$ for all values x such that $a \leq x \leq b$. Illustrating from the preceding example, we would have

$$P(15 \leq X \leq 20) = p(15) + p(20)$$
$$= 4/12 + 2/12$$
$$= 6/12.$$

In other words, the probability that the total sum of money selected is either 15 or 20 cents is 6/12, or .5.

EXPECTED VALUE

A probability distribution is the distribution of a population. Consider, for example, the probability distribution shown in Table 5.3, where the random variable X represents the payoff (in dollars) from a proposed investment of $25.

TABLE 5.3   *PROBABILITY DISTRIBUTION OF X*

x	$p(x)$
20	1/2
40	1/4
60	1/4

We can conceive of the underlying population in the following way. Imagine a barrel containing an infinitely large number of chips, of which one-half are labeled 20, one-quarter are labeled 40, and one-quarter are labeled 60. If X denotes the label on a chip that is randomly selected from the population of chips, the probability distribution of X is as shown in Table 5.3.

Now, consider the population of labels on all chips. We may wish to find the mean of this population, just as we did with the populations encountered back in Chapter 3, where we defined the *mean of a population* of N values of X to be

$$\mu = \frac{\sum_{i=1}^{N} x_i}{N} = \sum_{i=1}^{N} x_i \cdot \frac{1}{N}.$$

For the infinitely large population of labels, however, we must replace $1/N$ with the probability, or relative frequency, with which x_i occurs. The mean of such a population, called the **mean value** of X, is therefore given by

$$\mu = \sum x \cdot p(x),$$

where the sum is taken over all values of X. This is also referred to as the **expected value** of X, written $E(X)$. Hence, the expected value of the payoff from the $25 investment is

$$E(X) = \mu$$
$$= 20\left(\frac{1}{2}\right) + 40\left(\frac{1}{4}\right) + 60\left(\frac{1}{4}\right) = \$35.$$

In general, we have the following definition.

Expected Value

Given a discrete random variable X with values $x_1, x_2, \ldots, x_n$ that occur with probabilities $p(x_i)$, the **expected value** of X is

$$E(X) = \sum_{i=1}^{n} x_i \cdot p(x_i).$$

The expected value of a random variable X is the weighted average of the possible values that X may assume, where the weights are the probabilities of occurrence of those values. The expected value of X should be interpreted simply as a weighted average of the possible values of X, rather than as a value that X is expected to assume. In fact, as the preceding example illustrates, $E(X)$ may not even be a possible value of X.

An alternative interpretation of the expected value of X employs the long-run relative frequency approach to probability described in Chapter 4. If the investment in the foregoing example were undertaken repeatedly a large number of times, the expected value of X, $35, would be a good approximation of the average payoff resulting from the many investments.

VARIANCE

The expected value of a random variable X is a weighted average of the values of X; it therefore provides us with a measure of the central location of the distribution of X. It does not tell us, however, whether the values of X are clustered closely about the expected value or are widely scattered. Thus, the mean, or expected value, of a random variable does not by itself adequately describe the random variables. Just as was the case in Chapter 3, we need a measure of dispersion.

Recall that a popular measure of the dispersion of a population of N measurements $x_1, \ldots, x_N$ is the variance, given by

$$\sigma^2 = \frac{\sum_{i=1}^{N}(x_i - \mu)^2}{N} = \sum_{i=1}^{N}(x_i - \mu)^2 \cdot \frac{1}{N}.$$

The variance of a random variable X is defined in a similar manner, with $1/N$ being replaced by $p(x_i)$. We may then describe the variance of a random variable X as the weighted average of the squared deviations of the values of X from their mean μ, with the weight attached to $(x_i - \mu)^2$ being $p(x_i)$—the probability with which that squared deviation occurs. In other words, the variance of X is the expected value of the random variable $(X - \mu)^2$.

Variance

Let X be a discrete random variable with possible values $x_1, x_2, \ldots, x_N$, which occur with probabilities $p(x_i)$, and let $E(X) = \mu$. The **variance** of X is defined to be

$$\sigma^2 = E[(X - \mu)^2] = \sum_{i=1}^{N}(x_i - \mu)^2 \cdot p(x_i).$$

Notice that a variance is always nonnegative, since each item in the summation is nonnegative. Alternative notations for the variance of X are σ_x^2 and $V(X)$, both of which are useful for indicating the random variable in question.

As an illustration of the computation of variance, consider once again the probability distribution (see Table 5.3) for X, the payoff from an investment of \$25. The variance of the payoffs is

$$\sigma_x^2 = (20 - 35)^2\left(\frac{1}{2}\right) + (40 - 35)^2\left(\frac{1}{4}\right) + (60 - 35)^2\left(\frac{1}{4}\right)$$

$$= 275 \text{ (dollars)}^2.$$

A variance, considered by itself, is somewhat difficult to interpret. The notion of variance is therefore chiefly used to compare the variabilities of different distributions, which may (for example) represent the possible outcomes of alternative courses of action under consideration. One important application arises in finance, where variance is the most popular numerical measure of risk; the underlying assumption is that a larger variance corresponds to a higher level of risk.

Let Y represent the payoff from a second proposed investment of $25. The possible payoffs in this case are $10, $40, and $80, occurring with probabilities 1/2, 1/4, and 1/4, respectively. The expected value of Y can be shown to be $35—the same as the expected value of X—but the variance of Y is 825 (dollars)^2, as you can verify. If the riskiness of the investments is measured by the variance of their payoffs, the second proposed investment is riskier than the first, since $\sigma_y^2 > \sigma_x^2$. This risk assessment is consistent with the intuitive impression you would probably obtain from a casual comparison of the distributions of X and Y.

The variance of X is defined to be $E[(X - \mu)^2]$. By expanding $(X - \mu)^2$, we can confirm that an alternative formulation of the variance of X is as follows.

Shortcut for Computing Variance

$$\sigma_x^2 = E(X^2) - \mu^2.$$

This shortcut for computing the variance is useful because the calculation of $E(X^2)$ is often simpler than the direct computation of σ_x^2, which involves squared deviations. Like that of any other random variable, the expected value of the random variable X^2 is obtained by taking a weighted average of its possible values:

$$E(X^2) = \sum_{i=1}^{N} x_i^2 \cdot p(x_i).$$

As was the case in Chapter 3 with a set of measurement data, we may wish to express the variability of X in terms of a measure that has the same units as X. Once again, this is accomplished by taking the positive square root of the variance.

Standard Deviation

The **standard deviation** of a random variable X, denoted σ, is the positive square root of the variance of X.

For instance, the standard deviation of X, the payoff from the first proposed investment, is

$$\sigma_X = \sqrt{275} = \$16.58.$$

EXAMPLE 5.1

Now that the new models are available, a car dealership has lowered its prices on last year's models in order to clear its holdover inventory. With prices slashed, a young and aggressive salesman estimates the probability distribution of X, the total number of cars he'll sell in the next week:

x	0	1	2	3	4
$p(x)$	.05	.15	.35	.25	.20

Determine the expected value and standard deviation of X.

Solution.   The expected value, variance, and standard deviation of X can be calculated directly from their definitions:

$$E(X) = \mu = \sum_{i=1}^{5} x_i \cdot p(x_i)$$

$$= 0(0.5) + 1(.15) + 2(.35) + 3(.25) + 4(.20)$$

$$= 2.40$$

$$V(X) = \sigma^2 = \sum_{i=1}^{5} (x_i - 2.4)^2 \cdot p(x_i)$$

$$= (0 - 2.4)^2(.05) + (1 - 2.4)^2(.15) + (2 - 2.4)^2(.35)$$

$$+ (3 - 2.4)^2(.25) + (4 - 2.4)^2(.20)$$

$$= 1.24$$

$$\sigma = \sqrt{1.24} = 1.11.$$

The expected number of cars that the young salesman will sell next week is 2.4, with a standard deviation of 1.11.

A convenient alternative for computational purposes is to record the probability distribution of X (and subsequent computations) in a table such as Table 5.4. Rather than having a column for $(x - \mu)^2$, we have chosen to use the shortcut formula for variance, which entails finding the expected value of X^2. Therefore, from Table 5.4,

---

TABLE 5.4   COMPUTATIONS FOR $E(X)$ AND $E(X^2)$

x	$p(x)$	$xp(x)$	x^2	$x^2p(x)$
0	.05	0	0	0
1	.15	.15	1	.15
2	.35	.70	4	1.40
3	.25	.75	9	2.25
4	.20	.80	16	3.20
TOTAL		$2.40 = E(X)$		$7.00 = E(X^2)$

$$E(X) = \mu = 2.4$$
$$V(X) = E(X^2) - \mu^2$$
$$= 7 - (2.4)^2 = 1.24$$
$$\sigma = \sqrt{1.24} = 1.11.$$

 **EXERCISES**

LEARNING THE TECHNIQUES

5.1 Consider a random variable X with the following probability distribution:

x	p(x)
−4	.2
0	.3
1	.4
2	.1

Find the following probabilities:

a. $P(X > 0)$ c. $P(0 \leq X \leq 1)$ e. $P(X = -2)$

b. $P(X \geq 0)$ d. $P(X = -4)$ f. $P(X < 2)$

5.2 Consider a random variable X with the following probability distribution:

$$p(x) = .1x, \qquad x = 1, 2, 3, \text{ or } 4$$

Express the probability distribution in tabular form, and use it to find the following probabilities:

a. $P(X \geq 1)$ d. $P(X = 4)$

b. $P(X > 1)$ e. $P(X = 3.5)$

c. $P(2 \leq X \leq 3)$

5.3 Determine which of the following are not valid probability distributions, and explain why not.

a. x	p(x)
1	.2
2	.2
3	.3
4	.4

b. x	p(x)
0	−.1
2	.2
4	.3
5	.4

c. x	p(x)
−2	.1
−1	.1
1	.1
2	.7

5.4 Let X be the number of spots turning up when a six-sided die is tossed.

a. Express the probability distribution of X in tabular form.

b. Express the probability distribution of X in graphical form.

5.5 Let X be the number of times a fair coin comes up heads when it is flipped three times.

a. Express the probability distribution of X in tabular form.

b. Express the probability distribution of X in graphical form.

5.6 Let X be a random variable with the following probability distribution:

x	1	2	3	4
p(x)	.4	.3	.2	.1

a. Find $E(X)$ and $V(X)$.

b. Is $E(X)$ a possible value of X?

5.7 Let X be a random variable with the following probability distribution:

x	−4	0	1	2
p(x)	.2	.3	.4	.1

a. Find μ and σ.

b. Is μ a possible value of X?

c. Find $E(X^2)$.

5.8 Let X be a random variable with the following probability distribution:

x	5	10	15	20	25
p(x)	.05	.30	.25	.25	.15

a. Find the expected value and variance of X.

b. Find the expected value and variance of $Y = 4X$.

5.9 Let X be a random variable with the following probability distribution:

x	-10	-5	0	5	10
$p(x)$	.10	.20	.20	.20	.30

a. Find the mean and standard deviation of X.

b. Find the mean and standard deviation of $2X$.

5.10 Let X be a random variable with the following probability distribution:

x	0	5	10	20
$p(x)$	.2	.3	.3	.2

a. Find the mean and standard deviation of X.

b. Find $E(X^2)$.

APPLYING THE TECHNIQUES

5.11 Let X represent the number of people in an American household. According to the *Statistical Abstract of the United States: 1988*, the probability distribution of X is as follows (rounded to two decimal places):

x	1	2	3	4	5	6	7
$p(x)$	.23	.31	.18	.16	.07	.03	.02

a. Express the probability distribution in graphical form.

b. Comment on the symmetry or skewness of the distribution.

c. What is the most likely number of people in a household?

d. What is the probability of a household's having fewer than four people? More than seven people?

Self-Correcting Exercise (See Appendix 5.A for the solution.)

5.12 Let X represent the number of children under 18 years old in an American family. According to the *Statistical Abstract of the United States: 1989*, the probability distribution of X is as follows:

x	0	1	2	3	4	5
$p(x)$	.50	.21	.19	.07	.02	.01

a. Express the probability distribution of X in graphical form.

b. Comment on the symmetry or skewness of the distribution.

c. What is the most likely number of children in a family?

d. What is the probability of a family's having more than two children?

5.13 Using historical data, the personnel manager of a plant has determined that the probability distribution of X, the number of employees absent on any given day, is as follows:

x	0	1	2	3	4	5	6	7
$p(x)$	.005	.025	.310	.340	.220	.080	.019	.001

a. Express the probability distribution of X in graphical form.

b. Comment on the symmetry or skewness of the distribution.

c. Find the probability that $2 \le X \le 4$.

d. Find the plant's probability of having more than one absentee on a given day.

5.14 A mutual fund saleswoman has arranged to call upon three households tomorrow. Based on past experience, she feels that there is a 20% chance of closing a sale on each call, and that the outcome of each call is independent of the others. Let X represent the number of sales that she closes tomorrow.

a. Find the probability distribution of X.

b. Express the probability distribution of X graphically.

c. What is the probability that more than one sale will be closed tomorrow?

5.15 Let X represent the number of times a student visits a nearby pizza parlor in a one-month period. Assume that the following table is the probability distribution of X.

x	$p(x)$
0	.1
1	.3
2	.4
3	.2

a. Find the mean (μ) and the standard deviation (σ) of this distribution.

b. What is the probability that the student will visit the pizza parlor at least twice in the next month?

c. Find $P(X \geq 1.5)$.

d. Construct a graph of the probability distribution, and locate μ and the interval $\mu \pm \sigma$ on the graph.

Self-Correcting Exercise (See Appendix 5.A for the solution.)

5.16 The owner of a small firm has just purchased a microcomputer, which he expects will serve him for the next two years. The owner has been told that he "must" buy a surge suppressor to provide protection for his new hardware against possible surges or variations in the electrical current. His son David, a recent university graduate, advises that an inexpensive suppressor could be purchased that would provide protection against one surge only. He notes that the amount of damage without a suppressor would depend on the extent of the surge. David conservatively estimates that, over the next two years, there is a 1 percent chance of incurring $400 damage and a 2 percent chance of $200 damage. The probability of incurring $100 damage is .1; that of incurring no damage is .87.

a. How much should the owner be willing to pay for a surge suppressor?

b. Determine the standard deviation of the possible amounts of damage.

5.17 In Exercise 4.32, it was noted that insurance companies rely heavily on probability theory when computing the premiums to charge for various life insurance and annuity products. Suppose that a 40-year-old male purchases a $100,000 10-year term life policy from an insurance company, meaning that the insurance company must pay out $100,000 if the insured male dies within the next 10 years.

a. Use the accompanying life table to determine the insurance company's expected payout on this policy.

b. What would the expected payout be if the same policy were taken out by a 50-year-old male?

NUMBER OF DEATHS AT VARIOUS AGES OUT OF 100,000 AMERICAN MALES BORN ALIVE

Age Interval*	Number of Deaths
0–1	1,527
1–10	495
10–20	927
20–30	1,901
30–40	2,105
40–50	4,502
50–60	10,330
60–70	19,954
70–80	28,538
80 and over	29,721
TOTAL	100,000

* Interval contains all ages from lower limit up to (but not including) upper limit.

SOURCE: *Life Tables, Vital Statistics of the United States* (1978), U.S. Department of Health and Human Services.

5.18 Suppose that you have the choice of receiving $500 in cash or receiving a gold coin that has a face value of $100. The actual value of the gold coin depends on its gold content. You are told that the coin has a 40% chance of being worth $400, a 30% chance of being worth $900, and and a 30% chance of being worth its face value. If you base your decision on expected value, which should you choose?

5.19   In order to examine the effectiveness of their four annual promotions, a mail-order company has sent a questionnaire to each of its customers, asking how many of the prior year's promotions prompted orders that would not otherwise have been made. The following table summarized the data received, where the random variable X is the number of promotions indicated in the customers' responses.

x	$p(x)$
0	.10
1	.25
2	.40
3	.20
4	.05

a. Assuming that the responses received were accurate evaluations of individual effectiveness,

and that customer behavior in the coming year will not change, what is the expected number of promotions each customer will take advantage of by ordering goods that would not otherwise be purchased next year?

b. What is the variance of X?

c. A previous analysis of historical data has found that the mean value of orders for promotional goods is $12.50, with the company earning a gross profit of 20% on each order. The fixed cost of conducting the four promotions next year is estimated to be $15,000, with a variable cost of $3.00 per customer for mailing and handling costs. Assuming that the survey results can be used as an accurate predictor of behavior for existing and potential customers, how large a customer base must the company have to cover the costs of the promotions?

BINOMIAL DISTRIBUTION

Having covered the basic properties of probability distributions in general, we now consider in detail the binomial distribution—the first of three important specific probability distributions. The binomial distribution is probably the single most important discrete distribution. An important characteristic of the underlying binomial random experiment is that there are only two possible outcomes. Experiments having such a dichotomy of outcomes are numerous: a coin flip results in heads or tails, an election candidate is favored or not; a product is defective or nondefective; an employee is male or female; and an invoice being audited is correct or incorrect. It is conventional to apply the generic labels **success** and **failure** to the two possible outcomes. Binomial experiments of practical interest usually involve several repetitions or trials of the basic experiment, and these trials must satisfy the conditions outlined in the definition of a binomial experiment.

Binomial Experiment

A **binomial experiment** possesses the following properties:

1. The experiment consists of a fixed number n of trials.
2. The result of each trial can be classified into one of two categories: success or failure.

3. The probability p of a success remains constant for each trial.

4. Each trial of the experiment is independent of the other trials.*

An example of a binomial experiment consists of flipping a coin ten times and observing the result of each flip. Which of the two possible outcomes of each trial (flip) is designated as a success is arbitrary, but we will designate the appearance of heads as a success. Assuming that the coin is fair, the probability of a success is $p = .5$ for each of the ten trials. Clearly, each trial is independent of the others. Our main interest in a binomial experiment such as this is the number of successes (heads) observed in the ten trials. The random variable that records the number of successes (heads) observed in the $n = 10$ trials is called the **binomial random variable.**

Binomial Random Variables

The **binomial random variable** indicates the number of successes in the n trials of a binomial experiment.

A binomial random variable is therefore a discrete random variable that can take on any one of the values $0, 1, 2, \ldots, n$. The probability distribution of this random variable, called the **binomial probability distribution,** gives us the probability that a success will occur x times in the n trials, for $x = 0, 1, 2, \ldots, n$. Using a probability tree to work out binomial probabilities from scratch each time would be tedious. Fortunately, a general formula exists that can be used to calculate the probabilities associated with any binomial experiment.

Probability Distribution of a Binomial Experiment

If the random variable X is the number of successes in the n trials of a binomial experiment that has probability p of a success on any given trial, the probability distribution of X is given by

$$P(X = x) = p(x) = C_x^n p^x q^{n-x}, \qquad \text{where } q = 1 - p$$

$$= \left(\frac{n!}{x!(n-x)!} \right) p^x q^{n-x}, \qquad x = 0, 1, \ldots, n.$$

where

$$n! = n(n-1)(n-2) \cdots (2)(1)$$
$$0! = 1.$$

---

* Two trials are independent if the result from one trial does not affect the outcome of the other trial.

FIGURE 5.3   GRAPHS OF THREE BINOMIAL DISTRIBUTIONS

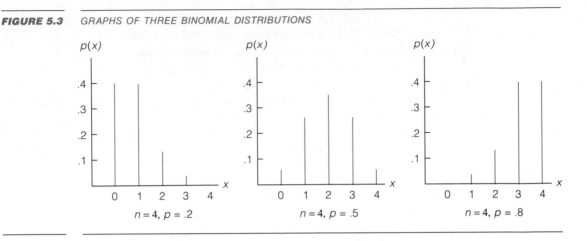

$n = 4, p = .2$ $n = 4, p = .5$ $n = 4, p = .8$

The notation $n!$ is read "n factorial." With $n = 4$, for example, we obtain $4! = 4 \cdot 3 \cdot 2 \cdot 1 = 24$. A common alternative to the notation C_x^n used here to represent the **binomial coefficient** is $\binom{n}{x}$.*

Each pair of values (n, p) determines a distinct binomial distribution. Graphical representations of three binomial distributions are shown in Figure 5.3. Each of the $(n + 1)$ possible values of a binomial random variable X has a positive probability of occurring. The fact that some possible values of X do not have a vertical line above them in Figure 5.3 simply means that the probability that those values will occur is too small to be displayed on the graph. A binomial distribution is symmetrical whenever $p = .5$; it is asymmetrical otherwise.

EXAMPLE 5.2

The quality-control department of a manufacturer tested the most recent batch of 1,000 catalytic converters produced and found 50 of them to be defective. Subsequently, an employee unwittingly mixed the defective converters with the nondefective ones. If a sample of 3 converters is randomly selected from the mixed batch, what is the probability distribution of the number of defective converters in the sample?

Solution.   The first thing to do is to make sure that the conditions for a binomial experiment are satisfied. The experiment consists of a fixed number of $n = 3$ trials, with each trial resulting in one of two possible outcomes: a defective converter (success) or a nondefective converter (failure). The probability p of selecting a defective converter does not remain constant for each trial, however, since the probability of selecting a defective converter on a given trial depends on the results of the previous trials. In other words, the trials are not independent. The probability of selecting a defective on the

---

* The binomial coefficient C_x^n is the number of ways of choosing x objects from a total of n objects. Thus, it is the number of *combinations* that can be formed.

TABLE 5.5   BINOMIAL DISTRIBUTION ($n = 3$, $p = .05$)

x	$p(x)$
0	.8574
1	.1354
2	.0071
3	.0001

first trial is $\frac{50}{1000} = .05$. But if a defective converter is selected on the first trial, the (conditional) probability of selecting a defective converter on the second trial is $\frac{49}{999} = .049$.

In practical situations, this slight violation of the conditions of a binomial experiment is often treated as negligible. While p does vary from trial to trial, it remains quite close to .05. The violation would become important, however, if we were sampling from a batch of 100 widgets of which only 5 were defective. In this case, p would change appreciably from trial to trial—especially if one of the defective widgets were selected on an earlier trial—and the binomial model should not be used.

Returning to the original problem, let's assume that the binomial model adequately describes the situation and that $p = .05$ for each trial. Let X be the binomial random variable indicating the number of defective converters in the sample of three. We may then compute:

$$P(X = 0) = p(0) = \frac{3!}{0!3!} \cdot (.05)^0 \cdot (.95)^3 = .8574$$

$$P(X = 1) = p(1) = \frac{3!}{1!2!} \cdot (.05)^1 \cdot (.95)^2 = .1354$$

$$P(X = 2) = p(2) = \frac{3!}{2!1!} \cdot (.05)^2 \cdot (.95)^1 = .0071$$

$$P(X = 3) = p(3) = \frac{3!}{3!1!} \cdot (.05)^3 \cdot (.95)^0 = .0001.$$

We thereby obtain the probability distribution of the number of defective converters in the sample of three, as shown in Table 5.5.

USING THE BINOMIAL TABLES

Calculating binomial probabilities by means of the formula, as illustrated in Example 5.2, is time-consuming and unwieldy when n is large. Fortunately, tables identifying these probabilities are available. One such table is Table 1 in Appendix B at the back

TABLE 5.6   PARTIAL REPRODUCTION OF TABLE 1: BINOMIAL PROBABILITIES FOR $n = 5$*

				p				
k	.01	.05	.10	.20	.25	.30	.40	.50
0	.951	.774	.591	.328	.237	.168	.078	.031
1	.048	.204	.328	.410	.396	.360	.259	.156
2	.001	.021	.073	.205	.264	.309	.346	.312
3	.000	.001	.008	.051	.088	.132	.230	.312
4	.000	.000	.000	.006	.015	.028	.077	.156
5	.000	.000	.000	.000	.001	.002	.010	.031

k	.60	.70	.75	.80	.90	.95	.99 ·
0	.010	.002	.001	.000	.000	.000	.000
1	.077	.028	.015	.006	.000	.000	.000
2	.230	.132	.088	.051	.008	.001	.000
3	.346	.309	.264	.205	.073	.021	.001
4	.259	.360	.396	.410	.328	.204	.048
5	.078	.168	.237	.328	.591	.774	.951

* Tabulated values are $P(X = k) = p(k)$. (Entries are rounded to three decimal places.)

of this book, which presents binomial distributions for various values of n and p. (Although the probabilities in the preceding example were computed to four decimal places, the binomial probabilities provided by Table 1 are rounded to three decimal places.) A partial reproduction of this table, for $n = 5$, is shown in Table 5.6. The 15 columns in Table 5.6, corresponding to 15 different values of p, represent 15 distinct binomial distributions. Individual tabulated values are of the form

$$P(X = k) = p(k).$$

To find the probability of obtaining exactly three successes in $n = 5$ trials of a binomial experiment with $p = .2$, we locate the entry corresponding to $k = 3$ and $p = .2$:

$$P(X = 3) = p(3) = .051.$$

To find the probability that X will assume some value within a range of values, using Table 1, we must locate and sum together several probabilities. For example, the probability of *at most* three successes in $n = 5$ trials of a binomial experiment with $p = .2$ is obtained as follows:

$$P(X \le 3) = \sum_{x=0}^{3} p(x)$$
$$= p(0) + p(1) + p(2) + p(3)$$
$$= .328 + .410 + .205 + .051$$
$$= .994.$$

We have just seen how to use Table 1 in Appendix B to save time in finding binomial probabilities. There is also a time-saving procedure for finding the mean and the variance of a binomial random variable. While these two parameters could be calculated in the usual time-consuming way—using the definitional formulas involving summations—it can be shown that the mean and the variance of a binomial random variable are given by the following pair of formulas.

Mean and Variance of Binomial Random Variables

If X is a binomial random variable, the mean and variance of X are

$$E(X) = \mu = np$$
$$V(X) = \sigma^2 = npq$$

where

$$q = 1 - p.$$

USING THE CUMULATIVE BINOMIAL TABLES*

An alternative way of presenting the binomial distribution ($n = 3$, $p = .05$) in Table 5.5 is depicted in Table 5.7. The difference here is that the probabilities in Table 5.7 are **cumulative probabilities** representing the sum of binomial probabilities from $x = 0$ to $x = k$.

TABLE 5.7   *CUMULATIVE BINOMIAL DISTRIBUTION ($n = 3$, $p = .05$)*

k	$\sum_{x=0}^{k} p(x)$
0	.8574
1	.9928
2	.9999
3	1.0000

* Coverage of this section is optional. Some students feel that the difficulty of learning how to use cumulative binomial tables outweighs the benefits derived from them.

If $k = 1$, for example, we have

$$P(X \leq 1) = \sum_{x=0}^{1} p(x) = p(0) + p(1)$$

$$= .8574 + .1354$$

$$= .9928.$$

The advantage of working with such a table of cumulative binomial probabilities is that it enables us to find, more quickly, the probability that X will assume some value within a range of values.

Individual binomial probabilities are obtained from Table 5.7 by subtraction. For example, the probability of obtaining exactly two successes is

$$p(2) = P(X \leq 2) - P(X \leq 1)$$

$$= \sum_{x=0}^{2} p(x) - \sum_{x=0}^{1} p(x)$$

$$= .9999 - .9928$$

$$= .0071.$$

Table 2 in Appendix B at the back of this book presents cumulative binomial distributions for various values of n and p. (Like the values in Table 1 of Appendix B, the cumulative binomial probabilities provided by Table 2 are rounded to three decimal places.) A partial reproduction of this table, for $n = 5$, is shown in Table 5.8.

TABLE 5.8 *PARTIAL REPRODUCTION OF TABLE 2: BINOMIAL PROBABILITIES FOR n = 5**

				p				
k	.01	.05	.10	.20	.25	.30	.40	.50
0	.951	.774	.590	.328	.237	.168	.078	.031
1	.999	.977	.919	.737	.633	.528	.337	.188
2	1.000	.999	.991	.942	.896	.837	.683	.500
3	1.000	1.000	1.000	.993	.984	.969	.913	.812
4	1.000	1.000	1.000	1.000	.999	.998	.990	.969
k	.60	.70	.75	.80	.90	.95	.99	
0	.010	.002	.001	.000	.000	.000	.000	
1	.087	.031	.016	.007	.000	.000	.000	
2	.317	.163	.104	.058	.009	.001	.000	
3	.663	.472	.367	.263	.081	.023	.001	
4	.922	.832	.763	.672	.410	.226	.049	

* Tabulated values are $P(X \leq k) = \sum_{x=0}^{k} p(x)$. Entries are rounded to three decimal places.

The 15 columns in Table 5.8, corresponding to 15 different values of p, represent 15 distinct binomial distributions. Individual tabulated values are of the form

$$P(X \le k) = \sum_{x=0}^{k} p(x).$$

To find the probability of at most three successes in $n = 5$ trials of a binomial experiment with $p = .2$, we locate the entry corresponding to $k = 3$ and $p = .2$:

$$
\begin{aligned}
P(X \le 3) &= \sum_{x=0}^{3} p(x) \\
&= p(0) + p(1) + p(2) + p(3) \\
&= .993.^{*}
\end{aligned}
$$

Notice that the final probability in each column (distribution) of the table—that is, reading horizontally, the row corresponding to $k = n$—has been omitted. This probability will always be equal to 1, since, for $k = n$,

$$P(X \le k) = P(X \le n) = 1.$$

EXAMPLE 5.3

A shoe store's records show that 30% of customers making a purchase use credit cards to make payment. This morning, 20 customers purchased shoes from the store.

a. Using Table 1 (or Table 2) of Appendix B, find the probability that at least 12 of the customers used credit cards.

b. What is the probability that at least 3 customers, but not more than 6, used credit cards?

c. What is the expected number of customers who used credit cards?

d. Find the probability that exactly 14 customers did not use credit cards.

e. Find the probability that at least 9 customers did not use credit cards.

Solution.   If making payment with a credit card is designated as a success, we have a binomial experiment with $n = 20$ and $p = .3$. Let X denote the number of customers who used credit cards.

a. Using Table 1, we obtain

$$
\begin{aligned}
P(X \ge 12) &= P(X = 12) + P(X = 13) + P(X = 14) + \cdots + P(X = 20) \\
&= .004 + .001 + .000 + \cdots + .000 \\
&= .005.
\end{aligned}
$$

Alternatively, we could use Table 2. But to do so, we must first express the required probability in terms of probabilities of the form $P(X \le k)$, since this is the form in which probabilities are tabulated in Table 2:

$$
\begin{aligned}
P(X \ge 12) &= P(X = 12) + P(X = 13) + \cdots + P(X = 20) \\
&= P(X \le 20) - P(X \le 11).
\end{aligned}
$$

---

*The fact that this differs from the value of .994 obtained (on page 145) using Table 1 is due to rounding errors.

Since the probabilities in a binomial distribution must sum to 1, $P(X \leq 20) = 1$. From Table 1, $P(X \leq 11) = .995$. Therefore,

$$P(X \geq 12) = 1 - .995 = .005.$$

The probability that at least 12 customers used credit cards is .005.

b. From Table 1, we have

$$P(3 \leq X \leq 6) = P(X = 3) + P(X = 4) + P(X = 5) + P(X = 6)$$
$$= .072 + .130 + .179 + .192$$
$$= .573.$$

Alternatively, we could use Table 2. Expressing the probability we seek in terms of the types of probabilities tabulated in Table 2, we have

$$P(3 \leq X \leq 6) = P(X = 3) + P(X = 4) + P(X = 5) + P(X = 6)$$
$$= P(X \leq 6) - P(X \leq 2)$$
$$= .608 - .035 = .573.$$

The probability that the number of customers who used credit cards was between 3 and 6 is .573.

c. The expected number of customers who used a credit card is

$$E(X) = np = 20(.3) = 6.$$

d. Let Y denote the number of customers who did not use a credit card. The probability that a credit card was not used by a customer is $(1 - .3) = .7$. This part of the example can be solved in either of two ways:

   i. You can interchange the designations of success and failure, and work with $p = .7$

   ii. You can express the required probability in terms of the number of customers who did use a credit card, and proceed with $p = .3$.

Method (i) is probably easier when you are using the tables in the text. In many cases, however, binomial tables with p values above .5 are not available, and method (ii) must be used.

Using method (i) begins with recognizing that, since the original assignment of the designations *success* and *failure* was arbitrary, we may choose to interchange them. If not using a credit card is designated as a success, then $p = .7$. From Table 1, with $n = 20$, and $p = .7$, we find that

$$P(Y = 14) = .192.$$

Alternatively, using Table 2, we obtain

$$P(Y = 14) = P(Y \leq 14) - P(Y \leq 13) = .584 - .392$$
$$= .192.$$

In method (ii) we retain the original designation, so using a credit card is a success and $p = .3$. If 14 customers did not use a credit card, then $(20 - 14) = 6$ customers did use one. Hence, from Table 1,

$$P(Y = 14) = P(X = 6)$$
$$= .192.$$

Using either method, we find that the probability that exactly 14 customers did not use a credit card is .192.

e. Again, let Y denote the number of customers who did not use a credit card. If not using a credit card is designated as a success, then $p = .7$. Expressing the required probability in terms of values listed in Table 1, we have

$$P(Y \geq 9) = 1 - P(Y \leq 8)$$
$$= 1 - [P(Y = 0) + \cdots + P(Y = 6) + P(Y = 7) + P(Y = 8)]$$
$$= 1 - [.000 + \cdots + .000 + .001 + .004]$$
$$= 1 - .005 = .995.$$

Alternatively, using Table 2, we obtain

$$P(Y \geq 9) = 1 - P(Y \leq 8)$$
$$= 1 - .005$$
$$= .995.$$

The probability that at least 9 customers did not use credit cards is .995.

EXERCISES

LEARNING THE TECHNIQUES

5.20   Evaluate the following binomial coefficients:

a. C_2^5 b. C_2^6 c. C_4^6 d. C_0^7 e. C_7^7

5.21   Consider a binomial random variable X with $n = 4$ and $p = .6$.

a. Find the probability distribution of X, and graph it.

b. Find $P(X \leq 2)$.

c. Find the mean and the variance of X.

5.22   Let X be a binomial random variable. Use the formula to compute the following probabilities, where the relevant distribution is identified by its two parameters.

a. $P(X = 2)$ if $n = 8$, $p = .1$

b. $P(X = 5)$ if $n = 9$, $p = .5$

c. $P(X = 9)$ if $n = 10$, $p = .95$

5.23   Use Table 1 (or Table 2) in Appendix B to check your answers to Exercise 5.22.

5.24   Let X be a binomial random variable. Use the formula to compute the following probabilities.

a. $P(X = 3)$ if $n = 5$ and $p = .2$

b. $P(X = 2)$ if $n = 6$ and $p = .3$

c. $P(X = 5)$ if $n = 7$ and $p = .75$

5.25   Use Table 1 (or Table 2) in Appendix B to check your answers to Exercise 5.24.

5.26   Given a binomial random variable X with $n = 15$ and $p = .3$, find the following probabilities, using Table 1 (or Table 2) in the Appendix.

a. $P(X \leq 2)$ d. $P(4 \leq X \leq 8)$

b. $P(X \geq 7)$ e. $P(X \geq 12)$

c. $P(X = 6)$ f. $P(7 < X < 10)$

5.27   Given a binomial random variable X with $n = 25$ and $p = .6$, find the following probabilities, using Table 1 (or Table 2) in Appendix B.

a. $P(X \leq 10)$

b. $P(X \geq 12)$

c. $P(X = 15)$

d. $P(18 \leq X \leq 21)$

e. $P(18 < X < 21)$

5.28   A sign on the gas pumps of a certain chain of gasoline stations encourages customers to have their oil checked, claiming that one out of every four cars should have its oil topped up.

a. Of the next 10 cars entering a station, what is the probability that exactly 3 of them should have their oil topped up?

b. What is the probability that at least half of the next 10 cars entering a station should have their oil topped up? At least half of the next 20 cars?

APPLYING THE TECHNIQUES

5.29   A student majoring in accounting is trying to decide upon the number of firms to which she should apply. Given her work experience, grades, and extracurricular activities, a placement counselor estimates that she can expect to receive a job offer from 80 percent of the firms to which she applies. Wanting to save time, the student applies to five firms only. Assuming that the counselor's estimate is correct, find the probability that the student receives:

a. no offers

b. at most two offers

c. between two and four offers (inclusive)

d. five offers

Self-Correcting Exercise (See Appendix 5.A for the solution.)

5.30   A multiple-choice quiz has 15 questions. Each question has five possible answers, of which only one is correct.

a. What is the probability that sheer guesswork will yield at least seven correct answers?

b. What is the expected number of correct answers by sheer guesswork?

5.31   An auditor is preparing for a physical count of inventory as a means of verifying its value. Items counted are reconciled with a list prepared by the storeroom supervisor. Normally 20% of the items counted cannot be reconciled without reviewing invoices.

a. If the auditor selects ten items, find the following probabilities.
    i. Up to four items cannot be reconciled.
    ii. At least six items cannot be reconciled.
    iii. Between four and six items (inclusive) cannot be reconciled.

b. If it normally takes 20 minutes to review the invoice for an item that cannot be reconciled and one hour for the balance of the count, how long should the auditor expect the physical count to take?

5.32   Flight delays at major American airports are an increasing source of exasperation to executives, who may miss important appointments as a result. About 190,000 flights were delayed by more than 15 minutes during the first six months of 1984, with many of the delays lasting hours (*Fortune,* 1 October 1984). During this period, 13% of all arrivals and departures at New York's LaGuardia Airport experienced delays of at least 15 minutes. The corresponding percentage for Denver's Stapleton Airport was about 5%. Suppose that an executive made three round trips from Denver to New York during this period.

a. Find the probability that the executive experienced at least four delays of 15 minutes or more at Stapleton Airport during arrival or departure.

b. Find the probability that the executive experienced no delays of 15 minutes or more upon arrival at or departure from LaGuardia Airport during the three trips.

c. Find the probability that the executive experienced no delays of 15 minutes or more during the three round trips.

d. What assumptions have you made in solving the first three parts of this exercise?

<table>
<tr><td>SECTION
5.4</td><td># POISSON DISTRIBUTION</td></tr>
</table>

A second important discrete distribution is the Poisson distribution. Whereas a binomial random variable counts the number of successes that occur in a fixed number of trials, a Poisson random variable counts the number of "rare" events (successes) that occur in a specified time interval or a specified spatial region. Activities to which the Poisson distribution can be successfully applied include counting the number of telephone calls received by a switchboard in a specified time period, counting the number of arrivals at a service location (such as a service station, tollbooth, or grocery checkout counter) in a given time period, and counting the number of bacteria in a specified culture. In order for application of the Poisson distribution to be appropriate in situations such as these, three conditions must be satisfied, as enumerated in the accompanying box. In the following description of a Poisson experiment, *success* refers to the occurrence of the event of interest, and *interval* refers to either an interval of time or an interval of space (such as an area or region).

Poisson Experiment

A **Poisson experiment** possesses the following properties:

1. The number of successes that occur in any interval is independent of the number of successes that occur in any other interval.
2. The probability of a success occurring in an interval is the same for all intervals of equal size, and is proportional to the size of the interval.
3. The probability of two or more successes occurring in an interval approaches zero as the interval becomes smaller.

Less formally, then, the Poisson model is applicable when the events of interest occur *randomly, independent* of one another, and *rarely,* as specified by the preceding conditions. In particular, condition 3 specifies what is meant by *rarely.* The arrival of individual diners at a restaurant, for example, would not fit the Poisson model, because diners usually arrive with companions, violating the independence condition.

Poisson Random Variable

The **Poisson random variable** indicates the number of successes during a given time interval or in a specified region in a Poisson experiment.

Probability Distribution of Poisson Random Variable

If X is a Poisson random variable, the **probability distribution of X** is given by

$$P(X = x) = p(x) = \frac{e^{-\mu} \cdot \mu^x}{x!}, \; x = 0, 1, 2, \ldots$$

where μ is the average number of successes occurring in the given time interval or region, and $e = 2.71828 \ldots$ is the base of the natural logarithms.

Notice that, since μ (the average number of successes occurring in a specified interval) appears in the formula for the Poisson probability $p(x)$, we must have an estimate of μ—usually from historical data—before we can apply the Poisson distribution. Care must be taken to ensure that the intervals specified in the definitions of X and μ are the same size, and that the same units are used for each.

Although the computation of a Poisson probability may be performed by using the formula, it requires us to calculate $e^{-\mu}$. If your calculator will not perform this calculation, you must resort to tabulated values of $e^{-\mu}$. But this becomes impractical when you wish to find the probability that a Poisson random variable will assume any one of a large number of specified values. Fortunately, there is an easier method. To ease the computation of Poisson probabilities, tabulated values of Poisson probabilities are given in Table 3 of Appendix B. In addition, tabulated values of *cumulative* Poisson probabilities are given in Table 4 of Appendix B. The use of Table 4 is optional; just as with the binomial distribution, you may find these cumulative probabilities more convenient when finding the probability that a variable will assume some value within a range of values.

There is no limit to the number of possible values that a Poisson random variable can assume. The Poisson random variable is a discrete random variable with infinitely many possible values—unlike the binomial random variable, which has only a finite number. If X is a Poisson random variable for which μ is the average number of successes occurring in a specified interval, it can be shown that the expected value of X and the variance of X have the same value:

$$E(X) = V(X) = \mu.$$

The graphs of three specific Poisson distributions are shown in Figure 5.4.

FIGURE 5.4   GRAPHS OF THREE POISSON DISTRIBUTIONS

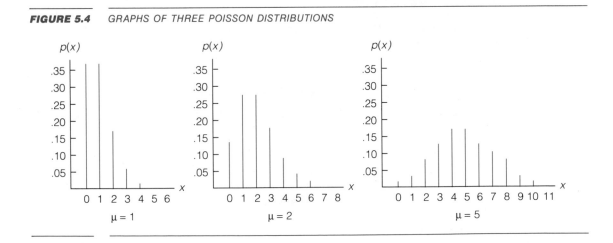

EXAMPLE 5.4

A tollbooth operator has observed that cars arrive randomly at a rate of 360 cars per hour.

a. Using the formula, calculate the probability that only 2 cars will arrive during a specified 1-minute period.

b. Using Table 3 (or Table 4) of Appendix B, find the probability that only 2 cars will arrive during a specified 1-minute period.

c. Using Table 3 (or Table 4), find the probability that at least 4 cars will arrive during a specified 1-minute period.

Solution.   Let X denote the number of arrivals during the 1-minute period. Then the mean value of X is $\mu = 360/60 = 6$ cars per minute. Notice that we have defined both X and μ in terms of the same time interval: 1 minute.

a. According to the formula for a Poisson probability, the probability of exactly two arrivals is

$$P(X = 2) = \frac{(e^{-6})(6^2)}{2!} = \frac{(.00248)(36)}{2 \cdot 1}$$
$$= .0446.$$

The value of e^{-6} was obtained by using a calculator.

b. Using Table 3 with $\mu = 6$, the probability of exactly two arrivals is
$$P(X) = .045.$$

Alternatively, according to the cumulative Poisson probabilities given in Table 4 of Appendix B, the probability of exactly two arrivals is
$$P(X = 2) = P(X \le 2) - P(X \le 1)$$
$$= .062 - .017 = .045.$$

c. Finding the probability of at least four arrivals, using Table 3, is simplified if we apply the complement rule:
$$P(X \ge 4) = 1 - P(X \le 3)$$
$$= 1 - [P(X = 0) + P(X = 1) + P(X = 2) + P(X = 3)]$$
$$= 1 - [.003 + .015 + .045 + .089]$$
$$= 1 - .152 = .848.$$

Alternatively, based on the cumulative probabilities in Table 4, the probability of at least four arrivals is
$$P(X \ge 4) = 1 - P(X \le 3)$$
$$= 1 - .151 = .849.*$$

---

* The slight difference in the values obtained using Table 3 and Table 4 is due to rounding errors.

████████████   **EXERCISES**

LEARNING THE TECHNIQUES

5.33 Compute the following Poisson probabilities, using the formula.

a. $P(X = 4)$ if $\mu = 1$

b. $P(X \le 1)$ if $\mu = 1.5$

c. $P(X \ge 2)$ if $\mu = 2$

5.34 Repeat Exercise 5.33, using Table 3 (or Table 4) of Appendix B.

5.35 Let X be a Poisson random variable with $\mu = 5$. Use Table 3 (or Table 4) to find the following probabilities:

a. $P(X \le 5)$ b. $P(X = 5)$ c. $P(X \ge 7)$

5.36 Suppose that X is a Poisson random variable whose distribution has a mean of 2.5. Use Table 3 (or Table 4) to find the following probabilities:

a. $P(X \le 3)$

b. $P(X = 6)$

c. $P(X \ge 2)$

d. $P(X > 2)$

5.37 Graph the probability distribution of a Poisson random variable with $\mu = .5$.

APPLYING THE TECHNIQUES

Self-Correcting Exercise (See Appendix 5.A for the solution.)

5.38 The marketing manager of a company has noticed that she usually receives 10 complaint calls from customers during a week (which has five working days), and that the calls occur at random. Find the probability of her receiving exactly 5 such calls in a single day.

5.39 The number of calls received by a switchboard operator between 9 and 10 A.M. has a Poisson distribution with a mean of 12. Find the probability that the operator received at least 5 calls during the following periods:

a. between 9 and 10 A.M.

b. between 9 and 9:30 A.M.

c. between 9 and 9:15 A.M.

5.40 The number of accidents that occur on an assembly line has a Poisson distribution, with an average of 3 accidents per week.

a. Find the probability that a particular week will be accident-free.

b. Find the probability that at least 3 accidents will occur in a week.

c. Find the probability that exactly 5 accidents will occur in a week.

5.41 During the summer months (June to August inclusive), an average of 5 marriages per month take place in a small city. Assuming that these marriages occur randomly and independently of one another, find the following probabilities.

a. Fewer than 4 marriages will occur in June.

b. At least 14 but not more than 18 marriages occur during the entire 3 months of summer.

c. Exactly 10 marriages occur during the 2 months of July and August.

5.42 The number of arrivals at a service counter between 1:00 and 3:00 P.M. has a Poisson distribution with a mean of 14.

a. Find the probability that the number of arrivals between 1:00 and 3:00 P.M. is at least 8.

b. Find the probability that the number of arrivals between 1:30 and 2:00 P.M. is at least 8.

c. Find the probability of there being exactly 1 arrival between 2:00 and 3:00 P.M.

5.43 A snow-removal company bills its customers on a per snowfall basis, rather than at a flat monthly rate. Based on the fee it charges per snowfall, the company will just break even in a month that has exactly 6 snowfalls. Suppose that the average number of snowfalls per month (during the winter) is 8.

a. What is the probability that the company will just break even in a given winter month?

b. What is the probability that the company will make a profit in a given winter month?

5.44 An experimental laboratory receives a shipment of developing frogs each week. The biologist

at the laboratory has noted that, over the past 1-year period, these shipments have contained a total of 26 mutated frogs. What is the probability that next week's shipment will contain at least 1 mutated frog?

SECTION 5.5

CONTINUOUS PROBABILITY DISTRIBUTIONS

Up to this point, we have focused our attention on discrete distributions—distributions of random variables that have either a finite number of possible values (for example: $x = 0, 1, 2, \ldots, n$) or a countably infinite number of values ($x = 0, 1, 2, \ldots$). In contrast, a continuous random variable has an uncountably infinite number of possible values and can assume any value in the interval between two points a and b ($a < x < b$). Whereas discrete random variables typically involve counting, continuous random variables involve the measurement of attributes such as length, weight, time, and temperature.

One major distinction between a continuous random variable and a discrete one involves the numerical events of interest. We can list all of the possible values of a discrete random variable, and it is meaningful to consider the probability that an individual value will be assumed. On the other hand, we cannot list all of the values of a continuous random variable—since there is always another possible value between any two of its values—so the only meaningful events for a continuous random variable are intervals.

The probability that a continuous random variable X will assume any particular value is zero. While this may appear strange at first, it seems reasonable when you consider that you could not possibly assign a positive probability to each of the (uncountably) infinitely many values of X and still have the probabilities sum to one. This situation is analogous to a line segment: while the segment has a positive length, no point on it does. For a continuous random variable X, then, it is only meaningful to talk about the probability that the value assumed by X falls within some interval of values.

We first encountered continuous data in Chapter 2, when we measured the durations of long-distance telephone calls. The relative frequency histogram for telephone call durations (Figure 2.2) is reproduced in Figure 5.5, with one slight alteration. The heights of the rectangles have been scaled down so that the total area under the histogram is equal to 1. The area under a rectangle now represents the proportion of measurements falling into that class. For example, the area under the first rectangle is $(3)(\frac{3}{90}) = \frac{3}{30}$, which is the proportion of telephone call durations falling between 2 and 5 minutes. If we have taken a very large sample of measurements, the the resulting relative frequency histogram would closely approximate the relative frequency histogram of the entire population of telephone call durations, and the proportion represented by the area of a rectangle would be a very good approximation of the true probability of obtaining a measurement in the class interval corresponding to that rectangle. Experience has shown that, as the size of the sample of measurements becomes larger and as the class width is reduced, the outline of the relative frequency

FIGURE 5.5 RELATIVE FREQUENCY HISTOGRAM

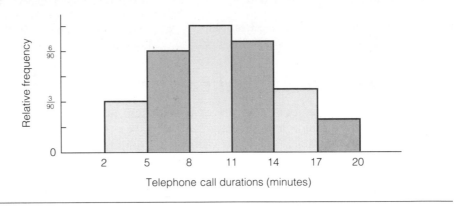

histogram tends toward a smooth curve. That is, the relative frequency polygon (adjusted to have a total area of 1) for the entire population of measurements progressively approaches a smooth curve.

When dealing with continuous data, we attempt to find a function $f(x)$, called a **probability density function,** whose graph approximates the relative frequency polygon for the population. A probability density function $f(x)$ must satisfy two conditions:

1. $f(x)$ must be nonnegative.
2. The total area under the curve representing $f(x)$ must be 1. It is important to note that $f(x)$ is not a probability. That is, $f(x) \neq P(X = x)$. As previously mentioned, the probability that X will take any specific value is zero: $P(X = x) = 0$. Given a probability density function $f(x)$, the area under the graph of $f(x)$ between two values a and b is the probability that X will take a value between a and b. This area is the shaded area in Figure 5.6.

A continuous random variable X has an expected value and variance, just as a discrete random variable does. Earlier in this chapter, we saw how to compute the

FIGURE 5.6 PROBABILITY DENSITY FUNCTION f(x) (SHADED AREA IS P(a < X < b))

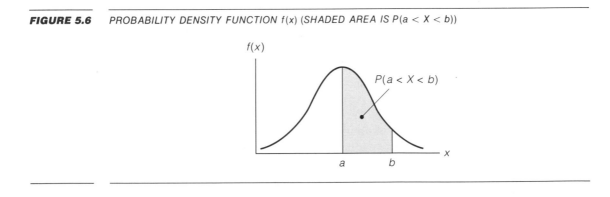

expected value and variance of any discrete random variable; we also saw that, when dealing with a well-known discrete distribution such as the binomial or the Poisson, we need not calculate the expected value and the variance from their definitions, since these parameters are well known. Similarly, most continuous distributions used in practice are familiar ones having expected values and variances that are well known and therefore need not be computed.

EXERCISES

5.45 Consider a random variable X having a probability density function described by

$$f(x) = -.5x + 1, \qquad 0 \le x \le 2.$$

a. Graph the density function $f(x)$.

b. Verify that $f(x)$ is a probability density function.

c. Find $P(X \ge 1)$.

d. Find $P(X \le .5)$.

e. Find $P(X = 1.5)$.

Self-Correcting Exercise (See Appendix 5.A for the solution.)

5.46 A continuous distribution that has appeal due to its descriptive simplicity, but limited practical application, is the **uniform distribution** (or rectangular distribution). The general formula for the probability density function of a uniform random variable X is

$$f(x) = \frac{1}{b - a}, \qquad a \le x \le b.$$

Consider a random variable X having the uniform density function $f(x)$ with $a = 20$ and $b = 30$.

a. Define and graph the density function $f(x)$.

b. Verify that $f(x)$ is a probability density function.

c. Determine $P(22 \le X \le 30)$, by finding the corresponding area under the curve.

d. Find $P(X = 25)$.

5.47 Consider a random variable X with a probability density function described by

$$f(x) = \begin{cases} .2 + .04x, & -5 \le x \le 0 \\ .2 - .04x, & 0 \le x \le 5. \end{cases}$$

a. Graph the density function $f(x)$.

b. Verify that $f(x)$ is a probability density function.

c. Find $P(X \ge -2)$.

d. Find $P(X \le 3)$.

e. Find $P(3 \le X \le 5)$.

5.48 A hospital receives a pharmaceutical delivery each morning at a time that varies uniformly between 7:00 A.M. and 8:00 A.M. (The uniform distribution was described in Exercise 5.48.)

a. If X represents the time of delivery on a given morning, define and graph the density function $f(x)$.

b. Find the probability that the delivery on a given morning will occur between 7:15 and 7:30 A.M.

c. Find the probability that the delivery on a given morning will occur between 7:25 and 7:49 A.M.

SECTION 5.6   NORMAL DISTRIBUTION

The normal distribution is the most important specific continuous distribution that we will consider in detail. Other important continuous distributions (most of which we will encounter in later chapters) include the Student t distribution, the chi-square distribution, and the F distribution. The graph of the normal distribution is the familiar symmetrical, bell-shaped curve shown in Figure 5.7. One reason for the importance of the normal distribution is that it usefully models or describes the distributions of

---

FIGURE 5.7   SYMMETRICAL, BELL-SHAPED NORMAL DISTRIBUTION

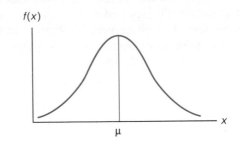

---

numerous random variables that arise in practice, such as the heights or weights of a group of people, the total annual sales of a firm, the grades of a class of students, and the measurement errors that arise during the performance of an experiment. In examples such as these, the observed measurements tend to cluster in a symmetrical fashion about the central value, giving rise to a bell-shaped distribution curve.

A second reason for the normal distribution's importance is that this distribution provides a useful approximation to many other distributions, including discrete distributions such as the binomial distribution. Finally, as we will see in Chapter 8, the normal distribution is the cornerstone distribution of statistical inference, representing the distribution of the possible estimates of a population parameter that may arise from different samples. This last point, in fact, is primarily responsible for the importance of the normal distribution.

Normal Distribution

A random variable X, with mean μ and variance σ^2, is normally distributed if its probability density function is given by

$$f(x) = \left(\frac{1}{\sigma\sqrt{2\pi}}\right)e^{-(1/2)[(x-\mu)/\sigma]^2}, \qquad -\infty < x < \infty$$

where $\pi = 3.14159\ldots$ and $e = 2.71828.\ldots$

A random variable that is normally distributed is called a **normal random variable.** A normal random variable can take on any real value from $-\infty$ to $+\infty$; the normal probability density function $f(x)$ is continuous and has a positive value for all values of x. Like that of any other probability density function, the value of $f(x)$ is not the probability that X assumes the value x, but an expression of the height of the curve at the value x. Moreover, the entire area under the curve depicting $f(x)$ must equal 1.

It is apparent from the formula for the probability density function that a normal distribution is completely determined once the two parameters μ and σ^2 are specified. That is, a whole family of different normal distributions exists, but one differs from

FIGURE 5.8   *NORMAL DISTRIBUTIONS WITH THE SAME VARIANCE BUT DIFFERENT MEANS*

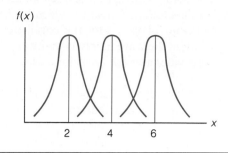

FIGURE 5.9   *NORMAL DISTRIBUTIONS WITH THE SAME MEAN BUT DIFFERENT VARIANCES*

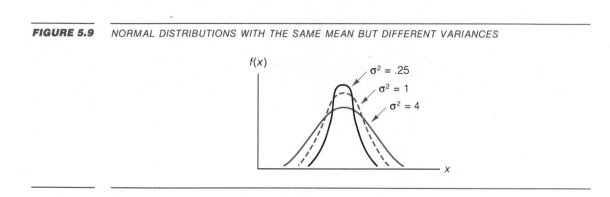

another only in the location of its mean μ and in the variance σ^2 of its values; all normal distributions have the same general symmetrical, bell-shaped appearance. Figure 5.8 depicts three normal distributions having the same variance but different means, while Figure 5.9 shows three normal distributions having the same mean but different variances. Notice in the latter figure that the shape of the distribution becomes flatter and more spread out as the variance becomes larger.

FINDING NORMAL PROBABILITIES

Once we determine that a situation can be modeled appropriately by using a normal distribution, we'll want to find various normal probabilities, which are represented by areas under the normal curve. The procedure for finding normal probabilities is illustrated in the following example.

Suppose that the length of time students take in writing a standard entrance examination is known to be normally distributed, with a mean of 60 minutes and a standard deviation of 8 minutes. If we observe the time taken by a particular student, what is the probability that the student's time will be between 60 and 70 minutes?

Given that X denotes the time taken to write the entrance examination, the probability we seek is written $P(60 < X < 70)$. This probability is given by the area under the normal curve between 60 and 70, depicted by the shaded region in Figure 5.10(a). The actual calculation of such an area (probability) is difficult, however, so we resort to the tabulated areas provided by Table 5 in Appendix B.

Since each pair of values for the parameters μ and σ^2 gives rise to a different normal distribution, there are infinitely many possible normal distributions, making it impossible to provide tables of areas for each one. Fortunately, we can make do with just one table.

The particular normal distribution for which Table 5 in Appendix B has been constructed is the normal distribution with $\mu = 0$ and $\sigma = 1$, called the **standard normal distribution.** The corresponding normal random variable, with a mean of 0 and a standard deviation of 1, is called the **standardized normal random variable** and is denoted Z. Thus, before using Table 5, we must convert or transform our normal random variable X into the standardized normal random variable Z. This is accomplished by applying the following transformation.

Standard Normal Random Variable

$$Z = \frac{X - \mu_x}{\sigma_x}$$

FIGURE 5.10   *SHADED AREA IS $P(60 < X < 70) = P(0 < Z < 1.25)$*

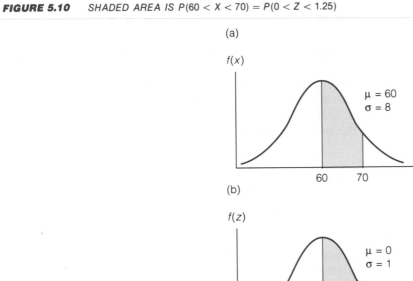

(a)

$\mu = 60$
$\sigma = 8$

(b)

$\mu = 0$
$\sigma = 1$

For our example, we obtain

$$Z = \frac{X - 60}{8}.$$

It can be shown that Z is a normally distributed random variable with a mean of 0 and a standard deviation of 1.

In order to find the desired probability, $P(60 < X < 70)$, we must first determine the interval of z-values corresponding to the interval of x-values of interest: $60 < x < 70$. Using elementary algebra, we know that

$$60 < x < 70$$

holds whenever

$$\frac{60 - 60}{8} < \frac{x - 60}{8} < \frac{70 - 60}{8}$$

or

$$0 < z < 1.25.$$

We therefore obtain

$$P(60 < X < 70) = P(0 < Z < 1.25).$$

Thus, we can find the required area (probability) by finding the corresponding area under the standard normal curve, which is depicted by the shaded area in Figure 5.10(b). Areas such as this one, which correspond to probabilities of the form $P(0 < Z < z_0)$, are tabulated in Table 5 in Appendix B. Table 5 is reproduced here as Table 5.9.

In Table 5 (and in Table 5.9), a value of z correct to the first decimal place is found in the left-hand column; the second decimal place is located across the top row. We need to find $P(0 < Z < 1.25)$, which is represented by the area over the interval from 0 to 1.25. To find this area corresponding to $z = 1.25$, first locate 1.2 in the left-hand column, and then move across that row until you reach the column with .05 at the top. The area corresponding to $z = 1.25$ is .3944, so

$$P(60 < X < 70) = P(0 < Z < 1.25)$$
$$= .3944.$$

The probability that a particular student will take between 60 and 70 minutes to write the entrance exam is therefore .3944.

We repeat that the z-value corresponding to a given value x_0 has an important interpretation. Since $(x_0 - \mu)$ expresses how far x_0 is from the mean, the corresponding z-value

$$z_0 = \frac{x_0 - \mu}{\sigma}$$

tells us how many standard deviations x_0 is from the mean. Moreover, if z_0 is positive, then x_0 lies to the right of its mean; and conversely, if z_0 is negative, then x_0 lies to the

TABLE 5.9   REPRODUCTION OF TABLE 5: STANDARD NORMAL CURVE AREAS

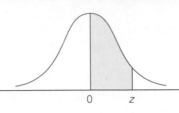

z	.00	.01	.02	.03	.04	.05	.06	.07	.08	.09
0.0	.0000	.0040	.0080	.0120	.0160	.0199	.0239	.0279	.0319	.0359
0.1	.0398	.0438	.0478	.0517	.0557	.0596	.0636	.0675	.0714	.0753
0.2	.0793	.0832	.0871	.0910	.0948	.0987	.1026	.1064	.1103	.1141
0.3	.1179	.1217	.1255	.1293	.1331	.1368	.1406	.1443	.1480	.1517
0.4	.1554	.1591	.1628	.1664	.1700	.1736	.1772	.1808	.1844	.1879
.05	.1915	.1950	.1985	.2019	.2054	.2088	.2123	.2157	.2190	.2224
.06	.2257	.2291	.2324	.2357	.2389	.2422	.2454	.2486	.2517	.2549
.07	.2580	.2611	.2642	.2673	.2704	.2734	.2764	.2794	.2823	.2852
.08	.2881	.2910	.2939	.2967	.2995	.3023	.3051	.3078	.3106	.3133
0.9	.3159	.3186	.3212	.3238	.3264	.3289	.3315	.3340	.3365	.3389
1.0	.3413	.3438	.3461	.3485	.3508	.3531	.3554	.3577	.3599	.3621
1.1	.3643	.3665	.3686	.3708	.3729	.3749	.3770	.3790	.3810	.3830
1.2	.3849	.3869	.3888	.3907	.3925	.3944	.3962	.3980	.3997	.4015
1.3	.4032	.4049	.4066	.4082	.4099	.4115	.4131	.4147	.4162	.4177
1.4	.4192	.4207	.4222	.4236	.4251	.4265	.4279	.4292	.4306	.4319
1.5	.4332	.4345	.4357	.4370	.4382	.4394	.4406	.4418	.4429	.4441
1.6	.4452	.4463	.4474	.4484	.4495	.4505	.4515	.4525	.4535	.4545
1.7	.4554	.4564	.4573	.4582	.4591	.4599	.4608	.4616	.4625	.4633
1.8	.4641	.4649	.4656	.4664	.4671	.4678	.4686	.4693	.4699	.4706
1.9	.4713	.4719	.4726	.4732	.4738	.4744	.4750	.4756	.4761	.4767
2.0	.4772	.4778	.4783	.4788	.4793	.4798	.4803	.4808	.4812	.4817
2.1	.4821	.4826	.4830	.4834	.4838	.4842	.4846	.4850	.4854	.4857
2.2	.4861	.4864	.4868	.4871	.4875	.4878	.4881	.4884	.4887	.4890
2.3	.4893	.4896	.4898	.4901	.4904	.4906	.4909	.4911	.4913	.4916
2.4	.4918	.4920	.4922	.4925	.4927	.4929	.4931	.4932	.4934	.4936
2.5	.4938	.4940	.4941	.4943	.4945	.4946	.4948	.4949	.4951	.4952
2.6	.4953	.4955	.4956	.4957	.4959	.4960	.4961	.4962	.4963	.4964
2.7	.4965	.4966	.4967	.4968	.4969	.4970	.4971	.4972	.4973	.4974
2.8	.4974	.4975	.4976	.4977	.4977	.4978	.4979	.4979	.4980	.4981
2.9	.4981	.4982	.4982	.4983	.4984	.4984	.4985	.4985	.4986	.4986
3.0	.4987	.4987	.4987	.4988	.4988	.4989	.4989	.4989	'.4990	.4990

SOURCE: Abridged from Table 1 of A. Hald, *Statistical Tables and Formulas* (New York: John Wiley & Sons, Inc.), 1952.
Reproduced by permission of A. Hald and the publisher, John Wiley & Sons, Inc.

left of the mean. Thus, in the preceding example, the value 70 lies 1.25 standard deviations to the right of the mean value of 60. That is, $70 = 60 + 1.25(8)$.

As we have just seen, we can obtain desired probabilities for any normal distribution from probabilities tabulated for the standard normal distribution. A table of probabilities for just one normal distribution supplies us with all the information we need, because normal distributions differ from one another only in their means and variances. The probability that the variable assumes a value within z_0 standard deviations of the mean remains constant from one normal random variable to the next. In other words, if X is any normal random variable with mean μ and standard deviation σ, then

$$P(\mu - z_0\sigma < X < \mu + z_0\sigma) = P(-z_0 < Z < z_0).$$

We first caught a glimpse of this concept when we took up the Empirical Rule in Chapter 3. According to this rule, about 68% of the values from a mound-shaped distribution (such as the normal distribution) lie within one standard deviation of the mean, about 95% of the values lie within two standard deviations of the mean, and almost 100% of the values lie within three standard deviations.*

Therefore, probabilities of the form $P(-z_0 < Z < z_0)$ need only be tabulated for one normal distribution, since they are the same for all others. In fact, since a normal distribution is symmetrical, it suffices to tabulate probabilities of the form $P(0 \le Z \le z_0)$. The probabilities found in Table 5 in Appendix B, then, are of the form $P(0 \le Z \le z_0)$, for values of z_0 from 0.00 to 3.09. Given that the total area under the normal curve equals 1, any desired probability may be obtained by adding and subtracting probabilities of this form.

EXAMPLE 5.5

Determine the following probabilities:

   a. $P(Z \ge 1.47)$

   b. $P(-2.25 \le Z \le 1.85)$

   c. $P(.65 \le Z \le 1.36)$

Solution

   a. It is advisable to begin by sketching a diagram and indicating the area of interest under the normal curve, as shown in Figure 5.11. In part (a), area A_1 corresponds to the required probability, and A_2 is the area between $z = 0$ and $z = 1.47$. Since the entire area under the normal curve equals 1, and since the curve is symmetrical about $z = 0$, the entire area to the right of $z = 0$ is .5; so

        $A_1 + A_2 = .5.$

   Area A_2 is of the form that can be found in Table 5. Locating $z = 1.47$ in Table 5, we find that area A_2 is .4292, so $P(0 \le Z \le 1.47) = .4292$. The required

---

* For the special mound-shaped distribution called the *normal distribution,* Table 5 in Appendix B identifies the precise percentages as 68.26, 95.44, and 99.74, respectively.

FIGURE 5.11   SHADED AREAS ARE $P(0 < Z < 1.47)$ AND $P(Z \geq 1.47)$ IN EXAMPLE 5.5a

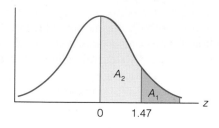

probability is therefore

$$P(Z \geq 1.47) = A_1$$
$$= .5 - A_2$$
$$= .5 - .4292 = .0708.$$

b. Whenever the area of interest straddles the mean, as in part (b), we must express it as the sum of the portions to the left and to the right of the mean. The required probability $P(-2.25 \leq Z \leq 1.85)$ corresponds to the sum of the areas A_1 and A_2 in Figure 5.12. That is,

$$P(-2.25 \leq Z \leq 1.85) = A_1 + A_2.$$

From Table 5, we find that $A_2 = .4678$. Because the normal distribution is symmetrical, we can write

$$A_1 = P(-2.25 \leq Z \leq 0) = P(0 \leq Z \leq 2.25).$$

Locating $z = 2.25$ in Table 5, we find that $A_1 = .4878$. Therefore, the required probability is

$$P(-2.25 \leq Z \leq 1.85) = A_1 + A_2$$
$$= .4878 + .4678 = .9556.$$

c. In part (c), $P(.65 \leq Z \leq 1.36)$ corresponds to the shaded area A in Figure 5.13. Since Table 5 only provides areas from 0 up to some positive value of Z, we must express A as the difference between two such areas. If A_1 is the area between $z = 0$

FIGURE 5.12   SHADED AREA IS $P(-2.25 \leq Z \leq 1.85)$ IN EXAMPLE 5.5b

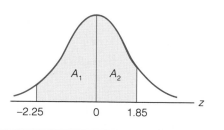

FIGURE 5.13   SHADED AREA IS P(.65 < Z < 1.36) IN EXAMPLE 5.5c

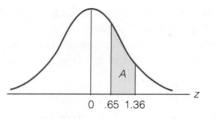

and $z = 1.36$, then $A_1 = .4131$ (from Table 5). Similarly, if A_2 is the area between $z = 0$ and $z = .65$, then $A_2 = .2422$. Therefore,

$$P(.65 \leq Z \leq 1.36) = A$$
$$= A_1 - A_2$$
$$= P(0 \leq Z \leq 1.36) - P(0 \leq Z \leq .65)$$
$$= .4131 - .2422 = .1709.$$

EXAMPLE 5.6

If Z is a standard normal variable, determine the value z_0 for which $P(Z \leq z_0) = .6331$.

Solution.   Since the area to the left of $z = 0$ is .5, z_0 must be a positive number, as indicated in Figure 5.14. If A is the area between $z = 0$ and $z = z_0$, then

$$.6331 = .5 + A,$$

so

$$A = .6331 - .5 = .1331.$$

Locating the area .1331 in the body of Table 5, we find the corresponding value of z_0 to be $z_0 = .34$. Therefore,

$$P(z \leq .34) = .6331.$$

FIGURE 5.14   SHADED AREA IS P(0 ≤ Z ≤ z₀) IN EXAMPLE 5.6

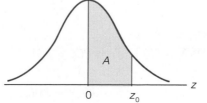

EXAMPLE 5.7: FINDING $Z_{\alpha/2}$

This example introduces some useful notation that you will use frequently in statistical inference, beginning in Chapter 8. If Z is a standard normal random variable and α is any probability, then $z_{\alpha/2}$ represents that value for which the area under the standard normal curve to the right of $z_{\alpha/2}$ is $\alpha/2$. In other words,

$$P(Z > z_{\alpha/2}) = \alpha/2.$$

Thus, because the normal distribution is symmetrical, $-z_{\alpha/2}$ represents that value for which the area under the standard normal curve to the left of $-z_{\alpha/2}$ is $\alpha/2$. Determine $z_{.025}$.

Solution. If A denotes the area in Figure 5.15 between $z = 0$ and $z = z_{.025}$, then the desired valued $z_{.025}$ is the z-value in Table 5 corresponding to the area A. Since the area under the curve to the right of $z_{.025}$ is .025,

$$A = .5 - .025 = .475.$$

From Table 5, we find that the z-value corresponding to the area .475 is

$$Z_{.025} = 1.96,$$

so

$$P(Z > 1.96) = .025.$$

From symmetry, we know that the area to the left of $z = -1.96$ is also .025. That is,

$$P(Z < -1.96) = .025.$$

EXAMPLE 5.8

A venture capital company feels that the rate of return (X) on a proposed investment is approximately normally distributed with a mean of 30% and a standard deviation of 10%.

   a. Find the probability that the return will exceed 55%.

   b. Find the probability that the return will be less than 22%.

Solution

   a. Figure 5.16 shows the required area A_1, together with values of Z corresponding to selected values of X. The value of Z corresponding to $x = 55$ is

$$z = \frac{x - \mu}{\sigma} = \frac{55 - 30}{10} = 2.5.$$

Therefore,

$$P(X > 55) = A_1 = P(Z > 2.5)$$
$$= .5 - P(0 \leq Z \leq 2.5)$$
$$= .5 - .4938 = .0062.$$

The probability that the return will exceed 55% is .0062.

FIGURE 5.15   LOCATING $z_{.025}$ IN EXAMPLE 5.7

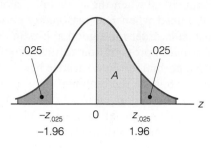

FIGURE 5.16   CORRESPONDING VALUES OF X AND Z FOR EXAMPLE 5.8

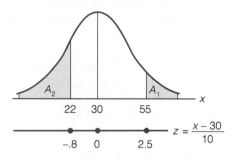

b. Figure 5.16 shows the required area A_2. By the same logic that was used in part (a),

$$P(X < 22) = A_2 = P\left(Z < \frac{22 - 30}{10}\right)$$

$$= P(Z < -.8) = P(Z > .8)$$

$$= .5 - P(0 \le Z \le .8)$$

$$= .5 - .2881 = .2119.$$

The probability that the return will be less than 22% is .2119.

NORMAL APPROXIMATION TO THE BINOMIAL

The normal distribution can be used to approximate a number of other probability distributions, including the binomial distribution. The normal approximation to the binomial is useful whenever the number of trials n is so large that the binomial tables cannot be used. Since the normal distribution is symmetrical, it best approximates binomial distributions that are reasonably symmetrical. And since a binomial distribution is symmetrical when the probability p of a success equals .5, the best approximation is obtained when p is reasonably close to .5. The farther p is from .5, the larger n must be in order for a good approximation to result.

The normal approximation to the binomial distribution works best when the approximating normal random variable has only a very small probability of assuming a value that falls outside the binomial range ($0 \le X \le n$). Generally, this is satisfied if $np \ge 5$ and $nq \ge 5$; so a conventional rule of thumb is that the normal distribution will provide an adequate approximation of a binomial distribution if $np \ge 5$ and $nq \ge 5$.

Given a binomial distribution with n trials and probability p of a success on any trial, the mean of the binomial distribution is $\mu = np$ and the variance is $\sigma^2 = npq$. We therefore choose the normal distribution with $\mu = np$ and $\sigma^2 = npq$ to be the approximating distribution.

To see how the approximation works, consider the binomial distribution with $n = 20$ and $p = .5$, the graph of which is shown in Figure 5.17. Although it is not necessary to use the normal approximation in this case, we have purposely chosen n to be small enough that the binomial tables can be used as a check against the normal approximation. We will approximate the binomial probabilities, using the normal distribution with mean $\mu = (20)(.5) = 10$ and variance $\sigma^2 = 20(.5)(.5) = 5$ (or standard deviation $\sigma = 2.24$). Let X *denote the binomial random variable* and Y *the normal random variable.* The binomial probability $P(X = 10)$, represented by the height of the line above $x = 10$ in Figure 5.17, is equal to the area of the rectangle erected above the interval from 9.5 to 10.5. This area (or probability) is approximated by the area under the normal curve between 9.5 and 10.5. That is,

$$P(X = 10) \cong P(9.5 \le Y \le 10.5).$$

The .5 that is added to and subtracted from 10 is called the *continuity correction factor;* it corrects for the fact that we are using a continuous distribution to approximate a discrete one. To check the accuracy of this particular approximation, we can use the binomial tables to obtain

$$P(X = 10) = .176.$$

FIGURE 5.17   *NORMAL APPROXIMATION TO BINOMIAL DISTRIBUTION*

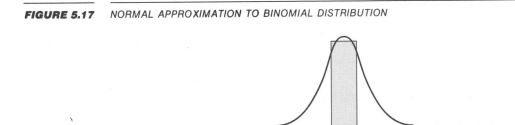

9.5 10.5

From Table 5, the normal approximation is

$$P(9.5 \le Y \le 10.5) = P\left(\frac{9.5 - 10}{2.24} \le Z \le \frac{10.5 - 10}{2.24}\right)$$

$$= P(-.22 \le Z \le .22)$$

$$= 2(.0871)$$

$$= .1742.$$

The approximation for any other value of X would proceed in the same manner. In general, the binomial probability $P(X = x_0)$ is approximated by the area under the normal curve between $(x_0 - .5)$ and $(x_0 + .5)$.

Suppose, in the preceding example, that we wish to approximate the binomial probability $P(5 \le X \le 12)$. This probability would be approximated by the area under the normal curve between 4.5 and 12.5. That is,

$$P(5 \le X \le 12) \cong P(4.5 \le Y \le 12.5)$$

$$= P\left(\frac{4.5 - 10}{2.24} \le Z \le \frac{12.5 - 10}{2.24}\right)$$

$$= P(-2.46 \le Z \le 1.12)$$

$$= P(0 \le Z \le 2.46) + P(0 \le Z \le 1.12)$$

$$= .4931 + .3686$$

$$= .8617.$$

As a check, the binomial tables yield

$$P(5 \le X \le 12) = .862.$$

Including the continuity correction factor when finding the probability associated with an interval becomes less important as n becomes larger. In subsequent chapters, we will ignore the continuity correction factor when n exceeds 25.

EXERCISES

LEARNING THE TECHNIQUES

5.49 Use Table 5 of Appendix B to find the area under the standard normal curve between the following values:

a. $z = 0$ and $z = 2.3$

b. $z = 0$ and $z = 1.68$

c. $z = .24$ and $z = 1.33$

d. $z = -2.58$ and $z = 0$

e. $z = -2.81$ and $z = -1.35$

f. $z = -1.73$ and $z = .49$

5.50 Use Table 5 to find the following probabilities:

a. $P(Z \ge 1.7)$ d. $P(Z \le 2.43)$

b. $P(Z \ge -.95)$ e. $P(-2.97 \le Z \le -1.38)$

c. $P(Z \le -1.96)$ f. $P(-1.14 \le Z \le 1.55)$

5.51 Use Table 5 to find the value z_0 for which:

a. $P(0 \le Z \le z_0) = .41$

b. $P(Z \ge z_0) = .025$

c. $P(Z \ge z_0) = .9$

d. $P(Z \le z_0) = .95$

e. $P(Z \leq z_0) = .2$

f. $P(-z_0 \leq Z \leq z_0) = .88$

5.52 Determine $z_{\alpha/2}$, and locate its value on a graph of the standard normal distribution, for each of the following values of α:

a. .01   b. .02   c. .10

5.53 Let X be a normal random variable with a mean of 50 and a standard deviation of 8. Find the following probabilities:

a. $P(X \geq 52)$ d. $P(X > 40)$

b. $P(X < 40)$ e. $P(35 < X \leq 64)$

c. $P(X = 40)$ f. $P(32 \leq X \leq 37)$

5.54 If X is a normal random variable with a mean of 50 and a standard deviation of 8, how many standard deviations away from the mean is each of the following values of X?

a. $x = 52$ d. $x = 64$

b. $x = 40$ e. $x = 32$

c. $x = 35$ f. $x = 37$

5.55 Let X be a binomial random variable with $n = 100$ and $p = .6$. Approximate the following probabilities, using the normal distribution:

a. $P(X = 65)$

b. $P(X \leq 70)$

c. $P(X > 50)$

APPLYING THE TECHNIQUES

Self-Correcting Exercise (See Appendix 5.A for the solution.)

5.56 The time required to assemble an electronic component is normally distributed with a mean of 12 minutes and a standard deviation of 1.5 minutes. Find the probability that a particular assembly takes:

a. more than 14 minutes

b. more than 8 minutes

c. less than 14 minutes

d. less than 10 minutes

e. between 10 and 15 minutes

5.57 The lifetime of a certain brand of tires is approximately normally distributed, with a mean of 45,000 miles and a standard deviation of 2,500 miles. The tires carry a warranty for 40,000 miles.

a. What proportion of the tires will fail before the warranty expires?

b. What proportion of the tires will fail after the warranty expires but before they have lasted for 41,000 miles?

5.58 A firm's marketing manager believes that total sales for the firm next year can be modeled by using a normal distribution with a mean of $2.5 million and a standard deviation of $300,000.

a. What is the probability that the firm's sales will exceed $3 million?

b. What is the probability that the firm's sales will fall within $150,000 of the expected level of sales?

c. In order to cover fixed costs, the firm's sales must exceed the break-even level of $1.8 million. What is the probability that sales will exceed the break-even level?

d. Determine the sales level that has only a 9% chance of being exceeded next year.

5.59 Empirical studies have provided support for the belief that a common stock's annual rate of return is approximately normally distributed. Suppose that you have invested in the stock of a company for which the annual return has an expected value of 16% and a standard deviation of 10%.

a. Find the probability that your one-year return will exceed 30%.

b. Find the probability that your one-year return will be negative.

c. Suppose that this company embarks on a new high-risk, but potentially highly profitable, venture. As a result, the return on the stock now has an expected value of 25% and a standard deviation of 20%. Answer parts (a) and (b) in light of the revised estimates concerning the stock's return.

d. As an investor, would you approve of the company's decision to embark on the new venture?

5.60 A steel fabricator produces pipes with a diameter that is approximately normally distributed with a mean of 10 cm and a variance of .01 cm^2.

a. Suppose that the tolerance limit for these pipes is .2 cm, so that pipes with a diameter falling within the interval $10 \pm .2$ cm are acceptable. What proportion of the pipes produced will be acceptable?

b. Suppose that pipes with too small a diameter can be reworked, but pipes with too large a diameter must be scrapped. Suppose also that the tolerance has been reduced to .1 cm. What proportion of the pipes must be scrapped?

5.61 a. Mensa is an organization whose members possess IQs in the top 2% of the population.

a. If IQs are normally distributed with a mean of 100 and a standard deviation of 16, what is the minimum IQ necessary for admission?

b. If three individuals are chosen at random from the general population, what is the probability that all three satisfy the minimum requirement for admission to Mensa?

c. If two individuals are chosen at random from the general population, what is the probability that at least one of them exceeds the minimum requirement for admission to Mensa?

5.62 Universities throughout the United States and Canada are concerned about the aging of their faculty members, as the average age of professors is at a historic high. A very large number of faculty members will retire within the next decade, making it difficult to find adequate replacements to fill all of the positions that will become available. In 1989, Canadian professors had a median age of 46.4 years, and 36% of them were at least 50 years of age (*Globe and Mail,* 29 March 1989, p. Al). Assume that the ages of these professors are normally distributed.

a. Determine the standard deviation of the ages.

b. Assume that there are currently 40,000 professors at Canadian universities and that the mandatory retirement age is 65. What is the minimum number of professors who will retire during the next decade?

5.63 The maintenance department of a city's electric power company finds that it is cost efficient to replace all streetlight bulbs at once, rather than to replace the bulbs individually as they burn out. Assume that the lifetime of a bulb is normally distributed, with a mean of 3,000 hours and a standard deviation of 200 hours.

a. If the department wants no more than 1% of the bulbs to burn out before they are replaced, after how many hours should all of the bulbs be replaced?

b. If two bulbs are selected at random from among those that have been replaced, what is the probability that at least one of them has burned out?

5.64 Companies are interested in the demographics of the listening audience for radio programs they sponsor. A radio station has determined that only 20% of listeners phoning into a morning talk program are male. During a particular week, 200 calls are received by this program.

a. What is the probability that at least 50 of these 200 callers are male?

b. What is the probability that more than half of these 200 callers are female?

c. There is a 30% chance that the number of males among these 200 callers does not exceed what?

5.65 Due to an increasing number of nonperforming loans, a Texas bank now insists that several stringent conditions be met before a customer is granted a consumer loan. As a result, 60% of all customers applying for a loan are rejected. If 40 new loan applications are selected at random, calculate the following probabilities.

a. At least 12 are accepted.

b. At least half of them are accepted.

c. No more than 16 are accepted.

d. The number of applications rejected is between 20 and 30, inclusive.

5.66 Historical data collected at a paper mill reveal that 40% of sheet breaks are due to water drops, which result from the condensation of steam. Suppose that the causes of the next 50 sheet breaks are monitored and that the sheet breaks are independent of one another.

a. Find the expected value and the standard deviation of the number of sheet breaks that are caused by water drops.

b. What is the probability that at least 25 of these breaks are due to water drops?

c. What is the probability that the number of breaks due to water drops is between 10 and 25, inclusive?

SUMMARY

The concept of a random variable permits us to summarize the results of an experiment in terms of numerical-valued events. Specifically, a random variable assigns a numerical value to each simple event of an experiment. A random variable is discrete if it can assume at most a countably infinite number of values; it is continuous if it can take any of infinitely many values within some interval of values. Once the probability distribution of a random variable is known, we can determine its expected value, its variance, and the probability that it will assume various values. These abilities will stand us in good stead when we reach statistical inference and want to determine the probability that any particular sample will be selected from a population over which the random variable is defined.

Two discrete random variables that frequently arise in real-world applications are the binomial and the Poisson. We described the characteristics of random experiments that give rise to each of these random variables, and we gave the formulas for their probability distributions. The normal probability distribution is the most important continuous distribution. Besides approximating the distribution of numerous random variables that arise in practice, the normal distribution is the cornerstone distribution of statistical inference.

IMPORTANT TERMS

Random variable
Discrete random variable
Continuous random variable
Discrete probability distribution
Expected value of a discrete random variable
Variance of a discrete random variable
Standard deviation of a random variable
Binomial experiment

Binomial random variable
Binomial probability distribution
Poisson experiment
Poisson random variable
Poisson probability distribution
Normal probability distribution
Normal random variable
Standardized normal random variable

SUMMARY OF FORMULAS

$$\mu = E(X) = \sum_{i=1}^{N} x_i \cdot p(x_i).$$

$$\sigma^2 = \sum_{i=1}^{N} (x_i - \mu)^2 \cdot p(x_i).$$

Binomial

$$P(X = x) = p(x) = C_x^n \cdot p^x \cdot q^{n-x}, \quad \text{where } q = 1 - p$$

$$= \left(\frac{n!}{x!(n-x)!} \right) p^x \cdot q^{n-x}, \quad x = 0, 1, \dots, n$$

$$E(X) = \mu = np$$

$$V(X) = \sigma^2 = npq$$

Poisson

$$P(X = x) = p(x) = \frac{e^{-\mu} \cdot \mu^x}{x!}, \quad x = 0, 1, 2, \dots$$

$$E(X) = V(X) = \mu$$

Standardized Normal Random Variable

$$Z = \frac{X - \mu}{\sigma}$$

SUPPLEMENTARY EXERCISES

5.67 Let X be a random variable with the following probability distribution.

x	0	2	4	6	8
$p(x)$	.10	.20	.25	.30	.15

a. Find the expected value and the standard deviation of X.

b. Find $E(X^2)$.

5.68 Two coins are selected from a box of four coins: a nickel, two dimes, and a quarter. Let X be the number of dimes selected.

a. Express the probability distribution of X in tabular form.

b. Express the probability distribution of x in graphical form.

5.69 A large manufacturer has purchased an insurance policy for $500,000 per year to insure itself against 4 specific types of losses. The costs associated with each type of loss and their probabilities are listed in the accompanying table. The probability that no loss will occur is .63, and it is assumed that at most one type of loss will occur in a given year. Of the total cost of the policy, 20% is to cover administrative expenses.

Cost	Probability
$100,000	.15
$800,000	.10
$1,500,000	.08
$2,500,000	.04

a. What is the expected *profit* to the insurance company on this policy?

b. What is the standard deviation of the profits to the insurance company?

5.70 Let X, Y, and W be three random variables with the following probability distributions:

x	$p(x)$	y	$p(y)$	w	$p(w)$
2	1/4	2	1/8	1	1/4
4	1/4	4	3/8	4	1/4
6	1/4	6	3/8	6	1/4
8	1/4	8	1/8	9	1/4

a. Determine the means of X, Y, and W simply by inspection.

b. Verify your answers to part (a) by calculating the means.

c. Without performing any calculations, determine which of the three distributions has the smallest variance and which has the largest. Explain your reasoning. (HINT: Compare X with Y and X with W.)

d. Verify your answer to part (c) by computing the variances.

5.71 Exercise 5.6 gave the probability distribution of the number of children in American families. Use the data in that exercise to find the probability distribution of the number of children in families with at least one child. (This is called a **conditional probability distribution.**)

5.72 Let X be a binomial random variable with $n = 20$ and $p = .4$. Use Table 1 (or Table 2) to find the following probabilities:

a. $P(X \le 3)$ d. $P(X > 9)$

b. $P(X = 3)$ e. $P(5 \le X \le 8)$

c. $P(X \ge 6)$ f. $P(7 \le X \le 9)$

5.73 The BDW Car Dealership sells one sports model, the FX500. Of the customers who buy this model, 50% choose fire-engine red as the color, 30% choose snow white, and 20% choose jet black.

a. What is the probability that at least 6 of the next 10 customers who buy an FX500 model choose red cars?

b. On average, a customer who buys a red FX500 orders options worth $3,000. Customers who buy white FX500 models buy only $2,000 worth of options and those who buy black FX500 models buy $1,500 worth of options. What is the expected value of the options bought by a customer who buys an FX500?

5.74 Financing acquisitions often takes the form of a leveraged buyout (LBO), in which case a substantial portion of the purchase price is financed by debt. Bankers look at a number of factors when evaluating an LBO proposal. In the United States, it's estimated that 70 percent of all LBO proposals are not accepted by bankers (*Canadian Business,* August 1985). If 25 LBO proposals are randomly selected for consideration by a bank, find the following probabilities.

a. Not more than eight are accepted.

b. Exactly eight are accepted.

c. More than eight are accepted.

d. At least five but less than twelve are accepted.

5.75 What assumptions did you make in order to answer Exercise 5.74?

5.76 ACME Plumbing Supply has just received a shipment of 5,000 stainless steel valves that are designed for use in chemical plants producing acidic chemicals that corrode regular steel valves. Minutes after receiving the valves, the supplier calls to inform ACME that one of its employees inadvertently included 100 regular steel valves in the shipment. Unfortunately there is no way to distinguish the regular valves without extensive testing. At about the same time, ACME receives an emergency order for 5 of the stainless steel valves from one of its largest customers.

a. If ACME decides to fill the order for 5 stainless steel valves, what is the probability that one or more will be a regular steel valve?

b. If ACME explains its predicament to the customer and ships 6 valves, which the customer will test prior to use, what is the probability that at least 5 of those valves will be stainless steel?

5.77 Suppose that a machine breaks down occasionally due to a particular part that wears out, and suppose that these breakdowns occur randomly and independently. The average number of breakdowns per 8-hour day has been established to be 4. Assume that the distribution of breakdowns is stable over the 8-hour day.

a. Find the probability that no breakdowns occur during a given day.

b. Find the probability that at most 2 breakdowns occur during the first hour of the day.

c. What is the minimum number of spare parts that management should have on hand on a given day if it wishes to be at least 90% sure that the machine will not be idle at any time during the day due to a lack of parts?

5.78 The MacTell toy company produces toy firetrucks. Suppose that records kept on the number of imperfections per firetruck show that many of the trucks had no imperfections, a few had two imperfections, and so on. That is, the distribution of the number of imperfections approximated a Poisson distribution. The records also indicate that the firetrucks are produced with a mean imperfection rate of .5 per truck.

An order for 1,000 toy firetrucks has been received. The cost department must estimate the total cost of repairing the trucks before the work begins. Past experience indicates that the first imperfection on each firetruck costs 20¢ to repair, while each subsequent imperfection on a firetruck costs 10¢ to repair. (Thus a truck with three imperfections costs 40¢ to repair.) Find the total expected repair cost for the order for 1,000 firetrucks.

5.79 The sales manager for a national women's apparel distributor claims that 20% of the company's orders are for a low-end line of apparel, 70% are for a medium line, and 10% are for a high-end line.

a. If the next 5 orders are independent of one another, what is the probability that at least 3 of them will be for a medium line of apparel?

b. If the next 15 orders are independent of one another, what is the probability that at most 8 of them will be for a low-end line of apparel?

c. Suppose that 30% of orders for a low-end line of apparel include an order for accessories (such as hats or jewelry), 50% of orders for a medium line include an order for accessories, and 40% of orders for a high-end line include an order for accessories. What is the probability that an order for accessories will be included in the next order for an apparel line?

5.80 A boat broker in Florida receives an average of 26 orders per year for an exotic model of cruiser. Assuming that the demand for this model is uniform throughout the year, calculate the following probabilities.

a. The boat broker receives exactly 1 order for this model in a given week.

b. The boat broker receives exactly 2 orders for this model over a given 2-week period.

c. The boat broker receives exactly 4 orders for this model over a given 4-week period.

5.81 A maintenance worker in a large paper-manufacturing plant knows that, on average, the main pulper (which beats solid materials to a pulp) breaks down 6 times per 30-day month. Find the probability that, on a given day, she will have to repair the pulper:

a. exactly once

b. at least once

c. at least once but not more than twice

5.82 The scheduling manager for a certain hydro-electric power utility knows that an average of 12 emergency calls regarding power failures are received per month. Assume that a month consists of 30 days.

a. Find the probability that the utility will receive at least 12 emergency calls during a specified month.

b. Suppose that the utility company can handle a maximum of 3 emergency calls per day. What is the probability that on a given day, there will be more emergency calls than the utility can handle?

5.83 Use Table 5 in Appendix B to find the following probabilities:

a. $P(\geq 1.64)$

c. $P(Z < .52)$

b. $P(1.23 \leq Z \leq 2.71)$

d. $P(-.68 \leq Z \leq 2.42)$

5.84 Use Table 5 in Appendix B to find the following probabilities, where X has a normal distribution with $\mu = 24$ and $\sigma = 4$:

a. $P(X > 30)$

c. $P(X \leq 26)$

b. $P(25 \leq X \leq 27)$

d. $P(18 \leq X \leq 23)$

5.85 Suppose that the actual amount of instant coffee that a filling machine puts into 6-ounce cans varies from can to can, so that the actual fill may be looked upon as a random variable having a normal distribution with a standard deviation of .04 ounces. If only 2 out of every 100 cans are to contain less than 6 ounces of coffee, what must be the mean fill of these cans?

5.86 A soft-drink bottling plant uses a machine that fills bottles with drink mixture. The fluid volume of the filled bottles is normally distributed, with a mean of 16 ounces and a variance of 4 $(oz)^2$. Determine the fluid volume exceeded by only the fullest 10% of the filled bottles.

5.87 Consumer advocates frequently complain about the large variation in prices charged by different pharmacies for the same medication. A survey of pharmacies in Chicago by one such advocate revealed that the prices charged for 100 tablets of Tylenol 3 were normally distributed, with about 90% of the prices ranging between $8.25 and $11.25. The mean price charged was $9.75. What proportion of the pharmacies charged over $10.25 for the prescription?

5.88   Suppose that the height of men is normally distributed with a mean of 5 feet 9 inches and a standard deviation of 2 inches. Find the minimum height of the ceiling of an airplane such that at most 2% of the men walking down the aisle will have to duck their heads.

5.89   Suppose that X is a binomial random variable with $n = 100$ and $p = .20$. Use the normal approximation to find the probability that X takes a value between 22 and 25 (inclusive).

5.90   Venture capital firms provide financing for small, high-risk enterprises that have the potential to become highly profitable. A successful venture capital firm notes that it provides financing for only 10% of the proposals that it reviews. Of the 200 proposals submitted this year, what is the probability that more than 30 will receive financing?

CASE 5.1   *Calculating Probabilities Associated with the Stock Market*

The Value Line Investment Survey is a stock market advisory service that is well known for its fine performance record. Value Line follows 1,700 stocks. Each week it assigns each stock a ranking from 1 (best) to 5 (worst), indicating the stock's timeliness for purchase. There are always 100 stocks in the (top) Rank 1 group.

Suppose that, at the beginning of a calendar year, a portfolio (called the passive Rank 1 portfolio) consisting of the 100 Rank 1 stocks is formed and is held (unchanged) for one year. At the end of the year, the rate of return on this passive Rank 1 portfolio is compared to the return on the market portfolio, which consists of all 1,700 stocks. Holloway observed that the Passive Rank 1 portfolio outperformed the market portfolio in each of the 14 years from 1965 to 1978, with the exception of 1970.* The probability that this would occur by chance is .00085. After noting that the performances of the two portfolios were almost identical in two of the years (1975 and 1976), Holloway stated: "Even if we count these two years as failures, the probability of obtaining the Value Line results by *chance* is only .0286." Subsequently, Gregory took exception to this statement and wrote: "That observation is a misuse of statistics."† He pointed out that, while the probability of .0286 would be correct if applied to an advisory service selected at random, Value Line was selected *because* of its fine performance record. Gregory then noted that "out of a population of, say, 20 investment advisory services, the probability of finding at least one with 3 [or fewer] bad years out of 14 is .44." In other words, it isn't all that surprising to find one advisory service with such a good performance record.

Holloway also examined an active portfolio strategy, in which the Rank 1 portfolio was "updated weekly to consist always of the 100 Rank 1 stocks." This

---

* Clark Holloway, "A Note on Testing an Aggressive Investment Strategy Using Value Line Ranks," *Journal of Finance* 36(3) (1981): 711–19.

† N. A. Gregory, "Testing an Aggressive Investing Strategy Using Value Line Ranks: A Comment," *Journal of Finance* 38(1) (1983): 257–70.

strategy "outperformed the market in each of the 14 consecutive years" from 1965 to 1978, neglecting the brokerage commission incurred whenever a stock was bought or sold. Although the probability of achieving this performance by chance is only .000061, analysis of results that included brokerage commissions indicated that performance under this active strategy was not significantly superior to the performance of the passive Rank 1 portfolio.

In another phase of Holloway's study, the 100 Rank 1 stocks were partitioned into 5 subportfolios. Holloway monitored the performance of each of the 5 sub-portfolios over the 4 years from 1974 to 1977, thereby observing 20 returns. These were compared with the 20 corresponding returns from a passive (buy-and-hold) strategy. The active strategy performed better than the passive strategy in 17 of these 20 cases, when brokerage commissions were not considered, but it was superior in only 12 of these cases when brokerage costs were included. Are either of these two results significantly different from what could be expected to happen simply by chance?

Verify the values of the four different probabilities mentioned in this case.

SOLUTIONS TO SELF-CORRECTING EXERCISES

5.12 a. $p(x)$

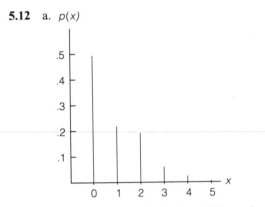

b. The distribution is positively skewed (skewed to the right).

c. The most likely number of children in a family is 0, which occurs with probability .5.

d. $P(X > 2) = P(X \geq 3) = .10$.

5.16 Let X represent the amount of damage incurred.

x	$p(x)$	$xp(x)$	x^2	$x^2p(x)$
0	.87	0	0	0
100	.10	10	10,000	1,000
200	.02	4	40,000	800
400	.01	4	160,000	1,600
TOTAL		$18 = E(X)$		$3,400 = E(X^2)$

a. The owner should be willing to pay up to $18, which is the expected amount of damage to be incurred.

b. $V(X) = E(X^2) - \mu^2 = 3,400 - (18)^2 = 3.076$
$\sigma = \sqrt{3,076} = \$55.46$.

5.30 Let X be the number of correct answers for $n = 15$ questions, with $p = .2$.

a. $P(X \geq 7) = 1 - P(X \leq 6) = 1 - .982 = .018$.

b. The expected number of correct answers is $E(X) = np = 15(.2) = 3$.

5.38 Let X denote the number of calls in a day, with $\mu = 10/5 = 2$. From Table 4,

$P(X = 5) = P(X \leq 5) - P(X \leq 4)$
$= .983 - .947$
$= .036$.

5.46   a. $f(x) = 1/(30 - 20) = .1$
(for $20 \leq x \leq 30$)
   $f(x) = 0$ (elsewhere).

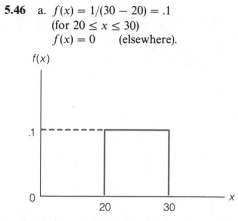

b. $f(x)$ is a probability density function, since:
   (1) $f(x) \geq 0$ for all values of x.
   (2) The total area under the curve representing
      $f(x)$ is $(10)(.1) = 1$.

c. $P(22 \leq X \leq 30) =$ (Base)(Height)
   $= (30 - 22)(.1)$
   $= (8)(.1)$
   $= .8$.

d. $P(X = 25) = 0$.

5.56   Let X be the time required to assemble a
component, where $\mu = 12$ and $\sigma = 1.5$.

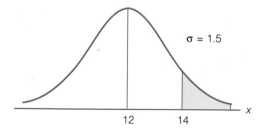

a. $P(X > 14) = P\left(Z > \dfrac{14 - 12}{1.5}\right)$
   $= P(Z > 1.33)$
   $= .5 - P(0 \leq Z \leq 1.33)$
   $= .5 - .4082$
   $= .0918$.

b. $P(X > 8) = P\left(Z > \dfrac{8 - 12}{1.5}\right)$
   $= P(Z > -2.67)$
   $= .5 + P(0 \leq Z \leq 2.67)$
   $= .5 + .4962$
   $= .9962$.

c. $P(X < 14) = 1 - P(X \geq 14)$
   $= 1 - .0918$ (from part (a))
   $= .9082$.

d. $P(X < 10) = P\left(Z > \dfrac{10 - 12}{1.5}\right)$
   $= P(Z < -1.33)$
   $= P(Z > 1.33)$
   $= .0918$ (from part (a)).

e. $P(10 \leq X \leq 15)$
   $= P\left(\dfrac{10 - 12}{1.5} \leq Z \leq \dfrac{15 - 12}{1.5}\right)$
   $= P(-1.33 \leq Z \leq 2)$
   $= P(0 \leq Z \leq 2) + P(0 \leq Z \leq 1.33)$
   $= .4772 + .4082$
   $= .8854$

SAMPLING AND SAMPLING DISTRIBUTIONS

INTRODUCTION

The material in this chapter acts as a link between the probability distributions presented in Chapter 5 and statistical inference, which is introduced in Chapter 7 and continues to the end of the book. In Chapter 5 we discussed how to make probability statements about an individual member of a population, given that we knew the probability distribution and the population parameters. For example, suppose that household incomes in this country are normally distributed, with population parameters $\mu = \$25,000$ and $\sigma = \$5,000$. We can use this knowledge to calculate the probability that the household income of a randomly selected family exceeds (for example) $30,000. That is, we compute

$$P(x > 30,000) = P\left(\frac{x - \mu}{\sigma} > \frac{30,000 - 25,000}{5,000}\right)$$
$$= P(z > 1)$$
$$= .1587.$$

In this chapter we will discuss sampling distributions, which allow us to compute probabilities associated with sample statistics. In Section 6.4 we will present the sampling distribution of the sample mean $\bar{x}$. This will enable us to compute the probability that the sample mean falls within a specific range of values. For instance, we will be able to determine the probability that 50 randomly selected families have a mean income in excess of $30,000. That is, we can find

$$P(\bar{x} > 30,000).$$

The importance of sampling distributions lies in what we're about to do starting in Chapter 7. In that chapter we begin studying statistical inference, whose objective is to learn something about unknown population parameters from sample statistics. Working inside the ivy-covered walls of a university or within the covers of a statistics textbook, we may assume that population parameters are known. In real life, however, calculating parameters becomes prohibitive because populations tend to be quite large. As a result, most population parameters are unknown. For example, in order to determine the mean annual income of North American blue-collar workers, we would have to ask each North American blue-collar worker what his or her income is, and then calculate the mean of all the responses. Because this population consists of several million people, the task is both expensive and impractical. If we are willing to accept less than 100% accuracy, we can use statistical inference to obtain an estimate.

Rather than investigating the entire population, we take a sample, determine the annual income of the workers in this group, and calculate the sample mean $\bar{x}$. While there is very little chance that the sample mean is identical to the population mean, we would expect $\bar{x}$ to be reasonably close to μ; and sampling distributions allow us to measure how close the value of the sample statistic is likely to be to the value of the population parameter. The sampling distribution plays a critical role in statistics because the measure of proximity it provides is the key to statistical inference. In Section 6.4 we will discuss the sampling distribution of the sample mean; and in later chapters we will present other sampling distributions, as they are needed. To begin, however, we need to discuss the concepts and techniques of sampling itself.

SAMPLING

The chief motive for examining a sample rather than a population is cost. Statistical inference permits us to draw conclusions about a population parameter based on a sample that is quite small in comparison to the size of the population. For example, television executives want to know the proportion of television viewers who watch their network's programs. Since 100 million people may be watching television in the United States on a given evening, determining the actual proportion of the population watching certain programs is impractical and prohibitively expensive. The Nielsen ratings provide approximations of the desired information by observing what a sample of 1,000 television viewers watch. Thus they estimate the population proportion by calculating the sample proportion.

The field of quality control illustrates yet another reason for sampling. In order to ensure that a production process is operating properly, the operations manager needs to know the proportion of defective units that are being produced. If the quality-control technician must destroy the unit in order to determine whether or not it is defective, there is no alternative to sampling; a complete inspection of the population would destroy the entire output of the production process.

We know that the sample proportion of television viewers or of defective items is probably not exactly equal to the population proportion we want it to estimate. Nonetheless, the sample statistic can come quite close to the parameter it is designed to estimate, if the **target population** (the population about which we want to draw inferences) and the **sampled population** (the population from which we've actually taken a sample) are the same. In practice these may not be the same.

For example, the Nielsen ratings are supposed to provide information about the television shows that all Americans are watching. Hence, the target population is the television viewers of the United States. If the sample of 1,000 viewers were drawn exclusively from the state of New York, however, the sampled population would be the television viewers of New York. In this case, the target population and the sampled population are not the same, and no valid inferences about the target population can be drawn. To allow proper estimation of the proportion of all American television viewers watching a specific program, the sample should contain men and women of varying ages, incomes, occupations, and residences in a pattern similar to that of the target population. The importance of sampling from the target population cannot be overestimated, since the consequences of drawing conclusions from improperly selected samples can be costly. One of the most spectacular examples of how not to conduct a survey took place in 1936.

The *Literary Digest* was a popular magazine of the 1920s and 1930s, which had correctly predicted the outcomes of several presidential elections. In 1936, the *Digest* predicted that the Republican candidate, Alfred Landon, would defeat the Democrat incumbent, Franklin D. Roosevelt, by a 3–2 margin. But in that election, Roosevelt won a landslide victory, garnering the support of 62% of the electorate. The source of this blunder was the sampling procedure: the *Digest* sent out 10 million sample ballots to prospective voters, but only 2.3 million ballots were returned, resulting in a self-selected sample.

Self-selected samples are almost always biased, because the individuals who participate in them are more keenly interested in the issue than are the other members of the population. You often see similar surveys conducted today when radio stations ask people to call and give their opinion on an issue of interest. Again, only those who are concerned about the topic and have enough patience to get through to the station will be included in the sample. Hence, the sampled population is composed entirely of people who are interested in the issue, whereas the target population is made up of all the people within the listening radius of the radio station. As a result, the conclusions drawn from such surveys are frequently wrong. Unfortunately, because the true value of the parameter being estimated is never known (unlike the situation in a political survey, where the election provides the true parametric value), these surveys give the impression of providing useful information. In fact, the results of such surveys are likely to be no more accurate than the results of the 1936 *Literary Digest* poll.*

In the next section, we discuss a number of different ways in which populations can be surveyed. In all cases, we assume that the surveys are properly performed and that the target population and the sampled population are very similar.

■■■■■■ EXERCISES

6.1 For each of the following sampling plans, indicate why the target population and the sampled population are not the same.

a. In order to determine the opinions and attitudes of customers who regularly shop at a particular mall, a surveyor stands outside a large department store in the mall and randomly selects people to participate in the survey.

b. A library wishes to estimate the proportion of its books that have been damaged. They decide to select one book per shelf as a sample, by measuring 12 inches from the left edge of each shelf and selecting the book in that location.

c. A political surveyor visits 200 residences and asks the eligible voters present in the house at the time whom they intend to vote for. The visits take place during the afternoon.

---

* Many statisticians ascribe the *Literary Digest*'s statistical debacle to the wrong causes. For a better understanding of what really happened, read Maurice C. Bryson, "The *Literary Digest* Poll: Making of a Statistical Myth," *American Statistician* 30(4) (November 1976): 184–85.

SAMPLING PLANS

Our objective in this section is to introduce several different sampling plans. We begin our presentation with the most basic design.

SIMPLE RANDOM SAMPLING

> **Simple Random Sample**
>
> A **simple random sample** is a sample in which each member of the population is equally likely to be included.

One way to conduct a simple random sample is to assign a number to each element in the population, write these numbers on individual slips of paper, toss them into a hat, and draw the required number of slips (the sample size, n) from the hat. This procedure is the kind used in raffles, when all of the ticket stubs go into a large rotating drum from which the winners are selected.

Sometimes the elements of the population are already numbered. For example, virtually all adults have social security numbers; all employees of large corporations have employee numbers; many people have driver's license numbers, medical plan numbers, student numbers, and so on. In such cases, choosing the procedure to use is simply a matter of deciding how to select from among these numbers.

In other cases, a common form of numbering has built-in flaws that make it inappropriate as a source of samples. Not everyone has a phone number, for example, so the telephone book does not list all of the people in a given area. Some people do not have phones, others have unlisted phones, and others have more than one phone number; each of these differences means that the individual members of the population do not have an equal probability of being selected.

Once each member or element of the chosen population has been assigned a unique number, sample numbers can be selected at random. It is usual to employ a computer-generated random numbers table, such as Table 10 in Appendix B, for this purpose.

Conceptually the numbers are derived as follows. There are only ten digits: 0 through 9. Working from a rectangular probability distribution, wherein each of these ten numbers has the same probability of being selected, the computer picks a number at random and records it. These individual integers are then formatted to be printed in columns of 5 or 10 integers, with 50 or 100 rows per page.

Using the tables involves picking a row and a column at random, and then reading off the numbers systematically from that point on. For example, we might proceed horizontally to the right or left, or vertically downward or upward. If you are making extensive use of a random numbers table, you should replace it every so often. Human nature is such that each of us has a propensity to start in about the same place and to proceed in a similar manner repeatedly. Repeated use of the same table, therefore, can lead to selection of the same string of random numbers.

EXAMPLE 6.1

A department store audit involves checking a random sample from a population of 30 outstanding credit-account balances. The 30 accounts are listed in the accompanying table.

Account No.	Balance	Account No.	Balance	Account No.	Balance
1	25	11	918	21	159
2	0	12	801	22	279
3	605	13	227	23	115
4	1,010	14	0	24	27
5	527	15	47	25	27
6	34	16	0	26	291
7	245	17	102	27	16
8	59	18	215	28	0
9	67	19	429	29	402
10	403	20	197	30	17

Use a random numbers table to select 5 accounts at random.

Solution.   Going to our random numbers table, we select row 1, column 8 as our starting point. We shall go down that column, selecting the first two digits as our random numbers. The random numbers are reproduced here for convenience.

Random Numbers		Random Numbers	
22	✓	19	✓
17	✓	51	
83		39	
57		59	
27	✓	84	
54		20	✓

Notice that we had to select more than five numbers, since some of them were of no use to us.

The following 5 accounts, therefore, are to be audited:

Random Number (account number)	Balance
22	$279
17	$102
27	$16
19	$429
20	$197

This yields a sample mean of $\bar{x} = \$204.60$, which is quite close to the population mean of $\mu = \$241.47$.

MINITAB RANDOM NUMBERS

Instead of using a random numbers table, we can use Minitab to generate the random numbers. The commands

```
RANDOM 100 C1;
INTEGERS 0 99.
```

will generate 100 random numbers between 0 and 99 and store them in column 1. To produce the 5 random numbers required in Example 6.1 we could type

```
RANDOM 5 C1;
INTEGERS 1 30.
```

These commands would store 5 random numbers between 1 and 30 in column 1. However, since some of the numbers may be identical we should generate more numbers than we actually need. When we inputted the commands

```
RANDOM 10 C1;
INTEGERS 1 30.
PRINT C1
```

the computer printed the following:

```
18 16 21 7 12 1 15 1 21 9
```

Consequently we selected as our random sample the following balances:

Random Number (account number)	Balance
18	$215
16	$0
21	$159
7	$245
12	$801

This sample produced a mean of $\bar{x} = \$284.00$.

STRATIFIED RANDOM SAMPLING

In making inferences about a population, we attempt to extract as much information as possible from a sample. The basic sampling plan, simple random sampling, often accomplishes this goal at low cost. Other methods, however, can be used to increase the amount of information about the population. One such procedure is stratified random sampling.

> **Stratified Random Sample**
>
> A **stratified random sample** is obtained by separating the population into mutually exclusive sets or strata and then drawing simple random samples from each stratum.

Examples of criteria for separating a population into strata (and the strata themselves) are as follows:

1. Sex: male
   female
2. Age: under 20
   20–30
   31–40
   41–50
   51–60
   over 60
3. Occupation: professional
   clerical
   blue-collar
   other

Any stratification must be done so that the strata are mutually exclusive. This means that each member of the population must be assigned to exactly one stratum. Once the population has been stratified in this way, we can employ simple random sampling to generate the complete sample.

As you'll see later in this book, we can improve the quality of the statistical inference by reducing the variability associated with the sample. One advantage of this sampling procedure is that, if the strata are relatively homogeneous (similar), the variability within each stratum and the overall variability are reduced. A second advantage is that we can draw inferences about each stratum individually. For example, suppose that we wanted to estimate the average annual individual income of people living in a large city, on the basis of a sample of 1,000. We could generate a simple random sample by randomly selecting a sample of 1,000 individuals. With stratified random sampling, we can improve our estimation by stratifying the population in a number of ways. We can, for instance, stratify by age; that is, we can separate the population into the age categories

under 20

21–40

41–60

over 60

and draw random samples of 250 from each of the subgroups. The advantage of this approach is that the incomes within each age group are likely to be somewhat similar, and as a result our estimate will be better. Additionally, we can estimate the average income for each age group.

CLUSTER SAMPLING

Cluster Sample

A **cluster sample** is a simple random sample of groups or clusters of elements.

This sampling plan is particularly useful when it is difficult or costly to develop a complete list of the population members (making it difficult or costly to generate a simple random sample). It is also useful whenever the population elements are widely dispersed geographically. For example, suppose that we wanted to estimate the average annual household income in a large city. In order to use simple random sampling, we would need a complete list of households in the city from which to sample. To use stratified random sampling, we would again need the list of households, and we would also need to have each household categorized by some other variable (such as age of household head) in order to develop the strata. A less expensive alternative would be to let each block within the city represent a cluster. A sample of clusters could then be randomly selected, and every household within these clusters could be interviewed to determine income. By reducing the distances the surveyor must cover to gather the data, cluster sampling reduces the cost.

SECTION 6.4

SAMPLING DISTRIBUTION OF THE SAMPLE MEAN

As you might guess, a sampling distribution is created by sampling. That is, we start with a population whose probability distribution and parameters are known. Then we draw a large number of samples of size n from that population. In each sample, we compute the sample statistic; in this section, we compute the sample mean. The sampling distribution is depicted by drawing a histogram of the sample means.

To illustrate, suppose that it is known that monthly sales at gasoline stations are normally distributed with mean $\mu = 18,000$ gallons and standard deviation $\sigma = 3,000$ gallons. Figure 6.1 depicts this distribution. To create the sampling distribution of the sample mean $\bar{x}$, we can take random samples of size $n = 25$ from the population. For each sample, we determine the sample mean $\bar{x}$. Suppose that we actually drew 50 different samples of size $n = 25$, and that the sample means were computed and listed as in Table 6.1. The first thing to notice is that the values of $\bar{x}$ vary: they are not all the same. This means that $\bar{x}$ can be treated as a random variable. To see how this new random variable is distributed, we drew a histogram (see Figure 6.2).

There are several important points to notice about the values of $\bar{x}$. First, from Figure 6.2 we can see that $\bar{x}$ appears to be normally distributed. Naturally, the histogram is not perfectly bell-shaped, since we only have 50 values of $\bar{x}$ and not the complete population of $\bar{x}$. If we had begun with a much larger number of values, we would have produced a considerably more bell-shaped histogram. Second, it appears that the mean of the 50 values of $\bar{x}$ is approximately 18,000, the mean of the population from which we've sampled. (The actual value of the mean of $\bar{x}$, calculated from Table 6.1 is 17,992.7.) Third, the distribution of $\bar{x}$ is considerably narrower than that of the original population. In the original population most values of x would lie between 12,000 and 24,000. (Recall that 95% of the observations from a normal population would lie within two standard deviations of the mean. That is, 95% of the values of x would fall between $\mu - 2\sigma$ and $\mu + 2\sigma$.) As Table 6.1 reveals, the smallest observed value of $\bar{x}$ is 16,967 and the largest is 19,321.

FIGURE 6.1   *DISTRIBUTION OF MONTHLY GASOLINE SALES*

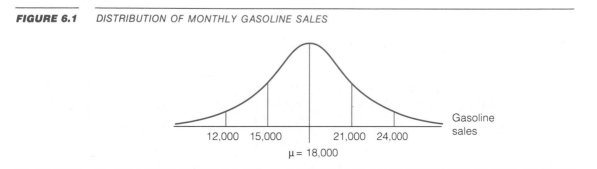

FIGURE 6.2   HISTOGRAM OF 50 VALUES OF $\bar{x}$

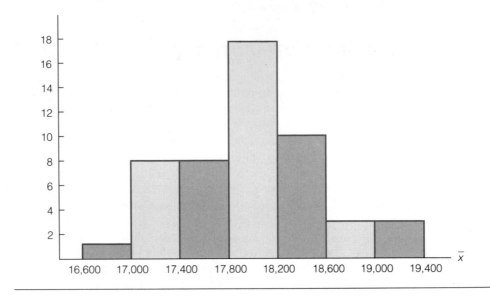

TABLE 6.1   FIFTY VALUES OF $\bar{x}$

Sample	$\bar{x}$	Sample	$\bar{x}$	Sample	$\bar{x}$	Sample	$\bar{x}$
1	17,386	14	17,836	27	17,935	40	18,303
2	17,002	15	17,735	28	17,636	41	17,976
3	18,068	16	17,295	29	18,150	42	17,712
4	18,561	17	18,817	30	17,106	43	17,558
5	18,287	18	17,318	31	18,254	44	18,128
6	19,231	19	18,139	32	17,973	45	18,432
7	17,838	20	17,887	33	18,391	46	18,479
8	18,267	21	18,543	34	17,222	47	19,041
9	17,509	22	17,318	35	18,014	48	18,012
10	17,643	23	18,132	36	18,308	49	18,860
11	17,428	24	17,920	37	17,313	50	17,895
12	17,839	25	17,978	38	16,967		
13	18,953	26	17,718	39	19,321		

Table 6.1 and Figure 6.2 illustrate how the sampling distribution is created and make three important points about the sampling distribution of the sample mean. Using some basic rules of mathematics we can prove the following relationships:

1. The mean of the sampling distribution of $\bar{x}$ (labeled $\mu_{\bar{x}}$) is equal to the mean of the population from which we've sampled. That is,

   $$\mu_{\bar{x}} = \mu.$$

   In our illustration, both means equal 18,000.

2. The variance of the sampling distribution (labeled $\sigma_{\bar{x}}^2$) is equal to the variance of the population, divided by the sample size. That is,

   $$\sigma_{\bar{x}}^2 = \frac{\sigma^2}{n}.$$

3. The standard deviation of $\bar{x}$ is called the **standard error of the mean** (labeled $\sigma_{\bar{x}}$). The standard error of the mean in our example is

   $$\sigma_{\bar{x}} = \frac{\sigma}{\sqrt{n}} = \frac{3,000}{\sqrt{25}} = 600.$$

From Table 6.1 we computed the standard deviation of the 50 values of $\bar{x}$ to be 561.3, which is quite close to the theoretical standard deviation of $\bar{x}$.

By using more sophisticated mathematics, we can also learn something about the form of the sampling distribution of $\bar{x}$. The mathematics that produces this discovery is called the Central Limit Theorem.

Central Limit Theorem

If samples of size n are drawn from any population, the sample means are approximately normally distributed for large values of n. The sample size necessary to provide a good approximation depends on the extent of nonnormality of the population.

Without question, this is one of the most important theorems in the development of statistical inference. Its importance will be reflected in the number of times in future chapters we refer to the sampling distribution of $\bar{x}$.

The Central Limit Theorem tells us that, no matter what the original population random variable's distribution looks like, the sampling distribution of $\bar{x}$ will be approximately normal for large enough sample sizes. If x follows a distribution that is approximately normal, then $\bar{x}$ will also be approximately normal even for small values of n. As a matter of fact, if x is normal, then $\bar{x}$ is also normal for any value of n. If x is quite nonnormal, however, $\bar{x}$ will be approximately normal only for relatively large values of n.

What we know about the sampling distribution of the sample mean can be summarized in three points.

FIGURE 6.3 SAMPLING DISTRIBUTION OF $\bar{x}$

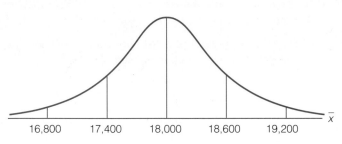

16,800	17,400	18,000	18,600	19,200

Sampling Distribution of $\bar{x}$

1. $\bar{x}$ is either normal or approximately normal.

2. $\mu_{\bar{x}} = \mu$.

3. $\sigma_{\bar{x}} = \dfrac{\sigma}{\sqrt{n}}$.

Figure 6.3 depicts the sampling distribution of $\bar{x}$ for samples of size $n = 25$ from the population of service stations ($\mu = 18,000$ and $\sigma = 3,000$).

EXAMPLE 6.2

The foreman of a bottling plant has observed that the amount of soda pop in each "32-ounce" bottle is actually a normally distributed random variable, with a mean of 32.2 ounces and a standard deviation of .3 ounces.

  a. Find the probability that, if a customer buys one bottle, that bottle will contain less than 32 ounces.

  b. Find the probability that, if a customer buys a carton of four bottles, the mean of the four will be less than 32 ounces.

Solution

  a. Since the random variable is the amount of fill of one bottle, we want to find

$$P(x < 32)$$

where x is normally distributed, with $\mu = 32.2$ and $\sigma = .3$. Hence,

$$P(x < 32) = P\left(\frac{x - \mu}{\sigma} < \frac{32 - 32.2}{.3}\right)$$
$$= P(z < -.67)$$
$$= .2514.$$

b. Now we want to find the probability that the mean of four fills is less than 32 ounces. That is, we want

$$P(\bar{x} < 32).$$

From our previous analysis and from the Central Limit Theorem, we know the following:

1. $\bar{x}$ is normally distributed.

2. $\mu_{\bar{x}} = \mu = 32.2$.

3. $\sigma_{\bar{x}} = \dfrac{\sigma}{\sqrt{n}} = \dfrac{.3}{\sqrt{4}} = .15.$

Hence,

$$P(\bar{x} < 32) = P\left(\frac{\bar{x} - \mu_{\bar{x}}}{\sigma_{\bar{x}}} < \frac{32 - 32.2}{.15}\right)$$
$$= P(z < -1.33)$$
$$= .0918.$$

Figure 6.4 describes the distributions used in this example.

In Example 6.2 we began with the assumption that both the mean and the standard deviation were known. Then, using the sampling distribution, we made a

FIGURE 6.4   *DISTRIBUTION OF x AND SAMPLING DISTRIBUTION OF $\bar{x}$ IN EXAMPLE 6.2*

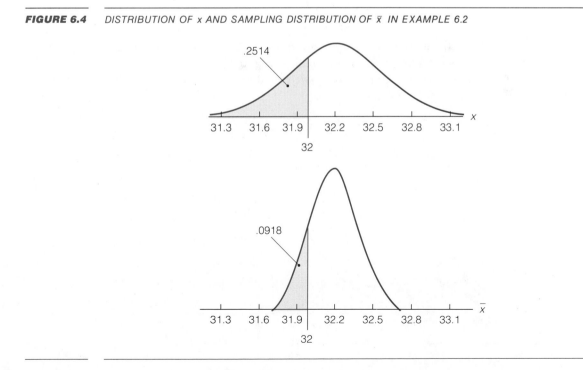

probability statement about $\bar{x}$. This use of the sampling distribution is of no great interest to us, since the values of the parameters μ and σ are generally unknown. We can, however, use the sampling distribution to infer something about the unknown value of the population mean on the basis of a sample mean.

EXAMPLE 6.3

The dean of the business school claims that the average weekly income of graduates of his school one year after graduation is $700.

a. If the dean's claim is correct and if weekly incomes are normally distributed with a standard deviation of $60, what is the probability that 36 randomly selected graduates have an average weekly income of less than $675?

b. If a random sample of 36 graduates had an average weekly income of $675, what would you conclude about the validity of the dean's claim?

Solution

a. We want to find

$$P(\bar{x} < 675).$$

Since $\bar{x}$ is normally distributed, with $\mu_{\bar{x}} = 700$ and $\sigma_{\bar{x}} = 60/\sqrt{36} = 10$,

$$P(\bar{x} < 675) = P\left(\frac{\bar{x} - \mu_{\bar{x}}}{\sigma_{\bar{x}}} < \frac{675 - 700}{10}\right)$$

$$= P(z < -2.5)$$

$$= .0062.$$

b. The probability of observing a sample mean as low as $675 when the population mean is $700 is extremely small, as Figure 6.5 indicates. Since this event is quite rare and thus quite unlikely, we would have to conclude that the dean's claim is probably unjustified.

FIGURE 6.5   SAMPLING DISTRIBUTION OF $\bar{x}$ FOR EXAMPLE 6.3

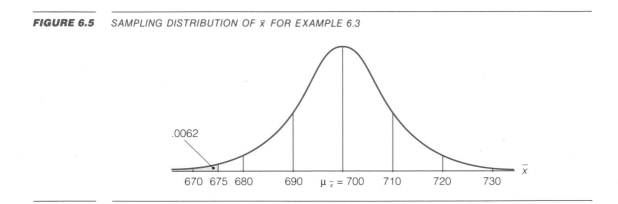

Our conclusion in part (b) of Example 6.3 illustrates a form of statistical inference called **hypothesis testing.** Another form of inference is **estimation,** which we will now use to answer part (b) in a different way. We know that about 95% of the values of $\bar{x}$ will fall within two standard errors of the population mean. Thus 95% of the values of $\bar{x}$ will fall within \$20 of μ. As a result, we would infer that the population mean lies somewhere between \$655 and \$695. Since the dean claimed that $\mu = \$700$, which does not fall into this interval, we would conclude that the claim is not supported by the statistical result.

As you've just seen, the sampling distribution allows us to draw inferences about population parameters. In Chapters 8 through 18, we will use various sampling distributions to test and estimate several different parameters. In each application, the sampling distribution is a critical component of the technique.

SECTION
6.5

SUMMARY

Because most populations are so large, it is extremely costly and impractical to investigate each member of the population to determine the values of the parameters. As a practical alternative, we sample the population and use the sample statistics to draw inferences about the parameters. Care must be taken to ensure that the target population is the same as the sampled population.

There are several different sampling plans, including simple random sampling, stratified random sampling, and cluster sampling. The sampling distribution represents the probability distribution created by repeated sampling and by calculation of the sample statistics. This allows us to calculate the probability that a statistic falls into a range of values, given that we know the population parameters.

The Central Limit Theorem states that the sampling distribution of $\bar{x}$ is approximately normal (for large n), with mean μ and variance σ^2/n. The sampling distribution of $\bar{x}$ and other sampling distributions (developed in later chapters) play a crucial role in statistics by providing a probability link between the sample statistics and the population parameters.

IMPORTANT TERMS

Sample	Cluster sample
Target population	Sampling distribution
Sampled population	Sampling distribution of the sample mean
Simple random sample	Standard error of the same mean
Stratified random sample	Central Limit Theorem

FORMULAS

$\mu_{\bar{x}} = \mu$

$\sigma_{\bar{x}}^2 = \sigma^2/n$

$\sigma_{\bar{x}} = \sigma/\sqrt{n}$

EXERCISES

6.2 A sample of $n = 100$ observations is drawn from a normal population, with $\mu = 1,000$ and $\sigma = 200$. Find the following probabilities.

a. $P(\bar{x} > 1,050)$

b. $P(\bar{x} < 960)$

c. $P(\bar{x} > 1,100)$

6.3 Suppose that the sample size in Exercise 6.2 was 16. Find the following probabilities.

a. $P(\bar{x} > 1,050)$

b. $P(\bar{x} < 960)$

c. $P(\bar{x} > 1,100)$

6.4 Given a large population whose mean is 1,000 and whose standard deviation is 200, find the probability that a random sample of 400 has a mean that lies between 995 and 1,020.

6.5 An automatic machine in a manufacturing process is operating properly if the lengths of an important subcomponent are normally distributed, with mean $\mu = 117$ cm and standard deviation $\sigma = 2.1$ cm.

a. Find the probability that one randomly selected unit has a length greater than 120 cm.

b. Find the probability that, if three units are randomly selected, all three have lengths exceeding 120 cm.

c. Find the probability that, if three units are randomly selected, their mean length exceeds 120 cm.

6.6 The manufacturer of cans of salmon that are supposed to have a net weight of 6 ounces tells you that the net weight is actually a random variable with a mean of 6.05 ounces and a standard deviation of .18 ounces. Suppose that you take a random sample of 36 cans.

a. Find the probability that the sample mean will be less than 5.97 ounces.

b. Suppose that your random sample of 36 cans produces a mean of 5.95 ounces. Comment on the statement made by the manufacturer.

6.7 A large shipment of cereal boxes is delivered to a supermarket. The manager is told that the weights of the cereal boxes are normally distributed, with a mean of 16.5 ounces and a standard deviation of .5 ounces.

a. Find the probability that a random sample of 100 boxes has a mean weight of between 16.49 and 16.51 ounces.

b. Repeat part (a), but assume that the size of the random sample is 400.

c. Comment on the effect that the sample size has on the probability.

6.8 The sign on an elevator in a large skyscraper states, "Maximum capacity 2,500 pounds or 16 persons." A professor of statistics wonders what the probability is that 16 people would weigh more than 2,500 pounds. If the weights of the people who use the elevator is normally distributed, with a mean of 150 pounds and a standard deviation of 20 pounds, what is the probability that the professor seeks?

STATISTICAL INFERENCE: INTRODUCTION

INTRODUCTION

Much of the remainder of this book deals with problems that attempt to say something about the properties of a population. Because populations are generally quite large, the information we usually have available to work with comes from a relatively small sample taken from the population. The process of drawing conclusions about the properties of a population based on information obtained from a sample is called **statistical inference.**

Examples of statistical inference include the following: estimating the mean annual household income of families in New York; determining whether or not a new advertising campaign has increased the proportion of customers who buy a company's product; estimating the average monthly sales of home computers for next year; and determining whether or not a fuel additive is actually effective in increasing the gas mileage of automobiles. In each case, we are interested in a specific characteristic of the population in question. Most of these characteristics can be determined by using the numerical descriptive measures presented in Chapter 3. Recall from Chapter 1 that descriptive measures of a population are called *parameters,* while descriptive measures calculated from a sample are called *statistics.* In many applications of statistical inference, we draw conclusions about a parameter of a population by using sample statistics.

In the course of this textbook, we will present about three dozen different statistical techniques that have proved useful to business managers and economists. You will find that the arithmetic needed for each method is quite simple; the only mathematical operations required are addition, subtraction, multiplication, division, and the calculation of squares and square roots. Even these skills may be less in demand if you use a calculator to do much of the work; and if you use a computer, virtually no mathematics is needed. In fact, because of the availability of inexpensive computers and software, many students find that they do very few computations by hand. This is certainly true in real-life (defined as anything outside a college or university) applications of statistics.

Thus the real challenge of the subject of statistics relates to your ability to determine which technique is the most appropriate one to use in answering a given question. Most students who are taking their first course in statistics have some difficulty in recognizing the particular kind of statistical problem involved in practice exercises—and hence the appropriate statistical technique to use. This difficulty intensifies when you must apply statistical techniques to real-life practical problems, where the questions to be addressed may themselves be vague and ill-defined. In this textbook, most of the exercises and examples depict situations in which the data have already been gathered, and your task is simply to answer a specific question by applying one of the statistical techniques you've studied. In a real-life situation, you will probably have to design the experiment, define the questions, and perform and interpret the statistical computations yourself. The difficulty of determining what to do can be formidable.

Because people encounter such difficulty both during and after studying this subject, we have adopted a systematic approach that is designed to help you identify the statistical problem.

**SECTION
7.2** ## DATA TYPE AND PROBLEM OBJECTIVE

A number of factors determine which statistical technique should be used, but two of these are especially important: the type of data being measured, and the purpose of the statistical inference.

In Chapter 2, we defined the two types of data: qualitative and quantitative. Recall that qualitative data have values that are categorical and are usually defined verbally. For example, if in a survey people are asked to identify their marital status, they may respond as follows:

Single

Married

Divorced

Widowed

Other examples of qualitative statistical variables are race (Asian, Black, Caucasian, Hispanic, Other), university degree (B.A., B.Sc., B.B.A., B.Eng., Other), occupation, and sex. To help record the responses, we sometimes assign numbers to the possible answers. Since these numbers are assigned arbitrarily, however, any calculations performed with them would be meaningless. All we can do with qualitative data is count the number of times each value has occurred, and then calculate proportions.

Quantitative statistical variables are variables whose outcomes are real numbers. For instance, the possible responses to the survey question "What is your monthly income?" are the numbers ranging from zero to several thousand. Other examples of quantitative variables are as follows:

Age

Height

Weight

Amount of time devoted to weekly exercise

Number of children

In each case the values of the variables represent meaningful numbers that are not arbitrarily assigned. As a result we are permitted to calculate descriptive statistics such as means and variances from them.

It is important to realize that we can treat a quantitative variable as a qualitative one. For example, suppose that we wanted to measure the weights of bags of potato chips that are supposed to weigh 8 ounces. (You should recognize at once that the variable is quantitative.) Suppose further that our only interest in this experiment is to find the bags that weigh less than 8 ounces, which are considered unacceptable. As a result, for each bag of potato chips, the outcome of the experiment is either acceptable or unacceptable—outcomes that identify the variable as qualitative. However, we cannot reverse the process and treat a qualitative variable as a quantitative one.

The second key factor in determining the appropriate statistical technique to use is the purpose behind the work. You will find that every statistical method has some specific objective. We will now identify and describe five such objectives.

1. *Description of a Single Population.*   Our objective here is to describe some property of a population of interest. The decision about which property to describe is generally dictated by the type of data to be considered. For example, suppose that the population of interest consists of all purchasers of home computers. If we are interested in the purchasers' incomes (for which the data are quantitative), we may calculate the mean or the variance to describe that aspect of the population. But if we are interested in the brand of computer that has been bought (for which the data are qualitative), all we can do is compute the proportion of the population that purchases each brand.

2. *Comparison of Two Populations.*   In this case, our goal is to compare a property of one population with a corresponding property of a second population. For example, suppose that the populations of interest are male and female purchasers of computers. We could compare the means and variances of their incomes, or we could compare the proportion of each population that purchases a certain brand. Once again, the type of data generally determines what kind of properties we compare.

3. *Comparison of Two or More Populations.*   We may wish to compare the average or the variance of incomes in each of several locations, in order (for example) to decide where to build a new shopping center. Or we may wish to compare the proportions of defective items in a number of production lines, to determine which line is the best. In each case, the problem objective involves comparing two or more populations.

4. *Analysis of the Relationship Between Two Variables.*   In many instances we want to know how one variable is related to another. Governments need to know what effect rising interest rates have on the unemployment rate. Companies want to investigate how the size of their advertising budget influences sales volume. In most of the problems we deal with in this introductory text, the two variables to be analyzed will be of the same type: either both will be quantitative or both will be qualitative.

5. *Analysis of the Relationship Among Two or More Variables.*   Our objective here is usually to forecast one variable (called the *dependent variable*) on the basis of several other variables (called *independent variables*). We will deal with this problem only in situations in which all of the variables are quantitative.

SECTION
7.3

HOW, WHEN, AND WHY OF STATISTICAL INFERENCE

In Chapters 8 through 18 of this textbook, we present a number of different statistical techniques. In the course of developing them, we answer three types of questions pertaining to each: how, when, and why the statistical method is performed.

For the most part, knowing *how* to calculate the relevant statistics involves nothing more than understanding simple arithmetic. If you can add, subtract, multiply, and divide, you will be able to perform most of the necessary computations. Nonetheless, several techniques are so time-consuming that computers are used almost exclusively to solve problems with them. The recent trend is toward using computers on a greater variety of problems, including ones that could easily be done on an inexpensive calculator. If you have ready access to a computer and the appropriate software, you may not need to do the calculations by hand. Nonetheless, in order to understand the logic of the technique, you probably should do several problems of each type by hand or with the aid of a calculator.

The most difficult issue for students is to determine *when* to apply each technique. Using our systematic approach should alleviate this difficulty. We have observed that graduates of statistics courses hesitate to use statistical techniques because they remain uncertain about the appropriateness of a method. To combat this problem, we detail all of the required conditions that must be satisfied in using a method.

The question of *why* statistical methods are used is somewhat more difficult to answer. This is not because of any shortage of real-life applications of statistics—we could easily produce a long list of such applications as they pertain to the areas of accounting, finance, production, marketing, and organizational behavior—but because statistics plays so integral a role in many managerial decisions that the statistical application is often difficult to show by itself, outside the wider context of the manager's decision problem. Moreover, real-life problems often involve several different techniques, in which case understanding the complete problem necessitates understanding a number of methods. This circumstance conflicts somewhat with the step-by-step approach necessary in a statistics book.

We propose to deal with the why issue in several ways. In most of the worked examples, we set up the problem in a decision context; and even though some are quite simplistic, they should give you some idea of the motivation for using statistics. Many of the exercises also stress the reason for the application. We acknowledge that these reasons are frequently simplified; but as we progress, the assumptions become much more reasonable, and problems that in practice involve the use of several methods can be addressed. In Chapter 19, where we review all of the techniques covered in the statistical inference part of the book, we provide as exercises several cases that deal with real studies (as reported in magazines and journals) and real data. Solving these not infrequently requires applying several different techniques. As such, the cases are as real-life as we can make them.

SECTION 7.4   SUMMARY TABLE

In the next eleven chapters, we develop approximately 30 statistical techniques, each of which will be identified by problem objective and data type. Table 7.1 shows the five problem objectives and the two types of data. For each combination of objective and data type, one or more techniques are used to answer questions, and Table 7.1 identifies the chapter and section where these techniques are described.

TABLE 7.1 GUIDE TO STATISTICAL TECHNIQUES, SHOWING CHAPTERS AND SECTIONS WHERE EACH TECHNIQUE IS INTRODUCED

Problem Objective	Quantitative Data	Qualitative Data
Description of a Single Population	Sec. 8.3, 8.4 Sec. 10.3, 10.5	Sec. 8.5 Sec. 10.6 Sec. 14.2
Comparison of Two Populations	Sec. 9.2, 9.3 Sec. 11.2 Sec. 18.3	Sec. 9.4 Sec. 11.3
Comparison of Two or More Populations	Chap. 13 Sec. 18.4	Sec. 14.3
Analysis of the Relationship Between Two Variables	Chap. 15	Sec. 14.3
Analysis of the Relationship Among Two or More Variables	Chap. 16	—

Where possible, we will group the statistical techniques according to their common problem objectives. Because of similarities in some of the techniques, however, this order of presentation cannot always be strictly adhered to. Table 7.1 should help you keep track of the order of presentation.

EXERCISES

7.1 Provide two examples each of qualitative data and quantitative data.

7.2 Discuss the difference between qualitative data and quantitative data.

7.3 Identify the data type of the following items:

a. numbers on the backs of baseball players' uniforms

b. identification numbers of students enrolled in a university

c. prices of objects in a department store

d. the time it takes for runners to complete the Boston Marathon

7.4 For each of the following experiments, identify the type of data being measured.

a. Annual surveys measure trends in the popularity of televised baseball games. Individuals are asked whether or not they regularly watch baseball on television.

b. A government agency randomly selects containers of packaged goods to make certain that the packages weigh what their manufacturers advertise.

c. A breakfast cereal manufacturer surveys customers to determine which of three new package designs is most popular.

d. A fast-food franchiser wants to know if the position of items on the menu board influences sales. He organizes an experiment in which the sales of an item are counted during a week when the item appears in one position on the board and during a second week when the item appears in another position.

7.5 For each of the following, identify the problem objective.

a. A firm wishes to determine whether increasing the advertising budget will result in an increase in sales volume. Analysts determine the monthly advertising expenses and the monthly sales volume for the past 12 months.

b. In the recent recession, a number of workers had to work reduced hours. An economist wants to determine whether differences exist among five industries in the average number of hours of work per week.

c. In order to design advertising campaigns, a marketing manager needs to know whether different segments of the population prefer her company's product to competing products. She decides to perform a survey that will determine whether different proportions of people in five separate age categories purchase the product.

d. The same marketing manager as in part (c) wants to know whether the proportion of men purchasing the product is different from the proportion of women.

e. The production manager of a large plant is contemplating changing the process by which a certain product is produced. Since workers in this plant are paid on the basis of their output, it is essential to demonstrate that the rate of assembling a unit will increase under the new system. Ten workers are randomly selected to participate in an experiment in which each worker assembles one unit under the old process and one unit under the new process.

ESTIMATION: DESCRIBING A SINGLE POPULATION

INTRODUCTION

In Chapter 6, where we briefly introduced statistical inference, we pointed out that we can make inferences about populations in two ways: by estimating the unknown population parameter, or by testing its value. In this chapter we will deal with the problem of estimating parameters that describe single populations. The actual parameter of interest will be determined by the type of data. If the data type is quantitative, we will be interested in estimating the population mean μ. If the data type is qualitative, however, the parameter is the population proportion p.

Here are some examples illustrating the estimation of parameters of a single population:

1. A federal inspector wanted to know whether the actual weight of tins of tuna were at least as large as the weight shown on the label. Since she cannot weigh every single can of tuna, she draws a random sample of cans and uses the sample data to estimate the *mean* of all cans of tuna.

2. One week before election day an incumbent senator wants to know if he will win the upcoming election. A survey of 500 registered voters is conducted wherein voters are asked who they will vote for. The results allow the senator to estimate the *proportion* of all voters who support him.

3. An education psychologist would like to show how well students from households with the lowest 25% of incomes perform in post-secondary educational institutions. Since he can't investigate the complete population, he takes a random sample of such households. He can use the sample data to estimate the *proportion* of young adults aged 18–24 who take advantage of post-secondary education. He can also estimate the grade-point *average* of those who attend.

ESTIMATION

There are two types of estimators: point estimators and interval estimators.

Point Estimator

A **point estimator** draws inferences about a population by estimating the value of an unknown parameter, using a single value or point.

For example, we will use the sample mean to estimate the population mean. Later in this chapter you will see that we estimate a population proportion by calculating the sample proportion. One of the disadvantages associated with a point estimator is that we have no way of knowing how close the estimate is likely to be to the parameter. Suppose, for instance, that we estimate that the mean annual income of first-year accountants is $22,000. This information is useful, but we have no idea how close the entire population mean is to $22,000. As a result, we usually prefer to use an interval estimator.

> **Interval Estimator**
>
> An **interval estimator** is a range of values within which the parameter likely lies.

Thus, we may estimate that the mean annual income of first-year accountants lies in the range $19,000 to $25,000. This interval estimate provides us with additional information about how low and how high the true population mean income is likely to be. As you will see shortly, this additional information is quite a bit more useful than the information supplied by the point estimate alone.

In the preceding discussion we used the terms **estimator** and **estimate.** We distinguish between them by noting that an estimate is the calculation of a specific value of the estimator. For example, we say that the sample mean is an estimator of a population mean. However, once we compute the value of the sample mean, that value represents the estimate of the population mean.

SECTION 8.3   ESTIMATING THE POPULATION MEAN WHEN THE VARIANCE IS KNOWN

In this section we discuss how to estimate an unknown population mean μ when the population variance σ^2 is known. Let us at once concede that this is quite unrealistic; if the population mean is unknown, it is quite unlikely that we would know the value of the population variance. However this approach allows us to introduce the subject and then progress to more realistic situations later.

In order to proceed, recall our discussion of sampling distributions in Chapter 6. At that time we showed that, if we repeatedly draw samples of size n from a population whose mean and variance are μ and σ^2, respectively, the sample mean $\bar{x}$ will be approximately normally distributed, with mean μ and variance σ^2/n. (Recall as well that the population is assumed to be normal; and if that is not the case, n must be large.) It follows, of course, that the standard deviation is $\sigma/\sqrt{n}$. This sampling distribution is described in Figure 8.1. Knowing the sampling distribution allows us to make probability statements about $\bar{x}$. For example, we can state that 95% of the values of $\bar{x}$ lie within 1.96 standard deviations of μ.

FIGURE 8.1   SAMPLING DISTRIBUTION OF THE SAMPLE MEAN

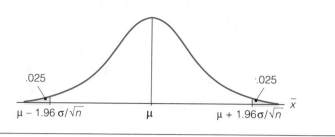

If you're wondering where the 1.96 came from, recall the normal distribution we presented in Chapter 5. We showed there that $z_{.025} = 1.96$, where $z_{.025}$ is the value of the standard normal random variable such that the area to its right under the standard normal curve is .025 (see Figure 8.2).

Another way of expressing the same thing is to say that 95% of the values of $\bar{x}$ will produce intervals of from $\bar{x} - 1.96\sigma/\sqrt{n}$ to $\bar{x} + 1.96\sigma/\sqrt{n}$ containing the poulation mean μ. This form of the probability statement is of great interest to us because it represents the interval estimator of μ. The range $\bar{x} - 1.96\sigma/\sqrt{n}$ to $\bar{x} + 1.96\sigma/\sqrt{n}$ is called the 95% **confidence interval estimator** of μ. A shortcut way of representing this interval is as

$$\bar{x} \pm 1.96\frac{\sigma}{\sqrt{n}}.$$

It is important to realize that we can use probabilities other than 95%. For instance, if we want 90% probability, the interval becomes

$$\bar{x} \pm 1.645\frac{\sigma}{\sqrt{n}}.$$

We can also represent the interval estimator of μ for any probability $1 - \alpha$.

FIGURE 8.2   STANDARD NORMAL DISTRIBUTION WITH $z_{.025} = 1.96$

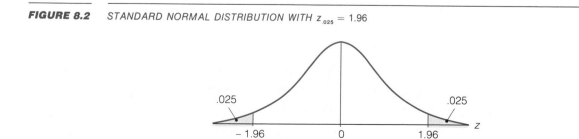

Confidence Interval Estimator of μ

$$\bar{x} \pm z_{\alpha/2} \frac{\sigma}{\sqrt{n}}$$

The probability $1 - \alpha$ is called the **confidence level.**

$\bar{x} - z_{\alpha/2} \dfrac{\sigma}{\sqrt{n}}$ is called the **lower confidence limit (LCL).**

$\bar{x} \pm z_{\alpha/2} \dfrac{\sigma}{\sqrt{n}}$ is called the **upper confidence limit (UCL).**

Notice that α represents the probability that the interval will not include the value of μ. However, to construct the confidence interval estimate, we must determine $z_{\alpha/2}$. A statistician may wish to use any value for the confidence level, and as a consequence you must be able to calculate $z_{\alpha/2}$ for any specified $1 - \alpha$. However, statisticians do use certain confidence levels more frequently than others. Table 8.1 lists five such values, together with their associated $z_{\alpha/2}$ values.

EXAMPLE 8.1

The sponsors of television shows targeted at the children's market wanted to know the amount of time children spend watching television, since the types and number of programs and commercials are greatly influenced by this information. As a result, a survey was conducted to estimate the average number of hours North American children spend watching television per week. From past experience, it is known that the population standard deviation σ is 8.0 hours. In a sample of 100 children, it was found that $\bar{x} = 27.5$ hours. Find the 95% confidence interval estimate of the average number of hours North American children spend watching television.

TABLE 8.1   *FIVE CONFIDENCE LEVELS AND $z_{\alpha/2}$*

Confidence Level $1 - \alpha$	α	$\alpha/2$	$z_{\alpha/2}$
.80	.20	.10	1.28
.90	.10	.05	1.645
.95	.05	.025	1.96
.98	.02	.01	2.33
.99	.01	.005	2.58

Solution.   The confidence interval estimator of a population mean is

$$\bar{x} \pm z_{\alpha/2} \frac{\sigma}{\sqrt{n}}.$$

The sponsors know from past experience that

$$\sigma = 8.0.$$

From the sample of $n = 100$ children, we have

$$\bar{x} = 27.5.$$

The specified confidence level is

$$1 - \alpha = .95,$$

so

$$z_{\alpha/2} = z_{.025} = 1.96.$$

The 95% confidence interval estimate is

$$\bar{x} \pm z_{\alpha/2} \frac{\sigma}{\sqrt{n}} = 27.5 \pm 1.96 \frac{8.0}{\sqrt{100}} = 27.5 \pm 1.57.$$

We therefore estimate that the average number of hours children spend watching television each week lies somewhere between

$$LCL = 25.93 \text{ hours} \quad \text{and} \quad UCL = 29.07 \text{ hours.}$$

From this estimate, a network executive may decide (for example) that, since the average child watches at least 25.93 hours of television per week, the number of commercials children see is sufficiently high to satisfy the programs' sponsors. A number of other decisions may follow from that one.

Of course, the point estimate ($\bar{x} = 27.5$ hours per week) alone would not provide enough information to the executive. He would also need to know how low the population mean is likely to be; and for other decisions, he might need to know how high the population mean is likely to be. A confidence interval estimate gives him that information.

MINITAB COMPUTER OUTPUT FOR EXAMPLE 8.1*

```
THE ASSUMED SIGMA = 8.000
        N      MEAN     STDEV    SE MEAN    95.0 PERCENT C.I.
C1    100     27.50     7.578     0.80      (25.93,    29.07)
```

The output includes the value of σ, the sample size, the mean, and the sample standard deviation (which is not needed for this interval estimate). Also printed is the standard error ($\sigma/\sqrt{n} = 0.80$) and of course the 95% confidence interval estimate.

---

* Appendix 8.A describes the instructions used to produce this output.

Clearly, the use of the confidence interval estimator in the preceding example is not at all difficult. The chief difficulty in applying statistical methods is knowing which one to use. But at this point you should have no problem in determining which method to use, since you only know one. However, in order to practice the systematic approach, we'll review how we know that the technique used above is the correct one.

If you reread Example 8.1, you'll see that the objective was to describe the population of hours children spend in front of the television set per week. The type of data is quantitative since what is being measured is the amount of time. To understand this point more fully, imagine that the 100 children in the sample were also asked whether or not they believed the commercials. Their responses to this question could be *yes* or *no*, and such responses produce qualitative data because the results are not numerical. Therefore, some other technique (to be discussed in Section 8.5) would have to be used to assess the data.

We can summarize the factors that determine when to use the *z*-interval estimator of μ as follows.

Factors That Identify the z-Interval Estimator of μ

1. *Problem objective:* Describe a single population.
2. *Data type:* quantitative
3. *Population variance:* known

Before doing another example, let's review the steps used to estimate a population mean when the population variance is known.

Steps in Estimating a Population Mean When the Population Variance Is Known

1. Determine the sample mean $\bar{x}$.
2. Determine the desired confidence level $1 - \alpha$, which in turn specifies α. From α and Table 5 in Appendix B, find $z_{\alpha/2}$.
3. Calculate

$$LCL = \bar{x} - z_{\alpha/2}\frac{\sigma}{\sqrt{n}}$$

$$UCL = \bar{x} + z_{\alpha/2}\frac{\sigma}{\sqrt{n}}.$$

EXAMPLE 8.2

To determine the mean waiting time for his customers, a bank manager took a random sample of 50 customers and found that the mean waiting time was 7.2 minutes.

Assuming that the population standard deviation is known to be 5 minutes, find the 90% confidence interval estimate of the mean waiting time for all of the bank's customers.

Solution.   We recognize that the problem objective is to describe the population of waiting times whose data type is quantitative. The confidence interval estimator we use is

$$\bar{x} \pm z_{\alpha/2} \frac{\sigma}{\sqrt{n}}.$$

We know that

$$\sigma = 5$$
$$n = 50$$
$$\bar{x} = 7.2.$$

The confidence level is

$$1 - \alpha = .90.$$

Hence,

$$z_{\alpha/2} = z_{.05} = 1.645.$$

The 90% confidence interval estimate is

$$\bar{x} \pm z_{\alpha/2} \frac{\sigma}{\sqrt{n}} = 7.2 \pm 1.645 \frac{5}{\sqrt{50}} = 7.2 \pm 1.16.$$

Therefore, we estimate that the mean customer waiting time is between

$$LCL = 6.04 \text{ minutes} \quad \text{and} \quad UCL = 8.36 \text{ minutes.}$$

This interval estimate may be useful in a number of decisions. For instance, the manager may determine that an average wait that may be as long as 8.36 minutes is excessive and may decide to hire more tellers.

INTERPRETING THE CONFIDENCE INTERVAL ESTIMATE

In Example 8.1, we found that the 95% confidence interval estimate of the mean number of hours that children watch television per week to be $LCL = 25.93$ and $UCL = 29.07$. Some people erroneously interpret this interval to mean that there is a 95% probability that the population mean lies between 25.93 and 29.07. This interpretation is wrong because it implies that the population mean is a variable about which we can make probability statements. In fact, the population mean is a fixed but unknown quantity. Consequently, we cannot interpret the confidence interval estimate of μ as a probability statement about μ.

To translate the interval estimate properly, we must recall that the interval estimator was derived from the sampling distribution, which enables us to make probability statements about the sample mean. Thus, we say that the 95% confidence interval estimator of μ implies that 95% of the values of $\bar{x}$ will create intervals that will contain the true value of the population mean. The other 5% of sample means will create intervals that do not include the population mean. (That is, 95% of the interval estimates will be right and 5% will be wrong.)

Refer to Table 6.1 on page 190. This table lists 50 sample means drawn from

TABLE 8.2   *95% CONFIDENCE INTERVAL ESTIMATES OF μ*

Sample	$\bar{x}$	$LCL =$ $\bar{x} - 1.96\sigma/\sqrt{n}$	$UCL =$ $\bar{x} + 1.96\sigma/\sqrt{n}$	Sample	$\bar{x}$	$LCL =$ $\bar{x} - 1.96\sigma/\sqrt{n}$	$UCL =$ $\bar{x} + 1.96\sigma/\sqrt{n}$
1	17,386	16,210	18,562	26	17,718	16,542	18,894
2	17,002	15,826	18,178	27	17,935	16,759	19,111
3	18,068	16,892	19,244	28	17,636	16,460	18,812
4	18,561	17,385	19,737	29	18,150	16,974	19,326
5	18,287	17,111	19,463	30	17,106	15,930	18,282
6	19,231	18,055	20,407	31	18,254	17,078	19,430
7	17,838	16,662	19,014	32	17,973	16,797	19,149
8	18,267	17,091	19,443	33	18,391	17,215	19,567
9	17,509	16,333	18,685	34	17,222	16,046	18,398
10	17,643	16,467	18,819	35	18,014	16,838	19,190
11	17,428	16,252	18,604	36	18,308	17,132	19,484
12	17,839	16,663	19,015	37	17,313	16,137	18,489
13	18,953	17,777	20,123	38	16,967	15,791	18,143
14	17,836	16,660	19,012	39	19,321	18,145	20,497
15	17,735	16,559	18,911	40	18,303	17,127	19,479
16	17,295	16,119	18,471	41	17,976	16,800	19,152
17	18,817	17,641	19,993	42	17,712	16,536	18,888
18	17,318	16,142	18,494	43	17,558	16,382	18,734
19	18,139	16,963	19,315	44	18,128	16,952	19,304
20	17,887	16,711	19,063	45	18,432	17,256	19,608
21	18,543	17,367	19,719	46	18,479	17,303	19,655
22	17,318	16,142	18,494	47	19,041	17,865	20,217
23	18,132	16,956	19,308	48	18,012	16,836	19,188
24	17,920	16,744	19,096	49	18,860	17,684	20,036
25	17,978	16,802	19,154	50	17,895	16,719	19,071

a normal population whose mean is $\mu = 18,000$ and whose standard deviation is $\sigma = 3,000$. If we now use each sample mean to construct 95% confidence interval estimates of the population mean, we produce 50 different confidence interval estimates of μ. These are listed in Table 8.2. Notice that all but two of the intervals include $\mu = 18,000$. Only samples 6 and 39 exclude $\mu = 18,000$. Students often react to this observation by asking, "What went wrong with samples 6 and 39?" The answer is *nothing.* Statistics does not promise 100% certainty. In fact, in this illustration we expected 95% of the intervals to include the actual value of the population mean and 5% to exclude it. Since we observed 50 sample means, we expected that 2.5 (5% of 50) intervals would not contain $\mu = 18,000$. We actually observed 2 such intervals.

In practice, only one sample will be drawn, and thus only one sample mean will be calculated. The resulting confidence interval estimate will either correctly include the population mean or incorrectly exclude it. In each case we do not know whether the interval estimate includes the population mean or not. All that we can say about a 95% confidence interval estimate is that, in the long run, 95% of such intervals will be correct.

EXERCISES

LEARNING THE TECHNIQUES

8.1 In a random sample of 400 observations from a population whose variance is $\sigma^2 = 100$, we calculated $\bar{x} = 75$. Find the 95% confidence interval estimate of the population mean μ.

8.2 Describe what happens to the width of a confidence interval estimate of μ when each of the following occurs.

a. The confidence level increases from 95% to 99%.

b. The sample size decreases.

c. The value of σ increases.

8.3 Suppose that a random sample of five observations was taken from a normal population whose variance is 25. The results are

8, 15, 12, 6, 7.

Find the 99% confidence interval estimate of the population mean.

8.4 A random sample of 400 observations from a population whose standard deviation is 90 produced $\bar{x} = 1,500$. Find the 90% confidence interval estimate of μ.

8.5 Given the following information, determine the 95% confidence interval estimate of μ:

$n = 1000$

$\sigma = 40$

$\bar{x} = 125$.

8.6 The following observations were drawn from a normal population whose variance is 100:

12, 8, 22, 15, 30, 6, 39, 48.

Determine the 90% confidence interval of the population mean.

8.7 Repeat Exercise 8.6, using a confidence level of 99%.

APPLYING THE TECHNIQUES

Self-Correcting Exercise (See Appendix 8.B for the solution.)

8.8 In a survey* conducted to determine, among other things, the costs of vacations, 164 individuals were randomly sampled. Each was asked to assess the total cost of his or her most recent vacation.

---

* P. K. Tat and J. R. Thompson, "An Exploratory Study of Brand Loyalty in Selecting Travel Destinations," *Developments in Marketing Science* 6 (1983): 562–65.

The average cost was $1,386. Assuming that the standard deviation was $400, estimate the population mean cost of vacations, with 99% confidence.

8.9   In an article about disinflation (*Newsweek,* 26 August 1985), various investments were examined. The investments included stocks, bonds, and housing. The annual compound rate of return was calculated for each for the period June 1980 to June 1985. Suppose that, in order to determine the rate of return for housing, a random sample of 50 residential properties sold during the period 1980 to 1985 was drawn. If the sample mean was 4.3%, estimate with 95% confidence the average rate of return of all houses between 1980 and 1985. (Assume that the standard deviation was 1%.)

8.10   A survey of 20 companies indicated that the average annual income of company presidents was $110,000. Assuming that the population standard deviation is $7,000 and that annual incomes are normally distributed, calculate the 90% confidence interval estimate of the average annual income of all company presidents.

8.11   In a random sample of 70 students in a large university, a dean found that the mean weekly time devoted to homework was 14.3 hours. If we assume that homework time is normally distributed, with a standard deviation of 4.0 hours, find the 99% confidence interval estimate of the weekly time spent doing homework for all the university's students.

SECTION
8.4

ESTIMATING THE POPULATION MEAN WHEN THE VARIANCE IS UNKNOWN

We now proceed to a more realistic type of problem. Again, when the population mean is unknown, the variance usually is, too. As a result, we cannot use the estimator

$$\bar{x} \pm z_{\alpha/2} \frac{\sigma}{\sqrt{n}}$$

in this section. But we still proceed as logically as possible through our options. Thus, since the population standard deviation σ is unknown, we will use the sample standard deviation s in its place. Unfortunately, when we do so, the sampling distribution of the sample mean (which was the source of the interval estimator presented in Section 8.3) is no longer normal. Therefore, we must instead use a sampling distribution called the **Student *t*.**

If repeated samples are drawn from a normal population, the sampling distribution of

$$t = \frac{\bar{x} - \mu}{s/\sqrt{n}}$$

is the Student *t* distribution, which has the following characteristics:

1. It is mound-shaped.
2. It is symmetrical about zero.
3. It is more widely dispersed than the standard normal distribution.
4. Its actual shape depends on the sample size *n*. A convenient way of representing this characteristic is to say that the *t*-statistic has $(n - 1)$ **degrees of freedom.**

FIGURE 8.3 STANDARD NORMAL DISTRIBUTION, *t* DISTRIBUTION WITH 2 DEGREES OF FREEDOM, AND *t* DISTRIBUTION WITH 25 DEGREES OF FREEDOM

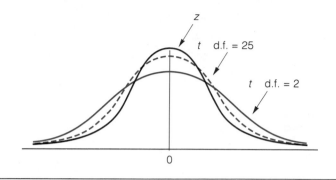

Figure 8.3 compares the distribution of z with that of a t-statistic with 2 degrees of freedom and with that of another t-statistic with 25 degrees of freedom. As you can see, the Student t distributions are more widely spread than the standard normal distribution; and among Student t distributions, those with a smaller number of degrees of freedom are more widely spread than those with a larger number of degrees of freedom. This is because using the sample standard deviation s in the Student t distribution (as compared to using σ in the standard normal distribution) results in a second source of variation. (The first source of variation is the sample mean $\bar{x}$.) In repeated sampling we expect not only that the sample means will vary from sample to sample, but that the sample standard deviations will, too. Consequently, the Student t distribution is more dispersed than the standard normal distribution. However, as the sample size and the degrees of freedom increase, s provides a more stable estimate of σ, causing the variability to decrease. In fact, for large (theoretically infinite) sample sizes the Student t and standard normal distributions are identical.

Table 6 in Appendix B specifies values for t_α (where t_α equals the value of t such that the area to its right under the t curve is equal to α). This table is reproduced here as Table 8.3. Observe that t_α values are provided for degrees of freedom (d.f.) ranging from 1 to 29 and for ∞. For example, if we want the t value with an area .05 to its right with d.f. = 5, we find the column headed by $t_{.05}$ and locate the row with d.f. = 5; the value you should find is $t_{.05} = 2.015$. If d.f. = 10, then $t_{.05} = 1.812$; and if d.f. = 25, then $t_{.05} = 1.708$. As d.f. increases, $t_{.05}$ grows smaller. When d.f. = 29, then $t_{.05} = 1.699$; and if d.f. = ∞, then $t_{.05} = 1.645$, which you should recognize as $z_{.05}$. This is not a coincidence. As was mentioned earlier, $t_\alpha = z_\alpha$ when d.f. is large.

You may be wondering why Table 8.3 does not show t_α with d.f. $\geq$ 30 (other than ∞). The reason is that t_α with d.f. $\geq$ 30 is approximately equal to t with d.f. = ∞ (that is, z_α). In fact, you can see for yourself that t_α with d.f. = 29 is already approximately equal to t_α with d.f. = ∞. We will let $t_{\alpha,v}$ represent the value of t_α with v degrees of freedom.

Using the same logic that produced the confidence interval estimator of the population mean when the variance is known, we can develop the confidence interval estimator of the population mean when the variance is unknown.

TABLE 8.3 CRITICAL VALUES OF THE STUDENT t DISTRIBUTION

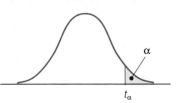

Degrees of Freedom	$t_{.100}$	$t_{.050}$	$t_{.025}$	$t_{.010}$	$t_{.005}$
1	3.078	6.314	12.706	31.821	63.657
2	1.886	2.920	4.303	6.965	9.925
3	1.638	2.353	3.182	4.541	5.841
4	1.533	2.132	2.776	3.747	4.604
5	1.476	2.015	2.571	3.365	4.032
6	1.440	1.943	2.447	3.143	3.707
7	1.415	1.895	2.365	2.998	3.499
8	1.397	1.860	2.306	2.896	3.355
9	1.383	1.833	2.262	2.821	3.250
10	1.372	1.812	2.228	2.764	3.169
11	1.363	1.796	2.201	2.718	3.106
12	1.356	1.782	2.179	2.681	3.055
13	1.350	1.771	2.160	2.650	3.012
14	1.345	1.761	2.145	2.624	2.977
15	1.341	1.753	2.131	2.602	2.947
16	1.337	1.746	2.120	2.583	2.921
17	1.333	1.740	2.110	2.567	2.898
18	1.330	1.734	2.101	2.552	2.878
19	1.328	1.729	2.093	2.539	2.861
20	1.325	1.725	2.086	2.528	2.845
21	1.323	1.721	2.080	2.518	2.831
22	1.321	1.717	2.074	2.508	2.819
23	1.319	1.714	2.069	2.500	2.807
24	1.318	1.711	2.064	2.492	2.797
25	1.316	1.708	2.060	2.485	2.787
26	1.315	1.706	2.056	2.479	2.779
27	1.314	1.703	2.052	2.473	2.771
28	1.313	1.701	2.048	2.467	2.763
29	1.311	1.699	2.045	2.462	2.756
∞	1.282	1.645	1.960	2.326	2.576

Confidence Interval Estimator of μ, with σ^2 Unknown

$$\bar{x} \pm t_{\alpha/2} \frac{s}{\sqrt{n}} \qquad \text{d.f.} = n - 1$$

It should be noted that this estimator can only be used if the random variable x is normally distributed. In practice, this means that we can use this formula as long as x is not extremely nonnormal or if the sample size is large.

   We now have two different interval estimators of the population mean. The basis for deciding which one to use is quite clear. If the population variance is known, the confidence interval estimator of the population mean is

$$\bar{x} \pm z_{\alpha/2} \frac{\sigma}{\sqrt{n}}.$$

If the population variance is unknown, the confidence interval estimator of the population mean is

$$\bar{x} \pm t_{\alpha/2} \frac{s}{\sqrt{n}}, \qquad \text{d.f.} = n - 1.$$

   When d.f. ≥ 30, $t_{\alpha/2}$ is approximately equal to $z_{\alpha/2}$. If σ^2 is unknown and d.f. ≥ 30, then $t_{\alpha/2}$ can be determined from the standard normal table. Bear in mind, however, that the interval estimate is still $\bar{x} \pm t_{\alpha/2} s/\sqrt{n}$, with $t_{\alpha/2}$ being approximated by $z_{\alpha/2}$. It should be noted that in most realistic applications where we wish to estimate a population mean, the population variance is unknown. Consequently, the interval estimator of the population mean that will be used most frequently in real life is

$$\bar{x} \pm t_{\alpha/2} \frac{s}{\sqrt{n}}$$

no matter what the sample size is.

EXAMPLE 8.3

The owner of a large fleet of taxis is trying to estimate his costs for next year's operations. One major cost is for fuel purchases. Because of the high cost of gasoline, the owner has recently converted his taxis to operate on propane. He needs to know what the average consumption will be; so he has taken a random sample of 8 taxis and measured the miles per gallon achieved by each. The results are as follows:

   28.1, 33.6, 42.1, 37.5, 27.6, 36.8, 39.0, 29.4.

Estimate, with 95% confidence, the mean propane mileage for all taxis in his fleet. (Assume that the distribution of mileage is normal.)

Solution.   The problem objective is to describe a single population (gas mileage of a fleet of taxis), and the data type is quantitative (miles driven per gallon of propane). Since we have no knowledge of the population variance, the correct confidence interval estimator is

$$\bar{x} \pm t_{\alpha/2} \frac{s}{\sqrt{n}}.$$

From the data, we compute

$$\bar{x} = 34.26$$
$$s^2 = 29.59$$
$$s = 5.44,$$

with

$$n = 8.$$

Since we want a 95% confidence level,

$$1 - \alpha = .95$$
$$t_{\alpha/2} = t_{.025} \quad (\text{d.f.} = n - 1 = 7) \quad = 2.365.$$

The 95% confidence interval estimate is

$$\bar{x} \pm t_{\alpha/2} \frac{s}{\sqrt{n}} = 34.26 \pm 2.365 \frac{5.44}{\sqrt{8}} = 34.26 \pm 4.55$$

or

$$LCL = 29.71 \quad \text{and} \quad UCL = 38.81.$$

We estimate that the average propane mileage for all taxis in the fleet falls between 29.71 and 38.81 miles per gallon. From this estimate the owner should be able to estimate the total propane mileage for the entire fleet and eventually predict next year's cost of operations.

MINITAB COMPUTER OUTPUT FOR EXAMPLE 8.3*

```
        N    MEAN    STDEV    SE MEAN    95.0 PERCENT C.I.
C1      8    34.26   5.44     1.92       (29.71,   38.81)
```

As you can see, Minitab prints the sample size, the sample mean and standard deviation, the standard error of the mean (which in this case is $s/\sqrt{n} = 1.92$), and the 95% confidence interval estimate of the population mean propane mileage.

To recognize when to use the confidence interval estimator of a population mean when the population variance is unknown, remember the following factors.

---

* See Appendix 8.A for the Minitab instructions needed to answer this question.

Factors That Identify the *t*-Interval Estimator of *μ*

1. *Problem objective:* Describe a single population.
2. *Data type:* quantitative
3. *Population variance:* unknown

   EXERCISES

LEARNING THE TECHNIQUES

8.12   A random sample of 75 observations from a normal population produced the following statistics:

$\bar{x} = 27.3$ $s = 7.8$.

Estimate the population mean, with 99% confidence.

8.13   The following data were drawn from a normal population:

   4, 8, 12, 11, 14, 6, 12, 8, 9, 5.

Estimate the population mean with 90% confidence.

8.14   Given the following statistics

$\bar{x} = 156.3$ $s = 14.9$ $n = 12,$

estimate the population mean, with 95% confidence.

8.15   What assumption must be made to answer Exercise 8.14?

8.16   Repeat Exercise 8.3, assuming that the population variance is unknown.

8.17   Explain the difference between the confidence interval estimates calculated in Exercises 8.3 and 8.16.

8.18   Repeat Exercise 8.6, assuming that the population variance is unknown.

8.19   Explain the difference between the confidence interval estimates calculated in Exercises 8.6 and 8.18.

APPLYING THE TECHNIQUES

Self-Correcting Exercise (See Appendix 8.B for the solution.)

8.20   A real-estate company appraised the market value of 20 homes in a prestigious district of San Francisco and found that the sample mean and sample standard deviation were $236,500 and $23,000, respectively. Estimate the mean appraisal value of all the homes in this area, with 90% confidence. (Assume that the appraised values are normally distributed.)

8.21   A federal agency responsible for enforcing laws concerning weights and measures routinely inspects packages to determine if the weight of the contents is at least as great as that advertised on the package. A random sample of 25 observations of a product whose container claims that the net weight is 10 ounces yielded the following statistics:

$\bar{x} = 10.52$ $s^2 = 1.43$.

Estimate with 95% confidence the mean weight of the container.

8.22   A manufacturer of a brand of designer jeans realizes that many retailers charge less than the suggested retail price of $40. A random sample of 20 retailers reveals that the mean and the standard deviation of the prices of the jeans are $32 and $2.50, respectively. Estimate with 90% confidence the mean retail price of the jeans.

8.23   An advertisement for a major home appliance manufacturer claims that its repairmen are the loneliest in the world because its appliances require the smallest number of service calls. To examine this claim, researchers drew a random sample of 100 owners of 5-year-old washing machines. The mean and the standard deviation of the number of service calls in the 5-year period were 4.3 and 1.8, respectively. Find the 90% confidence interval estimate for the mean number of service calls for all 5-year old washing machines.

ESTIMATING THE POPULATION PROPORTION

In Chapter 7 we pointed out that, when the data type is qualitative, the only computation permitted is one to determine the proportion of times each value occurs. If the problem objective is to describe a single population, the parameter of interest is the proportion p of times a certain outcome occurs. In keeping with the concepts and notation of the binomial experiment, we label the outcome of interest to us a *success*. Any other outcomes are labeled *failures*. Our task in this section is to develop the technique of estimating the proportion of successes in a binomial experiment.

Point Estimator of a Population Proportion

The point estimator of the population proportion is the **sample proportion,** which is defined as

$$\hat{p} = \frac{x}{n},$$

where x is the number of successes in n trials. ($\hat{p}$ is read p-hat.)

Recall from Chapter 5 that the number of successes in n independent trials is a binomial random variable. It follows that, since $\hat{p} = x/n$, $\hat{p}$ is also a binomial random variable. Hence, the sampling distribution of $\hat{p}$ is binomial. Unfortunately, the binomial distribution is awkward to use for statistical inference. In Chapter 5, we also showed that the binomial distribution can be approximated by the normal distribution, as long as n is large (np and nq must be at least 5). The mean of $\hat{p}$ is p, and the standard deviation is $\sqrt{pq/n}$. Recall, too, that $q = 1 - p$; in the notation that follows, $\hat{q} = 1 - \hat{p}$.

Sampling Distribution of $\hat{p}$

$\hat{p}$ is approximately normally distributed, with mean p and standard deviation $\sqrt{pq/n}$.

Using the same mathematical steps that were used to develop confidence interval estimators in the previous two sections, we can find the confidence interval estimate of a population proportion.

Confidence Interval Estimator of p

$$\hat{p} \pm z_{\alpha/2} \sqrt{\frac{\hat{p}\hat{q}}{n}}$$

The sample size n must be large enough so that

$$n\hat{p} \geq 5 \quad \text{and} \quad n\hat{q} \geq 5.$$

Notice that we use $\hat{p}$ and $\hat{q}$ in computing the standard deviation $\sqrt{\hat{p}\hat{q}/n}$ because the actual standard deviation $\sqrt{pq/n}$ is unknown. (Obviously, we don't know p and q; if we did, we wouldn't need to estimate p.)

EXAMPLE 8.4

A factory produces a component used in manufacturing computers. Each component is tested prior to shipment to determine whether or not it is defective. In a random sample of 400 units, 60 were found to be defective. Estimate with 99% confidence the true proportion of defective components produced by the factory.

Solution.   The problem objective is to describe the population of computer components produced by the factory. The data type is qualitative, because the values of the variable are *defective* and *nondefective*. It follows that we wish to estimate the population proportion p. The confidence interval estimator is

$$\hat{p} \pm z_{\alpha/2} \sqrt{\frac{\hat{p}\hat{q}}{n}}.$$

From the data we observe that

$$\hat{p} = \frac{60}{400} = .15$$

and

$$\hat{q} = 1 - \hat{p} = 1 - .15 = .85.$$

The confidence level is

$$1 - \alpha = .99,$$

so

$$z_{\alpha/2} = z_{.005} = 2.58.$$

The 99% confidence interval estimate is

$$\hat{p} \pm z_{\alpha/2} \sqrt{\frac{\hat{p}\hat{q}}{n}} = .15 \pm 2.58 \sqrt{\frac{(.15)(.85)}{400}} = .15 \pm .046.$$

The confidence limits are

$$LCL = .104 \quad \text{and} \quad UCL = .196.$$

The proportion of defectives is thus estimated to lie between 10.4% and 19.6%. The quality-control manager could use these results to decide that, since the proportion of defectives may be as high as 19.6%, some modification to the production process is necessary.

> **Factors That Identify the Interval Estimator of *p***
>
> 1. *Problem objective:* Describe a single population.
> 2. *Data type:* qualitative

 EXERCISES

LEARNING THE TECHNIQUES

8.24 Given that $\hat{p} = .84$ and $n = 600$, estimate p with 90% confidence.

8.25 In a random sample of 250, we found 75 successes. Estimate the population proportion of successes, with 99% confidence.

8.26 Estimate p with 95% confidence, given

$x = 27 \qquad n = 110$.

8.27 A statistician counted 100 successes in a random sample of 150. Estimate the population proportion of successes, with 90% confidence.

8.28 Estimate p with 95% confidence, given that a random sample of 100 produced $\hat{p} = .2$.

8.29 Repeat Exercise 8.28 for a confidence level of 90%.

8.30 Repeat Exercise 8.28 for $n = 1,000$.

8.31 Repeat Exercise 8.28 for $\hat{p} = .5$.

APPLYING THE TECHNIQUES

Self-Correcting Exercise (See Appendix 8.B for the solution.)
8.32 In a random sample of 1,000 picture tubes produced in a large plant, 80 were defective. Estimate with 95% confidence the true proportion of defective picture tubes produced at this plant.

8.33 In a survey of 250 voters prior to an election, 40% indicated that they would vote for the incumbent candidate. Estimate with 90% confidence the population proportion of voters who support the incumbent.

8.34 Surveyors asked a random sample of women what factor was the most important in deciding where to shop. The results, which appeared in the *Wall Street Journal* (5 February 1987) appear in the accompanying table. If the sample size was 1,200, estimate with 95% confidence the proportion of women who identified price and value as the most important factor.

Factor	Percentage
Price and value	44%
Quality and selection of merchandise	34%
Service	11%
Shopping environment	11%

SOURCE: Newspaper Advertising Bureau, Inc.

8.35 In a survey, 1,039 adults were asked, "How much respect and confidence do you have in the public school system?" The results, which were reported in the *Toronto Star* (26 September 1988), are shown in the accompanying table. Estimate with 90% confidence the proportion of all adults who answered "A great deal" or "Quite a lot."

Responses	Percentage
A great deal	12%
Quite a lot	30%
Some	35%
Very little	13%
No opinion	10%

SELECTING THE SAMPLE SIZE

As you've seen in the previous three sections, interval estimates can often provide useful information about the value of a parameter. If the interval is too wide, however, its use is quite limited. For example, estimating that the proportion of customers who will buy a new product lies in the interval 2% to 52% provides very little useful input to a manager. One way for statisticians to control the width of the interval is by determining the sample size necessary to produce narrow intervals. To do this, we must specify three factors:

1. The parameter to be estimated
2. The desired confidence level of the interval estimator
3. The bound of the error of estimation, where error of estimation is the absolute difference between the point estimate and the parameter

We denote the bound on the error of estimation by B. For the types of interval estimators discussed in this chapter and in Chapter 9, the interval estimator is

Point estimate $\pm B$.

DETERMINING THE SAMPLE SIZE FOR ESTIMATING A POPULATION MEAN

In order to determine the sample size required for estimating a population mean (with population variance known), we find the value of n such that

$$z_{\alpha/2} \frac{\sigma}{\sqrt{n}} = B.$$

Simplifying this equation, we get the following result.

Sample Size Necessary to Estimate μ with σ^2 Known

$$n = \frac{z_{\alpha/2}^2 \sigma^2}{B^2}$$

To solve for n, we have to use some value for σ. This value may be approximated from previous experiments or from prior knowledge about the population. A popular method of approximating the population standard deviation is to begin by approximating the range of the random variable. A conservative estimate of σ is then

$\sigma \approx \text{Range}/4.$

This method is quite effective because approximating the range is often easy.

━━━━━━━━━━ **EXAMPLE 8.5**

The operations manager of a large production plant would like to estimate the average amount of time a worker takes to assemble a new electronic component. After observing a number of workers assembling similar devices, she noted that the shortest time taken was 10 minutes, while the longest time taken was 22 minutes. How large a sample of workers should she take if she wishes to estimate the mean assembly time to within 20 seconds? Assume that the confidence level is to be 99%.

Solution.   The parameter to be estimated is the population mean μ. The confidence level is

$$1 - \alpha = .99.$$

Thus,

$$z_{\alpha/2} = z_{.005} = 2.58.$$

The error bound is

$$B = 20,$$

and the range is

$$\text{Range} = 22 - 10 = 12 \text{ minutes.}$$

As a result, we approximate σ as

$$\sigma \approx \text{Range}/4 = 12/4 = 3 \text{ minutes} = 180 \text{ seconds.}$$

We can now solve for n:

$$n = \frac{z_{\alpha/2}^2 \sigma^2}{B^2} = \frac{(2.58)^2(180)^2}{20^2} = 540.$$

The operations manager should randomly sample 540 workers in order to estimate the mean assembly time to within 20 seconds, with 99% confidence.

DETERMINING THE SAMPLE SIZE FOR ESTIMATING A POPULATION PROPORTION

To find the sample size for estimating p, we solve the equation

$$z_{\alpha/2}\sqrt{\frac{\widehat{p}\widehat{q}}{n}} = B$$

to obtain the following formula.

Sample Size Necessary to Estimate p

$$n = \frac{z_{\alpha/2}^2 \hat{p}\hat{q}}{B^2}$$

Unfortunately, since we haven't taken the sample yet, we don't know the values of $\hat{p}$ and $\hat{q}$. The best way of proceeding is to select the values of $\hat{p}$ and $\hat{q}$ that produce the largest possible value of n. Thus we set $\hat{p} = .5$ and $\hat{q} = .5$, and hence

$$n = \frac{z_{\alpha/2}^2 (.5)(.5)}{B^2} = \frac{z_{\alpha/2}^2 (.25)}{B^2}.$$

EXAMPLE 8.6

A market analyst wants to estimate the proportion of shoppers who will buy a new type of liquid detergent. How large a sample should he take in order to estimate that proportion to within .04, with 90% confidence?

Solution. The parameter to be estimated is the population proportion p. With a confidence level of $1 - \alpha = .90$,

$$z_{\alpha/2} = z_{.05} = 1.645.$$

The error bound is

$$B = .04.$$

Thus,

$$n = \frac{z_{\alpha/2}^2 (.25)}{B^2} = \frac{(1.645)^2 (.25)}{(.04)^2} = 423.$$

A sample of 423 shoppers should be taken to estimate the proportion of shoppers who will buy the new detergent to within .04, with 90% confidence.

EXERCISES

8.36 Find n, given that we wish to estimate μ to within 10 units, with 95% confidence, and assuming that $\sigma = 100$.

8.37 Determine the sample size necessary to estimate μ to within 10 units, with 99% confidence. We know that the range of the population is 200 units.

8.38 A medical statistician wants to estimate the average weight loss of people who are on a new diet plan. In a preliminary study, she found that the smallest weight loss was 3 pounds and the largest weight loss was 39 pounds. How large a sample should be drawn to estimate the mean weight loss to within 2 pounds, with 90% confidence?

8.39 A forester would like to estimate the mean tree diameter of a large tract of trees. He would like to estimate μ to within .5 inch, with 99% confidence. A quick survey reveals that the smallest tree has a diameter of 2 inches, while the largest tree has a diameter of 27 inches. How large a sample should he take?

8.40 How large a sample should be taken to estimate a population proportion to within .05, with 95% confidence?

8.41 How large a sample should be taken to estimate a population proportion to within .02, with 95% confidence?

8.42 A marketing manager is in the process of deciding whether to introduce a new product. He has concluded that he needs to perform a market survey in which he asks a random sample of people whether they will buy the product. How large a sample should he take if he wants to estimate the proportion of people who will buy the product to within 3%, with 99% confidence?

SECTION
8.7

SUMMARY

Estimation techniques are quite easy to apply. They require the statistician first to identify the parameter to be estimated and second to choose the appropriate formula. Table 8.4 summarizes the relevant formulas and the conditions required for their use.

We also discussed in this chapter how to determine the sample sizes required to estimate μ and p. These formulas are shown in Table 8.5.

IMPORTANT TERMS

Estimator	Lower confidence limit (LCL)
Point estimator	Upper confidence limit (UCL)
Interval estimator	Student t distribution
Sampling distribution	Degrees of freedom
Confidence interval estimator	Bound on the error of estimation
Confidence level	Sample size

TABLE 8.4   *SUMMARY OF INTERVAL ESTIMATORS OF μ AND p*

Parameter	Confidence Interval Estimator	Required Conditions
μ	$\bar{x} \pm z_{\alpha/2} \dfrac{\sigma}{\sqrt{n}}$	σ^2 is known; x is normally distributed or n is sufficiently large.
	$\bar{x} \pm t_{\alpha/2} \dfrac{s}{\sqrt{n}}$	σ^2 is unknown; x is normally distributed.
p	$\hat{p} \pm z_{\alpha/2} \sqrt{\dfrac{\hat{p}\hat{q}}{n}}$	$n\hat{p} \geq 5$ and $n\hat{q} \geq 5$.

TABLE 8.5   *SUMMARY OF SAMPLE SIZES FOR ESTIMATING μ AND p*

Parameter	Sample Size
μ	$n = \dfrac{z_{\alpha/2}^2 \sigma^2}{B^2}$
p	$n = \dfrac{z_{\alpha/2}^2 (.25)}{B^2}$

 SUPPLEMENTARY EXERCISES

8.43 A time study of a large production facility was undertaken to determine the average time required to assemble a widget. A random sample of 15 assemblies produced $\bar{x} = 12.2$ minutes, with a standard deviation of 2.4 minutes.

a. Assuming that the assembly times are normally distributed, estimate the mean assembly time, with 95% confidence.

b. How would your answer to part (a) change if the population standard deviation was known to be 2.0 minutes?

8.44 Suppose that annual household incomes in a certain city have a standard deviation of $3,000. A random sample of 50 families reveals that the mean annual income is $27,500.

a. Estimate the mean annual family income of all families in this city, with 95% confidence.

b. Without doing the calculations, specify what happens to the width of the interval in each of the following circumstances.
   i. σ is $5,000, not $3,000.
   ii. The confidence level is 90%, not 95%.
   iii. The sample mean is $30,000, not $27,500.

8.45 In a study to determine the size of loan requests at a suburban bank, the mean in a random sample of 25 requests was $7,500, with a standard deviation of $2,000. Assuming that loan requests are normally distributed, estimate with 95% confidence the mean loan request.

8.46 In a poll of 1,500 Americans, 30% stated that in 10 years' time the world will be a better place to live in than it is today (*Toronto Star,* 4 April 1985).

Estimate with 99% confidence the proportion of all Americans who believe that the world will be a better place to live in 10 years from now than it is today.

8.47 As a result of a recent Federal Trade Commission ruling, doctors are allowed to advertise. In a survey designed to examine this issue, 91 doctors were asked whether they believed that doctors should be allowed to advertise.* A total of 23 physicians supported advertising by doctors. Estimate with 90% confidence the proportion of all doctors who support advertising.

8.48 A large university wants to determine the average income their students earn during the summer. A random sample of 25 second-year business students produced the following statistics (where x is measured in hundreds of dollars):

$$\sum x_i = 826.6 \qquad \sum x_i^2 = 27,935.7$$

a. Estimate the mean summer employment income for all second-year business students, with 99% confidence.

b. Does the estimate in part (a) pertain to all business students? To all university students? Explain.

8.49 A firm's management is contemplating modifying one of its products. To help in making a decision, management representatives wish to conduct a market survey that will enable them to

---

* G. Riecker and G. Yavas, "Do Medical Professionals Favor Advertising?" *Developments in Marketing Science* 7 (1984): 239–43.

estimate the proportion of potential customers who would buy the new product. They wish to estimate this proportion to within 3%, with 99% confidence. How large a sample should be drawn?

8.50 A department store wants to estimate the average account of all its credit-card customers, to within $10.00, with 99% confidence. A quick analysis tells us that the smallest account shows $0 while the largest is $500.

a. Determine the sample size.

b. Suppose that a survey was performed, and the sample mean is $150. Find a 99% confidence interval estimate of μ, assuming that the value of σ used in part (a) is correct. (HINT: This question should take you no more than 5 seconds to answer.)

8.51 A large company is considering moving from its present downtown location to a location in the suburbs. One factor in this decision is the amount of time the company's employees spend getting to work. A random sample of 20 employees reveals that the mean and the standard deviation of the time required to get to work are 36.5 and 11.3 minutes, respectively. Estimate with 95% confidence the mean time to arrive at work for all of this company's employees.

8.52 In an examination of consumer loyalty in the travel business, 24 out of a total of 72 first-time visitors to a tourist attraction stated that they would not return.* Estimate with 95% confidence the proportion of all first-time visitors who would not return to the same destination.

8.53 A rock promoter is in the process of deciding whether or not to book a new band for a rock concert. He knows that this band appeals almost exclusively to teenagers. According to the latest census, there are 400,000 teenagers in the area. The promoter decides to do a survey to try to estimate the proportion of teenagers who will attend the concert. How large a sample should be taken in order to estimate the proportion to within .02 with 99% confidence?

---

* P. K. Tat and J. R. Thompson, "An Exploratory Study of Brand Loyalty in Setting Travel Destinations," *Developments in Marketing Science* 6 (1983): 563–65.

8.54 In Exercise 8.53, suppose that the promoter decides to draw a sample of size 600 (because of financial considerations). Of these 600, 75 respondents indicate that they would attend the concert. Estimate the population proportion, with 99% confidence.

8.55 Researchers asked a random sample of business executives how many days they take for vacations annually. The results, which were reported in the *Wall Street Journal* (6 February 1987) appear in the accompanying table (in percentages). If the sample size was 800, estimate with 99% confidence the mean number of days spent on vacation by business executives.

Days[†]	Frequency
0–5	9%
5–10	24%
10–15	31%
15–20	23%
20–25	13%

SOURCE: Karn/Ferry International.

[†] Each interval includes the lower limit but excludes the upper limit.

8.56 In a survey reported in the *Wall Street Journal* (9 February 1987), a random sample of the high-school class of 1972 was asked how many years it took for them to complete their bachelor's degrees in college. The results (in percentages) are shown below. If 1,000 graduates were surveyed, estimate with 95% confidence the mean number of years taken to complete the bachelor's degree.

Four years	49%
Five years	27%
Six years	9%
Seven years	15%

SOURCE: Center for Education Statistics.

8.57 In the 1988 presidential election campaign, George Bush and Michael Dukakis participated in a televised debate on September 25, 1988. In an ABC-TV poll, 639 registered voters were surveyed and asked who won the debate. The results (reported in the *Toronto Star*, 26 September 1988) are as follows:

George Bush   36%
Michael Dukakis   44%
Tie   20%

a. Estimate with 95% confidence the proportion of all registered voters who believed George Bush won.

b. Estimate with 95% confidence the proportion of all registered voters who believed Michael Dukakis won.

8.58 Refer to Exercise 8.57. A *Newsweek* poll of 337 registered voters had 42% saying that Michael Dukakis won and 41% saying that George Bush won. Do these results contradict the results of the ABC-TV poll?

CASE 8.1*   NATIONAL PATENT DEVELOPMENT CORPORATION

The National Patent Development Corporation (NPD) has recently acquired a new product that can be used to replace the dentist's drill. The product, called Caridex, is a solution that dissolves decayed matter in cavities without requiring drilling.

It is known that 100,000 dentists in the United States treat cavities. A preliminary analysis has revealed that 10% of all dentists would use Caridex in the first year after its introduction. However, Caridex is only effective on certain types of cavities. In a survey of 400 dentists, each was asked to estimate the number of cavities per week he or she would treat with Caridex. The mean and standard deviation of these estimates are 4.015 and 1.764, respectively.

The dispensing unit costs NPD $200, and it intends to sell the unit at cost. The solution costs $0.50 per cavity and will be sold to dentists at a price of $2.50 per cavity. Fixed annual costs are expected to be $4 million.

NPD would like an estimate of the profit it can expect in the first year of operation.

CASE 8.2†   AUTOMATIC TELLER MACHINE

The automatic teller machine (ATM), first introduced in the 1960s, was a major technological innovation. With it, a customer can make deposits, withdrawals, and other transactions without the aid of a teller. It is estimated that, for each transaction performed by an ATM instead of a teller, the banks saves about $1. In an effort to persuade as many customers as possible to use ATMs, banks install the machines in as many locations as are feasible. Because of installation and maintenance costs, however, the machines should only be placed in locations where the demand warrants it.

---

* Based on a report by Ladenburg Thalman—a large, New York–based investment firm. The survey is fictitious.

† Based on D. L. Varble and J. M. Hawes, "Profiling the Users of Automated Teller Machines," *Developments in Marketing Science* 9 (1986): 369–72.

In a survey to determine the frequency of use of a proposed ATM, 542 individuals who work in the building where the machine would be installed were asked how frequently they would use it. Their responses appear in the accompanying table. The bank would like to estimate the average annual use of the ATM. (Assume that those who state "less than once per month" would use the machine twice per year.) Given that the potential population of users numbers 10,000, the bank would also like to estimate the annual savings achieved by using the ATM in place of a bank teller.

FREQUENCY OF PROPOSED USE OF AN ATM

Use	Frequency
Twice per week	23
Once per week	37
Once per two weeks	18
Once per month	35
Less than once per month	44
Never	385
TOTAL	542

CASE 8.3   MIAMI HERALD SURVEY

Political surveys play such an important role in election campaigns that it's hard to imagine a recent election without extensive polling. Besides electing people to various political offices, voters also decide issues such as gun control and tax limitation. The November 4, 1986, ballot in the state of Florida contained questions about proposed casinos and lotteries, as well as choices for senator and governor. A survey of 959 registered voters, reported by the *Miami Herald* (30 October 1986), produced the following results.

Casinos

Q: If the election were held today, would you vote for or against the amendment to allow casino gambling in counties that want it?

For	35%
Against	60%
Don't Know	5%

U.S. Senate Race

Q: Suppose the election for U.S. Senate were held today. Would you vote for Paula Hawkins, the Republican, or Bob Graham, the Democrat?

Graham	47%
Hawkins	41%
Undecided	7%
Refused	5%

Governor's Race

Q: Suppose the election for governor were held today. Would you vote for Bob Martinez, the Republican, or Steve Pajcic, the Democrat?

Martinez	43%
Pajcic	40%
Undecided	14%
Refused	3%

Lottery

Q: If the election were held today, would you vote for or against a state-run lottery to help public education?

For	58%
Against	34%
Don't Know	8%

What conclusions can you draw from these data?

MINITAB INSTRUCTIONS

ESTIMATING μ WITH σ² KNOWN

To produce a 95% confidence interval estimate of μ, type

```
ZINTERVAL K1 C1
```

which specifies that $\sigma = $ K1 and that the data are stored in column 1. If you wish, you may use the NAME command to identify the variable in column 1. You may then use the variable name in the TINTERVAL command. Thus the commands

```
NAME C1 = 'x'
ZINTERVAL K1 'x'
```

would produce the same output as the preceding command, except the variable name x would appear in place of C1. The command

```
ZINTERVAL .90 25 C1
```

produces the 90% confidence interval estimate of μ when $\sigma = 25$. If the .90 is omitted, a 95% confidence interval estimate will be produced.

Suppose that the 100 observations alluded to in Example 8.1 are stored in column 1. The command

```
ZINTERVAL 8 C1
```

would produce the following output:

```
THE ASSUMED SIGMA = 8.000
        N     MEAN    STDEV    SEMEAN    95.0 PERCENT C.I.
C1     100    27.50    7.578     0.80     (25.93,    29.07)
```

ESTIMATING μ WITH σ^2 UNKNOWN

The command

```
TINTERVAL .95 C1
```

produces the 95% confidence interval estimate of μ (when σ^2 is unknown) from the data in column 1. Example 8.3 would be done by the computer as follows (since we show the data in the example, we'll show how the data are input here):

```
SET C1
28.1 33.6 42.1 37.5 27.6 36.8 39.0 29.4
END
TINTERVAL .95 C1
```

The output that would be produced is

```
       N     MEAN     STDEV     SE MEAN     95.0 PERCENT C.I.
C1     8     34.26    5.44      1.92        (29.71,   38.81)
```

SOLUTIONS TO SELF-CORRECTING EXERCISES

8.8 $\bar{x} \pm z_{\alpha/2} \dfrac{\sigma}{\sqrt{n}}$

$= 1386 \pm 2.58 \dfrac{400}{\sqrt{164}}$

$= 1{,}386 \pm 80.59.$

We estimate that the cost lies between 1,305.41 and 1,466.59.

8.20 $\bar{x} \pm t_{\alpha/2} \dfrac{s}{\sqrt{n}}$

$= 236{,}500 \pm 1.729 \dfrac{23{,}000}{\sqrt{20}}$

$= 236{,}500 \pm 8892.$

The mean market value is estimated to fall between 227,608 and 245,392.

8.32 $\hat{p} \pm z_{\alpha/2} \sqrt{\dfrac{\hat{p}\hat{q}}{n}}$

$= .08 \pm 1.96 \sqrt{\dfrac{(.08)(.92)}{1{,}000}}$

$= .08 \pm .017.$

The true proportion of defective picture tubes is estimated to be between 6.3% and 9.7%.

C H A P T E R **9**

ESTIMATION: COMPARING TWO POPULATIONS

INTRODUCTION

In Chapter 8 we discussed the basic principles of estimation and presented the confidence interval estimators used to describe a single population with both data types. In this chapter we extend our presentation to cover estimation methods when the objective involves comparing two populations. When the data type is quantitative, we will estimate the difference between two population means $\mu_1 - \mu_2$. When the data are qualitative, we will estimate the difference between two population proportions $p_1 - p_2$. We offer the following examples to illustrate applications of these estimation techniques.

1. Firms that use subcomponents manufactured by other companies in producing their own finished products are often concerned about the quality, reliability, and price of the subcomponents. If two competing suppliers of a component are available, the firm's manager may wish to compare the reliability of the two products. For example, a car manufacturer currently equips its product with a certain brand of tire. If a similarly priced brand of tire becomes available, the decision about which brand to use should be based on which tire, on average, lasts longer. In this situation, the data are quantitative (tire life is usually measured by the number of miles until wearout), and the problem objective is to compare the two populations of tires. The parameter to be estimated is $\mu_1 - \mu_2$.

2. Politicians are constantly concerned about how the voting public perceives their actions and behavior. Of particular interest are the extent to which constituents approve of a politician's behavior and the ways in which their approval changes over time. As a result, politicians frequently poll the public to determine the proportion of voters who support them and to gauge whether that support has changed since the previous survey. The data type is qualitative, since the responses are "I support the politician" or "I do not support the politician." The parameter of interest is $p_1 - p_2$, where p_1 is the proportion of support at present and p_2 is the proportion of support in the previous poll.

3. Operations managers of production facilities are always looking for ways of improving productivity in their plants. This can be accomplished by rearranging sequences of operations, acquiring new technology, or improving the training of workers. When one or more such changes are made, their effect on the operation of the entire plant is of interest. The manager can measure the effect by comparing productivity after the innovation with productivity before the innovation. In this case, the data type is quantitative (we often measure productivity in terms of the number of units produced), and the problem

objective is to compare two populations (the productivity before and after the change). It follows that the parameter of interest is $\mu_1 - \mu_2$.

SECTION
9.2

ESTIMATING THE DIFFERENCE BETWEEN TWO POPULATION MEANS WHEN THE VARIANCES ARE KNOWN

Once again, we begin with the simplest (and least realistic) procedure for estimating the difference between two population means. As Figure 9.1 depicts, we draw samples from each of the two populations of interest. From Population 1, we draw a random sample of size n_1 and compute $\bar{x}_1$. Similarly, we compute $\bar{x}_2$ from a random sample of size n_2 from Population 2. The estimator of the difference between the two unknown population means, $\mu_1 - \mu_2$, is the difference between the two sample means $\bar{x}_1 - \bar{x}_2$.

By extension of our work in Chapter 6, we discover that the sampling distribution of $\bar{x}_1 - \bar{x}_2$ is approximately normal, with mean $\mu_1 - \mu_2$ and variance $\sigma_1^2/n_1 + \sigma_2^2/n_2$. Using exactly the same set of arithmetic operations we used to develop the confidence interval estimations in Chapter 8, we determine the confidence interval estimator of the difference between two population means.

Confidence Interval Estimator of $\mu_1 - \mu_2$ with σ_1^2 and σ_2^2 Known

$$(\bar{x}_1 - \bar{x}_2) \pm z_{\alpha/2} \sqrt{\frac{\sigma_1^2}{n_1} + \frac{\sigma_2^2}{n_2}}$$

EXAMPLE 9.1

Periodically, coupons that can be used to purchase products at discount prices appear in newspapers. A supermarket chain has two different types of coupon for its own

---

FIGURE 9.1   SAMPLES FROM TWO POPULATIONS

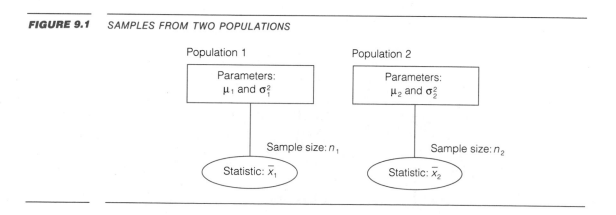

brand of bread. Coupon 1 offers two loaves for the price of one, and coupon 2 offers a 25¢ discount on the purchase of each loaf. In order to determine the relative selling power of the two plans, the supermarket chain performs the following experiment. The coupons appear in four consecutive weeks (coupon 1 in weeks 1 and 2, and coupon 2 in weeks 3 and 4) in the local newspaper. The company wants to estimate the average daily sales under each coupon plan. The average number of loaves sold per day during the first 14 days (supermarkets are open 7 days per week) was 153. The average number per day during the second 14 days was 142. Assuming that the population standard deviation was 10 loaves per week, estimate with 99% confidence the difference in mean daily sales under the two coupon plans. The number of loaves sold per day is normally distributed.

Solution.   The problem objective is to compare two populations, and the data type is quantitative. (We wish to compare daily sales using coupon 1 with daily sales using coupon 2.) Therefore, the parameter to be estimated is $\mu_1 - \mu_2$. We define

$\mu_1 =$ Mean daily sales using coupon 1

$\mu_2 =$ Mean daily sales using coupon 2.

The confidence interval estimator is

$$(\bar{x}_1 - \bar{x}_2) \pm z_{\alpha/2} \sqrt{\frac{\sigma_1^2}{n_1} + \frac{\sigma_2^2}{n_2}}.$$

We are given the following values:

$\bar{x}_1 = 153$

$\bar{x}_2 = 142$

$n_1 = n_2 = 14$

$\sigma_1 = \sigma_2 = 10.$

The confidence level is

$1 - \alpha = .99.$

Hence,

$z_{\alpha/2} = z_{.005} = 2.58.$

The 99% confidence interval estimate of $\mu_1 - \mu_2$ is

$$(\bar{x}_1 - \bar{x}_2) \pm z_{\alpha/2} \sqrt{\frac{\sigma_1^2}{n_1} + \frac{\sigma_2^2}{n_2}} = (153 - 142) \pm 2.58 \sqrt{\frac{10^2}{14} + \frac{10^2}{14}}$$

$$= 11 \pm 9.8.$$

The confidence limits are

$$LCL = 1.2 \qquad \text{and} \qquad UCL = 20.8.$$

We estimate that the difference between the two population mean daily sales lies between 1.2 and 20.8 loaves. Expressed another way, mean daily sales with coupon 1 are between 1.2 and 20.8 loaves more than mean daily sales with coupon 2. The management of the supermarket chain can be quite confident that coupon 1 generates greater sales than does coupon 2.

Here is a brief summary of the factors that tell us when to use the z-interval estimator of the difference between two population means.

Factors That Identify the z-Interval Estimator of $\mu_1 - \mu_2$

1. *Problem objective:* Compare two populations.
2. *Data type:* quantitative
3. *Population variances:* known

EXERCISES

LEARNING THE TECHNIQUES

9.1 Assume you are given the following information:

$n_1 = 100$ $n_2 = 200$

$\bar{x}_1 = 510$ $\bar{x}_2 = 480$

$\sigma_1 = 80$ $\sigma_2 = 90$.

Determine the 95% confidence interval estimate of $\mu_1 - \mu_2$.

9.2 A random sample of 25 observations from a normal population whose variance is 110 produced a sample mean of 45. A random sample of 40 from another normal population whose variance is 250 had a sample mean of 80. Estimate with 90% confidence the difference between the two population means.

9.3 The following information has been received:

$n_1 = 50$ $n_2 = 50$

$\bar{x}_1 = 175$ $\bar{x}_2 = 150$

$\sigma_1 = 40$ $\sigma_2 = 50$.

Estimate $\mu_1 - \mu_2$, with 99% confidence.

9.4 Repeat Exercise 9.3, with 95% confidence.

9.5 Repeat Exercise 9.3, with 90% confidence.

APPLYING THE TECHNIQUES

Self-Correcting Exercise (See Appendix 9.B for the solution.)

9.6 In order to help make a financial decision, an investor observes 25 returns on one type of investment and 35 returns on a second type of investment. The sample means are $\bar{x}_1 = 12.5$ and $\bar{x}_2 = 11.3$. Assume that the returns are normally distributed, with standard deviations $\sigma_1 = \sigma_2 = 5$. Estimate the difference in mean returns, with 95% confidence.

9.7 A survey of 200 second-year university business students revealed that their mean monthly income from summer jobs was $1,150. Another survey of 200 third-year university business students showed that their mean monthly summer-job income was $1,300. If incomes are normally distributed, with variances σ_1^2 (second-year) = 35,000 and σ_2^2 (third-year) = 42,000, estimate the difference in mean income between second- and third-year business students. Use a confidence level of 90%.

9.8 In order to compare the wages paid to workers in two large industries, random samples of 50 hourly wage earners are drawn from each.

The averages are $\bar{x}_1 = \$7.50$ and $\bar{x}_2 = \$7.90$. Assuming that $\sigma_1 = 2.00$ and $\sigma_2 = 1.80$, estimate with 95% confidence the difference in average wages between the two industries.

9.9 The management of a chain of department stores wants to know if there is a difference in the average annual income of potential customers at two possible sites for a new store. In one location, a random sample of 100 households showed a mean annual income of $27,000. In the other location, the mean annual income of 75 households was $29,000. Assuming that $\sigma_1 = \sigma_2 = 5,000$, estimate with 99% confidence the difference between average annual incomes in the two locations.

SECTION
9.3

ESTIMATING THE DIFFERENCE BETWEEN TWO POPULATION MEANS WHEN THE VARIANCES ARE UNKNOWN

Applications of inference about the difference between two population means when the population variances are known are quite rare, since it is unlikely that we would know the value of population variances but not know the population means. When the population variances are unknown, we proceed much as we did in Chapter 8 when we estimated the population mean for the case when the population variance is unknown. That is, we substitute the sample variances s_1^2 and s_2^2 for the unknown population variances. When the sample sizes are sufficiently large (each greater than 30), the sampling distribution remains approximately normal.

Confidence Interval Estimator of $\mu_1 - \mu_2$, with σ_1^2 and σ_2^2 Unknown, $n_1 > 30$ and $n_2 > 30$

$$(\bar{x}_1 - \bar{x}_2) \pm z_{\alpha/2} \sqrt{\frac{s_1^2}{n_1} + \frac{s_2^2}{n_2}}$$

EXAMPLE 9.2

In an effort to determine the effectiveness of a new type of fertilizer, agricultural researchers subdivided an 80-acre farm into 80 plots of 1 acre each. Of these, 40 plots were treated with the new fertilizer, and the remaining 40 were treated with the fertilizer that is currently used in the area. Wheat was planted on the farm, and at the end of the season the number of bushels reaped was measured. The means and variances were calculated to be as follows:

New Fertilizer	Current Fertilizer
Mean: $\bar{x}_1 = 27.08$	Mean: $\bar{x}_2 = 25.74$
Variance: $s_1^2 = 14.21$	Variance: $s_2^2 = 11.38$

Estimate with 95% confidence the difference in mean crop yield between the two kinds of fertilizer.

Solution.   We wish to compare two populations of crop yields. Hence, the problem objective is to compare two populations whose data type is quantitative. This tells us that the parameter to be estimated is $\mu_1 - \mu_2$. The population variances are unknown, and each sample size exceeds 30. (The two sample sizes are $n_1 = 40$ and $n_2 = 40$.) The confidence interval estimator is

$$(\bar{x}_1 - \bar{x}_2) \pm z_{\alpha/2} \sqrt{\frac{s_1^2}{n_1} + \frac{s_2^2}{n_2}}.$$

Because we wish to estimate with 95% confidence, we determine

$$z_{\alpha/2} = z_{.025} = 1.96.$$

Thus, the 95% confidence interval estimate of the difference in mean crop yields is

$$(\bar{x}_1 - \bar{x}_2) \pm z_{\alpha/2} \sqrt{\frac{s_1^2}{n_1} + \frac{s_2^2}{n_2}} = (27.08 - 25.74) \pm 1.96 \sqrt{\frac{14.21}{40} + \frac{11.38}{40}}$$

$$= 1.34 \pm 1.57.$$

The confidence limits are

$$LCL = -.23 \quad \text{and} \quad UCL = 2.91.$$

The difference in mean crop yield is thus estimated to fall between $-.23$ and 2.91 bushels. This tells us that the mean crop yield using the new fertilizer may be as low as .23 bushels *less* or as high as 2.91 bushels *more* than the mean crop yield produced using the current fertilizer. In other words, we cannot say with 95% confidence that one fertilizer is better than the other. This result suggests to farmers that the less expensive fertilizer should be used.

MINITAB COMPUTER OUTPUT FOR EXAMPLE 9.2*

```
TWOSAMPLE T FOR C1 VS C2
       N      MEAN      ST DEV     SE MEAN
C1    40     27.08      3.77        0.60
C2    40     25.74      3.37        0.53
95 PCT CI FOR MU C1-MU C2 (-0.23, 2.91)
T TEST MU C1 = MU C2 (VS NE): T = 1.68 P = 0.094 DF = 77.1
```

The output includes sample sizes, means, standard deviations, and standard errors $(s/\sqrt{n})$. The 95% confidence interval estimate of $\mu_1 - \mu_2$ is $(-0.23, 2.91)$. The last row of the printout refers to the test of hypothesis, which is discussed in Chapter 11.

---

* See Appendix 9.A for the Minitab commands that produced this printout.

Before proceeding to an example of another confidence interval estimator of the difference between two population means, let's review how to recognize when to use the z-interval estimator of $\mu_1 - \mu_2$ when the population variances are unknown.

Factors That Identify the z-Interval Estimator of $\mu_1 - \mu_2$

1. *Problem objective:* Compare two populations.
2. *Data type:* quantitative
3. *Population variances:* unknown
4. *Sample sizes:* $n_1 > 30$ and $n_2 > 30$.

The confidence interval estimator just developed is valid only if the sample sizes are large (both sample sizes must be greater than 30). If either sample size is small ($n_1 \leq 30$ or $n_2 \leq 30$), another interval estimator must be used. This estimator requires that the populations being compared be normally distributed and that the unknown population variances be equal. In other words, it is necessary that $\sigma_1^2 = \sigma_2^2$.

Confidence Interval Estimator of $\mu_1 - \mu_2$, with σ_1^2 and σ_2^2 unknown, $n_1 \leq 30$, or $n_2 \leq 30$

$$(\bar{x}_1 - \bar{x}_2) \pm t_{\alpha/2} \sqrt{s_p^2 \left(\frac{1}{n_1} + \frac{1}{n_2} \right)},$$

where

$$s_p^2 = \frac{(n_1 - 1)s_1^2 + (n_2 - 1)s_2^2}{n_1 + n_2 - 2}$$

and

$$\text{d.f.} = n_1 + n_2 - 2.$$

The quantity s_p^2, called the **pooled variance estimate,** is the weighted average of the two sample variances. It uses both samples combined to produce a single estimate of the population variance. This is made possible by the requirement that $\sigma_1^2 = \sigma_2^2$ so that the common variance can be estimated by pooling the two sample variances. The sampling distribution is Student t, with $n_1 + n_2 - 2$ degrees of freedom. Recall from Chapter 8 that a Student t distribution can only be used if the populations are normal.

We will encounter applications where at least one of the sample sizes is small (less than or equal to 30) but the number of degrees of freedom is 30 or greater. The confidence interval estimator presented here is the appropriate one to use. However, it should be noted that the value of $t_{\alpha/2}$ in such situations approximately equals $z_{\alpha/2}$. (Recall that $t \approx z$ for d.f. ≥ 30.) The quantity $t_{\alpha/2}$ can be read from either the Normal Table (Table 5 in Appendix B) or the Student t Table (Table 6 in Appendix B) (see Exercise 9.11).

<hr>

EXAMPLE 9.3

A nationally known manufacturer of replacement shock absorbers claims that its product lasts longer than does the type of shock absorber that the car manufacturer installs. To examine this claim, researchers equipped 8 cars with the original shock absorbers and equipped another 8 cars with the replacement shock absorbers. The cars were then driven until the shock absorbers were no longer effective. The number of miles until this happened in each case was recorded, and the results are shown in the accompanying table. Estimate with 90% confidence the difference in mean miles until the shock absorbers fail between the two types of products.

NUMBER OF MILES (1,000s)

Original Shock Absorber	Replacement Shock Absorber
39.6	35.7
34.2	52.0
47.0	46.8
40.9	58.5
50.6	45.7
27.5	52.4
43.5	41.3
36.3	43.8

Solution. The problem objective is to compare two populations whose data type is quantitative. (We compare the miles driven with the two kinds of shock absorbers.) The parameter to be estimated is $\mu_1 - \mu_2$. Because the population variances are unknown and the sample sizes are less than 30, the confidence interval estimator is

$$(\bar{x}_1 - \bar{x}_2) \pm t_{\alpha/2} \sqrt{s_p^2 \left(\frac{1}{n_1} + \frac{1}{n_2} \right)}.$$

From the data we computed the following statistics.

Original Shock Absorber	Replacement Shock Absorber
$\bar{x}_1 = 39.95$	$\bar{x}_2 = 47.03$
$s_1^2 = 54.02$	$s_2^2 = 51.22$

The pooled variance estimate is

$$s_p^2 = \frac{(n_1 - 1)s_1^2 + (n_2 - 1)s_2^2}{n_1 + n_2 - 2} = \frac{7(54.02) + 7(51.22)}{14} = 52.62.$$

The specified confidence level is

$$1 - \alpha = 90\%.$$

Hence we need to find $t_{\alpha/2} = t_{.05}$, with $n_1 + n_2 - 2 = 14$ degrees of freedom. From Table 6 in Appendix B, we find

$$t_{.05,14} = 1.761.$$

The 90% confidence interval estimate of the difference in mean longevity between the two kinds of shock absorbers is

$$(\bar{x}_1 - \bar{x}_2) \pm t_{\alpha/2}\sqrt{s_p^2\left(\frac{1}{n_1} + \frac{1}{n_2}\right)} = (39.95 - 47.03) \pm 1.761\sqrt{52.62\left(\frac{1}{8} + \frac{1}{8}\right)}$$

$$= -7.08 \pm 6.39.$$

Thus we find confidence limits of

$$LCL = -13.47 \quad \text{and} \quad UCL = -.69.$$

The difference in mean miles until shock absorber failure between the two types of shock absorbers is estimated to lie between -13.47 and $-.69$ thousand miles. That is, the replacement shock absorber is estimated to last on average between 690 and 13,470 miles longer than the original shock absorber. The manufacturer's claim appears to be believable.

MINITAB COMPUTER OUTPUT FOR EXAMPLE 9.3*

```
TWOSAMPLE T FOR C1 VS C2
        N     MEAN    ST DEV    SE MEAN
C1      8     39.95   7.35      2.6
C2      8     47.03   7.16      2.5
95 PCT CI FOR MU C1 - MU C2 (-14.9, 0.7)
T TEST MU C1 = MU C2 (VS NE): T = -1.95  P = 0.073  DF = 14.0
```

Unfortunately, Minitab produces only the 95% confidence interval estimate of $\mu_1 - \mu_2$. If you want any other confidence level you will have to compute it yourself, using the outputted means and standard deviations from Minitab.

---

* Appendix 9.A describes the Minitab commands that produced this output.

> **Factors That Identify the *t*-Interval Estimator of $\mu_1 - \mu_2$**
>
> 1. *Problem objective:* Compare two populations.
> 2. *Data type:* quantitative
> 3. *Population variance:* unknown but equal
> 4. *Sample sizes:* $n_1 \leq 30$ or $n_2 \leq 30$

EXERCISES

LEARNING THE TECHNIQUES

9.10 Assume that the following statistics were calculated from samples from two populations:

$$n_1 = 42 \qquad n_2 = 34$$
$$\bar{x}_1 = 115.6 \qquad \bar{x}_2 = 133.0$$
$$s_1 = 11.8 \qquad s_2 = 28.6.$$

Estimate with 99% confidence the difference between the two population means.

9.11 You are given the following information:

$$n_1 = 18 \qquad n_2 = 24$$
$$\bar{x}_1 = 7.63 \qquad \bar{x}_2 = 6.19$$
$$s_1 = .79 \qquad s_2 = .85.$$

a. Estimate $\mu_1 - \mu_2$, with 90% confidence.

b. What assumptions must you make in order to answer part (a)?

9.12 Suppose that random samples of size $n_1 = n_2 = 100$ from two normal populations produced the following statistics:

$$\bar{x}_1 = 592 \qquad \bar{x}_2 = 404$$
$$s_1 = 88 \qquad s_2 = 76$$

Estimate with 95% confidence the difference between the two population means.

9.13 Repeat Exercise 9.12, but change the sample sizes to 10.

9.14 The following random samples were drawn from two normal populations.

   Sample 1:   14, 29, 32, 18, 24
   Sample 2:   41, 36, 40, 27, 23, 32, 37

Estimate the difference between their population means, with 90% confidence.

9.15 Estimate $\mu_1 - \mu_2$ with 99% confidence, using the following statistics:

$$n_1 = 10 \qquad n_2 = 15$$
$$\bar{x}_1 = 245 \qquad \bar{x}_2 = 183$$
$$s_1 = 24 \qquad s_2 = 31.$$

9.16 Random samples of 15 observations from each of two normal populations were drawn, with the following results:

$$\bar{x}_1 = 1.48 \qquad \bar{x}_2 = 1.23$$
$$s_1 = .18 \qquad s_2 = .14.$$

Estimate the difference between the two population means with 90% confidence.

9.17 Repeat Exercise 9.16, but change the sample sizes to 31.

APPLYING THE TECHNIQUES

Self-Correcting Exercise (See Appendix 9.B for the solution.)

9.18 Three years ago, a 100-acre site was planted with 250,000 white spruce seedlings. Half the site was scarified (soil turned up) and the seedlings spot-fertilized; the other half was not fertilized. Random samples of 50 trees from each half of the site were taken and the foliage of each tree was weighed. The results are shown in the accompanying table. Estimate with 95% confidence the difference in mean foliage weight between fertilized and unfertilized trees.

Fertilized Trees	Unfertilized Trees
$\bar{x}_1 = 5.98$	$\bar{x}_2 = 4.79$
$s_1^2 = .61$	$s_2^2 = .77$

9.19 Until recently, most car salespeople have been men. However, in the past decade, numerous automobile dealers have hired women as salespeople in the hope that they will sell more cars to female customers. A researcher decided to examine how successful female salespeople are. She took a random sample of eight female and eight male salespeople and recorded their commission income for the preceding year. The results are shown in the accompanying table. Estimate with 95% confidence the difference in mean commission income between all male and female automobile salespeople.

COMMISSION INCOME (in $1,000s)

	Male Salespeople	Female Salespeople
	31	35
	12	27
	52	24
	51	22
	20	55
	19	49
	28	14
	29	44
MEAN	30.25	33.75
VARIANCE	210.79	208.50

9.20 The management of a chain of electronic products retailers is trying to decide on the location of its newest store. After some careful analysis the choice has been narrowed to two possibilities. To help make the decision, researchers measure one of the critical factors—the number of people passing each location. In a random sample of 10 days, the average and the standard deviation of the number of pedestrians per day for each location were calculated as follows.

Location 1	Location 2
$\bar{x}_1 = 2,741$	$\bar{x}_2 = 2,519$
$s_1 = 149$	$s_2 = 163$

Estimate with 90% confidence the difference in the mean number of passing pedestrians between the two locations.

9.21 A sporting goods manufacturer has developed a new type of golf ball that he is sure will travel farther than any other type of ball currently in use. In an experiment to verify his claim, he took 100 of his golf balls and 100 golf balls of a leading competitor to a local driving range, where he asked a variety of people to hit the balls with a driver. The distances were measured, and the statistics shown in the accompanying table were determined. Estimate with 90% confidence the difference between the mean distances of the two brands of golf balls.

DISTANCE TRAVELED (yards)

New Type of Golf Ball	Competitor's Golf Ball
$\bar{x}_1 = 193$	$\bar{x}_2 = 184$
$s_1 = 27$	$s_2 = 22$

9.22 A statistics professor was about to select a statistical software package for her course. One of the most important features, according to the professor, is the ease with which students learn to use the software. She has narrowed the selection down to two possibilities. To help make her decision, she selects 10 students at random from her second-year required Business Statistics course and arbitrarily assigns 5 students to use software package *A* and 5 to use software package *B*. She gives each student a statistics problem to solve by computer and the appropriate manual. The amount of time each student needed to complete the problem was recorded, and these times are listed in the accompanying table. Estimate the difference in mean completion time between the two software packages, using a confidence level of 90%.

COMPLETION TIMES (in minutes)

Software Package A	Software Package B
47	69
28	44
61	50
53	59
50	68

9.23 In assessing the value of radio advertisements, sponsors not only measure the total number of listeners but also record their ages. The 18–34 age group is considered to be the group that spends the most money. To examine this issue, the manager of an FM station commissioned a survey. One objective was to record the difference in listening habits between the age groups 18–34 and 35–50. The survey asked 500 people in each age category how many minutes per day they listened to FM radio. The results are summarized in the accompanying table. Estimate with 99% confidence the difference in the amount of time spent listening to FM radio by the two age groups.

TIME SPENT LISTENING TO FM RADIO (in minutes)

18–34	35–50
$\bar{x}_1 = 47.3$	$\bar{x}_2 = 59.8$
$s_1 = 11.4$	$s_2 = 15.7$

9.24 One factor in low productivity is the amount of time wasted by workers. Wasted time includes time spent cleaning up mistakes, waiting for more material and equipment, and performing any other activity not related to production. In a project to examine this problem, an operations management consultant took a survey of 200 workers in companies that were classified as successful (on the basis of their latest annual profit) and another 200 workers from unsuccessful companies. The amount of time wasted in a standard 40-hour work week was recorded for each worker. The accompanying table summarizes these data. Estimate with 90% confidence the difference in mean time wasted between the two types of firms.

WASTED TIME (in hours)

Successful Firms	Unsuccessful Firms
$\bar{x}_1 = 6.3$	$\bar{x}_2 = 11.5$
$s_1 = 2.0$	$s_2 = 3.9$

9.25 Cholesterol in the blood is one of the leading causes of heart attacks. Several drugs on the market reduce cholesterol levels. A researcher for a pharmaceutical company has recently developed a new drug that he hopes will be more effective than the drugs currently available. In a preliminary study, 50 men with cholesterol levels in excess of 220 were randomly selected. Half were given the new drug while the other half took one of the most commonly used drugs already on the market. After one month, the percentage cholesterol reduction was recorded. The statistics shown in the accompanying table were then computed.

PERCENTAGE CHOLESTEROL REDUCTION

New Drug	Most Popular Drug
$\bar{x}_1 = 5.6$	$\bar{x}_2 = 4.8$
$s_1 = 1.3$	$s_2 = 1.5$

Estimate with 95% confidence the difference in percentage cholesterol reduction between the two drugs.

ESTIMATING THE DIFFERENCE BETWEEN TWO POPULATION PROPORTIONS

As we've discussed before, we cannot calculate means and variances if the data type is qualitative. We can only count the number of occurrences of each qualitative outcome and report their proportions. When the problem objective is to compare two populations and the data type is qualitative, we do this by estimating the difference between the two population proportions $p_1 - p_2$.

The estimator of the parameter $p_1 - p_2$ is the difference between the two sample proportions $\hat{p}_1 - \hat{p}_2$. The sampling distribution of the statistic $\hat{p}_1 - \hat{p}_2$ is approximately normal, provided that the sample sizes are sufficiently large—that is, if $n_1\hat{p}_1 \geq 5$, $n_1\hat{q}_1 \geq 5$, $n_2\hat{p}_2 \geq 5$, and $n_2\hat{q}_2 \geq 5$.

The Confidence Interval Estimator of $p_1 - p_2$

$$(\hat{p}_1 - \hat{p}_2) \pm z_{\alpha/2}\sqrt{\frac{\hat{p}_1\hat{q}_1}{n_1} + \frac{\hat{p}_2\hat{q}_2}{n_2}}$$

EXAMPLE 9.4

A 1988 survey of 400 people found that 32% believed that the greenhouse effect would increase the earth's temperature. In 1990, another survey of 500 people discovered that the proportion of people who believed in the greenhouse effect was 35%. In order to determine the real size of the change, estimate with 90% confidence the difference between the 1988 and 1990 findings.

Solution. The problem objective is to compare two populations (beliefs in 1988 and in 1990). There are two possible responses to the survey: "yes, I believe in the greenhouse effect" and "no, I don't believe in the greenhouse effect." This makes the data type qualitative. The parameter to be estimated is $p_1 - p_2$. The confidence interval estimator is

$$(\hat{p}_1 - \hat{p}_2) \pm z_{\alpha/2}\sqrt{\frac{\hat{p}_1\hat{q}_1}{n_1} + \frac{\hat{p}_2\hat{q}_2}{n_2}},$$

where

p_1 = Proportion of the entire population in 1988 who believe in the greenhouse effect

p_2 = Proportion of the entire population in 1990 who believe in the greenhouse effect.

The sample proportions are

$\hat{p}_1 = .32 \quad$ (and $\hat{q}_1 = 1 - \hat{p}_1 = 1 - .32 = .68$)

$\hat{p}_2 = .35 \quad$ (and $\hat{q}_2 = 1 - \hat{p}_2 = 1 - .35 = .65$).

The confidence level is specified as 90%, so

$$z_{\alpha/2} = z_{.05} = 1.645.$$

The 90% confidence interval estimate of the difference between the 1988 and 1990 population proportions is

$$(\hat{p}_1 - \hat{p}_2) \pm z_{\alpha/2}\sqrt{\frac{\hat{p}_1\hat{q}_1}{n_1} + \frac{\hat{p}_2\hat{q}_2}{n_2}} = (.32 - .35) \pm 1.645\sqrt{\frac{(.32)(.68)}{400} + \frac{(.35)(.65)}{500}}$$

$$= -.03 \pm .052.$$

The confidence limits are

$$LCL = -.082 \qquad \text{and} \qquad UCL = .022.$$

It is estimated that the 1988 population proportion worried about the greenhouse effect is between 8.2% lower and 2.2% higher than the 1990 population proportion. We cannot be very confident that there has been a real change between 1988 and 1990.

Recognizing when to use the interval estimator of the difference between two population proportions involves only two factors.

> **Factors That Identify the Estimator of $p_1 - p_2$**
>
> 1. *Problem objective:* Compare two populations.
> 2. *Data type:* qualitative

 EXERCISES

LEARNING THE TECHNIQUES

9.26 Estimate $p_1 - p_2$ with 90% confidence, given the following:

$n_1 = 500 \qquad n_2 = 500$

$\hat{p}_1 = .56 \qquad \hat{p}_2 = .51.$

9.27 A random sample of $n_1 = 200$ from population 1 produced $x_1 = 50$ successes, and a random sample of $n_2 = 100$ from population 2 yielded $x_2 = 35$ successes. Estimate with 95% confidence the difference between the population proportions.

9.28 Given that $\hat{p}_1 = 110/300$ and $\hat{p}_2 = 96/400$, estimate $p_1 - p_2$, with 99% confidence.

9.29 Random samples of 1,000 from each of two populations yielded 300 successes from the first population and 200 successes from the second. Estimate the difference in population success rates between the two populations. Use a confidence level of 99%.

APPLYING THE TECHNIQUES

Self-Correcting Exercise (See Appendix 9.B for the solution.)

9.30 A market researcher employed by a chain of service centers offering no-wait oil and filter changes wants to know the difference in the fraction of male and female automobile owners who regularly use the service. Such information will be quite useful in designing advertising. In a random sample of 500 men, 42 indicated that they frequently have their cars serviced by this chain. A random sample of 300 women showed that 38 use the service. Estimate with 99% confidence the difference in the proportions of men and women who use the oil-change service.

9.31 An inspector for the Atlantic City Gaming Commission suspects that a particular blackjack dealer may be cheating when dealing at expensive tables. To test her belief she observed the dealer at the $100-limit table and noted that in 400 hands the dealer won 212 times. At the $3,000-limit table the same dealer won 295 out of 500 deals. Estimate the difference in winning percentage between the two tables. Use a confidence level of 90%.

9.32 An author of statistics textbooks lives in the East, while his publisher is located in the West. Because of the amount of material sent back and forth, speed of delivery is critical. Two couriers are regularly used. In 53 deliveries sent through courier 1, 12 were late (delivered past the promised delivery time) while in 41 deliveries by courier 2, 5 were late. Estimate with 90% confidence the difference in the fraction of late deliveries between the two couriers.

9.33 Have the attitudes of university freshmen changed much in the last 20 years? In annual surveys conducted by the American Council on Education and by the Higher Education Research Institute at the University of California at Los Angeles, freshmen were asked a variety of questions about their attitudes and goals. Following are some of the results.

	Percent of Freshman Who Identified Goal As "Essential" or "Very Important"		
Goal	1967	1977	1987
Develop a meaningful philosophy of life	81%	59%	39%
Be very well off financially	43%	58%	76%

Assuming that the annual sample size was 1,000, estimate with 99% confidence the following parameters:

a. The difference in the proportion of those who considered the development of a meaningful philosophy essential or very important between 1987 and 1967.

b. The difference in the proportion who considered being financially very well off essential or very important between 1987 and 1977.

9.34 In the survey referred to in Exercise 9.33, freshmen were asked about their political orientation. In 1977 13% considered themselves conservatives, while in 1987 18% said they were conservatives. Estimate with 90% confidence the increase in the proportion of freshman who claim to be politically conservative.

SECTION
9.5

SUMMARY

The statistical techniques used to estimate the difference between two population means and the difference between two population proportions were described in this chapter. The confidence interval estimator formulas are summarized in Table 9.1.

IMPORTANT TERMS

Difference between two population means
z-estimator of $\mu_1 - \mu_2$
t-estimator of $\mu_1 - \mu_2$

Pooled variance estimate
Difference between two population proportions
Estimator of $p_1 - p_2$

TABLE 9.1   *SUMMARY OF INTERVAL ESTIMATORS OF $\mu_1 - \mu_2$ AND $p_1 - p_2$*

Parameter	Confidence Interval Estimator	Required Conditions
$\mu_1 - \mu_2$	$(\bar{x}_1 - \bar{x}_2) \pm z_{\alpha/2}\sqrt{\dfrac{\sigma_1^2}{n_1} + \dfrac{\sigma_2^2}{n_2}}$	σ_1^2 and σ_2^2 are known; x_1 and x_2 are normally distributed, or n_1 and n_2 are large.
	$(\bar{x}_1 - \bar{x}_2) \pm z_{\alpha/2}\sqrt{\dfrac{s_1^2}{n_1} + \dfrac{s_2^2}{n_2}}$	σ_1^2 and σ_2^2 are unknown; x_1 and x_2 are normally distributed; $n_1 > 30$ and $n_2 > 30$.
	$(\bar{x}_1 - \bar{x}_2) \pm t_{\alpha/2}\sqrt{s_p^2\left(\dfrac{1}{n_1} + \dfrac{1}{n_2}\right)}$	σ_1^2 and σ_2^2 are unknown and equal ($\sigma_1^2 = \sigma_2^2$); x_1 and x_2 are normally distributed.
$p_1 - p_2$	$(\hat{p}_1 - \hat{p}_2) \pm z_{\alpha/2}\sqrt{\dfrac{\hat{p}_1\hat{q}_1}{n_1} + \dfrac{\hat{p}_2\hat{q}_2}{n_2}}$	$n_1\hat{p}_1$, $n_1\hat{q}_1$, $n_2\hat{p}_2$, and $n_2\hat{q}_2 \geq 5$.

SUPPLEMENTARY EXERCISES

9.35 An article in the *Wall Street Journal* (15 May 1989) discussed how managers divide their work week among a variety of activities. Suppose that 150 managers were interviewed. The companies that they work for were categorized as either successful or unsuccessful on the basis of their annual profit margins. It was found that, in the 96 successful firms, the mean and the standard deviation of the percentage of the managers' time spent on direct selling were 28.3% and 5.4%, respectively. For the 54 unsuccessful firms the mean and the standard deviation were 22.4% and 7.9%. Estimate the difference in mean percentage of time devoted to direct selling between successful and unsuccessful firms. Use a confidence level of 95%.

9.36 Physicians have been encouraging their patients to reduce smoking for many years. In a study to determine who smokes regularly, a random sample of 1,000 people were interviewed. Each was asked whether or not they smoke regularly, as well as a variety of questions relating to demographic characteristics (such as age and education). It was found that 248 respondents were university graduates. Of these, 52 smoked regularly. Of the remaining 752 respondents, 226 smoked regularly. Estimate with 90% confidence the difference in the fraction of smokers between university graduates and nongraduates.

9.37 The MBA program director of a large university was analyzing the performance of the program's part-time and full-time MBA students. One of the entrance criteria is the Graduate Management Admission Test (GMAT) which consists of verbal and quantitative scores. In a random sample of 50 full-time and 40 part-time students, the MBA program director found the statistics given in the accompanying table.

GMAT SCORE RESULTS

Portion	Full-time Students	Part-time Students
Verbal	$\bar{x}_1 = 563$ $s_1 = 68$	$\bar{x}_2 = 601$ $s_2 = 81$
Quantitative	$\bar{x}_1 = 652$ $s_1 = 75$	$\bar{x}_2 = 626$ $s_2 = 86$

a. Estimate with 95% confidence the difference in mean verbal GMAT scores between full-time and part-time students.

b. Estimate with 95% confidence the difference in mean quantitative GMAT scores between full-time and part-time students.

9.38 A major automobile manufacturer has plants in a number of countries. To examine productivity in the United States and Korea, a statistician counted the daily output for one randomly selected plant in the United States and a similar-sized plant in Korea. The mean and the standard deviation of the daily number of cars produced in 15 days were computed. These statistics are shown in the accompanying table. Estimate the difference in the mean number of cars produced between the plants in the United States and Korea. Use a confidence level of 99%.

DAILY CAR PRODUCTION

United States	Korea
$\bar{x}_1 = 365$	$\bar{x}_2 = 345$
$s_1 = 18$	$s_2 = 15$

9.39 Use the results in Exercise 9.38 to estimate the difference in annual production. Assume 250 working days per year.

9.40 Random samples of 1,000 people from each of the United States and Canada were drawn. Each person was asked "Do you think the NATO Alliance should be maintained or is this alliance not necessary any more?" The results are described in the accompanying table. Ignoring those who responded "No opinion," estimate with 99% confidence the difference in support for NATO between Canada and the United States.

Country	NATO Should Be Maintained	NATO Is Not Necessary	No Opinion
Canada	782	79	139
United States	749	98	153

SOURCE: *Toronto Star*, 26 October, 1989.

9.41 Because of the high costs of energy, homeowners in northern climates are always seeking ways to cut their heating costs. In an experiment to examine this issue, 150 houses in a large subdivision were recruited. Each house was built around 1970, with minimal insulation. All of the houses were two-story, four-bedroom homes with approximately 2,000 square feet of floor space. Half of the homes were then reinsulated (R20 in the walls and R32 in the attic) and the heating costs for last year were recorded. The resulting statistics are listed in the accompanying table. Estimate with 99% confidence the difference in mean monthly (January) heating costs between well-insulated and poorly insulated houses.

JANUARY HEATING COSTS

Reinsulated Houses	Poorly Insulated Houses
$\bar{x}_1 = \$121.50$	$\bar{x}_2 = \$183.70$
$s_1 = \$11.92$	$s_2 = \$21.88$

9.42 Every year North Americans spend billions of dollars attempting to lose weight. It is important for diet doctors and diet food companies to know how many people consider themselves overweight, because these people are potential customers. A Gallup survey (*Toronto Star*, 26 December 1989) of 1,044 individuals revealed that 37% believe that they are overweight. A similar survey in 1979 showed that 35% of the respondents stated that they were overweight. Estimate with 90% confidence the increase in the proportion of North Americans who believe that they are overweight between 1979 and 1989.

9.43 As a result of the public's perception of the health benefits of seafood, the retail seafood market in the United States has grown by about 36% since 1983 (*Wall Street Journal*, 27 June 1989). A survey of 500 Americans in 1982 revealed that the mean and standard deviation of annual seafood consumption were 12.2 and 4.8 pounds, respectively. A survey of 700 Americans in 1988 showed that the mean and the standard deviation of annual seafood consumption were 15.0 and 6.2 pounds, respectively. Estimate the difference in mean annual seafood consumption between 1988 and 1982. Use a confidence level of 90%.

9.44 In 1976 the United States signed into law the Metric Conversion Act, which asks industries and consumers to use the metric system instead of the English system for transactions using weights and measurements. In a 1986 survey, however, 58% of the respondents said that they opposed the use of the metric system. Among other results, the survey revealed that 153 out of 507 people 18 to 34 years old favored the adoption of metric, while 81 out of 398 individuals 55 years old or older favored metric. Estimate with 95% confidence the difference between the 18–34 age group and the 55 and over age group in the proportion who support the use of the metric system.

CASE 9.1*   ACCOUNTING COURSE EXEMPTIONS

One of the problems encountered in teaching accounting in a business program is the issue of what to do with students who have taken one or more accounting courses in high school. Should these students be exempted from the university accounting course, or can it be assumed that the high-school course does not cover sufficient material and that students with high-school accounting are not likely to outperform students without high-school accounting?

In order to examine this issue, students enrolled in the third year of the Bachelor of Commerce program at St. Mary's University were sampled. In the third year of this program, two introductory accounting half-credits are required: ACC 241 and ACC 242. Of the 638 students enrolled in ACC 241 in the fall semesters of 1982 and 1983, 374 were selected because of the similarities in their high-school backgrounds (excluding high-school accounting). Student files were examined for all 374 students, of whom 275 continued on to ACC 242 in the winter quarters of 1983 and 1984. Table A summarizes the high-school accounting background of these students. Assume that the 99 students who took ACC 241 but not ACC 242 failed ACC 241. The average grades for each group of students are shown in Table B. How much better grades are achieved by students who have taken accounting in high school? What exemption policy would you recommend?

TABLE A   *HIGH-SCHOOL ACCOUNTING BACKGROUNDS OF STUDENTS IN THE SAMPLE*

Years of High-school Accounting	Number of Students in ACC 241	Number of Students in ACC 242
0	296	210
1	24	15
2	54	50
ALL STUDENTS	374	275

---

* Adapted from E. Morash, G. Walsh, and N. M. Young, "Accounting for Performance: An Analysis of the Relationship Between Success in Introductory Accounting in University and Prior Study of Accounting in High School." *Proceedings of the 14th Annual Atlantic Schools of Business Conference* (1984), pp. 13–44.

TABLE B   *AVERAGE GRADES OF STUDENTS IN THE SAMPLE*

Years of High-school Accounting	Grades in ACC 241		Grades in ACC 242	
	Mean	Standard Deviation	Mean	Standard Deviation
0	2.0281	1.4189	2.2081	1.2721
1	2.0238	1.5611	1.9583	1.1172
2	2.7778	1.1313	2.1591	1.1653
ALL STUDENTS	2.1528	1.4089	2.1867	1.2426

MINITAB INSTRUCTIONS

ESTIMATING $\mu_1 - \mu_2$ WITH σ_1^2 AND σ_2^2 UNKNOWN

The following Minitab commands are designed to test hypotheses about $\mu_1 - \mu_2$. However, they also produce 95% confidence interval estimates of $\mu_1 - \mu_2$. The command

```
TWOSAMPLE T C1 C2
```

is used whenever the sample sizes are large ($n_1 > 30$ and $n_2 > 30$). To answer Example 9.2, we store the observations from sample 1 in column 1 and the observations from sample 2 in column 2. The command

```
TWOSAMPLE T C1 C2
```

produces the following output:

```
TWOSAMPLE T FOR C1 VS C2
        N     MEAN    STDEV    SE MEAN
C1     40    27.08     3.77     0.60
C2     40    25.74     3.37     0.53
95 PCT CI FOR MU C1-MU C2 (-0.23, 2.91)
T TEST MU C1=MU C2 (VS NE): T=1.68 P=0.094 DF=77.1
```

When at least one of the sample sizes is small ($n_1 \leq 30$ or $n_2 \leq 30$), the 95% confidence interval estimate is produced by adding the subcommand

```
POOLED
```

to the TWOSAMPLE T command. (Remember that the command must end with a semicolon and the subcommand must end with a period.) The POOLED subcommand instructs Minitab to calculate and use the pooled variance estimate s_p^2. To solve Example 9.3, we proceed as follows:

```
READ      C1  C2
39.6    35.7
34.2    52.0
47.0    46.8
40.9    58.5
50.6    45.7
27.5    52.4
43.5    41.3
36.3    43.8
END
TWOSAMPLE  T  C1  C2;
POOLED.
```

The output is

```
TWOSAMPLE  T  FOR  C1  VS  C2
      N     MEAN    STDEV    SE MEAN
C1    8    39.95    7.35     2.6
C2    8    47.03    7.16     2.5
95 PCT CI FOR MU C1-MU C2 (-14.9, 0.7)
T TEST MU C1=MU C2 (VS NE): T=-1.95 P=0.073 DF=14.0
```

SOLUTIONS TO SELF-CORRECTING EXERCISES

9.6 $(\bar{x}_1 - \bar{x}_2) \pm z_{\alpha/2} \sqrt{\dfrac{\sigma_1^2}{n_1} + \dfrac{\sigma_2^2}{n_2}}$

$= (12.5 - 11.3) \pm 1.96 \sqrt{\dfrac{5^2}{25} + \dfrac{5^2}{35}}$

$= 1.2 \pm 2.57.$

We estimate that the difference between the two mean returns lies between -1.37 and 3.77.

9.18 $(\bar{x}_1 - \bar{x}_2) \pm z_{\alpha/2} \sqrt{\dfrac{s_1^2}{n_1} + \dfrac{s_2^2}{n_2}}$

$= (5.98 - 4.79) \pm 1.96 \sqrt{\dfrac{.61}{50} + \dfrac{.77}{50}}$

$= 1.19 \pm .33.$

The difference in mean foliage weight between fertilized and unfertilized trees lies between .86 and 1.52.

9.30 $(\hat{p}_1 - \hat{p}_2) \pm z_{\alpha/2} \sqrt{\dfrac{\hat{p}_1 \hat{q}_1}{n_1} + \dfrac{\hat{p}_2 \hat{q}_2}{n_2}}$

$= (.084 - .127) \pm 2.58 \sqrt{\dfrac{(.084)(.916)}{500} + \dfrac{(.127)(.873)}{300}}$

$= -.043 \pm .059.$

The difference in proportions between male and female users of the oil-changing service lies between $-.102$ and $.016$.

HYPOTHESIS TESTING: DESCRIBING A SINGLE POPULATION

INTRODUCTION

In the previous two chapters, we've dealt with the estimation of various parameters. Now we're going to investigate the second type of statistical inference—hypothesis testing. The purpose of this type of inference is to determine whether enough statistical evidence exists for us to conclude that a belief or hypothesis about a parameter is reasonable. Examples of this type of inference include the following.

1. Companies often do surveys to help them make decisions concerning the effectiveness of their advertising. For example, suppose that a company has a 10% market share. To improve its position, it launches a new advertising campaign. At the campaign's completion the company wants to know if the campaign is likely to be successful in raising its market share. A random sample of purchasers of the product will provide an answer. Since the survey produces qualitative results ("Yes, I will buy the product", or "No, I won't"), the parameter to be tested is the proportion p.

2. The research and development departments of companies frequently develop new products. In order to ensure that a new product works at least as well as earlier versions, scientists may use statistical analysis. For instance, suppose that an agricultural products firm has produced a new fertilizer. To determine if it improves crop yields, researchers will use it to fertilize a random sample of farms. The resultant crop yields can be measured. The parameter of interest here is the mean crop yield μ.

3. The quality-control engineer's responsibility is to ensure that only a very small proportion of a firm's products are defective. Since a complete inspection is impractical, the engineer will base his or her decision on a sample of units. The data type in this experiment is qualitative ("defective" or "nondefective"), and hence the parameter of interest is the proportion p. The quality-control engineer may test to determine if there is sufficient evidence to justify concluding that the proportion of defective units is less than some critical amount.

In order to answer these and other questions, we must first develop the structure of hypothesis testing.

HYPOTHESIS TESTING

The tests of hypothesis that we present in this chapter (and in all others except Chapter 18) are called **parametric tests** because they test the value of a population parameter. These tests consist of four components:

1. Null hypothesis
2. Alternative hypothesis
3. Test statistic
4. Decision rule

NULL HYPOTHESIS

The null hypothesis, which is denoted H_0 (H-naught) always specifies one single value for the population parameter. For example, if we wish to test to determine whether the mean weight loss of people who participate in a new weight reduction program is 10 pounds, we would test

$H_0: \mu = 10.$

To test whether the proportion of defective stereos coming off a production line is equal to 3%, we would test

$H_0: p = .03.$

ALTERNATIVE HYPOTHESIS

This hypothesis, denoted H_A, is really the more important one, because it is the hypothesis that answers our question. If a company wants to know whether its 10% market share has increased as a result of a new advertising campaign, it would specify the alternative hypothesis as

$H_A: p > .10.$

If it wanted to know whether the campaign decreased sales, it would test

$H_A: p < .10.$

And if it wished to determine whether its market share had changed at all, the alternative hypothesis would be

$H_A: p \neq .10.$

In all of these cases the null hypothesis would be

$H_0: p = .10.$

There are two crucial things to remember about the two hypotheses. First, the null hypothesis must specify one single value for the parameter. Second, the alternative hypothesis must answer the researcher's question by specifying that the parameter is greater than, less than, or different from the value shown in the null hypothesis.

TEST STATISTIC

In any test we decide to *reject* or *not reject* the null hypothesis. (As we will explain later, we use the term *not reject* instead of *accept* because the latter can lead to an erroneous interpretation.)

> **Test Statistic**
>
> The criterion upon which we base our decision to reject or not reject the null hypothesis is called the **test statistic.**

The test statistic is based on the point estimator of the parameter to be tested. For example, to test a population mean when the variance is known, the test statistic is

$$z = \frac{\bar{x} - \mu}{\sigma/\sqrt{n}}.$$

To test a population proportion, we use

$$z = \frac{\hat{p} - p}{\sqrt{pq/n}}.$$

As we present each parameter's test, we will state what the test statistic is.

DECISION RULE

> **Decision Rule**
>
> The **decision rule** defines the range of values for the test statistic that leads to rejection of the null hypothesis. This is called the **rejection region.**

To understand how the decision rule is determined, it is important to realize that, since our conclusion is based on sample data, the possibility of making an error always exists. As indicated in Figure 10.1, the null hypothesis is either true or false, and we must decide either to reject or not to reject the null hypothesis. Therefore, two correct decisions are possible: not rejecting the null hypothesis when it is true, and rejecting the null hypothesis when it is false. Conversely, two incorrect decisions are possible: rejecting H_0 when it is true (this is called a **Type I error**), and not rejecting H_0 when it is

FIGURE 10.1   *RESULTS OF A TEST OF HYPOTHESIS*

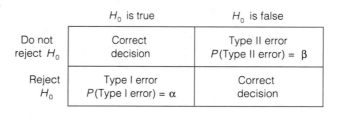

	H_0 is true	H_0 is false
Do not reject H_0	Correct decision	Type II error $P(\text{Type II error}) = \beta$
Reject H_0	Type I error $P(\text{Type I error}) = \alpha$	Correct decision

false (this is called a **Type II error**). We define the probability of a Type I error as α. The probability of a Type II error is β (Greek letter beta).

The decision rule is based on specifying the value of α, which is also called the **significance level.** We usually select a small value of α such as .01, .05, or .10. To illustrate, suppose that we want to test

$$H_0: \mu = 50$$
$$H_A: \mu \neq 50.$$

If we assume that the population variance is known, the test statistic is

$$z = \frac{\bar{x} - \mu}{\sigma/\sqrt{n}}.$$

We want to reject the null hypothesis whenever the test statistic is a large positive or a large negative number. The value of α selected determines what is considered "large." Figure 10.2 depicts the sampling distribution of the test statistic. If we set $\alpha = .05$, we want the total area of the rejection region to equal .05. Since we will reject the null hypothesis when z is either too large positive or too large negative, our decision rule is

Reject H_0 if $z > 1.96$ or if $z < -1.96$.

The values -1.96 and $+1.96$ are called **critical values.** This type of test is called a **two-tail test** because we will reject the null hypothesis if the test statistic lies in either of the two tails of the sampling distribution. For any value of α, the decision rule is

Reject H_0 if $z > z_{\alpha/2}$ or if $z < -z_{\alpha/2}$.

Another way of expressing this is to state

Reject H_0 if $|z| > z_{\alpha/2}$.

We use a **one-tail test** if the alternative hypothesis states either that the parameter is greater than or less than the value shown in the null hypothesis. For instance, if we test

FIGURE 10.2   *SAMPLING DISTRIBUTION OF THE TEST STATISTIC* $z = \dfrac{\bar{x} - \mu}{\sigma/\sqrt{n}}$

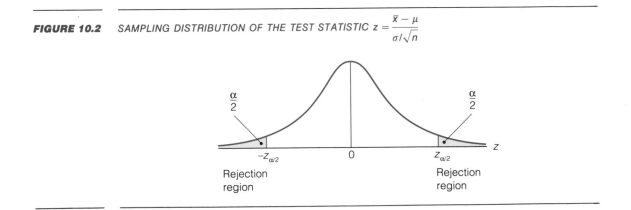

$$H_0: \mu = 1,000$$
$$H_A: \mu > 1,000,$$

we reject the null hypothesis only if the value of the test statistic is too large. In such a case the decision rule is

Reject H_0 if $z > z_\alpha$.

Notice that we use z_α rather than $z_{\alpha/2}$. That's because the entire area of the rejection region is located in one tail of the sampling distribution (see Figure 10.3).
If we test

$$H_0: \mu = 1,000$$
$$H_A: \mu < 1,000,$$

the decision rule is

Reject H_0 if $z < -z_\alpha$.

(See Figure 10.4.)

FIGURE 10.3 REJECTION REGION FOR A ONE-TAIL TEST

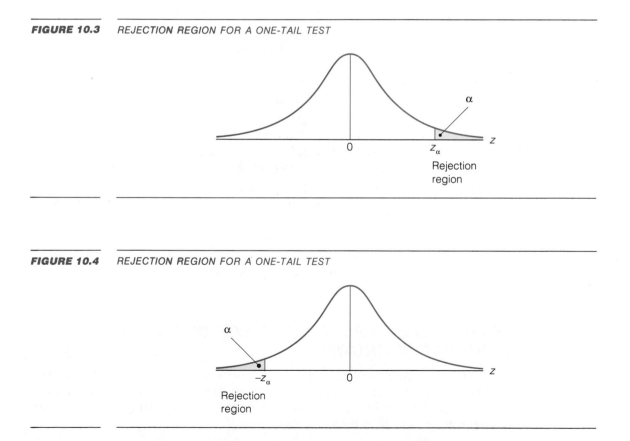

FIGURE 10.4 REJECTION REGION FOR A ONE-TAIL TEST

Many students have difficulty in determining when they should use a one- or two-tail test and, if it's a one-tail test, which tail to use. We will be stressing in this book that the alternative hypothesis is set up to answer the question posed. Thus, if we have been asked if we can conclude that the mean is different from (say) 500, then

$$H_A: \mu \neq 500,$$

and we use a two-tail test. If we have been asked if there is enough evidence to show that the mean is greater than 500, then

$$H_A: \mu > 500,$$

and we have a one-tail test (right tail of the sampling distribution). Finally, if we want to know if there is enough evidence to imply that the mean is less than 500, then

$$H_A: \mu < 500,$$

and again we use a one-tail test (left tail of the sampling distribution).

Six-Step Process for Testing Hypotheses

Step 1: Set up the null and alternative hypotheses.
NOTE: Since the alternative hypothesis answers the question, set this one up first. The null hypothesis will automatically follow.

Step 2: Determine the test statistic.
NOTE: Certain parameters have only one test statistic. Others may have two or three.

Step 3: Specify the significance level.
NOTE: We usually set $\alpha = .01, .05,$ or $.10$, but other values are possible.

Step 4: Define the decision rule.
NOTE: This involves using the appropriate statistical table from Appendix B to determine the range of values of the test statistic that result in rejection of the null hypothesis (rejection region).

Step 5: Calculate the value of the test statistic.
NOTE: Nonmathematicians need not fear. Only simple arithmetic is needed.

Step 6: Make a decision and answer the question.
NOTE: Remember to answer the original question. Making a decision about the null hypothesis is not enough.

SECTION 10.3

TESTING THE POPULATION MEAN WHEN THE VARIANCE IS KNOWN

In the previous section we discussed the main components of hypothesis testing. We are now going to use the method to test hypotheses about a population mean when the population variance is known. As you're about to see, the technique of hypothesis testing requires us to fill in the following blanks.

1. H_0: _____

   H_A: _____

2. *Test statistic:* _____

3. *Significance level:* _____

4. *Decision rule:* _____

5. *Value of the test statistic:* _____

6. *Conclusion:* _____

We will now demonstrate these steps with an example.

EXAMPLE 10.1

A manufacturer of a new, cheaper type of light bulb claims that his product is better than the higher-priced competitive light bulb. The average life of the other light bulb is known to be 5,000 hours. In a test to examine the manufacturer's claim, 100 of his bulbs are left on until they burn out. The average length of life in the sample is 5,100 hours. With a significance level of $\alpha = .05$, is there enough evidence to support the manufacturer's claim? Assume that $\sigma = 500$ hours.

Solution

Step 1: The question asks us to determine if the claim that $\mu > 5,000$ is supported by the statistical evidence. Therefore, the alternative hypothesis is

$$H_A: \mu > 5,000,$$

and the null hypothesis automatically follows as

$$H_0: \mu = 5,000.$$

Step 2: In a test of the population mean μ (with σ^2 known) the test statistic is

$$z = \frac{\bar{x} - \mu}{\sigma/\sqrt{n}}$$

(As was the case in Chapter 8, we assume that either the population is normal or n is sufficiently large.)

Step 3: The question specifies the significance level

$$\alpha = .05.$$

Step 4: Because the alternative hypothesis was one-sided, the test is a one-tail test. Thus the decision rule is

Reject H_0 if $z > z_\alpha$.

Since $z_\alpha = z_{.05} = 1.645$, our decision rule is

Reject H_0 if $z > 1.645$.

Step 5: The calculation of the value of the test statistic requires only arithmetic operations. We have

$$z = \frac{\bar{x} - \mu}{\sigma/\sqrt{n}} = \frac{5,100 - 5,000}{500/\sqrt{100}} = 2.0.$$

FIGURE 10.5   SAMPLING DISTRIBUTION FOR EXAMPLE 10.1

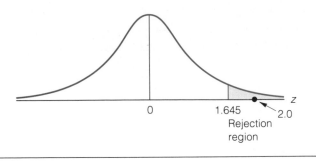

Notice that the value of μ in the test statistic is the value specified under the null hypothesis. This will always be the case.

Step 6: Since the value of the test statistic is 2.0, which is greater than 1.645, we reject H_0. We therefore conclude that sufficient evidence exists to support the manufacturer's claim that his light bulb lasts longer on average than his competitor's product.

It is quite helpful in such a case to draw the sampling distribution, which shows the rejection region and the value of the test statistic. Figure 10.5 depicts the sampling distribution for Example 10.1.

MINITAB COMPUTER OUTPUT FOR EXAMPLE 10.1*

```
TEST OF MU = 5000 VS MU G.T.  5000
THE ASSUMED SIGMA=500.0
        N      MEAN     STDEV    SE MEAN     Z     P VALUE
C1     100     5100     527.3      50.0     2.0     0.0228
```

The quantity P VALUE is the prob-value discussed in Section 10.4.

INTERPRETING THE RESULTS OF A TEST

In Example 10.1 we rejected the null hypothesis, but this did not prove that the alternative hypothesis was true. Since our conclusion is based on sample data (and not on the whole population) we can never prove anything by using statistical inference. As a result we say that enough statistical evidence exists to allow us to conclude that the alternative hypothesis is true.

In Example 10.1 suppose that $\bar{x} = 5{,}050$ and that, as a consequence, the value of the test statistic is $z = 1.0$. Now the value of the test statistic does not fall into the rejection region. (Recall the decision rule: Reject H_0 if $z > 1.645$.) This result does not

---

* See Appendix 10.A for the commands that produced this output.

allow us to conclude that sufficient evidence exists to show that the null hypothesis is true ($\mu = 5{,}000$). Unfortunately, we can never have enough statistical evidence to establish that a population parameter equals the value specified in the null hypothesis (unless we sample the complete population). Thus, if the value of the test statistic does not fall into the rejection region, then—rather than say that we accept H_0 (which implies that we are saying that the null hypothesis is true)—we state that we do not reject H_0, and we conclude that not enough evidence exists to show that the alternative hypothesis is true. Notice that, no matter the result of the test, the conclusion is based on the alternative hypothesis.

> **Rejecting and Not Rejecting H_0**
>
> If we reject H_0, we state that there is enough evidence to show that H_A is true.
> If we do not reject H_0, we state that there is not enough evidence to show that H_A is true.

Another example should help reinforce this technique and clarify how we interpret the results of a test.

EXAMPLE 10.2

In the midst of labor-management negotiations, the president of the union claims that her blue-collar workers (whose annual mean income is $20,000) are underpaid, since the average annual North American blue-collar income exceeds $20,000. Management claims that the workers are well paid, since the average annual North American blue-collar income is less than $20,000. To help resolve the impasse, an arbitrator decides to do a survey of 400 North American blue-collar workers to determine if their mean income is different from $20,000. Assuming that $\sigma = \$8{,}000$, can the arbitrator conclude at the 5% significance level that μ is different from 20,000 if the sample mean is $\bar{x} = 20{,}500$?

Solution. In this example we want to know if the mean annual income differs from $20,000. As a result we set up the alternative hypothesis as

$$H_A: \mu \neq 20{,}000$$

and the null hypothesis as

$$H_0: \mu = 20{,}000.$$

The test statistic is

$$z = \frac{\bar{x} - \mu}{\sigma/\sqrt{n}}.$$

Because the alternative hypothesis specifies that μ is not equal to 20,000, this test is a two-tail test. The decision rule is

$$\text{Reject } H_0 \text{ if } z > z_{\alpha/2} = z_{.025} = 1.96 \quad \text{or}$$
$$\text{if } z < -z_{\alpha/2} = -z_{.025} = -1.96.$$

A shortcut way of specifying this decision rule is to state

$$\text{Reject } H_0 \text{ if } |z| > z_{\alpha/2} = z_{.025} = 1.96.$$

The complete test is as follows:

$H_0: \mu = 20{,}000$

$H_A: \mu \neq 20{,}000$

Test statistic: $z = \dfrac{\bar{x} - \mu}{\sigma/\sqrt{n}}$

Significance level: $\alpha = .05$

Decision rule: Reject H_0 if $|z| > 1.96$.

Value of the test statistic: $z = \dfrac{\bar{x} - \mu}{\sigma/\sqrt{n}} = \dfrac{20{,}500 - 20{,}000}{8{,}000/\sqrt{400}} = 1.25$

Conclusion: Do not reject H_0.

There is not enough evidence to show that the mean income is different from 20,000.

Since there is not enough statistical evidence to indicate that the mean annual North American blue-collar income is different from $20,000, the arbitrator would assume that the union members' incomes are close to the North American average. Figure 10.6 describes the sampling distribution for this test.

FIGURE 10.6   SAMPLING DISTRIBUTION FOR EXAMPLE 10.2

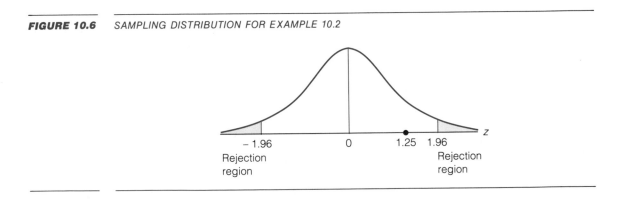

MINITAB COMPUTER OUTPUT FOR EXAMPLE 10.2

```
TEST OF MU = 20000 VS N.E. 20000
THE ASSUMED SIGMA = 8000.0
         N     MEAN    STDEV    SE MEAN     Z     P VALUE
C1     400    20500   8215.0       400    1.25    0.2112
```

The same factors that were used to recognize the interval estimator of a population mean with the variance known are involved in the test of μ.

> **Factors That Identify the z-Test of μ**
>
> 1. *Problem objective:* Describe a single population.
> 2. *Data type:* quantitative
> 3. *Population variance:* known

EXERCISES

LEARNING THE TECHNIQUES

10.1   Define the following terms:

a. Type I error

b. Type II error

c. significance level

d. rejection region

10.2   For each of the following tests of hypotheses about μ, determine the rejection region.

a. $H_0: \mu = 1{,}000$
   $H_A: \mu \neq 1{,}000$
   $\alpha = .05$

b. $H_0: \mu = 50$
   $H_A: \mu > 50$
   $\alpha = .01$

c. $H_0: \mu = 15$
   $H_A: \mu < 15$
   $\alpha = .10$

10.3   Sketch the sampling distribution and indicate the rejection region for each of the tests in Exercise 10.2.

10.4   A random sample of 200 observations from a normal population whose variance is 10,000 produced a mean of 150. Test the hypothesis $H_0: \mu = 160$ against the alternative hypothesis $H_A: \mu < 160$. Use $\alpha = .05$.

10.5   A machine that produces ball bearings is set so that the average diameter is .50 inch. In a sample of 100 ball bearings, it was found that $\bar{x} = .51$ inch. Assuming that the standard deviation is .05 inch, can we conclude (with $\alpha = .05$) that the mean diameter is not .50 inch?

10.6   For the following tests of hypotheses, determine the rejection regions in terms of $\bar{x}$.

a. $H_0: \mu = 500$
   $H_A: \mu > 500$
   $\alpha = .02 \qquad \sigma = 25 \qquad n = 100$

b. $H_0: \mu = 20$
   $H_A: \mu \neq 20$
   $\alpha = .07 \qquad \sigma = 2 \qquad n = 250$

c. $H_0: \mu = 1{,}000$
   $H_A: \mu \neq 1{,}000$
   $\alpha = .04 \qquad \sigma = 50 \qquad n = 20$

10.7   Given that

$$\bar{x} = 22.3 \qquad \sigma = 12 \qquad n = 100,$$

test the following hypotheses with $\alpha = .01$:

$H_0: \mu = 20$
$H_A: \mu \neq 20.$

10.8 Test the following hypotheses, given that a sample of size $n = 25$ from a normal population whose variance is 100 produced $\bar{x} = 115$:

$H_0: \mu = 110$
$H_A: \mu > 110.$

10.9 Repeat Exercise 10.8, changing n to 16.

APPLYING THE TECHNIQUES

Self-Correcting Exercise (See Appendix 10.B for the solution.)

10.10 A large university claims that the average GMAT score of applicants to its MBA program has increased during the past five years. Five years ago the mean and the standard deviation of GMAT scores of the university's MBA program applicants were 560 and 50, respectively. In a sample of 20 of this year's applicants for the MBA program, the mean GMAT was 575. At the 5% level of significance, can we conclude that the university's claim is true? (Assume that the standard deviation is unchanged.)

10.11 A study in the *Academy of Management Journal* reported that the average annual return on investment for American banks was 10.2%, with a standard deviation of .8%.* The article hypothesized that banks that exercised comprehensive planning would outperform the average bank. In a

* D. R. Wood and R. L. Laforge, "The Impact of Comprehensive Planning on Financial Performance," *Academy of Management Journal* 22(3) (1979): 516–26.

random sample of 26 banks that used comprehensive planning, the mean return on investment was 14.6%. Can we conclude, at the 5% level of significance, that the article's hypothesis is correct? (Assume that the standard deviation of the return on investment for banks that used comprehensive planning was also .8%.)

10.12 Past experience indicates that the monthly long-distance telephone bill is normally distributed with a mean of $10.12 and a standard deviation of $3.27. After an advertising campaign that encouraged people to use long-distance telephone more frequently, a random sample of 57 households revealed that the mean monthly long-distance bill was $10.98. Can we conclude at the 10% significance level that the advertising campaign was successful?

10.13 North Americans' obsession with sweets is blamed by nutritionists for a variety of ills, including cavities, diabetes, hyperactivity, and even violent crime (*Newsweek*, 26 August 1985). These problems, as well as the evergrowing use of sugar substitutes, have negative implications for sugar refiners. In 1975, the average per capita consumption of refined sugar in the United States was 89.2 pounds per year. Suppose that, in order to determine whether in 1984 there was a decrease in sugar consumption, the eating patterns of 100 Americans were surveyed. If the sample mean annual consumption of sugar was 87.5 pounds, can we conclude at the 10% significance level that there has been a decrease in annual per capita consumption of sugar in the United States? (Assume that $\sigma = 10$ pounds.)

SECTION
10.4

PROB-VALUE OF A TEST

One of the drawbacks of the testing procedure described in Section 10.3 is that the significance level selected can change the test's conclusion. For instance, in Example 10.1 the value of the test statistic $z = 2.0$ fell into the rejection region when we used $\alpha = .05$ (rejection region $z > 1.645$); but if we had set $\alpha = .01$ (rejection region $z = 2.33$), we would not reject the null hypothesis. One way of avoiding this problem is by reporting the **prob-value** of the test.

FIGURE 10.7   *CALCULATION OF THE PROB-VALUE FOR EXAMPLE 10.1*

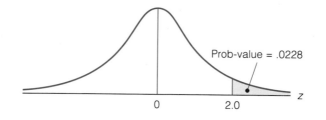

If in Example 10.1 the decision rule was

Reject H_0 if $z \geq 2.0$,

then the value of the test statistic $z = 2.0$ would just fall into the rejection region. The prob-value is simply the probability

$P(z \geq 2.0)$.

Using Table 5 in Appendix B, we find

Prob-value $= P(z \geq 2.0) = .0228$.

Figure 10.7 depicts this calculation.

For a two-tail test, we would multiply the tail-area probability by 2 to get the prob-value. In Example 10.2 we found that the value of the test statistic was $z = 1.25$. The probability

$P(z \geq 1.25) = .1056$

would be doubled to produce

Prob-value $= 2P(z \geq 1.25) = 2(.1056) = .2112$

(see Figure 10.8).

INTERPRETING THE PROB-VALUE

A small prob-value indicates that the value of the test statistic is either very large positive or very large negative. A small prob-value thus results in rejection of the

> **Prob-Value**
>
> The prob-value of a test is the value of α that would just result in the rejection of the null hypothesis.

FIGURE 10.8   *CALCULATION OF THE PROB-VALUE FOR EXAMPLE 10.2*

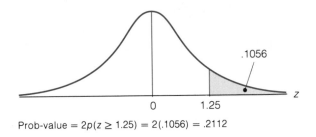

Prob-value $= 2p(z \geq 1.25) = 2(.1056) = .2112$

null hypothesis. The reader of the statistical result decides what is small enough. In Example 10.1 we found the prob-value to be .0228. If we decide that $\alpha = .05$ is small enough, then—since .0228 is less than .05—we reject the null hypothesis. If, however, we set $\alpha = .01$, then—since .0228 is greater than .01—we do not reject the null hypothesis.

> **Interpreting the Prob-Value**
>
> The smaller the prob-value the greater is the impetus to reject the null hypothesis.

EXERCISES

Self-Correcting Exercise (See Appendix 10.B for the solution.)

10.14 Determine the prob-value in Exercise 10.10.

10.15 Find the prob-value of the following test.

$H_0: \mu = 200$
$H_A: \mu > 200$
$z = 2.63$

10.16 Determine the prob-value in Exercise 10.11.

10.17 Find the prob-value of the following test.

$H_0: \mu = 500$
$H_A: \mu \neq 500$
$z = -1.76$

10.18 Determine the prob-value in Exercise 10.13.

10.19 Find the prob-value of the following test:

$H_0: \mu = 25$
$H_A: \mu \neq 25$
$\bar{x} = 29 \qquad \sigma = 15 \qquad n = 100$

10.20 In performing the following test of hypothesis, a statistician found $z = 1.75$. Find the prob-value of the test. (HINT: Be careful.)

$H_0: \mu = 600$
$H_A: \mu < 600$

10.21 The Minitab output of a statistical procedure is as shown in Figure E10.21.

a. What are the null and alternative hypotheses?

FIGURE E10.21

```
TEST OF MU=15 VS G.T. 15
THE ASSUMED SIGMA = 5.00
        N      MEAN     STDEV     SE MEAN     Z      P VALUE
C1     100     15.83     4.96       0.50     1.66    0.0485
```

b. If the statistician conducts the test at the 5% significance level, what conclusion should be drawn?

10.22   Almost everyone who regularly drives his or her car in a large North American city agrees that traffic is getting worse. A randomly selected sample of 50 cars had their speeds measured on a freeway during rush hour. The sample mean speed was 17.5 mph. Traffic engineers determined that two years ago the mean and the standard deviation of the speeds on the same freeway during rush hour were 18.6 and 6.2 mph, respectively. Find the prob-value to determine whether the sample results provide enough statistical evidence to allow the engineers to conclude that freeway traffic has worsened in the last two years.

SECTION 10.5   TESTING THE POPULATION MEAN WHEN THE VARIANCE IS UNKNOWN

In Section 10.3 we described the hypothesis test for a rather unlikely situation: testing the population mean when the population variance is known. In this section we progress to the more realistic case in which the population variance is unknown. As you are about to learn, the only difference between the two cases is the test statistic. In Section 10.3 the test statistic was

$$z = \frac{\bar{x} - \mu}{\sigma/\sqrt{n}}.$$

In this section we use

$$t = \frac{\bar{x} - \mu}{s/\sqrt{n}},$$

which is Student t distributed, with $n - 1$ degrees of freedom, as long as the population is normally distributed. The other five steps in the test are exactly the same as those described in Section 10.3. The following example illustrates this.

EXAMPLE 10.3

A manufacturer of television picture tubes has a production line that used to produce an average of 100 tubes per day. Because of new government regulations, a new safety device is installed, which the manufacturer believes will reduce average daily output.

After installation of the safety device, a random sample of 15 days' production was recorded, as follows:

93, 103, 95, 101, 91, 105, 96, 94, 101, 88, 98, 94, 101, 92, 95.

Assuming that the daily output is normally distributed, is there sufficient evidence to allow the manufacturer to conclude that average daily output has decreased following installation of the safety device? (Use $\alpha = .05$.)

Solution.   The problem objective is to describe the population of daily output. Since we count the number of units produced, the data type is quantitative. Thus the parameter to be tested is the population mean μ.

We specify the hypotheses as before. The alternative hypothesis is set up to answer the question. Since we want to know whether the mean production is now less than 100, we have

$$H_A: \mu < 100.$$

The null hypothesis must always specify a single value for the parameter. Hence,

$$H_0: \mu = 100.$$

In identifying the test statistic, we note that the population variance is not mentioned in the question, so we assume that it is unknown. As a consequence the test statistic is

$$t = \frac{\bar{x} - \mu}{s/\sqrt{n}},$$

which has a Student t distribution, with $n - 1$ degrees of freedom. From the 15 observations, we compute

$$\bar{x} = 96.47$$
$$s^2 = 23.55$$
$$s = 4.85.$$

Because of the way the alternative hypothesis is set up, this is a one-tail test. The decision rule is

$$\text{Reject } H_0 \text{ if } t < -t_{\alpha, n-1} = -t_{.05, 14} = -1.761.$$

The complete test is as follows:

$$H_0: \mu = 100$$
$$H_A: \mu < 100$$

Test statistic: $t = \dfrac{\bar{x} - \mu}{s/\sqrt{n}}$

Significance level: $\alpha = .05$

Decision rule: Reject H_0 if $t < -1.761$.

Value of the test statistic: $t = \dfrac{\bar{x} - \mu}{s/\sqrt{n}} = \dfrac{96.47 - 100}{4.85/\sqrt{15}} = -2.82$

Conclusion: Reject H_0.

There is enough evidence to indicate that mean daily production has decreased after the installation of the safety device.

The operations manager would be advised to look for ways to restore productivity with the safety device in place. Perhaps developing another safety device would help. Figure 10.9 describes the sampling distribution of this test.

MINITAB COMPUTER OUTPUT FOR EXAMPLE 10.3*

```
TEST OF MU=100.00 VS L.T. 100.00
       N    MEAN    STDEV    SE MEAN     T     P VALUE
C1    15    96.47    4.85      1.25    -2.82    0.0068
```

Notice that no decision is made by the computer. You are expected to make the decision yourself by judging whether the prob-value (P VALUE) is small enough.

Factors that Identify the *t*-Test of μ

1. *Problem objective:* Describe a single population.
2. *Data type:* quantitative
3. *Population variance:* unknown

FIGURE 10.9   SAMPLING DISTRIBUTION FOR EXAMPLE 10.3

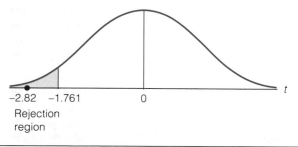

* Appendix 10.A describes the Minitab commands for this example.

■■■■ **EXERCISES**

LEARNING THE TECHNIQUES

10.23 In a random sample of 15 observations from a normal population, we found that $\bar{x} = 150$ and $s = 10$. Using $\alpha = .01$, test the hypotheses

$H_0: \mu = 160$
$H_A: \mu < 160$.

10.24 For each of the following tests of hypotheses about the mean of a normal population, determine whether or not the null hypothesis should be rejected.

a. $H_0: \mu = 10,000$
$H_A: \mu > 10,000$
$n = 10$ $\bar{x} = 11,500$ $s = 3,000$ $\alpha = .05$

b. $H_0: \mu = 75$
$H_A: \mu > 75$
$n = 29$ $\bar{x} = 77$ $s = 1$ $\alpha = .01$

c. $H_0: \mu = 200$
$H_A: \mu < 200$
$n = 25$ $\bar{x} = 175$ $s = 50$ $\alpha = .10$

10.25 A random sample of 75 observations from a normal population produced the following statistics:

$\bar{x} = 239.6$ $s^2 = 1,637.5$.

Test the following hypotheses, with $\alpha = .05$:

$H_0: \mu = 230$
$H_A: \mu \neq 230$.

10.26 Do the following data (drawn from a normal population) allow us to conclude, with $\alpha = .10$, that $\mu > 7$?

4, 8, 12, 11, 14, 6, 12, 8, 9, 5

10.27 The following data were drawn from a normal population. Can we conclude at the 5% significance level that the population mean is not equal to 32?

25, 18, 29, 33, 17

APPLYING THE TECHNIQUES

Self-Correcting Exercise (See Appendix 10.B for the solution.)

10.28 A diet doctor claims that the average North American is more than 10 pounds overweight. To test his claim, a random sample of 50 North Americans were weighed, and the difference between their actual weight and their ideal weight was calculated. The mean and the standard deviation of that difference were 11.5 and 2.2 pounds, respectively. Can we conclude, with $\alpha = .05$, that enough evidence exists to show that the doctor's claim is true?

10.29 A courier service advertises that its average delivery time is less than 6 hours for local deliveries. A random sample of the amount of time this courier takes to deliver packages to an address across town produced the following delivery times (rounded to the nearest hour):

7, 3, 4, 6, 10, 5, 6, 4, 3, 8.

a. Is this sufficient evidence to support the courier's advertisement, at the 5% level of significance?

b. What assumption must be made in order to answer part (a)?

10.30 A highway patrolman believes that the average speed of cars traveling over a certain stretch of highway exceeds the posted limit of 55 mph. The speeds of a random sample of 10 cars were measured by radar, with the following results (in mph):

71, 53, 62, 49, 59, 52, 58, 61, 85, 55.

a. Do these data provide sufficient evidence to support the highway patrolman's belief, at the 10% level of significance?

b. What assumption did you make in order to answer part (a)?

10.31 Ecologists have long advocated recycling newspapers as a way of saving trees and reducing landfills. In recent years a number of companies have gone into the business of collecting used newspapers from households and recycling them. A financial analyst for one such company has recently computed that the firm would make a profit if the mean weekly newspaper collection from each household exceeded 2 pounds. In a study to determine the feasibility of a recycling plant, a random sample of 100 households showed that the mean and the standard deviation of the weekly weight of newspapers discarded for recycling are

$$\bar{x} = 2.2 \text{ pounds} \qquad s = .7 \text{ pounds}.$$

Do these data provide sufficient evidence at the 1% significance level to allow the analyst to conclude that a recycling plant would be profitable?

10.32   One of the critical factors in choosing a location for a new men's clothing store is the mean clothing expenditure per household in the surrounding neighborhood. A survey of 20 households reveals that the mean and the standard deviation of annual expenditure on clothes are $387 and $60, respectively. Can we conclude at the 5% sig-

nificance level that the population mean annual expenditure is less than $400?

10.33   Municipal politicians in a large city have been concerned about the high cost of housing. It is known that 10 years ago the average cost of housing (mortgage payments or rent, plus heating, electricity, and water) represented 28% of the household income. In a survey of 25 households, pollsters found that the mean and the standard deviation of housing costs, expressed as a percentage of household income, are

$$\bar{x} = 31\% \qquad s = 7.8\%.$$

Do these results allow the politicians to conclude at the 1% significance level that housing costs relative to household income have increased in the last 10 years?

TESTING THE POPULATION PROPORTION

As you have seen in Chapter 7 and in Section 8.5, we cannot calculate means when the data type is qualitative. Instead, the parameter of interest is the population proportion. The point estimator of this parameter is the sample proportion $\hat{p}$, which under some rather reasonable conditions has an approximate normal sampling distribution.

> **Test Statistic for a Population Proportion**
>
> The test statistic used to test a population proportion is
>
> $$z = \frac{\hat{p} - p}{\sqrt{pq/n}}.$$

In order for this test statistic to be valid, the sample size must be large enough so that $np \geq 5$ and $nq \geq 5$. As was the case with previous tests of hypothesis, the value of the parameter in the test statistic is that specified in the null hypothesis. In this test statistic, the parameter p appears in both the numerator and the denominator; remember, too, that $q = 1 - p$.

EXAMPLE 10.4

After careful analysis, a company contemplating the introduction of a new product has determined that it must capture a market share of 10% to break even. Anything greater than 10% will result in a profit for the company. In a survey, 100 potential customers are asked whether or not they would purchase the product. If 14 people respond affirmatively, is this enough evidence to enable the company to conclude that the product will produce a profit? (Use $\alpha = .05$.)

Solution. The problem objective is to describe the population of shoppers. The data type is qualitative, since the possible responses to the survey question are "Yes, I would purchase this product" and "No, I would not purchase this product." The parameter of interest is the population proportion p. We want to know if there is enough evidence to allow us to conclude that the company will make a profit, so

$$H_A: p > .10$$

The complete test is as follows:

$$H_0: p = .10$$
$$H_A: p > .10$$

Test statistic: $z = \dfrac{\hat{p} - p}{\sqrt{pq/n}}$

Significance level: $\alpha = .05$

Decision rule: Reject H_0 if $z > z_\alpha = z_{.05} = 1.645$.

Value of the test statistic: $z = \dfrac{\hat{p} - p}{\sqrt{pq/n}} = \dfrac{.14 - .10}{\sqrt{(.10)(.90)/100}} = 1.33$

Conclusion: Do not reject H_0.

There is not enough evidence to allow us to conclude that the product will contribute a profit to the company.

Observe that we did find some evidence to support a conclusion that the population is greater than 10% (the sample proportion was 14%). But the evidence was not strong enough (at the 5% significance level) to allow us to say that the population proportion exceeds 10%. Figure 10.10 describes this test.

FIGURE 10.10 SAMPLING DISTRIBUTION FOR EXAMPLE 10.4

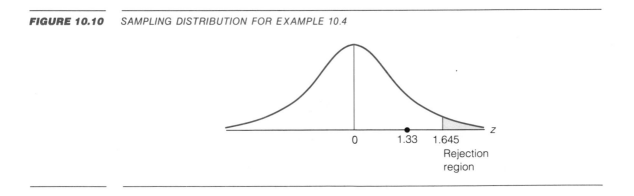

> **Factors That Identify the Test of *p***
>
> 1. *Problem objective:* Describe a single population.
> 2. *Data type:* qualitative

   **EXERCISES**

LEARNING THE TECHNIQUES

10.34   Test each of the following hypotheses:

a. $H_0: p = .45$
   $H_A: p \neq .45$
   $\alpha = .05 \quad n = 100 \quad \hat{p} = .40$

b. $H_0: p = .7$
   $H_A: p > .7$
   $\alpha = .01 \quad n = 1,000 \quad \hat{p} = .75$

c. $H_0: p = .25$
   $H_A: p < .25$
   $\alpha = .10 \quad n = 2,000 \quad \hat{p} = .23$

10.35   If $\hat{p} = .57$ and $n = 100$, can we conclude at the 5% level of significance that the population proportion *p* is greater than .50?

10.36   Repeat Exercise 10.35 with $n = 500$.

10.37   Suppose that, in a sample of 200, we observe 140 successes. Is this sufficient evidence at the 1% significance level to indicate that the population proportion of successes is at least 65%?

10.38   Test the following hypotheses, with $\alpha = .10$:

   $H_0: p = .05$
   $H_A: p < .05$
   $x = 1 \quad n = 100$.

10.39   Find the prob-value of the test in Exercise 10.38.

APPLYING THE TECHNIQUES

Self-Correcting Exercise (See Appendix 10.B for the solution.)

10.40   A tire manufacturer claims that more than 90% of her tires will last at least 50,000 miles. In a random sample of 200 tires, 10 tires wore out before reaching 50,000 miles. Do the data support the manufacturer's claim, with $\alpha = .01$?

10.41   A coin is flipped 100 times. If the number of heads that occur is 60, is this sufficient evidence at the 5% level of significance to justify concluding that the coin is unfair?

10.42   In a random sample of 100 units from an assembly line, 15 were defective. Does this constitute sufficient evidence at the 10% significance to conclude that the defective rate among all units exceeds 10%?

10.43   In a television commercial, the manufacturer of a toothpaste claims that 4 out of 5 dentists recommend its product. In order to test the claim, a consumer-protection group randomly samples 400 dentists and finds that 310 recommended that toothpaste. At the 5% level of significance, test to determine if sufficient evidence exists to refute the manufacturer's claim. (Interpret the claim to say that *at least* 4 out of 5 dentists recommend the product.)

10.44   What is the prob-value of the test in Exercise 10.43?

10.45   In a test to evaluate the effectiveness of a new drug for combating acne, a drug company found that the symptoms of 120 out of a random sample of 220 acne sufferers improved after treatment with this new preparation. The leading acne treatment has a 50% improvement rate. Can we conclude from the data that this new drug is more effective in treating acne? (Use $\alpha = .01$.)

10.46   What is the prob-value of the test in Exercise 10.45?

10.47   A professor of business statistics recently adopted a new textbook. At the completion of the course, 100 randomly selected students were asked to assess the book. The results are shown in the accompanying table.

Assessment	Number Responding
Excellent	61
Good	22
Adequate	10
Poor	7

a. Do these results allow us to conclude at the 5% significance level that more than 50% of all business students using this book would rate it as excellent?

b. Do these results allow us to conclude at the 5% significance level that more than 90% would rate it as at least adequate?

SECTION 10.7   SUMMARY

In this chapter we presented the hypothesis testing techniques that are used in describing a single population. As was the case with estimation, the statistician must identify the parameter to be tested and its test statistic. Other important steps in the process include setting up the hypotheses and specifying the decision rule. Table 10.1 shows the test statistics and the required conditions.

IMPORTANT TERMS

Test of hypothesis   Type II error
Null hypothesis   Significance level
Alternative hypothesis   Sampling distribution
Test statistic   Two-tail test
Decision rule   One-tail test
Rejection region   Prob-value
Type I error

TABLE 10.1   *SUMMARY OF TEST STATISTICS FOR μ AND p*

Parameter	Test Statistic	Required Conditions
μ	$z = \dfrac{\bar{x} - \mu}{\sigma/\sqrt{n}}$	σ^2 is known; x is normally distributed or n is sufficiently large.
	$t = \dfrac{\bar{x} - \mu}{s/\sqrt{n}}$	σ^2 is unknown; x is normally distributed.
p	$z = \dfrac{\hat{p} - p}{\sqrt{pq/n}}$	$np \geq 5$ and $nq \geq 5$.

SUPPLEMENTARY EXERCISES

10.48 Suppose that hourly wages in the chemical industry are normally distributed, with a mean of $7.60 and a standard deviation of $0.60. A large company in this industry took a random sample of 50 of its workers and determined that their average hourly wage was $7.50. Can we conclude at the 10% level of significance that this company's average hourly wage is less than that of the entire industry?

10.49 Refer to Exercise 10.48. What is the prob-value of this test?

10.50 The television networks often compete on the evening of the day of an election to be the first to identify the winner of the election correctly. One commonly used technique is the random sampling of voters as they exit the polling booth. Suppose that, in a two-candidate race, 55% of a random sample of 500 voters indicate that they voted Republican. Can we conclude at the 5% level of significance that the Republican candidate will win?

10.51 Refer to Exercise 10.50. What is the prob-value of this test?

10.52 For the past few years, the number of customers of a drive-in bank in New York has averaged 20 per hour, with a standard deviation of 3 per hour. This year, another bank 1 mile away opened a drive-in window. The manager of the first bank believes that this will result in a decrease in the number of customers. A random sample of 15 hours showed that the mean number of customers per hour was 18.7. Can we conclude at the 5% level of significance that the manager's belief is correct?

10.53 A manufacturer of computer chips claims that at least 90% of his product conforms to specifications. In a random sample of 1,000 chips drawn from a large production run, 125 were defective. Do the data provide sufficient evidence at the 1% level of significance to conclude that the manufacturer's claim is false? What is the prob-value of this test?

10.54 An automotive expert claims that the large number of self-serve gasoline stations has resulted in poor automobile maintenance, and that the average tire pressure is at least 4 pounds per square inch (psi) below its manufacturer's specification. As a quick test, ten tires are examined, and the number of pounds per square inch each tire is below specification is recorded. The resulting data (in psi) are as follows:

   7, 9, 2, 0, 5, 6, 3, 5, 8, 9.

Is there sufficient evidence, with $\alpha = .05$, to support the expert's claim?

10.55 A fast-food franchiser is considering building a restaurant at a certain location. Based on financial analysis, a site is acceptable only if the number of pedestrians passing the location averages at least 100 per hour. A random sample of 50 hours produced $\bar{x} = 110$ and $s = 12$ pedestrians per hour. Do these data provide sufficient evidence to establish that the site is acceptable? (Use $\alpha = .05$.)

10.56 Last year in an election, a politician received 58% of the ballots cast. Several months later, a survey of 700 people revealed that 54% now supported her. Is this sufficient evidence to allow us to conclude that her popularity has decreased? (Let $\alpha = .05$.)

10.57 Officials of Amtrak claim that less than 10% of all its trains are late. If a random sample of 70 trains shows that only 60 of them are on schedule, can we conclude that the claim is false? (Use $\alpha = .10$.)

10.58 The "just-in-time" policy of inventory control (developed by the Japanese) is growing in popularity. For example, General Motors recently announced that it intends to spend $2 billion on its Oshawa, Ontario, plant so that it will be less than one hour from most suppliers. Suppose that an automobile parts supplier claims to deliver parts to any manufacturer in an average time of less than one hour. In an effort to test the claim, a manufacturer recorded the times of 25 deliveries from this supplier. The sample mean and the sample standard deviation were $\bar{x} = 1.1$ hours and $s = .3$ hour. Can we conclude at the 5% level of significance that the supplier's assertion is incorrect?

10.59   In a large city 22% of the households had the afternoon newspaper delivered to their doors. After an aggressive marketing campaign to increase that figure, a random sample of 200 households was taken, and it was found that 61 households now have the paper delivered. Can we conclude at the 5% significance level that the campaign was a success?

10.60   An oil company sends out monthly statements to its customers who purchased gasoline and other items using the company's credit card. Until now, the company has not included a preaddressed envelope for returning payments. The average and the standard deviation of the number of days before payment is received are 10.5 and 3.3, respectively. As an experiment to determine whether enclosing preaddressed envelopes speeds up payment, 100 customers selected at random were sent preaddressed envelopes with their bills. The mean number of days to payment was 9.3, and the standard deviation was 2.2. Do the data provide sufficient evidence at the 5% level of significance to establish that enclosure of the preaddressed envelopes improves the average speed of payments?

10.61   The owner of a downtown parking lot suspects that the person she hired to run the lot is stealing some money. The receipts as provided by the employee indicate that the average number of cars parked in the lot is 125 per day and that, on average, each car is parked for 3.5 hours. In order to determine whether the employee is stealing, the owner watches the lot for 5 days. On those days the number of cars parked is as follows:

120, 130, 124, 127, 128.

For the 629 cars that the owner observed during the 5 days, the mean and the standard deviation of the time spent on the lot were 3.6 and 0.4 hours, respectively. Can the owner conclude at the 5% level of significance that the employee is stealing? (HINT: Since there are two ways to steal, two tests should be performed.)

CASE 10.1*   FACULTY ATTITUDES ABOUT STUDENT EVALUATIONS

Student evaluations of professors and instructors in colleges and universities are a common practice. These evaluations provide feedback so that professors can improve their classroom performance; they are also used as factors in considering salary increases, promotions, and tenure. Most students favor the evaluations because they hold potential for improving the overall quality of university and college instruction. Faculty members do not universally support the evaluations, however, for a variety of reasons.

In a study designed to determine the attitudes of faculty members toward student evaluations, 250 professors at a large university were randomly selected and asked whether or not they agreed with a number of statements concerning evaluations. One purpose of the research was to test the idea that the majority of faculty members would agree with each of the following views:

1. Student evaluations serve a useful purpose.

2. High evaluations are related to high grades.

3. High evaluations are related to the "entertaining personality."

4. Too much emphasis is placed on evaluations by superiors.

---

* Adapted from M. A. Stutts, "Faculty Perceptions of Student Evaluations," *Developments in Marketing Science* 9 (1985): 157–62.

5. Evaluations from freshmen and sophomores are lower than those from juniors and seniors.

6. Evaluations from large classes are lower than those from small classes.

7. Evaluations from quantitatively oriented courses are lower than those from qualitatively oriented classes.

8. Evaluations from required courses are lower than those from elective courses.

The number of respondents who agreed with each of these eight statements is shown in the accompanying table. Is there sufficient statistical evidence to support the idea that the eight views are shared by a majority of faculty members?

Statement	Respondents Agreeing
1	173
2	136
3	195
4	137
5	125
6	164
7	114
8	168

MINITAB INSTRUCTIONS

TESTING μ WITH σ^2 KNOWN

In order to perform a two-tail test of μ, type

ZTEST K1 K2 C1

where K1 is the value of μ under the null hypothesis, $\sigma =$ K2, and the data are in column 1. For example,

ZTEST 100 10 C1

tests

$$H_0: \mu = 100$$
$$H_A: \mu \neq 100,$$

when $\sigma = 10$.

     To perform a one-tail test, we employ the subcommand ALTERNATIVE. (Remember that, in order to use a subcommand, you must end the preceding command with a semicolon and you must end the subcommand with a period.) The subcommand

ALTERNATIVE 1

performs a one-tail test with

$$H_A: \mu > \text{K1}.$$

The subcommand

ALTERNATIVE -1

employs the alternative hypothesis

$$H_A: \mu < \text{K1}.$$

For example,

```
ZTEST 100 10 C1;
ALTERNATIVE -1.
```

tests

$$H_0: \mu = 100$$
$$H_A: \mu < 100,$$

when $\sigma = 10$. If the data for Example 10.1 were stored in column 1, the commands

```
ZTEST 5000 500 C1;
ALTERNATIVE 1.
```

would produce the following output:

```
TEST OF MU = 5000 VS MU G.T. 5000
THE ASSUMED SIGMA = 500.0
        N      MEAN    STDEV    SE MEAN     Z     P VALUE
C1     100     5100    527.3     50.0     2.00    0.0228
```

TESTING μ WITH σ^2 UNKNOWN

The command

```
TTEST K1 C1
```

performs a two-tail test. The subcommmand `ALTERNATIVE` allows us to perform a one-tail test. For example,

```
TTEST 40 C1;
ALTERNATIVE 1.
```

tests

$$H_0: \mu = 40$$
$$H_A: \mu > 40,$$

when σ^2 is unknown. The computer output includes the value of the test statistic t and the prob-value.

As an illustration, we now show how Example 10.3 is answered:

```
SET C1
93 103 95 101 91 105 96 94 101 88 98 94 101 92 95
END
TTEST 100 C1
ALTERNATIVE -1.
```

The output is

```
TEST OF MU = 100.00 VS MU L.T. 100.00
        N      MEAN    STDEV    SE MEAN      T      P VALUE
C1      15     96.47    4.85     1.25      -2.82    0.0068
```

SOLUTIONS TO SELF-CORRECTING EXERCISES

10.10 $H_0: \mu = 560$

$H_A: \mu > 560$

Test statistic: $z = \dfrac{\bar{x} - \mu}{\sigma/\sqrt{n}}$

Significance level: $\alpha = .05$

Decision rule: Reject H_0 if $z > z_\alpha = z_{.05} = 1.645$.

Value of the test statistic:

$z = \dfrac{\bar{x} - \mu}{\sigma/\sqrt{n}} = \dfrac{575 - 560}{50/\sqrt{20}} = 1.34$

Conclusion: Do not reject H_0.

There is not enough evidence to support the university's claim.

10.14 prob-value $= P(z > 1.34) = .0901$.

10.28 $H_0: \mu = 10$

$H_A: \mu > 10$

Test statistic: $t = \dfrac{\bar{x} - \mu}{s/\sqrt{n}}$

Significance level: $\alpha = .05$

Decision rule: Reject H_0 if $t > t_{\alpha, n-1} = t_{.05, 49} = 1.645$.

Value of the test statistic:

$t = \dfrac{\bar{x} - \mu}{s/\sqrt{n}} = \dfrac{11.5 - 10}{2.2/\sqrt{50}} = 4.82$

Conclusion: Reject H_0.

There is enough evidence to allow us to conclude that the average North American is more than 10 pounds overweight.

10.40 $H_0: p = .90$

$H_A: p > .90$

Test statistic: $z = \dfrac{\hat{p} - p}{\sqrt{pq/n}}$

Significance level: $\alpha = .01$

Decision rule: Reject H_0 if $z > z_\alpha = z_{.01} = 2.33$.

Value of the test statistic:

$z = \dfrac{\hat{p} - p}{\sqrt{pq/n}} = \dfrac{.95 - .90}{\sqrt{(.90)(.10)/200}} = 2.36$

Conclusion: Reject H_0.

There is sufficient evidence to support the claim that more than 90% of the tires will last at least 50,000 miles.

HYPOTHESIS TESTING: COMPARING TWO POPULATIONS

287

INTRODUCTION

In this chapter we continue our journey into the wonderful world of statistical inference. We will extend the range of techniques by discussing how to perform tests of hypothesis when the problem objective involves comparing two populations. When the data type is quantitative, we will test hypotheses about the difference between two population means, $\mu_1 - \mu_2$. When the data type is qualitative, we will test hypotheses about the difference between two population proportions, $p_1 - p_2$. Examples of the use of these methods include the following.

1. Market managers and advertisers are eager to know which segments of the population are buying their products. If they can determine these groups, they can target their advertising messages and tailor their products to these customers. For example, if advertisers determine that the decision to purchase a particular household product is made more frequently by men than by women, the interest and concerns of men will be the focus of most commercial messages. The choice of advertising media also depends on whether the product is of greater interest to men or to women. The most common way of measuring this factor is to find the difference in the proportions of men and women buying the product. In these situations, the parameter to be tested is $p_1 - p_2$.

2. Consumers who purchase televisions, major household appliances, and automobiles consider reliability a major factor in their brand choice. Reliability can be measured by the amount of time the product lasts. To compare two brands of televisions, we would test $\mu_1 - \mu_2$, the difference between the mean lifetimes of the two brands.

3. Production supervisors and quality-control engineers are responsible for measuring, controlling, and minimizing the number of defective units that are produced at a plant. Frequently, more than one method or machine can be used to perform the manufacturing function. The decision about which one of two machines to acquire and use often depends on which machine produces a smaller proportion of defective units—or in other words, on the parameter $p_1 - p_2$, the difference in the proportions of defective units from each machine.

TESTING THE DIFFERENCE BETWEEN TWO POPULATION MEANS

In Chapter 10 we presented the six-step process used to test hypotheses. We will go through these same six steps to test hypotheses in this chapter. Step 1 specifies the null and alternative hypotheses. In this section, of course, all hypotheses will feature $\mu_1 - \mu_2$. The null hypothesis will again specify that $\mu_1 - \mu_2$ is equal to some value D (usually zero), while the alternative hypothesis takes on one of the following three formats, depending on what the question asks:

1. $H_A: \mu_1 - \mu_2 \neq D$
2. $H_A: \mu_1 - \mu_2 > D$
3. $H_A: \mu_1 - \mu_2 < D$

The second step is to determine the test statistic. As you may recall from Chapter 9, we had access to three different confidence interval estimators of the difference between two population means; and the choice among them depended on several factors. Those same factors combine to produce three different test statistics. The test statistics and the factors that identify their use are as follows.

1. If σ_1^2 and σ_2^2 are known

$$\text{Test statistic: } z = \frac{(\bar{x}_1 - \bar{x}_2) - (\mu_1 - \mu_2)}{\sqrt{\dfrac{\sigma_1^2}{n_1} + \dfrac{\sigma_2^2}{n_2}}}$$

2. If σ_1^2 and σ_2^2 are unknown and $n_1 > 30$ and $n_2 > 30$

$$\text{Test statistic: } z = \frac{(\bar{x}_1 - \bar{x}_2) - (\mu_1 - \mu_2)}{\sqrt{\dfrac{s_1^2}{n_1} + \dfrac{s_2^2}{n_2}}}$$

3. If σ_1^2 and σ_2^2 are unknown and $n_1 \leq 30$ or $n_2 \leq 30$

$$\text{Test statistic: } t = \frac{(\bar{x}_1 - \bar{x}_2) - (\mu_1 - \mu_2)}{\sqrt{s_p^2 \left(\dfrac{1}{n_1} + \dfrac{1}{n_2} \right)}} \qquad \text{d.f.} = n_1 + n_2 - 2$$

Recall that s_p^2 is the pooled variance estimate, defined as

$$s_p^2 = \frac{(n_1 - 1)s_1^2 + (n_2 - 1)s_2^2}{n_1 + n_2 - 2}$$

and that, if d.f. ≥ 30, the test statistic is approximately normally distributed, allowing us to find the critical value of the rejection region from either Table 5 or Table 6 in Appendix B.

The remaining parts of the test are the same as in Chapter 10. That is, we proceed as follows:

Step 3: Specify the significance level.

Step 4: Define the decision rule.

Step 5: Calculate the value of the test statistic.

Step 6: Make a decision and answer the question.

The next three examples illustrate the procedure for testing $\mu_1 - \mu_2$.

EXAMPLE 11.1

The selection of a new store location depends on many factors, one of which is the level of household income in areas around the proposed site. Suppose that a large department-store chain is trying to decide whether to build a new store in Kitchener or in the nearby city of Waterloo. Building costs are lower in Waterloo, and the company decides it will build there unless the average household income is higher in Kitchener than in Waterloo. A survey of 100 residences in each of the cities found that the mean annual household income was $29,980 in Kitchener and $28,650 in Waterloo. From other sources, it is known that the population standard deviations of annual household incomes are $4,740 in Kitchener and $5,365 in Waterloo. At the 5% significance level, can it be concluded that the mean household income in Kitchener exceeds that of Waterloo? Assume that incomes are normally distributed.

Solution. The problem objective is to compare two populations whose data type is quantitative (income in two cities). This tells us that the parameter to be tested is $\mu_1 - \mu_2$ (where μ_1 = Mean annual household income in Kitchener, and μ_2 = Mean annual household income in Waterloo). Because we want to know if we can conclude that μ_1 exceeds μ_2, the alternative hypothesis is

$$H_A: (\mu_1 - \mu_2) > 0.$$

The population standard deviations are known ($\sigma_1 = 4,740$ and $\sigma_2 = 5,365$). Consequently the correct test statistic is

$$z = \frac{(\bar{x}_1 - \bar{x}_2) - (\mu_1 - \mu_2)}{\sqrt{\dfrac{\sigma_1^2}{n_1} + \dfrac{\sigma_2^2}{n_2}}}$$

The complete test follows:

$$H_0: (\mu_1 - \mu_2) = 0$$
$$H_A: (\mu_1 - \mu_2) > 0$$

Test statistic: $z = \dfrac{(\bar{x}_1 - \bar{x}_2) - (\mu_1 - \mu_2)}{\sqrt{\dfrac{\sigma_1^2}{n_1} + \dfrac{\sigma_2^2}{n_2}}}$

Significance level: $\alpha = .05$

Decision rule: Reject H_0 if $z > z_\alpha = z_{.05} = 1.645$.

Value of the test statistic: $z = \dfrac{(\bar{x}_1 - \bar{x}_2) - (\mu_1 - \mu_2)}{\sqrt{\dfrac{\sigma_1^2}{n_1} + \dfrac{\sigma_2^2}{n_2}}}$

$$= \frac{(29,980 - 28,650) - 0}{\sqrt{\dfrac{4,740^2}{100} + \dfrac{5,365^2}{100}}} = 1.86$$

FIGURE 11.1 SAMPLING DISTRIBUTION FOR EXAMPLE 11.1

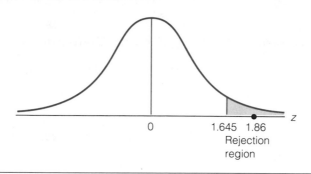

Conclusion: Reject H_0.

There is enough evidence to infer that the mean household income in Kitchener exceeds that of Waterloo.

Hence, despite lower building costs in Waterloo, we recommend locating the new store in Kitchener (see Figure 11.1).

Because three different possible test statistics can be used in testing the difference between two population means, you must be particularly careful in identifying factors that determine when to use the z-test of $\mu_1 - \mu_2$.

> **Factors That Identify the z-Test of $\mu_1 - \mu_2$**
>
> 1. *Problem objective:* Compare two populations.
> 2. *Data scale:* quantitative
> 3. *Population variances:* known

EXAMPLE 11.2

A senior at a prestigious eastern university is trying to decide whether to enter a one-year teacher's college and become a high-school teacher or go to graduate school, obtain an M.A. and Ph.D., and become a university professor. After careful consideration, he concludes that the decision should be made on the basis of the average annual income of the two groups ten years after getting the bachelor's degree. In particular, he will become a university professor unless there is enough evidence to allow him to conclude that high-school teachers earn more money. The senior takes a sample of 50 university professors and 50 high-school teachers, all of whom graduated with their bachelor's degrees ten years ago and determines their annual incomes. The results are summarized in the accompanying table.

MEAN AND VARIANCE OF ANNUAL INCOMES
(in $1,000s)

High-school Teachers	University Professors
$\bar{x}_1 = 43.7$	$\bar{x}_2 = 41.5$
$s_1^2 = 11.8$	$s_2^2 = 46.3$

At the 5% significance level, should he become a university professor or a high-school teacher?

Solution.   The problem objective is to compare two populations whose data type is quantitative (annual income of teachers and professors). Thus, the parameter to be tested is $\mu_1 - \mu_2$ (where μ_1 = Mean annual income of teachers, and μ_2 = Mean annual income of professors). Because the senior wants to know if there is enough evidence to show that teachers earn more, the alternative hypothesis is

$$H_A: (\mu_1 - \mu_2) > 0.$$

We have no knowledge of the population variances, and the sample sizes are large ($n_1 > 30$ and $n_2 > 30$). Consequently, the test statistic is

$$z = \frac{(\bar{x}_1 - \bar{x}_2) - (\mu_1 - \mu_2)}{\sqrt{\dfrac{s_1^2}{n_1} + \dfrac{s_2^2}{n_2}}}.$$

The complete test is as follows:

$$H_0: (\mu_1 - \mu_2) = 0$$
$$H_A: (\mu_1 - \mu_2) > 0$$

Test statistic: $z = \dfrac{(\bar{x}_1 - \bar{x}_2) - (\mu_1 - \mu_2)}{\sqrt{\dfrac{s_1^2}{n_1} + \dfrac{s_2^2}{n_2}}}$

Significance level: $\alpha = .05$

Decision rule: Reject H_0 if $z > z_\alpha = z_{.05} = 1.645$.

Value of the test statistic: $z = \dfrac{(\bar{x}_1 - \bar{x}_2) - (\mu_1 - \mu_2)}{\sqrt{\dfrac{s_1^2}{n_1} + \dfrac{s_2^2}{n_2}}}$

$$= \frac{(43.7 - 41.5) - 0}{\sqrt{\dfrac{11.8}{50} + \dfrac{46.3}{50}}} = 2.04$$

Conclusion: Reject H_0.

FIGURE 11.2   *SAMPLING DISTRIBUTION FOR EXAMPLE 11.2*

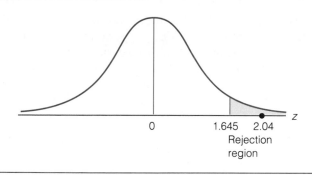

$$0 \qquad 1.645 \quad 2.04 \qquad z$$

Rejection
region

There is enough evidence to allow the senior to conclude that high-school teachers earn more money than university professors.

Thus, the senior will enter a teacher's college next fall. Figure 11.2 describes the sampling distribution of this test.

MINITAB COMPUTER OUTPUT FOR EXAMPLE 11.2*

```
TWOSAMPLE T FOR C1 VS C2
        N      MEAN      STDEV     SE MEAN
C1     50      43.7      3.44      0.486
C2     50      41.5      6.80      0.962
95 PCT CI FOR MU C1-MU C2 (0.09, 4.31)
T TEST MU C1 = MU C2 (VS GT): T = 2.04  P = .022  DF = 72.5
```

As you can see, Minitab prints the sample sizes, means, standard deviations, and standard errors of the mean. It also provides the 95% confidence interval estimate of $\mu_1 - \mu_2$ and the test statistic, which it labels T (T = 2.04). The prob-value is shown as P = .022. Ignore DF = 72.5.

Review Example 11.2 to ensure that you can recognize when to use the z-test of the difference between two population means, when the population variances are unknown.

Factors That Identify the z-Test of $\mu_1 - \mu_2$

1. *Problem objective:* Compare two populations.
2. *Data type:* quantitative
3. *Population variances:* unknown
4. *Sample sizes:* $n_1 > 30$ and $n_2 > 30$

---

* See Appendix 11.A for the Minitab instructions that produced this printout.

EXAMPLE 11.3

The manager of a large production facility believes that worker productivity is a function of, among other things, the design of the job, which refers to the sequence of worker movements involved. Two designs are being considered for the production of a new product. In an experiment, six workers using design A had a mean assembly time of 7.60 minutes, with a standard deviation of 2.36 minutes, for this product. (The six observations were 8.2, 5.3, 6.5, 5.1, 9.7, and 10.8). Eight workers using design B had a mean assembly time of 9.20 minutes, with a standard deviation of 1.35 minutes. (The eight observations were 9.5, 8.3, 7.5, 10.9, 11.3, 9.3, 8.8, and 8.0.) Can we conclude at the 5% significance level that the average assembly times differ between the two designs? Assume that the times are normally distributed.

Solution.   This question is identical to that posed in Example 11.2, except with respect to the sample sizes. That is, the problem objective is once again to compare two populations of quantitative data, where the population variances are unknown. In this example, however, the sample sizes are small ($n_1 = 6$ and $n_2 = 8$).

The test statistic is

$$t = \frac{(\bar{x}_1 - \bar{x}_2) - (\mu_1 - \mu_2)}{\sqrt{s_p^2 \left(\frac{1}{n_1} + \frac{1}{n_2} \right)}}.$$

Because we want to know if the two means are different, we test the alternative hypothesis

$$H_A: (\mu_1 - \mu_2) \neq 0.$$

The complete test follows.

$$H_0: (\mu_1 - \mu_2) = 0$$
$$H_A: (\mu_1 - \mu_2) \neq 0$$

Test statistic: $t = \dfrac{(\bar{x}_1 - \bar{x}_2) - (\mu_1 - \mu_2)}{\sqrt{s_p^2 \left(\frac{1}{n_1} + \frac{1}{n_2} \right)}}$

Significance level: $\alpha = .05$

Decision rule: Reject H_0 if $|t| > t_{\alpha/2, n_1 + n_2 - 2} = t_{.025, 12} = 2.179$.

Value of the test statistic: Since

$$s_p^2 = \frac{(n_1 - 1)s_1^2 + (n_2 - 1)s_2^2}{n_1 + n_2 - 2} = \frac{5(2.36)^2 + 7(1.35)^2}{12} = 3.38,$$

it follows that

$$t = \frac{(\bar{x}_1 - \bar{x}_2) - (\mu_1 - \mu_2)}{\sqrt{s_p^2 \left(\frac{1}{n_1} + \frac{1}{n_2} \right)}} = \frac{(7.60 - 9.20) - 0}{\sqrt{3.38 \left(\frac{1}{6} + \frac{1}{8} \right)}} = -1.61.$$

FIGURE 11.3   SAMPLING DISTRIBUTION FOR EXAMPLE 11.3

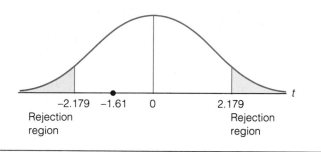

Conclusion: Do not reject H_0.

There is not enough evidence to allow us to infer that a difference in mean assembly times exists between designs A and B.

The decision about which design to use should be based on some other criterion (such as setup cost or labor preference). Figure 11.3 depicts the test's sampling distribution.

MINITAB COMPUTER OUTPUT FOR EXAMPLE 11.3*

```
TWOSAMPLE T FOR C1 VS C2
          N      MEAN      STDEV     SE MEAN
C1        6      7.60      2.36      0.96
C2        8      9.20      1.35      0.48
95 PCT CI FOR MU C1-MU C2: (-3.76, 0.56)
T TEST MU C1 = MU C2 (VS NE): T = -1.61 P = 0.13 DF = 12.0
```

The value of the test statistic is $t = -1.61$, and the prob-value is 0.13.

Following is a list of the critical factors that tell us when to use the t-test of the difference between two population means.

> **Factors That Identify the t-Test of $\mu_1 - \mu_2$**
>
> 1. *Problem objective:* Compare two populations.
> 2. *Data type:* quantitative
> 3. *Population variances:* unknown
> 4. *Sample sizes:* $n_1 \leq 30$ or $n_2 \leq 30$

* See Appendix 11.A for the commands that produced this output.

■■■■■■   **EXERCISES**

LEARNING THE TECHNIQUES

11.1   You are given the following information:

$n_1 = 50$ $n_2 = 100$

$\bar{x}_1 = 52.3$ $\bar{x}_2 = 49.0$

$\sigma_1 = 6.1$ $\sigma_2 = 7.9$.

Test

$H_0: (\mu_1 - \mu_2) = 0$
$H_A: (\mu_1 - \mu_2) \neq 0$
$\alpha = .05$.

11.2   Assume that, from samples drawn from two normal populations, we have

$n_1 = 15$ $n_2 = 10$

$\bar{x}_1 = 140$ $\bar{x}_2 = 150$

$\sigma_1 = 10$ $\sigma_2 = 15$.

Test

$H_0: (\mu_1 - \mu_2) = 0$
$H_A: (\mu_1 - \mu_2) < 0$
$\alpha = .01$.

11.3   Test the hypotheses

$H_0: (\mu_1 - \mu_2) = 0$
$H_A: (\mu_1 - \mu_2) > 0$,

given

$n_1 = 40$ $n_2 = 70$

$\bar{x}_1 = 27.3$ $\bar{x}_2 = 24.6$

$\sigma_1 = 7.2$ $\sigma_2 = 6.9$

$\alpha = .05$.

11.4   What is the prob-value of the test in Exercise 11.3?

11.5   Test the following hypotheses:

a. $H_0: (\mu_1 - \mu_2) = 0$
   $H_A: (\mu_1 - \mu_2) > 0$
   $n_1 = 10$ $n_2 = 8$
   $\bar{x}_1 = 200$ $\bar{x}_2 = 185$
   $s_1 = 20$ $s_2 = 15$
   $\alpha = .05$.

   (Assume that x_1 and x_2 are normally distributed.)

b. $H_0: (\mu_1 - \mu_2) = 0$
   $H_A: (\mu_1 - \mu_2) \neq 0$
   $n_1 = 50$ $n_2 = 70$
   $\bar{x}_1 = 21$ $\bar{x}_2 = 20$
   $s_1 = 2$ $s_2 = 3$
   $\alpha = .01$.

   (Assume that x_1 and x_2 are normally distributed.)

11.6   Suppose that samples of size $n_1 = 20$ and $n_2 = 15$ are drawn from two normal populations. The sample statistics are as follows:

$\bar{x}_1 = 110$ $\bar{x}_2 = 125$

$s_1^2 = 225$ $s_2^2 = 150$.

Can we conclude at the 5% level of significance that μ_1 is less than μ_2?

11.7   Samples of $n_1 = 60$ and $n_2 = 80$ were drawn from two normal populations. The following statistics were produced:

$\bar{x}_1 = 70.6$ $\bar{x}_2 = 68.3$

$s_1 = 14.9$ $s_2 = 12.3$.

Do these results allow us to conclude that μ_1 is greater than μ_2? (Use $\alpha = .10$.)

11.8   What is the prob-value of the test in Exercise 11.7?

11.9   The following two samples were drawn from two normal populations:

Sample 1: $n_1 = 20$ $\bar{x}_1 = 2.5$ $s_1 = 9.8$
Sample 2: $n_2 = 25$ $\bar{x}_2 = -1.6$ $s_2 = 7.8$.

Do these data provide sufficient evidence at the 5% significance level to allow us to conclude that μ_1 is not equal to μ_2?

11.10   Given the output in Figure E11.10, briefly describe what each number tells you.

11.11   The computer printout of a hypothesis test is shown in Figure E11.11. Specify the hypotheses being tested and the conclusion you would draw at the 1% significance level.

FIGURE E11.10

```
TWOSAMPLE T FOR C1 VS C2
        N     MEAN    STDEV    SE MEAN
C1     40    126.3     21.4     3.38
C2     70    132.4     25.3     3.02
95 PCT CI FOR MU C1-MU C2: (-14.99, 2.79)
T TEST MU C1 = MU C2 (VS LT): T = -1.34 P = .0917 DF = 92.7
```

FIGURE E11.11

```
TWOSAMPLE T FOR C1 VS C2
        N     MEAN    STDEV    SE MEAN
C1     12    29.3      5.8      1.67
C2      9    34.9      6.9      2.30
95 PCT CI FOR MU C1-MU C2: (-11.40, 0.20)
T TEST MU C1 = MU C2 (VS NE): T = -2.02 P = .0578 DF = 19
```

APPLYING THE TECHNIQUES

Self-Correcting Exercise (See Appendix 11.B for the solution.)

11.12 A baby-food producer claims that her product is superior to that of her leading competitor, in that babies gain weight faster with her product. As an experiment, 10 healthy newborn infants are randomly selected. For 2 months, 5 of the babies are fed the producer's product and the other 5 are fed the competitor's product. Each baby's weight gain (in ounces) is shown in the accompanying table.

WEIGHT GAIN (ounces)

Producer's Product	Competitor's Product
30	32
36	24
28	30
37	29
40	27

Can we conclude that the average weight gain for babies fed on the producer's baby food is greater than the average weight gain for babies fed on the competitor's baby food? (Use $\alpha = .05$.)

11.13 Kool Kat, a manufacturer of automobile air conditioners, is considering switching its supplier of condensors. Supplier *A*, the current producer of condensers for Kool Kat, prices its product 5% higher than supplier *B* does. Since Kool Kat wants to maintain its reputation for quality, however, Kool Kat wants to be sure that supplier *B*'s condensers last at least as long as supplier *A*'s do. The management of Kool Kat has decided to retain supplier *A* if there is sufficient statistical evidence that supplier *A*'s condensers last longer on the average than supplier *B*'s condensers. In an experiment, ten midsize cars were equipped with air conditioners using type *A* condensers while another ten midsize cars were equipped with type *B* condensers. The number of miles driven by each car before the condenser broke down was recorded, and the relevant statistics are listed in the accompanying table.

Type A Condensers	Type B Condensers
$\bar{x}_1 = 75{,}000$	$\bar{x}_2 = 70{,}000$
$s_1 = 6{,}000$	$s_2 = 5{,}000$

Assuming that the distance traveled is normally distributed, should Kool Kat retain supplier A? (Use $\alpha = .10$.)

11.14 Do students at four-year universities work harder than those at two-year junior colleges? To help answer this question, 47 randomly selected university students and 36 college students were asked how many hours per week they spent doing homework. The means and variances for both groups are shown next. Do these results allow us to answer our opening question affirmatively? (Use $\alpha = .01$.)

University Students	College Students
$\bar{x}_1 = 18.6$	$\bar{x}_2 = 14.7$
$s_1^2 = 22.4$	$s_2^2 = 20.9$

11.15 What is the prob-value of the test in Exercise 11.14?

11.16 Automobile insurance companies take many factors into consideration when setting rates. These factors include age, marital status, and miles driven per year. In order to determine the effect of gender, 100 male and 100 female drivers were surveyed. Each was asked how many miles he or she drove in the past year. The means and the standard deviations are shown in the accompanying table. Can we conclude at the 5% significance level that male and female drivers differ in the number of miles driven per year?

	Female Drivers	Male Drivers
Mean	9,117	10,014
Standard deviation	3,249	3,960

11.17 High blood pressure is a leading cause of strokes. Medical researchers are constantly seeking ways to treat patients suffering from this condition. A specialist in hypertension claims that regular aerobic exercise can reduce high blood pressure just as successfully as drugs, with none of the adverse side effects. To test the claim, 50 patients who suffer from high blood pressure were chosen to participate in an experiment. For 60 days half the sample exercised 3 times per week for one hour; the other half took the standard medication. The percentage reduction in blood pressure was recorded for each individual, and the resulting data are shown in the accompanying table. Can we conclude at the 1% significance level that exercise is at least as effective as medication in reducing hypertension?

PERCENTAGE REDUCTION IN BLOOD PRESSURE

Exercise	Medication
$\bar{x}_1 = 14.31$	$\bar{x}_2 = 13.28$
$s_1 = 1.63$	$s_2 = 1.82$

11.18 Companies that hire business students must often choose between undergraduates (BBAs) and graduates (MBAs). Typically, MBAs are more mature, have more experience, and demand higher salaries. To help determine future hiring practices, a consultant to a large corporation undertook a research project in which he randomly selected 50 MBAs and 75 BBAs who were hired last year. To measure how well they performed their jobs, he computed their percentage salary increase one year after their initial hiring. The summarized statistics are shown in the accompanying table. Can we conclude at the 5% significance level that BBAs performed at least as well as MBAs?

PERCENTAGE SALARY INCREASE

BBAs	MBAs
$\bar{x}_1 = 8.6$	$\bar{x}_2 = 8.1$
$s_1 = 1.4$	$s_2 = 1.0$

11.19 Find the prob-value of the test in Exercise 11.18.

11.20 Disposable batteries are expensive and they release dangerous chemicals when discarded. Consequently, many people are now using rechargeable batteries. However, some rechargeable batteries do not accept a full charge and as a result do not function as well as others. In an experiment to determine which batteries accept charges better, 100 D cells made by firm A and another 100 D cells made by firm B were randomly selected. Each battery was charged for 14 hours. The number of volts of power each was capable of producing was measured (D cells are supposed to produce 1.25 volts); the results are summarized in the accompanying table. Do these results allow us to conclude at the 1% significance level that the mean power differs between the two brands of batteries?

POWER OUTPUT (volts)

Firm A	Firm B
$\bar{x}_1 = 1.16$	$\bar{x}_2 = 1.21$
$s_1 = .08$	$s_2 = .10$

11.21 In designing advertising campaigns to sell magazines, it is important to know how much time each of a number of demographic groups spends reading magazines. In a preliminary study, 20 people were randomly chosen. Each was asked how much time per week he or she spent reading magazines; additionally, each was categorized by sex and by income level (high or low). The data are shown in the accompanying table.

a. Is there sufficient evidence at the 5% significance level to allow us to conclude that men and women differ in their magazine-reading habits?

b. Is there sufficient evidence at the 5% significance level to allow us to conclude that those whose incomes are higher devote more time to reading magazines than do lower-income individuals?

Respondent	Time Spent Reading Magazines	Sex	Income
1	80	M	L
2	125	M	H
3	150	F	H
4	140	M	H
5	105	F	L
6	85	F	H
7	70	F	H
8	90	M	L
9	80	M	L
10	65	F	L
11	150	M	H
12	75	F	L
13	90	F	H
14	110	M	H
15	115	M	L
16	125	F	H
17	90	F	L
18	80	F	L
19	130	F	H
20	150	M	H

SECTION 11.3

TESTING THE DIFFERENCE BETWEEN TWO POPULATION PROPORTIONS

When the problem objective is to compare two populations and the data type is qualitative, the parameter to be tested is $p_1 - p_2$, the difference between two population proportions. There are two different test statistics for this parameter; the choice of which one to use depends on the null hypothesis.

Case 1.   If the null hypothesis specifies that the difference between the two population proportions is zero $(H_0: (p_1 - p_2) = 0)$, the test statistic is

$$z = \frac{(\hat{p}_1 - \hat{p}_2) - (p_1 - p_2)}{\sqrt{\hat{p}\hat{q}\left(\dfrac{1}{n_1} + \dfrac{1}{n_2}\right)}}$$

The statistics are

$$\hat{p}_1 = \frac{x_1}{n_1} \qquad \text{(the proportion of successes in sample 1)}$$

$$\hat{p}_2 = \frac{x_2}{n_2} \qquad \text{(the proportion of successes in sample 2)}$$

$$\hat{p} = \frac{x_1 + x_2}{n_1 + n_2} \qquad \text{(the proportion of successes in both samples combined)}$$

$$\hat{q} = 1 - \hat{p}$$

The quantity $\hat{p}$ is called the **pooled proportion estimate.** Since under the null hypothesis we assume that the two population proportions are equal, we can produce a single estimate of that proportion to be used to estimate the standard deviation. As was the case when we computed the pooled variance estimate in Chapters 8 and 10, it is better to combine the data from two samples if possible. Notice that, under Case 2 (following), it is not possible to combine the sample data to estimate the standard deviation, because we assume there that the two population proportions differ.

Case 2.   If the null hypothesis states that the difference between the two population proportions is a nonzero value $(H_0: (p_1 - p_2) = D$ where $D \neq 0)$, the test statistic is

$$z = \frac{(\hat{p}_1 - \hat{p}_2) - (p_1 - p_2)}{\sqrt{\dfrac{\hat{p}_1\hat{q}_1}{n_1} + \dfrac{\hat{p}_2\hat{q}_2}{n_2}}}$$

In both cases, the sample sizes must be sufficiently large. That is, $n_1\hat{p}_1, n_1\hat{q}_1, n_2\hat{p}_2$, and $n_2\hat{q}_2$ must be greater than or equal to 5.

EXAMPLE 11.4

An insurance company is thinking about offering discounts on its life-insurance policies to nonsmokers. As part of its analysis, it randomly selects 200 men who are 50 years old and asks them if they smoke at least one pack of cigarettes per day and if they have ever suffered from heart disease. The results indicate that 20 out of 80 smokers and 15 out of 120 nonsmokers suffer from heart disease. Can we conclude at the 5% level of significance that smokers have a higher incidence of heart disease than nonsmokers?

Solution.   The problem objective is to compare two populations (50-year-old men who smoke, and 50-year-old men who don't smoke). The data type is qualitative, since the responses are "suffer from heart disease" and "don't suffer from heart disease." The parameter of interest is therefore $p_1 - p_2$ (where p_1 = Proportion of smokers who suffer from heart disease, and p_2 = Proportion of nonsmokers who suffer from heart disease. Since we want to know whether p_1 is greater than p_2, the alternative hypothesis is $H_A: (p - p_2) > 0$. As a result, the null hypothesis is $H_0: (p_1 - p_2) = 0$. It follows that the appropriate test statistic is shown in Case 1. That is,

$$z = \frac{(\hat{p}_1 - \hat{p}_2) - (p_1 - p_2)}{\sqrt{\hat{p}\hat{q}\left(\dfrac{1}{n_1} + \dfrac{1}{n_2}\right)}}.$$

The complete test is as follows:

$H_0: (p_1 - p_2) = 0$

$H_A: (p_1 - p_2) > 0$

Test statistic: $z = \dfrac{(\hat{p}_1 - \hat{p}_2) - (p_1 - p_2)}{\sqrt{\hat{p}\hat{q}\left(\dfrac{1}{n_1} + \dfrac{1}{n_2}\right)}}$

Significance level: $\alpha = .05$

Decision rule: Reject H_0 if $z > z_\alpha = z_{.05} = 1.645$.

Value of the test statistic: $\hat{p}_1 = \dfrac{20}{80} = .25$

$$\hat{p}_2 = \frac{15}{120} = .125$$

$$\hat{p} = \frac{20 + 15}{80 + 120} = \frac{35}{200} = .175$$

$$z = \frac{(\hat{p}_1 - \hat{p}_2) - (p_1 - p_2)}{\sqrt{\hat{p}\hat{q}\left(\dfrac{1}{n_1} + \dfrac{1}{n_2}\right)}}$$

$$= \frac{(.25 - .125) - 0}{\sqrt{(.175)(.825)\left(\dfrac{1}{80} + \dfrac{1}{120}\right)}} = 2.28$$

Conclusion: Reject H_0.

There is sufficient evidence to enable us to conclude that the proportion of smokers who suffer from heart disease is greater than the proportion of non-smokers who do.

Figure 11.4 describes this test.

FIGURE 11.4   SAMPLING DISTRIBUTION FOR EXAMPLE 11.4

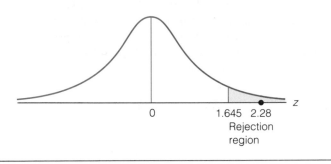

EXAMPLE 11.5

The process that is used to produce a complex component used in medical instruments typically results in defective rates in the 40% range. Recently two innovations have been developed. Innovation 1 appears to be more promising but is considerably more expensive to purchase and operate than innovation 2. After a careful analysis of the costs, management decides that it will adopt innovation 1 only if the proportion of defective components it produces is at least 8% smaller than that produced by innovation 2. In a random sample of 300 units produced by innovation 1, 33 are found to be defective. In sample of 300 components produced by innovation 2, 84 are found to be defective. At the 1% significance level, can we conclude that management should adopt innovation 1?

Solution.   The problem objective is to compare two populations (components produced by the two innovations), and the data type is qualitative (the value of the variable is either *defective* or *nondefective*). It follows that the parameter of interest is $p_1 - p_2$. Because we wish to know if there is sufficient statistical evidence to allow us to conclude that p_1 is at least .08 less than p_2, the alternative hypothesis is

$$H_A: (p_1 - p_2) < -.08$$

which means that the test statistic is described in Case 2. The complete test is as follows:

$$H_0: (p_1 - p_2) = -.08$$
$$H_A: (p_1 - p_2) < -.08$$

Test statistic: $z = \dfrac{(\hat{p}_1 - \hat{p}_2) - (p_1 - p_2)}{\sqrt{\dfrac{\hat{p}_1 \hat{q}_1}{n_1} + \dfrac{\hat{p}_2 \hat{q}_2}{n_2}}}$

Significance level: $\alpha = .01$

Decision rule: Reject H_0 if $z < -z_\alpha = -z_{.01} = -2.33$.

Value of the test statistic: $\hat{p}_1 = \dfrac{33}{300} = .11$

$$\hat{p}_2 = \frac{84}{300} = .28$$

$$z = \frac{(\hat{p}_1 - \hat{p}_2) - (p_1 - p_2)}{\sqrt{\dfrac{\hat{p}_1\hat{q}_1}{n_1} + \dfrac{\hat{p}_2\hat{q}_2}{n_2}}}$$

$$= \frac{(.11 - .28) - (-.08)}{\sqrt{\dfrac{(.11)(.89)}{300} + \dfrac{(.28)(.72)}{300}}} = -2.85$$

Conclusion: Reject H_0.

There is sufficient evidence to conclude that the proportion of defective components produced by innovation 1 is at least 8% smaller than the proportion of defective components produced by innovation 2. It follows that the firm should adopt innovation 1. Figure 11.5 describes this test.

The critical factors that tell us when to use the z-test of $p_1 - p_2$ are as follows.

Factors That Identify the z-Test of $p_1 - p_2$

1. *Problem objective:* Compare two populations.
2. *Data type:* qualitative

FIGURE 11.5   SAMPLING DISTRIBUTION FOR EXAMPLE 11.5

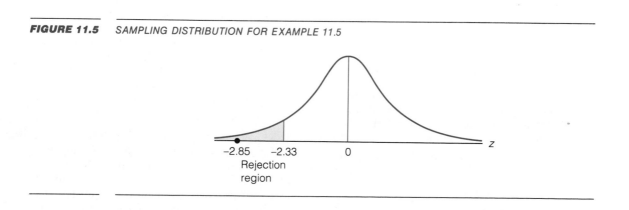

■■■■■■ **EXERCISES**

LEARNING THE TECHNIQUES

11.22 Test the following hypotheses:

a. $H_0: (p_1 - p_2) = 0$

$\quad H_A: (p_1 - p_2) \neq 0$

$\quad n_1 = 100 \qquad n_2 = 150 \qquad \alpha = .01$

$\quad x_1 = 50 \qquad x_2 = 90.$

b. $H_0: (p_1 - p_2) = .05$

$\quad H_A: (p_1 - p_2) > .05$

$\quad n_1 = 500 \qquad n_2 = 400 \qquad \alpha = .05$

$\quad x_1 = 200 \qquad x_2 = 100.$

11.23 Test the following hypotheses:

$H_0: (p_1 - p_2) = 0$

$H_A: (p_1 - p_2) > 0$

$n_1 = 250 \qquad n_2 = 400 \qquad \alpha = .01$

$\hat{p}_1 = .24 \qquad \hat{p}_2 = .17.$

11.24 Given $n_1 = 40$, $\hat{p}_1 = .25$, $n_2 = 50$, and $\hat{p}_2 = .32$, test to determine whether there is enough evidence at the 5% significance level to show that $p_2 > p_1$.

11.25 What is the prob-value of the test in Exercise 11.24?

11.26 A random sample of $n_1 = 1,000$ from population 1 produced $x_1 = 500$, and a random sample of $n_2 = 1,500$ from population 2 produced $x_2 = 500$. Can we conclude, with $\alpha = .10$, that p_1 exceeds p_2 by at least .10?

11.27 Test the following hypotheses:

$H_0: (p_1 - p_2) = .25$

$H_A: (p_1 - p_2) < .25$

$n_1 = 200 \qquad n_2 = 500 \qquad \alpha = .01$

$x_1 = 60 \qquad x_2 = 50.$

11.28 A random sample of $n_1 = 200$ from population 1 produced $x_1 = 50$, and a random sample of $n_2 = 100$ from population 2 yielded $x_2 = 35$. Can we conclude, with $\alpha = .10$, that $p_1 \neq p_2$?

11.29 Given the following data, can we conclude, with $\alpha = .01$, that $p_1 > p_2$?

$n_1 = 500 \qquad n_2 = 1000$

$x_1 = 150 \qquad x_2 = 200$

APPLYING THE TECHNIQUES

Self-Correcting Exercise (See Appendix 11.B for the solution.)

11.30 In a public opinion survey, 60 out of a sample of 100 high-income voters and 40 out of a sample of 75 low-income voters supported a decrease in sales tax. Can we conclude at the 5% level of significance that the proportion of voters favoring a sales tax decrease differs between high- and low-income voters?

11.31 A pharmaceutical company has produced a flu vaccine. In a test of its effectiveness, 1,000 people were randomly selected; of these, 500 were injected with the vaccine, and the other 500 went untreated. The number of people in each group who contracted the flu during the next three months is summarized in the accompanying table.

	Number of People	
Condition	Treated with Vaccine	Untreated
Developed the flu	80	120
Did not develop the flu	420	380

Do these data provide sufficient evidence that the vaccine is effective in preventing the flu? (Use $\alpha = .05$.)

11.32 In a random sample of 500 television sets from a large production line, there were 80 defective sets. In a random sample of 200 television sets from a second production line, there were 10 defective sets. Do these data provide sufficient evidence to establish that the proportion of defective sets from the first line exceeds the proportion of defective sets from the second line by at least 3%? (Use $\alpha = .05$.)

11.33 A survey (reported in the *Toronto Star*, 6 May 1985) to study the usefulness of computers used a sample of 330 managers, professionals, and executives. This group included 132 computer users, 102 people who did not use computers, and 96 who said they would use them relatively soon.

Asked if computers boost personal productivity, 50% of the nonusers and intenders said *no*, as did 25% of the users. Can we conclude from these data, at the 1% level of significance, that users and nonusers (including intenders) differ in their opinion of the usefulness of computers?

11.34 Surveys have been widely used by politicians in North America as a way of monitoring the opinions of the electorate. Six months ago, a survey was undertaken to determine the proportion of voters who supported a national leader. Of a sample of 1,100, 56% indicated that they would vote for this politician. This month, another survey of 800 voters indicated that 53% now support the leader. At the 5% level of significance, can we infer that the national leader's popularity has decreased?

SECTION 11.4

SUMMARY

The techniques used to test for differences between two populations were described in this chapter. When the data type is quantitative, the parameter we test is $\mu_1 - \mu_2$. The three test statistics for this parameter are listed in Table 11.1. When the data type is qualitative, the parameter of interest is $p_1 - p_2$. The two test statistics used for this parameter are also shown in Table 11.1.

TABLE 11.1 SUMMARY OF TEST STATISTICS FOR $\mu_1 - \mu_2$ AND $p_1 - p_2$

Parameter	Test Statistic	Required Conditions
$\mu_1 - \mu_2$	$z = \dfrac{(\bar{x}_1 - \bar{x}_2) - (\mu_1 - \mu_2)}{\sqrt{\dfrac{\sigma_1^2}{n_1} + \dfrac{\sigma_2^2}{n_2}}}$	σ_1^2 and σ_2^2 are known; x_1 and x_2 are normally distributed or n_1 and n_2 are large.
	$z = \dfrac{(\bar{x}_1 - \bar{x}_2) - (\mu_1 - \mu_2)}{\sqrt{\dfrac{s_1^2}{n_1} + \dfrac{s_2^2}{n_2}}}$	σ_1^2 and σ_2^2 are unknown; x_1 and x_2 are normally distributed; $n_1 > 30$ and $n_2 > 30$.
	$t = \dfrac{(\bar{x}_1 - \bar{x}_2) - (\mu_1 - \mu_2)}{\sqrt{s_p^2\left(\dfrac{1}{n_1} + \dfrac{1}{n_2}\right)}}$	σ_1^2 and σ_2^2 are unknown and equal ($\sigma_1^2 = \sigma_2^2$); x_1 and x_2 are normally distributed.
$p_1 - p_2$	$z = \dfrac{(\hat{p}_1 - \hat{p}_2) - (p_1 - p_2)}{\sqrt{\hat{p}\hat{q}\left(\dfrac{1}{n_1} + \dfrac{1}{n_2}\right)}}$	The null hypothesis is $H_0: (p_1 - p_2) = 0$; $n_1\hat{p}_1, n_1\hat{q}_1, n_2\hat{p}_2$ and $n_2\hat{q}_2 \geq 5$.
	$z = \dfrac{(\hat{p}_1 - \hat{p}_2) - (p_1 - p_2)}{\sqrt{\dfrac{\hat{p}_1\hat{q}_1}{n_1} + \dfrac{\hat{p}_2\hat{q}_2}{n_2}}}$	The null hypothesis is $H_0: (p_1 - p_2) = D$, where $D \neq 0$; $n_1\hat{p}_1, n_1\hat{q}_1, n_2\hat{p}_2$, and $n_2\hat{q}_2 \geq 5$.

IMPORTANT TERMS

z-test of $\mu_1 - \mu_2$ z-test of $p_1 - p_2$
t-test of $\mu_1 - \mu_2$ Pooled proportion estimate
Pooled variance estimate

SUPPLEMENTARY EXERCISES

11.35 A chicken farmer who supplies an international fast-food chain is experimenting with ways to make chickens grow faster. His latest scheme is to remove the feathers of young chickens so that the energy normally used to grow feathers will be used instead to make their bodies grow faster. In order to test his scheme, the farmer takes 20 young chickens and removes the feathers from 10 of them. He then treats them exactly alike for 2 months, at which point he measures their weight and calculates their percentage weight gain. The resulting statistics are shown in the accompanying table. Can we conclude from these statistics that the scheme is effective? (Use $\alpha = .05$.)

"Defeathered" Chickens	"Feathered" Chickens
$n_1 = 10$	$n_2 = 10$
$\bar{x}_1 = 112.5$	$\bar{x}_2 = 102.0$
$s_1^2 = 98.6$	$s_2^2 = 79.5$

11.36 In a widely publicized study, doctors discovered that aspirin seems to help prevent heart attacks. The research project, which was scheduled to last for five years, employed 22,000 American physicians. Half took an aspirin tablet three times per week while the other half took a placebo on the same schedule. After three years, researchers determined that 104 of those who took aspirin and 189 of those who took the placebo had had heart attacks.

a. At the .005 level of significance, do these results indicate that aspirin is effective in reducing the incidence of heart attacks?

b. A not-so-widely-publicized British study attempted to replicate the American research plan; however, it used only 5,000 men (2,500 took aspirin and 2,500 took the placebo). Suppose that the respective proportions of men who suffered heart attacks were exactly the same

as in the American study. Do such results allow us to draw the same conclusion, with $\alpha = .005$? If the appropriate conclusion is not the same in the British study as in the U.S. study, explain why not.

11.37 Over the past 30 years, the public has grown increasingly critical of the educational system. In a series of surveys between 1948 and 1982, people were asked: "Do you think children today are being better educated or worse educated than you were?" The results are shown in the accompanying table.

	Assessment of Educational System			
Year	Better	Worse	Same	Can't Say
1948	74%	12%	10%	4%
1971	63%	20	12	5
1976	49	33	13	5
1981	47	38	9	6
1982	52	31	12	6

Assuming that the 1981 and 1982 surveys were each based on 1,049 interviews, can we conclude that there is a significant difference in the proportion of those who responded "Better" between 1981 and 1982? (Use $\alpha = .10$, and omit those who responded "Can't say.")

11.38 A restaurant located in an office building decides to adopt a new strategy for attracting customers to the restaurant. Every week it advertises in the city newspaper. In the 10 weeks immediately prior to the advertising campaign, the average weekly gross was $10,500, with a standard deviation of $750. In the 8 weeks after the campaign began, the average weekly gross was $12,000, with a standard deviation of $1,000.

a. Assuming that the weekly grosses are normally

distributed, can we conclude, with $\alpha = .10$, that the advertising campaign was successful?

b. Assume that the net profit is 20% of the gross. If the ads cost $100 per week, can we conclude at the 10% significance level that the ads are worthwhile?

11.39 Have North Americans grown to distrust television and newspaper journalists? A survey was conducted in 1988 to compare what Americans thought of the press then versus what they said they thought in 1985. The results are shown in the accompanying table.

	Percent in Agreement	
Proposed Opinion	1985	1988
1. Press reports are "often inaccurate"	34%	48%
2. Press "tends to favor one side" when reporting on political and social issues	53%	59%
3. Press "often invades people's privacy"	73%	78%
4. Rate TV news "very favorably"	25%	18%
5. Rate daily newspaper "very favorably"	25%	21%

Can we conclude at the 5% significance level that Americans had become more distrustful of television and newspaper reporting in 1988 than they were in 1985? (Assume that the number of respondents in each survey was 400.)

11.40 The owners of two downtown restaurants (whose customers are mostly office workers on coffee breaks) each claim to serve more coffee than the other. To test their claims, the number of cups of coffee sold during 5 randomly selected days in Restaurant 1 and another 5 randomly selected days in Restaurant 2 were counted. The resulting data are presented in the accompanying table. (After some analysis, it is determined that the number of cups of coffee is normally distributed.) Can we conclude that there is a difference between the average coffee sales of the two restaurants? (Use $\alpha = .10$.)

NUMBER OF CUPS OF COFFEE SOLD

Restaurant 1	Restaurant 2
670	410
420	500
515	440
690	640
825	650

11.41 Company policies that force people who are 65 years old to retire are coming under attack from various sources. In a poll reported in the *Toronto Star* (20 January 1986), 1,025 people were interviewed and asked "Do you think that mandatory retirement at age 65 is or is not a good idea?" The survey was performed in January 1985 and repeated in December 1985. The results are given in the following table.

	Response		
Survey Date	Good Idea	Not a Good Idea	Don't Know
January 1985	492	492	41
December 1985	513	482	30

Referring only to those who expressed an opinion (that is, to those who did not respond "Don't know"), can we conclude at the 5% significance level that support for mandatory retirement increased during 1985?

11.42 In the December 1985 survey referred to in Exercise 11.41, the age categories of the interviewees were also recorded. Suppose that the responses by age were as shown in the accompanying table.

	Response		
Category	Good Idea	Not a Good Idea	Don't Know
18 to 29 years	168	187	11

(continued)

| | **Response** | | |
Category	Good Idea	Not a Good Idea	Don't Know
30 to 49 years	233	210	13
50 years & over	112	85	6

Is there sufficient evidence, with $\alpha = .05$, to conclude that people who are at least 50 years old more strongly support mandatory retirement than do people who are 30 to 49 years old? (Include only those who express an opinion for or against.)

11.43 In an effort to reduce absenteeism, an electronics company initiated a program under which employees could participate in a monthly lottery, provided that they had perfect attendance and punctuality during the month. A $10 cash prize was awarded to the winner of each monthly lottery. Approximately 80 employees participated in the program. In order to assess the impact of the program, comparisions were made between sick-leave expenditures for 8 randomly selected months before and 6 randomly selected months after the system was instituted. The results are shown in the accompanying table. Can we conclude at the 5% significance level that the mean monthly sick leave expenditure is lower after the institution of the program?

Prior Monthly Costs ($)	Post Monthly Costs ($)
903	746
812	775
1012	596
855	767
826	469
814	670
755	
690	

11.44 Have career expectations changed in the last five years? This question was addressed by a survey whose results were reported in *Newsweek* (27 January 1986). In the survey, 1,000 university freshmen were asked in 1980 and another 1,000 freshmen were asked in 1985 about their career expectations. The results appear in the accompanying table.

a. Can we conclude at the 5% significance level that the proportion of students who expect to become business executives has increased?

b. Can we conclude at the 5% significance level that the proportion of students who expect to become computer programmers or analysts has decreased?

Career	**1980**	**1985**
Accounting	58	63
Business executive	101	127
Computer programmer/analyst	53	44
Engineer	107	100
Lawyer/Judge	41	39
Military career	9	11
Physician	35	38
Teacher	38	38
Other/Undecided	558	540
TOTAL	1,000	1,000

11.45 In recent years a number of state governments have passed mandatory seat-belt laws. Although the use of seat belts is known to save lives and reduce serious injuries, compliance with seat-belt laws is not universal. In an effort to increase the use of seat belts, a government agency sponsored a two-year study. Among its objectives were to determine if there was enough evidence to justify the following conclusions:

a. Seat-belt usage increased between 1988 and 1989.

b. In 1989 seat belts were used more frequently by women than by men.

c. In 1989 seat belts were used more frequently during highway driving than during city driving.

What conclusions can be drawn from the results shown in Table E11.45? (Use $\alpha = .01$.)

TABLE E11.45

Wearers/ Wearing Conditions	1988		1989	
	Use Seat Belts	Don't Use Seat Belts	Use Seat Belts	Don't Use Seat Belts
All	1362	341	1615	346
Men	742	215	940	218
Women	620	126	675	128
Highway driving	532	87	621	107
City driving	830	254	994	239

11.46 Is oat bran an effective way of reducing cholesterol? Early studies indicated that eating oat bran daily reduces cholesterol levels by 5 to 10%. Reports of this study resulted in the introduction of many new breakfast cereals that contained various percentages of oat bran as an ingredient. However, a January 1990 experiment performed by medical researchers in Boston, Massachusetts, cast doubt on the effectiveness of oat bran. In that study 20 volunteers ate a breakfast cereal consisting of oat bran, while another 20 individuals ate another grain cereal for breakfast. At the end of 6 weeks, the percentage cholesterol reduction was computed for both groups. These results are shown in the accompanying table. What can we conclude at the 5% significance level from these results?

PERCENTAGE CHOLESTEROL REDUCTION

Oat Bran	Other Cereal
$\bar{x}_1 = 7.6$	$\bar{x}_2 = 7.1$
$s_1 = 1.1$	$s_2 = 0.8$

11.47 In October 1979, February 1981, and November 1981, 1,020 people were asked, "Do you favor or oppose capital punishment . . .

a. For the killing of a prison guard or an on-duty policeman?

b. For the killing of any innocent person?

c. For murders committed by terrorists?"

The results are shown in the accompanying table.

Category	Response		
	Favor	Oppose	Don't Know
Prison Guard/ Policeman:			
November 1981	730	210	80
February 1981	745	204	71
October 1979	714	224	82
Any Innocent Person:			
November 1981	704	235	81
February 1981	683	255	82
October 1979	690	240	90
Terrorists:			
November 1981	755	194	71
February 1981	755	184	81
October 1979	720	200	100

For each of the three categories (a, b, and c), can we conclude at the 5% significance level that the proportion of those who favor capital punishment has changed between October 1979 and November 1981? (Omit those who responded "Don't know.")

11.48 In a preliminary study to determine the effectiveness of a new cavity-fighting toothpaste, 16 10-year-old children were randomly selected. Of these, 8 were told to use the new product, while the other 8 continued to use one of the leading brands. The experiment began with all of the children visiting a dentist and having any cavities filled. After a year, the children visited their dentist again, and the number of new cavities were counted. It is assumed that the number of new cavities is a normally distributed variable. The results are shown in the accompanying table. Can we conclude at the 5% significance level that the new toothpaste is effective in reducing cavities?

NUMBER OF NEW CAVITIES

New Toothpaste	Leading Brand of Toothpaste
0	2
3	4
2	3
4	3
1	2
0	4
2	4
1	3

11.49 In a Gallup poll (reported in the *Toronto Star,* 4 April 1985) conducted in 16 nations, respondents were asked "Do you think for people like yourself, the world in 10 years' time will be a better place to live than it is now, a worse place, or just about the same as it is today?" The results are shown in Table E11.49.

a. Considering only the respondents who expressed one of the three defined opinions, is there statistical evidence at the 5% significance level that Americans are more optimistic than Canadians? (An optimistic respondent is one who responded "Better.")

b. Can we conclude that Americans are more optimistic than Brazilians? (Use $\alpha = .05$.)

TABLE E11.49   RESPONSES TO GALLUP POLL, BY NATION

Nation	Better	Worse	About Same	Can't Say	Approximate Sample Size
North America:					
Canada	19%	35%	41%	4%	(1,000)
United States	30	30	35	5	(1,500)
South America:					
Argentina					
(Buenos Aires only)	44	27	21	8	(700)
Brazil	27	48	17	8	(2,700)
Uruguay	54	23	15	9	(800)
Europe:					
Belgium	15	31	17	17	(1,000)
Germany	4	31	19	19	(1,000)
Great Britain	18	45	31	6	(1,000)
Greece	46	29	15	10	(1,000)
Netherlands	15	26	53	6	(1,000)
Portugal	16	37	9	38	(2,000)
Switzerland	23	33	40	4	(4,000)
Turkey	26	38	12	24	
Other:					
Australia	14	41	38	7	(1,000)
Japan	12	53	18	17	(1,400)
South Africa					
(white population only)	13	52	28	7	(1,000)

━━━━━━━ **CASE 11.1***   STUDENT SURROGATES IN
                     MARKET RESEARCH

Researchers in both the business world and the academic world often treat college students as representative of the adult population. This practice reduces sampling costs enormously, but its effectiveness is open to question. An experiment was performed to determine the suitability of using student surrogates in research. The study used three groups of people:

1. The first consisted of 59 adults (18 years of age or older) chosen so that they represented by age and occupation the adult population of a midwestern state.
2. The second consisted of 42 students enrolled in an introductory marketing course at a public university. Many of the students were registered in a business program, but few were marketing majors.
3. The third consisted of 33 students enrolled in an advanced marketing course, almost all of whom were marketing majors.

The experiment consisted of showing each group a sequence of three 30-second television advertisements dealing with financial institutions. Each respondent was asked to assess each commercial on the basis of believability and interest. The responses were recorded on a 10-point graphic rating scale, where a higher rating represented greater believability or interest. The sample means and standard deviations were then calculated, and these are shown in Tables A and B.

What conclusions can you draw regarding the suitability of using students as surrogates in marketing research?

TABLE A   COMPARISON OF RESPONSES OF INTRODUCTORY MARKETING STUDENTS, ADVANCED MARKETING STUDENTS, AND ADULTS: BELIEVABILITY OF AD

Advertisement	Introductory Marketing Students		Advanced Marketing Students		Adults	
	$\bar{x}$	s	$\bar{x}$	s	$\bar{x}$	s
1	6.7	2.5	6.6	3.1	6.9	2.7
2	7.3	2.6	7.2	2.3	6.1	3.0
3	5.9	2.7	6.6	2.8	7.0	2.9

* Adapted from R. Kesevan, D. G. Anderson, and O. Mascarenhas, "Students as Surrogates in Advertising Research," *Developments in Marketing Science* 7 (1984): 438–41.

TABLE B   COMPARISON OF RESPONSES OF INTRODUCTORY MARKETING STUDENTS, ADVANCED MARKETING STUDENTS, AND ADULTS: INTEREST IN AD

Advertisement	Introductory Marketing Students		Advanced Marketing Students		Adults	
	$\bar{x}$	s	$\bar{x}$	s	$\bar{x}$	s
1	4.5	3.2	4.3	2.8	5.9	2.4
2	6.0	2.7	6.1	2.5	4.5	2.9
3	4.0	2.6	4.3	2.8	5.8	3.1

CASE 11.2*   SPECIALTY ADVERTISING RECALL

Advertisers are extremely interested not only in having customers hear about their products but also in having consumers remember the product and its name. It is generally believed that, if an advertisement is seen only once, the amount of recall diminishes over time. In an experiment to study the amount of recall in specialty advertising, 355 people were randomly selected. Each received by mail three specialty items with imprinted advertising: a ball-point pen with the name American Airlines printed on it, a key ring with the letters TIW on it, and a note pad with the name General Electric imprinted on the cover. One week later, 164 of these people were asked if they remember the products received and if they could also recall the products' sponsors. One month after the products were received, the remaining 191 people were

TABLE A   PRODUCT RECALL

Product	Number Who Recalled Product	
	1 Week	1 Month
Ball-point pen	140	159
Key ring	141	125
Note pad	149	150

* Adapted from A. Raj, C. R. Stoner, and R. A. Schreiber, "Advertising Specialties: A Note on Recall," *Developments in Marketing Science* 8 (1985): 308–11.

TABLE B   SPONSOR'S NAME RECALL

Sponsor's Name	Number Who Recalled Sponsor's Name	
	1 Week	1 Month
American Airlines	74	63
TIW	45	36
General Electric	74	58

asked the same questions. The numbers of those who could recall the products and the sponsors' names are shown in tables A and B.

Do these data indicate that the level of recall about these specialty items decreases over time?

MINITAB INSTRUCTIONS

TESTING $\mu_1 - \mu_2$, WITH σ_1^2 AND σ_2^2 UNKNOWN

When the sample sizes are large ($n_1 > 30$ and $n_2 > 30$), we test $\mu_1 - \mu_2$ with the command

```
TWOSAMPLE T C1 C2
```

When the data from Example 11.2 were stored in columns 1 and 2, the TWOSAMPLE T C1 C2 command produced the following output:

```
TWOSAMPLE T C1 C2
          N    MEAN    STDEV    SE MEAN
   C1    50    43.7    3.44     0.486
   C2    50    41.5    6.80     0.962
95 PCT CI FOR MU C1-MU C2 (0.09, 4.31)
T TEST MU C1=MU C2 (VS GT): T=2.04 P=.022 DF=72.5
```

When the sample sizes are small ($n_1 \leq 30$ or $n_2 \leq 30$), the subcommand POOLED calculates and uses the pooled variance estimate s_p^2. We answer Example 11.3 as follows:

```
SET C1
8.2 5.3 6.5 5.1 9.7 10.8
END
SET C2
9.5 8.3 7.5 10.9 11.3 9.3 8.8 8.0
END
TWOSAMPLE T C1 C2;
POOLED.
```

(Remember to include the semicolon after the command and the period after the subcommand.) The output is

```
TWOSAMPLE T FOR C1 VS C2
        N    MEAN    STDEV    SE MEAN
 C1     6    7.60    2.36     0.96
 C2     8    9.20    1.35     0.48
95 PCT CI FOR MU C1-MU C2: (-3.76, 0.56)
T TEST MU C1=MU C2 (VS NE): T=-1.61 P=0.13 DF=12.0
```

SOLUTIONS TO SELF-CORRECTING EXERCISES

11.12 $H_0: (\mu_1 - \mu_2) = 0$
$H_A: (\mu_1 - \mu_2) > 0$

Test statistic:

$$t = \frac{(\bar{x}_1 - \bar{x}_2) - (\mu_1 - \mu_2)}{\sqrt{s_p^2 \left(\dfrac{1}{n_1} + \dfrac{1}{n_2}\right)}}$$

Significance level:

$\alpha = .05$

Decision rule: Reject H_0 if

$t > t_{\alpha, n_1 + n_2 - 2} = t_{.05, 8} = 1.860.$

Value of the test statistic:

$\bar{x}_1 = 34.2 \qquad \bar{x}_2 = 28.4$

$s_1^2 = 25.2 \qquad s_2^2 = 9.3 \qquad s_p^2 = 17.25$

$$t = \frac{(\bar{x}_1 - \bar{x}_2) - (\mu_1 - \mu_2)}{\sqrt{s_p^2 \left(\dfrac{1}{n_1} + \dfrac{1}{n_2}\right)}}$$

$$= \frac{(34.2 - 28.4) - 0}{\sqrt{17.25 \left(\dfrac{1}{5} + \dfrac{1}{5}\right)}} = 2.21$$

Conclusion: Reject H_0.

There is enough evidence to allow us to conclude that the average weight gain with the producer's product exceeds that with the competitor's product.

11.30 $H_0: (p_1 - p_2) = 0$
$H_A: (p_1 - p_2) \neq 0$

Test statistic:

$$z = \frac{(\hat{p}_1 - \hat{p}_2) - (p_1 - p_2)}{\sqrt{\hat{p}\hat{q} \left(\dfrac{1}{n_1} + \dfrac{1}{n_2}\right)}}$$

Significance level:

$\alpha = .05$

Decision rule: Reject H_0 if

$|z| > z_{\alpha/2} = z_{.025} = 1.96.$

Value of the test statistic:

$$\hat{p}_1 = \frac{60}{100} = .60 \qquad \hat{p}_2 = \frac{40}{75} = .53$$

$$\hat{p} = \frac{60 + 40}{100 + 75} = .57$$

$$z = \frac{(\hat{p}_1 - \hat{p}_2) - (p_1 - p_2)}{\sqrt{\hat{p}\hat{q} \left(\dfrac{1}{n_1} + \dfrac{1}{n_2}\right)}}$$

$$= \frac{(.60 - .53) - 0}{\sqrt{(.57)(.43)\left(\dfrac{1}{100} + \dfrac{1}{75}\right)}} = .93$$

Conclusion: Do not reject H_0.

There is not enough evidence to allow us to conclude that the proportions of high-income and low-income voters who support a sales tax decrease differ.

STATISTICAL INFERENCE: A REVIEW OF CHAPTERS 8 THROUGH 11

INTRODUCTION

In the preceding four chapters, we have introduced the methods of estimation and hypothesis testing and have applied them to two different problem objectives and both data types. This entire chapter is devoted to a review of the material in Chapters 8 through 11. We begin by summarizing our systematic method of identifying which of the techniques covered thus far should be used to answer a particular question. The exercises at the end of the chapter are of types you have already seen in the preceding four chapters. Since they are not identified by chapter, however, these exercises should give you some good practice in recognizing techniques.

GUIDE TO IDENTIFYING THE
CORRECT TECHNIQUE

As you have already seen, the two most important determinants of the appropriate technique to use are the problem objective and the type of data. When the data type is qualitative, only the problem objective needs to be identified in order to determine the correct confidence interval estimator and test statistic. For quantitative data, however, additional questions must be answered to determine the right method to use. Tables 12.1 and 12.2 describe the factors that must be recognized and the appropriate statistical techniques. Table 12.1 lists the confidence interval estimators, and Table 12.2 shows the test statistics.

Procedure for Determining the Statistical Technique

1. Decide if you wish to estimate the parameter's value or test it.

2. Identify the problem objective.

3. Identify the data type.

4. Based on your decisions in Steps 1, 2 and 3, proceed to the appropriate box in Table 12.1 or Table 12.2, and identify the parameter.

5. If any additional questions are asked, respond to them.

The correct formula to use should now be apparent.

The next example illustrates the use of the guide.

TABLE 12.1   CONFIDENCE INTERVAL ESTIMATORS

	Problem Objective	
Data Type	Description of Single Population	Comparison of Two Populations
Quantitative	*Parameter:* μ Question: Do we know the population variance? 1. Yes, σ^2 is known: $$\bar{x} \pm z_{\alpha/2}\frac{\sigma}{\sqrt{n}}.$$ 2. No, σ^2 is unknown: $$\bar{x} \pm t_{\alpha/2}\frac{s}{\sqrt{n}} \quad \text{d.f.} = n - 1.$$	*Parameter:* $\mu_1 - \mu_2$ Question: Do we know the population variances? 1. Yes, σ_1^2 and σ_2^2 are known: $$(\bar{x}_1 - \bar{x}_2) \pm z_{\alpha/2}\sqrt{\frac{\sigma_1^2}{n_1} + \frac{\sigma_2^2}{n_2}}.$$ 2. No, σ_1^2 and σ_2^2 are unknown. Question: Are the sample sizes large? 1. Yes, $n_1 > 30$ and $n_2 > 30$: $$(\bar{x}_1 - \bar{x}_2) \pm z_{\alpha/2}\sqrt{\frac{s_1^2}{n_1} + \frac{s_2^2}{n_2}}.$$ 2. No, $n_1 \leq 30$ or $n_2 \leq 30$: $$(\bar{x}_1 - \bar{x}_2) \pm t_{\alpha/2}\sqrt{s_p^2\left(\frac{1}{n_1} + \frac{1}{n_2}\right)}$$ $$\text{d.f.} = n_1 + n_2 - 2.$$
Qualitative	*Parameter:* p $$\hat{p} \pm z_{\alpha/2}\sqrt{\frac{\hat{p}\hat{q}}{n}}$$	*Parameter:* $p_1 - p_2$ $$(\hat{p}_1 - \hat{p}_2) \pm z_{\alpha/2}\sqrt{\frac{\hat{p}_1\hat{q}_1}{n} + \frac{\hat{p}_2\hat{q}_2}{n}}$$

EXAMPLE 12.1

The executives of an adhesive-manufacturing company whose product is used to attach heat-shield tiles to the space shuttle are concerned about the performance of their product. They find that the drying time is excessive and that the fraction of tiles requiring reattachment is too large. As a result, they're looking for an improved product. The research and development laboratory has produced a new adhesive that the company hopes is superior to the old one. To test the new adhesive, 25 tiles are attached using the old adhesive, and another 25 are attached using the new adhesive. The number of hours of drying time required and an expert's judgment as to whether or not the tile has been properly attached are then recorded, as shown in Table 12.3. Because of the cost of changing adhesives, the executives are willing to switch only if the new adhesive can be shown to be superior to the old one.

TABLE 12.2 TEST STATISTICS

Data Type	Problem Objective	
	Description of Single Population	Comparison of Two Populations
Quantitative	Parameter: μ Question: Do we know the population variance? 1. Yes, σ^2 is known $$z = \frac{\bar{x} - \mu}{\sigma/\sqrt{n}}.$$ 2. No, σ^2 is unknown: $$t = \frac{\bar{x} - \mu}{s/\sqrt{n}} \quad \text{d.f.} = n - 1.$$	Parameter: $\mu_1 - \mu_2$ Question: Do we know the population variances? 1. Yes, σ_1^2 and σ_2^2 are known $$z = \frac{(\bar{x}_1 - \bar{x}_2) - (\mu_1 - \mu_2)}{\sqrt{\dfrac{\sigma_1^2}{n_1} + \dfrac{\sigma_2^2}{n_2}}}.$$ 2. No, σ_1^2 and σ_2^2 are unknown. Question: Are the samples sizes large? 1. Yes, $n_1 > 30$ and $n_2 > 30$: $$z = \frac{(\bar{x}_1 - \bar{x}_2) - (\mu_1 - \mu_2)}{\sqrt{\dfrac{s_1^2}{n_1} + \dfrac{s_2^2}{n_2}}}.$$ 2. No, $n_1 \leq 30$ or $n_2 \leq 30$: $$t = \frac{(\bar{x}_1 - \bar{x}_2) - (\mu_1 - \mu_2)}{\sqrt{s_p^2\left(\dfrac{1}{n_1} + \dfrac{1}{n_2}\right)}}$$ d.f. $= n_1 + n_2 - 2$.
Qualitative	Parameter: p $$z = \frac{\hat{p} - p}{\sqrt{\dfrac{pq}{n}}}$$	Parameter: $p_1 - p_2$ $$z = \frac{(\hat{p}_1 - \hat{p}_2) - 0}{\sqrt{\hat{p}\hat{q}\left(\dfrac{1}{n_1} + \dfrac{1}{n_2}\right)}} \quad \text{or}$$ $$z = \frac{(\hat{p}_1 - \hat{p}_2) - (p_1 - p_2)}{\sqrt{\dfrac{\hat{p}_1\hat{q}_1}{n_1} + \dfrac{\hat{p}_2\hat{q}_2}{n_2}}}$$

a. At the 5% significance level, can we conclude that the new adhesive has a superior drying time?

b. At the 5% significance level, can we conclude that the new adhesive is superior in fraction of proper attachments?

TABLE 12.3   RECORDED DATA FOR EXAMPLE 12.1

	Old Adhesive			New Adhesive	
Tile	Drying Time (hours)	Properly Attached (Y or N)	Tile	Drying Time (hours)	Properly Attached (Y or N)
1	7.1	Y	1	8.3	Y
2	6.3	Y	2	8.5	Y
3	9.2	N	3	7.3	Y
4	8.6	Y	4	6.5	Y
5	5.5	N	5	7.0	Y
6	7.3	N	6	6.4	Y
7	6.6	Y	7	6.3	N
8	8.0	N	8	7.7	Y
9	7.7	Y	9	5.2	Y
10	8.9	N	10	7.6	N
11	9.1	Y	11	6.1	Y
12	8.6	N	12	5.7	Y
13	5.7	Y	13	6.3	Y
14	4.9	Y	14	7.0	N
15	6.0	N	15	8.8	Y
16	6.8	Y	16	6.9	Y
17	6.7	N	17	6.5	Y
18	7.5	Y	18	5.8	N
19	8.3	Y	19	4.3	Y
20	8.0	N	20	4.9	Y
21	6.1	Y	21	6.6	N
22	9.1	Y	22	6.8	Y
23	5.8	N	23	7.0	Y
24	6.0	Y	24	6.5	Y
25	7.3	N	25	6.0	Y

c. Estimate with 99% confidence the average drying time of the new adhesive.

d. Estimate with 99% confidence the fraction of proper attachments achieved by the new adhesive.

Solution.   The various parts of this example require a number of different statistical techniques.

a. The problem objective here is to compare two populations, and the data type is quantitative (the drying times of the two adhesives). The population standard deviations are unknown, and $n_1 \leq 30$ and $n_2 \leq 30$. As a result of these factors, we identify the t-test of $\mu_1 - \mu_2$ as the appropriate test.

   Since we want to know whether we can conclude that the mean drying time of the new adhesive (labeled μ_2) is less than the mean drying time of the old adhesive (labeled μ_1), the alternative hypothesis is

$$H_A: (\mu_1 - \mu_2) > 0$$

   In order to perform the t-test, we need $\bar{x}_1, \bar{x}_2, s_1^2, s_2^2,$ and s_p^2, which we now calculate. The resulting statistics appear in the accompanying table.

Old Adhesive	**New Adhesive**	
$\bar{x}_1 = 7.24$	$\bar{x}_2 = 6.64$	
$s_1^2 = 1.62$	$s_2^2 = 1.13$	$s_p^2 = 1.375$

The complete test is as follows:

$$H_0: (\mu_1 - \mu_2) = 0$$
$$H_A: (\mu_1 - \mu_2) > 0$$

Test statistic: $t = \dfrac{(\bar{x}_1 - \bar{x}_2) - (\mu_1 - \mu_2)}{\sqrt{s_p^2\left(\dfrac{1}{n_1} + \dfrac{1}{n_2}\right)}}$

Significance level: $\alpha = .05$

Decision rule: Reject H_0 if $t > t_{\alpha, n_1 + n_2 - 2} = t_{.05, 48} = 1.645.$

Value of the test statistic: $t = \dfrac{(7.24 - 6.64) - 0}{\sqrt{1.375\left(\dfrac{1}{25} + \dfrac{1}{25}\right)}} = 1.81$

Conclusion: Reject H_0.

   There is sufficient evidence to allow us to conclude that the new adhesive has a superior drying time.

b. The problem objective here is once again to compare two populations. But in this case the data type is qualitative, since the responses to the question are either *yes* (the tile is properly attached) or *no* (the tile is not properly attached). The correct technique is easily identified as the z-test of $p_1 - p_2$. To conduct this test, we need to know the proportions of tiles that are not properly attached. (Alternatively, we could perform this test by determining the proportions of properly attached tiles.) By counting, we find

$$\hat{p}_1 = 11/25 = .44$$
$$\hat{p}_2 = 5/25 = .20.$$

The pooled proportion estimate is

$$\hat{p} = \frac{11 + 5}{25 + 25} = \frac{16}{50} = .32$$

and

$$\hat{q} = 1 - \hat{p} = 1 - .32 = .68.$$

Since we want to know whether the proportion of tiles improperly attached with the new adhesive is smaller than the corresponding proportion for the old adhesive, the alternative hypothesis is

$$H_A : (p_1 - p_2) > 0.$$

The complete test is as follows:

$$H_0 : (p_1 - p_2) = 0$$
$$H_A : (p_1 - p_2) > 0$$

Test statistic: $z = \dfrac{(\hat{p}_1 - \hat{p}_2) - (p_1 - p_2)}{\sqrt{\hat{p}\hat{q}\left(\dfrac{1}{n_1} + \dfrac{1}{n_2}\right)}}$

Significance level: $\alpha = .05$

Decision rule: Reject H_0 if $z > z_\alpha = z_{.05} = 1.645.$

Value of the test statistic: $z = \dfrac{(.44 - .20) - 0}{\sqrt{(.32)(.68)\left(\dfrac{1}{25} + \dfrac{1}{25}\right)}} = 1.82$

Conclusion: Reject H_0.

There is enough evidence to allow us to conclude that the new adhesive is superior to the old adhesive in the fraction of proper attachments it achieves.

c. The problem here is to describe a single population, and the data type is quantitative. Hence we wish to estimate μ; and since σ^2 is unknown, the estimator is

$$\bar{x} \pm t_{\alpha/2}\frac{s}{\sqrt{n}} = 6.64 \pm 2.797\frac{1.06}{\sqrt{25}} = 6.64 \pm .59.$$

d. The problem objective here is to describe a single population, and the data type is qualitative. The interval estimator of p (the proportion of properly attached tiles) is

$$\hat{p} \pm z_{\alpha/2}\sqrt{\frac{\hat{p}\hat{q}}{n}} = .80 \pm 2.58\sqrt{\frac{(.80)(.20)}{25}} = .80 \pm .21.$$

We are 99% confident that the true proportion of properly attached tiles achieved by using the new adhesive lies between .59 and 1.0 (since p cannot exceed 1).

MINITAB COMPUTER OUTPUT FOR EXAMPLE 12.1*

Columns 1 and 3 are used to store the adhesive drying times, and columns 2 and 4 are used to store the code representing whether the tile has been properly attached (Yes = 1 and No = 0).

```
a. TWO SAMPLE T FOR C1 VS   C3
            N      MEAN      STDEV      SE MEAN
    C1     25      7.24      1.27       0.25
    C3     25      6.64      1.06       0.21
   95 PCT CI FOR MU C1-MU C3: (-0.06, 1.27)
   T TEST MU C1=MU C3 (VS GT): T=1.81 P=0.037 DF=48.0

b. ROWS    C2
              COUNT
       0       11
       1       14
     ALL       25
  ROWS    C4
              COUNT
       0        5
       1       20
     ALL       25
```

From this output we learn that:

$$\hat{p}_1 = 11/25 = .44$$

and

$$\hat{p}_2 = 5/25 = .20.$$

We can then compute the value of the z-test.

```
c.        N    MEAN    STDEV     SE MEAN    99.0 PERCENT C.I.
   C3    25   6.640    1.062     0.212      (6.046, 7.234)
```

d. The output for part (b) provides the statistic needed to answer this question.

EXERCISES

12.1 A real-estate company employs agents who work on a commission basis. It claims that, during their first year, agents will earn a mean commission of at least $25,000. In an examination of these claims, a random sample of 20 first-year employees is selected, and their commissions are recorded. The

---

* See Appendix 12.A for the Minitab commands used to produce this example.

sample mean and the standard deviation are $27,500 and $3,800, respectively. Test to determine whether the claim is true. (Use $\alpha = .05$.)

12.2 Random samples of two brands of whole milk are checked for their fat content (in grams), as follows: 33 half-gallon containers of each brand are selected, and the fat content is weighed (in grams). The resulting data are shown in the accompanying table.

Brand A			Brand B		
30	26	36	24	33	17
26	33	35	27	20	21
31	20	32	22	18	18
27	28	27	31	26	25
37	27	29	30	25	27
28	31	33	25	20	24
31	35	27	22	22	24
29	30	30	26	24	20
25	26	36	29	33	18
27	29	30	22	25	20
25	31	27	30	26	27
$\sum x_i = $ 974			$\sum x_i = $ 801		
$\sum x_i^2 = 29{,}200$			$\sum x_i^2 = 20{,}037$		

a. Estimate with 95% confidence the difference in mean fat content between brand A and brand B.

b. Any half-gallon container that contains 30 grams or more of fat is considered unacceptable. Is there enough evidence to allow us to conclude that brand A has a higher fraction of unacceptable containers than brand B? (Use $\alpha = .01$.)

c. The owner of brand B claims that no more than 10% of his containers are unacceptable. Is there sufficient evidence at the 5% significance level to refute the claim?

d. Estimate with 90% confidence the fraction of unacceptable brand A containers.

12.3 The Barbarian Ball Company of Baden produces ball bearings. The contract that Barbarian has requires that it produce ball bearings whose diameters are 1,010 microns, with a tolerance of ± 2.5 microns. That is, the diameters must fall between 1,007.5 and 1,012.5 microns. Any bearings whose diameters are outside this interval are considered to be defective. Barbarian owns two machines that produce ball bearings; in order to compare them, a sample of 25 ball bearings was drawn from each machine, and their diameters were measured. The samples are as follows (measured in microns):

Machine 1

1,007	1,011	1,012	1,010	1,011
1,009	1,007	1,006	1,010	1,011
1,012	1,008	1,009	1,013	1,015
1,009	1,010	1,009	1,011	1,012
1,006	1,010	1,009	1,010	1,011

$\sum x_i = 25{,}248$
$\sum x_i^2 = 25{,}498{,}570$

Machine 2

1,011	1,010	1,011	1,009	1,008
1,008	1,010	1,009	1,009	1,013
1,010	1,011	1,015	1,010	1,008
1,009	1,010	1,008	1,010	1,011
1,007	1,010	1,009	1,011	1,018

$\sum x_i = 25{,}255$
$\sum x_i^2 = 25{,}512{,}733$

a. Do these data provide sufficient evidence at the 1% significance level to allow us to conclude that the average diameters of ball bearings produced by the two machines differ?

b. Can we conclude (with $\alpha = .05$) that machine 2 has a lower defective rate than machine 1?

c. Estimate the fraction of defective ball bearings produced on machine 1, with 98% confidence.

12.4 In an attempt to increase business, a major credit-card company is thinking of offering a 1% discount on all monthly accounts that exceed $1,000. Currently, average monthly billings are $273. As an experiment, 100 cardholders were offered the discount. In the following month, the mean and the standard deviation of their billings were $285 and $53, respectively. Do these statistics provide sufficient evidence at the 5% significance level to indicate that the discount plan will increase business?

12.5 A random sample consisting of 20 McDonald's stores revealed a mean of 20.5 employees, with a standard deviation of 4.3. A random sample of 25 Wendy's stores had a mean of 16.7, with a standard deviation of 6.9. Do these results provide sufficient evidence at the 5% significance level that Wendy's and McDonald's employ an unequal average number of employees nationwide?

12.6 It's important for a politician to know if different groups within her constituency support her to a greater or lesser extent than others. If she finds support flagging in one group, she can take action to remedy the problem. Suppose that the politician discovers in a survey that 187 out of 417 men interviewed approve of her performance, while 225 out of 632 women approve of it. Can the politician conclude at the 1% significance level that men and women do not support her equally?

12.7 Laurier Trucking Company is trying to decide whether to purchase its tires from Alpha Tire Co. or Beta Tire Co. Laurier currently buys its tires from Alpha and will continue to do so unless the Beta's tires can be shown to last more than 5,000 miles longer (on average) than Alpha's. Laurier conducts an experiment by running 10 Alpha tires and 14 Beta tires until they wear out. The number of miles each traveled before wearing out was recorded, and the data were summarized with the following statistics:

Alpha	Beta
$\bar{x}_1 = $ 46,384	$\bar{x}_2 = $ 52,050
$s_1^2 = 985,000$	$s_2^2 = 856,000$

Is there sufficient evidence to allow Laurier to conclude that it should buy from Beta? (Use $\alpha = .05$, and assume that the miles traveled before wearing out are normally distributed.)

12.8 The past decade has seen a decrease in alcohol consumption among adults. In a study reported in the *Wall Street Journal* (14 June 1990), high-school seniors were asked whether they had drunk an alcoholic beverage in the previous 30 days. The results of surveys conducted in 1979 and 1989 are shown in the accompanying table. Assum-

ing that the sample sizes are 1,000 in each year, estimate with 99% confidence the decrease in the proportion of high-school seniors who had drunk an alcoholic beverage in the previous 30 days between 1979 and 1989.

Year	Percent Responding Yes
1979	71.8%
1989	60.1%

12.9 The management of a large pension fund is interested in studying the distribution of monthly rates of return on large, well-diversified portfolios of common stock. In particular, the management is interested in finding out whether the mean exceeds .5%. Intensive gathering of data yielded 90 monthly returns on various large and well-diversified portfolios. These returns are expressed as gross returns per $1,000 invested. The data have been classified into intervals, with the frequency distribution shown in the accompanying table.

FREQUENCY DISTRIBUTION OF GROSS RETURNS

Range*	Frequency
$960–970	4
$970–980	4
$980–990	10
$990–1,000	13
$1,000–1,010	16
$1,010–1,020	15
$1,020–1,030	13
$1,030–1,040	8
$1,040–1,050	5
$1,050–1,060	2

* Each closed interval includes the lower limit but excludes the upper limit.

Is there sufficient evidence to allow the management to conclude that the mean monthly return exceeds .5%? (Use $\alpha = .05$.)

12.10   The electric company in a large city is considering an incentive plan to encourage its customers to pay their bills promptly. The plan is to discount the bills 1% if the customer pays within 5 days, as opposed to the usual 25 days. As an experiment, 20 customers are offered the discount on their September bill. The mean and the variance of the number of days before payment is received from this group are 6.3 and 9.1, respectively. A random sample of 20 customers who were not offered the discount took an average of 23.1 days (with a variance of 26.3) to pay their bills. (Assume that the time elapsed before payment is normally distributed.)

a. Estimate with 99% confidence the difference between the mean payment periods for the two groups.

b. Calculate the 95% confidence interval estimate of the average number of days before payment for the group of customers who were not offered the discount to pay early.

12.11   North American Oil is considering sites for new gas stations. An estimate of the mean traffic flow (average number of passing cars per day) at each site is to be determined by taking traffic counts for a random sample of days. The mean for each site is to be estimated to within 5 cars per day, with 90% confidence. Experience at existing sites indicates that the standard deviation of the number of cars passing in a day is about 100. What sample size should be used?

12.12   An increasing number of managers are emphasizing their family life over their jobs. A survey of 216 human resource executives were asked whether they considered opportunities for advancement highly important now and whether such opportunities would be highly important in the future. The results, reported in the *Wall Street Journal* (18 June 1990) revealed that 68% of the executives believed that opportunities for advancement were highly important now, while only 48% believed that they would be highly important in the future. Estimate both population proportions with 95% confidence.

12.13   Amcar Motor Company has test-driven a random sample of 35 new Amcars. Gasoline mileage figures for the sample cars (in miles per gallon) are given in the accompanying table.

a. Construct a 95% confidence interval for the proportion of cars that get more than 20 miles per gallon.

b. Estimate with 99% confidence the mean gasoline mileage.

Gasoline Mileage (in mpg)						
15.4	18.1	19.0	19.8	20.6	21.3	21.8
16.3	18.3	19.1	20.1	20.8	21.4	22.0
16.7	18.7	19.3	20.4	20.9	21.5	22.5
17.2	18.7	19.4	20.4	21.0	21.6	23.2
17.8	19.0	19.4	20.5	21.0	21.8	25.0

$$\sum x_i = 700.0 \qquad \sum x_i^2 = 14{,}137.18$$

12.14   A firm that makes insecticide wants the percentage of impurities in its product not to exceed an average of 3%. A random sample of 28 1-gallon cans yields the following percentages of impurities:

```
3  3  1  1  0  2  2
4  2  2  4  2  5  3
4  5  3  1  3  1  1
1  1  1  3  3  2  4
```

On the basis of these data, can we conclude that the true average is less than 3%? (Let $\alpha = .05$.)

12.15   The administration at a large state university has proposed to the faculty a new policy for promotion. It is believed that the proportion favoring the proposal among untenured faculty is different from the proportion favoring the proposal among tenured faculty. In a sample of 64 faculty without tenure, it is found that only 20 favor the proposal; while in a sample of 36 tenured faculty, 18 favor the proposal. Can we conclude at the 10% level of significance that there is a difference in opinion between tenured and untenured faculty?

12.16   Many college and university professors have been accused of grade inflation over the past several years. This means that they assign higher grades now than they did in the past, even though students' work is of the same caliber. If grade inflation has occurred, the mean grade-point average of today's students should exceed the mean of 10 years ago. To test the grade inflation theory at one university, a business professor randomly selects 75 business majors who are graduating with the present class and 50 who graduated 10 years ago. The results are shown in the accompanying table. Test to see whether or not the data support the hypothesis of grade inflation in the business school of this university. (Use $\alpha = .05$.)

Present	10 Years Ago
$\bar{x}_1 = 3.04$	$\bar{x}_2 = 2.82$
$s_1 = .38$	$s_2 = .43$
$n_1 = 75$	$n_2 = 50$

12.17 A cereal manufacturer has recently redesigned its product's container. In a random sample of 1,000 households prior to the switch, the manufacturer found that 220 purchased its brand of cereal. After the switch, a survey of 1,000 households determined that 250 bought that brand. Estimate with 99% confidence the difference in the cereal's market share before and after the design change.

12.18 An entomologist wants to determine the extent of a spruce budworm infestation. This is done by counting the number of budworm larvae on a representative sampling of 18-inch branch tips. If the entomologist believes that the variance of the number of larvae per branch tip is 400, determine how many branch tips should be sampled to estimate the mean number of budworm larvae per branch tip to within 2, with 95% confidence.

12.19 Suppose that in Exercise 12.18 the mean and the variance of the sample taken were $\bar{x} = 41.0$ and $s^2 = 352.0$.

a. Estimate with 95% confidence the mean number of spruce budworm larvae per branch tip.

b. If the policy of the Forestry Service is to spray the spruce trees when sufficient evidence exists (with $\alpha = .01$) to indicate that the average number of larvae per branch tip exceeds 38.0, should the trees be sprayed?

12.20 The chief of police wishes to estimate the mean number of accidents per weekend at a busy intersection. In a sample of 50 randomly selected weekends, the police found 2 weekends with two accidents, 18 weekends with one accident, and the remainder with no accidents. Estimate with 96.4% confidence the true mean number of accidents per weekend at this intersection.

12.21 The federal government is interested in determining whether men's salaries differ from women's salaries. Suppose that random samples of 15 women and 22 men are drawn from the population of first-level managers in the private sector. The information is summarized in the accompanying table. Test whether the salaries differ, at the 10% level of significance.

Women	Men
$\bar{x}_1 = \$18,400$	$\bar{x}_2 = \$19,700$
$s_1 = \$2,300$	$s_2 = \$3,100$
$n_1 = 15$	$n_2 = 22$

12.22 Suppose that you want to estimate the mean percentage of gain in per-share value for growth-type mutual funds over a specific 2-year period. For 10 mutual funds randomly selected from the population of all commonly listed funds, the percentage gain figures are as follows:

$$12 \quad -3 \quad 7 \quad 6 \quad -2$$
$$4 \quad 8 \quad 18 \quad 9 \quad 3$$

Find a 90% confidence interval for the mean percentage of gain for the population of funds. (Assume that the gains are normally distributed.)

12.23 Last year a local television station determined that 70% of the people who watch news at 11:00 P.M. watch its station. The station's management believes that the current audience share may have changed. In an attempt to determine whether or not this is so, the station questions a random sample of 80 local viewers and finds that 60 watch its news show. Does the sample evidence support the management's belief that its audience share has changed? (Test at the $\alpha = .10$ level of significance.)

12.24 A recent U.S. survey (reported in the *Toronto Star*, 6 December 1989), reported that 53% of a sample of 1,000 people eat spaghetti by winding it on a fork, while 47% cut the strands before eating them. (Not included in the study were those who slurp the strands directly from the plate without using dining implements at all.) Can we conclude at the 5% significance level that, in the whole population of spaghetti eaters, more people wind on forks than cut the strands?

12.25 In the period 1987–1988 several Wall Street scandals focused attention on the Yuppie (Young Urban Professionals) lifestyle and particularly on greed versus family life and charity work. In a survey performed by the Gallup Organization by telephone, 16–17 December 1987, and reported in *Newsweek* (4 January 1988), 606 adults were asked a series of questions, which were also asked in several earlier surveys. Two of the questions and the results of this survey, together with the results of the earlier surveys, are reported next. Can we conclude at the 5% significance level that the following assertions are true?

a. The ideal number of children to have has increased between 1980 and 1987.

b. There has been an increase in charity or social service activities between 1980 and 1987.

Q: What is the ideal number of children for a family to have?

	1987	1980
None	6	18
One	24	12
Two	315	333
Three	170	121
Four	61	55
Five	12	12
No answer	18	55

Q: Are you involved in any charity or social service activities, such as helping the poor, the sick, or the elderly?

	1987	1980
Yes	49%	29%
No	51%	71%

CASE 12.1*   COMPREHENSIVE PLANNING FOR BANKS

Wood and Laforge examined a number of banks to test their belief that "large U.S. banks that had more comprehensive planning would financially outperform those that had less comprehensive planning." A total of 61 banks were involved in the study. Of this total, 26 had comprehensive formal plans, 6 had partial formal plans, and 9 had no formal planning system. The remaining 20 banks represented a random sample of all banks.

The financial performance over a five-year period (1972–1976) was analyzed with respect to two different performance measures: growth in net income, and return on owner's investment. Both were measured in terms of average annual percentage. The results appear in Tables A and B. What conclusions can you draw from these data?

---

* Adapted from D. R. Wood Jr., and R. L. Laforge, "The Impact of Comprehensive Planning on Financial Performance," *Academy of Management Journal* 22(3) (1979): 516–26.

TABLE A   *AVERAGE ANNUAL PERCENT INCREASE IN NET INCOME*

Bank Group	Mean	Standard Deviation	Sample Size
Comprehensive formal planners	11.928	3.865	26
Partial formal planners	9.972	7.470	6
No formal planning system	2.098	10.838	9
Random sample of all banks	4.936	4.466	20

TABLE B   *AVERAGE ANNUAL PERCENT RETURN ON OWNER'S INVESTMENT*

Bank Group	Mean	Standard Deviation	Sample Size
Comprehensive formal planners	12.780	0.603	26
Partial formal planners	13.596	0.992	6
No formal planning system	10.080	1.141	9
Random sample of all banks	10.232	0.761	20

CASE 12.2*   HOST SELLING AND ANNOUNCER COMMERCIALS

A study was undertaken to compare the effects of host selling commercials and announcer commercials on children. Announcer commercials are straightforward commercials in which the announcer describes to viewers why they should buy a particular product. Host selling commercials feature a children's show personality or television character who extols the virtues of the product. In 1975, the National Association of Broadcasters prohibited using show characters to advertise during the same program in which they appear. This was overturned in 1982, however, by a judge's decree.

The objective of the study was to determine whether the two types of advertisements have different effects on children viewing them. The experiment utilized two groups of children, ranging in age from 6 to 10. One group of 121 children watched a program in which two host selling commercials appeared. (The commercials tried to sell Canary Crunch, a breakfast cereal.) A second group of 121 children watched the same program, but this group was exposed to two announcer commercials for the same product. Immediately after the show the children were given a questionnaire that tested their memory concerning the commercials they had watched. Each child was marked

---

* Adapted from J. H. Miller, "An Empirical Evaluation of the Host Selling Commercial and the Announcer Commercial When Used on Children," *Developments in Marketing Science* 8 (1985): 276–78.

(on a scale of 10) on their ability to remember details of the commercial. In addition, each child was offered a free box of cereal. The children were shown four different boxes of cereal—Froot Loops, Boo Berries, Kangaroo Hops, and Canary Crunch (the advertised cereal)—and asked to pick the one they wanted.

The summarized results of the experiment are shown in tables A and B. What conclusions can be drawn from these data?

TABLE A   CHILDREN'S RECALL (10-POINT SCALE)

Type of Commercial	
Host	Announcer
$\bar{x} = 7.81$	$\bar{x} = 7.28$
$s^2 = 2.87$	$s^2 = 1.94$

TABLE B   CHILDREN'S CHOICE OF BREAKFAST CEREAL

	Type of Commercial	
Cereal	Host	Announcer
Froot Loops	28	35
Boo Berries	15	11
Kangaroo Hops	34	38
Canary Crunch	44	37

CASE 12.3*   *EFFECT OF THE DEATH OF KEY EXECUTIVES ON STOCK MARKET RETURNS*

How does the death of a key executive affect a company? This question was addressed by two researchers. In particular they wanted to know how the stock market would react to the deaths of the chief executive officer and/or chairman of the board of companies whose stock trades over the counter. A sample of 21 companies whose CEO or chairman died during a 17-year period from 1966 to 1982 was selected. For each company the weekly stock returns were recorded for 55 weeks prior to the executives' deaths and for 5 weeks after. A market model was used to determine expected returns, and the difference between the actual and expected returns was calculated. These are

---

* Adapted from D. L. Warnell and W. N. Davidson, III, "The Death of Key Executives in Small Firms: Effects on Investor Wealth," *Journal of Small Business Management* 27(2) (April 1989): 10–16.

called **abnormal returns.** The abnormal returns for each company for the period 3 weeks prior to the deaths and 5 weeks after are shown in the accompanying table.

Under stable conditions the average abnormal return should equal zero, and we should observe an equal number of positive and negative abnormal returns. The researchers believed that, in the weeks before the deaths ($t = -3, -2, -1$), the abnormal returns would indicate stable conditions. After the deaths ($t = 0, 1, 2, 3, 4, 5$), however, these returns would be negative, reflecting the effects of bad news. What conclusions can you draw from the data?

ABNORMAL RETURNS (%) FOR WEEKS $t = -3, -2, \ldots, 5$

Company	$t = -3$	-2	-1	0	1	2	3	4	5
1	−2.73	−6.03	6.67	2.50	−11.63	5.59	−4.53	−2.09	−2.65
2	−1.01	−3.30	−0.69	7.97	−4.37	1.63	−0.98	4.14	2.31
3	−2.53	6.89	−2.03	−7.17	−1.01	−1.51	−4.97	−1.48	0.27
4	−3.87	−2.53	−2.60	−0.45	−0.32	6.91	−2.19	3.12	−1.62
5	7.22	−1.21	2.19	−0.02	−1.52	−2.36	−5.16	−8.31	1.45
6	9.88	6.51	−1.17	−5.04	−1.26	0.03	3.05	−4.10	4.01
7	2.20	−6.26	9.93	−5.32	−4.14	−4.45	−5.97	11.54	3.67
8	−1.72	3.40	−2.68	−0.59	−0.11	−4.93	2.12	−1.59	1.89
9	3.68	−6.36	10.41	−0.22	5.71	−3.63	−1.01	0.65	−4.54
10	−5.90	2.58	−1.34	−1.90	−0.83	8.51	−1.80	0.73	−1.75
11	0.15	6.09	−0.16	−0.73	−3.10	−3.31	6.05	−3.89	−0.27
12	−1.19	−0.87	−0.26	−2.48	3.42	4.54	4.33	−0.44	3.66
13	−2.06	4.32	1.67	−0.62	−0.66	0.08	3.57	6.79	1.91
14	1.60	1.22	−4.04	−1.33	−0.85	0.66	−4.72	−2.49	0.84
15	6.82	5.94	6.46	3.08	−0.68	−2.71	9.19	0.14	0.98
16	2.40	−1.39	2.94	−3.19	−10.91	8.11	3.99	4.27	−0.68
17	3.51	−3.49	7.32	−5.53	−2.13	−0.49	0.55	1.49	−3.80
18	−5.03	0.32	−2.49	−7.46	−0.66	0.14	1.35	1.44	−2.35
19	−6.02	1.68	−1.26	−7.51	1.19	−2.67	−0.67	−0.13	−1.85
20	−0.54	0.68	−0.17	−5.33	−2.38	−7.56	1.10	1.21	0.26
21	−8.65	1.22	7.06	−0.75	1.77	−1.96	5.99	−1.64	−2.32
MEAN	−.180	.448	1.703	−2.004	−1.641	.030	.442	.446	−.028
STANDARD DEVIATION	4.715	4.189	4.460	3.840	3.939	4.431	4.229	4.160	2.470

CASE 12.4*   ALTERING REPORTED INCOMES

It is often in the interest of companies to report incomes in a favorable light. A recent study investigated the extent to which firms make minor alterations in their reported figures to improve the appearance of the results. Psychologists have noted that humans have a tendency to simplify numbers by rounding them up or down. Changing one or two digits in a number may make an important difference since there are often rewards for managers who meet goals as opposed to those who fall just short. Managers in such situations may take steps to create the appearance that goals are being met. For instance, an income figure of $298,086 may be increased to $301,086 because the latter figure appears so much larger than the former. It is possible to detect this phenomenon by observing the second digit. If small changes of this sort are being made, the result will be a greater number of zeros and a smaller number of nines than expected in the second digit.

It would seem logical that the proportion of times any digit will occur in a given place in a number would be 1/9 for the first digit (which cannot be zero) and 1/10 for all other digits. However, this is not the case. By a complex mathematical formula, the expected frequencies of the first and second digits were computed, as shown in Table A.[†]

A random sample of financial statements from 220 firms during the years 1981 to 1985 was selected. Statements acknowledging losses were excluded, resulting in a usable sample of 805 statements. The number of occurrences of each first and second digit for ordinary and net income is shown in Table B. The data and expected frequencies of the first digits are shown to ensure that the formulas that produced the expected frequencies in Table A are reasonable.

What conclusions can you draw from these data?

TABLE A   *EXPECTED FREQUENCIES OF FIRST AND SECOND DIGITS*

	Expected Frequencies	
Digit	First Digit	Second Digit
0	—	.120
1	.301	.114
2	.176	.109
3	.125	.104
4	.097	.100

(continued)

* C. A. P. N. Carslaw, "Anomalies in Income Numbers: Evidence of Goal-Oriented Behavior," *Accounting Review* 63(2) (April 1988): 321–27.

† See W. Feller, *An Introduction to Probability Theory,* Vol. 2 (New York: John Wiley & Sons, 1966), pp. 62–63.

Digit	Expected Frequencies	
	First Digit	Second Digit
5	.079	.097
6	.067	.093
7	.058	.090
8	.051	.088
9	.046	.085
Total	1	1

TABLE B   ACTUAL FREQUENCIES OF FIRST AND SECOND DIGITS IN REPORTED ORDINARY AND NET INCOME

Digit	First Digits		Second Digits	
	Ordinary Income	Net Income	Ordinary Income	Net Income
0	—	—	133	129
1	262	235	95	89
2	119	123	78	87
3	110	119	86	82
4	82	82	72	68
5	55	56	70	74
6	53	60	76	71
7	45	42	76	72
8	43	46	68	77
9	36	42	51	56
Total	805	805	805	805

MINITAB
INSTRUCTIONS

In this appendix we use the Minitab statistical application package to answer Example 12.1. We begin by typing in the data. Columns 1 and 3 are the values of the drying times of the old and new adhesives, respectively. Columns 2 and 4 represent the qualitative data specifying whether the tile has been properly attached; we arbitrarily let Yes = 1 and No = 0. The commands we enter for this part of Example 12.1 are as follows:

```
READ  C1-C4
7.1        1        8.3        1
6.3        1        8.5        1
9.2        0        7.3        1
8.6        1        6.5        1
5.5        0        7.0        1
7.3        0        6.4        1
6.6        1        6.3        0
8.0        0        7.7        1
7.7        1        5.2        1
8.9        0        7.6        0
9.1        1        6.1        1
8.6        0        5.7        1
5.7        1        6.3        1
4.9        1        7.0        0
6.0        0        8.8        1
6.8        1        6.9        1
6.7        0        6.5        1
7.5        1        5.8        0
8.3        1        4.3        1
8.0        0        4.9        1
```

(continued)

```
6.1       1       6.6       0
9.1       1       6.8       1
5.8       0       7.0       1
6.0       1       6.5       1
7.3       0       6.0       1
END
```

a. To test

$$H_0: (\mu_1 - \mu_2) = 0$$

$$H_A: (\mu_1 - \mu_2) > 0,$$

we type the commands

```
TWOSAMPLE T C1 C3;
POOLED;
ALTERNATIVE 1.
```

The output is

```
TWOSAMPLE T FOR C1 VS C3
          N      MEAN      STDEV      SE MEAN
C1        25     7.24      1.27       0.25
C3        25     6.64      1.06       0.21
95 PCT CI FOR MU C1-MU C3: (-0.06, 1.27)
T TEST MU C1=MU C3 (VS GT): T=1.81 P=0.037 D=48.0
```

b. In order to answer this part, we test

$$H_0: (p_1 - p_2) = 0$$

$$H_A: (p_1 - p_2) > 0.$$

Although there is no direct test for these hypotheses, we can instruct Minitab to count the number of times each value of the variables occurs. This involves using the TABLE command for columns 2 and 4. That is, the command

```
TABLE C2
```

causes the computer to print

```
ROWS C2
            COUNT
0           11
1           14
ALL         25
```

Similarly, the command

```
TABLE C4
```

prints

```
ROWS  C4
          COUNT
0             5
1            20
ALL          25
```

c. The command

```
TINTERVAL .99 C3
```

outputs

```
        N    MEAN    STDEV   SE MEAN    99.0 PERCENT C.I.
C3     25   6.640    1.062    0.212    (6.046, 7.234)
```

C H A P T E R **13**

ANALYSIS OF VARIANCE

INTRODUCTION

This chapter addresses problems whose objective is to compare two or more populations when the data type is quantitative. The parameters to be compared are the population means. Ironically the technique used analyzes the sample variance in order to test and estimate means, and for this reason the method is called the **analysis of variance.** Examples of applications of the analysis of variance include the following:

1. A supermarket chain-store executive needs to determine whether or not sales of a new product are affected by the aisle in which the product is stored. Given that there are eight aisles in the store, the experiment consists of locating the product in a different aisle in each of eight weeks and recording the weekly sales. The test would assess whether or not the mean weekly sales differ.

2. A farm products manufacturer wants to determine whether the yield of a crop is different when the soil is treated with various fertilizers. Similar plots of land are planted with the same type of seed but are fertilized differently. At the end of the growing season, the mean yields from the sample plots can be compared. Historically, this type of experiment was one of the first to use the analysis of variance, and the terminology of the original experiment is still used. No matter what the experiment, the test is designed to determine whether significant differences exist among the **treatment means.**

TESTING FOR DIFFERENCES AMONG TWO OR MORE POPULATION MEANS

The experiment is performed by drawing random samples from each of the populations to be compared. Each population has mean μ_j and variance σ_j^2, where both parameters are unknown. For each sample of size n_j, we calculate the sample mean $\bar{x}_j$ and the sample variance s_j^2. The number of populations to be compared is denoted k. Figure 13.1 depicts this process.

We'll explore how to perform the analysis of variance in the following example.

EXAMPLE 13.1

An apple juice manufacturer has developed a new product—a liquid concentrate that, when mixed with water, produces 1 liter of apple juice. After careful analysis she has decided to market the product in one of three ways: emphasizing convenience, emphasizing quality, or emphasizing price. In order to help make a decision, she con-

FIGURE 13.1   *SAMPLING FOR THE ANALYSIS OF VARIANCE*

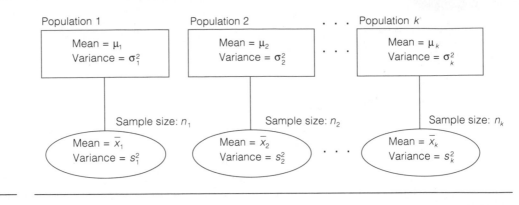

ducts an experiment. She launches the product in three different small cities, with advertising stressing convenience in one city, quality in the second city, and price in the third city. The number of packages sold weekly is recorded for the eight weeks following the beginning of the campaign; these data are shown in the accompanying table. Can we conclude at the 5% significance level that there are differences in the weekly sales of the product among the three cities?

WEEKLY SALES (100s OF UNITS)

City 1 (convenience)	City 2 (quality)	City 3 (price)
15	10	13
17	12	18
22	15	19
20	17	16
18	12	17
16	13	16
14	15	15
19	16	18

Solution.   You should confirm that the data are quantitative (weekly sales) and that the problem objective is to compare three populations (the three types of advertising).

Following the same pattern we used to conduct tests in Chapters 10 and 11, we now proceed to conduct this test. We begin with the null and alternative hypotheses. The null hypothesis states that there are no differences among the population means. Hence,

$$H_0: \mu_1 = \mu_2 = \mu_3.$$

The alternative hypothesis, as usual, answers the question being addressed. Since we'd like to know if there is evidence of a difference among the population means, the alternative hypothesis states

H_A: At least two means differ.

The next step is to determine the test statistic, which is a somewhat more involved process than was the case with the test statistics we developed previously.

Test Statistic.   The test statistic is computed in accordance with the following rationale. If the null hypothesis were true, the population means would all be equal to each other. We would then expect that the sample means would be close to one another. If the alternative hypothesis were true, however, some of the sample means would exhibit relatively large differences. The calculation that measures the proximity of the sample means to each other is called the **between-treatments variability,** denoted *SST* (sum of squares for treatments), where

$$SST = \sum_{j=1}^{k} n_j(\bar{x}_j - \bar{\bar{x}})^2.$$

The quantity $\bar{\bar{x}}$, called the **grand mean,** is the mean of all the observations. As you can deduce from this formula, if the sample means are close to each other, all sample means are close to the grand mean and consequently *SST* is small. In fact, *SST* achieves its smallest possible value (zero) when all of the sample means are equal. That is, if

$$\bar{x}_1 = \bar{x}_2 = \cdots = \bar{x}_k,$$

then

$$SST = 0.$$

It follows that a small value of *SST* tends to support the null hypothesis.

In our example, we compute the sample means and the grand mean as

$$\bar{x}_1 = \frac{(15 + 17 + \cdots + 19)}{8} = \frac{141}{8} = 17.625$$

$$\bar{x}_2 = \frac{(10 + 12 + \cdots + 16)}{8} = \frac{110}{8} = 13.75$$

$$\bar{x}_3 = \frac{(13 + 18 + \cdots + 18)}{8} = \frac{132}{8} = 16.5$$

$$\bar{\bar{x}} = \frac{(15 + 17 + \cdots + 18)}{24} = \frac{383}{24} = 15.9583.$$

Then

$$SST = \sum_{j=1}^{3} n_j(\bar{x}_j - \bar{\bar{x}})^2$$
$$= 8(17.625 - 15.9583)^2 + 8(13.75 - 15.9583)^2 + 8(16.5 - 15.9583)^2$$
$$= 63.59.$$

If large differences exist among the sample means, at least some sample means differ considerably from the grand mean, producing a large value of *SST*. It is then reasonable to reject the null hypothesis in favor of the alternative. The key question to be answered in this test (as in all of the tests we've encountered thus far) is, how large must *SST* be in order for us to be justified in rejecting the null hypothesis? In our example, $SST = 63.59$. Is this value large enough to indicate that the population means differ? To answer this question, we compare *SST* to the variability within the treatments. The **within-treatments variability** offers a measure of the degree of variability we can expect from the random variable we're measuring. This process is basically the same one we employed in testing the difference between two population means in Chapter 11, where we judged the difference between the two sample means by using the sample variances.

To understand this concept, examine Tables 13.1 and 13.2. Table 13.1 describes an example in which the variability within each sample is quite small—and hence by

---

TABLE 13.1   *RELATIVELY LARGE VARIABILITY BETWEEN SAMPLES*

Treatment 1	Treatment 2	Treatment 3
10	15	20
10	16	20
11	14	20
10	16	20
9	14	20
$\bar{x}_1 = 10$	$\bar{x}_2 = 15$	$\bar{x}_3 = 20$

TABLE 13.2   *RELATIVELY SMALL VARIABILITY BETWEEN SAMPLES*

Treatment 1	Treatment 2	Treatment 3
1	19	33
12	31	5
20	4	20
10	9	30
7	12	12
$\bar{x}_1 = 10$	$\bar{x}_2 = 15$	$\bar{x}_3 = 20$

comparison SST is relatively large. Table 13.2 depicts a case in which, because the variability within the samples is large, the same value of SST could by comparison be considered small. The term that measures the amount of variability within the samples is the **sum of squares for error,** denoted SSE, where

$$SSE = \sum_{j=1}^{k} \sum_{i=1}^{n_j} (x_{ij} - \bar{x}_j)^2.$$

When SSE is partially expanded, we get

$$SSE = \sum_{i=1}^{n_1} (x_{i1} - \bar{x}_1)^2 + \sum_{i=1}^{n_2} (x_{i2} - \bar{x}_2)^2 + \cdots + \sum_{i=1}^{n_k} (x_{ik} - \bar{x}_k)^2.$$

If you examine each of the k components of SSE, you'll see that each individually is a measure of the variability of that sample. If we divide each component by $n_j - 1$, the results of our computations are the sample variances of each sample. We can express this by rewriting SSE as

$$SSE = (n_1 - 1)s_1^2 + (n_2 - 1)s_2^2 + \cdots + (n_k - 1)s_k^2,$$

where s_j^2 is the sample variance of sample j. SSE is thus the combined or pooled variability of all k samples. This is an extension of a calculation we made in Section 9.3, where we determined the pooled estimate of the equal population variance (denoted s_p^2). In that case, it was a required condition that the population variances be equal. That same condition is now necessary in order for us to use SSE. That is, we require that

$$\sigma_1^2 = \sigma_2^2 = \cdots = \sigma_k^2.$$

Returning to the example, we compute the following:

Sample 1

$$s_1^2 = \frac{\sum(x_i - \bar{x})^2}{n - 1},$$

which can be computed, using the shortcut method described in Chapter 3, as

$$s_1^2 = \frac{\sum x_i^2 - \dfrac{(\sum x_i)^2}{n}}{n - 1} = \frac{2535 - \left(\dfrac{141}{8}\right)^2}{7} = 7.125.$$

Sample 2

$$s_2^2 = \frac{1552 - \left(\dfrac{110}{8}\right)^2}{7} = 5.643.$$

Sample 3

$$s_3^2 = \frac{2204 - \left(\dfrac{132}{8}\right)^2}{7} = 3.714.$$

Within-Treatments Variability

$$SSE = (n_1 - 1)s_1^2 + (n_2 - 1)s_2^2 + (n_3 - 1)s_3^2$$
$$= 7(7.125) + 7(5.643) + 7(3.714)$$
$$= 49.875 + 39.500 + 26.000 = 115.375.$$

The next step is to compute the **mean squares.** The mean square for treatments is

$$MST = \frac{SST}{k - 1},$$

and the mean square for errors is (where n is the total sample size)

$$MSE = \frac{SSE}{n - k}.$$

The test statistic is

$$F = \frac{MST}{MSE}.$$

In our example we find

$$MST = \frac{SST}{k - 1} = \frac{63.59}{3 - 1} = 31.80$$

$$MSE = \frac{SSE}{n - k} = \frac{115.375}{24 - 3} = 5.49,$$

and

$$F = \frac{MST}{MSE} = \frac{31.80}{5.49} = 5.79.$$

Sampling Distribution of the Test Statistic.   The test statistic we have just defined is labeled F because it follows a distribution known as the **F distribution.** The actual shape of the distribution depends on two sets of degrees of freedom: $v_1 = k - 1$ and $v_2 = n - k$. Table 7 in Appendix B provides values of F_{α,v_1,v_2}, where F_{α,v_1,v_2} is the value of F with v_1 and v_2 degrees of freedom such that the probability that this value is exceeded is α. Figure 13.2 describes the F distribution and this notation.

Part of Table 7 is reproduced here as Table 13.3. Notice for example, that, with 5 numerator degrees of freedom (v_1) and 7 denominator degrees of freedom (v_2),

$$F_{.05,5,7} = 3.97.$$

The order of the degrees of freedom is very important. Observe that

$$F_{.05,7,5} = 4.88.$$

The use of the F distribution requires that the population random variable be normally distributed. Accordingly we will apply the analysis of variance technique only when the populations are at least approximately normal.

FIGURE 13.2   F DISTRIBUTION

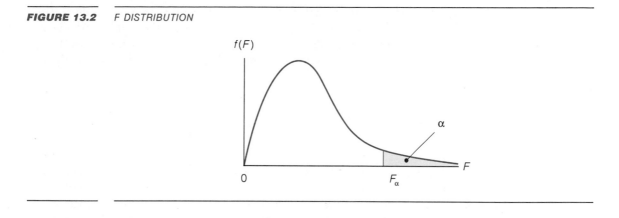

TABLE 13.3   CRITICAL VALUES OF THE F DISTRIBUTION, WITH $\alpha = .05$

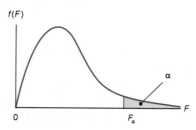

v_2 \ v_1	\multicolumn{9}{c}{**Numerator Degrees of Freedom**}
	1	**2**	**3**	**4**	**5**	**6**	**7**	**8**	**9**
1	161.4	199.5	215.7	224.6	230.2	234.0	236.8	238.9	240.5
2	18.51	19.00	19.16	19.25	19.30	19.33	19.35	19.37	19.38
3	10.13	9.55	9.28	9.12	9.01	8.94	8.89	8.85	8.81
4	7.71	6.94	6.59	6.39	6.26	6.16	6.09	6.04	6.00
5	6.61	5.79	5.41	5.19	5.05	4.95	4.88	4.82	4.77
6	5.99	5.14	4.76	4.53	4.39	4.28	4.21	4.15	4.10
7	5.59	4.74	4.35	4.12	3.97	3.87	3.79	3.73	3.68
8	5.32	4.46	4.07	3.84	3.69	3.58	3.50	3.44	3.39
9	5.12	4.26	3.86	3.63	3.48	3.37	3.29	3.23	3.18
10	4.96	4.10	3.71	3.48	3.33	3.22	3.14	3.07	3.02

Denominator Degrees of Freedom

Decision Rule.   The purpose of calculating the F-statistic is to help us determine whether the value of SST is large enough to allow us to reject the null hypothesis. As you can see from the formula of the test statistic, if SST is large, then F is also large. It follows that we reject the null hypothesis only if F is large enough. Specifically, we reject H_0 only if

$$F > F_{\alpha, k-1, n-k}.$$

The rejection region for the present example is

$$F > F_{\alpha, k-1, n-k} = F_{.05, 2, 21} = 3.47.$$

Figure 13.3 depicts the sampling distribution, which shows the rejection region and the value of the test statistic. Since the value of the test statistic $F = 5.79$ falls into the rejection region, we reject the null hypothesis and conclude that differences exist in the weekly sales of the product among the three cities. If we assume that the three cities are similar in all respects, we may infer that there are differences in effectiveness among the three marketing approaches. The company should perform more analyses in the hope of determining which approach is likely to be the most successful.

The results of an analysis of variance test are usually reported in an analysis of variance (ANOVA) table. Table 13.4 shows the general organization of the ANOVA table, and Table 13.5 shows the specific ANOVA table for Example 13.1.

Notice that the ANOVA table reports the sum of SST and SSE. Not surprisingly, this quantity is called the **total sum of squares,** which is denoted $SS(\text{Total})$. That is,

$$SS(\text{Total}) = \sum_{j=1}^{k} \sum_{i=1}^{n_j} (x_{ij} - \bar{\bar{x}})^2,$$

and

$$SS(\text{Total}) = SST + SSE.$$

FIGURE 13.3   *SAMPLING DISTRIBUTION FOR EXAMPLE 13.1*

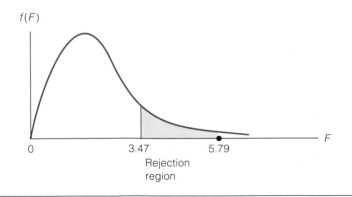

TABLE 13.4 GENERAL ORGANIZATION OF THE ANOVA TABLE

Source of Variability	Degrees of Freedom	Sum of Squares	Mean Squares	F-ratio
Between treatments	$k - 1$	SST	$MST = SST/(k - 1)$	$F = \dfrac{MST}{MSE}$
Within treatments	$n - k$	SSE	$MSE = SSE/(n - k)$	
TOTAL	$n - 1$	$SS(\text{Total})$		

TABLE 13.5 ANOVA TABLE FOR EXAMPLE 13.1

Source of Variability	Degrees of Freedom	Sum of Squares	Mean Squares	F-ratio
Between treatments	2	63.59	31.80	5.79
Within treatments	21	115.375	5.49	
TOTAL	23	178.965		

$SS(\text{Total})$ does not play any part in the test statistic. Its inclusion in the ANOVA table merely emphasizes that the test is based on decomposing the total variation of the data into two sources of variability: SST, which measures the variability between samples; and SSE, which measures the variability within samples.

Before doing another example let's summarize what we know about the analysis of variance.

Factors that Identify the Analysis of Variance

1. *Problem objective:* compare two or more populations
2. *Data type:* quantitative

Hypotheses
$$H_0: \mu_1 = \mu_2 = \cdots = \mu_k.$$
H_A: At least two means differ.

Test Statistic

$$SST = \sum_{j=1}^{k} n_j(\bar{x}_j - \bar{\bar{x}})^2$$

$$SSE = \sum_{j=1}^{k} (n_j - 1)s_j^2$$

$$MST = \frac{SST}{k-1}$$

$$MSE = \frac{SSE}{n-k}$$

$$F = \frac{MST}{MSE}$$

Decision Rule

Reject H_0 if $F > F_{\alpha, k-1, n-k}$.

EXAMPLE 13.2

A department-store chain is considering building a new store at one of four different sites. One important factor in the decision is the average annual household income of the residents of the four areas. Suppose that, in a preliminary study, various residents in each area are asked what their annual household incomes are. The results of this survey are shown in the accompanying table. Is there sufficient evidence to allow us to conclude that differences exist in average annual household incomes among the four communities? (Use $\alpha = .01$.)

ANNUAL HOUSEHOLD INCOMES ($1,000s)

Area 1	Area 2	Area 3	Area 4
25	32	27	18
27	35	32	23
31	30	48	29
17	46	25	26
29	32	20	42
30	22	12	
	19	18	
	51		
	27		

Solution. The problem objective is to compare four populations, and the data type is quantitative. The appropriate statistical technique to be used is the analysis of variance, as follows:

$H_0: \mu_1 = \mu_2 = \mu_3 = \mu_4.$

$H_A:$ At least two means differ.

Significance level: $\alpha = .01$

Decision Rule: Reject H_0 if $F > F_{\alpha, k-1, n-k} = F_{.01, 3, 23} = 4.76.$

Value of the Test Statistic:

Sample 1

$$\sum x_i = 159 \qquad \sum x_i^2 = 4345$$

$$\bar{x}_1 = \frac{159}{6} = 26.5$$

$$s_1^2 = \frac{4345 - \left(\frac{159}{6}\right)^2}{5} = 26.3.$$

Sample 2

$$\sum x_i = 294 \qquad \sum x_i^2 = 10,464$$

$$\bar{x}_2 = \frac{294}{9} = 32.67$$

$$s_2^2 = \frac{10,464 - \left(\frac{294}{9}\right)^2}{8} = 107.5.$$

Sample 3

$$\sum x_i = 182 \qquad \sum x_i^2 = 5550$$

$$\bar{x}_3 = \frac{182}{7} = 26.0$$

$$s_3^2 = \frac{5550 - \left(\frac{182}{7}\right)^2}{6} = 136.33.$$

Sample 4

$$\sum x_i = 138 \qquad \sum x_i^2 = 4134$$

$$\bar{x}_4 = \frac{138}{5} = 27.6$$

$$s_4^2 = \frac{4134 - \left(\frac{138}{5}\right)^2}{4} = 81.3.$$

Grand Mean

$$\bar{\bar{x}} = \frac{159 + 294 + 182 + 138}{6 + 9 + 7 + 5} = \frac{773}{27} = 28.63.$$

Between-Treatments Variation

$$SST = \sum_{j=1}^{4} n_j(\bar{x}_j - \bar{\bar{x}})^2$$

$$= 6(26.5 - 28.63)^2 + 9(32.67 - 28.63)^2$$
$$+ 7(26.0 - 28.63)^2 + 5(27.6 - 28.63)^2$$

$$= 227.84.$$

Within-Treatments Variation

$$SSE = \sum_{j=1}^{4} (n_j - 1)s_j^2$$

$$= 5(26.3) + 8(107.5) + 6(136.33) + 4(81.3)$$

$$= 2134.68.$$

Mean Squares

$$MST = \frac{SST}{k-1} = \frac{227.84}{4-1} = 75.95$$

$$MSE = \frac{SSE}{n-k} = \frac{2134.68}{27-4} = 92.81.$$

F-Statistic

$$F = \frac{MST}{MSE} = \frac{75.95}{92.81} = .82.$$

Conclusion: Do not reject H_0.

There is not enough evidence to allow us to conclude that average annual household incomes differ among the four communities. The department-store chain's management would be advised to ignore household income as a factor in its decision about the new store location. Figure 13.4 depicts this test.

FIGURE 13.4   SAMPLING DISTRIBUTION FOR EXAMPLE 13.2

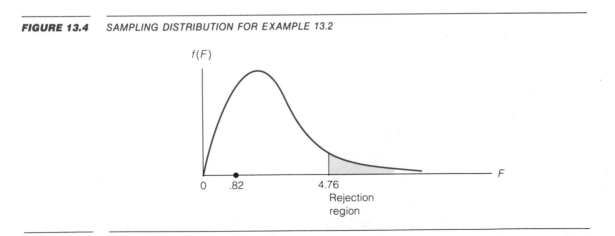

MINITAB COMPUTER OUTPUT FOR EXAMPLE 13.2*

```
ANALYSIS OF VARIANCE
SOURCE    DF      SS       MS      F
FACTOR     3     227.6    75.9    0.82
ERROR     23    2134.7    92.8
TOTAL     26    2362.3


LEVEL     N     MEAN     STDEV
  C1      6    26.500    5.128
  C2      9    32.667   10.368
  C3      7    26.000   11.676
  C4      5    27.600    9.017
```

The first part of the output includes the ANOVA table. The between-treatments variability is called the `FACTOR`; the within-treatments variability is labeled `ERROR`. The second half of the output shows the sample sizes n_j, the sample means $\bar{x}_j$, and the sample standard deviations s_j.

▬▬▬▬▬▬   **EXERCISES**

LEARNING THE TECHNIQUES

13.1 Application of the analysis of variance to a particular problem has resulted in the following ANOVA table:

Source	DF	SS	MS	F
Treatment	2	457.1241	228.5621	52.74
Error	17	117.0165	4.3339	

Complete the test at a significance level of 5%.

13.2 Complete the following ANOVA table, and test with $\alpha = .01$.

Source	DF	SS	MS	F
Treatment	2	1.0214		
Error	12	1.2159		

13.3 Given the following information, complete the ANOVA table; then conduct the F-test with $\alpha = .05$:

$SST = 581.6$

$SSE = 470.4$

$\quad k = 3$

$n_1 = n_2 = n_3 = 10.$

13.4 Given the following information, complete the test of the analysis of variance at a significance level of 1%:

$SST = 254.57$

$SSE = 214.29$

$\quad k = 4$

$n_1 = n_2 = n_3 = n_4 = 7.$

---

* See Appendix 13.A for the Minitab commands that produced this printout.

13.5   Given the following information, perform an analysis of variance test with $\alpha = .05$:

	Treatment		
	1	2	3
n	26	31	18
$\sum x_i$	537	718	454
$\sum x_i^2$	13,470	19,256	13,007

13.6   An analysis of variance experiment produced the statistics that follow. Determine the ANOVA table.

		Treatment		
	1	2	3	4
n	16	16	16	16
$\bar{x}$	158.6	149.2	151.3	157.6
s^2	95.3	102.1	96.8	99.1

13.7   The following statistics were generated by sampling from four normal populations. Do these statistics provide enough evidence at the 5% significance level to allow us to conclude that differences exist among the four population means?

		Treatment		
	1	2	3	4
n	11	11	11	11
$\sum x_i$	653	712	507	698
$\sum x_i^2$	40,975	48,210	25,493	46,431

13.8   Using the following statistics, test with $\alpha = .01$ to determine whether differences exist among the population means:

$n_1 = 49$ $n_2 = 45$ $n_3 = 29$

$\bar{x}_1 = 8.36$ $\bar{x}_2 = 7.91$ $\bar{x}_3 = 9.03$

$s_1 = 2.98$ $s_2 = 3.15$ $s_3 = 3.62$.

13.9   Given the following statistics, test at the 1% significance level to determine whether differences exist among the population means.

$n_1 = 31$ $n_2 = 31$ $n_3 = 31$ $n_4 = 31$

$\bar{x}_1 = 122$ $\bar{x}_2 = 159$ $\bar{x}_3 = 144$ $\bar{x}_4 = 139$

$s_1 = 22$ $s_2 = 31$ $s_3 = 33$ $s_4 = 28$.

APPLYING THE TECHNIQUES

Self-Correcting Exercise (See Appendix 13.B for the solution.)

13.10   The management of a computer company that has previously specialized in the home computer market wishes to expand into business applications. In order to determine which areas of business are most likely to purchase their computers and software, a preliminary survey was performed. A total of 150 middle managers were randomly selected, 50 of whom were in the banking industry, 50 from resource-based companies, and the remaining 50 from retail companies. Each was asked how many hours per week he or she spent working on a computer at the office. The computer company's management has decided that, if there is no evidence of differences among the industries, the company's marketing strategy will be to attempt to sell to all industries. If there are differences, however, it will tailor marketing and advertising toward the industry that uses the computer most. Based on the following statistics, what would you recommend? (Use $\alpha = .05$.)

$SST = 73.18$

$SSE = 1548.70$

13.11   An engineering student who is about to graduate decided to survey various firms in Silicon Valley to see which offered the best chance for early promotion and career advancement. In approaching 18 different high-tech firms, the student asked (among other things) how much time must elapse after the initial hiring before a really good technician can receive a promotion. Suspecting that there might be differences depending on whether it was a small new firm, a medium-size firm, or a large international firm, the student grouped the data by size of firm, as follows:

NUMBER OF WEEKS UNTIL FIRST PROMOTION

Small Firms	Medium Firms	Large Firms
30	30	49
26	34	42
30	32	43
38	25	48
32	36	40
24		49
32		

$\bar{x}_1 = 30.3$ $\bar{x}_2 = 31.4$ $\bar{x}_3 = 45.2$

$s_1 = 4.536$ $s_2 = 4.219$ $s_3 = 3.971$

Do these data provide sufficient evidence at the 1% significance level to indicate differences among the three sizes of firms?

13.12 The Internal Revenue Service (IRS) is always looking for ways to improve the wording and format of its tax return forms. Three new formats have been developed recently. To determine which, if any, are superior to the current form, 20 individuals were asked to participate in an experiment. Each of the three new forms and the old form were filled out by 5 different people. The amount of time taken by each person to complete the task is recorded in the accompanying table. At the 10% significance level, can we conclude that differences in completion times exist among the four forms?

COMPLETION TIMES (HOURS)

	New Forms		Current Form
A	B	C	D
9.2	12.6	7.5	6.3
8.6	10.9	9.3	9.8
10.3	11.8	8.8	10.1
11.4	10.8	7.8	8.5

	New Forms		Current Form
A	B	C	D
8.5	10.1	9.1	7.1
Sample means	9.60	11.24	8.50	8.36
Sample variances	1.525	.943	.645	2.739

13.13 Repeat Exercise 13.12 to test at the 10% significance level whether a difference exists between forms B and D.

13.14 Another way of determining the effectiveness of tax returns is to count the number of errors made by the taxpayer in filling out his or her return. An IRS tax auditor examined each of the 20 returns described in Exercise 13.12 and computed the number of errors. These data are shown next. At the 10% significance level, can we conclude that there are differences in the number of errors among the four forms?

NUMBER OF ERRORS

	New Forms		Current Form
A	B	C	D
3	1	6	4
5	3	8	1
6	2	3	0
2	4	3	6
1	1	2	2
$\sum x_i$ 17	11	22	13
$\sum x_i^2$ 75	31	122	57

13.15 Repeat Exercise 13.14 to test at the 10% significance level whether a difference exists between forms C and D.

13.16 Repeat Exercise 13.15, using the technique presented in Chapter 11.

ESTIMATING THE POPULATION MEANS

Although the primary function of the analysis of variance is to test for differences in treatment means, the results can also be used to estimate single population means and the difference between two means. In Chapter 8, we developed the confidence interval estimate of the population mean μ, when σ^2 is unknown. That formula is

$$\bar{x} \pm t_{\alpha/2, n-1} \frac{s}{\sqrt{n}},$$

where s is the estimator of the unknown population standard deviation σ.

We can use this formula to estimate each of the k population means that we dealt with in the analysis of variance. For example, we can determine $\bar{x}_1$ and s_1 and use these statistics to estimate μ_1 in Example 13.1. Turning back to Example 13.1 we find

$$\bar{x}_1 = 17.625$$

and

$$s_1 = 2.67.$$

The 95% confidence interval estimate of μ_1 is

$$\bar{x}_1 \pm t_{\alpha/2, n_1-1} \frac{s_1}{\sqrt{n}} = 17.625 \pm 2.365 \frac{2.67}{\sqrt{8}} = 17.625 \pm 2.23.$$

It is possible to improve on this estimate by using the calculations in the analysis of variance. Because we assumed that there was a common but unknown population variance, we calculated the common or pooled variability of the data, denoted SSE. When SSE is divided by its degrees of freedom, the result (MSE) is an estimator of the population variance. Since it is based on a larger sample size, however, the confidence interval estimator of μ_1 based on MSE is likely to be a better estimator than the one based solely on the data in the sample drawn from population 1. The confidence interval estimator of μ_1 based on all of the data is (note that the degrees of freedom are $n - k$)

$$\bar{x}_1 \pm t_{\alpha/2, n-k} \sqrt{\frac{MSE}{n_1}}.$$

Hence, the 95% confidence interval estimate of μ_1 is

$$17.625 \pm 2.080 \sqrt{\frac{5.49}{8}} = 17.625 \pm 1.72.$$

Notice that the interval that incorporates MSE is narrower (and thus better) than the one based on s_1.

Confidence Interval Estimate of μ_j

$$\bar{x}_j \pm t_{\alpha/2, n-k} \sqrt{\frac{MSE}{n_j}}.$$

We can also use all of the data to estimate the difference between two population means.

Confidence Interval Estimator of $\mu_j - \mu_m$

$$(\bar{x}_j - \bar{x}_m) \pm t_{\alpha/2, n-k} \sqrt{MSE\left(\frac{1}{n_j} + \frac{1}{n_m}\right)}$$

For example, the 95% confidence interval estimate of $\mu_1 - \mu_2$ from Example 13.1 is

$$(\bar{x}_1 - \bar{x}_2) \pm t_{.025, 21} \sqrt{MSE\left(\frac{1}{n_1} + \frac{1}{n_2}\right)}$$

$$= (17.625 - 13.75) \pm 2.080 \sqrt{5.49\left(\frac{1}{8} + \frac{1}{8}\right)}$$

$$= 3.875 \pm 2.44.$$

Thus, the 95% confidence interval estimate of $\mu_1 - \mu_2$ is

$$LCL = 1.435 \qquad \text{and} \qquad UCL = 6.315$$

▬▬▬▬▬▬ **EXERCISES**

LEARNING THE TECHNIQUES

13.17 Suppose that you are given the following treatment means and sample sizes:

$\bar{x}_1 = -2.150 \qquad n_1 = 5$

$\bar{x}_2 = 5.147 \qquad n_2 = 7$

$\bar{x}_3 = 6.021 \qquad n_3 = 6.$

With $MSE = 44.8101$, compute 95% confidence intervals for μ_1, μ_2, and μ_3.

13.18 For Exercise 13.3, suppose that we've calculated the following sample means:

$\bar{x}_1 = 17.6 \qquad \bar{x}_2 = 8.8 \qquad \bar{x}_3 = 18.6.$

Compute the 99% confidence interval estimates of

a. μ_1

b. μ_2

c. $\mu_1 - \mu_2$

d. $\mu_1 - \mu_3$

13.19 For Exercise 13.4, suppose that the following sample means were computed:

$\bar{x}_1 = 23.714 \qquad \bar{x}_2 = 29.714$

$\bar{x}_3 = 31.000 \qquad \bar{x}_4 = 25.286.$

Find the 90% confidence interval estimates of

a. μ_1

b. μ_3

c. $\mu_1 - \mu_2$

d. $\mu_2 - \mu_3$

13.20 Suppose that you are given the following statistics:

$\bar{x}_1 = 3.21 \qquad n_1 = 5$

$\bar{x}_2 = 5.78 \qquad n_2 = 8$

$\bar{x}_3 = 4.19 \qquad n_3 = 7$

$\bar{x}_4 = 6.01 \qquad n_4 = 4.$

With $MSE = 34.12$, compute 95% confidence interval estimates of

a. μ_1 c. $\mu_2 - \mu_3$

b. μ_4 d. $\mu_2 - \mu_4$

13.21 The observations that follow were drawn from three normally distributed populations whose variances are equal.

Treatment		
1	2	3
7	15	8
9	11	15
16	12	21
3	4	18
	8	19
	6	

The following statistics were produced:

$SST = 168.9 \qquad SSE = 274.9.$

Compute 90% confidence interval estimates of

a. μ_1

b. $\mu_1 - \mu_3$

13.22 For Exercise 13.21, use the formulas shown in Chapters 8 and 10 to find 90% confidence interval estimates of

a. μ_1

b. $\mu_1 - \mu_3$

13.23 Compare the results of Exercises 13.21 and 13.22.

APPLYING THE TECHNIQUES

Self-Correcting Exercise (See Appendix 13.B for the solution.)

13.24 Refer to Exercise 13.10. The sample means were computed as follows:

Small Firms	Medium Firms	Large Firms
$\bar{x}_1 = 13.163$	$\bar{x}_2 = 12.308$	$\bar{x}_3 = 14.018$

a. Estimate with 90% confidence the mean promotion time for large firms.

b. Estimate with 90% confidence the differences in mean promotion times between large and small firms.

13.25 In attempting to compare the returns on four different types of stocks trading on the New York Stock Exchange, an investor selected a random sample from each category and computed the rates of return. Prior to conducting an analysis of variance test, he computed the following statistics:

$SST = 438.1$

$SSE = 2,834.4$

$\bar{x}_1 = 11.04 \quad \bar{x}_2 = 14.51 \quad \bar{x}_3 = 7.12 \quad \bar{x}_4 = 12.88$

$n_1 = 14 \qquad n_2 = 20 \qquad n_3 = 12 \qquad n_4 = 18.$

a. Do these data provide sufficient evidence to allow the investor to conclude that the rates of return differ among the four stock types? (Use $\alpha = .05$.)

b. Suppose that the investor decides to invest in type 3 stocks. Determine a 99% confidence interval estimate of the mean percentage return for this type of stock.

c. After further consideration, the investor decides that type 2 stocks are less risky than type 3 stocks. He would therefore like to know the difference between their mean returns. Determine a 90% confidence interval estimate of the difference between the mean returns of type 2 and type 3 stocks.

13.26 For Exercise 13.12, estimate with 99% confidence

a. the mean completion time for the current form

b. the difference in mean completion time between form C and the current form

---

SECTION 13.4

SUMMARY

The analysis of variance allows us to test for differences among populations when the data are quantitative. We report the results in an analysis of variance table, which among other things shows the value of the F-statistic. The results can also be used to produce confidence interval estimates of the population means and the difference between any two population means.

IMPORTANT TERMS

Analysis of variance
Treatment means
Grand mean
Between-treatments variability
Sum of squares for treatments
Within-treatments variability
Sum of squares for errors

Total sum of squares
Mean squares
Mean square for treatments
Mean square for errors
F-distribution
F-statistic
ANOVA table

FORMULAS

$$SST = \sum_{j=1}^{k} n_j(\bar{\bar{x}}_j - \bar{x})^2$$

$$SSE = \sum_{j=1}^{k} \sum_{i=1}^{n_j} (x_{ij} - \bar{x}_j)^2 = \sum_{j=1}^{k} (n_j - 1)s_j^2$$

$$MST = \frac{SST}{n - k}$$

$$MSE = \frac{SSE}{k - 1}$$

$$F = \frac{MST}{MSE} \qquad \begin{array}{l} v_1 = k - 1 \\ v_2 = n - k \end{array}$$

$$\bar{x}_j \pm t_{\alpha/2, n-k}\sqrt{\frac{MSE}{n_j}}$$

$$(\bar{x}_j - \bar{x}_m) \pm t_{\alpha/2, n-k}\sqrt{MSE\left(\frac{1}{n_j} + \frac{1}{n_m}\right)}$$

SUPPLEMENTARY EXERCISES

13.27 Police cars, ambulances, and other emergency vehicles are required to carry road flares. One of the most important features of flares is their burning time. In a preliminary study to help decide which of four brands of flares to use, a police laboratory measured the burning times of 5 flares of each brand. The results, recorded to the nearest minute, are shown in the accompanying table. Is there sufficient evidence at the 5% significance level to indicate that differences exist among the four brands?

BURNING TIME *(minutes)*

	Brand		
1	2	3	4
16	15	14	18
19	20	19	22
22	18	16	19
21	16	12	23

	Brand		
1	2	3	4
23	14	15	20
$\bar{x}$ 20.2	16.6	15.2	20.4
s 2.775	2.408	2.588	2.074

13.28 For Exercise 13.27, estimate the following with 90% confidence

a. the mean burning time for brand 4

b. the difference in mean burning times between brands 3 and 4

13.29 In marketing children's products, it's extremely important to produce television commercials that hold the attention of the children who view them. A psychologist hired by a marketing research firm wants to determine whether differences in generated attention span exist among advertisements for different types of products. Fifteen children under 10 years of age are asked to watch one 60-second commercial for one of three types of products, and their attention spans are measured in seconds. The results are shown next. Do these data provide enough evidence to conclude that there are differences in generated attention span among the three products advertised? (Use $\alpha = .05$.)

CHILDREN'S ATTENTION SPANS (seconds)

Type of Product Advertised		
Toys/Games	Food/Candy	Children's Clothing
42	55	30
45	58	35
48	52	42
40	60	32
50	57	38

$SST = 1{,}105.20$

$SSE = 196.40$

13.30 Henry Blank is trying to choose a university to attend in order to get his MBA. Since money is the only thing that matters to him, he has decided to judge schools on the basis of the average annual salary their graduates receive one year after graduation. If there are differences, Henry will attend the university with the highest average income. If there is no evidence of a difference, he will select the U. of A., because he likes the school song. A random sample of the annual salaries of graduates of each of the four universities that have accepted him is shown in the accompanying table. What should Henry do? (Use $\alpha = .05$.)

ANNUAL SALARY ($1,000s)

U. of A.	U. of B.	U. of C.	U. of D.
24	41	27	19
18	38	26	22
19	29	29	33
28	24	33	40
22	28	22	27

U. of A.	U. of B.	U. of C.	U. of D.
33	18	25	26
27	22	31	19
21		27	33
43			32
			21
			20

$SST = 28.56$

$SSE = 1{,}507.33$

13.31 The possible imposition of a residential property tax has been a sensitive political issue in a large city that consists of five boroughs. Currently, property tax is based on an assessment system that dates back to 1950. This system has produced numerous inequities whereby newer homes tend to be assessed higher values than older homes. A new system has been proposed that is based on the market value of the house. Opponents of the plan argue that residents of some boroughs would have to pay considerably more on the average, while residents of other boroughs would pay less. As part of a study examining this issue, several homes in each borough were assessed under both plans. The percentage increase or decrease in each case is recorded in the accompanying table. Can we conclude at the 5% significance level that there are differences in the effect the new assessment system would have on the five boroughs?

PERCENTAGE CHANGE IN ASSESSMENT

Borough				
1	2	3	4	5
7	22	7	−2	7
16	18	10	12	10
5	10	12	18	15
17	14	11	14	11
8	9	18	0	14
14	16	21	20	12
12	18	14	16	18

Borough				
1	2	3	4	5
-1	11	10	12	7
3	7	11	15	0
	12	15	11	9
	15	17	19	8
		16		-3

$SST = 244.38$

$SSE = 1,594.38$

13.32 For many years automobile insurance companies have charged young men especially high premiums, reflecting this group's relatively poor driving record. An executive in the insurance industry believes that different premiums should be charged according to age for all drivers, because drivers in some age groups drive considerably more than others. To examine this issue, 50 young (25–40), 50 middle-age (40–55) and 50 older (over 55) drivers were questioned concerning the number of miles they drove in the previous 12 months. The results are summarized in the following table. Do these data allow us to conclude at the 1% significance level that there are differences in miles driven among the three age groups?

MILES DRIVEN (1,000s), BY AGE

	Age of Driver		
	Young	Middle-age	Older
$\sum x_i$	830.3	855.4	548.8
$\sum x_i^2$	14,263.7	15,049.1	6,599.1

13.33 For Exercise 13.32 estimate the following with 95% confidence:

a. the mean miles driven by young drivers

b. the difference in mean miles driven between young and older drivers

13.34 An economist wants to determine whether differences exist among the salaries of university professors in different departments. In a prelimi-

nary study, she took a random sample of six professors from each of the departments of business, history, and psychology. These data are shown in the following table. Can she conclude at the 5% significance level that differences exist among the salaries in the three departments?

SALARIES ($1,000s)

	Business	History	Psychology
	48	28	37
	56	48	43
	33	62	28
	41	45	48
	60	39	51
	52	43	40
$\bar{x}$	48.333	44.167	41.167
s	9.973	11.161	8.232

$SST = 155.4$

$SSE = 1,459.0$

13.35 For Exercise 13.34, estimate the following with 95% confidence:

a. the mean salary of business professors

b. the difference in mean salary between business and psychology professors

13.36 In a recent report, a group of scientists claimed that Americans consume an excessive amount of selenium in their diets. The National Science Foundation has stated that the safe upper limit is 200 micrograms per day. In order to determine the extent of the problem, researchers drew samples of people from each of five widely separated cities and measured their daily consumption of selenium. The researchers decided that, if there were no differences among the cities, there must be numerous sources of selenium in the diet. On the other hand, if differences exist, the sources may be quite localized. From the data in Table E13.36, what conclusions can be drawn? (Use $\alpha = .05$.)

TABLE E13.36 DAILY SELENIUM INTAKE (MICROGRAMS)

	New York	Minneapolis	San Diego	Dallas	Atlanta
	227	181	175	221	183
	183	163	166	183	225
	219	175	188	195	228
	248	189	195	188	203
	163	193	175	203	195
	175	188	171	201	198
$\bar{x}$	202.50	181.50	178.33	198.50	205.33
s	33.58	11.10	10.95	13.38	17.69

$SST = 3,718$

$SSE = 9,315$

13.37 Some restaurants seem to prefer to hire older waiters and waitresses, while others seem to prefer younger ones. To help establish hiring policies for a large restaurant chain, a management consultant wanted to determine whether restaurant customers generally prefer younger or older waiters and waitresses. She decided that a reasonable measure of a customer's satisfaction is the size of the tip that the customer leaves. The consultant took a random sample of seven young (20–30), seven middle-age (40–50), and seven older (55–65) waiters and waitresses and measured the percentage of the total bill left as a tip during one evening. The resulting data appear in the accompanying table. Can the consultant conclude at the 10% significance level that there are differences in the tips left to the three age groups?

PERCENTAGE TIPS

	Young	Middle-age	Older
	14.5	13.3	9.8
	10.9	16.5	10.6
	11.6	12.4	8.5
	9.8	10.9	10.6
	11.9	11.6	11.1
	12.6	13.5	9.8
	11.1	12.8	9.2
$\bar{x}$	11.771	13.000	9.943
s	1.487	1.796	0.902

$SST = 33.13$

$SSE = 37.51$

■■■■■■■ **CASE 13.1*** **DIVERSIFICATION STRATEGY FOR**
MULTINATIONAL COMPANIES

One of the many goals of management researchers is to identify factors that differentiate between success and failure and among different levels of success in businesses. In this way it may be possible to help more businesses become successful. Among

---

* Adapted from J. M. Geringer, P. W. Beamish, and R. C. da Costa, "Diversification Strategy and Internationalization: Implications for MNE Performance," *Strategic Management Journal* 10 (1989): 109–19.

multinational enterprises (MNEs), two factors to be examined are the degree of product diversification and the degree of internationalization. *Product diversification* refers to efforts by companies to increase the range and the variety of products produced. The more unrelated the products are, the greater is the degree of diversification created. *Internationalization* is a term for expressing geographic diversification. Companies that sell their products to many countries are said to employ a high degree of internationalization.

Three management researchers set out to examine these issues. In particular they wanted to test two hypotheses:

1. MNEs employing strategies that result in more product diversification outperform those with less product diversification.
2. MNEs employing strategies that result in more internationalization outperform those with less internationalization.

Company performance was measured in two ways:

1. *Profit-to-sales* is the ratio of profit to total sales, expressed as a percentage.
2. *Profit-to-assets* is the ratio of profit to total assets, expressed as a percentage.

A random sample of 189 companies was selected. For each company, the profit-to-sales and profit-to-assets ratios were measured. In addition, each company was judged to have a low (1), medium (2), or high (3) level of diversification. The degree of internationalization was measured on a 5-point scale, where 1 = Lowest level and 5 = Highest level. For each diversification category and each internationalization category, the mean and the variance of profit-to-sales and profit-to-assets were computed. The resulting statistics are shown in the accompanying tables. What do these results tell you about the researchers' hypotheses?

TABLE A   PROFIT-TO-SALES

	Diversification		
	1	2	3
Sample size	41	85	63
Mean	4.884	3.554	2.291
Variance	11.343	8.521	19.184

TABLE B   PROFIT-TO-SALES

	Internalization				
	1	2	3	4	5
Sample size	53	63	39	22	12
Mean	3.194	3.084	3.552	4.634	3.553
Variance	14.304	15.390	8.283	11.662	20.757

TABLE C PROFIT-TO-ASSETS

	Diversification		
	1	2	3
Sample size	41	85	63
Mean	6.030	4.630	3.320
Variance	20.803	11.972	27.563

TABLE D PROFIT-TO-ASSETS

	Internalization				
	1	2	3	4	5
Sample size	53	63	39	22	12
Mean	4.088	4.388	4.798	4.969	5.034
Variance	17.356	25.150	22.877	8.497	18.276

MINITAB INSTRUCTIONS

The command

```
AOVONEWAY C1-C3
```

performs the analysis of variance to compare the population means for the sample data stored in columns 1, 2, and 3. The following series of keyboard entries will perform the analysis of variance for Example 13.2:

```
SET C1
25 27 31 17 29 30
END
SET C2
32 35 30 46 32 22 19 51 27
END
SET C3
27 32 48 25 20 12 18
END
SET C4
18 23 29 26 42
END
AOVONEWAY C1-C4
```

The resulting output is

```
ANALYSIS OF VARIANCE
SOURCE     DF        SS       MS       F
FACTOR     3      227.6     75.9    0.82
ERROR     23     2134.7     92.8
TOTAL     26     2362.3
```

SOLUTIONS TO SELF-CORRECTING EXERCISES

13.10 $H_0: \mu_1 = \mu_2 = \mu_3$.

H_A: At least two means differ.

Test statistic: $F = \dfrac{MST}{MSE}$

Significance level: $\alpha = .05$

Decision rule: Reject H_0 if

$F > F_{\alpha, k-1, n-k} = F_{.05, 2, 147} \approx 3.07$

Value of the test statistic:

Source	DF	SS	MS	F
Treatments	2	73.18	36.59	3.47
Error	147	1548.70	10.54	

Conclusion: Reject H_0.

There is enough evidence to allow us to conclude that differences in computer use exist among the three industries surveyed.

13.24 a. $\bar{x}_3 \pm t_{\alpha/2, n-k} \sqrt{\dfrac{MSE}{n_3}}$

$= 14.018 \pm 1.645 \sqrt{\dfrac{10.54}{50}}$

$= 14.018 \pm .755$.

The mean promotion time for large firms is estimated to lie between 13.263 and 14.773 weeks.

b. $(\bar{x}_3 - \bar{x}_1) \pm t_{\alpha/2, n-k} \sqrt{MSE\left(\dfrac{1}{n_3} + \dfrac{1}{n_1}\right)}$

$= (14.018 - 13.163) \pm 1.645 \sqrt{10.54\left(\dfrac{1}{50} + \dfrac{1}{50}\right)}$

$= .855 \pm 1.068$.

The difference in mean promotion times between large and small firms is estimated to lie between $-.213$ and 1.923 weeks.

CHI-SQUARE TESTS

INTRODUCTION

This chapter develops two statistical techniques that involve qualitative data. The first is a **goodness-of-fit test** applied to data produced by a multinomial experiment—which is a generalization of a binomial experiment. The second uses data arranged in a table (called a **contingency table**) to determine whether or not two classifications of a population of qualitative data are statistically independent; this test can also be interpreted as a comparison of two or more populations.

The sampling distribution of the test statistics in both tests is identical—the chi-square distribution, which is presented in the next section.

Following are two examples of situations in which chi-square tests could be applied:

1. Firms periodically estimate the proportion (or market share) of consumers who prefer their product, as well as the market shares of competitors. These market shares may change over time as a result of advertising compaigns or the introduction of new and improved products. To determine whether the actual current market shares are in accord with its beliefs, a firm might sample several consumers and compute, for each of k competing companies, the proportion of consumers sampled who prefer that company's product. Such an experiment, in which each consumer is classified as perferring one of the k companies, is called a *multinomial experiment*. If only two companies were considered ($k = 2$), we would be dealing with the familiar binomial experiment. After computing the proportion of consumers preferring each of the k companies, a goodness-of-fit test could be conducted to determine whether or not the sample proportions (or market shares) differ significantly from those hypothesized by the firm. The problem objective is to describe the population of consumers, and the data are qualitative.

2. For advertising and other purposes, it is important for a company to understand which segments of the market prefer which of its products. For example, it would be helpful for an automotive manufacturer to know if there is a relationship between the buyer preferences for its various models and the sex of the consumer. After conducting a survey to solicit consumers' preferences, the firm could classify each respondent according to two qualitative variables: model preferred and sex. A test could then be conducted to determine whether consumers' preferences are independent of their sex. Rather than interpreting this test as a test of the independence of two qualitative variables defined over a single population, we could view male and female consumers as representing two different populations.

Then we could interpret the test as testing for differences in preferences between these two populations.

CHI-SQUARE TEST OF A MULTINOMIAL EXPERIMENT

This section presents another test designed to describe a single population of qualitative data. The first such test was presented in Chapter 10, where we discussed inferences concerning the population proportion p. In that case, the data for the statistical tests were provided by a binomial experiment. Recall that the result of each trial of a binomial experiment is measured on the basis of categories such as defective or nondefective and favor or disfavor. In some important experiments (called *multinomial experiments*), however, the result of each trial is measured by qualitative data involving more than two categories. For example, apparel produced by a machine may be classified as having a tear, improper stitching, or no defects. Or a consumer might prefer product A, B, C, or D. A **multinomial experiment** is a generalized version of a binomial experiment that allows for more than two possible outcomes on each trial of the experiment.

> **Multinomial Experiment**
>
> A **multinomial experiment** is one possessing the following properties:
>
> 1. The experiment consists of a fixed number n of trials.
> 2. The outcome of each trial can be classified into exactly one of k categories, called **cells.**
> 3. The probability p_i that the outcome of a trial will fall into cell i remains constant for each trial, for $i = 1, 2, \ldots, k$. Moreover, $p_1 + p_2 + \cdots + p_k = 1$.
> 4. Each trial of the experiment is independent of the other trials.

Just as we count the number of successes and failures in the n trials of a binomial experiment, we count the number of outcomes falling into each of the k cells in a multinomial experiment. We thereby obtain a set of observed frequencies $O_1, O_2, \ldots, O_k$, where O_i is the **observed frequency** of outcomes falling into cell i, for $i = 1, 2, \ldots, k$. Since an outcome must fall into some cell,

$$O_1 + O_2 + \cdots + O_k = n$$

These observed frequencies may then be used to test hypotheses about the values of the probabilities $p_i (i = 1, 2, \ldots, k)$.

As an illustration, consider Willy Winn, the bookie, who is searching for ways to improve the profitability of his business. He regularly establishes odds and accepts bets on races at the local racetrack, which runs six horses in each race. Willy believes that some post positions may be more favorable than others, so that horses starting in these post positions win more frequently than horses starting in other positions. If this hunch is correct, he can use the information to advantage in setting his odds.

The population in question is the population of winning post positions for all races at this track. Although the data may appear at first glance to be quantitative, they are in fact qualitative. The numbers from one to six simply give unique names to each of the post positions. The relevant parameters are the probabilities $p_1, p_2, \ldots, p_6$ that post positions 1 to 6 are the winning positions. To test Willy's belief, we will have the null hypothesis specify that each post position is equally likely to win. That means that each of the probabilities $p_1, p_2, \ldots, p_6$ equals $1/6$. Thus,

$$H_0: p_1 = 1/6, \ p_2 = 1/6, \ p_3 = 1/6, \ p_4 = 1/6, \ p_5 = 1/6, \ p_6 = 1/6.$$

Because we want to know if at least one post position wins more frequently than the others, the alternative hypothesis is:

H_A: At least one p_i is not equal to the specified value.

To test these hypotheses, Willy has obtained the results of a random sample of 300 races and counted the number of times each post position was the winning position. These observed frequencies O_i are recorded in Table 14.1. We proceed, as usual, by assuming that the null hypothesis is true. In that case, we would expect each of the post positions to win one-sixth of the time; and since $n = 300$, our expectation under H_0 would be that each position won $300(1/6) = 50$ times. In general, the **expected frequency** for each post position is given by

$$E_i = np_i.$$

This expression is based on the formula for the expected value of a binomial random variable:

$$E(X) = np.$$

TABLE 14.1   RESULTS OF 300 RACES

Post Position i	Observed Frequency O_i
1	44
2	65
3	42
4	60
5	46
6	43
TOTAL	300

TEST STATISTIC

Table 14.2 summarizes the observed frequencies O_i and the expected frequencies E_i. If the null hypothesis is true, the observed and expected frequencies should be similar. (Because we're dealing with random variables, they wouldn't be required—or expected—to be identical.) If there are large differences between the observed and expected frequencies, however, this would cast doubt on the null hypothesis, and we would reject H_0 in favor of H_A. The test statistic for judging this is

$$\chi^2 = \sum_{i=1}^{k} \frac{(O_i - E_i)^2}{E_i}.$$

SAMPLING DISTRIBUTION OF THE TEST STATISTIC

The test statistic we have just defined is labeled χ^2 because it follows a distribution known as the χ^2 **distribution.** The shape of the distribution depends on the number of degrees of freedom it possesses, which in this application is

d.f. $= k - 1$,

where k is the number of values of the qualitative variable. (In this case $k = 6$ post positions.) Figure 14.1 depicts several chi-square distributions with different degrees of freedom. We use the same type of notation that we previously used for the standard normal and Student t distributions. That is, we let $\chi^2_{\alpha,v}$ represent the χ^2 value (with v degrees of freedom) such that the area to its right is equal to α (see Figure 14.2).

Table 8 in Appendix B, reproduced here as Table 14.3, provides values of $\chi^2_{\alpha,v}$ for various degrees of freedom and values of α. For example,

$$\chi^2_{.05,2} = 5.99147$$

is the χ^2 value with 2 degrees of freedom such that the area to its right is .05.

TABLE 14.2 COMPUTATION OF χ^2 FOR 300 HORSE RACES

Post Position i	Observed Frequency O_i	Expected Frequency E_i	$(O_i - E_i)^2$	$\dfrac{(O_i - E_i)^2}{E_i}$
1	44	50	36	.72
2	65	50	225	4.50
3	42	50	64	1.28
4	60	50	100	2.00
5	46	50	16	.32
6	43	50	49	.98
TOTAL	300	300		$\chi^2 = 9.80$

FIGURE 14.1   CHI-SQUARE DISTRIBUTIONS

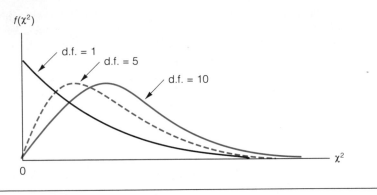

FIGURE 14.2   CHI-SQUARE DISTRIBUTION SHOWING χ_α^2

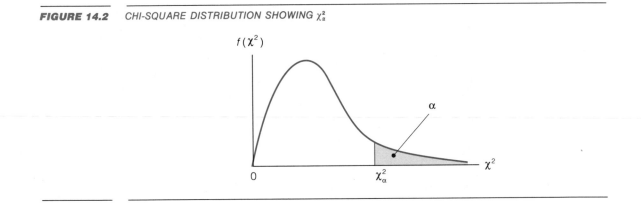

DECISION RULE

The test statistic

$$\chi^2 = \sum_{i=1}^{k} \frac{(O_i - E_i)^2}{E_i}$$

is small if the observed and expected values are similar. Hence a small χ^2 supports the null hypothesis. A large value of χ^2 is the result of some large differences between the observed and expected values. Thus we wish to reject the null hypothesis whenever χ^2 is too large. The decision rule is

Reject H_0 if $\chi^2 > \chi_{\alpha, k-1}^2$.

In this example, we reject H_0 if

$$\chi^2 > \chi_{.05, 5}^2 = 11.0705$$

TABLE 14.3   CRITICAL VALUES OF THE χ^2 DISTRIBUTION

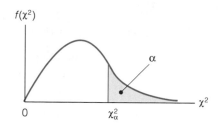

Degrees of Freedom	$\chi^2_{.100}$	$\chi^2_{.050}$	$\chi^2_{.025}$	$\chi^2_{.010}$	$\chi^2_{.005}$
1	2.70554	3.84146	5.02389	6.63490	7.87944
2	4.60517	5.99147	7.37776	9.21034	10.5966
3	6.25139	7.81473	9.34840	11.3449	12.8381
4	7.77944	9.48773	11.1433	13.2767	14.8602
5	9.23635	11.0705	12.8325	15.0863	16.7496
6	10.6446	12.5916	14.4494	16.8119	18.5476
7	12.0170	14.0671	16.0128	18.4753	20.2777
8	13.3616	15.5073	17.5346	20.0902	21.9550
9	14.6837	16.9190	19.0228	21.6660	23.5893
10	15.9871	18.3070	20.4831	23.2093	25.1882
11	17.2750	19.6751	21.9200	24.7250	26.7569
12	18.5494	21.0261	23.3367	26.2170	28.2995
13	19.8119	22.3621	24.7356	27.6883	29.8194
14	21.0642	23.6848	26.1190	29.1413	31.3193
15	22.3072	24.9958	27.4884	30.5779	32.8013
16	23.5418	26.2962	28.8454	31.9999	34.2672
17	24.7690	27.5871	30.1910	33.4087	35.7185
18	25.9894	28.8693	31.5264	34.8053	37.1564
19	27.2036	30.1435	32.8523	36.1908	38.5822
20	28.4120	31.4104	34.1696	37.5662	39.9968
21	29.6151	32.6705	35.4789	38.9321	41.4010
22	30.8133	33.9244	36.7807	40.2894	42.7956
23	32.0069	35.1725	38.0757	41.6384	44.1813
24	33.1963	36.4151	39.3641	42.9798	45.5585
25	34.3816	37.6525	40.6465	44.3141	46.9278

(continued)

Degrees of Freedom	$\chi^2_{.100}$	$\chi^2_{.050}$	$\chi^2_{.025}$	$\chi^2_{.010}$	$\chi^2_{.005}$
26	35.5631	38.8852	41.9232	45.6417	48.2899
27	36.7412	40.1133	43.1944	46.9630	49.6449
28	37.9159	41.3372	44.4607	48.2782	50.9933
29	39.0875	42.5569	45.7222	49.5879	52.3356
30	40.2560	43.7729	46.9792	50.8922	53.6720
40	51.8050	55.7585	59.3417	63.6907	66.7659
50	63.1671	67.5048	71.4202	76.1539	79.4900
60	74.3970	79.0819	83.2976	88.3794	91.9517
70	85.5271	90.5312	95.0231	100.425	104.215
80	96.5782	101.879	106.629	112.329	116.321
90	107.565	113.145	118.136	124.116	128.299
100	118.498	124.342	129.561	135.807	140.169

From Table 14.2 we find, by using Willy's data, that the value of the test statistic is

$$\chi^2 = \frac{(44-50)^2}{50} + \frac{(65-50)^2}{50} + \cdots + \frac{(43-50)^2}{50} = 9.80.$$

Since the computed value of 9.80 does not exceed the critical value of 11.0705, insufficient evidence exists to allow us to conclude that some post positions are more favorable than others, at the 5% level of significance. Therefore, Willy cannot use the post position to help predict the winner of the race.

While it is common to test for no differences in the cell probabilities $p_1, p_2, \ldots, p_k$ (as we did in the foregoing example), we are not restricted to this formulation. Based on prior expectations, we may hypothesize a different value for each p_i, as long as they sum to 1. The following example illustrates such a test, in which the null hypothesis specifies values for the cell probabilities that differ from one another.

EXAMPLE 14.1

Two companies, A and B, have recently conducted aggressive advertising campaigns in order to maintain and possibly increase their respective shares of the market for a particular product. These two companies enjoy a dominant position in the market. Before the advertising campaigns began, the market share of company A was $p_1 = .45$, while company B had a market share of $p_2 = .40$. Other competitors accounted for the remaining market share of $p_3 = .15$. To determine whether these market shares changed after the advertising campaigns, a marketing analyst solicited the preferences

---

TABLE 14.4   RESULTS OF MARKET SURVEY

Company	Observed Frequency O_i
A	100
B	85
Others	15
TOTAL	200

---

of a random sample of 200 consumers of this product. Of the 200 consumers, 100 indicated a preference for company A's product, 85 preferred company B's product, and the remainder preferred one or another of the products distributed by the competitors. Table 14.4 reproduces the relevant data. Conduct a test to determine, at the 5% level of significance, whether the market shares have changed from the levels they were at before the advertising campaigns occurred.

Solution.   There is only one population (the population of preferences of all consumers), and the data are qualitative. The parameters of interest are the proportions of consumers preferring the product marketed by A, by B, and by the other competitors. Since we wish to determine whether or not the proportions have changed from their previous values, the alternative hypothesis states that at least one proportion has changed. We therefore have

$H_0: p_1 = .45, p_2 = .40, p_3 = .15$

H_A: At least one p_1 is not equal to its specified value.

Test statistic:

$$\chi^2 = \sum_{i=1}^{3} \frac{(O_i - E_i)^2}{E_i} \qquad \text{d.f.} = k - 1 = 3 - 1 = 2$$

Significance level: $\alpha = .05$

Decision rule: Reject H_0 if $\chi^2 > \chi^2_{\alpha, k-1} = \chi^2_{.05, 2} = 5.99147$.

Value of the test statistic: The expected values are

$E_1 = np_1 = 200(.45) = 90$

$E_2 = np_2 = 200(.40) = 80$

$E_3 = np_3 = 200(.15) = 30.$

The test statistic is

$$\chi^2 = \sum_{i=1}^{3} \frac{(O_i - E_i)^2}{E_i} = \frac{(100 - 90)^2}{90} + \frac{(85 - 80)^2}{80} + \frac{(15 - 30)^2}{30} = 8.92.$$

FIGURE 14.3   *SAMPLING DISTRIBUTION FOR EXAMPLE 14.1*

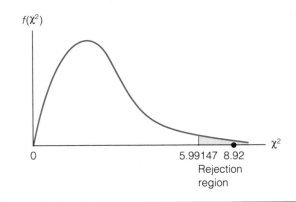

Conclusion: Reject H_0.

There is sufficient evidence at the 5% level of significance to allow us to conclude that the market shares have changed from the levels they were at before the advertising campaigns occurred. Figure 14.3 depicts this test.

RULE OF FIVE

The test statistic used to compare the relative sizes of observed and expected frequencies is

$$\chi^2 = \sum_{i=1}^{k} \frac{(O_i - E_i)^2}{E_i}.$$

We previously stated that this test statistic has an approximate chi-square distribution. In fact, the actual distribution of this test statistic is discrete, but it can be conveniently approximated by using a continous chi-square distribution when the sample size n is large, just as we approximated the discrete binomial distribution by using the normal distribution. This approximation may be poor, however, if the expected cell frequencies are small. For the (discrete) distribution of the test statistic χ^2 to be adequately approximated by the (continuous) chi-square distribution, the conventional (and conservative) rule—known as the **rule of five**—is to *require that the expected frequency for each cell be at least 5.** Where necessary, cells should be combined in order to satisfy this condition. The choice of cells to be combined should be made in such a way that meaningful categories result from the combination.

---

* To be on the safe side, this rule of thumb is somewhat conservative. A discussion of alternatives to the rule of five can be found in W. J. Conover, *Practical Nonparametric Statistics* (New York: John Wiley, 1971), p. 152, and in S. Siegel, *Nonparametric Statistics for the Behavioral Sciences* (New York: McGraw-Hill, 1956), p. 178.

Consider the following modification of Example 14.1. Suppose that three companies (A, B, and C) have recently conducted aggressive advertising campaigns; the market shares prior to the campaigns were $p_1 = .45$ for company A, $p_2 = .40$ for company B, $p_3 = .13$ for company C, and $p_4 = .02$ for other competitors. In a test to see if market shares changed after the advertising campaigns, the null hypothesis would now be

$$H_0: p_1 = .45, p_2 = .40, p_3 = .13, p_4 = .02.$$

Hence, if the preferences of a sample of 200 consumers were solicited, the expected frequencies would be

$E_1 = 90$

$E_2 = 80$

$E_3 = 26$

$E_4 = 4$

Since the expected cell frequency E_4 is less than 5, the rule of five requires that it be combined with one of the other expected frequencies (say, E_3) to obtain a combined cell frequency of (in this case) 30. Although E_4 could have been combined with E_1 or E_2, we have chosen to combine it with E_3 so that we still have a separate category representing each of the two dominant companies (A and B). After this combination is made, the null hypothesis reads

$$H_0: p_1 = .45, p_2 = .40, p_3 = .15.$$

where p_3 now represents the market share of all competitors of companies A and B. Therefore, the appropriate number of degrees of freedom for the chi-square test statistic would be $k - 1 = 3 - 1 = 2$, where k is the number of cells after some have been combined to satisfy the rule of five.

EXERCISES

LEARNING THE TECHNIQUES

14.1 Describe the properties of a multinomial experiment. How do they compare with the properties of a binomial experiment?

14.2 Describe an example of a multinomial experiment Formulate a pair of hypotheses that could be tested by using the data from this experiment.

14.3 Determine the decision rule for a test of hypothesis based on the results of a multinomial experiment with:

a. $k = 5$ and $\alpha = .05$

b. $k = 8$ and $\alpha = .01$

c. $k = 10$ and $\alpha = .10$

14.4 Consider a multinomial experiment involving $n = 300$ trials and $k = 5$ cells. The observed frequencies resulting from the experiment are shown in the accompanying table, and the null hypothesis to be tested is

$$H_0: p_1 = .1, p_2 = .2, p_3 = .3, p_4 = .2, p_5 = .2.$$

Test the hypothesis at the 1% significance level.

Cell	1	2	3	4	5
Frequency	24	65	86	70	55

14.5 Consider a multinomial experiment involving $n = 150$ trials and $k = 4$ cells. The observed frequencies resulting from the experiment are shown in the accompanying table, and the null hypothesis to be tested is

$$H_0: p_1 = .3, p_2 = .3, p_3 = .2, p_4 = .2.$$

Cell	1	2	3	4
Frequency	38	50	38	24

a. State the alternative hypothesis.

b. Test the hypotheses, using $\alpha = .05$.

14.6 For Exercise 14.5, retest the hypotheses, assuming that the experiment involved twice as many trials ($n = 300$) and that the observed frequencies were twice as high as before, as shown in the accompanying table. (Use $\alpha = .05$.)

Cell	1	2	3	4
Frequency	76	100	76	48

14.7 Explain what is meant by the *rule of five*.

APPLYING THE TECHNIQUES

Self-Correcting Exercise (See Appendix 14.B for the solution.)

14.8 To determine whether a single die is balanced, or fair, the die was rolled 600 times. The observed frequencies with which each of the six sides of the die turned up are recorded in the following table. Is there sufficient evidence to allow you to conclude, at the 5% level of significance, that the die is not fair?

Face	Observed Frequency
1	114
2	92
3	84
4	101
5	107
6	102

14.9 For Exercise 14.8, suppose that the die was rolled 1,200 times and that the observed frequencies were twice as high as before, as recorded in the accompanying table. Is there now sufficient evidence to conclude, at the 5% level of significance, that the die is not fair?

Face	Observed Frequency
1	228
2	184
3	168
4	202
5	214
6	204

14.10 Grades assigned by an economics instructor have historically followed a symmetrical distribution: 5% A's, 25% B's, 40% C's, 25% D's, and 5% F's. This year, a sample of grades revealed 11 A's, 32 B's, 62 C's, 29 D's, and 16 F's. Can you conclude, at the 1% level of significance, that this year's grades are distributed differently from grades in the past?

14.11 A firm has been accused of engaging in prejudicial hiring practices. According to the most recent census, the percentages of whites, blacks, and Hispanics in the community where the firm is located are 70%, 12%, and 18%, respectively. A random sample of 200 employees of the firm revealed that 165 were white, 14 were black, and 21 were Hispanic. What would you conclude, at the 5% level of significance?

14.12 Financial managers are interested in the speed with which customers who make purchases on credit pay their bills. In addition to calculating the average number of days that unpaid bills (called accounts receivable) remain outstanding, they often prepare an aging schedule. An aging schedule classifies outstanding accounts receivable according to the time that has elapsed since billing and records the proportion of accounts receivable belonging to each classification. A large firm has estimated its current aging schedule on the basis of a sample of 250 of its accounts receivable. With the economy moving into a recession, the firm wishes to determine whether the distribution of its current aging schedule differs from what it was one year ago. Using the data in the accompanying table, conduct an appropriate test at the 5% level of significance.

Number of Days Outstanding	Proportion of Accounts Receivable	
	Year Ago	Current
0–29	.72	.64
30–59	.15	.14
60–89	.10	.18
90 and over	.03	.04

CHI-SQUARE TEST OF A CONTINGENCY TABLE

This section deals with a test that addresses the relationship between two variables for which the data are qualitative. Defining qualitative variables over a population amounts to classifying the items in the population according to two different criteria. Specifically, the test discussed here investigates whether a relationship exists between two variables or whether the variables are statistically independent.

To see how the test for statistical independence is conducted, consider the following example. A certain cola company sells four types of cola throughout North America. To help determine if the same marketing approach used in the United States can be used in Canada and in Mexico, one of the firm's marketing analysts wishes to ascertain if there is an association between the type of cola preferred and the nationality of the consumer. She first classifies the population of cola drinkers according to the type of cola preferred: regular (A), both caffeine- and sugar-free (B), caffeine-free only (C), or sugar-free only (D). Her second classification consists of three nationalities: American (N_1), Canadian (N_2), and Mexican (N_3). The marketing analyst then interviews a random sample of 250 cola drinkers from the three countries, classifies each according to the two criteria and records the observed frequency of drinkers falling into each of the 12 possible cells (see Table 14.5). A rectangular table such as this, in which items from a population are classified according to two characteristics, is called a **contingency table.**

TABLE 14.5   CONTINGENCY TABLE CLASSIFYING COLA DRINKERS

Nationality	Cola Preference				Total
	A	B	C	D	
N_1	72	8	12	23	115
N_2	26	10	16	33	85
N_3	7	10	14	19	50
TOTAL	105	28	42	75	250

Since the marketing analyst wishes to determine whether there is an association between cola preference and nationality, the hypotheses to be tested are

H_0: The two classifications are independent.

H_A: The two classifications are dependent.

The appropriate test statistic is the same chi-square test statistic used for the multinomial experiment. Here, however, the null hypothesis doesn't specify values for the cell probabilities, which are needed if we are to calculate the expected cell frequencies. As a result, we must estimate the cell probabilities—and hence the expected frequencies—from the sample data.

Let A represent the event that a cola drinker prefers type A cola. Let events B, C, and D be defined similarly. Let N_i denote the event that a drinker belongs to nationality N_i, for $i = 1, 2,$ and 3.

As before, the expected cell frequencies will be obtained by multiplying the sample size n by the cell probabilities. But before we can do that, we must estimate the cell probabilities. This is achieved by estimating the marginal column probabilities (the probabilities of drinkers preferring each type of cola) and the marginal row probabilities (the proportions of drinkers belonging to each nationality).

The marginal column probabilities are estimated by dividing the column sums by the total sample size:

$$P(A) \cong \frac{105}{250} \qquad P(B) \cong \frac{28}{250} \qquad P(C) \cong \frac{42}{250} \qquad P(D) \cong \frac{75}{250}.$$

The notation $\cong$ indicates that these probabilities are only approximations (because they are determined on the basis of sample data).

In a similar manner, the marginal row probabilities are estimated by dividing the row sums by the total sample size:

$$P(N_1) \cong \frac{115}{250} \qquad P(N_2) \cong \frac{85}{250} \qquad P(N_3) \cong \frac{50}{250}.$$

Having estimated the marginal column and row probabilities, we can proceed to estimate the cell probabilities. Recall from Chapter 4 that, if events A and B are independent, $P(A \cap B) = P(A) \cdot P(B)$. Thus, assuming the null hypothesis to be true, we may apply this multiplication rule for independent events to obtain the joint probability that a cola drinker falls into the first cell:

$$P(A \cap N_1) = P(A) \cdot P(N_1) \cong \left(\frac{105}{250}\right)\left(\frac{115}{250}\right).$$

By multiplying this joint probability by the sample size, we obtain the expected number of drinkers who fall into the first cell:

$$E_{11} = n \cdot P(A \cap N_1) = 250\left(\frac{105}{250}\right)\left(\frac{115}{250}\right) = \frac{(105)(115)}{250}.$$

Observe that E_{11} was calculated by multiplying the total of column 1 by the total of row 1 and dividing by n. The other expected frequencies are estimated in a similar manner, using the following general formula for the expected frequency of the cell in row i and column j:

$$E_{ij} = \frac{(\text{Row } i \text{ total}) \cdot (\text{Column } j \text{ total})}{\text{Sample size}}.$$

The expected cell frequencies for the cola drinkers example are shown in parentheses in Table 14.6. Since the row and column sums of the expected frequencies must be the same as the corresponding sums for the observed frequencies, a quick means of checking the accuracy of the expected frequency calculations is available. As in the case of multinomial experiments, the expected frequencies here should satisfy the rule of five (discussed in the previous section).

Having determined the observed and expected cell frequencies, we use the same chi-square test statistic here as in the multinomial experiment to assess whether the differences between them are sufficiently great to allow us to reject the null hypothesis. For convenience of notation, we will continue to use single subscripts to denote observed and expected frequencies in the test statistic. From the calculations in Table 14.7, we obtain

$$\chi^2 = \sum_{i=1}^{12} \frac{(O_i - E_i)^2}{E_i}$$
$$= \frac{(72 - 48.30)^2}{48.30} + \frac{(26 - 35.70)^2}{35.70} + \cdots + \frac{(19 - 15.00)^2}{15.00}$$
$$= 42.75.$$

We must now locate the critical value and define the decision rule. To locate the critical value, we have to know the appropriate number of degrees of freedom for the chi-square distribution of the test statistic. The number of degrees of freedom for a contingency table with r rows and c columns is

$$\text{d.f.} = (r - 1)(c - 1)$$

The chi-square distribution for the test statistic in the cola drinkers example, therefore, has $(3 - 1)(4 - 1) = 6$ degrees of freedom. If we take $\alpha = .01$, then the criti-

---

TABLE 14.6 CONTINGENCY TABLE CLASSIFYING COLA DRINKERS

Nationality	Cola Preference				Total
	A	B	C	D	
N_1	72(48.30)	8(12.88)	12(19.32)	23(34.50)	115
N_2	26(35.70)	10(9.52)	16(14.28)	33(25.50)	85
N_3	7(21.00)	10(5.60)	14(8.40)	19(15.00)	50
TOTAL	105	28	42	75	250

TABLE 14.7   COMPUTATION OF χ^2 FOR COLA DRINKERS

Cell i	Observed Frequency O_i	Expected Frequency E_i	$(O_i - E_i)^2$	$\dfrac{(O_i - E_i)^2}{E_i}$
1	72	48.30	561.69	11.63
2	26	35.70	94.09	2.64
3	7	21.00	196.00	9.33
4	8	12.88	23.81	1.85
5	10	9.52	.23	.02
6	10	5.60	19.36	3.46
7	12	19.32	53.58	2.77
8	16	14.28	2.96	.21
9	14	8.40	31.36	3.73
10	23	34.50	132.25	3.83
11	33	25.50	56.25	2.21
12	19	15.00	16.00	1.07
TOTAL	250	250.00		$\chi^2 = 42.75$

cal value is $\chi^2_{.01,6} = 16.8119$. Since the computed value of our test statistic is 42.75, we reject the null hypothesis that the two classifications are independent. Based on the sample data, we conclude at the 1% level of significance that there is a relationship between the preferences of cola drinks and their nationality.

COMPARISON OF TWO OR MORE POPULATIONS

When analyzing the data in a contingency table, we are interested in determining whether or not two qualitative variables, or classifications, are statistically independent. But the results of a chi-square test for independence can also be interpreted in terms of a different problem objective: the comparison of two or more populations of qualitative data. In such a comparison, each of the categories belonging to one of the two classifications is considered to be a population. In the cola drinkers example, for instance, we could think of the three nationalities as representing three distinct populations with respect to cola preference.

The null hypothesis stated that nationality and cola preference were independent. If that were the case, we could state that

$$P(A \,|\, N_1) = P(A)$$
$$P(A \,|\, N_2) = P(A)$$
$$P(A \,|\, N_3) = P(A)$$

or equivalently,

$$P(A \,|\, N_1) = P(A \,|\, N_2) = P(A \,|\, N_3).$$

This would mean that the preference for cola A is the same for all three populations (American, Canadian, and Mexican). We could make similar statements of independence for colas B, C, and D:

$$P(B \,|\, N_1) = P(B \,|\, N_2) = P(B \,|\, N_3)$$
$$P(C \,|\, N_1) = P(C \,|\, N_2) = P(C \,|\, N_3)$$
$$P(D \,|\, N_1) = P(D \,|\, N_2) = P(D \,|\, N_3).$$

The alternative hypothesis in the cola-drinkers example asserted that the two variables were dependent. If this were true, the statement of independence would not hold for one of the colas—say, cola A. That is, at least one of $P(A \,|\, N_1)$, $P(A \,|\, N_2)$, and $P(A \,|\, N_3)$ would not be equal to $P(A)$. Hence, there would be differences in the preferences for cola A among the three populations.

From the preceding discussion, it should be clear that testing for differences between two or more qualitative populations is equivalent to testing for dependence between qualitative variables. The only differences are in the interpretation and in the problem objective.

EXAMPLE 14.2

The foreman at a shirt manufacturer, which operates three shifts daily, wishes to determine whether there are differences in the quality of workmanship among the three shifts. After an inspection of the 600 shirts produced on a particular day, the foreman compiled the data in Table 14.8, showing the number of seconds (shirts with flaws) produced by each shift. Do these data indicate that there are differences in the quality of workmanship among the three shifts? (Use $\alpha = .10$.)

Solution.   We can view the 600 shirts as representing a sample from a single population, classified both according to the shift that produced them and according to their

TABLE 14.8   CONTINGENCY TABLE CLASSIFYING SHIRTS

Shirt Condition	Shift			Total
	1	2	3	
Flawed	10	9	11	30
No flaws	240	191	139	570
TOTAL	250	200	150	600

condition. The data are qualitative. We may then conduct a chi-square test to determine whether these two classifications are statistically independent. Alternatively, we may view the data as consisting of three populations: the populations of shirts produced on each of the three shifts. In this regard, notice that, if the two classifications are independent, the shift producing the shirt and the shirt's condition are unrelated—meaning that there are no differences in workmanship among the shifts. The alternative hypothesis states that the shift and the shirt condition are related, and hence that there are differences in workmanship among the shifts.

H_0: The two classifications are independent.

H_A: The two classifications are dependent.

Test statistic:

$$\chi^2 = \sum_{i=1}^{6} \frac{(O_i - E_i)^2}{E_i} \qquad \text{with d.f.} = (r-1)(c-1) = (1)(2) = 2.$$

Significance level: $\alpha = .10$

Decision rule: Reject H_0 if $\chi^2 > \chi^2_{\alpha,(r-1)(c-1)} = \chi^2_{.10,2} = 4.60517.$

Value of the test statistic: The expected cell frequencies, which are estimated in the same way as in the preceding cola drinkers example, are shown in parentheses in Table 14.9. Therefore,

$$\chi^2 = \frac{(10-12.5)^2}{12.5} + \frac{(240-237.5)^2}{237.5} + \cdots + \frac{(139-142.5)^2}{142.5} = 2.36.$$

Conclusion: Do not reject H_0.

We cannot reject the hypothesis that the two classifications are independent: there is insufficient evidence to allow us to conclude, at the 10% level, that differences in workmanship exist among the three shifts (see Figure 14.4).

TABLE 14.9   CONTINGENCY TABLE AND EXPECTED VALUES FOR EXAMPLE 14.2

Shirt Condition	Shift			Total
	1	2	3	
Flawed	10(12.5)	9(10)	11(7.5)	30
No flaws	240(237.5)	191(190)	139(142.5)	570
TOTAL	250	200	150	600

FIGURE 14.4   SAMPLING DISTRIBUTION FOR EXAMPLE 14.2

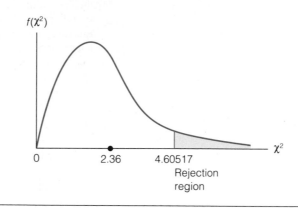

MINITAB COMPUTER OUTPUT FOR EXAMPLE 14.2*

Expected counts are printed below observed counts

```
          C1        C2        C3      Total
1         10         9        11        30
          12.5      10.0       7.5
2        240       191       139       570
         237.5     190.0     142.5
Total    250       200       150       600
ChiSq = 0.50 + 0.10 + 1.63 + 0.03 + 0.01 + 0.09 = 2.36
df = 2
```

The output includes observed and expected values, the test statistic, and the degrees of freedom.

EXERCISES

LEARNING THE TECHNIQUES

14.13   Consider a chi-square test of statistical independence.

a. What is the problem objective?

b. What is the data type?

c. What is meant by *statistical independence?*

14.14   A test of statistical independence is to be conducted, using the data in a contigency table with r rows and c columns. Determine the decision rule if:

a. $r = 3, c = 3$, and $\alpha = .01$

b. $r = 4, c = 6$, and $\alpha = .05$

14.15   A test of statistical independence is to be conducted, using the data in a contingency table with r rows and c columns. Determine the decision rule if:

a. $r = 4, c = 4$, and $\alpha = .025$

b. $r = 3, c = 5$, and $\alpha = .10$

14.16   Conduct a test to determine whether the two classifications L and M are independent, using the data in the accompanying contingency table and $\alpha = .01$.

---

* Appendix 14.A describes the Minitab commands that produced this output.

	M	
L	M_1	M_2
L_1	29	67
L_2	56	38

14.17 Conduct a test to determine whether the two classifications R and C are independent, using the data in the accompanying contingency table and $\alpha = .10$.

	C		
R	C_1	C_2	C_3
R_1	40	32	48
R_2	30	48	52

APPLYING THE TECHNIQUES

Self-Correcting Exercise (See Appendix 14.B for the solution.)

14.18 The trustee of a company's pension plan has solicited the opinions of a sample of the company's employees toward a proposed revision of the plan. A breakdown of the responses is shown in the accompanying table. Is there evidence that the responses differ among the three groups of employees? (Test at the 5% level of significance.)

Responses	Blue-collar Workers	White-collar Workers	Managers
For	67	32	11
Against	63	18	9

14.19 To determine if commercials viewed during happy television programs are more effective than those viewed during sad television programs, a study was conducted in which a random sample of students viewed an upbeat segment from *Real People* with commercials, while another random sample of students viewed a very sad segment from *Sixty Minutes* with commercials. The students were then asked what they were thinking during the final commercial. From their responses, they were categorized as thinking primarily about the commercial, thinking primarily about the program, or thinking about both. The results are summarized in the table. Do commercials viewed during happy television programs appear to be more effective than those viewed during sad television programs? (Test using $\alpha = .01$.)

Program Viewed	**What Viewers Were Thinking About**		
	Commercial	Program	Both
Real People	50	15	8
Sixty Minutes	11	42	25

SOURCE: Adapted from Marvin E. Goldberg and Gerald J. Gorn, "Happy and Sad TV Programs: How They Affect Reactions to Commercials," *Journal of Consumer Research* 14 (1987): 387–403.

14.20 In a study comparing characteristics of television commercials in the United States, Mexico, and Australia, characters from a random sample of commercials in the three countries were cross-classified, as shown in Table E14.20. For each of the three countries, conduct a test to determine whether men and women are portrayed in significantly different settings in commercials. (Test using $\alpha = .01$.)

14.21 The study referred to in Exercise 14.20 also cross-classified characters in commercials according to age and gender, as shown in Table E14.21. For each of the three countries, conduct a test to determine whether women are significantly more likely than men to be portrayed in commercials as being young. (Test using $\alpha = .005$.)

14.22 A market survey was conducted for the purpose of forming a demographic profile of individuals who would like to own a compact disk player. This profile will help to establish the target market for compact disk players, which in turn will be used in developing an advertising strategy. The data collected that relate to the consumer's gender are summarized in the accompanying table. Is there sufficient evidence to allow you to conclude that the desire to own a compact disk player is related to the consumer's gender? (Test using $\alpha = .05$.)

TABLE E14.20

Setting	United States		Mexico		Australia	
	Women	Men	Women	Men	Women	Men
Home	57	30	31	21	15	8
Store	15	9	19	14	3	7
Occupational	6	20	1	3	0	2
Outdoors	19	10	14	19	3	7
Other	72	63	55	45	31	25

SOURCE: Adapted from Mary C. Gilly, "Sex Roles in Advertising: A Comparison of Television Advertisements in Australia, Mexico and the United States," *Journal of Marketing* 52 (1988): 75–85.

TABLE E14.21

Age	United States		Mexico		Australia	
	Women	Men	Women	Men	Women	Men
Under 35	68	26	85	21	37	15
35–50	86	82	28	74	13	32
Over 50	15	24	7	7	2	2

SOURCE: Adapted from Mary C. Gilly, "Sex Roles in Advertising: A Comparison of Television Advertisements in Australia, Mexico and the United States," *Journal of Marketing* 52 (1988): 75–85.

Response	Men	Women
Want player	32	20
Don't want player	118	130

14.23 The Equal Credit Opportunity Act forbids lenders in the United States from soliciting the marital status of women who are applying for personal loans. Many women feel that this act should be extended to include business loans. They cite instances in which women have received business loans only after the lender determined they were married to men who had good credit ratings (*Business Week,* 27 May 1985). Suppose that a women's group has collected data on the business loan applications of 600 women, and that the results are as summarized in the accompanying table. Is there evidence of bias on the part of lenders regarding marital status? (Use $\alpha = .05$.)

Marital Status	Loan Granted	Loan Denied
Single	253	119
Married	181	47

SUMMARY

This chapter describes two statistical tests that are based on samples taken from a single population of qualitative data. The first is a goodness-of-fit test, used to determine the validity of a hypothesis concerning the multinomial distribution of a single population of qualitative data. The second test uses data arranged in a contingency table to determine whether or not two classifications of a population of qualitative data are statistically independent. Both tests are based on the same test statistic, which has an approximate chi-square distribution. In order for this approximation to be adequate, the sample must be sufficiently large so that no expected cell frequency is less than 5. The test for statistical independence can also be interpreted as a comparison of two or more populations of qualitative data.

IMPORTANT TERMS

Goodness-of-fit test	Expected frequency
Contingency table	Chi-square distribution
Multinomial experiment	Rule of five
Cells	Independent classification
Observed frequency	Dependent classification

FORMULAS

$$E_i = np_i$$

$$\chi^2 = \sum_{i=1}^{k} \frac{(O_i - E_i)}{E_i}$$

$$\text{d.f.} = k - 1$$

$$E_{ij} = \frac{(\text{Row } i \text{ total}) \cdot (\text{Column } j \text{ total})}{\text{Sample size}}$$

$$v = (r - 1)(c - 1)$$

SUPPLEMENTARY EXERCISES

14.24 Consider a multinomial experiment involving $n = 200$ trials and $k = 4$ cells. The observed frequencies resulting from the experiment are shown in the accompanying table, and the null hypothesis to be tested is

$$H_0: p_1 = .4, p_2 = .3, p_3 = .2, p_4 = .1.$$

Cell	1	2	3	4
Frequency	96	54	28	22

a. State the alternative hypothesis.

b. Test the hypothesis, using $\alpha = .05$.

14.25 An organization dedicated to ensuring fairness in television game shows is investigating *Wheel of Fortune*. In this show, three contestants are required to solve puzzles by selecting letters. Each contestant gets to select the first letter and continues selecting until he or she chooses a letter that is not in the phrase, place, or name. The order of contestants is random. However, contestant 1 gets to start game 1, contestant 2 starts game 2, and so on. The contestant who wins the most money is declared the winner and he or she is given an opportunity to win a grand prize. Usually, more than three games are played per show, and as a result it appears that contestant 1 has an advantage: contestant 1 will start 2 games while contestant 3 will start only one game. To see if this is the case, a random sample of 30 shows was taken and the starting position of the winning contestant for each show was recorded. These are shown in the following table.

Starting Position	Number of Winners
1	14
2	10
3	6

Do the tabulated results allow us to conclude that the game is unfair? (Use $\alpha = .05$.)

14.26 Econetics Research Corporation, a well-known Montreal-based consulting firm, desires to test how it can influence the proportion of questionnaires returned from surveys. Believing that the inclusion of an inducement to respond may be important, it sends out 1,000 questionnaires: 200 promise to send respondents a summary of the survey results, 300 indicate that 20 respondents (selected by lottery) will be awarded gifts, and 500 are accompanied by no inducements. Of these, 80 questionnaires promising a summary, 100 questionnaires offering gifts, and 120 questionnaires offering no inducements are returned. What can you conclude, at the 1% level of significance?

14.27 It has been estimated that employee absenteeism costs North American companies more than $100 billion per year. As a first step in addressing the rising cost of absenteeism, the personnel department of a large corporation recorded the weekdays during which individuals in a sample of 362 absentees were away over the past several months. Do these data suggest that absenteeism is higher on some days of the week than on others? (Use $\alpha = .05$.)

Day of the week	Mon	Tues	Wed	Thurs	Fri
Number absent	87	62	71	68	74

14.28 Suppose that the personnel department in Exercise 14.27 continued its investigation by categorizing absentees according to the shift on which they worked, as shown in the accompanying table. Is there evidence of a relationship between the days on which employees were absent and the shift on which the employees worked? (Use $\alpha = .10$.)

Shift	Mon	Tues	Wed	Thurs	Fri
Day	52	28	37	31	33
Evening	35	34	34	37	41

14.29 A relationship has long been suspected between smoking and susceptibility to having a stroke. Strong statistical evidence on this issue has been lacking, however, since a convincing study would involve monitoring a large number of individuals over a long period of time. The *Toronto Star* (March 1987) reported that one such study has now been conducted, involving over 2,000 residents outside Boston who were studied over a 26-year period. Because of the large number of individuals observed, researchers were able to maintain reasonable sample sizes even after segmenting the observed group to control for factors other than smoking that might influence the individual susceptibility to a stroke, such as gender and blood-pressure level. Suppose that the results for men with low blood-pressure levels were as shown in the accompanying table. What would you conclude at the 5% level of significance?

Individual	Stroke	No Stroke
Smoker	37	183
Nonsmoker	21	274

14.30 Acute otitis media, an infection of the middle ear, is a very common childhood illness. Although it is normally treated with amoxicillin, emerging resistance to the antibiotic has promoted the search for an alternative. Your friend David has just read about a study that tested the efficacy of one such alternative: trimethoprimsulfamethoxazole. In this study, 203 "patients were randomly assigned to receive either amoxicillin or trimethoprimsulfamethoxazole by means of a computer-generated table of random numbers." The data are summarized in the accompanying table. Being a specialist, David's interest in the study centered on the reported gastrointestinal side effects of the two drugs. But his inquisitive nature induced him to seek your help in understanding the chi-square test that was conducted on the tabulated data.

a. Conduct a test to determine if there are differences, at the 10% level of significance, in the outcomes for children treated with amoxicillin and for children treated with trimethoprimsulfamethoxazole.

b. The chi-square test was reported to have a prob-value of .42. For David's benefit, explain what this means.

Outcome	Treatment	
	Amoxicillin	Trimethoprim-sulfamethoxazole
Cure	60	65
Improvement	31	22
Treatment Failure	12	13

SOURCE: William Feldman, Joanne Momy, and Corinne Dulberg, "Trimethoprimsulfamethoxazole v. Amoxicillin in the Treatment of Acute Otitis Media," *Canadian Medical Association Journal* 139 (1988): 961–64.

14.31 Research into the meaning of object ownership and consumption may improve our understanding of demand and consumer behavior. Two researchers have conducted a study involving 298 individuals that, among other things, investigated "differences between Southwest American men and women in the selection of favorite objects." From the researchers' data, shown in the following table, would you conclude that men and women exhibit differences in the type of object that is their favorite? (Test using $\alpha = .01$.)

Favorite Object	Female	Male
Functional (chair, clock)	24	48
Entertainment (stereo, TV)	28	36
Personal item	27	15
Art piece	11	18
Photograph	18	6

Favorite Object	Female	Male
Plant	8	16
Handicraft	18	7
Antique	14	4

SOURCE: Adapted from Melanie Wallendorf and Eric J. Arnould, "My Favorite Things: A Cross-Cultural Inquiry into Object Attachment, Possessiveness and Social Linkage," *Journal of Consumer Research* 14 (1988): 531–47.

14.32 The researchers mentioned in Exercise 14.31 also investigated the relationship between age and favorite object. On the basis of their data, which are shown in the accompanying table, what would you conclude at the 1% level of significance? (Some object categories have been combined to satisfy the rule of five.)

FAVORITE OBJECTS OF SOUTHWEST AMERICANS, BY AGE GROUP

Favorite Object	Age Group			
	18–24	25–35	36–44	45+
Functional	14	29	13	10
Entertainment	9	32	11	9
Personal item/Art	7	20	19	21
Photograph/Plant	9	18	5	10
Handicraft/Antique	6	15	14	6

SOURCE: Adapted from Melanie Wallendorf and Eric J. Arnould, "My Favorite Things: A Cross-Cultural Inquiry into Object Attachment, Possessiveness and Social Linkage," *Journal of Consumer Research* 14 (1988): 531–47.

14.33 A management behavior analyst has been studying the relationship between male/female reporting structures in the workplace and the level of employees' job satisfaction. The results of a recent survey are shown in Table E14.33. Using $\alpha = .10$, conduct a test to determine whether the level of job satisfaction depends on the boss/employee gender relationship.

TABLE E14.33

Level of Satisfaction	Boss/Employee				Total
	Female/Male	Female/Female	Male/Male	Male/Female	
Satisfied	20	25	50	75	170
Neutral	40	50	50	40	180
Dissatisfied	30	45	10	15	100
TOTAL	90	120	110	130	450

14.34 A discount video shop sells televisions, video cassette recorders, and video cameras. The store's manager wishes to determine whether there is a relationship between the method of payment and the item purchased. The relevant data on last month's purchases are shown in the accompanying table. Using $\alpha = .10$, test to see if the data in the table suggest such a relationship.

Payment Method	VCR	TV	Camera
Cash	11	4	7
Credit Card	52	19	12
Installment	27	32	11

▬▬▬▬▬ CASE 14.1* AUDITOR SWITCHING IN FAILING COMPANIES

The phenomenon of auditor switching has broad implications for the auditing profession, and the Securities and Exchange Commission has expressed its concern over this issue (see, for example, SEC ASR No. 165 [1974]). There may be a variety of reasons behind any switch in auditor. In a study designed to examine the issue, the following factors were hypothesized to influence auditor switching:

The financial health of the company

The desire for a more prestigious auditor when the company is failing

Receipt of a qualified opinion from the current auditor in a failing company

A change in the company management in a failing company

The experiment consisted of examining a random sample of 132 companies that went bankrupt in the period from 1974 to 1982 and another 132 similar but financially

---

* Adapted from K. B. Schwartz and K. Menon, "Auditor Switches by Failing Firms," *Accounting Review* (April 1985): 248–61.

healthy companies. Each company was asked if it had switched CPA firms and (if so) whether the switch involved a Big Eight CPA firm, whether their audit statements were qualified, and whether the firm changed management. The results are laid out in the accompanying tables.

Comment on the factors that influence an auditor switch.

TABLE A   ASSOCIATION BETWEEN FINANCIAL DISTRESS AND AUDITOR SWITCHES

Action Taken	Bankrupt	Nonbankrupt
Switched CPA firms	35	13
Did not switch CPA firms	97	119

TABLE B   DIRECTION OF AUDITOR SWITCHES BY FAILING COMPANIES

Action Taken	Switched to Big Eight CPA Firm	Switched to Non-Big Eight CPA Firm
Switched from Big Eight CPA firm	11	10
Switched from non-Big Eight CPA firm	12	2

TABLE C   ASSOCIATION BETWEEN AUDIT QUALIFICATION AND AUDITOR SWITCHES FOR FAILING COMPANIES

Action Taken	Qualified	Not Qualified
Switched CPA firms	14	17
Did not switch CPA firms	63	34

TABLE D   ASSOCIATION BETWEEN MANAGEMENT CHANGES AND AUDITOR SWITCHES FOR FAILING COMPANIES

Action Taken	Changed Management	Did Not Change Management
Switched CPA firms	13	18
Did not switch CPA firms	34	64

![CASE 14.2] **LOTTO 6/49**

Lotto 6/49 is a lottery that operates as follows. Players select six different numbers between 1 and 49 for each $1.00 ticket. Several times each month, the corporation that runs the lottery selects seven numbers at random between 1 and 49. Winners are determined by how many numbers on their tickets agree with the drawn numbers. In selecting their numbers, players often look at past patterns as a way to help them predict future drawings. A regular feature that appears in the newspaper identifies the number of times each number has occurred in the previous year. The data recorded in the accompanying table appeared in the January 21 edition of the *Toronto Star*.

What would you recommend to anyone who believes that past patterns of the lottery numbers are useful in predicting future drawings?

DRAWING FREQUENCY OF LOTTO NUMBERS

Lotto Number	Number of Times Drawn in the Last Year	Lotto Number	Number of Times Drawn in the Last Year
1	12	26	11
2	9	27	13
3	10	28	2
4	13	29	8
5	8	30	14
6	12	31	13
7	13	32	14
8	9	33	13
9	16	34	9
10	7	35	10
11	11	36	10
12	9	37	3
13	7	38	10
14	8	39	11
15	5	40	10
16	6	41	11
17	6	42	7
18	13	43	10
19	16	44	10
20	12	45	16

(continued)

Lotto Number	Number of Times Drawn in the Last Year	Lotto Number	Number of Times Drawn in the Last Year
21	15	46	13
22	8	47	12
23	9	48	6
24	12	49	8
25	7		

MINITAB INSTRUCTIONS

CHI-SQUARE TEST OF A CONTINGENCY TABLE

The command

```
CHISQUARE C1-C3
```

causes Minitab to calculate the chi-square statistic for a contingency table whose columns are stored in columns 1 to 3. To illustrate, we solve Example 14.2 by entering the following Minitab instructions:

```
READ C1-C3
 10      9     11
240    191    139
END
CHISQUARE C1-C3
```

The output is:

```
Expected counts are printed below observed counts

            C1       C2       C3      Total
     1      10        9       11        30
           12.5     10.0      7.5
     2     240      191      139       570
          237.5    190.0    142.5
Total      250      200      150        600
ChiSq = 0.50+0.10+1.63+0.03+0.01+0.09 = 2.36
df = 2
```

The CHISQUARE command can be used whenever the contingency table has been determined; if the contingency table has not been determined, another command must be employed. If the first column lists the values of the first qualitative variable and the second column lists the values of the second qualitative variable, the command

```
CONTINGENCY TABLE C1 C2
```

will elicit output of the observed and expected values and of the test statistic. If we had the raw data in Example 14.2 (where variable Shift = 1, 2, or 3 and variable Condition = 1 [Flawed] or 2 [No flaws]), we would proceed as follows:

```
READ C1 C2
3     2
2     1
1     1
.     .
.     .
.     .
2     2
END
CONTINGENCY TABLE C1 C2
```

This output is almost identical to the output produced by the previous CHISQUARE command.

SOLUTIONS TO SELF-CORRECTING EXERCISES

14.8 Let p_i be the probability that side i will turn up on any one roll ($i = 1, 2, \ldots, 6$).

H_0: $p_1 = p_2 = p_3 = p_4 = p_5 = p_6 = 1/6$.
H_A: At least one p_i is not equal to its specified value.

Test statistic: $\chi^2 = \sum\limits_{i=1}^{6} \dfrac{(O_i - E_i)^2}{E_i}$

Significance level: $\alpha = .05$

Decision rule: Reject H_0 if
$\chi^2 > \chi^2_{\alpha, k-1} = \chi^2_{.05,5} = 11.0705$.

Value of the test statistic:

$$\chi^2 = \sum_{i=1}^{6} \frac{(O_i - E_i)^2}{E_i}$$
$$= \frac{(114 - 100)^2}{100} + \frac{(92 - 100)^2}{100} + \frac{(84 - 100)^2}{100}$$
$$+ \frac{(101 - 100)^2}{100} + \frac{(107 - 100)^2}{100}$$
$$+ \frac{(102 - 100)^2}{100} = 5.70$$

Conclusion: Do not reject H_0.

There is not sufficient evidence to allow us to conclude that the die is not fair.

14.18 H_0: The two classifications are independent.
H_A: The two classifications are dependent.

Test statistic: $\chi^2 = \sum\limits_{i=1}^{6} \dfrac{(O_i - E_i)^2}{E_i}$

Significance level: $\alpha = .05$

Decision rule: Reject H_0 if
$\chi^2 > \chi^2_{\alpha,(r-1)(c-1)} = \chi^2_{.05,2} = 5.99147$.

Value of test statistic:

$$\chi^2 = \frac{(67 - 71.5)^2}{71.5} + \frac{(63 - 58.5)^2}{58.5} + \frac{(32 - 27.5)^2}{27.5}$$
$$+ \frac{(18 - 22.5)^2}{22.5} + \frac{(11 - 11)^2}{11} + \frac{(9 - 9)^2}{9}$$
$$= 2.27$$

Conclusion: Do not reject H_0.

There is not sufficient evidence to allow us to conclude that the responses differ among the three groups of employees.

SIMPLE LINEAR REGRESSION AND CORRELATION

INTRODUCTION

The techniques presented in this chapter address problems whose objective is to analyze the relationship between two variables whose data types are quantitative. The statistical technique we will discuss is called *regression analysis.*

One of the reasons for the importance of regression, particularly in business and economics applications, is that it can be used to forecast variables. As you can easily appreciate, almost all companies and governmental institutions frequently forecast variables such as product demand, interest rates, inflation rates, prices of raw materials, and labor costs. While several different forecasting techniques can be used, regression analysis is one of the most popular.

The technique involves developing a mathematical equation that analyzes the relationship between the variable to be forecast and the variable that the statistician believes is related to the forecast variable. The variable to be forecast is called the **dependent variable** and is denoted y, while the related variable is called the **independent variable** and is denoted x.

The following examples illustrate uses of regression analysis:

1. A real-estate agent wants to develop a more accurate method of predicting the selling price of houses. She believes that the most important factor is the size of the house. The house price is labeled y, and the house size is labeled x. She will gather data about x and y to develop the model.

2. A government economist is assigned the task of analyzing the relationship between interest rates and unemployment. Because high interest rates generally cause higher unemployment, he denotes the unemployment rate y and the interest rate x. Observing monthly values of x and y will enable the economist to produce a model to assist in the analysis.

3. The president of a national chain of print shops is reevaluating the company's prices. The president needs to know how prices affect gross sales. Consequently he labels gross sales y and the price per copy x. Gathering annual data for x and y for several different outlets across the country is the next step in the procedure.

MODEL

The first step is to develop a mathematical model that represents the relationship between the two variables. A mathematical model is an equation that represents an actual relationship. For example, an appliance repair company charges its customers (for labor only) according to the following schedule:

| First hour | $70 |
| Each additional quarter hour | $10 |

We can represent this schedule by the equation

$$y = 70 + 10x,$$

where

y = Total charge

x = Number of quarter hours after the first hour.

Suppose that we recorded the following times (in quarter hours after the first hour) and labor charges for six randomly selected customers of this company:

Customer	x	y
1	4	110
2	0	70
3	3	100
4	6	130
5	2	90
6	8	150

Figure 15.1 depicts the graph of these data. Notice that the six points fall exactly along the straight line $y = 70 + 10x$. This type of model is called **deterministic**, because

FIGURE 15.1   TOTAL CHARGE VERSUS NUMBER OF QUARTER HOURS

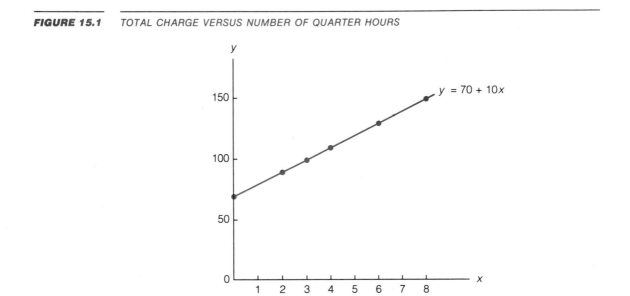

knowing the value of x allows us to determine the exact value of y. In many practical applications deterministic models are unrealistic. Is it reasonable, for example, to believe that we can determine the selling price of a house solely on the basis of its size? Unquestionably the size of a house affects its price, but so do many other variables, some of which may not be measurable. What must be included in most practical models is a method for representing the randomness that is part of a real-life process. Such a model is called **probabilistic.** To create a probabilistic model we start with a deterministic model that approximates the relationship we wish to model. We then add a random term that measures the error of the deterministic component.

For example, suppose that, in the example described earlier, the real-estate agent knows that the cost of building a new house is about $40 per square foot and that most lots sell for about $10,000. Then the approximate selling price would be

$$y = 10,000 + 40x,$$

where

y = Selling price

x = Size of the house (in square feet).

A house of 2,000 square feet would therefore be estimated to sell for

$$y = 10,000 + 40(2,000) = \$90,000.$$

We know, however, that the selling price is not likely to be exactly $90,000. Prices may actually range from $70,000 to $200,000. In other words, the deterministic model is not really suitable. To represent this situation properly, we should use the probabilistic model

$$y = 10,000 + 40x + \varepsilon,$$

where ε (the Greek letter epsilon) represents the random term—the difference between the actual selling price and the estimated price based on the size of the house. The random term thus accounts for all of the variables—measurable and unmeasurable—that are not part of the model.

This model is called the **simple linear regression model.**

Simple Linear Regression Model

$$y = \beta_0 + \beta_1 x + \varepsilon$$

where

y = Dependent variable

x = Independent variable

β_0 = y-intercept

β_1 = Slope of the line (defined as the ratio Rise/Run)

ε = Random error term

FIGURE 15.2 *SIMPLE LINEAR REGRESSION MODEL: DETERMINISTIC COMPONENT*

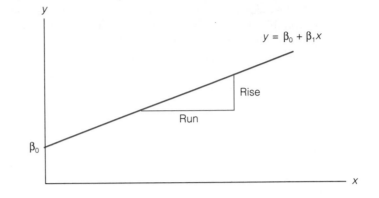

Figure 15.2 depicts the deterministic component of the model.

The problem objective addressed by the model is to analyze the relationship between two variables, x and y, both of which must be quantitative. To define the relationship between x and y, we need to know the value of the coefficients of the model β_0 and β_1. However, these coefficients are population parameters, which are almost always unknown. In the next section, we discuss how to estimate them, and in later sections we discuss a number of statistical techniques that allow us to draw inferences about the model. For these methods to be valid, a number of conditions about the error variable must be satisfied. These are as follows:

Required Conditions for ε

1. The probability distribution of ε is normal.
2. The mean of the distribution of ε is zero; that is, $E(\varepsilon) = 0$.
3. The variance of ε is σ_ε^2 (which is a constant, no matter what the value of x is).
4. The errors associated with any two values of y are independent. As a result, the value of the error variable at one point does not affect the value of the error variable at another point.

Requirements 1, 2, and 3 can be interpreted in another way: for each value of x, y is a normally distributed random variable whose mean is

$$E(y) = \beta_0 + \beta_1 x$$

and whose variance is σ_ε^2. Notice that the mean of y depends on x. To reflect this, the expected value is sometimes expressed as

$$E(y \mid x) = \beta_0 + \beta_1 x.$$

FIGURE 15.3   DISTRIBUTION OF THE ERROR VARIABLE

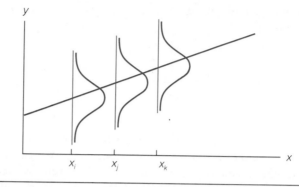

The variance however, is not influenced by x, since it is a constant over all values of x. Figure 15.3 depicts this interpretation.

EXERCISES

15.1   Graph each of the following straight lines. Identify the intercept and the slope on the graph.

a. $y = 2 + 3x$

b. $y = 5 - 2x$

c. $y = -2 + 4x$

d. $y = x$

e. $y = 4$

15.2   For each of the following data sets, plot the points on a graph to determine whether the simple linear regression model is reasonable.

a.

x	2	3	5	7	9
y	6	9	4	7	8

b.

x	1	3	5	4	7
y	5	7	10	9	16

c.

x	7	9	2	3	6
y	4	1	6	10	5

15.3   Graph the following observations of x and y.

x	1	2	3	4	5	6
y	4	6	7	7	9	11

Draw a straight line through the data. What are the intercept and the slope of the line you drew?

SECTION 15.3

LEAST SQUARES METHOD

We estimate the parameters β_0 and β_1 much as we do all other parameters discussed in this book—by drawing a random sample from the populations of interest and calculating the sample statistics that we need. Because β_0 and β_1 represent the coefficients of a straight line, their estimators are based on drawing a straight line through the sample data. To see how this is done, consider the following example.

EXAMPLE 15.1

Given the following six observations of variables x and y, determine the straight line that fits these data.

x	2	4	8	10	13	16
y	50	38	26	25	7	2

Solution.   As a first step we graph the data, as shown in Figure 15.4. This graph is called a **scatter diagram** or **scattergram.** The scattergram usually reveals whether or not a straight line model fits the data reasonably well. Evidently, in this case a linear model is justified. Notice, however, that the points do not align themselves perfectly in a straight line. Our task is to draw a straight line that provides the best possible fit.

We can define what we mean by *best* in various ways. For example, we can draw the line that minimizes the sum of the differences between the line and the points. But because some of the differences will be positive (points above the line) and others will be negative (points below the line), a canceling effect may produce a straight line that does not fit the data at all. To eliminate the positive and negative differences, we will draw the line that minimizes the sum of the squared differences. Hence, we wish to minimize

$$\sum_{i=1}^{n} (y_i - \hat{y}_i)^2,$$

where y_i represents the observed value of y and $\hat{y}_i$ represents the value of y calculated from the line. That is,

$$\hat{y}_i = \hat{\beta}_0 + \hat{\beta}_1 x_i.$$

FIGURE 15.4   SCATTERGRAM FOR EXAMPLE 15.1

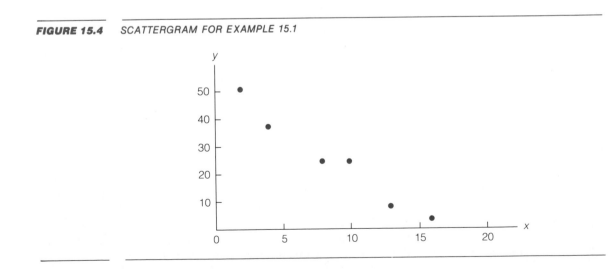

The technique that produces this line is called the **least squares method.** The line itself is called the **least squares line,** the **fitted line,** or the **regression line.** The hats on the coefficients remind us that they are estimators of the parameters β_0 and β_1.

By using calculus, we developed formulas for $\hat{\beta}_0$ and $\hat{\beta}_1$.

Calculation of $\hat{\beta}_0$ and $\hat{\beta}_1$

$$\hat{\beta}_1 = \frac{SS_{xy}}{SS_x},$$

where

$$SS_{xy} = \sum (x_i - \bar{x})(y_i - \bar{y}) = \sum x_i y_i - \frac{(\sum x_i)(\sum y_i)}{n}$$

and

$$SS_x = \sum (x_i - \bar{x})^2 = \sum x_i^2 - \frac{(\sum x_i)^2}{n}.$$

$$\hat{\beta}_0 = \bar{y} - \hat{\beta}_1 \bar{x},$$

where

$$\bar{y} = \frac{\sum y_i}{n}$$

and

$$\bar{x} = \frac{\sum x_i}{n}.$$

Notice that there are two formulas each for SS_{xy} and SS_x. The second formula in each pair is the shortcut version. You should realize, however, that SS_x is nothing more than the numerator when the sample variance of x is computed. The shortcut procedure for computing the sample variance of x is described in Chapter 3.

Applying these formulas to Example 15.1, we can compute

$$\sum x_i = 53$$
$$\sum x_i^2 = 609$$
$$\sum y_i = 148$$
$$\sum x_i y_i = 833.$$

From these summations, we find

$$SS_{xy} = \sum x_i y_i - \frac{(\sum x_i)(\sum y_i)}{n} = 833 - \frac{(53)(148)}{6} = -474.333$$

$$SS_x = \sum x_i^2 - \frac{(\sum x_i)^2}{n} = 609 - \frac{(53)^2}{6} = 140.833$$

$$\bar{y} = \frac{\sum y_i}{n} = \frac{148}{6} = 24.667$$

$$\bar{x} = \frac{\sum x_i}{n} = \frac{53}{6} = 8.833.$$

Finally, we calculate

$$\hat{\beta}_1 = \frac{SS_{xy}}{SS_x} = \frac{-474.333}{140.833} = -3.368$$

and

$$\hat{\beta}_0 = \bar{y} - \hat{\beta}_1\bar{x} = 24.667 - (-3.368)(8.833) = 54.417.$$

Thus, the least squares line is

$$\hat{y} = 54.417 - 3.368x.$$

Figure 15.5 describes the regression line for Example 15.1. As you can see, the line fits the data quite well. We can measure how well by computing the value of the minimized sum of squared differences. The differences between the points and the line are called **residuals,** denoted e_i. That is,

$$e_i = y_i - \hat{y}_i.$$

The residuals are the observed values of the error variable. Thus, the minimized sum of squared differences is called the **sum of squares for error,** denoted SSE.

Sum of Squares for Error

$$SSE = \sum(y_i - \hat{y}_i)^2$$

TABLE 15.1   CALCULATION OF SSE FOR EXAMPLE 15.1

Observation	Observed Value		Calculated Value	Residuals	Residuals Squared
i	x_i	y_i	$\hat{y}_i = 54.417 - 3.368x$	$y_i - \hat{y}_i$	$(y_i - \hat{y}_i)^2$
1	2	50	47.681	2.319	5.378
2	4	38	40.945	−2.945	8.673
3	8	26	27.473	−1.476	2.179
4	10	25	20.737	4.263	18.173
5	13	7	10.633	−3.633	13.199
6	16	2	.529	1.471	2.164
					$\sum(y_i - \hat{y}_i)^2 = 49.765$

FIGURE 15.5   REGRESSION LINE FOR EXAMPLE 15.1

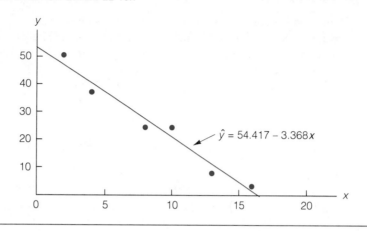

The calculation of *SSE* for Example 15.1 is shown in Figure 15.6. Notice that we compute $\hat{y}_i$ by substituting x_i into the regression line. The residuals are the differences between the values y_i from the sample and $\hat{y}_i$ from the line. Table 15.1 lists specific values of the variables for Example 15.1.

Thus,

$$SSE = 49.765$$

No other straight line will produce a sum of squared errors as small as 49.765. In that sense, the regression line fits the data best.

Let's now apply the technique to a more practical problem.

FIGURE 15.6   MEASURING THE RESIDUALS IN EXAMPLE 15.1

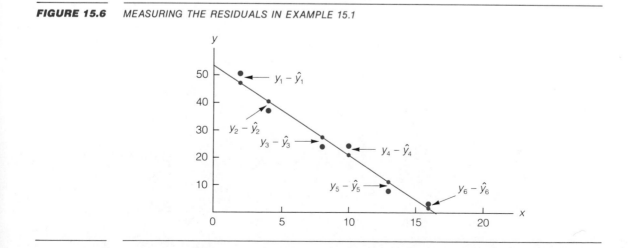

EXAMPLE 15.2

A real-estate agent would like to predict the selling price of single-family homes. After careful consideration, she concludes that the variable likely to be most closely related to selling price is the size of the house. As an experiment, she takes a random sample of 15 recently sold houses and records the selling price (in $1,000s) and the size (in 100 ft^2) of each. These are shown in the accompanying table. Find the sample regression line for these data.

House Size (100 ft^2) x	Selling Price ($1,000s) y
20.0	89.5
14.8	79.9
20.5	83.1
12.5	56.9
18.0	66.6
14.3	82.5
27.5	126.3
16.5	79.3
24.3	119.9
20.2	87.6
22.0	112.6
19.0	120.8
12.3	78.5
14.0	74.3
16.7	74.8

FIGURE 15.7   SCATTERGRAM FOR EXAMPLE 15.2

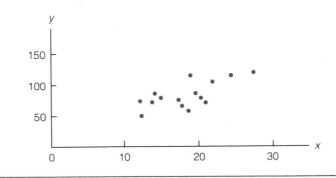

Solution. Both variables are quantitative. Since we want to predict the selling price, this variable is labeled y and house size is labeled x. The scattergram in Figure 15.7 seems to indicate that a linear model is suitable. The various required summations are shown in the following table. We have also calculated $\sum y_i^2$, which is not necessary now but will be useful later.

x	y	x^2	y^2	xy
20.0	89.5	400.00	8,010.25	1,790.00
14.8	79.9	219.04	6,384.01	1,182.52
20.5	83.1	420.25	6,905.61	1,703.55
12.5	56.9	156.25	3,237.61	711.25
18.0	66.6	324.00	4,435.56	1,198.80
14.3	82.5	204.49	6,806.25	1,179.75
27.5	126.3	756.25	15,951.69	3,473.25
16.5	79.3	272.25	6,288.49	1,308.45
24.3	119.9	590.49	14,376.01	2,913.57
20.2	87.6	408.04	7,673.76	1,769.52
22.0	112.6	484.00	12,678.76	2,477.20
19.0	120.8	361.00	14,592.64	2,295.20
12.3	78.5	151.29	6,162.25	965.55
14.0	74.3	196.00	5,520.49	1,040.20
16.7	74.8	278.89	5,595.04	1,249.16
$\sum x_i = 272.6$	$\sum y_i = 1{,}332.6$	$\sum x_i^2 = 5{,}222.24$	$\sum y_i^2 = 124{,}618.42$	$\sum x_i y_i = 25{,}257.97$

From these summations, we produce

$$SS_{xy} = \sum x_i y_i - \frac{\left(\sum x_i\right)\left(\sum y_i\right)}{n} = 25{,}257.97 - \frac{(272.6)(1{,}332.6)}{15} = 1{,}040.18$$

$$SS_x = \sum x_i^2 - \frac{\left(\sum x_i\right)^2}{n} = 5{,}222.24 - \frac{(272.6)^2}{15} = 268.19$$

$$\bar{y} = \frac{\sum y_i}{n} = \frac{1{,}332.6}{15} = 88.84$$

$$\bar{x} = \frac{\sum x_i}{n} = \frac{272.6}{15} = 18.17.$$

It then follows that

$$\hat{\beta}_1 = \frac{SS_{xy}}{SS_x} = \frac{1{,}040.18}{268.19} = 3.88$$

FIGURE 15.8   GRAPH OF EXAMPLE 15.2

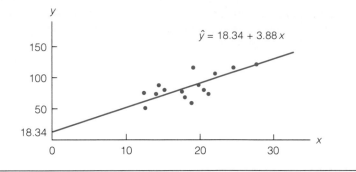

and

$$\hat{\beta}_0 = \bar{y} - \hat{\beta}_1\bar{x} = 88.84 - 3.88(18.17) = 18.34.$$

The sample regression line is

$$\hat{y} = 18.34 + 3.88x.$$

Figure 15.8 graphs the points and the regression line.

Interpreting the Coefficients.   The coefficient $\hat{\beta}_1$ is equal to 3.88 (in \$1,000s) which means that, for each additional 100 square feet, the price of the house increases by an average of \$3,880. If we change the units, $\hat{\beta}_1$ tells us that each additional square foot increases the price by \$38.80.

The intercept is $\hat{\beta}_0 = 18.34$. Technically the intercept is the point at which the regression line and the y-axis intersect. This means that, when $x = 0$ (no house), $\hat{y} = 18.34$ (in \$1,000s). We might be tempted to interpret this to mean that the lot the house is built on is worth \$18,340, on average; however, it is often misleading to interpret $\hat{\beta}_0$ in this way. Since our sample did not include the sale of any empty lots, we really have no basis for concluding that the lots are worth \$18,340. As a general rule, we cannot interpret the value of y for a value of x that is far outside the observed range of values of x. In this example, the range of x was

$$12.3 \le x \le 27.5.$$

Since $x = 0$ is not in the range, we cannot safely interpret the value of y when $x = 0$.

MINITAB COMPUTER OUTPUT FOR EXAMPLE 15.2*

As you will see shortly, several different statistics are typically computed as part of regression analysis. We will show the complete printout here; as you proceed through

---

* See Appendix 15.A for the Minitab commands that produced this printout.

this chapter, refer back to it whenever we discuss how Minitab presents the different components of regression analysis.

```
The regression equation is

Y=18.4+3.88 X

Predictor    Coef      Stdev     t-ratio
Constant     18.35     14.81     1.24
       X     3.8786    0.7936    4.89

s=13.00    R-sq=64.8%    R-sq(adj)=62.0%

Analysis of Variance

SOURCE        DF      SS        MS
Regression     1    4034.4    4034.4
Error         13    2195.8     168.9
Total         14    6230.2
```

Minitab presents the sample regression line at the top of the printout. Thus, we have

$$y = 18.4 + 3.88 \ X$$

EXERCISES

LEARNING THE TECHNIQUES

15.4 Given the following six points, find the least squares regression line:

x	-5	-2	0	3	4	7
y	15	9	7	6	4	1

15.5 Find the least squares regression for the following data:

x	15	6	27	19	14	24	20
y	10	3	21	13	10	11	8

15.6 A set of 10 observations to be analyzed by a regression model yields the following summations:

$$\sum x = 31 \qquad \sum y = 37 \qquad \sum xy = 75$$
$$\sum x^2 = 103 \qquad \sum y^2 = 445.$$

Find the least squares regression line.

15.7 A set of 25 observations of two variables x and y produced the following summations:

$$\sum x = 62.5 \qquad \sum y = 129.0 \qquad \sum xy = 141.1$$
$$\sum x^2 = 317.8 \qquad \sum y^2 = 936.4.$$

Find the least squares regression line.

APPLYING THE TECHNIQUES

Self-Correcting Exercise (See Appendix 15.B for the solution.)

15.8 The accompanying table exhibits, for 8 grocery stores, the annual profit per dollar of sales y (measured in cents) and the number of employees per store x.

x	3	6	4	5	2	5	4	1
y	22	30	20	25	18	26	22	19

a. Find the least squares regression line to help predict profit per sales dollar on the basis of the number of employees.

b. Plot the points, and graph the regression line.

c. Does it appear that a straight line model is reasonable?

d. Make an economic interpretation of the slope.

15.9 A custom jobber of specialty fiberglass-bodied cars wished to estimate overhead expenses (labeled y and measured in \$1,000s) as a function of the number of cars (x) it produced monthly. A random sample of 12 months was recorded and the following statistics calculated.

$$\sum x = 157 \qquad \sum y = 57 \qquad \sum xy = 987$$
$$\sum x^2 = 4{,}102 \qquad \sum y^2 = 413$$

Find the least squares regression line and interpret the value of $\hat{\beta}_1$.

15.10 Twelve secretaries were asked to take a special 3-day intensive course to improve their typing skills. They were given a particular 2-page letter and asked to type it flawlessly at the beginning and again at the end of the course. The data shown in the following table were recorded.

Typist	Number of Years of Experience x	Improvement (words per minute) y
A	2	9
B	6	11
C	3	8
D	8	12
E	10	14
F	5	9
G	10	14
H	11	13
I	12	14
J	9	10
K	8	9
L	10	10
	$\sum x = 94$	$\sum y = 133$ $\sum xy = 1{,}102$
	$\sum x^2 = 848$	$\sum y^2 = 1{,}529$

a. Find the equation of the regression line.

b. As a check of your calculations in part (a), plot the 12 points and graph the line.

c. Does it appear that the typists' experience is linearly related to their typing improvement?

15.11 Students in a small class were polled by a surveyor attempting to establish a relationship between hours of study in the week immediately preceding a major midterm exam and the marks received on the exam. The surveyor gathered the data listed in the accompanying table.

Hours of Study (x)	Exam Score (y)
25	93
12	57
18	55
26	90
19	82
20	95
23	95
15	80
22	85
8	61
$\sum x = 188$	$\sum y = 793$ $\sum xy = 15{,}540$
$\sum x^2 = 3{,}832$	$\sum y^2 = 65{,}143$

a. Find the equation of the regression line to help predict the exam score on the basis of study hours.

b. As a check of your calculations in part (a), plot the 10 points and graph the line.

c. Interpret the meaning of the coefficients.

d. Is the sign of the slope logical? If the slope had the opposite sign, what would that tell you?

15.12 Advertising is often touted as the key to success. In seeking to determine just how influential advertising is, the management of a recently set-up retail chain has collected data over the previous 15 weeks on sales revenue and advertising expenditures, with the results shown in the accompanying table.

Advertising Expenditures ($1,000s) x	Sales ($1,000s) y
3	50
5	250
7	700
6	450
6.5	600
8	1,000
3.5	75
4	150
4.5	200
6.5	550
7	750

Advertising Expenditures ($1,000s) x	Sales ($1,000s) y
7.5	800
7.5	900
8.5	1,100
7	600

$\sum x = 91.5$ $\sum y = 8,175$ $\sum xy = 57,787.5$
$\sum x^2 = 598.75$ $\sum y^2 = 6,070,625$

a. Find the coefficients of the regression line, using the least squares method.

b. Make an economic interpretation of the slope.

c. If the sign of the slope were negative, what would that say about the advertising?

d. What does the value of the intercept tell you?

SECTION 15.4

ASSESSING THE MODEL: ESTIMATING σ_ε^2

The least squares method produces the best straight line (where *best* is defined as minimizing the sum of squared errors). At this point, however, we do not know whether there is a linear relationship between x and y. If no linear relationship exists, the use of a linear model will produce poor forecasts. Hence it is important to assess the model. If it is poor, we would do better to discard it and search for a better one.

Three different methods can be used to evaluate the model. In this section we will discuss assessing the model by analyzing the error variable ε.

If the linear regression line fits the data well, there will be mostly small deviations between the data points and the line (see Figure 15.9). Consequently most of the residuals (the differences between the actual value of y and the computed value of y) will be close to their mean value of zero. In such a case the variance of the error variable will be small. If the model's fit is poor, some of the residuals will be large, and as a result the variance of ε will be large (see Figure 15.10). Thus, we can assess the model by determining the variance of the error variable σ_ε^2. Unfortunately, σ_ε^2 is a population parameter, and its value is usually unknown. Still, σ_ε^2 can be estimated from the data in the random sample. Recall from Section 15.3 that the minimum sum of squared errors is labeled *SSE*. The sample statistic

$$s_\varepsilon^2 = \frac{SSE}{n-2}$$

FIGURE 15.9 STRAIGHT LINE AS A GOOD FIT

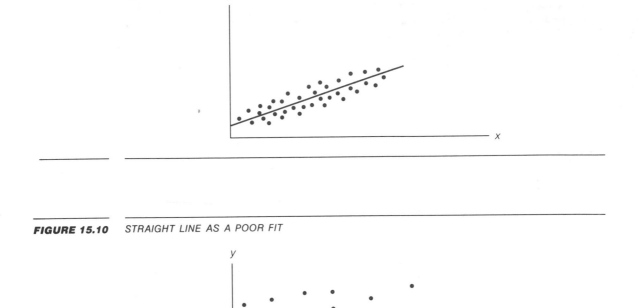

FIGURE 15.10 STRAIGHT LINE AS A POOR FIT

is the estimator of σ_ε^2. The square root of s_ε^2 is called the **standard error of estimate.**

Standard Error of Estimate

$$s_\varepsilon = \sqrt{\frac{SSE}{n-2}}$$

In order to compute s_ε^2, we need to calculate SSE. Recall that we determined SSE in Example 15.1 by calculating $\hat{y}_i$ from the regression line, taking the difference between the observed y_i and $\hat{y}_i$, squaring the differences, and summing the squares. When the sample size is large, this process is extremely time-consuming. Fortunately a shortcut method is available.

Shortcut Calculation of SSE

$$SSE = SS_y - \frac{SS_{xy}^2}{SS_x},$$

where

$$SS_y = \sum (y_i - \bar{y})^2 = \sum y_i^2 - \frac{(\sum y_i)^2}{n}.$$

In anticipation of this equation, we computed $\sum y_i^2$ in the table accompanying Example 15.2.

EXAMPLE 15.3

From the data developed in Example 15.2, determine the estimate of σ_{ε}^2 and the standard error of estimate.

Solution.   We begin by calculating SS_y. In the course of Example 15.2, we found

$$\sum y_i^2 = 124{,}618.42$$

and

$$\sum y_i = 1{,}332.6.$$

From these, we find

$$SS_y = \sum y_i^2 - \frac{(\sum y_i)^2}{n} = 124{,}618.42 - \frac{(1{,}332.6)^2}{15} = 6{,}230.24.$$

While calculating $\hat{\beta}_1$ in Example 15.2, we found

$$SS_{xy} = 1{,}040.18$$

and

$$SS_x = 268.19.$$

Thus, we have

$$SSE = SS_y - \frac{SS_{xy}^2}{SS_x} = 6{,}230.24 - \frac{(1{,}040.18)^2}{268.19} = 2{,}195.88$$

and

$$s_{\varepsilon}^2 = \frac{SSE}{n-2} = \frac{2{,}195.88}{15-2} = 168.91.$$

The estimate of σ_{ε}^2 is $s_{\varepsilon}^2 = 168.91$. The standard error of estimate is

$$s_{\varepsilon} = \sqrt{168.91} = 13.00.$$

Interpreting the Value of s_ε. The smallest value that s_ε can assume is zero, which occurs when $SSE = 0$ (that is, when all the points fall on the regression line). Therefore, if the standard error of estimate is close to zero, the fit is excellent, and the linear model is likely to be a useful and effective analytical and forecasting tool. If the standard error of estimate is large, the model is a poor one, and the statistician should attempt to find a better one.

We judge the value of s_ε by comparing it to the values of the dependent variable y or (more particularly) to the sample mean $\bar{y}$. In this case, because $s_\varepsilon = 13.00$ and $\bar{y} = 88.84$, we would say that s_ε is not very small. Since there is no predefined upper limit on the standard error of estimate, however, it is difficult to assess the model definitively in this way (except when s_ε is close to zero). In general, the standard error of estimate cannot be used as an absolute measure of the model's utility.

Nonetheless, s_ε is useful in comparing models. If the statistician has several models to choose from, the one with the smallest value of s_ε generally should be the one used. As you'll see in subsequent sections of this chapter, the standard error of estimate is also an important statistic in the other techniques associated with regression analysis. It will be used in Section 15.5 to test the model, and it will be used later in the chapter to estimate and predict the value of y.

MINITAB COMPUTER OUTPUT FOR EXAMPLE 15.3

Refer to page 409 to examine the Minitab computer output for Example 15.2. Minitab denotes the standard error of estimate s and prints

s = 13.00

 EXERCISES

LEARNING THE TECHNIQUES

15.13 A set of 15 observations to be analyzed by regression analysis yields the following summations:

$\sum x = 75$ $\sum y = 525$ $\sum xy = 3{,}145$
$\sum x^2 = 455$ $\sum y^2 = 25{,}146.$

Compute the standard error of estimate (s_ε).

15.14 For Exercise 15.4, calculate the sum of squared errors (SSE) by computing each value of $\hat{y}$, subtracting y, squaring the differences, and summing the squared differences. To check your computation, calculate SSE by the shortcut method.

15.15 For Exercise 15.5, calculate SSE by computing each value of $\hat{y}$, subtracting y, squaring the differences, and summing the squared differences. Then compute SSE by the shortcut method, and compare the results.

15.16 In a study of the relationship between two variables x and y, the following summations were computed:

$\sum x = 105$ $\sum y = 4{,}414$ $\sum xy = 37{,}525$
$\sum x^2 = 956$ $\sum y^2 = 1{,}818{,}421$ $n = 15.$

Compute SSE, s_ε^2, and s_ε.

15.17 Calculate SSE and s_ε for Exercise 15.6.

15.18 Provide an example of five observations of x and y for which $s_\varepsilon = 0$.

15.19 Calculate SSE and s_ε for Exercise 15.7.

APPLYING THE TECHNIQUES

Self-Correcting Exercise (See Appendix 15.B for the solution.)

15.20   For Exercise 15.8, find the standard error of estimate. What does this value tell you about the linear regression model?

15.21   An economist wanted to investigate the relationship between office rents and vacancy rates. She took a random sample of the monthly office rents per square foot and the percentage of vacant office space in 10 different cities. The results are shown in the following table.

City	Vacancy Rate x	Monthly Rent y
1	3	5.00
2	11	2.50
3	6	4.75
4	5	4.50
5	9	3.00
6	2	4.50
7	5	4.00
8	7	3.00
9	10	3.25
10	8	2.75
	$\sum x = 66$	$\sum y = 37.25$ $\sum xy = 225.0$
	$\sum x^2 = 514$	$\sum y^2 = 146.44$

a. Compute the least squares regression line.

b. Calculate the standard error of estimate. How well does the linear model fit the data?

15.22   Calculate the standard error of estimate in Exercise 15.10, in order to determine how well the model fits the data.

15.23   A new profit-sharing plan was introduced at an automobile parts manufacturing plant last year. Both management and union representatives are interested in determining how a worker's years of experience influence his or her productivity gains. After the plan had been in effect for a while, the following data were collected.

Worker	Years on Assembly Line x	Number of Units Manufactured Daily y
1	15.1	110
2	7.0	105
3	18.6	115
4	23.7	127
5	11.5	98
6	16.4	103
7	6.3	87
8	15.4	108
9	19.9	112
	$\sum x = 133.9$ $\sum y = 965$ $\sum xy = 14,801.2$	
	$\sum x^2 = 2,258.73$ $\sum y^2 = 104,469$	

a. Find the least squares regression line.

b. Calculate the standard error of estimate.

c. What does the value of s_ε tell you about the relationship between x and y?

15.24   Calculate the standard error of estimate for Exercise 15.12. What does this value tell you about the relationship between sales and advertising expenditures?

SECTION 15.5   ## ASSESSING THE MODEL: DRAWING INFERENCES ABOUT β_1

A second method of assessing the model involves determining whether a linear relationship actually exists between x and y. Suppose that in Example 15.2 we had

---

FIGURE 15.11   POPULATION REGRESSION LINE REVEALING NO LINEAR RELATIONSHIP

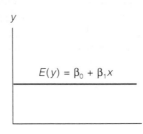

---

examined the relationship between the selling price and the house size for all houses in the region. We could then determine the population regression line

$$E(y) = \beta_0 + \beta_1 x.$$

Notice that, since we are dealing in this case with the entire population, we refer to the population parameters β_0 and β_1 (no hats).

Suppose that, when drawn, the regression line produces the graph shown in Figure 15.11. The line here is horizontal, which means that the value of y is unaffected by the value of x. A horizontal straight line has a slope of zero; hence, $\beta_1 = 0$ means that no linear relationship exists and that the linear model is inappropriate.

In general, however, β_1 is unknown, because it's a population parameter. Thus, once again, we must use the sample slope $\hat{\beta}_1$ to make inferences about the population slope β_1.

TESTING β_1

The process of testing hypotheses about β_1 is identical to the process of testing any other parameter. We begin with the hypotheses. As usual we can test any one of three alternative hypotheses:

1. If we want to test the slope, in order to determine whether some linear relationship exists between x and y, we test

    $H_A: \beta_1 \neq 0.$

2. If we want to test for a positive linear relationship, we test

    $H_A: \beta_1 > 0.$

3. If we want to test for a negative linear relationship, we test

    $H_A: \beta_1 < 0.$

In all cases, the null hypothesis specifies that no linear relationship exists. That is,

$H_0: \beta_1 = 0.$

The test statistic is as follows.

Test Statistic for β_1

$$t = \frac{\hat{\beta}_1 - \beta_1}{s_{\hat{\beta}_1}}$$

where $s_{\hat{\beta}_1}$ is the standard deviation of $\hat{\beta}_1$ (also called the *standard error* of $\hat{\beta}_1$) and is equal to

$$s_{\hat{\beta}_1} = \frac{s_\varepsilon}{\sqrt{SS_x}}$$

Assuming that the error variable ε is normally distributed, the test statistic follows a Student t distribution, with $n - 2$ degrees of freedom.

EXAMPLE 15.4

Using the data in Example 15.2, can we conclude at the 1% level of significance that the size of a house is linearly related to its selling price?

Solution.   We wish to test the following hypotheses:

$H_0: \beta_1 = 0.$

$H_A: \beta_1 \neq 0.$

Test statistic:

$$t = \frac{\hat{\beta}_1 - \beta_1}{s_{\hat{\beta}_1}}$$

Significance level: $\alpha = .01$

Decision rule: Reject H_0 if $|t| > t_{\alpha/2, n-2} = t_{.005, 13} = 3.012.$

Value of the test statistic: From previous work, we have

$$\hat{\beta}_1 = 3.88$$

$$s_{\hat{\beta}_1} = \frac{s_\varepsilon}{\sqrt{SS_x}} = \frac{13.00}{\sqrt{268.19}} = .794.$$

Therefore,

$$t = \frac{\hat{\beta}_1 - \beta_1}{s_{\hat{\beta}_1}} = \frac{3.88 - 0}{.794} = 4.89.$$

Conclusion: Reject H_0.

There is sufficient evidence to indicate that house size linearly affects selling price (see Figure 15.12).

FIGURE 15.12   SAMPLING DISTRIBUTION FOR EXAMPLE 15.4

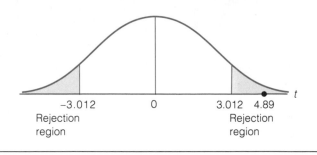

In effect, we are saying that a linear relationship does exist and that the slope of the line is significantly different from zero. If we had not been able to reject the null hypothesis, our conclusion would have been that there was insufficient evidence to show that the slope is not equal to zero, and consequently that there may be no linear relationship between x and y.

MINITAB COMPUTER OUTPUT FOR EXAMPLE 15.4

The Minitab system allows you to test β_0 and β_1. As we've pointed out before, however, interpreting the value of the y-intercept can lead to erroneous conclusions. As a result, we will not test β_0. The output from Minitab includes the standard deviation of $\hat{\beta}_1$ ($s_{\hat{\beta}_1}$) and the t-statistic. To see where in the printout these values appear, again refer to the computer output for Example 15.2 on page 409.

The relevant part of the printout is

```
Predictor    Coef      Stdev     t-ratio
Constant    18.35      14.81      1.24
       X     3.8786     0.7936     4.89
```

The standard deviation (`Stdev`) of $\hat{\beta}_1$ is .7936, and the value of the test statistic

$$t = \frac{\hat{\beta}_1 - \beta_1}{s_{\hat{\beta}_1}}$$

is 4.89.

EXERCISES

LEARNING THE TECHNIQUES

15.25   Test each of the following hypotheses:

a. $H_0: \beta_1 = 0$.
     $H_A: \beta_1 \neq 0$.
     $\hat{\beta}_1 = 1.87$ $s_{\hat{\beta}_1} = .63$ $n = 25$ $\alpha = .05$

b. $H_0: \beta_1 = 0$.
     $H_A: \beta_1 < 0$.
     $\hat{\beta}_1 = -26.32$ $s_{\hat{\beta}_1} = 14.51$ $n = 100$
     $\alpha = .01$

c. $H_0: \beta_1 = 0.$
$H_A: \beta_1 > 0.$
$\beta_1 = .056 \qquad s_{\hat{\beta}_1} = .021 \qquad n = 10 \qquad \alpha = .05$

15.26 Test with $\alpha = .05$ to determine whether there is evidence of a linear relationship, given the following results:

$\sum x = 55 \qquad \sum y = 325 \qquad \sum xy = 929$
$\sum x^2 = 175 \qquad \sum y^2 = 6{,}051 \qquad n = 20$

15.27 Test with $\alpha = .01$ to determine whether there is evidence of a linear relationship for the following data:

x	7	12	0	-2	5
y	9	6	12	15	10

15.28 Twelve observations of x and y produced the following summations:

$\sum x = 65 \qquad \sum y = 515 \qquad \sum xy = 3{,}085$
$\sum x^2 = 445 \qquad \sum y^2 = 24{,}815.$

Is there sufficient evidence at the 1% significance level to determine whether a positive linear relationship exists between x and y?

15.29 For Exercise 15.5, test with $\alpha = .10$ to determine whether there is enough evidence to allow us to conclude that a linear relationship exists between x and y.

APPLYING THE TECHNIQUES

Self-Correcting Exercise (See Appendix 15.B for the solution.)

15.30 Frank Jones is a student in the class referred to in Exercise 15.11. He doesn't believe that more hours of study result in a higher exam score. Using the data in Exercise 15.11, produce a test with $\alpha = .05$ to convince Frank that he's wrong.

15.31 To get a better idea of some of the determinants of medical expenditures by families, a social worker collected data on family size and average monthly medical bills, with the results shown in the following table.

Family Size x	Monthly Medical Expenses (in dollars) y
2	20
2	28
4	52
5	50
7	78
3	35
8	102
10	88
5	51
2	22
3	29
5	49
2	25
$\sum x = 58$ $\sum x^2 \doteq 338$	$\sum y = 629$ $\sum y^2 = 38{,}797$ $\sum xy = 3{,}582$

Do these data present sufficient evidence (with $\alpha = .05$) that larger families have larger monthly medical expenses?

15.32 The owner of the company alluded to in Exercise 15.12 does not believe that his advertising is effective in increasing sales. Perform an appropriate test, with $\alpha = .01$, to examine the problem.

15.33 Physicians have been recommending more exercise for their patients, particularly those who are overweight. One benefit of regular exercise appears to be a reduction in cholesterol, a substance associated with heart disease. In order to study the relationship more carefully, a physician took a random sample of 8 patients who did not exercise. He measured their cholesterol levels and then started them on regular exercise programs. After 4 months he asked each patient how many minutes per week (on the average) he or she exercised, and he again measured their cholesterol levels. The results are shown in the accompanying table. Can the physician conclude at the 5% significance level that more exercise leads to greater cholesterol reduction?

Patient	Weekly Exercise (minutes)	Cholesterol Level Before	Cholesterol Level After
1	75	240	180
2	80	210	195
3	105	230	200
4	40	220	200
5	20	235	230
6	150	205	180
7	60	190	180
8	90	200	185

15.34 Corporate sponsors of television commercials want people who see their commercials to remember at least the brand name of the product. A marketing manager of a major computer manufacturer believes that, all other things being equal, the more frequently the name of the product is mentioned in a television commercial, the greater the percentage of people who remember the name will be. To examine this potentially important phenomenon, she prepares 5 commercials that are essentially identical except in the number of times they mention the name of the computer company. Each commercial is shown to five different groups of 100 people. (At the same time, each group is also shown various other products' commercials.) Three days later they are asked to name the computer that was advertised. The number of correct responses from each group was recorded. The results are shown in the following table. Do these data support the marketing manager's belief? (Use $\alpha = 10$.)

Number of Times Product Mentioned	Number of People Identifying Product Name
2	40
3	45
5	41
7	48
8	55

SECTION
15.6

ASSESSING THE MODEL: MEASURING THE STRENGTH OF THE LINEAR RELATIONSHIP

The test of β_1 discussed in the previous section only addresses the question of whether there is enough evidence to allow us to conclude that a linear relationship does exist. In many cases, however, it is also useful to measure the strength of the linear relationship. This is particularly important when we wish to compare different models to see which one fits the data best. In this section, we present two such measures: the coefficient of correlation and the coefficient of determination.

COEFFICIENT OF CORRELATION

The **coefficient of correlation,** denoted ρ (the Greek letter rho), measures the similarity of the changes in the values of x and y. Its range is

$$-1 \leq \rho \leq +1.$$

If (in general) y increases when x increases, ρ is positive. If y generally decreases when x increases, ρ is negative. If y is unaffected by x, then $\rho = 0$. The absolute value of ρ measures how closely changes in x mirror changes in y. When $|\rho| = 1$, for example, a change in the value of x is reflected by a perfectly predictable change in the value of y, and every point falls on the regression line. When $\rho = 0$, the values of x and y are not correlated, which is equivalent to saying that there is no linear relationship between x and y.

Figure 15.13 depicts examples of different values of ρ. When $\rho = +1$, the slope is positive and all data points fall exactly on the line; when $\rho = -1$, the slope is negative but again all data points fall exactly on the line; when $\rho = 0$, the line is horizontal and no linear relationship exists between the two variables. Other values of ρ must be interpreted within the framework established by these three values. For example, $\rho = +.90$ tells us that there is a strong (but not perfect) positive linear relationship; similarly, $\rho = -.30$ indicates a weak negative relationship.

FIGURE 15.13   GRAPHICAL PRESENTATIONS OF FIVE VALUES OF CORRELATION COEFFICIENTS (ρ)

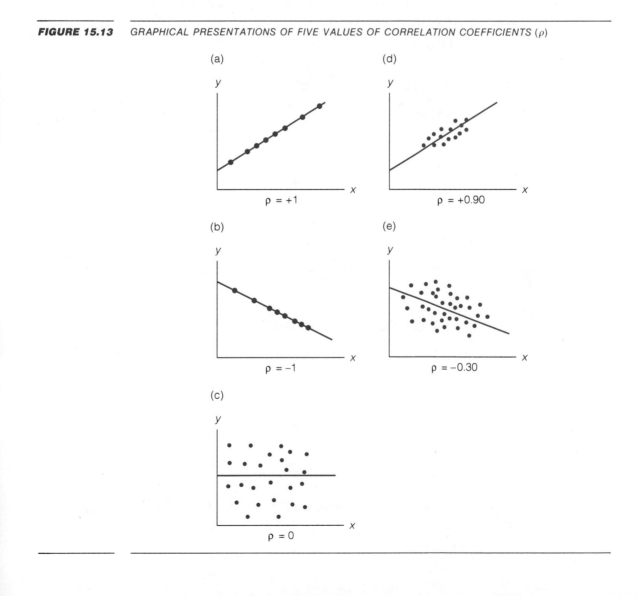

Since ρ is a population parameter, we estimate its value from the data, using the sample coefficient of correlation, denoted r.

Sample Coefficient of Correlation

$$r = \frac{SS_{xy}}{\sqrt{SS_x \cdot SS_y}}$$

Since each component has been previously calculated, r can quickly be determined. In Example 15.2 we found

$$SS_{xy} = 1{,}040.18$$
$$SS_x = 268.19,$$

and in Example 15.3 we found

$$SS_y = 6{,}230.24.$$

Hence,

$$r = \frac{SS_{xy}}{\sqrt{SS_x \cdot SS_y}} = \frac{1{,}040.18}{\sqrt{(268.19)(6{,}230.24)}} = .805.$$

The coefficient of correlation tells us two things. First because it is positive, the slope of the regression line is also positive. Second, since .805 is close to 1, the fit is fairly good. Unfortunately, when interpreting the value of r, we can only use vague terms such as close or fairly good. Except when $r = +1$, -1, or 0, we cannot interpret r precisely. This shortcoming will be remedied by the coefficient of determination.

COEFFICIENT OF DETERMINATION

The **coefficient of determination,** denoted r^2, is defined as the coefficient of correlation squared.

Sample Coefficient of Determination

$$r^2 = \frac{SS_{xy}^2}{SS_x \cdot SS_y}$$

If we perform some algebraic manipulations on the formula for r^2, we can rewrite it as

$$r^2 = \frac{SS_y - SSE}{SS_y},$$

where

$$SS_y = \sum(y_i - \bar{y})^2$$

measures the variation in the dependent variable y (you should recognize this statistic as the numerator in a calculation of the sample variance of y), and

$$SSE = \sum(y_i - \hat{y}_i)^2$$

measures the variation between the observed values of y and the calculated (from the regression line) values of $\hat{y}$. The difference between SS_y and SSE is denoted SSR, the sum of squares for regression. That is,

$$SSR = SS_y - SSE.$$

As a result,

$$r^2 = \frac{SSR}{SS_y}.$$

The sum of squares for regression SSR measures the amount of variation in y that is explained by the variation in x. (The sum of squares for error SSE represents the unexplained variation.) Consequently we interpret the coefficient of determination as the proportion of the variation in the dependent variable y that is explained by the variation in the independent variable x. We can illustrate this interpretation by examining two extreme cases.

Suppose that we have developed a regression line along which all the sample points fall. Parts (a) and (b) of Figure 15.13 depict this case. As you can see, we would compute

$$SSE = 0;$$

and since

$$r^2 = \frac{SS_y - SSE}{SS_y},$$

it follows that

$$r^2 = \frac{SS_y - 0}{SS_y} = 1.$$

Thus a coefficient of determination of 100% indicates a relationship in which any change in x results in a perfectly predictable change in y.

Part (c) of Figure 15.13 illustrates the case in which no linear relationship exists between x and y. In this case SSE achieves its maximum possible value, which is SS_y. It follows that

$$SSR = 0$$

and

$$r^2 = \frac{SSR}{SS_y} = 0.$$

Hence, no part of the variation in y is explained by the variation in x. Expressed differently, we say that, when $r^2 = 0$, the regression line has no explanatory power and is useless.

In Example 15.2 we found

$r = .805.$

Hence the coefficient of determination is

$r^2 = (.805)^2 = .648$

This means that 64.8% of the variation in house prices is explained by the houses' differences in size. The remaining 35.2% is unexplained.

MINITAB COMPUTER OUTPUT SHOWING THE COEFFICIENT OF DETERMINATION

Minitab prints the coefficient of determination as

`R-sq=64.8%`

Minitab also prints a second coefficient of determination, as

`R-sq(adj)=62.0%`

but we will not be discussing this statistic, so we recommend that you ignore it.

MINITAB COMPUTER OUTPUT SHOWING THE SUMS OF SQUARES

The last part of the computer output shown on page 409 is actually provided for another statistical technique, which will be discussed in Chapter 16. However, it does provide some useful information for our objectives in this chapter. It looks like this:

SOURCE	DF	SS	MS
Regression	1	4034.4	4034.3
Error	13	2195.8	168.9
Total	14	6230.2	

According to this tabulation, the sum of squares for regression is $SSR = 4,034.4$, the sum of squares for error is $SSE = 2,195.8$, and the total variation in y is $SS_y = 6,230.2$. Thus we can recompute the coefficient of determination as follows:

$$r^2 = \frac{SS_y - SSE}{SS_y} = \frac{SSR}{SS_y} = \frac{4,034.4}{6,230.2} = .648.$$

EXERCISES

LEARNING THE TECHNIQUES

15.35 A set of data consisting of 12 observations yields the following results:

$\sum x = 35 \qquad \sum y = 84 \qquad \sum xy = 185$

$\sum x^2 = 190 \qquad \sum y^2 = 719.$

a. Calculate the coefficient of correlation.

b. Calculate the coefficient of determination.

15.36 Given the following observations, determine the coefficient of correlation:

x	0	5	-1	0	3	2	4
y	3	10	2	4	6	5	7

15.37 Compute the coefficients of correlation and determination for Exercise 15.4.

15.38 Given the following summations calculated from 20 observations, find the coefficients of correlation and determination:

$$\sum x = 15.3 \qquad \sum y = 106.3 \qquad \sum xy = 61.0$$
$$\sum x^2 = 18.6 \qquad \sum y^2 = 725.1.$$

15.39 Given the following sums of squares, find the proportion of total variation explained by the regression model:

$$SSR = 650 \qquad SSE = 350 \qquad SS_y = 1,000.$$

15.40 Invent some values of x and y (about five pairs) that have a correlation of:

a. $+1$

b. -1

c. 0

15.41 Explain what the sign of the correlation coefficient means, and state how you would interpret the magnitude of r.

APPLYING THE TECHNIQUES

Self-Correcting Exercise (See Appendix 15.B for the solution.)

15.42 Calculate the coefficients of correlation and determination for Exercise 15.11. What do these values tell you?

15.43 A supermarket chain performed a survey to help determine desirable locations for new stores. The management of the chain wanted to know whether a linear relationship exists between weekly take-home pay and weekly food expenditures. A random sample of 8 households produced the data shown in the accompanying table.

Family	Weekly Take-home Pay (x)	Weekly Food Expenditures (y)
1	300	160
2	200	110
3	270	150
4	180	90
5	250	130
6	360	200
7	225	120
8	340	180

a. Find the least squares regression line.

b. Compute the standard error of estimate.

c. Do these data provide sufficient evidence (with $\alpha = .01$) to allow us to conclude that a linear relationship exists between x and y?

d. Calculate the coefficients of correlation and determination.

e. What does the value of r^2 tell you about the strength of the linear relationship?

15.44 A computer-manufacturing plant offers one year of free service with the sale of each computer. As part of an internal cost-control program, checks are being made to ascertain the time needed for a customer service call and the number of tape drives that customers ask to have adjusted. The results of this study (shown in the accompanying table) should result in better time use and in cost reduction.

No. of Tape Drives x	Minutes on Service Call y
5	310
3	240
7	380
2	120
1	90
9	510

(continued)

No. of Tape Drives	Minutes on Service Call
x	*y*
8	450
6	320
5	410
3	390

a. Determine the least squares regression line.

b. Interpret the coefficients.

c. Calculate *SSE* and the standard error of estimate.

d. Can we conclude that a positive linear relationship exists between *x* and *y*? (Use $\alpha = .05$.)

e. Compute the coefficient of determination, and comment on what it says about the strength of the linear relationship.

15.45   In order to determine a realistic price for a new product that a company wishes to market, the company's research department selected 10 sites thought to have essentially identical sales potential and offered the product in each at a different price. The resulting sales are recorded in the accompanying table.

Location	Price *x*	Sales ($1,000s) *y*
1	15.00	15
2	15.50	14
3	16.00	16
4	16.50	9
5	17.00	12
6	17.50	10
7	18.00	8
8	18.50	9
9	19.00	6
10	19.50	5

a. Find the equation of the regression line.

b. Is there sufficient evidence at the 10% significance level to allow us to conclude that a negative linear relationship exists between price and sales?

c. Calculate the coefficients of correlation and determination.

15.46   Calculate the coefficient of determination for Exercise 15.31. What does this value tell you about the strength of the linear relationship?

SECTION
15.7

USING THE REGRESSION EQUATION

As we pointed out in Section 15.1, the regression model can be used for forecasting and analysis. By analyzing the regression equation in Example 15.2, for instance, we learned that, for each additional square foot, the selling price of the house increases (on average) by $38.80. This information may be useful to real-estate agents, property tax assessors, banks (in determinating mortgage limits), and insurance agents (in calculating replacement costs).

We can also use the regression model to predict and estimate values of *y*. Again referring to Example 15.2, suppose that a real-estate agent wanted to predict the selling price of a house that occupies 2,000 square feet. Using the regression equation, with $x = 20$ (because the unit of measurement of *x* is hundreds of square feet), we get

$$\hat{y} = 18.34 + 3.88x = 18.34 + 3.88(20) = 95.94.$$

Thus, she would predict that the house will sell for $95,940 (since the unit of measurement of *y* is thousands of dollars).

By itself, however, this value does not provide any information about how closely it will match the true selling price of a 2,000-square-foot house. To discover that information, we must use a confidence interval. In fact, we can use one of two intervals: the prediction interval (for a particular value of y), or the confidence interval estimate (for the expected value of y).

PREDICTING THE PARTICULAR VALUE OF *y* FOR A GIVEN *x*

The first confidence interval we will discuss is used whenever we want to predict one particular value of the dependent variable, given a specific value of the independent variable. This confidence interval is often called the **prediction interval.**

> **Prediction Interval**
>
> $$\hat{y} \pm t_{\alpha/2, n-2} s_{\varepsilon} \sqrt{1 + \frac{1}{n} + \frac{(x_g - \bar{x})^2}{SS_x}}$$
>
> where x_g is the given value of x and
>
> $$\hat{y} = \hat{\beta}_0 + \hat{\beta}_1 x_g$$

EXAMPLE 15.5

Predict with 95% confidence the selling price of a house that occupies 2,000 square feet.

Solution.   From previous calculations, we have

$$\hat{y} = 18.34 + 3.88x_g = 18.34 + 3.88(20) = 95.94$$
$$s_{\varepsilon} = 13.00$$
$$SS_x = 268.19$$
$$\bar{x} = 18.17$$
$$t_{.025, 13} = 2.160.$$

The 95% prediction interval is

$$\hat{y} \pm t_{\alpha/2, n-2} s_{\varepsilon} \sqrt{1 + \frac{1}{n} + \frac{(x_g - \bar{x})^2}{SS_x}}$$

$$= 95.94 \pm (2.160)(13.00) \sqrt{1 + \frac{1}{15} + \frac{(20 - 18.17)^2}{268.19}}$$

$$= 95.94 \pm 29.17,$$

or

$$LCL = 66.77 \quad \text{and} \quad UCL = 125.11.$$

We predict that the selling price will fall between \$66,770 and \$125,110.

If you think that this interval is awfully wide, you're right. Even though there is sufficient evidence of a linear relationship, and even though we have determined that the coefficient of determination is .648, the size of the interval apparently makes the value of the model dubious. Bear in mind, however, that this sample is quite small—likely much smaller than the sample that would be used in a real application. More important, restricting the number of independent variables to one precluded us from producing a better model and hence a better prediction.

ESTIMATING THE EXPECTED VALUE OF y FOR A GIVEN x

The required conditions described in Section 15.2 imply that, for a given value of x, there is a population of values of y whose mean is

$$E(y) = \beta_0 + \beta_1 x.$$

To estimate this value, we would use the formula for a confidence interval estimator.

> **Confidence Interval Estimator of the Expected Value of y**
>
> $$\hat{y} \pm t_{\alpha/2, n-2} s_\varepsilon \sqrt{\frac{1}{n} + \frac{(x_g - \bar{x})^2}{SS_x}}$$

This formula produces a narrower estimate than that of the prediction interval. This is reasonable, given that predicting a single value is more difficult than estimating the average of a population of values.

EXAMPLE 15.6

In a certain part of the city, a developer built several thousand houses whose floor plans and exteriors differ, but whose sizes are all 2,000 square feet. To date they've been rented, but the builder now wishes to sell them and wants to know approximately how much money in total he can expect from the sale of the houses. Help him by producing a 95% confidence interval estimate of the mean selling price of the houses.

Solution. Since we now want to estimate the expected value of a large population of selling prices, we use the following formula:

$$\hat{y} \pm t_{\alpha/2, n-2} s_\varepsilon \sqrt{\frac{1}{n} + \frac{(x_g - \bar{x})^2}{SS_x}}.$$

Substituting the values previously calculated, we have

$$\hat{y} \pm t_{\alpha/2, n-2} s_\varepsilon \sqrt{\frac{1}{n} + \frac{(x_g - \bar{x})^2}{SS_x}}$$

$$= 95.94 \pm (2.160)(13.00) \sqrt{\frac{1}{15} + \frac{(20 - 18.17)^2}{268.19}}$$

$$= 95.94 \pm 7.90.$$

or

$$LCL = 88.04 \quad \text{and} \quad UCL = 103.84.$$

Thus, the mean selling price is estimated to lie between $88,040 and $103,840.

From the interval calculated in Example 15.5, we predicted that the price of each house will be between $66,770 and $125,110; now we estimate, in addition, that the mean price of all the houses will be between $88,040 and $103,840. Notice that, because predicting a single value is relatively difficult, the prediction interval for one house is wider than the confidence interval estimate of the expected value of all the houses.

MINITAB COMPUTER OUTPUT FOR EXAMPLE 15.5 and 15.6*

```
Fit      Stdev. Fit        95% C.I.            95% P.I.
95.92        3.66      (88.03, 103.82)    (66.75, 125.10)
```

The output includes the calculated value of $\hat{y}$, which is listed as `Fit` (`95.92`), the standard deviation of y (`3.66`), which is

$$s_\varepsilon \sqrt{\frac{1}{n} + \frac{(x_g - \bar{x})^2}{SS_x}},$$

the 95% confidence interval estimate of the expected value of y (`88.03, 103.82`), and the 95% prediction interval (`66.75, 125.10`).

EXERCISES

LEARNING THE TECHNIQUES

15.47 On the basis of 8 observations of x and y, the following summations were computed:

$$\sum x = 40 \qquad \sum y = 100 \qquad \sum xy = 600$$
$$\sum x^2 = 250 \qquad \sum y^2 = 2,000.$$

a. Determine a 95% confidence interval for the expected value of y when $x = 6$.

b. Determine a 95% prediction interval for the value of y when $x = 3$.

15.48 Consider the following statistics based on 25 observations:

$$\hat{\beta}_0 = 6.5 \qquad \hat{\beta}_1 = -2.0 \qquad s_\varepsilon = 5.0$$
$$SS_x = 100 \qquad \bar{x} = 25.0.$$

a. Find the 90% prediction interval for the value of y when $x = 22.0$.

b. Find the 99% confidence interval estimate of the expected value of y when $x = 27.0$.

15.49 For Exercise 15.5, find the 95% prediction interval for the value of y when $x = 12.0$.

15.50 What happens to the prediction interval and the confidence interval when $SSE = 0$?

15.51 Suppose that you are given the following six observations:

x	3	6	5	4	3	8
y	10	8	6	9	9	4

a. Determine a 99% confidence interval for the expected value of y when $x = 8$.

b. Determine a 99% prediction interval for the value of y when $x = 3$.

APPLYING THE TECHNIQUES

Self-Correcting Exercise (See Appendix 15.B for the solution.)

15.52 For Exercise 15.12, predict with 90% confidence the sales when advertising expenditures equal $5,000.

---

* See Appendix 15.A for the Minitab commands used to produce this output.

TABLE E15.53	Year	Disposable Income ($billions) x	Company Sales ($millions) y
	1970	137	202
	1971	154	212
	1972	175	221
	1973	196	233
	1974	209	245
	1975	224	259
	1976	245	273
	1977	270	285
	1978	291	294
	1979	310	303
	1980	341	313
	1981	375	323
	1982	402	335
	1983	441	350
	1984	487	368

$$\sum x = 4{,}257 \qquad \sum y = 4{,}216 \qquad \sum xy = 1{,}273{,}299$$
$$\sum x^2 = 1{,}369{,}249 \qquad \sum y^2 = 1{,}222{,}430$$

15.53 The E-Z Sleepwear Company decided to examine whether personal disposable income nationwide was a decisive factor in predicting overall company sales. Data collected over 15 recent years yielded the information shown in Table E15.53.

a. Find the equation of the regression line.

b. Use the equation you found in part (a) to produce a 90% prediction interval of company sales when disposable income is $500 billion.

c. What assumptions are being made about the data?

15.54 Use your regression equation to predict with 95% confidence the exam score of a student who studied for 21 hours, in Exercise 15.11.

15.55 Find the 95% confidence interval estimate of the mean exam score of all students who have studied for 21 hours, in Exercise 15.11.

15.56 Briefly explain the difference between your answers to Exercises 15.54 and 15.55.

15.57 The different interest rates charged by some financial institutions may reflect how stringent their standards are for their loan appraisals: the lower the rate, the higher the standards (and hence, the lower the default rate). The following data were collected from a sample of 9 financial companies selected at random:

Interest Rate (%) x	Default Rate (per 1,000 loans) y
7.0	38
6.6	40
6.0	35
8.5	46

Interest Rate (%) x	Default Rate (per 1,000 loans) y
8.0	48
7.5	39
6.5	36
7.0	37
8.0	44

$\sum x = 65.1 \qquad \sum y = 363 \qquad \sum xy = 2,652.25$

$\sum x^2 = 476.31 \qquad \sum y^2 = 14,811$

a. Find the least squares regression line.

b. Do these data provide sufficient evidence to indicate that there is a positive linear relationship between the interest rate and the default rate? (Use $\alpha = .10$.)

c. Calculate the coefficients of correlation and determination.

d. Find a 95% prediction interval for the default rate when the interest rate is 8%.

15.58 Estimate with 95% confidence the mean monthly medical expenses of all families of 4 people in Exercise 15.31.

15.59 A family of 8 people is trying to produce a budget. Help them by determining a 90% prediction interval for their monthly medical expenses (Exercise 15.31).

SECTION 15.8 COMPLETE EXAMPLE

EXAMPLE 15.7

Car dealers across North America use the "Red Book" to help them determine the value of used cars that their customers trade in when purchasing new cars. The book, which is published monthly, lists average trade-in values for all basic models of North American, Japanese, and European cars. These averages are determined on the basis of the amounts paid at recent used-car auctions. The book indicates alternate values of each car model according to its condition and optional features, but it does not inform dealers of how the odometer reading affects the trade-in value. In an experiment to determine whether the odometer reading should be included in the Red Book, an interested student of statistics and used cars randomly selects ten 3-year-old cars of the same make, condition, and optional features. The trade-in value and mileage for each are shown in the accompanying table.

Car	Odometer Reading (1,000 miles) x	Trade-in Value ($100s) y
1	59	37
2	92	31
3	61	43
4	72	39

(continued)

Car	Odometer Reading (1,000 miles) x	Trade-in Value ($100s) y
5	52	41
6	67	39
7	88	35
8	62	40
9	95	29
10	83	33

a. Find the sample regression line for determining how the odometer reading affects the trade-in value of the car.

b. What does the regression line tell us about the relationship between the two variables?

c. Find the standard error of estimate.

d. Can we conclude at the 5% significance level that, for all cars of the type described in this experiment, higher mileage results in a lower trade-in value?

e. Measure the strength of the linear relationship, by calculating the coefficients of correlation and determination.

f. Predict with 95% confidence the trade-in value of a car that has been driven 60,000 miles.

g. A large national courier company has a policy of selling its cars once the odometer reaches 75,000 miles. The company is about to sell a large number of 3-year-old cars, each equipped with the same optional features and in the same condition as the 10 cars described in the original experiment. The company president would like to know the cars' mean trade-in price. Determine the 95% confidence interval estimate of the expected value of all the cars that have been driven 75,000 miles.

Solution, Part (a). The problem objective is to analyze the relationship between two variables whose data are quantitative. Because we want to determine how the odometer reading influences trade-in value, we identify trade-in value as the dependent variable y and odometer reading as the independent variable x.

From the data, we compute the following summations:

$$\sum x_i = 731$$
$$\sum x_i^2 = 55,545$$
$$\sum y_i = 367$$
$$\sum y_i^2 = 13,657$$
$$\sum x_i y_i = 26,265$$

We then find the sum of squares:

$$SS_x = \sum x_i^2 - \frac{(\sum x_i)^2}{n} = 55{,}545 - \frac{(731)^2}{10} = 2{,}108.9$$

$$SS_y = \sum y_i^2 - \frac{(\sum y_i)^2}{n} = 13{,}657 - \frac{(367)^2}{10} = 188.1$$

$$SS_{xy} = \sum x_i y_i - \frac{(\sum x_i)(\sum y_i)}{n} = 26{,}265 - \frac{(731)(367)}{10} = -562.7.$$

Finally, we calculate the coefficients:

$$\hat{\beta}_1 = \frac{SS_{xy}}{SS_x} = \frac{-562.7}{2{,}108.9} = -.267$$

$$\hat{\beta}_0 = \bar{y} - \hat{\beta}_1 \bar{x} = \frac{367}{10} - (-.267)\frac{731}{10} = 56.203.$$

The sample regression line is

$$\hat{y} = 56.203 - .267x.$$

Solution, Part (b).   The intercept is the value of y when $x = 0$. Obviously, no 3-year-old cars have no mileage on the odometer, so we cannot realistically interpret the value of $\hat{\beta}_0$.

The slope ($\hat{\beta}_1 = -.267$) tells us that, for each additional 1,000 miles driven, the car's value decreases by an average of .267 (in \$100s) or \$26.70. By altering the units, we find that each additional mile results in an average reduction of 2.67 cents in trade-in value.

Solution, Part (c).   We want to calculate

$$s_\varepsilon = \sqrt{\frac{SSE}{n-2}}.$$

Using our shortcut method, we find

$$SSE = SS_y - \frac{SS_{xy}^2}{SS_x} = 188.1 - \frac{(-562.7)^2}{2{,}108.9} = 37.96.$$

Hence,

$$s_\varepsilon = \sqrt{\frac{37.96}{10-2}} = 2.18.$$

Therefore, the standard error of estimate is 2.18.

Solution, Part (d).   This question is answered by testing the population slope β_1. Since we want to know whether sufficient evidence exists to indicate a negative linear relationship, the alternative hypothesis is $H_A: \beta_1 < 0$. The complete test is as follows:

$$H_0: \beta_1 = 0.$$
$$H_A: \beta_1 < 0.$$

Test statistic:

$$t = \frac{\hat{\beta}_1 - \beta_1}{s_{\hat{\beta}_1}}$$

Significance level: $\alpha = .05$

Decision rule: Reject H_0 if $t < -t_{\alpha, n-2} = -t_{.05,8} = -1.860$.

Value of the test statistic: From the calculations in parts (a) and (c), we have

$$\hat{\beta}_1 = -.267$$
$$s_\varepsilon = 2.18$$
$$SS_x = 2,108.9$$

$$s_{\hat{\beta}_1} = \frac{s_\varepsilon}{\sqrt{SS_x}} = .047.$$

Hence,

$$t = \frac{\hat{\beta}_1 - \beta_1}{s_{\hat{\beta}_1}} = \frac{-.267 - 0}{.047} = -5.68.$$

Conclusion: Reject H_0.

There is sufficient evidence to allow us to conclude that higher mileage results in a lower trade-in value.

Solution, Part (e).   The coefficient of correlation is

$$r = \frac{SS_{xy}}{\sqrt{SS_x \cdot SS_y}} = \frac{-562.7}{\sqrt{(2,108.9)(188.1)}} = -.893.$$

The coefficient of determination is

$$r^2 = (-.893)^2 = .798.$$

The value of the coefficient of determination tells us that 79.8% of the variability in trade-in values is explained by the variability in odometer readings. The remaining 20.2% is unexplained. This indicates a strong linear relationship.

Solution, Part (f).   Since we want to predict the value of only one car, the prediction interval is

$$\hat{y} \pm t_{\alpha/2, n-2} s_\varepsilon \sqrt{1 + \frac{1}{n} + \frac{(x_g - \bar{x})^2}{SS_x}},$$

where

$$\hat{y} = 56.203 - .267x_g = 56.203 - .267(60) = 40.19$$
$$s_\varepsilon = 2.18$$
$$x_g = 60$$

$$\bar{x} = 73.1$$
$$SS_x = 2,108.9$$
$$t_{\alpha/2, n-2} = t_{.025,8} = 2.306.$$

The 95% prediction interval is

$$\hat{y} \pm t_{\alpha/2, n-2} s_\varepsilon \sqrt{1 + \frac{1}{n} + \frac{(x_g - \bar{x})^2}{SS_x}}$$

$$= 40.19 \pm 2.306(2.18) \sqrt{1 + \frac{1}{10} + \frac{(60 - 73.1)^2}{2,108.9}}$$

$$= 40.19 \pm 5.46,$$

which simplifies to

$$LCL = 34.73$$
$$UCL = 45.65.$$

We therefore predict that the trade-in value of the car will be between $3,473 and $4,565.

Solution, Part (g).   Since we now want to estimate the mean value of a large number of cars, the confidence interval estimator is

$$\hat{y} \pm t_{\alpha/2, n-2} s_\varepsilon \sqrt{\frac{1}{n} + \frac{(x_g - \bar{x})^2}{SS_x}},$$

where

$$\hat{y} = 56.203 - .267(75) = 36.19.$$

The 95% confidence interval estimate of the expected value is

$$\hat{y} \pm t_{\alpha/2, n-2} s_\varepsilon \sqrt{\frac{1}{n} + \frac{(x_g - \bar{x})^2}{SS_x}}$$

$$= 36.19 \pm 2.306(2.18) \sqrt{\frac{1}{10} + \frac{(75 - 73.1)^2}{2,108.9}}$$

$$= 36.17 \pm 1.60,$$

which simplifies to

$$LCL = 34.59$$
$$UCL = 37.79.$$

We therefore predict that the mean price of the cars will be between $3,459 and $3,779.

MINITAB COMPUTER OUTPUT FOR EXAMPLE 15.7

```
The regression equation is

Y=56.2-0.267 X

Predictor     Coef        Stdev       t-ratio
Constant      56.205      3.535       15.90
       X      -0.26682    0.04743     -5.63

s=2.178    R-sq=79.8%    R-sq (adj)=77.3%

Analysis of Variance

SOURCE        DF      SS          MS
Regression    1       150.14      150.14
Error         8       37.96       4.74
Total         9       188.10
```

Separate subcommands are used to answer parts (f) and (g). For part (f), the output is

```
  Fit       Stdev. Fit       95% C.I.            95% P.I.
40.195      0.928        (38.056, 42.335)    (34.734, 45.657)
```

The 95% prediction interval (95% P.I.) is

$$LCL = 34.734 \quad \text{and} \quad UCL = 45.657.$$

For part (g), the output is

```
  Fit       Stdev. Fit       95% C.I.            95% P.I.
36.193      0.695        (34.591, 37.795)    (30.919, 41.467)
```

The 95% confidence interval estimate (95% C.I.) of the mean trade-in value of all such cars with 75,000 miles is

$$LCL = 34.591 \quad \text{and} \quad UCL = 37.795.$$

SUMMARY

Simple linear regression and correlation are techniques for analyzing the relationship between two quantitative variables. Regression analysis assumes that the two variables are linearly related. The least squares method produces estimates of the intercept and the slope of the regression line. Considerable effort is required for assessing how well the linear model fits the data. We calculate the standard error of estimate, which is the standard deviation of the error variable. We test the population slope to determine whether there is evidence of a linear relationship. The strength of the linear association is measured by the coefficents of correlation and determination. When we're satisfied that the model provides a good fit, we can use it to predict the particular value and to estimate the expected value of the dependent variable.

IMPORTANT TERMS

Dependent variable

Independent variable

Deterministic model

Probabilistic model

Simple linear regression model

Error variable

y-intercept

Slope

Scatter diagram

Scattergram

Least squares method

Least squares line

Fitted line

Regression line

Residuals

Sum of squares for error

Standard error of estimate

Coefficient of correlation

Coefficient of determination

Sum of squares for regression

Predicting the particular value
   of y for a given x

Prediction interval

Estimating the expected value
   of y for a given x

FORMULAS

$$SS_x = \sum x_i^2 - \frac{\left(\sum x_i\right)^2}{n}$$

$$SS_y = \sum y_i^2 - \frac{\left(\sum y_i\right)^2}{n}$$

$$SS_{xy} = \sum x_i y_i - \frac{\left(\sum x_i\right)\left(\sum y_i\right)}{n}$$

$$\hat{\beta}_1 = \frac{SS_{xy}}{SS_x}$$

$$\hat{\beta}_0 = \bar{y} - \hat{\beta}_1 \bar{x}$$

$$SSE = SS_y - \frac{SS_{xy}^2}{SS_x}$$

$$s_\varepsilon = \sqrt{\frac{SSE}{n-2}}$$

$$s_{\hat{\beta}_1} = \frac{s_\varepsilon}{\sqrt{SS_x}}$$

$$t = \frac{\hat{\beta}_1 - \beta_1}{s_{\hat{\beta}_1}}$$

$$r = \frac{SS_{xy}}{\sqrt{SS_x \cdot SS_y}}$$

$$r^2 = \frac{SS_{xy}^2}{SS_x \cdot SS_y} = \frac{SS_y - SSE}{SS_y}$$

$$\hat{y} = \hat{\beta}_0 + \hat{\beta}_1 x_g$$

$$\hat{y} \pm t_{\alpha/2, n-2} s_\varepsilon \sqrt{1 + \frac{1}{n} + \frac{(x_g - \bar{x})^2}{SS_x}}$$

$$\hat{y} \pm t_{\alpha/2, n-2} s_\varepsilon \sqrt{\frac{1}{n} + \frac{(x_g - \bar{x})^2}{SS_x}}$$

SUPPLEMENTARY EXERCISES

15.60 The store manager of Colonial Furniture Inc. has been reviewing quarterly advertising expenditures. TV spot ads in particular caught her eye, because they were the major expenditure item. In order to maximize cost-effectiveness, she would like to get a better idea of the relationship between the TV spot advertising she sponsors and the number of people (adults) who visit her store because of them. To this end, she has compiled the data contained in the accompanying table.

Quarterly Number of TV Ads x	Quarterly Number of People y
7	42
5	32
1	10

(continued)

Quarterly Number of TV Ads x	Quarterly Number of People y
8	40
10	61
2	8
6	35
7	39
8	48
9	51
5	30
7	45
8	41
2	7
6	37
5	33

$\sum x = 96 \qquad \sum y = 559 \qquad \sum xy = 3{,}930$

$\sum x^2 = 676 \qquad \sum y^2 = 23{,}037$

a. Find the sample regression line that expresses the number of people coming to the store as a function of the number of TV ads run.

b. Is there enough evidence to allow the manager to conclude that a linear relationship exists between the two variables? (Use $\alpha = .10$.)

c. What proportion of the variability in the number of people coming into the store is explained by the variability in the number of TV ads?

d. Find a 99% prediction interval for the number of people entering the store if the store manager intends to sponsor 5 TV ads this quarter.

15.61 In recent years, fishermen on both the east and west coasts have suffered financial hardship because of shortened fishing seasons, reduced catches, and lower market prices. Moreover, fishermen have complained about price fluctuations and have called for a system of minimum prices. One suggestion made was that the size of the catch had an immediate impact on prices, and that this relationship should be clarified before potential solutions were discussed.

In an investigation of this issue, a random 12-week period was selected to study the price of fish versus the average daily catch. The following data were collected for analysis.

Average Daily Catch (100 pounds) x	Price per Pound ($) y
357	1.95
621	1.05
485	2.15
927	.55
520	1.70
645	1.40
515	1.60
395	1.00
485	1.75
615	1.15
695	1.10
710	1.05

$\sum x = 6{,}970 \qquad \sum y = 16.45 \qquad \sum xy = 8{,}972.8$

$\sum x^2 = 4{,}315{,}894 \qquad \sum y^2 = 24.94$

a. Determine the sample regression line that shows the price per pound as a function of average daily catch.

b. Calculate the standard error of estimate. What does this value tell you about the relationship between the two variables?

c. Do these data provide sufficient evidence at the 5% significance level to allow you to conclude that large catches result in lower prices?

d. Calculate the coefficient of determination. What does this value tell you about the relationship between the two variables?

e. Find a 90% confidence interval estimate for the expected value of the price per pound if the daily catch is 75,000 pounds.

15.62 The head office of a medium-sized New England life-insurance company believed that regional managers should have weekly meetings with their salesmen, not only to keep them abreast of current market trends but also to provide them with important facts and figures that would help them in their sales. Furthermore, the company felt that these meetings should be used for pep talks. One of the points management felt strongly about was the high value of new contact initiation and follow-up phone calls. To dramatize the importance of phone calls on prospective clients and (ultimately) on sales, the company undertook the following small study.

Twenty randomly selected life-insurance salesmen were surveyed to determine the number of weekly sales calls they made and the number of policy sales they concluded. The data shown in the accompanying table were collected.

Weekly Calls x	Weekly Sales y
66	20
43	15
57	18
32	12
18	2
59	21
61	18
32	8
48	14
39	12
58	17
54	16
48	13
37	9
29	9
21	5
43	12
62	18
51	17
44	14

$\sum x = 902 \qquad \sum y = 270 \qquad \sum xy = 13,432$

$\sum x^2 = 44,318 \qquad \sum y^2 = 4,120$

a. Find the least squares regression line that expresses the number of sales as a function of the number of calls.

b. What do the coefficients tell you?

c. Is there enough evidence (with $\alpha = .05$) to indicate that, the larger the number of calls, the larger the number of sales?

d. What proportion of the variability in the number of sales can be attributed to the variability in the number of calls?

e. Find a 90% confidence interval estimate of the mean number of sales made by all the salesmen who make 50 calls each.

f. Predict with 99% confidence the number of sales concluded by a salesman who makes 30 calls.

15.63 In order to control maintenance costs more effectively, the production manager at a factory divided the machines on the floor into five age classes and for each class selected three machines at random for which to investigate maintenance costs over the preceding 3 months. The data compiled appear in the accompanying table.

Age (months)	Monthly Costs ($)		
6	51.27	24.50	48.00
12	102.50	140.70	125.00
18	227.00	185.90	200.20
24	285.50	265.30	205.10
30	352.75	333.80	359.90

a. Do these data provide sufficient evidence at the 10% significance level to indicate that older machines incur higher monthly maintenance costs?

b. Estimate with 95% confidence the mean monthly maintenance cost of all machines that are 2 years old.

c. Predict with 99% confidence next month's maintenance cost of a machine that is 12 months old.

15.64 The Miami Beach Hotel Association has expressed concern about increased pollution in the area and the deterioration of some beaches. As part of its overall study of the problem, the MBHA wishes to determine the relationship between beach attendance and mean daily temperature. The following data were obtained for a random sample of weekends last summer in the local area.

Mean Daily Temperature (°F)	Number of People on Beach
72°F	270
68	170
85	430
80	400
78	420
89	380
78	400
80	440
82	480

a. Find the slope and intercept of the least squares regression line for these data.

b. Plot the data and draw the regression line.

c. Test the hypothesis (with $\alpha = .10$) of a linear relationship, and compare this to your graphical evidence.

d. Predict with 99% confidence the number of people on the beach when the mean daily temperature is 88°F.

e. Calculate the coefficients of correlation and determination. What do these values tell you about the relationship between the two variables?

15.65 Baseball fans are intensely interested in statistics about their favorite sport. Of particular interest is any statistic that might help them predict a team's winning percentage. A major newspaper (*Toronto Star,* 17 June 1986) published the data shown in Table E15.65.

TABLE E15.65 AMERICAN LEAGUE TEAMS

Team	Team Batting Average x	Team Winning Percentage y
Baltimore	.266	.574
Boston	.269	.661
California	.256	.508
Chicago	.246	.410
Cleveland	.271	.500
Detroit	.259	.467
Kansas City	.250	.508
Milwaukee	.271	.525
Minnesota	.274	.403
New York	.268	.587
Oakland	.252	.422
Seattle	.246	.391
Texas	.263	.548
Toronto	.270	.500

$\sum x = 3.661$ $\sum y = 7.004$ $\sum xy = 1.8365$
$\sum x^2 = .9586$ $\sum y^2 = 3.5826$

a. Can you conclude from these results that a team's batting average is linearly related to its winning percentage? (Use $\alpha = .10$.)

b. Predict with 90% confidence the winning percentage of a team whose batting average is .275.

15.66 An agriculture student at Texas A&M has pulled from his father's farm records some data relating crop yield to amount of fertilizer used, mean seasonal rainfall, mean number of hours of sunshine, and mean daily temperature. As a first approximation, he wishes to regress crop yield on amount of fertilizer used, based on the data provided in the following table.

Fertilizer (pounds/acre) x	Crop Yield (tons/acre) y
220	36
450	72
250	48
320	51
500	80
250	40
330	55
430	72
240	39
280	45
370	62
400	71
410	79
450	75

$\sum x = 4{,}900$ $\sum y = 825$ $\sum xy = 307{,}190$
$\sum x^2 = 1{,}825{,}600$ $\sum y^2 = 51{,}891$

a. Graph the data, and comment on the suitability of using a linear regression model.

b. Find the least squares regression line for these data.

c. Test to determine whether a linear relationship exists between the two variables. (Use $\alpha = .05$.)

d. Compute the coefficient of determination, and interpret its value.

e. Forecast the crop yield, with 99% confidence, based on using 500 pounds of fertilizer. How does this compare to the actual yield when 500 pounds were used?

15.67 In response to both students' and parents' complaints about the high cost of school materials, the local school board has attempted to keep track of students' cost of supplies. It has selected 3 students at random from each of the four grades (9–12) in high school, with the result shown in the following table.

Grade	Annual Cost ($) Student 1	2	3
9	$215	$200	$210
10	210	205	220
11	210	220	235
12	225	225	215

a. Find the equation of the regression line.

b. Do these data provide enough evidence to indicate that students in higher grades incur higher costs? (Use $\alpha = .10$.)

c. Predict with 95% confidence the annual cost of sending a child to grade 11.

d. Estimate with 98% confidence the mean annual cost of sending children to grade 9.

15.68 A homebuilders' association lobbying for various home subsidy programs argued that, during periods of high interest rates, the number of building permits issued decreased drastically, which in turn reduced the availability of new housing. The raw data in Table E15.68 on the next page (grouped monthly) were presented as part of their argument.

a. Find the equation of the regression line.

b. What is the exact meaning of the slope coefficient?

c. Test to see whether evidence exists of a linear relationship. (Use $\alpha = .05$.)

d. Calculate the coefficient of determination, and comment about its meaning.

e. Predict with 90% confidence the number of building permits that will be issued if the interest rate is 16%.

TABLE E15.68

Interest Rates (%) x	Building Permits y
18.00%	427
10.75	1,189
15.25	825
12.45	904
15.56	800
14.25	880
13.95	950
16.85	628
11.45	1,027
16.95	610
17.50	582
17.00	600

$\sum x = 179.96$ $\sum y = 9,422$ $\sum xy = 135,609.75$

$\sum x^2 = 2,764.48$ $\sum y^2 = 7,930,728$

CASE 15.1*   *DO TALLER MBAs EARN MORE THAN SHORTER ONES?*

One general belief held by observers of the business world is that taller people earn more than shorter ones. In a University of Pittsburgh study, MBA graduates were polled and asked their monthly incomes and their heights. Suppose that 30 of the observations are as listed in the accompanying table. What can we conclude about the relationship between height and income?

HEIGHTS AND INCOMES OF MBA GRADUATES

MBA Graduate	Height (inches)	Monthly Income
1	70	$2,990
2	67	2,870
3	69	2,950
4	70	3,140
5	65	2,790
6	73	3,230

* Adapted from an article that appeared in the *Wall Street Journal*, 30 December 1986.

HEIGHTS AND INCOMES OF MBA GRADUATES

MBA Graduate	Height (inches)	Monthly Income
7	64	2,880
8	70	3,140
9	69	3,000
10	73	3,170
11	68	2,910
12	66	2,840
13	71	3,180
14	68	3,020
15	73	3,220
16	73	3,370
17	70	3,180
18	71	3,340
19	69	2,970
20	73	3,240
21	75	3,150
22	68	2,860
23	69	2,930
24	76	3,210
25	71	3,180
26	66	2,670
27	69	3,050
28	65	2,750
29	67	2,960
30	70	3,050

CASE 15.2   BASEBALL TEAM SALARIES AND WINNING PERCENTAGES

A well-known cliché states that money can't buy happiness. However, this may not be true if you are the owner of a major league baseball team. With the goal of winning pennants and World Series, some owners have participated in bidding wars for the services of expensive free agents and have offered lucrative contracts to keep star players. In 1988, the National League's division playoff participants (New York Mets and Los Angeles Dodgers) had the highest player payrolls in their respective divisions. The following table lists all major league baseball teams, the winning percentage of each, and the average salary each paid per player during the 1988 season. Upon analysis of these data, can you conclude that money can buy successful teams and thus, to some degree, happiness?

WINNING PERCENTAGES AND AVERAGE SALARIES OF MAJOR
LEAGUE BASEBALL TEAMS IN 1988

American League

Division	Team	Winning Percentage	Average Salary
East	Boston Red Sox	.549	610,172
	Detroit Tigers	.543	612,326
	Toronto Blue Jays	.537	484,427
	Milwaukee Brewers	.537	385,335
	New York Yankees	.528	718,670
	Cleveland Indians	.482	305,841
	Baltimore Orioles	.335	424,568
West	Oakland Athletics	.642	424,581
	Minnesota Twins	.562	446,598
	Kansas City Royals	.522	522,555
	California Angels	.463	417,278
	Chicago White Sox	.441	226,392
	Texas Rangers	.435	241,389
	Seattle Mariners	.422	242,880

National League

Division	Team	Winning Percentage	Average Salary
East	New York Mets	.617	605,895
	Pittsburgh Pirates	.531	307,088
	Montreal Expos	.500	343,047
	Chicago Cubs	.475	472,008
	St. Louis Cardinals	.469	522,296
	Philadelphia Phillies	.404	501,954
West	Los Angeles Dodgers	.584	573,441
	Cincinnati Reds	.540	304,647
	San Diego Padres	.516	409,930
	San Francisco Giants	.512	403,567
	Houston Astros	.506	545,595
	Atlanta Braves	.338	384,641

SOURCE: Creative Statistics Company.

MINITAB INSTRUCTIONS

The command

```
REGRESS 'Y' 1 'X'
```

computes the linear regression line

$$\hat{y} = \hat{\beta}_0 + \hat{\beta}_1 x.$$

   In this application we use the variable names rather than the column numbers in the REGRESS command to improve the clarity of the output. Thus, it is necessary to label the columns using the NAME command. The term   refers to the use of only one independent variable. For Example 15.2, the following data and commands were input:

```
READ C1 C2
 89.5    20.0
 79.9    14.8
 83.1    20.5
 56.9    12.5
 66.6    18.0
 82.5    14.3
126.3    27.5
 79.3    16.5
119.9    24.3
 87.6    20.2
112.6    22.0
120.8    19.0
 78.5    12.3
 74.3    14.0
 74.8    16.7
END
```

```
NAME C1='Y', C2='X'
REGRESS 'Y' 1 'X'
```

The output is as follows:

```
The regression equation is
```

$$Y = 18.4 + 3.88 \ X$$

```
Predictor     Coef.        Stdev      t-ratio
Constant      18.35        14.81        1.24
    X          3.8786       0.7936      4.89


s = 13.00    R-sq = 64.8%    R-sq (adj) = 62.0%

Analysis of Variance

SOURCE         DF      SS         MS
Regression      1    4034.4     4034.4
Error          13    2195.8      168.9
Total          14    6230.2
```

The subcommand PREDICT is used to produce the 95% confidence interval estimate of the expected value of y for a given x and the 95% prediction interval of y for a given x. To answer Examples 15.5 and 15.6, we would type the following:

```
REGRESS 'Y' 1 'X';
PREDICT 60.
```

Notice that we specify that given value of x in the PREDICT subcommand. The computer would print

```
Fit      St Dev. Fit     95% C.I.            95% P.I.
95.92        3.66      (88.03, 103.82)    (66.75, 125.10)
```

SOLUTIONS TO SELF-CORRECTING EXERCISES

15.8 a. $SS_{xy} = 724 - \dfrac{(30)(182)}{8} = 41.5$

$SS_x = 132 - \dfrac{(30)^2}{8} = 19.5$

$\hat{\beta}_1 = \dfrac{41.5}{19.5} = 2.13$

$\hat{\beta}_0 = 22.75 - (2.13)(3.75) = 14.77.$

The regression line is

$\hat{y} = 14.77 + 2.13x.$

d. For each additional employee, the average profit per dollar of sales increases by 2.13 cents.

15.20 $\sum y_i = 182, \sum y_i^2 = 4{,}254$

$SS_y = 4{,}254 - \dfrac{(182)^2}{8} = 113.5$

$SSE = 113.5 - \dfrac{(41.5)^2}{19.5} = 25.18$

$s_\varepsilon^2 = \dfrac{25.18}{8 - 2} = 4.20.$

The standard error of estimate is

$s_\varepsilon = 2.05.$

15.30 $SS_y = 65{,}143 - \dfrac{(793)^2}{10} = 2{,}258.1$

$SSE = 2{,}258.1 - \dfrac{(631.6)^2}{297.6} = 917.65$

$s_\varepsilon = \sqrt{\dfrac{917.65}{10 - 2}} = 10.71$

$s_{\hat{\beta}_1} = \dfrac{10.71}{\sqrt{297.6}} = .62.$

$H_0: \beta_1 = 0.$

$H_A: \beta_1 > 0.$

Test statistic: $t = \dfrac{\hat{\beta}_1 - \beta_1}{s_{\hat{\beta}_1}}$

Significance level: $\alpha = .05$

Decision rule: Reject H_0 if $t > t_{\alpha, n-2} = t_{.05, 8} = 1.860.$

Value of the test statistic:

$t = \dfrac{\hat{\beta}_1 - \beta_1}{s_{\hat{\beta}_1}} = \dfrac{2.12 - 0}{.62} = 3.418$

Conclusion: Reject H_0.

There is sufficient evidence to indicate that more hours of study results in higher exam scores.

15.42 $r = \dfrac{631.6}{\sqrt{(297.6)(2{,}258.1)}} = .770$

$r^2 = (.770)^2 = .593$

15.52 $SS_y = 6{,}070{,}625 - \dfrac{(8{,}175)^2}{15}$

$= 1{,}615{,}250$

$$SSE = 1,615,250 - \frac{(7,920)^2}{40.6} = 70,264.8$$

$$s_\varepsilon = \sqrt{\frac{70,264.8}{15-2}} = 73.52$$

$$\hat{y} = -644.95 + 195.07(5) = 330.4$$

$$\hat{y} \pm t_{\alpha/2} s_\varepsilon \sqrt{1 + \frac{1}{n} + \frac{(x_g - \bar{x})^2}{SS_x}}$$

$$= 330.4 \pm (1.771)(73.52)$$

$$\times \sqrt{1 + \frac{1}{15} + \frac{(5 - 6.1)^2}{40.6}}$$

$$= 330.4 \pm 136.3$$

We predict that, when advertising expenditures equal \$5,000, sales will be between \$194,100 and \$466,700.

MULTIPLE REGRESSION

INTRODUCTION

In this chapter we extend the statistical technique introduced in Chapter 15. In thaι chapter we used the simple regression model to analyze how one variable (the dependent variable y) is affected by another variable (the independent variable x). Although the simple linear regression model is useful in many real-life situations, the limitation of using only one independent variable restricts the value of this model.

In this chapter we develop models that can use any number of independent variables to predict the value of the dependent variable. In doing so, we expect to improve our forecasting ability. The improved performance of the multiple regression model, however, is not cost-free. Because additional variables are included, calculating the required statistics becomes quite lengthy. Fortunately, the availability of computer software designed for this purpose enables us to avoid having to perform these calculations ourselves. Hence, our focus in this chapter is on recognizing and interpreting computer output.

MODEL

We now assume that k independent variables are potentially related to the dependent variable. Thus, the model is represented by the equation

$$y = \beta_0 + \beta_1 x_1 + \beta_2 x_2 + \cdots + \beta_k x_k + \varepsilon,$$

where y is the dependent variable, $x_1, x_2, \ldots, x_k$ are the independent variables, $\beta_0, \beta_1, \ldots, \beta_k$ are the regression coefficients, and ε is the error variable. The independent variables may actually be functions of other variables. For example, we may define some of the independent variables as follows:

$$x_2 = x_1^2$$
$$x_3 = x_1 \cdot x_2$$
$$x_5 = \log(x_4).$$

The error variable is retained because—even though we have included additional independent variables—deviations between values in the model and the actual values of y will still occur. Incidentally, when more than one independent variable is present in the regression analysis, we refer to the graphical depiction of the equation as a **response surface** rather than as a straight line. Figure 16.1 depicts such a surface when $k = 2$. Of course, when $k > 2$, we can only imagine the curve; we cannot draw it.

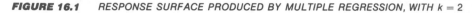

FIGURE 16.1   RESPONSE SURFACE PRODUCED BY MULTIPLE REGRESSION, WITH $k = 2$

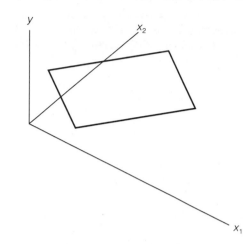

Our initial goal is to determine the value of the coefficients $\beta_0, \beta_1, \ldots, \beta_k$. Since these are population parameters, we estimate their values from a random sample by using the least squares method. That is, we calculate the estimates of the coefficients, $\beta_0, \beta_1, \ldots, \beta_k$ by minimizing

$$SSE = \sum(y_i - \hat{y}_i)^2.$$

Unlike the computations you encountered in applying simple regression, however, the calculations involved in applying multiple regression are so time-consuming that—except for those with masochistic tendencies—no one ever does the analysis by hand (even with the aid of a calculator). Instead, all of the analyses are performed by statistical application packages.

Consistent with the way we've presented computer output thus far, we will show the Minitab printout for the examples and exercises in this chapter. Appendix 16.A presents instructions for using Minitab in multiple regression applications.

SECTION 16.3

INTERPRETING AND TESTING THE COEFFICIENTS

EXAMPLE 16.1

In Example 15.2, we described the problem of a real-estate agent who wanted to predict the selling price of single-family homes. In order to use the simple regression model, she gathered the prices and sizes of 15 recently sold houses. In the analysis that followed, we found that the standard error of estimate was

$$s_\varepsilon = 13.00$$

TABLE 16.1 DATA FOR EXAMPLE 16.1

House	Selling Price ($1,000s) y	House Size (100s ft^2) x_1	Age (years) x_2	Lot Size (1,000s ft^2) x_3
1	89.5	20.0	5	4.1
2	79.9	14.8	10	6.8
3	83.1	20.5	8	6.3
4	56.9	12.5	7	5.1
5	66.6	18.0	8	4.2
6	82.5	14.3	12	8.6
7	126.3	27.5	1	4.9
8	79.3	16.5	10	6.2
9	119.9	24.3	2	7.5
10	87.6	20.2	8	5.1
11	112.6	22.0	7	6.3
12	120.8	19.0	11	12.9
13	78.5	12.3	16	9.6
14	74.3	14.0	12	5.7
15	74.8	16.7	13	4.8

and the coefficient of determination was

$$r^2 = .648.$$

The coefficient of determination indicates that 64.8% of the variation in selling price is explained by the variation in house size. The remaining 35.2% is unexplained. To reduce the proportion of unexplained variation and reduce the standard error of estimate, the agent decides to include two additional independent variables: the age of the house (in years) and the lot size (in 1,000s of square feet). All of these data are exhibited in Table 16.1. The model being proposed is

$$y = \beta_0 + \beta_1 x_1 + \beta_2 x_2 + \beta_3 x_3 + \varepsilon.$$

Estimate the coefficients, and interpret the results.

Solution. From the computer printout that we will present shortly, we find the following estimates of the coefficients:

$$\hat{\beta}_0 = -16.06$$
$$\hat{\beta}_1 = 4.146$$

$$\hat{\beta}_2 = -.236$$
$$\hat{\beta}_3 = 4.831.$$

Thus, the sample regression line is

$$\hat{y} = -16.06 + 4.146x_1 - .236x_2 + 4.831x_3.$$

The intercept $\hat{\beta}_0 = -16.06$ represents the value of y when $x_1 = x_2 = x_3 = 0$. As we observed in Chapter 15, it is often misleading to try to interpret the value of the intercept, particularly when the range of values of the independent variables does not include zero.

The relationship between x_1 and y is measured by $\hat{\beta}_1 = 4.146$. This indicates that, in this model, for each additional 100 square feet, the price of the house increases (on average) by \$4,146 (assuming that the other independent variables are fixed).

The coefficient $\hat{\beta}_2 = -.236$ specifies that, for each additional year in the age of the house, the price decreases by an average of \$236 (as long as the values of the other independent variables do not change).

Finally the coefficient $\hat{\beta}_3 = 4.831$ means that, for each additional 1,000 square feet of lot size, the price increases by an average of \$4,831 (assuming that x_1 and x_2 remain the same).

MINITAB COMPUTER OUTPUT FOR EXAMPLE 16.1*

The regression equation is

Y = -16.1 + 4.15 X1 - 0.236 X2 + 4.83 X3

Predictor	Coef	Stdev	t-ratio
Constant	-16.06	19.07	-0.84
X1	4.1462	0.7512	5.52
X2	-0.2361	0.8812	-0.27
X3	4.8309	0.9011	5.36

s = 6.894   R-sq = 91.6%   R-sq (adj) = 89.3%

Analysis of Variance

SOURCE	DF	SS	MS
Regression	3	5707.4	1902.5
Error	11	522.8	47.5
Total	14	6230.2	

---

* Appendix 16.A provides details about how Minitab performs the analysis for this example.

TESTING THE COEFFICIENTS

In Chapter 15, we tested hypotheses about β_1 to determine whether sufficient evidence existed of a linear relationship between the dependent and independent variables. The test statistic was

$$t = \frac{\hat{\beta}_1 - \beta_1}{s_{\hat{\beta}_1}},$$

which is Student t distributed with $n - 2$ degrees of freedom.

In multiple regression, we have more than one independent variable; and for each such variable, we can test to determine whether evidence exists of a linear relationship between it and y.

Testing the Coefficients

For $i = 1, 2, \ldots, k$,

$H_0: \beta_i = 0$.

$H_A: \beta_i \neq 0$.

The test statistic is

$$t = \frac{\hat{\beta}_i - \beta_i}{s_{\hat{\beta}_i}}, \qquad \text{which is Student } t \text{ distributed with d.f.} = n - k - 1.$$

We may also test for a positive linear relationship between x_i and y by specifying the alternative hypothesis

$$H_A: \beta_i > 0$$

or a negative linear relationship by specifying

$$H_A: \beta_i < 0.$$

Care should be taken in interpreting the results of these tests. We may find that in one model enough statistical evidence exists to show that a particular independent variable is linearly related to y, while in another model not enough evidence exists to establish such a linear relationship. As a result, whenever we do not reject H_0, we will state that there is not enough evidence to show that the independent variable and y are linearly related in the model currently being analyzed.

▬▬▬▬▬ **EXAMPLE 16.2**

Using the data developed in Example 16.1, test at the 5% level of significance to determine whether we can conclude that sufficient evidence exists of a linear relationship between x_1 and y, x_2 and y, and x_3 and y.

Solution. The tests that follow are performed just as all preceding tests in this book have been. We set up the hypotheses, define the decision rule, and identify the value of the test statistic. The only difference is that here the value of the test statistic comes from the computer printout.

For each independent variable, we test

$H_0: \beta_i = 0.$

$H_A: \beta_i \neq 0.$

The test statistic is

$$t = \frac{\hat{\beta}_i \div \beta_i}{s_{\hat{\beta}_i}},$$

for $i = 1, 2, 3$. The decision rule is

Reject H_0 if $|t| > t_{\alpha/2, n-k-1} = t_{.025, 11} = 2.201$.

From the computer output for Example 16.1, we find the value of the test statistics for each coefficient (other than β_0).

Test of β_1
Value of the test statistic: t = 5.52
Conclusion: Reject H_0.

There is enough evidence to allow us to conclude that a linear relationship exists between house price and house size.

Test of β_2
Value of the test statistic: t = −.27
Conclusion: Do not reject H_0.

There is not enough evidence to allow us to conclude that a linear relationship exists between age and price (in this model).

Test of β_3
Value of the test statistic: t = 5.36
Conclusion: Reject H_0.

There is enough evidence to allow us to conclude that lot size and price are linearly related.

Thus we have discovered that the size of the house and the lot size are linearly related to the price, while the age of the house is not necessarily linearly related to the price. If the real-estate agent has confidence in the reliability of these results, he will not make the age of the house a factor in recommending a price to either the buyer or the seller of the property.

 **EXERCISES**

LEARNING THE TECHNIQUES

16.1   Can we conclude the following, with $\alpha = .01$, from the output in the accompanying table?

a. x_1 and y are positively correlated.

b. x_2 and y are negatively correlated.

	Coefficients	Standard Error
Constant	125.6	52.0
x_1	12.3	3.9
x_2	−6.1	1.6

$k = 2$ $n = 30$

16.2   Do the results in the following table allow us to conclude that linear relationships exist between each of x_1, x_2, and x_3 and y? (Use $\alpha = .05$.)

	Coefficients	Standard Error
Constant	−30.0	10.0
x_1	−7.5	4.2
x_2	18.0	10.1
x_3	−0.5	0.2

$k = 3$ $n = 100$

16.3   Suppose that, in an effort to estimate the equation

$$y = \beta_0 + \beta_1 x_1 + \beta_2 x_2 + \varepsilon,$$

18 observations produced the following estimates and standard deviations:

$\hat{\beta}_0 = 5.5$ $s_{\hat{\beta}_0} = 2.0$
$\hat{\beta}_1 = 2.4$ $s_{\hat{\beta}_1} = .8$
$\hat{\beta}_2 = 6.0$ $s_{\hat{\beta}_2} = 3.6.$

Test the following hypotheses, with $\alpha = .01$:

a. $H_0: \beta_1 = 0.$
   $H_A: \beta_1 \neq 0.$
b. $H_0: \beta_2 = 0.$
   $H_A: \beta_2 \neq 0.$

16.4   From 25 observations of the variables y, x_1, x_2 and x_3, output on coefficients and standard errors of coefficients was produced in an attempt to estimate the model

$$y = \beta_0 + \beta_1 x_1 + \beta_2 x_2 + \beta_3 x_3 + \varepsilon.$$

Here are the output data:

$\hat{\beta}_0 = 51.2$ $s_{\hat{\beta}_0} = 10.6$
$\hat{\beta}_1 = 48.6$ $s_{\hat{\beta}_1} = 12.8$
$\hat{\beta}_2 = 19.3$ $s_{\hat{\beta}_2} = 14.3$
$\hat{\beta}_3 = −22.5$ $s_{\hat{\beta}_3} = 5.6.$

Test the following hypotheses, with $\alpha = .05$:

a. $H_0: \beta_1 = 0.$
   $H_A: \beta_1 \neq 0.$
b. $H_0: \beta_2 = 0.$
   $H_A: \beta_2 > 0.$
c. $H_0: \beta_3 = 0.$
   $H_A: \beta_3 < 0.$

16.5   In estimating the regression model

$$y = \beta_0 + \beta_1 x_1 + \beta_2 x_2 + \beta_3 x_3 + \beta_4 x_4 + \varepsilon$$

with 50 observations, a statistician observed the computer output shown in Figure E16.5.

FIGURE E16.5

```
The regression equation is

Y = 110.5 + 32.8 X1 - 56.3 X2 + 85.0 X3 - 27.6 X4

Predictor    Coef    Stdev    t-ratio
Constant    110.5    52.1      2.12
     X1      32.8    12.6      2.60
     X2     -56.3    48.5     -1.16
     X3      85.0    69.1      1.23
     X4     -27.6     5.6     -4.93
```

a. Do these data allow us to conclude at the 5% significance level that a linear relationship exists between x_1 and y?

b. Can we conclude (with $\alpha = .01$) that there is a negative linear relationship between x_2 and y?

c. Can we conclude at the 10% significance level that there is a positive linear relationship between x_3 and y?

APPLYING THE TECHNIQUES

Self-Correcting Exercise (See Appendix 16.B for the solution.)

16.6 The owner of a drywall-manufacturing plant wants to predict the monthly demand for drywall (in 100s of 4×8 sheets) as a function of the number of building permits issued in the county, the 5-year-term mortgage rates, and overall economic activity as measured by per capita GNP (in $1,000s). Taking monthly data over the last three years, he produced the results shown in Figure E16.6.

a. Interpret the coefficients $\hat{\beta}_1$, $\hat{\beta}_2$, and $\hat{\beta}_3$.

b. Test to determine whether a linear relationship exists between each of the independent variables and the dependent variable. (Use $\alpha = .05$.)

16.7 A meat packer wanted to improve his understanding of the variables that influence the price of beef in the state. After some thought, he produced the following list of four variables that he believes affect the price of beef (in hundred weights, on the hoof):

Average beef consumption
Price of chicken
Price of pork
Price of lamb

Using data from the last 120 months and a computer package, he produced the following statistics:

Variable	Coefficient $\hat{\beta}_i$	Standard Error $s_{\hat{\beta}_i}$	t-statistic
Beef	1.259	.397	3.174
Chicken	1.214	.601	2.020
Pork	2.386	2.708	.881
Lamb	1.366	.544	2.513
Constant	5.260	7.982	.659

a. Are the signs of $\hat{\beta}_1$, $\hat{\beta}_2$, $\hat{\beta}_3$, and $\hat{\beta}_4$ in the expected direction?

b. Which of the four independent variables are linearly related to the dependent variable? (Test with $\alpha = .05$.)

16.8 A developer who specializes in summer cottage properties is considering purchasing a large tract of land adjoining a lake, approximately 60 miles from a large urban area. The current owner of the tract has already subdivided the land into separate building lots and has prepared the lots by removing some of the trees. The developer wants to forecast the value of each lot. From previous experience, she knows that the most important factors affecting the price of a lot (in $1,000s) are lot size (in square feet), number of mature trees remaining, and distance to the lake (in feet). From a nearby area, she gathers relevant data about 60 recently sold lots. Using Minitab computer software, she produces the output shown in Figure E16.8 on the next page.

a. What do the values of $\hat{\beta}_0$, $\hat{\beta}_1$, $\hat{\beta}_2$, and $\hat{\beta}_3$ tell you?

FIGURE E16.6

```
Predictor    Coef     Stdev    t-ratio
Constant     5.127    1.325     3.869
 PERMITS     0.062    0.030     2.067
 RATES      -1.212    0.659    -1.839
 GNP         0.022    0.005     4.400
```

FIGURE E16.8

```
The regression equation is

PRICE = 8.242 + 0.102 SIZE + 1.248 TREES - 2.137 DISTANCE

Predictor     Coef     Stdev    t-ratio
Constant      8.242    3.257     2.531
   SIZE       0.102    0.048     2.125
   TREES      1.348    0.513     2.628
   DISTANCE  -2.137    0.676    -3.161
```

b. Is there sufficient evidence to indicate that price and size are linearly related? (Use $\alpha = .05$.)

c. Do these data provide enough evidence to enable the developer to conclude, at the 1% significance level, that price and distance from the lake are negatively linearly related?

16.9 Why do some door-to-door salespeople perform better than others? To investigate the factors that lead to successful selling, the general manager of a cosmetics company that sells its products door-to-door took a random sample of 50 salespeople in 50 different districts. For each he determined the dollar sales last month (the dependent variable), the number of homes visited by the salesperson, and the density of the district (the number of residences per square mile). Relevant statistics from the computer output of the multiple regression model appear next. Can the general manager conclude at the 5% significance level that the number of homes visited and the district density are both linearly related to monthly sales?

Variable	Coefficient $\hat{\beta}_i$	Standard Error $s_{\hat{\beta}_i}$	t-statistic
Visits	0.36	0.14	2.57
Density	0.15	0.06	2.50
Constant	3.62	1.23	2.94

ASSESSING THE MODEL

In almost all applications of regression analysis, it is important (for at least two reasons) that we assess or judge the usefulness of the model. First, we frequently have more than one model available that we could use; thus, we need a measure that allows us to compare the appropriateness of competing models. Second, we need to know whether the model selected is likely to be useful in forecasting and analyzing relationships. In this section, we discuss three methods of assessing the model: the standard error of estimate (s_ε), the coefficient of determination (r^2), and the analysis of variance F-test.

STANDARD ERROR OF ESTIMATE

Recall that σ_ε is the standard deviation of the error variable ε and that, since σ_ε is a population parameter, it is necessary to estimate its value by using s_ε. In multiple regression, the standard error of estimate is defined as follows.

Standard Error of Estimate

$$s_\varepsilon = \sqrt{\frac{SSE}{n - k - 1}}$$

By examining the output for Example 16.1 on page 453, we can see that Minitab prints the standard error of estimate as

s = 6.894

In the simple regression model in Chapter 15 (Example 15.2), we found $s_\varepsilon = 13.00$. Obviously, including the two additional variables x_2 and x_3 has improved the model.

COEFFICIENT OF DETERMINATION

The coefficient of determination is defined as follows.

Coefficient of Determination

$$r^2 = \frac{SS_y - SSE}{SS_y}$$

As the value for the coefficent of determination in the present case, Minitab outputs

R-sq = 91.6%

This means that 91.6% of the variation in house prices is explained by the three independent variables, while 8.4% remains unexplained. The simple regression model produced $r^2 = 64.8\%$.

TESTING THE UTILITY OF THE MODEL

In Section 16.3, we tested the individual coefficients to determine whether there was sufficient evidence to allow us to conclude that a linear relationship existed between each independent variable and the dependent variable. As we saw in Chapter 15, if there is only one dependent variable, the t-test of β_1 also tests whether the model is useful. When there is more than one independent variable, however, we need another technique for testing the overall utility of the model. This technique is called the **analysis of variance.**

When we discussed the coefficient of determination in Chapter 15, we noted that the variability of the dependent variable (measured by SS_y) can be decomposed into two parts: the explained variability (measured by SSR) and the unexplained variability (measured by SSE). That is,

$$SS_y = SSR + SSE.$$

Furthermore, we established that, if SSR is large relative to SSE, the coefficient of determination r^2 is high, signifying a good model. On the other hand, if SSE is large, most of the variation of y remains unexplained, which indicates that the model provides a poor fit and consequently has little utility.

The hypotheses to be tested are:

H_0: $\beta_1 = \beta_2 = \cdots = \beta_k = 0$.

H_A: At least one β_i is not equal to zero.

If the null hypothesis is true, none of the independent variables $x_1, x_2, \ldots, x_k$ is linearly related to y, and therefore the model is useless. If at least one β_i is not equal to zero, the model has some utility.

The test statistic is basically the same one we encountered in Chapter 13, where we tested for the equivalence of k population means. In order to judge whether SSR is large enough relative to SSE to allow us to conclude that at least one $\beta_i \neq 0$, we compute the ratio of the two mean squares. (Recall that the **mean square** is the sum of squares divided by the degrees of freedom; recall too, that the ratio of the mean squares is F-distributed, as long as the underlying population is normal—a required condition of this application.) The calculation of the test statistic is summarized in an analysis of variance table, which in general appears as follows:

Source of Variation	Degrees of Freedom	Sum of Squares	Mean Squares	F-ratio
Regression	k	SSR	$MSR = SSR/k$	$F = \dfrac{MSR}{MSE}$
Error	$n - k - 1$	SSE	$MSE = SSE/(n - k - 1)$	
Total	$n - 1$	SS_y		

Again, using Minitab we get the following analysis of variance table for Example 16.1 (see page 453).

Source of Variation	Degrees of Freedom	Sum of Squares	Mean Squares	F-ratio
Regression	3	5,707.4	1,902.5	40.053
Error	11	522.8	47.5	
Total	14	6,230.2		

A large value of F indicates that most of the variation of y is explained by the regression equation and that the model is useful. A small value of F indicates that most of the variation of y remains unexplained. The rejection region allows us to determine whether F is large enough to justify our rejecting H_0. For our test, the decision rule is

Reject H_0 if $F > F_{\alpha, k, n-k-1}$.

Therefore, in Example 16.1, the decision rule is (assuming that $\alpha = .05$)

Reject H_0 if $F > F_{\alpha, k, n-k-1} = F_{.05, 3, 11} = 3.59$.

Since the computed value of F is 40.053, we reject H_0. We conclude that at least one β_i is not equal to zero and that the model can be useful.

F-TEST, r^2, AND s_ε

Although each of the assessment measurements offers a different perspective, they agree in their assessment of how well the model fits the data. This is because they are all based on the sum of squares for error SSE. The standard error of estimate is

$$s_\varepsilon = \sqrt{\frac{SSE}{n - k - 1}},$$

and the coefficient of determination is

$$r^2 = \frac{SS_y - SSE}{SS_y}.$$

When the curve hits every single point,

$$SSE = 0.$$

Hence,

$$s_\varepsilon = 0$$
$$r^2 = 1.$$

If the model provides a poor fit, we know that SSE is large (its maximum value is SS_y), s_ε is large, and (since SSE is close to SS_y) r^2 is close to zero.

The F-statistic also depends on SSE. That is,

$$F = \frac{(SS_y - SSE)/k}{SSE/(n - k - 1)}.$$

When $SSE = 0$,

$$F = \frac{SS_y/k}{0/(n - k - 1)},$$

which is infinitely large. When SSE is large, SSE is close to SS_y and F is quite small.

The relationship among s_ε, r^2, and F is summarized in the accompanying table.

SSE	s_ε	r^2	F	Assessment of Model
0	0	1	∞	Perfect
Small	Small	Close to 1	Large	Good
Large	Large	Close to 0	Small	Poor
SS_y	$\sqrt{\dfrac{SS_y}{n - k - 1}}$ *	0	0	Useless

* When n is large and k is small, this quantity is approximately equal to the standard deviation of y.

████████ **EXERCISES**

LEARNING THE TECHNIQUES

16.10 Suppose that, in an attempt to estimate the model

$$y = \beta_0 + \beta_1 x_1 + \beta_2 x_2 + \beta_3 x_3 + \beta_4 x_4 + \varepsilon,$$

a researcher obtained 28 observations, which produced the following analysis of variance table:

Source	DF	SS	MS
Regression	4	126.30	31.58
Error	23	269.10	11.70
TOTAL	27	395.40	

Test (with $\alpha = .01$) the following hypotheses:

$H_0: \beta_1 = \beta_2 = \beta_3 = \beta_4 = 0.$
$H_A:$ At least one $\beta_i \neq 0.$

16.11 In analyzing a multiple regression model, with $n = 70$ and $k = 8$, a statistician found

$SS_y = 1,526.3 \qquad SSE = 1,162.2.$

Determine the following:

a. s_ε b. r^2 c. F

16.12 A random sample of 34 observations of five variables produced the following summations:

$SSR = 2,512.6 \qquad SSE = 4,509.2.$

Do these data provide sufficient evidence to indicate that the model is useful? (Test the appropriate hypothesis with $\alpha = .10$.)

16.13 In calculations undertaken to estimate the model

$$y = \beta_0 + \beta_1 x_1 + \beta_2 x_2 + \varepsilon,$$

50 observations of the variables y, x_1, and x_2 produced the following statistics:

$SS_y = 321.2 \qquad SSE = 259.0$

a. Find SSR.

b. Calculate the standard error of estimate.

c. Calculate the coefficient of determination.

d. Test the overall utility of the model, with $\alpha = .01$.

16.14 A random sample of 100 observations was taken to estimate the regression model

$$y = \beta_0 + \beta_1 x_1 + \beta_2 x_2 + \varepsilon.$$

Minitab was employed to produce the output shown in the accompanying table. Because of a printer malfunction, however, some values from the analysis of variance table are missing; at present, these are replaced by the letters (a) through (f). Fill in the missing values.

Source	DF	SS	MS
Regression	(a)	573.6	(e)
Error	(b)	(d)	(f)
TOTAL	(c)	925.9	

16.15 In Exercise 16.14, test with $\alpha = .05$ to determine whether the model is useful.

APPLYING THE TECHNIQUES

Self-Correcting Exercise (See Appendix 16.B for the solution.)

16.16 A Florida hardware cooperative wanted to study advertising effectiveness by relating the total dollar volume of sales at individual stores to dollar expenditures on localized direct mailings, local newspaper ads, and local TV spot ads. The results of the analysis are shown in the computer printout shown in Figure E16.16.

a. What does the value of the coefficient of determination tell you?

b. Test the overall utility of the model, with $\alpha = .01$.

16.17 For Exercise 16.16 find SSR, SSE, and SS_y. From these values (and from their degrees of freedom), calculate r^2 and s_ε. Confirm that these values are the same as those shown in the computer output.

16.18 In an effort to explain to customers why their electricity bills have been so high lately and how, specifically, they could save money by reducing the thermostat settings on both space heaters and water heaters, an electric utility company has collected total kilowatt consumption figures for last year's winter months, as well as average thermostat settings on space heaters and water heaters. These data are shown in the accompanying table.

Consumption (KWH/100)	Thermostat Settings (°F)	
y	Space Heater x_1	Water Heater x_2
20	70°	125°
24	72	130
16	68	120
28	74	135
32	75	140
19	68	120
24	71	130
29	72	135
35	75	140

Minitab generated the computer output shown in Figure E16.18 on the next page.

a. What does the value of the standard error of estimate tell you about the fit of the model?

b. What proportion of the variability in consumption is not explained by the model?

c. Is there sufficient evidence, with $\alpha = .05$, to allow you to conclude that consumption is affected by both space heater and water heater use?

16.19 The Christmas break (December 10–January 5) is a critical period for the tourist industry of Miami Beach. If relatively few people visit during this time period, the hotels, restaurants, and other tourist attractions suffer financial losses. A marketing analyst hired by the chamber of commerce to promote more tourism wants to analyze the factors that influence people to come to Miami Beach during Christmas break. She believes that the crucial factors affecting hotel vacancy rates are tied to weather conditions in the previous year. As a result, she proposed the model

$$y = \beta_0 + \beta_1 x_1 + \beta_2 x_2 + \varepsilon,$$

where

y = Vacancy rate during Christmas break in year i

FIGURE E16.16

```
The regression equation is

Y = -2.572 + 3.422 X1 + 5.216 X2 + 7.314 X3

Predictor    Coef     Stdev    t-ratio
Constant    -2.572    2.543    -1.011
     X1      3.422    1.744     1.962
     X2      5.216    2.542     2.052
     X3      7.314    3.448     2.121

s = 9.319    R-sq = 12.7%    R-sq (adj) = 9.8%

Analysis of Variance

SOURCE        DF      SS        MS
Regression     3    1115.25   371.75
Error         88    7641.89    86.84
Total         91    8757.14
```

FIGURE E16.18

```
The regression equation is

Y = -68.88 - 0.395 X1 + 0.937 X2

Predictor       Coef      Stdev     t-ratio
Constant     -68.8847    26.0721     -2.642
      X1      -0.3947     0.9086     -0.434
      X2       0.9375     0.3184      2.944

s = 1.480    R-sq = 95.9%   R-sq (adj) = 94.5%

Analysis of Variance

SOURCE         DF      SS        MS
Regression      2    304.42    152.21
Error           6     13.14      2.19
Total           8    317.56
```

x_1 = Mean daily high temperature (in degrees Fahrenheit) during Christmas break in year $i - 1$

x_2 = Number of rainy days during Christmas break in year $i - 1$.

The results for 15 recent years are as follows:

Year	y	x_1	x_2
1988	6	75	1
1987	12	68	4
1986	11	67	3
1985	8	73	2
1984	13	65	3
1983	9	71	4
1982	6	73	1
1981	8	74	1
1980	4	76	2
1979	10	73	3
1978	8	69	3
1977	9	71	4

Year	y	x_1	x_2
1976	8	66	2
1975	12	64	4
1974	2	73	5

The complete Minitab output is shown in Figure E16.19.

a. At the 5% significance level, can we conclude that the model is useful?

b. At the 5% significance level, can we conclude that y and x_2 are linearly related?

16.20 The administrator of a school board in a large southern state was analyzing the average mathematics score in the schools in his district. He noticed that there were enormous differences in scores among schools. In an attempt to determine some of the factors that influenced student performance on mathematics tests, he took a random sample of 30 high schools across the state and determined the mean mathematics score (y), the percentage of mathematics teachers who have at least one university degree in mathematics (x_1), the mean age of the mathematics teachers (x_2), and the

FIGURE E16.19

```
The regression equation is

Y = 53.4 - 0.627 X1 - 0.267 X2

Predictor      Coef       Stdev      t-ratio
Constant      53.38      12.60        4.24
   X1         -0.6272     0.1693     -3.71
   X2         -0.2672     0.5080     -0.53

s = 2.195    R-sq = 55.4%    R-sq (adj) = 47.9%

Analysis of Variance

SOURCE         DF        SS        MS
Regression      2      71.766    35.883
Error          12      57.834     4.820
Total          14     129.600
```

mean annual salary of the teachers (x_3). Part of the resulting computer output is as follows:

```
s = 8.16    R-sq = 7.6%

Analysis of Variance

SOURCE         DF        SS        MS
Regression      3      141.4     47.13
Error          26     1732.2     66.62
Total          29     1873.6
```

a. What proportion of the variability in mathematics scores is not explained by the model?

b. What is the value of the standard error of estimate? What does it tell you about the model's fit?

c. Can we conclude at the 10% significance level that the model is useful in predicting mean mathematics scores?

SECTION 16.5   USING THE REGRESSION EQUATION

As was the case with simple linear regression (Chapter 15), the multiple regression equation can be used in two ways: we can produce the prediction interval for a particular value of y; and we can produce the confidence interval estimate of the expected value of y. Like the other computations associated with multiple regression, however, the formulas for the prediction interval and the confidence interval estimate are usually too complicated for us to calculate by hand. Instead, we call on the computer to produce the results we want.

Suppose that in Example 16.1 we wanted to produce a 95% confidence interval estimate of the expected value of y and a 95% prediction interval of y, when the ground area of the house is 2,000 square feet $(x_1 = 20)$, the house is 10 years old $(x_2 = 10)$, and the lot size is 10,000 square feet $(x_3 = 10)$. Minitab would produce the following output:

```
   Fit      Stdev. Fit        95% C.I.            95% P.I.
 112.81        3.58       (104.94, 120.69)    (95.71, 129.91)
```

As you can see, the 95% confidence interval estimate (C.I.) of the expected value of y is (104.94, 120.69), and the 95% prediction interval (P.I.) of y is (95.71, 129.91).

SECTION
16.6

SUMMARY

In this chapter we discussed the multiple regression technique. With this technique, because of the difficulty of performing the calculations by hand, we must use the computer extensively in estimating and testing the parameters. The computer output also includes the standard error of estimate, the coefficient of determination, and the analysis of variance (which allows us to test the utility of the model).

IMPORTANT TERMS

Response surface
Dependent variable
Independent variables
Regression coefficients
Sum of squares for error
Standard error of estimate
Coefficient of determination

Analysis of variance
Mean squares
ANOVA table
Predicting the particular value of y for a
  given x
Estimating the expected value of y for a
  given x

FORMULAS

$$t = \frac{\hat{\beta}_i - \beta_i}{s_{\hat{\beta}_i}}$$

$$s_\varepsilon = \sqrt{\frac{SSE}{n - k - 1}}$$

$$r^2 = \frac{SS_y - SSE}{SS_y} = \frac{SSR}{SS_y}$$

$$MSR = \frac{SSR}{k}$$

$$MSE = \frac{SSE}{n - k - 1}$$

$$F = \frac{MSR}{MSE}$$

$$v_1 = k$$

$$v_2 = n - k - 1$$

SUPPLEMENTARY EXERCISES

16.21 The president of a national real-estate company wanted to know why certain branches of the company outperformed others. He felt that the key factors in determining total annual sales (in $millions) y were the advertising budget (in $1,000s) x_1 and the number of sales agents x_2. To analyze the situation, he took a sample of 15 offices and ran the data in the accompanying table through the Minitab software system. The output is shown in Figure E16.21.

Office	Annual Sales ($millions) y	Advertising ($1,000s) x_1	Number of Agents x_2
1	32	249	15
2	47	292	18
3	18	183	14
4	25	201	16

Office	Annual Sales ($millions) y	Advertising ($1,000s) x_1	Number of Agents x_2
5	49	310	21
6	41	248	20
7	52	246	18
8	38	241	14
9	36	288	13
10	29	191	15
11	43	248	21
12	28	210	18
13	24	256	20
14	36	275	16
15	41	241	19

a. Interpret the coefficients.

b. Test to determine whether a linear relationship exists between each independent variable and the dependent variable, with $\alpha = .05$.

c. Test the overall utility of the model, with $\alpha = .05$.

16.22 An auctioneer of semiantique and antique Persian rugs kept records of his weekly auctions in order to determine the relationships among price, age of carpet or rug, number of people attending the auction, and number of times the winning bidder had previously attended his auctions. He felt that, with this information, he could plan his auctions better, serve his steady customers better, and make a higher profit overall for himself. The results shown in the accompanying table were obtained.

Price y	Age x_1	Audience Size x_2	Previous Attendance x_3
1,080	80	40	1
2,540	150	80	12
1,490	85	55	3
960	55	45	0
2,100	140	70	8
1,820	95	65	5

(continued)

FIGURE E16.21

```
The regression equation is

Y = -19.50 + 0.158 X1 + 0.962 X2

Predictor      Coef       Stdev      t-ratio
Constant      -19.47      15.84      -1.23
     X1        0.15838    0.05613     2.82
     X2        0.9625     0.7781      1.24

s = 7.362    R-sq = 52.4%    R-sq (adj) = 44.5%

Analysis of Variance

SOURCE        DF      SS        MS
Regression     2    716.58    358.29
Error         12    650.35     54.20
Total         14   1366.93
```

Price y	Age x_1	Audience Size x_2	Previous Attendance x_3	Price y	Age x_1	Audience Size x_2	Previous Attendance x_3
2,230	140	80	7	2,950	175	120	10
1,490	80	60	9	2,370	150	115	10
1,620	90	65	10	1,240	55	55	3
1,260	60	55	8	1,620	70	75	5
1,880	90	70	7	2,120	120	100	0
2,080	100	100	5	1,090	50	50	8
2,150	120	85	3	1,850	65	65	9
1,940	95	80	0	2,220	125	95	7
1,860	90	80	6	1,420	60	45	8
2,240	135	90	8	2,140	115	95	5

The Minitab statistical application package was used to estimate the model

$$y = \beta_0 + \beta_1 x_1 + \beta_2 x_2 + \beta_3 x_3 + \varepsilon.$$

The resulting output is shown in Figure E16.22.

a. What proportion of the variance in y is explained by the independent variables?

b. Test the utility of the overall regression model, with $\alpha = .05$.

c. What price would you forecast for a 100-year-

FIGURE E16.22

```
The regression equation is

Y = 239.5 + 7.380 X1 + 10.181 X2 + 17.309 X3

Predictor      Coef      Stdev     t-ratio
Constant     239.533    108.88      2.20
    X1         7.380      1.459     5.06
    X2        10.181      2.273     4.48
    X3        17.309      9.041     1.92

s = 144.53    R-sq = 92.3%    R-sq (adj) = 91.3%

Analysis of Variance

SOURCE        DF        SS           MS
Regression     3     5530974.6    1843658.2
Error         22      459579.3      20890.0
Total         25     5990553.9
```

old rug, given an audience size of 120 that had on average attended three of the auctioneer's auctions before?

16.23 Economists have stated that the willingness of individuals to hold cash in safety deposit boxes or non-interest-bearing checking accounts is a function of an individual's income x_1 and of the prevailing interest rate x_2. A bank executive has decided to test this theory. He has selected a random sample of individuals at different times during the past 2 years and has gathered from them the relevant data. With the assistance of the Minitab system, he produced the output shown in Figure E16.23.

a. Do these data provide sufficient evidence to support the theory? (Test with $\alpha = .01$.)

b. Would you conclude that the prevailing interest rate is very important to an individual's willingness to hold cash? (Test with $\alpha = .01$.)

16.24 Stock market analysts are keenly interested in determining what factors influence the price of a stock. After some examination, a statistician hypothesized that a stock price would be affected by its quarterly dividends x_1, its price/earnings ratio x_2, and the interest rate of treasury bills x_3. The values of the relevant variables were observed for a period of 40 quarters. When the data were run on the Minitab computer system, the output shown in Figure E16.24 on the next page was created.

a. Test the overall utility of the model, with $\alpha = .05$.

b. Is the stock price explained by quarterly dividends? (Test with $\alpha = .05$.)

c. Is the stock price negatively related to the price/earnings ratio? (Test with $\alpha = .05$.)

16.25 The sales manager of a large retail chain has been given the task of determining why certain stores have been performing more poorly than expected. She believes that part of the problem is that some stores appear to be the victims of an inefficient distribution system. Other possible factors include the size of the population in the surrounding area and the amount of advertising used. She decides to take a sample of 50 stores, and for each she determines the following variables:

y = Total sales last year (in $1,000s)

x_1 = Population (in millions)

x_2 = Advertising expenditures (in $1,000s)

x_3 = Distribution efficiency index, ranging from

FIGURE E16.23

```
The regression equation is

Y = 15.7 + 1.63 X1 + 2.11 X2

Predictor     Coef      Stdev     t-ratio
Constant     15.721    10.256     1.533
     X1       1.634     0.431     3.791
     X2       2.112     1.742     1.212

s = 16.555   R-sq = 73.0%   R-sq (adj) = 72.1%

Analysis of Variance

SOURCE       DF       SS        MS
Regression    2     42320.1   21160.0
Error        57     15621.3     274.1
Total        59     57941.4
```

FIGURE E16.24

The regression equation is

Y = 17.393 + 41.299 X1 - 0.416 X2 + 0.571 X3

Predictor	Coef	Stdev	t-ratio
Constant	17.393	5.525	3.15
X1	41.299	7.502	5.51
X2	-0.416	0.523	-0.80
X3	0.571	0.408	1.40

s = 2.237   R-sq = 74.2%   R-sq (adj) = 72.0%

Analysis of Variance

SOURCE	DF	SS	MS
Regression	3	516.904	172.301
Error	36	180.137	5.004
Total	39	697.041	

1 = Poor distribution to 10 = Excellent distribution.

The data were run on the Minitab software package, with the results shown in Figure E16.25.

FIGURE E16.25

The regression equation is

Y = 13.6 + 34.1 X1 + 0.126 X2 - 0.993 X3

Predictor	Coef	Stdev	t-ratio
Constant	13.623	6.720	2.027
X1	34.079	4.114	8.284
X2	0.126	0.106	1.184
X3	-0.993	0.655	-1.516

s = 6.905   R-sq = 58.1%   R-sq (adj) = 55.4%

Analysis of Variance

SOURCE	DF	SS	MS
Regression	3	3046.165	1015.388
Error	46	2193.298	47.680
Total	49	5239.463	

a. Can we conclude at the 5% significance level that this model is useful in analyzing annual sales?

b. Do these data provide sufficient evidence at the 5% significance level to enable us to conclude that the distribution efficiency index is a factor in determining total annual sales?

c. Does the amount of advertising influence sales? (Test with $\alpha = .05$.)

16.26 In preparing for upcoming union–management talks about pensions, benefits, and other nonsalary items, a labor union wishes to determine the relationships among hourly wages, years of schooling, and years of experience on the job. Selecting a random sample of workers on a production line, the union recorded the accompanying data.

Hourly Wages y	Years of Schooling x_1	Years of Experience x_2
10.00	8	3
11.00	8	4
12.50	9	5
14.00	12	8

Hourly Wages y	Years of Schooling x_1	Years of Experience x_2
10.50	10	2
13.25	11	4
15.20	10	10
12.10	9	6
11.75	8	5
10.85	8	4
12.35	10	7
14.55	12	10
13.80	10	9
13.60	12	8

Using the Minitab statistical application package, the union then generated the output shown in Figure E16.26.

a. Is there sufficient evidence to allow you to conclude that the linear model as a whole is significant? (Test with $\alpha = .10$.)

b. What do the values of $\hat{\beta}_1$ and $\hat{\beta}_2$ tell you?

FIGURE E16.26

```
The regression equation is

Y = 6.76 + 0.317 X1 + 0.439 X2

Predictor    Coef     Stdev     t-ratio
Constant     6.759    1.162     5.817
      X1     0.317    0.141     2.248
      X2     0.439    0.0824    5.328

s = 0.621    R-sq = 87.2%    R-sq (adj) = 84.9%

Analysis of Variance

SOURCE        DF    SS        MS
Regression     2    28.919    14.459
Error         11     4.239     0.385
Total         13    33.158
```

16.27 The capital asset pricing model is an extremely important tool for financial analysts. The model, which allows analysts to assess the risk associated with portfolios of stocks, is based on constructing a regression line for which the dependent variable is the return of a particular stock and the independent variables are various stock-market indices. A business student decided to develop her own model, using the following variables:

y = Price of stock

x_1 = TSE (Toronto Stock Exchange) Composite Price-Earnings Ratio

x_2 = TSE300 Index.

The following data from 21 months in 1977 and 1978 were gathered:

Month	Stock Price ($)	TSE Composite Price/Earnings Ratio	TSE300 Index
1977 J	8 7/8	8.80	996.6
F	9	8.85	1,008.9
M	8 3/4	8.96	1,022.1
A	8 5/8	8.48	994.8

Month	Stock Price ($)	TSE Composite Price/Earnings Ratio	TSE300 Index
M	8 1/2	8.19	981.2
J	9 3/8	8.62	1,031.2
J	9 5/8	8.70	1,033.5
A	9 3/8	8.31	1,003.3
S	9 1/8	8.20	1,000.1
O	8 7/8	7.93	970.5
N	9 3/8	7.90	1,017.5
D	9 3/4	8.24	1,059.6
1978 J	9 1/4	7.64	998.4
F	9 5/8	7.65	1,005.7
M	10	8.09	1,063.3
A	10 1/8	8.06	1,081.5
M	10 7/8	8.25	1,128.8
J	10 7/8	8.23	1,126.2
J	10 1/8	8.58	1,193.8
A	11 3/8	8.66	1,232.2
S	11 1/2	9.12	1,284.7

FIGURE E16.27

```
The regression equation is

Y = 2.625 - 0.573PE + 0.0112 TSE300

Predictor      Coef      Stdev     t-ratio
Constant      2.625     1.090       2.41
      PE     -0.573     0.140      -4.09
   TSE300     0.0112   0.00066     16.91

s = 0.235    R-sq = 94.3%    R-sq (adj) = 93.6%

Analysis of Variance

SOURCE        DF       SS        MS
Regression     2    16.324     8.162
Error         18     0.993     0.0552
Total         20    17.317
```

FIGURE E16.28

```
The regression equation is

Y = 12432 + 11.643 X1 + 6.114 X2

Predictor    Coef      Stdev      t-ratio
Constant     12432     6346.5      1.96
      X1     11.643     2.788      4.18
      X2      6.114     1.570      3.89

s = 8.578    R-sq = 60.7%    R-sq (adj) = 53.5%

Analysis of Variance

SOURCE         DF      SS        MS
Regression      2    1249.3    624.7
Error          11     809.3     73.6
Total          13    2058.6
```

The data were input, and the Minitab system was used to produce the printout shown in Figure E16.27.

a. Test the overall usefulness of the model, at $\alpha = .05$.

b. Test each of the coefficients for significance, at $\alpha = .05$.

16.28 An electronic parts manufacturing firm can cost out a particular job easily in terms of direct labor and direct materials costs. Allocating indirect costs, however, is somewhat more difficult. In an effort to come to grips with this problem, the firm's controller instructed one of the accountants to regress total manufacturing overhead costs on the number of direct labor hours used (x_1) and on the quantity of direct materials used (x_2). The Minitab software package was then used to produce the results shown in Figure E16.28.

a. Is there sufficient evidence (with $\alpha = .05$) to indicate that total costs and direct labor are linearly related?

b. Is there sufficient evidence (with $\alpha = .05$) to indicate that total costs and direct materials are linearly related?

c. Test the overall usefulness of the regression model, with $\alpha = .05$.

d. Interpret the coefficient of determination.

| | **CASE 16.1*** | **RISK ASSESSMENT FROM FINANCIAL REPORTS** |

Investors are interested in assessing the riskiness of a company's common stock, as well as its expected rate of return. It is therefore desirable to potential investors that a company's financial reports provide information to help them assess the company's risk.

* Gail E. Farrelly, Kenneth R. Ferris, and William R. Reichenstein, "Perceived Risk, Market Risk and Accounting-Determined Risk Measures," *Accounting Review* 60 (1985): 278–88.

Farrelly, Ferris, and Reichenstein conducted an investigation into the relationship between seven accounting-determined measures of risk and the average risk assessment of financial analysts. The seven accounting-determined measures of risk (all of which could be computed from a company's financial reports) and their definitions are as follows:

Dividend payout = (Cash dividends)/(Earnings)

Current ratio = (Current assets)/(Current liabilities)

Asset size = Log(Total assets)*

Asset growth = Average growth rate in asset size for the years 1977–1981

Leverage = (Total senior debt)/(Total assets)

Variability in earnings = Standard deviation of the price-earnings ratio for the years 1977–1981

Covariability in earnings = Strength of the relationship between a firm's price–earnings ratio and the average price–earnings ratio of the market overall.

These seven measures were computed for 25 well-known stocks, based on data from the companies' annual reports from 1977 to 1981. The results are summarized in the accompanying table.

The names of the 25 stocks were then sent to a random sample of 500 financial analysts, who "were requested to assess the risk of each of the 25 companies on a scale of 1 (low) to 9 (high), assuming that the stock was to be added to a diversified portfolio." The mean rating assigned by the 209 financial analysts who responded is recorded for each of the 25 stocks. This measure of the financial analysts' risk perception was taken to be a reasonable surrogate for the (market) risk of each stock. The data were then used to estimate a multiple regression model. The data and the Minitab output are shown in the computer printout that follows. What conclusions can you draw about the usefulness of the information provided by financial reports for the purpose of assessing a company's risk?

SUMMARY DATA FOR SELECT STUDY VARIABLES

Name of Stock	Dividend Payout x_1	Current Ratio x_2	Asset Size x_3	Asset Growth x_4	Leverage x_5	Variability Earnings x_6	Covariability Earnings x_7	Mean Risk Assessment y
American Telephone	.63	.70	11.83	.093	.165	1.09	.62	1.89
Procter & Gamble	.47	1.76	8.85	.106	.318	2.79	.46	2.36
IBM	.61	1.41	10.30	.103	.338	1.95	.21	2.39
General Electric	.43	1.24	9.95	.111	.468	1.29	.97	2.69
Exxon	.47	1.34	11.33	.165	.277	2.25	.56	2.70

* In this definition, log is the natural logarithm.

Name of Stock	Dividend Payout x_1	Current Ratio x_2	Asset Size x_3	Asset Growth x_4	Leverage x_5	Variability Earnings x_6	Covariability Earnings x_7	Mean Risk Assessment y
Commonwealth Edison	.88	.72	9.32	.128	.620	1.76	.21	3.20
Dow Jones & Co.	.40	.78	6.28	.177	.477	2.96	.67	3.57
McDonald's	.15	.50	7.97	.150	.413	2.32	.62	3.87
Sears Roebuck	.66	1.24	10.24	.177	.573	1.42	.67	3.91
DuPont	.60	2.05	10.08	.244	.508	1.64	.67	4.11
Safeway	.59	1.08	8.21	.093	.691	2.01	.55	4.28
Citicorp	.36	1.47	11.69	.124	.467	1.52	.87	4.30
Dr. Pepper	.54	2.17	5.11	.121	.215	2.26	.31	4.32
General Motors	2.24	1.09	10.57	.093	.422	2.79	.32	4.59
Xerox	.42	1.74	8.95	.102	.397	1.04	.21	4.69
American Broadcasting	.31	2.63	7.37	.127	.370	.47	.16	4.86
Holiday Inns	.20	.87	7.43	.155	.536	1.34	.36	5.13
Tandy	.00	3.48	6.84	.168	.225	3.27	.31	5.54
Litton Industries	.17	1.53	8.21	.117	.552	2.52	1.00	5.66
RCA	.58	1.18	8.97	.143	.855	2.79	.51	5.67
Georgia Pacific	.80	1.48	8.53	.134	.450	3.13	.67	5.88
Emery Air Freight	.83	1.78	5.62	.135	.697	2.28	.46	5.92
E. F. Hutton	.18	1.47	8.64	.181	.467	1.80	.82	6.37
U.S. Homes	1.30	1.47	6.63	.136	.467	20.18	.10	7.23
International Harvester	8.58	1.48	8.58	.081	.704	2.79	.51	8.78

```
The regression equation is

Y = 2.19 + 0.443 X1 + 0.864 X2 - 0.248 X3 + 1.96 X4 + 3.59 X5 + 0.136 X6
    + 1.05 X7


Predictor     Coef      Stdev     t-ratio
Constant      2.19      1.87       1.17
    X1        0.443     0.142      3.12
    X2        0.864     0.373      2.32
    X3       -0.248     0.132     -1.88
    X4        1.96      6.25       0.31
    X5        3.59      1.44       2.50
    X6        0.135     0.0598     2.25
    X7        1.05      0.938      1.11

s = 0.981    R-sq = 74.2%    R-sq (adj) = 63.5%
```

Analysis of Variance

SOURCE	DF	SS	MS
Regression	7	47.037	6.720
Error	17	16.372	0.963
Total	24	63.409	

CASE 16.2*   *TESTING POPULAR BELIEFS ABOUT GOVERNMENT LOTTERIES*

Lotteries have become important sources of revenue for governments. Many people have criticized lotteries, however—often referring to them as a tax on the poor or a tax on the uneducated. In an examination of this issue, a random sample of 100 people were asked how much they spend on lottery tickets and were interviewed about various sociodemographic variables. The purpose of this work was to test the following beliefs:

1. Relatively poor people spend a greater proportion of their income on lotteries than do relatively rich people.
2. Older people buy more lottery tickets than do younger people.
3. People who have children spend more on lotteries than do those without children.
4. Relatively uneducated people spend more on lotteries than do relatively educated people.

As part of the study, the following model was proposed:

$$y = \beta_0 + \beta_1 x_1 + \beta_2 x_2 + \beta_3 x_3 + \beta_4 x_4 + \varepsilon.$$

In this model,

y = Amount spent on lottery tickets as a percentage of total household income

x_1 = Number of years of education

x_2 = Age

x_3 = Number of children

x_4 = Personal income.

The data were run on a statistical applications package, with the results shown in the accompanying table.

---

* This minicase is based on several different studies.

COMPUTER-GENERATED DATA RESULTS

Variable	Coefficients	t-Statistic
Constant	-7.35	-4.58
x_1	$-.46$	-2.83
x_2	$.55$	2.61
x_3	$.09$	$.71$
x_4	-5.81	-6.05

$r^2 = .41$

$F = 89.0$

Comment on the validity of the enumerated beliefs, in light of the statistical results.

MINITAB INSTRUCTIONS

The command

`REGRESS 'Y' 2 'X1' 'X2'`

will produce the regression equation

$$\hat{y} = \hat{\beta}_0 + \hat{\beta}_1 x_1 + \hat{\beta}_2 x_2.$$

The 2 in the command specifies the number of independent variables in the equation. The output includes the coefficients, t-statistics, s_ε, r^2, and the analysis of variance. The subcommand

`PREDICT X1, X2`

will produce the 95% confidence intervals and prediction intervals of y, when the given values of the independent variables are X1 and X2.

In Example 16.1, the following data are input:

```
READ C1-C4
    89.5    20.0     5     4.1
    79.9    14.8    10     6.8
    83.1    20.5     8     6.3
    56.9    12.5     7     5.1
    66.6    18.0     8     4.2
    82.5    14.3    12     8.6
   126.3    27.5     1     4.9
    79.3    16.5    10     6.2
   119.9    24.3     2     7.5
    87.6    20.2     8     5.1
   112.6    22.0     7     6.3
   120.8    19.0    11    12.9
```

```
 78.5    12.3    16    9.6
 74.3    14.0    12    5.7
 74.8    16.7    13    4.8
END
NAME C1='Y', C2='X1', C3='X2', C4='X3'
REGRESS 'Y' 3 'X1' 'X2' 'X3'
```

The following output is produced:

```
The regression equation is

Y = -16.1 + 4.14 X1 - 0.236 X2 + 4.83 X3

Predictor      Coef       Stdev      t-ratio
Constant     -16.06      19.07        -0.84
    X1         4.1462     0.7512        5.52
    X2        -0.2361     0.8812       -0.27
    X3         4.8309     0.9011        5.36


s = 6.894    R-sq = 91.6%    R-sq (adj) = 89.3%


Analysis of Variance

SOURCE         DF       SS        MS
Regression      3     5707.4    1902.5
Error          11      522.8      47.5
Total          14     6230.2
```

We can use the subcommand PREDICT to produce the 95% confidence interval estimate of the expected value of y and the 95% prediction interval of y. Thus, the commands

```
REGRESS 'Y' 3 'X1' 'X2' 'X3';
PREDICT 20 10 10.
```

will elicit the following statistical results:

```
Fit       Stdev.Fit       95% C.I.          95% P.I.
112.81       3.58      (104.94, 120.69)   (95.71, 129.91)
```

SOLUTIONS TO SELF-CORRECTING EXERCISES

16.6 a. $\hat{\beta}_1 = .062$. For each additional building permit issued, the drywall demand increases by .062 hundred sheets (on the average).

$\hat{\beta}_2 = -1.212$. For each 1-point increase in the mortgage rate, drywall demand decreases by 1.212 hundred sheets (on the average).

$\hat{\beta}_3 = .022$. For each \$1,000 increase in per capita GNP, drywall demand increases by .022 hundred sheets (on the average).

b. *Decision rule:* Reject H_0 if
$$|t| > t_{\alpha/2, n-k-1} = t_{.025, 32} = 1.96.$$

(i) *Test of β_1:* $t = 2.067$
Reject H_0.

(ii) *Test of β_2:* $t = -1.839$
Do not reject H_0.

(iii) *Test of β_3:* $t = 4.400$
Reject H_0.

There is evidence of a linear relationship between the number of building permits and between increases in per capita GNP and drywall demand.

16.16 a. $r^2 = 12.7\%$. Thus, 12.7% of the variation in sales volume is explained by the variation in the independent variables.

b. $H_0: \beta_1 = \beta_2 = \beta_3 = 0$.
H_A: At least one β_i is not equal to zero.

Decision rule: Reject H_0 if
$$F > F_{\alpha, k, n-k-1} = F_{.01, 3, 88} \approx 4.13.$$

Test statistic: $F = \dfrac{371.75}{86.84} = 4.28$

Conclusion: Reject H_0.

There is sufficient evidence to indicate that the model is useful.

TIME SERIES
ANALYSIS AND
FORECASTING

INTRODUCTION

Any variable that is measured over time in sequential order is called a **time series.** Our objective in this chapter is to analyze time series in order to detect patterns that will enable us to forecast the future value of the time series. The number of such applications in management and economics is almost infinite. For example:

1. Governments want to know future values of interest rates, unemployment rates, and percentage increases in the cost of living.

2. Housing industry economists must forecast mortgage interest rates, demand for housing, and the cost of building materials.

3. Many companies attempt to predict the demand for their product and their share of the market.

4. Universities and colleges often try to forecast how many students will be applying to be accepted at post-secondary-school institutions.

There are many different forecasting techniques. Some of these (including the ones we presented in the chapters on regression analysis) are based on developing a model that attempts to analyze the relationship between a dependent variable and one or more independent variables. The forecasting methods to be discussed in this chapter, however, are all based on time series analysis. The first step is to analyze the components of a time series, which we discuss in the next section. In Sections 17.3 through 17.6, we deal with methods for detecting and measuring which components exist. Once we uncover this information, we can develop forecasting tools.

Be forewarned that we will only scratch the surface of this topic. Our objective is to expose you to the concepts of forecasting and to introduce some of the simpler techniques. The level of this textbook precludes our investigating the more complicated methods.

COMPONENTS OF TIME SERIES

A time series may consist of four different components.

Components of a Time Series

1. Long-term trend (T)
2. Cyclical effect (C)

3. Seasonal effect (*S*)
4. Random variation (*R*)

A **trend** (also known as a *secular trend*) is a long-term relatively smooth pattern or direction that the series exhibits. Its duration is more than one year. For example, the population of the United States during the past 40 years has exhibited a trend of relatively steady growth from 147 million in 1948 to 246 million in 1988 (see Figure 17.1).

The trend of a time series is not always linear. For example, Figure 17.2 describes U.S. beer consumption per person (over the age of 20) from 1970 to 1987. As you can see, such consumption grew between 1970 and 1980, then leveled off, and for the last 5 years decreased.

A **cycle** is a wavelike pattern about a long-term trend that is generally apparent over a number of years. By definition, it has a duration of more than one year. Examples of cycles include the well-known business cycles that record periods of economic recession and inflation, long-term product-demand cycles, and cycles in the monetary and financial sectors.

Figure 17.3 displays a series of regular cycles. Unfortunately, in practice, cycles are seldom regular and often appear in company with other components. The

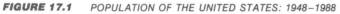

FIGURE 17.1   *POPULATION OF THE UNITED STATES: 1948–1988*

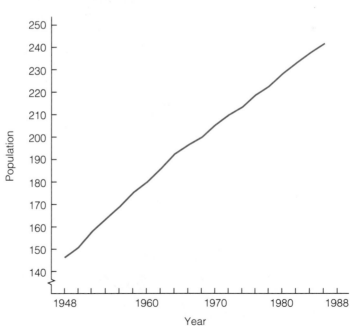

SOURCE: *Statistical Abstract of the United States.*

FIGURE 17.2 U.S. BEER CONSUMPTION PER PERSON OVER 20

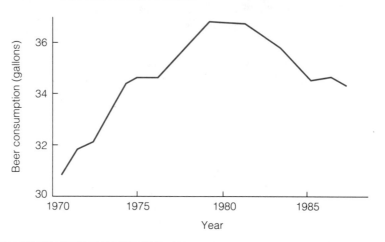

percentage change in U.S. domestic imports between 1970 and 1986 is depicted in Figure 17.4. There appear to be three irregular cycles and a long-term decrease in this time series.

Seasonal variations are like cycles, but they occur over short repetitive calendar periods and, by definition, have durations of less than one year. The term *seasonal variation* may refer to the four traditional seasons or to systematic patterns that occur during the period of one week or even over the course of one day. Stock-market prices, for example, often show highs and lows at particular times during the day.

An illustration of seasonal variation is provided in Figure 17.5, which graphs

FIGURE 17.3 CYCLICAL VARIATION IN A TIME SERIES

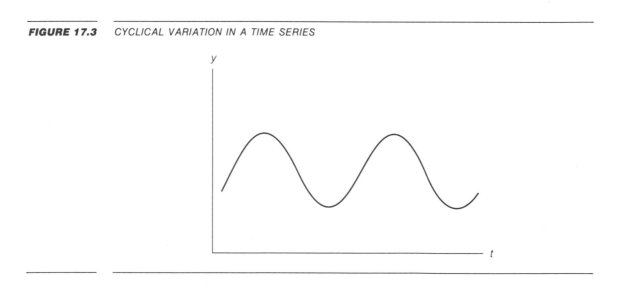

FIGURE 17.4   *PERCENTAGE CHANGE IN U.S. DOMESTIC IMPORTS*

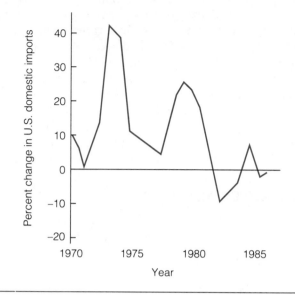

SOURCE: *Statistical Abstract of the United States.*

FIGURE 17.5   *TRAFFIC VOLUME IN BILLIONS OF MILES*

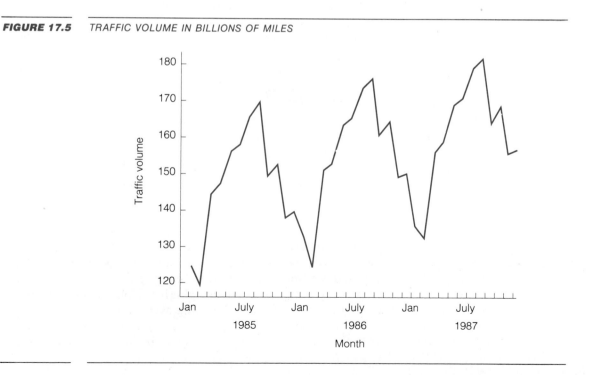

monthly U.S. traffic volume (in billions of miles). It is obvious from the graph that Americans drive more during the summer months than during the winter.

Random variation comprises the irregular changes in a time series that are not caused by any other component. Such variation tends to hide the existence of the other, more predicable components; and because it exists in almost all time series, you will benefit from learning how to remove the random variation, thereby allowing you to describe and measure the other components and ultimately to make accurate forecasts. If you examine Figures 17.1, 17.2, 17.4, and 17.5 you will detect some degree of random variation; because of it, even if we know precisely the contributions of the other components, we cannot predict the time series with 100% confidence. If you've learned anything from the previous 16 chapters in this book, you will recognize that this is not something new. Statisticians must always live with the fact of imperfect results.

TIME SERIES MODELS

The time series model is generally expressed either as an **additive model,** in which case the value of the time series at time t (denoted y_t) is specified as

$$y_t = T_t + C_t + S_t + R_t,$$

or as a **multiplicative model,** in which case the value of the time series at time t is specified as

$$y_t = T_t \cdot C_t \cdot S_t \cdot R_t.$$

Both models may be equally acceptable. However, it is frequently easier to understand the techniques associated with time series analysis if we refer to the multiplicative model. In the next four sections, we will present ways of determining which components are present in the time series.

SECTION 17.3

SMOOTHING TECHNIQUES

If we can determine which components actually exist in a time series, we can develop a better forecast. Unfortunately the existence of the random variation component often hides the other components. One of the simplest ways of removing the random fluctuation is to smooth the time series. In this section we will describe two methods of doing this: moving averages and exponential smoothing.

MOVING AVERAGES

A **moving average** for a time period is the simple arithmetic average of the values in that time period and those close to it. For example, to compute the three-period moving average for any time period, we would sum the value of the time series in that time period, the value in the previous time period, and the value in the following time period, and divide by 3. We calculate the three-period moving average for all time periods except the first and the last. To compute the five-period moving average, we average the value in that time period, the values in the two previous time periods, and the values in the two following time periods. We can choose any number of periods for which to calculate moving averages.

As part of an effort to forecast future gasoline sales, an operator of five independent gas stations recorded the quarterly gasoline sales (in 1,000s of gallons) for the past 4 years. These are shown in the accompanying table. Calculate the 3-quarter and 5-quarter moving averages. Then graph the quarterly sales and the moving averages.

QUARTERLY REGIONAL GASOLINE SALES

Time Period	Year	Quarter	Gasoline Sales (1,000s of gallons)
1	1	1	39
2		2	37
3		3	61
4		4	58
5	2	1	18
6		2	56
7		3	82
8		4	27
9	3	1	41
10		2	69
11		3	49
12		4	66
13	4	1	54
14		2	42
15		3	90
16		4	66

Solution.   To compute the 3-quarter moving averages, we group the gasoline sales in periods 1, 2, and 3, and then we average them. Thus, the first moving average is

$$\frac{39 + 37 + 61}{3} = \frac{137}{3} = 45.7.$$

---

* Appendix 17.A presents the Minitab commands used to produce the moving averages for this example.

The second moving average is calculated by dropping the first period's sales (39), adding the fourth period's sales (58), and then computing the new average. Thus, the second moving average is

$$\frac{37 + 61 + 58}{3} = \frac{156}{3} = 52.0.$$

The process continues as shown in the following table. Similar calculations are used to produce the 5-quarter moving averages shown in the table.

Time Period	Gasoline Sales	3-Quarter Moving Average	5-Quarter Moving Average
1	39	–	–
2	37	45.7	–
3	61	52.0	42.6
4	58	45.7	46.0
5	18	44.0	55.0
6	56	52.0	48.2
7	82	55.0	44.8
8	27	50.0	55.0
9	41	45.7	53.6
10	69	53.0	50.4
11	49	61.3	55.8
12	66	56.3	56.0
13	54	54.0	60.2
14	42	62.0	63.6
15	90	66.0	–
16	66	–	–

Notice that we place the moving averages in the center of the group of values that are being averaged. It is for this reason that we prefer to use an odd number of periods in calculating moving averages. Later in this section we will discuss how to deal with an even number of periods.

To see how the moving averages remove some of the random variation, examine Figures 17.6 and 17.7. Figure 17.6 depicts the quarterly gasoline sales. It is difficult to discern any of the time series components, because of the large amount of random variation. Now consider the 3-quarter moving average in Figure 17.7. You should be able to detect a seasonal pattern that exhibits peaks in the third quarter of each year (periods 3, 7, 11, and 15) and valleys in the first quarter of each year (periods 5, 9, and 13). There is also a small but discernible long-term trend of increasing sales.

FIGURE 17.6    QUARTERLY GASOLINE SALES

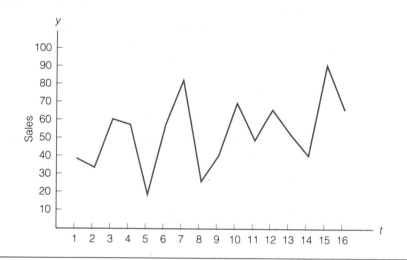

FIGURE 17.7   QUARTERLY GASOLINE SALES AND THE 3-QUARTER AND 5-QUARTER MOVING AVERAGES

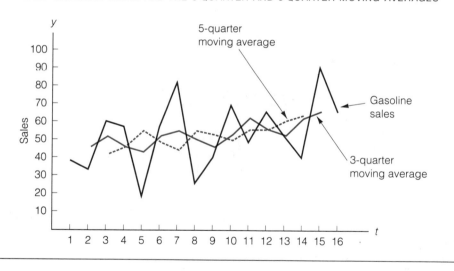

Notice also in Figure 17.7 that the 5-quarter moving average produces more smoothing than the 3-quarter moving average. In general, the longer the time period over which we average, the smoother the series becomes. Unfortunately, in this case we've smoothed too much, since the seasonal pattern is no longer apparent in the 5-quarter moving average. All that we can see is the long-term trend. It is important to realize that our objective is to smooth the time series sufficiently to remove the random variation and to reveal the other components (trend, cycle, and/or season) present. With too little smoothing, the random variation disguises the real pattern. With too much smoothing, however, some or all of the other effects may be eliminated along with the random variation.

CENTERED MOVING AVERAGES

If we use an even number of periods in calculating the moving averages, we have to figure out where to place the moving averages in a graph. For example, suppose that we calculate the four-period moving average of the data in the following table.

Period	Time Series
1	15
2	27
3	20
4	14
5	25
6	11

The first moving average is

$$\frac{15 + 27 + 20 + 14}{4} = \frac{76}{4} = 19.0.$$

However, since this value represents time periods 1, 2, 3, and 4, we must place this value between periods 2 and 3. The next moving average is

$$\frac{27 + 20 + 14 + 25}{4} = \frac{86}{4} = 21.5,$$

and it must be placed between periods 3 and 4. The moving average that falls between periods 4 and 5 is

$$\frac{20 + 14 + 25 + 11}{4} = \frac{70}{4} = 17.5.$$

Having the moving averages fall between the time periods causes various problems, including the difficulty of graphing. Centering the moving averages corrects the problem. This is performed by computing the two-period moving average of the moving averages. Thus, the **centered moving average** for period 3 is

$$\frac{19.0 + 21.5}{2} = 20.25.$$

Similarly, the centered moving average for period 4 is

$$\frac{21.5 + 17.5}{2} = 19.50.$$

The following table summarizes our results.

Period	Time Series	Four-period Moving Average	Four-period Centered Moving Average
1	15		–
2	27	–	–
3	20	19.0	20.25
4	14	21.5	19.50
5	25	17.5	–
6	11	–	–

Because of the extra computation involved in centering a moving average, we prefer to use an odd number of periods. However, in some situations we're required to use an even number of periods. Such cases are discussed in Section 17.6.

EXPONENTIAL SMOOTHING

Two drawbacks are associated with the moving average method of smoothing a time series. First, we do not have moving averages for the first and last sets of time periods. If the time series has few observations, the missing values may constitute an important loss of information. Second, the moving average "forgets" most of the previous time series values. For example, in the 5-month moving average described in Example 17.1, the average for month 4 reflects months 2, 3, 4, 5, and 6 but is not affected by month 1. Similarly the moving average for month 5 forgets months 1 and 2. Both of these problems are addressed by **exponential smoothing.**

The exponentially smoothed time series is defined next.

Exponential Smoothed-Time Series

$$S_t = wy_t + (1 - w)S_{t-1} \qquad \text{for } t \geq 2,$$

where

S_t = Exponentially smoothed time series at time t

y_t = Time series at time t

S_{t-1} = Exponentially smoothed time series at time $t - 1$

w = Smoothing constant, where $0 \leq w \leq 1$.

FIGURE 17.8   *ORIGINAL TIME SERIES AND TWO EXPONENTIALLY SMOOTHED SERIES*

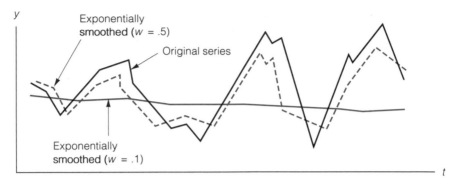

We begin by setting

$$S_1 = y_1.$$

The smoothing constant w is chosen on the basis of how much smoothing is required. A small value of w produces a great deal of smoothing. A large value of w results in very little smoothing. Figure 17.8 depicts a time series and two exponentially smoothed series with $w = .1$ and $w = .5$.

EXAMPLE 17.2

Apply the exponential smoothing technique with $w = .2$ and $w = .7$ to the data in Example 17.1, and graph the results.

Solution.   The exponentially smoothed values are calculated from the formula

$$S_t = wy_t + (1 - w)S_{t-1}$$

The results with $w = .2$ and $w = .7$ are shown in the following table.

Time Period	Gasoline Sales	Exponentially Smoothed Sales (with $w = .2$)	Exponentially Smoothed Sales (with $w = .7$)
1	39	$= 39$	$= 39$
2	37	$.2(37) + .8(39) = 38.6$	$.7(37) + .3(39) = 37.6$
3	61	$.2(61) + .8(38.6) = 43.1$	$.7(61) + .3(37.6) = 54.0$
4	58	$.2(58) + .8(43.1) = 46.1$	$.7(58) + .3(54.0) = 56.8$
5	18	$.2(18) + .8(46.1) = 40.5$	$.7(18) + .3(56.8) = 29.6$
6	56	$.2(56) + .8(40.5) = 43.6$	$.7(56) + .3(29.6) = 48.1$
7	82	$.2(82) + .8(43.6) = 51.2$	$.7(82) + .3(48.1) = 71.8$

Time Period	Gasoline Sales	Exponentially Smoothed Sales (with $w = .2$)	Exponentially Smoothed Sales (with $w = .7$)
8	27	$.2(27) + .8(51.2) = 46.4$	$.7(27) + .3(71.8) = 40.4$
9	41	$.2(41) + .8(46.4) = 45.3$	$.7(41) + .3(40.4) = 40.8$
10	69	$.2(69) + .8(45.3) = 50.1$	$.7(69) + .3(40.8) = 60.6$
11	49	$.2(49) + .8(50.1) = 49.8$	$.7(49) + .3(60.6) = 52.5$
12	66	$.2(66) + .8(49.8) = 53.1$	$.7(66) + .3(52.5) = 61.9$
13	54	$.2(54) + .8(53.1) = 53.3$	$.7(54) + .3(61.9) = 56.4$
14	42	$.2(42) + .8(53.3) = 51.0$	$.7(42) + .3(56.4) = 46.3$
15	90	$.2(90) + .8(51.0) = 58.8$	$.7(90) + .3(46.3) = 76.9$
16	66	$.2(66) + .8(58.8) = 60.2$	$.7(66) + .3(76.9) = 69.3$

Figure 17.9 depicts the graph of the original time series and the exponentially smoothed series. As you can see, $w = .7$ results in very little smoothing, while $w = .2$ results in perhaps too much smoothing. In both smoothed time series, it is difficult to discern the seasonal pattern that we detected by using moving averages. A different value of w (perhaps $w = .5$) would likely produce more satisfactory results.

Moving averages and exponential smoothing are relatively crude methods of removing random variations in order to discover the existence of other components. In the next three sections, we will attempt to measure the components more precisely.

FIGURE 17.9   *QUARTERLY GASOLINE SALES AND EXPONENTIALLY SMOOTHED SALES WITH $w = .2$ AND $w = .7$*

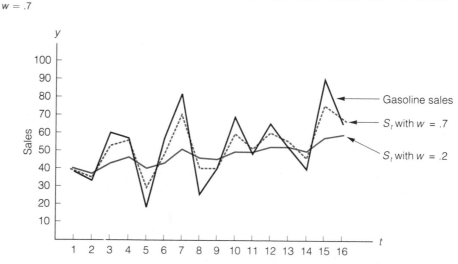

████████ **EXERCISES**

LEARNING THE TECHNIQUES

17.1 For the following time series, compute the three-period moving averages:

Period t	y
1	48
2	41
3	37
4	32
5	36
6	31
7	43
8	52
9	60
10	48
11	41
12	30

17.2 For Exercise 17.1, compute the five-period moving averages.

17.3 For Exercises 17.1 and 17.2, graph the time series and the two moving averages.

17.4 Compute the four-period centered moving averages for the following time series:

Period t	y
1	44
2	42
3	49
4	56
5	66
6	62
7	63
8	49

17.5 Apply exponential smoothing with $w = .1$ to help detect the components of the following time series:

Period t	y
1	12
2	18
3	16
4	24
5	17
6	16
7	25
8	21
9	23
10	14

17.6 Repeat Exercise 17.5, with $w = .8$

17.7 For Exercises 17.5 and 17.6, draw the time series and plot the two sets of exponentially smoothed values. Does there appear to be a trend component in the time series?

APPLYING THE TECHNIQUES

Self-Correcting Exercise (See Appendix 17.B for the solution.)

17.8 The following daily sales figures have been recorded in a medium-size merchandising firm.

Day	Week 1	Week 2	Week 3	Week 4
Monday	43	51	40	64
Tuesday	45	41	57	58
Wednesday	22	37	30	33
Thursday	25	22	33	38
Friday	31	25	37	25

a. Plot the series on a graph.

b. Calculate the 3-day moving averages, and superimpose them on the same graph.

c. Does there appear to be a seasonal (weekly) pattern?

17.9   For Exercise 17.8, compute the 5-day moving averages and superimpose them on the same graph. Does this help you answer part (c)?

17.10   The quarterly sales of a department store chain were recorded for the past 4 years. These figures are shown in the accompanying table.

a. Graph the time series.

b. Calculate the 4-quarter centered moving averages, and superimpose them on the time series graph.

c. What can you conclude from your time series smoothing?

Year	Quarter	Sales ($millions)
1986	1	18
	2	33

Year	Quarter	Sales ($millions)
	3	25
	4	41
1987	1	22
	2	20
	3	36
	4	33
1988	1	27
	2	38
	3	44
	4	52
1989	1	31
	2	26
	3	29
	4	45

17.11   Repeat Exercise 17.10, using exponential smoothing with $w = .4$.

SECTION 17.4

TREND ANALYSIS

In the last section we investigated how a time series can be smoothed to give us a clearer picture of which components are present. In order to forecast, however, we often need more precise measurements about trend, cyclical effects, and seasonal effects. In this section we will discuss methods that allow us to describe trend. In subsequent sections we will consider how to measure cyclical and seasonal effects.

As we noted earlier, a trend can be linear or nonlinear and, indeed, can take on a whole host of other functional forms. The easiest way of isolating the long-term trend is by regression analysis, where the independent variable is time. If we believe that the long-term trend is essentially linear, we use the following model.

> **Linear Model for Long-term Trend**
>
> $$y = \beta_0 + \beta_1 t + \varepsilon$$
>
> where t is the time period.

Although various nonlinear models are available, we will consider only the polynomial model, which can be used to describe many nonlinear time series.

FIGURE 17.10   POLYNOMIAL MODEL

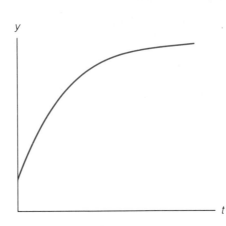

Polynomial Model for Long-term Trend

$$y = \beta_0 + \beta_1 t + \beta_2 t^2 + \varepsilon$$

Figure 17.10 depicts one form of the polynomial model. This may apply, for example, to a new product that has experienced a rapid early growth rate followed by the inevitable leveling off. Examples 17.3 and 17.4 illustrate how and when these models are used.

EXAMPLE 17.3

Annual sales (in millions of dollars) for a pharmaceutical company have been recorded for the past 10 years. These data are shown in the accompanying table. The management of the company believes that the trend over this period is basically linear. Use regression analysis to measure the trend.

Year	Sales ($millions)	Year	Sales ($millions)
1980	18.0	1985	21.1
1981	19.4	1986	23.5
1982	18.0	1987	23.2
1983	19.9	1988	20.4
1984	19.3	1989	24.4

Solution. It is easier (though not necessary) to change the times from years 1980 through 1989 to time periods 1 through 10. When that was done, the Minitab software package was used to estimate the model.

MINITAB COMPUTER OUTPUT FOR EXAMPLE 17.3

```
The  regression  equation  is

Y = 17.3 + 0.625  TIME

Predictor        Coef      Stdev     t-ratio
Constant      17.2800     0.9236      18.71
TIME           0.6255     0.1488       4.20


s = 1.352    R-sq = 68.8%    R-sq (adj) = 64.9%

Analysis  of  Variance

SOURCE         DF       SS        MS
Regression      1     32.273    32.273
Error           8     14.623     1.828
Total           9     46.896
```

The fit of the line is relatively poor with $r^2 = 68.8\%$. Because of the possible presence of cyclical and seasonal effects and because of random variation, we do not usually expect a very good fit. Remember, we're only measuring the trend in this analysis—not any other components.

The time series is shown graphically in Figure 17.11. The regression trend line that we just estimated is superimposed on the graph, showing a clear upward trend to the right.

One of the purposes of isolating the trend, as we suggested before, is to use it for forecasting. For example, we could use it for forecasting one year in advance, through 1990 ($t = 11$). From our trend equation, we get

$$\hat{y} = 17.28 + .6255t = 17.28 + .6255(11) = 24.1605.$$

This value, however, represents the forecast based only on trend. If we believe that a cyclical pattern also exists, we should incorporate that into the forecast, as well.

EXAMPLE 17.4

Americans are among the world's greatest consumers of beef. In the last decade, however, because of health concerns, many Americans have either decreased their consumption of beef or eliminated beef from their diets altogether. The effect has been serious for farmers and processors of meat products. To help analyze the problem, the

FIGURE 17.11   *TIME SERIES AND TREND LINE FOR EXAMPLE 17.3*

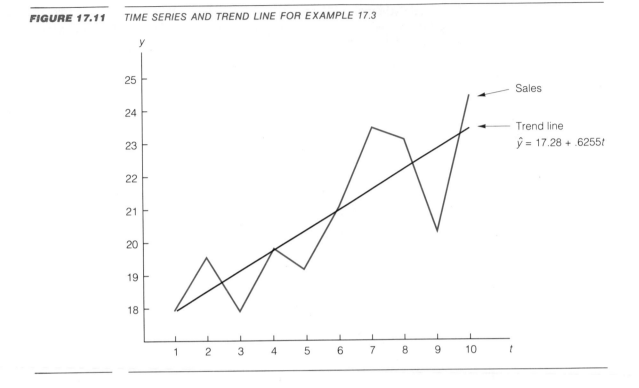

civilian per capita consumption of beef in the United States has been recorded for the period 1960–1982. These data are shown in the accompanying table. To help forecast future consumption of beef, apply regression analysis to determine the trend. A graph of the data suggests that a polynomial model might be best.

Year	t	**Annual Civilian per Capita Consumption of Beef (pounds)** y_t
1960	1	85.0
1961	2	87.8
1962	3	88.8
1963	4	94.3
1964	5	99.8
1965	6	99.5
1966	7	104.0

| | | Annual Civilian per Capita Consumption of Beef (pounds) |
Year	t	y_t
1967	8	106.2
1968	9	109.7
1969	10	110.8
1970	11	113.5
1971	12	113.0
1972	13	116.1
1973	14	109.6
1974	15	116.8
1975	16	118.8
1976	17	127.6
1977	18	123.9
1978	19	117.9
1979	20	105.5
1980	21	103.4
1981	22	104.3
1982	23	104.4

SOURCE: *Statistical Abstract of the United States.*

Solution.   The model

$$y = \beta_0 + \beta_1 t + \beta_2 t^2 + \varepsilon$$

was estimated, using the Minitab statistical system, with the following results.

MINITAB COMPUTER OUTPUT FOR EXAMPLE 17.4

```
The regression equation is

Y = 75.9 + 5.48 TIME - 0.185 TIME2

Predictor      Coef      Stdev     t-ratio
Constant       75.929    3.148      24.12
TIME            5.4802   0.6043      9.07
TIME2          -0.1846   0.0244     -7.55
```

```
s = 4.601    R-sq = 84.6%    R-sq(adj) = 83.0%
```

Analysis of Variance

SOURCE	DF	SS	MS
Regression	2	2322.3	1161.2
Error	20	423.4	21.2
Total	22	2745.8	

All the statistics (r^2, F, t-values) indicate that the polynomial model fits the data quite well. Thus, the trend is measured by

$$\hat{y} = 75.929 + 5.4802t - .1846t^2.$$

To forecast the per capita beef consumption for 1983, we use the regression equation with $t = 24$. Thus,

$$\hat{y} = 75.929 + 5.4802(24) - .1846(24^2) = 101.124.$$

The actual 1983 per capita beef consumption turned out to be 106.4. Figure 17.12 describes the time series and the trend line for this example.

FIGURE 17.12   TIME SERIES AND POLYNOMIAL TREND FOR EXAMPLE 17.4

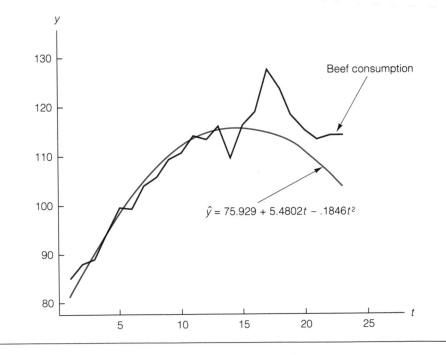

$\hat{y} = 75.929 + 5.4802t - .1846t^2$

Beef consumption

EXERCISES

LEARNING THE TECHNIQUES

17.12 Plot the following time series. Which model (linear or polynomial) would fit better?

Time Period t	y
1	.5
2	.6
3	1.3
4	2.7
5	4.1
6	6.9
7	10.8
8	19.2

17.13 Plot the following time series to determine which model appears to fit better.

Time Period t	y
1	55
2	57
3	53
4	49
5	47
6	39
7	41
8	33
9	28
10	20

APPLYING THE TECHNIQUES

17.14 Enrollment in institutions of higher education has grown phenomenally since World War II. Forecasting this enrollment pattern, however, has been difficult. As a preliminary step, various attempts have been made to improve our understanding of the historical trend. One particular example consists of historical data on post-secondary enrollment in one midwestern state over 11 recent years. These data are shown in the accompanying table.

Year	t	Enrollment (1,000s)
1980	1	185
1981	2	198
1982	3	213
1983	4	225
1984	5	235
1985	6	240
1986	7	242
1987	8	243
1988	9	250
1989	10	248
1990	11	253

a. Plot the time series.

b. Which of the trend models appears to fit better? Explain.

17.15 In Exercise 17.14, the linear trend line was found to be

$\hat{y} = 192 + 6.31t \qquad (t = 1, 2, \ldots, 11)$.

a. Plot this line on the graph.

b. Forecast the enrollment for 1991 and 1992.

17.16 In Exercise 17.14, the polynomial trend line is

$\hat{y} = 171 + 16.4t - .837t^2 \qquad (t = 1, 2, \ldots, 11)$.

a. Plot this line on the graph.

b. Forecast the enrollment for 1991 and 1992.

17.17 From the time series plot in Exercise 17.14 and from the graphs of the two trend lines, judge which model fits better.

17.18 Exports are an important component of the exchange rate and, domestically, are an important indicator of employment and profitability in certain industries. The value of merchandise exports, in particular, seems to have increased dramatically in the 20-year period described in the accompanying table.

Year	t	Exports ($millions)
1961	1	20,188
1962	2	20,973
1963	3	22,472
1964	4	25,690
1965	5	26,961
1966	6	29,379
1967	7	30,934
1968	8	34,063
1969	9	37,332
1970	10	42,659
1971	11	43,549
1972	12	49,199
1973	13	70,823
1974	14	97,908
1975	15	107,589
1976	16	115,150

Year	t	Exports ($millions)
1977	17	121,150
1978	18	143,681
1979	19	181,860
1980	20	220,630

SOURCE: U.S. Department of Commerce, Bureau of Economic Analysis, Business Statistics. Biennial supplement to the *Survey of Current Business* (1984).

a. Plot the time series.

b. Which trend model is likely to fit better? Explain.

17.19   In Exercise 17.18, the linear trend line is

$$\hat{y} = -22,393 + 8,999t \qquad (t = 1, 2, \ldots, 20).$$

Plot this line on the graph.

17.20   Refer to Exercise 17.18. The polynomial trend line is

$$\hat{y} = 36,858 - 7,160t + 769.5t^2 \qquad (t = 1, 2, \ldots, 20).$$

Plot this line on the graph.

17.21   Which of the two trend models in Exercises 17.19 and 17.20 appears to provide the better fit?

SECTION
17.5

MEASURING THE CYCLICAL EFFECT

The fundamental difference between cyclical and seasonal variations lies in the length of the time period under consideration. In addition, however, seasonal effects are felt to be predictable, whereas cyclical effects (except in the case of certain well-known economic and business cycles) are often viewed as being unpredictable. Nevertheless, cycles can be isolated, and the procedure we will use to identify cyclical variation is the **percentage of trend.**

The percentage of trend is calculated in the following way:

1. Determine the trend line (usually by regression).
2. For each time period, compute the trend value $\hat{y}$.
3. The percentage of trend is $[(y/\hat{y}) \cdot 100]$

Consider the following example.

EXAMPLE 17.5

The annual demand for energy in the United States is affected by various factors, including price availability, and the state of the economy. To help analyze the changes that have taken place and to develop a prediction, researchers recorded the annual total consumption for the United States (measured in quadrillions of Btu) for the period 1970–1986. These data are shown in the accompanying table. Assuming that a linear trend exists, calculate the percentage of trend for each year.

Year	Time Period t	Annual Energy Consumption y_t
1970	1	66.4
1971	2	69.7
1972	3	72.2
1973	4	74.3
1974	5	72.5
1975	6	70.6
1976	7	74.4
1977	8	76.3
1978	9	78.1
1979	10	78.9
1980	11	76.0
1981	12	74.0
1982	13	70.8
1983	14	70.5
1984	15	74.1
1985	16	74.0
1986	17	73.9

SOURCE: *Statistical Abstract of the United States.*

Solution.   Minitab* was used to produce the trend line and the percentage of trend. From the output (not shown), we observe that the trend line is

$$\hat{y} = 71.313 + .2248t.$$

For each value of $t(t = 1, 2, \ldots, 17)$, the predicted values y and the percentage of trend were determined as follows.

---

* See Appendix 17.A for the Minitab commands used to produce the accompanying table.

Year	Time Period t	Energy Consumption y	Trend $\hat{y} = 71.313 + .2248t$	Percentage of Trend $(y/\hat{y}) \cdot 100$
1970	1	66.4	71.5378	92.819
1971	2	69.7	71.7626	97.127
1972	3	72.2	71.9874	100.296
1973	4	74.3	72.2122	102.892
1974	5	72.5	72.4370	100.088
1975	6	70.6	72.6618	97.164
1976	7	74.4	72.8866	102.078
1977	8	76.3	73.1114	104.363
1978	9	78.1	73.3362	106.497
1979	10	78.9	73.5610	107.259
1980	11	76.0	73.7858	103.002
1981	12	74.0	74.0106	99.987
1982	13	70.8	74.2354	95.374
1983	14	70.5	74.4602	94.683
1984	15	74.1	74.6850	99.218
1985	16	74.0	74.9098	98.787
1986	17	73.9	75.1346	98.358

Figure 17.13 describes the time series and the trend line. The percentage of trend represents the extent to which the actual energy consumption lies above or below the line. Figure 17.14 is another way of depicting these values. The trend line now appears as the 100% line.

The problem we face when trying to interpret Figure 17.14 is that of distinguishing between random variation and a cyclical pattern. If what appears to be a random collection of percentage of trend values exists above and below the 100% line, we conclude that its cause is random and not cyclical. However, if we see alternating groups of percentage of trend values above and below the 100% line and the patterns are regular, we would confidently identify the cyclical effect. In Figure 17.14 there appears to be a cyclical pattern, although it is not very regular. This highlights the major problem in forecasting time series that possess a cyclical component: the cyclical effect is often quite clearly present but too irregular to forecast with any degree of accuracy. Forecasting methods for this type of problem are available, but they are too advanced for our use. We will be satisfied simply to identify and measure the cyclical component of time series.

FIGURE 17.13   TIME SERIES AND TREND LINE FOR EXAMPLE 17.5

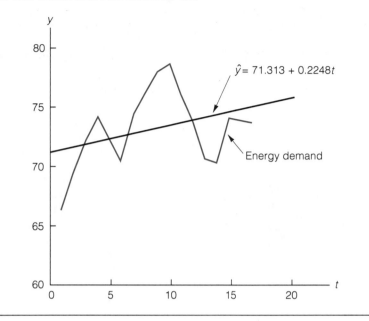

$\hat{y} = 71.313 + 0.2248t$

Energy demand

FIGURE 17.14   PERCENTAGE OF TREND FOR EXAMPLE 17.5

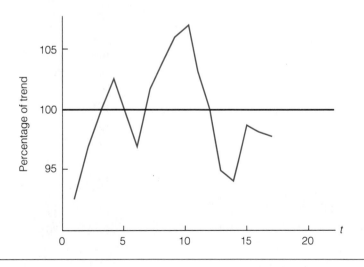

■■■■■■ **EXERCISES**

LEARNING THE TECHNIQUES

17.22 Consider the time series shown in the following table.

t	y	t	y
1	30	9	41
2	27	10	38
3	24	11	43
4	21	12	36
5	23	13	29
6	27	14	24
7	33	15	20
8	38		

The linear trend line is

$\hat{y} = 27.8 + .311t \qquad (t = 1, 2, \ldots, 15).$

a. Calculate the percentage of trend for each time period.

b. Plot the percentage of trend.

17.23 The time series shown in the following table was recorded.

t	y	t	y
1	6	7	20
2	11	8	22
3	21	9	18
4	17	10	17
5	27	11	12
6	23	12	15

The linear trend line is

$\hat{y} = 15.9 + .234t \qquad (t = 1, 2, \ldots, 12).$

a. Plot the time series.

b. Plot the trend line.

c. Calculate the percentage of trend.

d. Plot the percentage of trend.

APPLYING THE TECHNIQUES

Self-Correcting Exercise (See Appendix 17.B for the solution.)

17.24 One interesting phenomenon of the past several decades is the extent to which certain classes of assets have kept up with inflation while certain others have not. In terms of nominal interest rates, domestic corporate bond yields in the United States between 1961 and 1980 have assumed the values shown in the accompanying table.

Year	t	Domestic Corporate Bond Yields (annual averages; Moody's Aaa rating)
1961	1	4.35
1962	2	4.33
1963	3	4.26
1964	4	4.40
1965	5	4.49
1966	6	5.13
1967	7	5.51
1968	8	6.18
1969	9	7.03
1970	10	8.04
1971	11	7.39
1972	12	7.21
1973	13	7.44
1974	14	8.57
1975	15	8.83
1976	16	8.43
1977	17	8.02
1978	18	8.73
1979	19	9.63
1980	20	11.94

SOURCE: U.S. Department of Commerce, Bureau of Economic Analysis, Business Statistics. Biennial supplement to the *Survey of Current Business* (1984).

The linear trend line was computed as

$$\hat{y} = 3.42 + .340t \qquad (t = 1, 2, \ldots, 20).$$

a. Plot the time series, and graph the trend line.

b. Calculate the percentage of trend.

c. Plot the percentage of trend. Does there appear to be a cyclical effect?

17.25 As a preliminary step in forecasting future values, a large mail-order retail outlet has recorded the sales figures shown in the accompanying table.

Year	t	Sales ($millions)
1970	1	6.7
1971	2	7.4
1972	3	8.5
1973	4	11.2
1974	5	12.5
1975	6	10.7
1976	7	11.9
1977	8	11.4

Year	t	Sales ($millions)
1978	9	9.8
1979	10	11.5
1980	11	14.2
1981	12	18.1
1982	13	16.0
1983	14	11.2
1984	15	14.8
1985	16	15.2
1986	17	14.1
1987	18	12.2
1988	19	15.7

a. Plot the time series.

b. The trend line is

$$\hat{y} = 8.30 + .397t \qquad (t = 1, 2, \ldots, 19).$$

Graph this line.

c. Compute the percentage of trend.

SECTION 17.6 MEASURING THE SEASONAL EFFECT

Seasonal variation may occur within a year or within an even shorter time interval, such as a month, week, or day. In order to measure the seasonal effect, we shall construct **seasonal indices,** which attempt to measure the degree to which the seasons differ from one another. One requirement for this method is that we have a time series sufficiently long to allow us to observe several occurrences of each season. For example, if our seasons are the quarters of a year, we need to observe the time series over a number of years. Similarly, if the seasons are the days of the week, our time series should be observed for a number of weeks.

Seasonal indices are computed in the following way:

1. Remove the effect of seasonal and random variations by calculating the moving averages. Set the number of periods equal to the number of types of season. For example, we compute 12-month moving averages if the months of the year represent the seasons. A 5-day moving average is used if the seasons are the working days of the week. If the number of periods in the moving average is even, we compute centered moving averages. The effect of moving averages is seen in the multiplicative model of time series:

$$y_t = T_t \cdot C_t \cdot S_t \cdot R_t.$$

The moving averages remove S_t and R_t, leaving
$$MA_t = T_t \cdot C_t.$$

2. Compute the ratio of the time series over the moving averages. Thus, we have
$$\frac{y_t}{MA_t} = \frac{T_t \cdot C_t \cdot S_t \cdot R_t}{T_t \cdot C_t} = S_t \cdot R_t.$$

The result is a measure of seasonal and random variation.

3. For each type of season, calculate the average of the ratios in Step 2. This procedure removes most (but seldom all) of the random variation. The resulting average is a measure of the seasonal differences.

4. The seasonal indices are the average ratios from step 3 adjusted to ensure that the average seasonal index is 1.

EXAMPLE 17.6

The tourist industry is subject to enormous seasonal variation. A hotel in Bermuda has recorded its occupancy rate for each quarter during the past 5 years. These data are shown in the accompanying table. Calculate the seasonal indices for each quarter, to measure the amount of seasonal variation.

Year	Quarter	Hotel Occupancy	Year	Quarter	Hotel Occupancy
1985	1	.561	1987	3	.729
	2	.702		4	.600
	3	.800	1988	1	.622
	4	.568		2	.708
1986	1	.575		3	.806
	2	.738		4	.632
	3	.868	1989	1	.665
	4	.605		2	.835
1987	1	.594		3	.873
	2	.738		4	.670

Solution. Since there are 4 quarters (seasons) per year, we will calculate a 4-quarter centered moving average to remove the seasonal and random effects.

To calculate the 4-quarter centered moving averages, we first determine the 4-quarter moving averages and then compute the two-period moving averages of these values. So, for example, the moving average that falls between quarters 2 and 3 is

$$\frac{.561 + .702 + .800 + .568}{4} = \frac{2.631}{4} = .658.$$

Similarly, the moving average that falls between quarters 3 and 4 is

$$\frac{.702 + .800 + .568 + .575}{4} = \frac{2.645}{4} = .661.$$

Therefore, the third-quarter centered moving average is

$$\frac{.658 + .661}{2} = \frac{1.319}{2} = .660.$$

The next step is to find the ratio of the occupancy rates divided by the centered moving averages. The outcomes of the first two operations are shown in the accompanying table.

Year	Quarter	Occupancy y_t	Centered MA	Ratio y/MA
1985	1	.561	–	–
	2	.702	–	–
	3	.800	.660	1.213
	4	.568	.666	.853
1986	1	.575	.679	.847
	2	.738	.692	1.067
	3	.868	.699	1.242
	4	.605	.701	.863
1987	1	.594	.684	.869
	2	.738	.666	1.108
	3	.729	.669	1.090
	4	.600	.669	.898
1988	1	.622	.675	.922
	2	.708	.688	1.029
	3	.806	.697	1.156
	4	.632	.719	.879
1989	1	.665	.743	.895
	2	.835	.756	1.105
	3	.873	–	–
	4	.670	–	–

If we now group the ratios by quarter, we can see the similarities within each type of quarter and the differences between different types of quarter. For example, the ratios for quarter 1 are .847, .869, .922, and .895, whereas for quarter 3 they are 1.213,

1.242, 1.090, and 1.156. By averaging these values, we remove most of the random variation. The last step is to adjust the averages by dividing each average by the total 4.008 and multiplying by 4.000. The seasonal indices are these adjusted averages. The following table summarizes steps 3 and 4.

| | Quarter | | | | |
Year	1	2	3	4	Total
1985	–	–	1.213	.853	
1986	.847	1.067	1.242	.863	
1987	.869	1.108	1.090	.898	
1988	.922	1.029	1.156	.879	
1989	.895	1.105	–	–	
Average	.883	1.077	1.175	.873	4.008
Seasonal Index	.881	1.075	1.173	.871	4.000

The seasonal indices tell us that, on average, the occupancy rates in the first and fourth quarters are below the annual average, while the occupancy rates in the second and third quarters are above the annual average. That is, we expect the occupancy rate

FIGURE 17.15 *TIME SERIES AND MOVING AVERAGES FOR EXAMPLE 17.6*

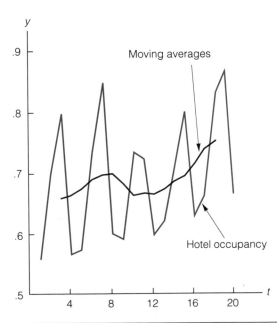

in the first quarter to be 11.9% below the annual rate. The second and third quarters' rates are expected to be 7.5% and 17.3%, respectively, above the annual rate. The fourth quarter's rate is 12.9% below the annual rate. Figure 17.15 depicts the time series and the moving averages for this example.

 **EXERCISES**

LEARNING THE TECHNIQUES

17.26 Compute the 5-day moving averages for the following time series, to remove the seasonality and random variations.

	Week			
Day	1	2	3	4
Monday	12	11	14	17
Tuesday	18	17	16	21
Wednesday	16	19	16	20
Thursday	25	24	28	24
Friday	31	27	25	32

17.27 For Exercise 17.26, calculate the seasonal (daily) indices.

17.28 Given the following time series, compute the 4-quarter centered moving averages.

	Year				
Quarter	1	2	3	4	5
1	50	41	43	36	30
2	44	38	39	32	25
3	46	37	39	30	24
4	39	30	35	25	22

17.29 For Exercise 17.28, compute the seasonal (quarterly) indices.

APPLYING THE TECHNIQUES

Self-Correcting Exercise (See Appendix 17.B for the solution.)

17.30 The quarterly earnings of a large soft-drink company have been recorded for the past 4 years. These data are shown in the accompanying table. Using an appropriate moving average, measure the quarterly variation by computing the seasonal (quarterly) indices.

EARNINGS ($millions)

	Year			
Quarter	1986	1987	1988	1989
1	52	57	60	66
2	67	75	77	82
3	85	90	94	98
4	54	61	63	67

17.31 Cable TV subscriptions over the past few years have grown dramatically, although sometimes somewhat erratically. In one southwestern state, the data shown in the accompanying table were observed.

Year	Quarter	Cable Subscribers (thousands)
1985	1	184
	2	173
	3	160
	4	189
1986	1	191
	2	185

(continued)

Year	Quarter	Cable Subscribers (thousands)
	3	184
	4	200
1987	1	205
	2	192
	3	200
	4	229
1988	1	236
	2	219
	3	211
	4	272
1989	1	280
	2	261
	3	275
	4	322

a. Plot the time series.

b. Calculate the 4-quarter centered moving averages.

c. Plot the moving averages.

17.32 Compute the seasonal quarterly indices, using the time series and moving averages in Exercise 17.31.

17.33 In order to forecast the number of pizzas she will sell each day, the owner of a pizzeria records the number sold daily during the past 4 weeks. These data are shown in the accompanying table. Calculate the seasonal (daily) indices, using a 7-day moving average.

NUMBER OF PIZZAS SOLD

Day	Week 1	2	3	4
Sunday	240	221	235	219
Monday	85	80	86	91
Tuesday	93	75	74	102
Wednesday	106	121	100	89
Thursday	125	110	117	105
Friday	188	202	205	192
Saturday	314	386	402	377

17.34 A manufacturer of ski equipment is in the process of reviewing his accounts receivable. He has noticed that there appears to be a seasonal pattern. Accounts receivable increase in the winter months and decrease during the summer. The quarterly accounts receivable for the past 4 years are shown in the accompanying table. Use a 4-quarter centered moving average to compute the seasonal (quarterly) indices.

ACCOUNTS RECEIVABLE ($millions)

Quarter	Year 1986	1987	1988	1989
1	106	115	114	121
2	92	100	105	111
3	65	73	79	82
4	121	135	140	163

SECTION 17.7 TIME SERIES FORECASTING WITH EXPONENTIAL SMOOTHING

In Section 17.3, we investigated smoothing techniques whose function is to reduce random fluctuation, thereby enabling us to identify the time series components. One of these methods, exponential smoothing, can also be used for forecasting. Recall the exponential smoothing formula

$$S_t = wy_t + (1 - w)S_{t-1},$$

where the choice of the smoothing constant w determines the degree of smoothing. A value of w close to 1 results in very little smoothing, whereas a value of w close to 0 results in a great deal of smoothing.

When a time series exhibits a gradual trend and no evidence of cyclical or seasonal effects, exponential smoothing can be a useful approach to forecasting. Suppose that t represents the current time period and we've computed the smoothed value S_t. This value is then the forecast value at time $t + 1$. That is,

$$F_{t+1} = S_t.$$

If we wish, we can forecast 2 or 3 or any number of time periods into the future:

$$F_{t+2} = S_t$$
$$F_{t+3} = S_t.$$

As long as we're dealing with a time series that possesses no cyclical or seasonal effects, we can produce reasonably accurate forecasts once we've eliminated the random variation.

◼◼◼◼◼ EXAMPLE 17.7

An important measure of a nation's manufacturing activity is earnings as a percentage of value added, which is calculated by dividing total nominal earnings of employees by the nominal value added. This shows labor's share of income generated in the manufacturing sector. The accompanying table lists Canada's earnings as a percentage of value added for each year from 1970 to 1984. Use exponential smoothing to forecast for 1985.

Year	Earnings as a Percentage of Value Added	Year	Earnings as a Percentage of Value Added
1970	53.1	1978	48.8
1971	52.4	1979	46.8
1972	51.7	1980	47.4
1973	49.5	1981	47.3
1974	46.7	1982	51.4
1975	49.5	1983	48.7
1976	51.2	1984	48.7
1977	50.4		

SOURCE: *World Tables* (1987).

Solution.   A plot of the time series (see Figure 17.16) reveals no long-term trend or distinct cyclical pattern. Consequently, exponential smoothing is an appropriate forecasting method. We choose $w = .3$. The results are shown in the following table.

FIGURE 17.16 TIME SERIES, EXPONENTIAL SMOOTHING, AND FORECAST FOR EXAMPLE 17.7

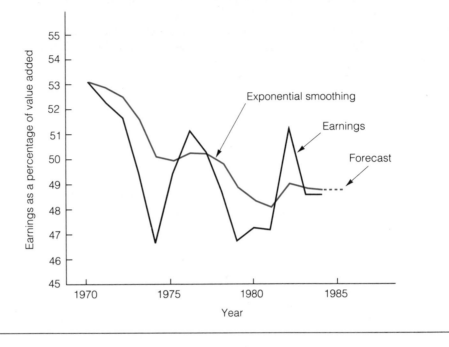

Year	Earnings as a Percentage of Value Added y_t	$S_t = wy_t + (1 - w)S_{t-1}: w = .3$
1970	53.1	53.1
1971	52.4	52.89
1972	51.7	52.53
1973	49.5	51.62
1974	46.7	50.15
1975	49.5	50.00
1976	51.2	50.33
1977	50.4	50.35
1978	48.8	49.88
1979	46.8	48.96
1980	47.4	48.49
1981	47.3	48.13
1982	51.4	49.11
1983	48.7	48.99
1984	48.7	48.90

The 1985 forecast is

$$F_{1985} = S_{1984} = 48.90.$$

The actual 1985 earnings as a percentage of value added turned out to be 49.0.

EXERCISES

LEARNING THE TECHNIQUES

17.35 Use exponential smoothing, with $w = .6$, to forecast the next value of the following time series:

t	y
1	23
2	18
3	26
4	27
5	24
6	22

17.36 Use exponential smoothing, with $w = .3$, to forecast the value of the following time series at time $t = 8$:

t	y
1	12
2	20
3	16
4	19
5	15
6	11
7	14

17.37 Use the following time series for the years 1980–1985 to develop forecasts for 1986–1989, with:

a. $w = .3$

b. $w = .6$

c. $w = .7$

Year	y
1980	110
1981	103
1982	111
1983	117
1984	126
1985	115

APPLYING THE TECHNIQUES

Self-Correcting Exercise (See Appendix 17.B for the solution.)

17.38 The following table lists U.S. earnings as a percentage of value added (see Example 17.7). Use exponential smoothing, with $w = .7$, to forecast earnings for 1985.

Year	Earnings as a Percentage of Value Added
1975	43.1
1976	41.7
1977	41.4
1978	41.3
1979	39.9
1980	40.9
1981	40.8
1982	41.4
1983	40.1
1984	40.0

SOURCE: *World Table* (1987).

17.39 The increased awareness among consumers of the health effects of cigarettes is expected to have an adverse impact on the tobacco industry. To help analyze the problem, a tobacco industry executive wants to forecast future production of cigarettes. The production amounts for the period 1977–1986 are shown in the accompanying table. Because of the relatively small changes that have taken place, it was decided to use exponential smoothing. Forecast the 1987 cigarette production, using a smoothing constant of $w = .5$.

Year	Cigarette Production (Billions)
1977	673
1978	688
1979	707
1980	702
1981	744
1982	711
1983	688
1984	657
1985	665
1986	652

SOURCE: *Statistical Abstract of the United States.*

17.40 Plywood is used in a number of industries, including housing and furniture. Annual U.S. production of plywood for the years 1971–1980 is listed in the accompanying table. Using exponential smoothing, with $w = .7$, predict U.S. production for 1981.

Year	U.S. Plywood Production (1,000s of cubic meters)
1971	16,184
1972	17,746
1973	18,054
1974	15,172
1975	14,579
1976	16,726
1977	17,981
1978	17,056
1979	18,200
1980	16,000

SOURCE: *Yearbook of Industrial Statistics.*

SECTION
17.8

FORECASTING SEASONAL TIME SERIES

In this section we will demonstrate how to forecast the future values of a time series that is composed of a long-term trend and a seasonal effect. We will use the linear model

$$y = \beta_0 + \beta_1 t + \varepsilon$$

to describe the trend, and we will use the seasonal indices to measure the seasonal variation. When we combine these two measures, we produce the following forecasting technique.

> **Forecast of Trend and Seasonality**
>
> $$F_t = [\hat{\beta}_0 + \hat{\beta}_1 t]SI_t,$$
>
> where
>
> F_t = Forecast for period t
>
> SI_t = Seasonal index for period t.

The process we use to forecast with seasonal indices is as follows:

1. Use simple linear regression to find the trend line
$$\hat{y} = \hat{\beta}_0 + \hat{\beta}_1 t.$$
2. Use the appropriate moving averages to calculate the seasonal indices.
3. For the future time period t, find the trend value
$$\hat{y} = \hat{\beta}_0 + \hat{\beta}_1 t.$$
4. Multiply the trend value $\hat{y}$ by the seasonal index for the season to be forecasted.
$$F_t = \hat{y} \cdot SI_t.$$

EXAMPLE 17.8

In Example 17.6, we computed the seasonal (quarterly) indices for the hotel occupancy rates. Compute the linear trend line, and use the seasonal indices to forecast each quarter's occupancy rate for 1990.

Solution.   Using the Minitab software system, we find the trend line
$$\hat{y} = .639 + .00525t.$$

The seasonal indices computed in Example 17.6 are as follows:

SEASONAL INDICES

Quarter			
1	2	3	4
.881	1.075	1.173	.871

The forecasts for 1990 are as follows:

Year	Quarter	Time Period t	Trend Value $\hat{y} = .639 + .00525t$	Seasonal Index	Forecast $F_t = \hat{y} \cdot SI_t$
1990	1	21	.749	.881	.660
	2	22	.755	1.075	.812
	3	23	.760	1.173	.891
	4	24	.765	.871	.666

Thus we forecast that the quarterly occupancy rates during 1990 will be .660, .812, .891, and .666.

▬▬▬▬▬ **EXAMPLE 17.9**

At the end of 1985, a major builder of residential houses in the northeastern United States wanted to predict the number of housing units to be started in 1986. This information would be extremely useful in determining a number of variables, including housing demand, availability of labor, and the prices of building materials. To assist them in developing an accurate forecasting model, researchers collected information on the number of housing starts for the previous 60 months (1981–1985). These numbers (in 1,000s of units) are shown in the accompanying table. Forecast the housing starts for the 12 months of 1986.

HOUSING STARTS IN THE NORTHEASTERN UNITED STATES (1,000s)

						Month						
Year	Jan.	Feb.	Mar.	Apr.	May	June	July	Aug.	Sept.	Oct.	Nov.	Dec.
1981	5.5	2.8	8.5	10.2	12.0	11.2	16.0	11.6	12.0	12.0	7.6	7.8
1982	2.6	3.3	7.3	8.7	11.9	10.0	11.3	12.9	15.9	11.0	14.0	7.8
1983	5.5	7.4	13.1	13.7	17.2	17.8	17.5	21.5	14.6	16.2	13.8	9.3
1984	7.2	8.8	11.1	17.1	18.1	22.8	19.9	21.1	19.5	22.2	21.6	14.2
1985	9.5	7.4	16.3	25.6	24.7	27.0	22.7	25.3	24.1	32.3	19.9	17.0

SOURCE: *Standard and Poor's Industry Surveys.*

Solution. The data display a very clear seasonal pattern. This is as might be expected, since much construction activity ceases during the winter months. Minitab was used to identify the linear trend line as

$$\hat{y} = 6.15 + 0.267t.$$

Minitab was also used to compute the following seasonal (monthly) indices:

Month	**Seasonal Indices**	**Month**	**Seasonal Indices**
January	.425	July	1.303
February	.474	August	1.308
March	.830	September	1.231
April	1.071	October	1.164
May	1.198	November	1.041
June	1.239	December	.718

The seasonal indices confirm our observation that there are more starts in the summer and far fewer in the winter.

FIGURE 17.17   TIME SERIES, TREND, AND FORECASTS FOR EXAMPLE 17.9

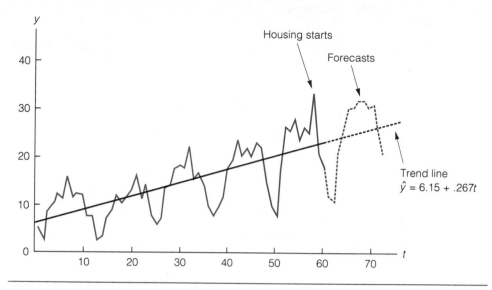

The 1986 forecasts are made by computing the trend line value for each month in 1986 and multiplying these values by the monthly seasonal indices. The resulting values are shown in the accompanying table. Figure 17.17 depicts the time series, the trend line, and the forecasted values.

FORECASTS

Year	Month	Time Period t	Trend Value $\hat{y} = 6.15 + .267t$	Seasonal Index	Forecast $F_t = \hat{y}_t \cdot SI_t$
1986	January	61	22.437	.425	9.5
	February	62	22.704	.474	10.8
	March	63	22.971	.830	19.1
	April	64	23.238	1.071	24.9
	May	65	23.505	1.198	28.2
	June	66	23.772	1.239	29.5
	July	67	24.039	1.303	31.3
	August	68	24.306	1.308	31.8
	September	69	24.573	1.231	30.2
	October	70	24.840	1.164	28.9
	November	71	25.107	1.041	26.1
	December	72	25.374	.718	18.2

When we examine the actual 1986 monthly housing starts, we see that the forecasts were quite accurate. The following table offers a comparison of the two.

Year	Month	Forecast F_t	Actual Housing Starts
1986	January	9.5	14.1
	February	10.8	12.3
	March	19.1	20.6
	April	24.9	29.3
	May	28.2	27.5
	June	29.5	27.5
	July	31.3	28.1
	August	31.8	34.0
	September	30.2	29.1
	October	28.9	27.2
	November	26.1	21.7
	December	18.2	19.1

EXERCISES

LEARNING THE TECHNIQUES

17.41 The following trend line and seasonal indices were computed from 10 years of quarterly observations:

$\hat{y} = 150 + 3t \quad (t = 1, 2, \ldots, 40).$

Quarter	SI
1	.7
2	1.2
3	1.5
4	.6

Forecast the next 4 quarters.

17.42 A time series has exhibited seasonal variation and a linear trend. The trend line and the seasonal (quarterly) indices are as follows:

$\hat{y} = 1000 - 5t \quad (t = 1, 2, \ldots, 20).$

Quarter	SI
1	1.25
2	1.05
3	.80
4	.90

Forecast the next 4 quarters.

17.43 The following trend line and seasonal indices were computed from 4 years of quarterly data:

$\hat{y} = 5.6 + .3t \quad (t = 1, 2, \ldots, 16).$

Quarter	SI
1	.85
2	.85
3	1.30
4	1.00

Forecast results for the next 4 quarters.

17.44 The linear trend line for the data in Exercise 17.26 is

$$\hat{y} = 16.8 + .366t \qquad (t = 1, 2, \ldots, 20).$$

Use the seasonal indices computed in Exercise 17.27 and the trend line to forecast results for the next 5 days.

17.45 The linear trend line for the data in Exercise 17.28 is

$$\hat{y} = 47.7 - 1.19t \qquad (t = 1, 2, \ldots, 20).$$

Use the seasonal indices calculated in Exercise 17.29 and the trend line to forecast results for the next 4 quarters.

APPLYING THE TECHNIQUES

Self-Correcting Exercise (See Appendix 17.B for the solution.)

17.46 The linear trend line for the data in Exercise 17.30 is

$$\hat{y} = 61.7 + 1.18t \qquad (t = 1, 2, \ldots, 16).$$

Use this trend line and the seasonal indices to forecast the earnings for the 4 quarters of 1990.

17.47 Forecast the number of cable subscribers in the 4 quarters of 1990, using the results of Exercise 17.32 and the trend line

$$\hat{y} = 150 + 6.53t \qquad (t = 1, 2, \ldots, 20).$$

17.48 Forecast the daily sales of pizzas in Exercise 17.33, given that the trend line is

$$\hat{y} = 145 + 1.66t \qquad (t = 1, 2, \ldots, 28).$$

17.49 Forecast the quarterly accounts receivable for 1990, using the results of Exercise 17.34 and the trend line

$$\hat{y} = 90.4 + 2.02t \qquad (t = 1, 2, \ldots, 16).$$

SECTION 17.9 SUMMARY

In this chapter, we discussed the classical time series and its decomposition into long-term trend and cyclical, seasonal, and random variation. Moving averages and exponential smoothing were used to remove some of the random fluctuation, enabling us to identify the time series' other components. The long-run trend was measured more scientifically by two regression models—linear and polynomial. The cyclical and seasonal effects are more clearly detected through calculation of percentage of trend and seasonal indices.

Once the components of a time series have been identified, we can select one of many available methods of forecasting the time series. When there is no or very little trend, cyclical variation, and seasonal variation, exponential smoothing is recommended. When trend and seasonality are present, we can use regression analysis with seasonal indices to make predictions.

IMPORTANT TERMS

Time series	Centered moving averages
Trend	Exponential smoothing
Cycle	Smoothing constant
Seasonal variation	Trend analysis
Random variation	Linear model
Additive model	Polynomial model
Multiplicative model	Percentage of trend
Smoothing	Seasonal indices
Moving averages	Forecasting

FORMULAS

$$S_t = wy_t + (1 - w)S_{t-1}$$
$$F_t = [\hat{\beta}_0 + \hat{\beta}_1 t]SI_t$$

SUPPLEMENTARY EXERCISES

17.50 The cost of healthcare in the United States has been increasing rapidly. The accompanying table lists annual per capita national health expenditures for 1970–1986.

a. Plot the time series.

b. Based on the linear trend line

$$\hat{y} = 80.1 + 96.4t \qquad (t = 1, 2, \ldots, 17),$$

compute the percentage of trend.

Year	t	Per Capita National Health Expenditures
1970	1	349
1971	2	384
1972	3	428
1973	4	467
1974	5	521
1975	6	590
1976	7	665
1977	8	743
1978	9	822
1979	10	921
1980	11	1,054
1981	12	1,207
1982	13	1,348
1983	14	1,473
1984	15	1,597
1985	16	1,710
1986	17	1,837

SOURCE: *Statistical Abstract of the United States.*

17.51 The number of hospital beds is a function of various factors including medical costs, popula-

tion age, and economic conditions. The number of beds available in the United States between 1975 and 1985 is recorded in the accompanying table. Use exponential smoothing, with $w = .4$, to forecast the number of hospital beds available in 1986.

Year	Number of Hospital Beds (1,000s)
1975	1,466
1976	1,434
1977	1,407
1978	1,381
1979	1,372
1980	1,365
1981	1,362
1982	1,360
1983	1,350
1984	1,339
1985	1,309

SOURCE: *Statistical Abstract of the United States.*

17.52 An important measure of a country's economic health is the difference between the value of its exports and the value of its imports. This quantity is sometimes called the *resource balance*. Canada's resource balance for the past 10 years is shown next. Use exponential smoothing, with $w = .4$, to forecast the 1987 figure.

Year	Resource Balance ($billions)
1977	6.17
1978	11.09

(continued)

Year	Resource Balance ($billions)
1979	7.18
1980	5.65
1981	2.51
1982	13.43
1983	13.28
1984	16.58
1985	15.64
1986	13.84

SOURCE: *World Tables* (1987).

Exercises 17.53 through 17.56 are based on the following problem.

The revenues of a chain of ice cream stores is listed for each quarter during the past 5 years.

REVENUES ($millions)

Quarter	Year 1984	1985	1986	1987	1988
1	16	14	17	18	21
2	25	27	31	29	30
3	31	32	40	45	52
4	24	23	27	24	32

17.53 Plot the time series.

17.54 Discuss why exponential smoothing is not recommended as a forecasting method in this case.

17.55 Calculate the 4-quarter centered moving averages, and use them to calculate the seasonal (quarterly) indices.

17.56 Regression analysis produced the trend line $\hat{y} = 20.2 + .732t$ $(t = 1, 2, \ldots, 20)$.

Using this trend line and the seasonal indices computed in Exercise 17.55, forecast quarterly revenues for 1989.

CASE 17.1 FORECASTING UNEMPLOYMENT RATES

The monthly unemployment rate in Canada typically displays a great deal of seasonal variation, partly because of the country's climate. This factor plays an important role when governments attempt to forecast unemployment. The monthly unemployment rates for 1984–1987 are listed in the accompanying table.

Use whatever forecasting technique you judge to be appropriate to forecast the 1988 monthly unemployment rates. We suggest using a computer for this case.

Month	Year 1984	1985	1986	1987	Month	Year 1984	1985	1986	1987
January	12.7	12.6	10.1	10.8	July	9.8	9.0	8.0	7.2
February	12.2	11.9	10.1	10.4	August	9.9	8.5	7.5	7.6
March	12.1	12.3	9.8	10.4	September	10.6	8.7	7.8	7.6
April	12.0	11.3	9.5	9.4	October	10.0	8.9	8.0	7.0
May	11.2	9.7	9.0	7.7	November	10.2	9.7	8.2	7.3
June	10.4	9.3	8.5	7.5	December	10.9	9.2	9.0	7.7

MINITAB INSTRUCTIONS

TIME SERIES PLOTTING

To plot the time series stored in column 1, type

```
TSPLOT C1
```

For example, the time series plot for Example 17.1 appears as shown in Figure 17.A.1.

MOVING AVERAGES

Minitab does not calculate moving averages directly. However, by using several commands, we can induce Minitab to compute moving averages based on any number of periods. To illustrate, we'll redo Example 17.1. We begin by inputting the time series in column 1:

```
SET C1
39 37 61 58 18 56 82 27 41 69 49 66 54 42 90 66
END
```

To calculate the 3-quarter moving averages, we copy column 1 into columns 2 and 3:

```
LET C2 = C1
LET C3 = C1
```

Next, we delete the first observation in column 2 and the first two observations in column 3.

```
DELETE 1   C2
DELETE 1:2   C3
```

FIGURE 17.A.1   *TIME SERIES PLOT FOR EXAMPLE 17.1*

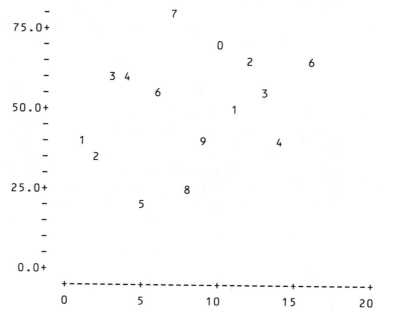

If you now print the 3 columns (PRINT C1-C3), you'll observe

39	37	61
37	61	58
61	58	18
58	18	56
18	56	82
56	82	27
82	27	41
27	41	69
41	69	49
69	49	66
49	66	54
66	54	42
54	42	90
42	90	66
90	66	
66		

As you can see, the first row contains observations 1, 2, and 3 of the time series. The mean of these values is the first moving average. The mean of the second row is the second moving average, and so on. The command

```
RMEAN C1-C3 C4
```

calculates the mean for each row in columns 1 to 3 and stores these means in column 4.

The command

```
PRINT C4
```

produces the following output:

```
45.6667    52.0000    45.6667    44.0000    52.0000    55.0000    50.0000
45.6667    53.0000    61.3333    56.3333    54.0000    62.0000    66.0000
78.0000    66.0000
```

Care should be taken when interpreting these values. The first value (45.6667) is the moving average for period 2. (Remember, there is no moving average for period 1.) The second value (52.000) is the moving average for period 3. The last two values (78.000) and (66.000) have no meaning and should be ignored.

You can present the moving averages in a more useful form by deleting the last two values in column 4 and inserting an asterisk (which represents missing data) in the first row:

```
DELETE 15:16 C4
INSERT  0   1 C4
*
END
PRINT   C1   C4
```

The output is

```
ROW    C1    C4
  1    39    *
  2    37    45.6667
  3    61    52.0000
  4    58    45.6667
  5    18    44.0000
  6    56    52.0000
  7    82    55.0000
  8    27    50.0000
  9    41    45.6667
 10    69    53.0000
 11    49    61.3333
 12    66    56.3333
 13    54    54.0000
 14    42    62.0000
 15    90    66.0000
 16    66
```

To produce the 5-quarter moving average in Example 17.1, we would type the following commands (after inputting the time series in column 1):

```
LET   C2=C1
LET   C3=C1
LET   C4=C1
LET   C5=C1
DELETE   1   C2
DELETE   1:2   C3
DELETE   1:3   C4
DELETE   1:4   C5
RMEAN   C1-C5   C6
PRINT   C6
```

The output is

```
42.6 46.0 55.0 48.2 44.8 55.0 53.6 50.4 55.8 56.0 60.2
63.6 63.0 66.0 78.0 66.0
```

The first value (42.6) is the moving average for period 3. The last four values (63.0, 66.0, 78.0, and 66.0) should be ignored. Again, we can make the results more presentable by instructing Minitab in the following way:

```
DELETE 13:16   C4
INSERT 0   1   C4
*
*
END
```

To calculate the centered moving averages we employ our procedure twice. To illustrate, consider the time series from page 490.

Period	Time Series
1	15
2	27
3	20
4	14
5	25
6	11

To compute the 4-period centered moving average, we type the following commands:

```
SET   C1
15   27   20   14   25   11
END
```

```
LET   C2=C1
LET   C3=C1
LET   C4=C1
DELETE   1   C2
DELETE   1:2   C3
DELETE   1:3   C4
RMEAN   C1-C4   C5
LET   C6=C5
DELETE   1   C6
RMEAN   C5-C6 C7
PRINT   C7
```

The output is

20.2500   19.5000   17.0833   17.3333   14.5000   11.0000

The centered moving averages for periods 3 and 4 are 20.25 and 19.5, respectively. Ignore the remaining four values.

MEASURING THE CYCLICAL EFFECT

To measure the cyclical effect, we begin by finding the trend line using regression analysis. The LET command is used to calculate the trend values, as well as the percentage of trend. The results for Example 17.5 are produced as follows:

```
READ    C1 C2
  1      66.4
  2      69.7
  3      72.2
  4      74.3
  5      72.5
  6      70.6
  7      74.4
  8      76.3
  9      78.1
 10      78.9
 11      76.0
 12      74.0
 13      70.8
 14      70.5
 15      74.1
 16      74.0
 17      73.9
END
REGRESS C2 1 C1
```

The regression results are

`C2 = 71.3131 + 0.2248C1`

The trend values are computed by

`LET C3 = 71.313 + 0.2248 * C1`

The percentage of trend values are determined by

`LET C4 = (C2/C3) * 100`

`PRINT C1-C4` outputs the following:

1	66.4	71.5378	92.819
2	69.7	71.7626	97.127
3	72.2	71.9874	100.296
4	74.3	72.2122	102.892
5	72.5	72.4370	100.088
6	70.6	72.6618	97.164
7	74.4	72.8866	102.078
8	76.3	73.1114	104.363
9	78.1	73.3362	106.497
10	78.9	73.5610	107.259
11	76.0	73.7858	103.002
12	74.0	74.0106	99.987
13	70.8	74.2354	95.374
14	70.5	74.4602	94.683
15	74.1	74.6850	99.218
16	74.0	74.9098	98.787
17	73.9	75.1346	98.358

We can then plot the results to duplicate Figure 17.14.

SOLUTIONS TO SELF-CORRECTING EXERCISES

17.8

Time Period	Sales	3-Day Moving Average
1	43	–
2	45	$(43 + 45 + 22)/3 = 36.7$
3	22	$(45 + 22 + 25)/3 = 30.7$
4	25	$(22 + 25 + 31)/3 = 26.0$
5	31	$(25 + 31 + 51)/3 = 35.7$
6	51	$(31 + 51 + 41)/3 = 41.0$
7	41	$(51 + 41 + 37)/3 = 43.0$
8	37	$(41 + 37 + 22)/3 = 33.3$
9	22	$(37 + 22 + 25)/3 = 28.0$
10	25	$(22 + 25 + 40)/3 = 29.0$
11	40	$(25 + 40 + 57)/3 = 40.7$
12	57	$(40 + 57 + 30)/3 = 42.3$
13	30	$(57 + 30 + 33)/3 = 40.0$
14	33	$(30 + 33 + 37)/3 = 33.3$
15	37	$(33 + 37 + 64)/3 = 44.7$
16	64	$(37 + 64 + 58)/3 = 53.0$
17	58	$(64 + 58 + 33)/3 = 51.7$
18	33	$(58 + 33 + 38)/3 = 43.0$
19	38	$(33 + 38 + 25)/3 = 32.0$
20	25	–

17.24

Time Period t	Yields y	Trend $\hat{y}$	Percentage of Trend $(y/\hat{y}) \cdot 100$
1	4.35	3.76	115.7
2	4.33	4.10	105.6
3	4.26	4.44	95.9
4	4.40	4.78	92.1
5	4.49	5.12	87.7
6	5.13	5.46	94.0
7	5.51	5.80	95.0
8	6.18	6.14	100.7
9	7.03	6.48	108.5
10	8.04	6.82	117.9
11	7.39	7.16	103.2
12	7.21	7.50	96.1
13	7.44	7.84	94.9
14	8.57	8.18	104.8
15	8.83	8.52	103.6
16	8.43	8.86	95.1
17	8.02	9.02	87.2
18	8.73	9.54	91.5
19	9.63	9.88	97.5
20	11.94	10.22	116.8

17.30

Period t	Earnings y	4-Quarter Moving Average	4-Quarter Centered Moving Average	Ratio y/MA
1	52	—	—	—
2	67		—	—
		64.50		
3	85		65.125	1.305
		65.75		
4	54		66.750	.809
		67.75		
5	57		68.375	.834
		69.00		
6	75		69.875	1.073
		70.75		
7	90		71.125	1.265
		71.50		
8	61		71.750	.850
		72.00		
9	60		72.500	.828
		73.00		
10	77		73.250	1.051
		73.50		
11	94		74.250	1.266
		75.00		
12	63		75.625	.833
		76.25		
13	66		76.750	.860
		77.25		
14	82		77.750	1.055
		—		
15	98		—	—
		—		
16	67		—	—

Year	Quarter				Total
	1	2	3	4	
1986	—	—	1.305	.809	
1987	.834	1.073	1.265	.850	
1988	.828	1.051	1.266	.833	
1989	.860	1.055	—	—	
Average	.841	1.060	1.279	.831	4.011
Seasonal index	.839	1.057	1.275	.829	4.000

17.38

Year	Earnings as a Percentage of Value Added y_t	$S_t = wy_t + (1 - w)S_{t-1}$ with $w = .7$
1975	43.1	$S_{1975} = 43.1$
1976	41.7	$S_{1976} = .7(41.7) + .3(43.1) = 42.1$
1977	41.4	$S_{1977} = .7(41.4) + .3(42.1) = 41.6$
1978	41.3	$S_{1978} = .7(41.3) + .3(41.6) = 41.4$
1979	39.9	$S_{1979} = .7(39.9) + .3(41.4) = 40.4$
1980	40.9	$S_{1980} = .7(40.9) + .3(40.4) = 40.7$
1981	40.8	$S_{1981} = .7(40.8) + .3(40.7) = 40.8$
1982	41.4	$S_{1982} = .7(41.4) + .3(40.8) = 41.2$
1983	40.1	$S_{1983} = .7(40.1) + .3(41.2) = 40.4$
1984	40.0	$S_{1984} = .7(40.0) + .3(40.4) = 40.1$

The 1985 forecast is $F_{1985} = S_{1984} = 40.1$.

17.46

Year	Quarter	Time Period t	Trend Value $\hat{y} = 61.7 + 1.18t$	Seasonal Index	Forecast $F_t = \hat{y}_t \cdot SI_t$
1990	1	17	81.76	.839	68.597
	2	18	82.94	1.057	87.668
	3	19	84.12	1.275	107.253
	4	20	85.30	.829	70.714

NONPARAMETRIC STATISTICS

INTRODUCTION

Throughout the first 17 chapters of this book we have discussed statistical techniques for both quantitative and qualitative data. There is, however, a third data type—one that we have ignored up to now. It is the product of a ranking procedure, and as a result we call it **ranked data** or **ordinal data.** As we explain in greater detail in Section 18.2, ranked data combines some of the characteristics of quantitative data with some of those of qualitative data. As a consequence, the calculation of the mean of ranked data is generally meaningless. Hence, the techniques we introduce in this chapter will not test specific parameters; instead we will test characteristics of populations without referring to parameters. For this reason, these techniques are called **nonparametric techniques.** Rather than testing the difference between two population means, for example, we will test to determine whether the population locations are different.

Although the nonparametric methods presented here are designed to test ranked data, they have another, perhaps more important area of application. In Chapters 11 and 13 we employed the t-test and the F-test. One of the required conditions for using these methods is that the populations be normally distributed. If the data are not normal, the results of these methods are invalid and meaningless. However, nonparametric methods can be used instead.

In Section 18.3, we present a nonparametric technique for comparing two populations when the population variances are unknown. The parametric counterpart of this test is the t-test of $\mu_1 - \mu_2$ when σ_1^2 are σ_2^2 are unknown but equal (Section 11.2). In Section 18.4 the problem objective to be handled nonparametrically is to compare two or more populations. The parametric counterpart to this technique is the analysis of variance (Chapter 13).

RANKED DATA

There are many practical applications of statistics that can be expressed as ranked data. For example, suppose that, in a market survey for a new soft drink, respondents are asked to taste the product and identify which of the following represents their opinion:

   (a) Excellent
   (b) Good
   (c) Fair
   (d) Poor

At first glance it would appear that the responses are qualitative. If that were so, we could assign any unique numerical value to each of the four possible responses for the purpose of recording them. But if numerical values are assigned completely arbitrarily, we lose information about the hierarchical order of the responses. To keep this from happening, we will use a numerical system that maintains such order. For example, we could assign values in the following way:

Excellent = 4
Good   = 3
Fair   = 2
Poor   = 1

Of course, since the assigned values are arbitrary, we can use any set of numbers as long as the hierarchical order is maintained. Hence, another equally valid system is

Excellent = 10
Good   = 8
Fair   = 4
Poor   = 1

It is important to realize that the difference between each value is not meaningful. Consequently, we cannot compute means and variances for ranked data. The only valid statistical techniques that can be applied to ranked data are ones that are themselves based on a ranking process.

SECTION
18.3

WILCOXON RANK SUM TEST

The test we develop in this section deals with problems in which the following conditions are satisfied:

1. The problem objective is to compare two populations.
2. The data type is either ranked or quantitative but nonnormal.

We will use the **Wilcoxon rank sum test** to determine whether the locations of the two populations are different. The two population locations differ if all or most of the values of one population exceed those of the other.

Figure 18.1 depicts a situation in which the two population locations differ, while Figure 18.2 shows two populations whose locations are about the same. Notice that, since we don't know (or care) anything about the shape of the distribution, we represent them as completely nonnormal. For this reason, nonparametric techniques are often (perhaps more accurately) called **distribution-free statistics.**

As we've done in all previous tests, we begin by specifying the hypotheses. The null hypothesis states that the two population locations are the same; the alternative hypothesis can take any one of three different forms:

FIGURE 18.1 POPULATION LOCATIONS DIFFER

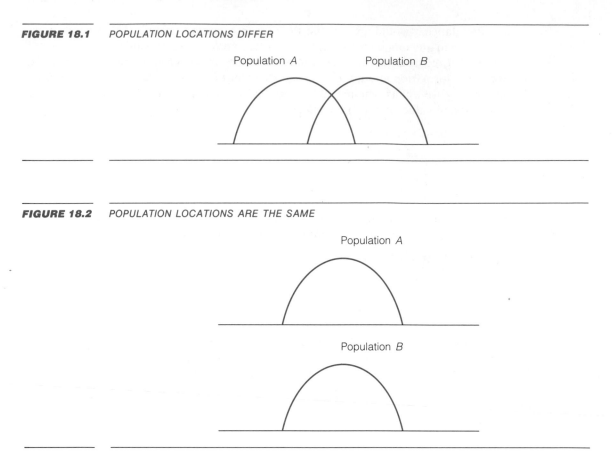

FIGURE 18.2 POPULATION LOCATIONS ARE THE SAME

1. If we want to know whether sufficient evidence exists to show a difference between the two populations, the alternative hypothesis is

H_A: The location of population A is different from the location of population B.

2. If we want to know whether we can conclude that population A is larger in general than population B, the alternative hypothesis is

H_A: The location of population A is to the right of the location of population B.

3. If we want to know whether we can conclude that population A is smaller in general than population B, the alternative hypothesis is

H_A: The location of population A is to the left of the location of population B.

The process of testing these hypotheses is basically the same as the process of testing hypotheses used in earlier chapters. The next steps in the procedure are to determine the appropriate test statistic and to determine the decision rule, based on its sampling distribution. You will find that these calculations are simpler and less time-consuming than any of the techniques previously encountered. In fact, they're so simple that you may wish to use them instead of the parametric tests presented in Chapters 11 and 13. When you are testing normally distributed quantitative data, however, parametric tests are better. (In general they are less susceptible to Type II errors.) Thus, nonparametric methods should only be applied to quantitative data that are not normally distributed or to ranked data.

TEST STATISTIC

We illustrate the calculation of the test statistic with an example.

EXAMPLE 18.1

Suppose that we wish to determine whether the following observations drawn from two populations allow us to conclude, with $\alpha = .05$, that the location of population A is to the right of the location of population B.

A	B
18	20
28	21
23	14
29	18
32	14

Solution.   We wish to test the hypotheses

H_0: The two population locations are the same.

H_A: The location of population A is to the right of the location of population B.

Calculating the Test Statistic.   The first step is to rank all 10 observations, where rank 1 is assigned to the smallest observation and rank 10 is assigned to the largest.

A	Rank	B	Rank
18	3.5	20	5
28	8	21	6
23	7	14	1.5
29	9	18	3.5
32	10	14	1.5
	$T_A = 37.5$		$T_B = 17.5$

Observe that the value 14 appears twice and occupies ranks 1 and 2. Where ties exist, we average the ranks; both observations of 14 are therefore assigned the rank of 1.5. The next larger observation is 18; and since there are two of these, both are assigned ranks of 3.5 (the average of ranks 3 and 4). The process continues until all of the observations have been ranked. Because there are 10 observations, the largest one is ranked 10.

The second step is to calculate the sum of ranks of each sample. The rank sum of sample A, denoted T_A, is 37.5. The rank sum of sample B, denoted T_B, is 17.5. (You should confirm that $T_A + T_B$ equals the sum of the integers 1 through 10, which is 55.) In applications of this test, we will arbitrarily select as the test statistic the rank sum of the sample with the fewer observations. For convenience, we will label that sample A and the other sample B. In this example, since both sample sizes are 5, we do not have to change labels. The test statistic is denoted T. Hence, $T = T_A$.

Decision Rule.   A large value of T indicates that most of the larger observations are in sample A and that most of the smaller ones are in sample B. This would imply that the location of population A is to the right of the location of population B, as shown in Figure 18.3. But in order for us to conclude statistically that this is the case, T must be large enough. The definition of "large enough" comes from the sampling distribution of T, the critical values of which appear in Table 9 in Appendix B and are repeated in Table 18.1.

Table 18.1 provides values of T_L (lower critical value of T) and T_U (upper critical value of T) for various combinations of sample sizes. The values of T_L and T_U in part (a) of the table are such that

$$P(T \leq T_L) = P(T \geq T_U) = .025.$$

The value of T_L and T_U in part (b) of the table are such that

$$P(T \leq T_L) = P(T \geq T_U) = .05.$$

Part (a) is used either in a two-tail test for which $\alpha = .05$ or in a one-tail test for which $\alpha = .025$. Part (b) is used either in a two-tail test for which $\alpha = .10$ or in a one-tail test for which $\alpha = .05$. Because no other values are provided, we are restricted to those two values of α. In addition, since n_1 (sample size of A) must be less than or equal to n_2 (sample size of B), we do not show values of T_L and T_U when $n_1 > n_2$.

FIGURE 18.3   LOCATION OF POPULATION A TO THE RIGHT OF THE LOCATION OF POPULATION B

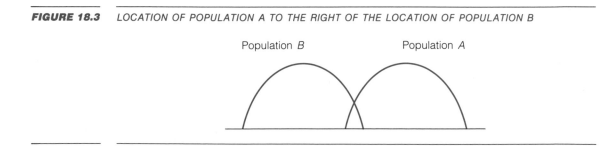

In our example, the null hypothesis is rejected in favor of the alternative hypothesis if T is too large. Thus, we reject H_0 if

$$T \geq T_U$$

where

$$P(T \geq T_U) = \alpha.$$

TABLE 18.1 *CRITICAL VALUES OF THE WILCOXON RANK SUM TEST*

a. $\alpha = .025$ *One-tail;* $\alpha = .05$ *Two-tail*

n_2 \ n_1	3		4		5		6		7		8		9		10	
	T_L	T_U	T_L	T_U	T_L	T_U	T_L	T_U	T_L	T_U	T_L	T_U	T_L	T_U	T_L	T_U
3	5	16														
4	6	18	11	25												
5	6	21	12	28	18	37										
6	7	23	12	32	19	41	26	52								
7	7	26	13	35	20	45	28	56	37	68						
8	8	28	14	38	21	49	29	61	39	73	49	87				
9	8	31	15	41	22	53	31	65	41	78	51	93	63	108		
10	9	33	16	44	24	56	32	70	43	83	54	98	66	114	79	131

b. $\alpha = .05$ *One-tail;* $\alpha = .10$ *Two-tail*

n_2 \ n_1	3		4		5		6		7		8		9		10	
	T_L	T_U	T_L	T_U	T_L	T_U	T_L	T_U	T_L	T_U	T_L	T_U	T_L	T_U	T_L	T_U
3	6	15														
4	7	17	12	24												
5	7	20	13	27	19	36										
6	8	22	14	30	20	40	28	50								
7	9	24	15	33	22	43	30	54	39	66						
8	9	27	16	36	24	46	32	58	41	71	52	84				
9	10	29	17	39	25	50	33	63	43	76	54	90	66	105		
10	11	31	18	42	26	54	35	67	46	80	57	95	69	111	83	127

SOURCE: F. Wilcoxon and R. A. Wilcox, "Some Rapid Approximate Statistical Procedures" (1964), pp. 20–23. Reproduced with permission of the American Cyanamid Company.

FIGURE 18.4   *SAMPLING DISTRIBUTION AND REJECTION REGION FOR EXAMPLE 18.1*

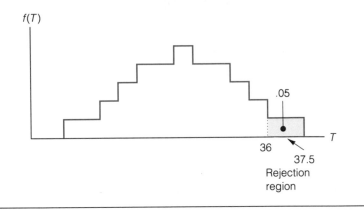

Since, $n_1 = 5$, $n_2 = 5$, and $\alpha = .05$ in the present example, we find from Table 18.1 (or from Table 9 in Appendix B) that

$$T_U = 36.$$

It follows that we should reject H_0 if $T \geq 36$. Therefore, since $T = 37.5$, we reject H_0 and conclude that enough evidence exists to show that the location of population A is to the right of the location of population B.

   Figure 18.4 depicts the sampling distribution of T and the rejection region for this test.* The unusual shape of this distribution is due to the fact that T is a discrete random variable (whereas the test statistics used previously have all been continuous random variables).

DECISION RULE FOR OTHER ALTERNATIVE HYPOTHESES

As was the case throughout Chapters 10 and 11, the alternative hypothesis dictates how the decision rule is determined. Thus, if we wish to determine whether the location of population A is to the left of the location of population B, we reject H_0 if

$$T \leq T_L,$$

where T_L is defined as

$$P(T \leq T_L) = \alpha.$$

For example, if $n_1 = 7$ and $n_2 = 9$ with $\alpha = .025$, the one-tail (left-tail) rejection region determined from Table 18.1 (a) is

---

* The actual shape of the sampling distributions of T depends on n_1 and n_2. For values of n_1 and $n_2 > 4$, it is extremely time-consuming to draw the exact distribution. Consequently, Figure 18.4 and other figures depicting discrete sampling distributions in this section are not drawn completely accurately.

FIGURE 18.5   REJECTION REGION FOR LEFT-TAIL HYPOTHESIS TEST WITH $n_1 = 7$ AND $n_2 = 9$, WITH $\alpha = .025$

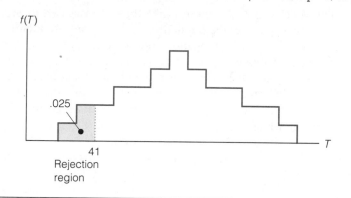

$$T \leq 41,$$

as shown in Figure 18.5.

If we wish to determine whether the two population locations differ, we reject H_0 if

$$T \leq T_L \text{ or } T \geq T_U,$$

where T_L and T_U are such that

$$P(T \leq T_L) = P(T \geq T_U) = \alpha/2.$$

For example, suppose that we want to test for a difference in locations in samples of $n_1 = 4$ and $n_2 = 8$, at the 10% significance level. From Table 18.1 (b) we find the following decision rule:

Reject H_0 if $T \leq 16$ or $T \geq 36$.

Figure 18.6 describes this rejection region.

FIGURE 18.6   REJECTION REGION FOR TWO-TAIL HYPOTHESIS TEST WITH $n_1 = 4$ AND $n_2 = 8$, WITH $\alpha = .10$

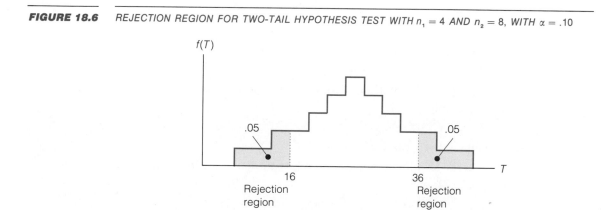

REQUIRED CONDITIONS

The Wilcoxon rank sum test (like the test discussed in Section 18.4) actually tests to determine whether the population distributions are identical. This means that it tests not only for identical locations but for identical spreads (dispersions) and shapes as well. Unfortunately, this in turn means that rejection of the null hypothesis may not necessarily signify a difference in population locations. Rejection of H_0 may instead be due to a difference in distribution shapes and/or spreads. To avoid this problem, we will require that the two probability distributions be identical except with respect to location, which then becomes the sole focus of the test. This requirement applies to the tests described in this and the next section.

Let's review what we have learned thus far about the Wilcoxon rank sum test.

Summary of Wilcoxon Rank Sum Test

Factors to Identify
Problem objective: Comparison of two populations
Data type: Ranked or quantitative

Calculation of the Test Statistic
Step 1: Rank all observations, where 1 = Smallest observation and n = Largest observation. Average the ranks of tied observations. Note that $n = n_1 + n_2$, where n_1 and n_2 are the sample sizes drawn from populations A and B, respectively. The label A is arbitrarily assigned to the population with the smaller sample size.
Step 2: Calculate the rank sums of the two samples T_A and T_B. As a check, confirm that

$$T_A + T_B = n(n + 1)/2.$$

The test statistic is $T = T_A$.

Decision Rule
Case 1. Alternative hypothesis:

H_A: The location of population A is different from the location of population B.

Reject H_0 if $T \leq T_L$ or $T \geq T_U$.

Case 2. Alternative hypothesis:

H_A: The location of population A is to the right of the location of population B.

Reject H_0 if $T \geq T_U$.

Case 3. Alternative hypothesis:

H_A: The location of population A is to the left of the location of population B.

Reject H_0 if $T \leq T_L$.

Required Condition
The two population distributions are identical in shape and spread.

The next two examples demonstrate how and (more importantly) where to use the Wilcoxon rank sum test.

EXAMPLE 18.2

A pharmaceutical company is planning to introduce a new pain-killer. In an experiment to determine its effectiveness, 20 people were randomly selected, of whom 10 were given the new pain-killer and 10 were given aspirin. All 20 were told to use the drug when headaches or other minor pains occurred and to rate the product's effectiveness on a 7-point scale. (On this scale, 1 represents least effective, and 7 represents most effective.) The results were as shown in the accompanying table.

RATINGS

Aspirin	New Pain-killer
4	6
3	4
4	5
2	7
2	3
3	6
2	4
3	3
4	5
5	4

Do these data provide sufficient evidence, at the 5% significance level, to allow us to conclude that the new pain-killer is perceived as being more effective?

Solution. The data are ranked (the results rate the level of effectiveness), and the problem objective is to compare two populations (ratings of the new pain-killer and of aspirin). Recognizing these two factors allows us to identify the appropriate technique as the Wilcoxon rank sum test.

The sample sizes are the same ($n_1 = n_2 = 10$), so we arbitrarily label the aspirin ratings A and the new pain-killer ratings B. Because we want to know whether the new pain-killer generally has higher ratings (and thus whether aspirin has lower ratings), the alternative hypothesis is

H_A: The location of population A is to the left of the location of population B.

The complete test is as follows:

H_0: The two population locations are the same.

H_A: The location of population A is to the left of the location of population B.

Significance level: $\alpha = .05$

Decision rule: With $n_1 = 10$ and $n_2 = 10$, we need to find T_L such that

$$P(T \leq T_L) = .05.$$

From Table 9 in Appendix B, we find $T_L = 83$. Thus, we reject H_0 if $T \leq 83$.
Value of the test statistic:

Population A (Aspirin)		Population B (New Pain-killer)	
Rating	Rank	Rating	Rank
4	11.5	6	18.5
3	6	4	11.5
4	11.5	5	16
2	2	7	20
2	2	3	6
3	6	6	18.5
2	2	4	11.5
3	6	3	6
4	11.5	5	16
5	16	4	11.5
	$T_A = 74.5$		$T_B = 135.5$

Thus we find $T = T_A = 74.5$

Conclusion: Reject H_0.

There is enough evidence to show that the new pain-killer is perceived as being more effective than aspirin. The company should consider using this experiment and others like it as the basis for its advertising. Figure 18.7 depicts this test.

FIGURE 18.7   *SAMPLING DISTRIBUTION FOR EXAMPLE 18.2*

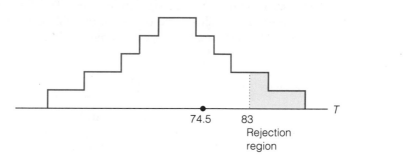

74.5   83
Rejection
region

MINITAB COMPUTER OUTPUT FOR EXAMPLE 18.2*

```
C1   N=10   MEDIAN=3.0000
C2   N=10   MEDIAN=4.5000
POINT ESTIMATE FOR ETA1-ETA2 IS -0.9999
95.5 PCT C.I. For ETA1-ETA2 IS (-2.99, 0.00)
W=74.5
TEST OF ETA1=ETA2 VS  ETA1 N.E. ETA2 IS SIGNIFICANT AT 0.0233
```

Minitab preforms the Mann–Whitney test rather than the Wilcoxon test. However, the two tests are equivalent and quite similar. The only difference between them is that the Mann–Whitney test calculates

$$U_A = n_1 n_2 + \frac{n_1(n_1 + 1)}{2} - T_A$$

and

$$U_B = n_1 n_2 + \frac{n_2(n_2 + 1)}{2} - T_B.$$

The conclusion in this case is based on judging whether U_A (or U_B, depending on the alternative hypothesis) is too small. In the preceding printout, ETA represents the population median. The results include a point estimate and a confidence interval estimate of the difference between the two medians. It also includes the value of the test statistic W (=74.5), which is the value of the Wilcoxon rank sum test statistic. That is,

$$T = W = 74.5.$$

In addition to knowing the value of the test statistic, we also have the two-tail prob-value (0.0233). Since we're performing a one-tail test, the prob-value is $\frac{.0233}{2} = .0117.$

---

* See Appendix 18.A for the Minitab commands that produced this printout.

As was pointed out in the introduction to this chapter, the Wilcoxon rank sum test is used to compare two populations when the data are either quantitative or ranked. Example 18.2 illustrated the use of the Wilcoxon rank sum test when the data were ranked. In the next example, we demonstrate the use of this test when the data are quantitative.

EXAMPLE 18.3

The manager of a large production facility believes that worker productivity is a function of (among other things) the design of the job — that is, the sequence of worker movements involved in performing it. Two designs are being considered for the production of a new product. In an experiment, the assembly times posted by 6 workers using design A and 8 workers using design B were recorded; these are shown in the following table. Can we conclude at the 5% significance level that the assembly times differ for the two designs? Assume that the times are not normally distributed.

ASSEMBLY TIMES (MINUTES)

Design A	Design B
8.2	9.5
5.3	8.3
6.5	7.5
5.1	10.9
9.7	11.3
10.8	9.3
	8.8
	8.0

Solution. The problem objective is to compare two populations (assembly times for designs A and B). The data type is quantitative; but the condition required to test $\mu_1 - \mu_2$ is not satisfied, because the assembly times are not normally distributed. Notice that, in all other respects, this example is the same as Example 11.3. The appropriate technique is the Wilcoxon rank sum test. Because we wish to know whether adequate evidence of a difference between the assembly times exists, the alternative hypothesis is

H_A: The location of population A is different from the location of population B.

The complete test is as follows:

H_0: The two population locations are the same.

H_A: The location of population A is different from the location of population B.

Significance level: $\alpha = .05$

Decision rule: Reject H_0 if $T \le T_L = 29$ or $T \ge T_U = 61$.

Value of the test statistic:

Design A		Design B	
Time	Rank	Time	Rank
8.2	6	9.5	10
5.3	2	8.3	7
6.5	3	7.5	4
5.1	1	10.9	13
9.7	11	11.3	14
10.8	12	9.3	9
		8.8	8
		8.0	5
	$T_A = 35$		$T_B = 70$

Thus we have $T = T_A = 35$.

Conclusion: Do not reject H_0.

There is not enough evidence to allow us to conclude that a difference in assembly times exists between designs *A* and *B*. You may recall that we drew a similar conclusion when the data were assumed to be normally distributed and we used the *t*-test of $\mu_1 - \mu_2$.

Figure 18.8 depicts the sampling distribution of this test.

FIGURE 18.8   SAMPLING DISTRIBUTION FOR EXAMPLE 18.3

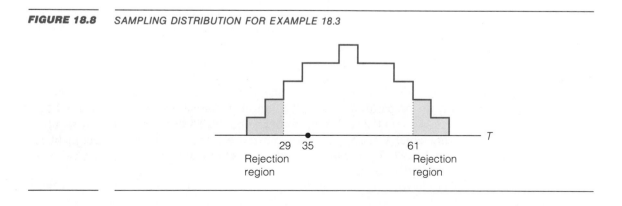

LARGE SAMPLE SIZES

You may have noticed that the values on n_1 and n_2 in Table 9 of Appendix B are less than or equal to 10. If n_1, n_2, or both exceed 10, the sampling distribution of T is approximately normal, with mean $E(T)$ and standard deviation σ_T calculated, respectively, as

$$E(T) = \frac{n_1(n_1 + n_2 + 1)}{2}$$

and

$$\sigma_T = \sqrt{\frac{n_1 n_2(n_1 + n_2 + 1)}{12}}.$$

When either of the sample sizes is large, the test statistic is

$$z = \frac{T - E(T)}{\sigma_T},$$

which is standard normally distributed. The rejection region is one of the following:

$|z| > z_{\alpha/2}$ (two-tail test)

$z > z_\alpha$ (one-tail test)

$z < -z_\alpha$ (one-tail test).

In most practical applications of the Wilcoxon rank sum test when the sample sizes are large, statisticians turn to the computer to produce some or all of the needed statistics. As you've already seen from the computer output for Example 18.2, Minitab gives you the value of the test statistic.

EXAMPLE 18.4

Because of the high cost of hiring and training new employees, employers would like to ensure that they retain highly qualified workers. To help develop a hiring program, the personnel manager of a large company wanted to compare how long business and nonbusiness university graduates worked for the company before quitting to accept a position elsewhere. The manager selected a random sample of 100 business and 80 nonbusiness graduates who had quit during the preceding 5 years. The amount of elapsed time between the day they were hired and the day they quit was determined. Analysis of the results revealed that the times were not normally distributed. Subsequently, in preparation for application of a nonparametric technique, all the times were ranked and the rank sums were computed. These results are shown in the accompanying table. At the 5% level of significance, is the personnel manager justified in concluding that a difference in the duration of employment exists between business and nonbusiness graduates?

Business Graduates	Nonbusiness Graduates
Sample size $= 100$	Sample size $= 80$
Rank sum $= 8,398$	Rank sum $= 7,892$

Solution. The problem objective is to compare two populations whose data are quantitative. However, the data are not normally distributed, precluding use of the t-test of $\mu_1 - \mu_2$. Thus the appropriate technique is the Wilcoxon rank sum test. Since the sample sizes are large (greater than 10), we will use the test statistic

$$z = \frac{T - E(T)}{\sigma_T}.$$

Because the sample of nonbusiness graduates is smaller than the sample of business graduates, we label the nonbusiness sample A and the business sample B. Thus, $n_1 = 80$ and $n_2 = 100$. The test proceeds as follows:

H_0: The two population locations are the same.

H_A: The location of population A is different from the location of population B.

Test statistic: $z = \dfrac{T - E(T)}{\sigma_T}$

Significance level: $\alpha = .05$

Decision rule: Reject H_0 if $|z| > z_{\alpha/2} = z_{.025} = 1.96$.

Value of the test statistic:

$$T = T_A = 7,892$$

$$E(T) = \frac{n_1(n_1 + n_2 + 1)}{2} = \frac{80(181)}{2} = 7,240$$

$$\sigma_T = \sqrt{\frac{n_1 n_2(n_1 + n_2 + 1)}{12}} = \sqrt{\frac{(80)(100)(181)}{12}} = 347.4$$

$$z = \frac{T - E(T)}{\sigma_T} = \frac{7,892 - 7,240}{347.4} = 1.88.$$

Conclusion: Do not reject H_0.

There is not enough evidence at the 5% significance level to establish that a difference in duration of employment exists between business and nonbusiness graduates. Figure 18.9 shows the sampling distribution of this test.

FIGURE 18.9 SAMPLING DISTRIBUTION FOR EXAMPLE 18.4

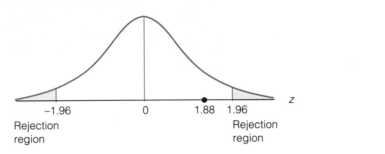

EXERCISES

LEARNING THE TECHNIQUES

18.1 Specify the test statistic and the decision rule for each of the following Wilcoxon rank sum tests.

a. H_0: The two population locations are the same.
  H_A: The location of population A is to the right of the location of population B.

  $$n_A = 8 \qquad n_B = 9 \qquad \alpha = .05$$

b. H_0: The two population locations are the same.
  H_A: The location of population A is to the left of the location of population B.

  $$n_A = 4 \qquad n_B = 6 \qquad \alpha = .025$$

c. H_0: The two population locations are the same.
  H_A: The location of population A is different from the location of population B.

  $$n_A = 20 \qquad n_B = 25 \qquad \alpha = .01$$

18.2 Use the Wilcoxon rank sum test on the data in the following table to determine whether the location of population A is to the left of the location of population B. (Use $\alpha = .05$.)

A	B
75	90
60	70
75	100
65	80
80	80

18.3 Perform the Wilcoxon rank sum test on the data in the following table to determine whether the location of population A is different from the location of population B. (Use $\alpha = .05$.)

A	B
5	7
12	10
11	15
10	12
9	16
	20

18.4 Use the Wilcoxon rank sum test on the data in the following table to determine whether the location of population A is to the right of the location of population B. (Use $\alpha = .05$.)

A	B
27	29
38	24
26	23
33	28
39	26
41	22
	20
	25

18.5 Perform the Wilcoxon rank sum test, with $\alpha = .05$, to determine whether the two population locations differ, given the following information.

Sample	Sample Size	Rank Sum
1	9	90
2	6	30

18.6 Using the Wilcoxon rank sum test, with $\alpha = .05$, test to determine whether there is enough evidence to indicate that the location of population A differs from that of population B, given the following information.

Sample	Sample Size	Rank Sum
1	30	1,162
2	40	1,323

18.7 Given the results that follow, conduct the Wilcoxon rank sum test to determine whether the location of population 1 is to the left of the location of population 2. (Use $\alpha = .025$.)

Sample	Sample Size	Rank Sum
1	50	2,120
2	40	1,975

APPLYING THE TECHNIQUES

Self-Correcting Exercise (See Appendix 18.B for the solution.)

18.8 In recent years, insurance companies offering medical coverage have given discounts to companies that are committed to improving the health of their employees. To help determine whether this policy is reasonable, the general manager of one large insurance company organized a study of a random sample of 10 workers who regularly participate in their company's lunchtime exercise program and 10 workers who do not. Over a two-year period he observed the total dollar amount of medical expenses for each individual. Do the resulting data allow the manager to conclude at the 5% significance level that companies that provide exercise programs should be given discounts? (Assume that the data are not normally distributed.)

MEDICAL CLAIMS ($)

Employees Who Exercise	Employees Who Do Not Exercise
$403	$229
38	99
0	385
55	526
121	415
354	367
183	504
106	298
95	601
210	422

18.9 To producers of household products, the question of who does the housework is important because of the way advertising campaigns are designed. One of many issues that affect advertising campaigns is the extent to which women are doing less housework and men are doing more. Suppose that, in a 1988 study, 10 women were asked how many hours of work around the home they perform weekly, and that these results are to be compared with the results of a similar 1985 survey that included 14 women. If we know that the data are not normally distributed, can we conclude at the 5% significance level that women are doing less housework in 1988 than in 1985?

WEEKLY HOURS OF HOUSEWORK

1985	1988
23	17
18	21
27	16

(continued)

1985	1988
14	20
17	14
26	13
19	18
22	10
28	12
18	15
15	
21	
25	
18	

18.10 Repeat Exercise 11.12, but assume that the weight gains are not normally distributed.

18.11 Repeat Exercise 11.48, but assume that the numbers of new cavities are not normally distributed.

18.12 Certain drugs differ in their side effects, depending on the gender of the patient. In a study to determine whether men or women suffer more serious side effects when taking a powerful penicillin substitute, 8 men and 8 women were given the drug. Each was asked to evaluate the level of stomach upset that occurred, on a 7-point scale where $1 =$ No effect and $7 =$ Very badly upset. The results were as shown in the following table. Can we conclude at the 10% significance level that men and women experience different levels of stomach upset from the drug?

Men	Women
6	2
3	2
5	4
4	7
1	3
3	3
5	2
6	1

SECTION 18.4

KRUSKAL–WALLIS TEST

The Kruskal–Wallis test is applied to problems with the following characteristics:

1. The problem objective is to compare two or more populations.
2. The data type is either ranked or quantitative but nonnormal.

   The null and alternative hypotheses are

   H_0: The locations of all populations are the same.

   H_A: At least two population locations differ.

EXAMPLE 18.5

A manufacturer of high-quality calculators is trying to decide which one of three types of battery to include with each calculator sold. The two key determinants of the decision are the cost and the length of life of the battery. In order to assess the latter factor, 5 calculators were equipped with type 1 batteries, another 5 calculators were equipped with type 2 batteries, and yet another 5 calculators were equipped with type 3 batteries. The 15 calculators were then run until the batteries wore out. The times until battery wearout were recorded, and they are reproduced in the following table.

HOURS UNTIL BATTERY WEAROUT

Type 1	Type 2	Type 3
15.5	20.5	13.3
17.2	18.3	18.9
13.3	21.2	19.5
20.6	15.7	15.2
19.2	16.3	13.8

At the 5% level of significance, is there a difference in the length of life of the three batteries? Assume that the wearout times are not normally distributed.

Solution.   The problem objective is to compare three populations, the data are quantitative, and the condition necessary to perform the analysis of variance is not satisfied (the data are not normally distributed). The appropriate technique is the Kruskal–Wallis test. The null and alternative hypotheses automatically follow:

H_0: The locations of all three populations are the same.

H_A: At least two population locations differ.

The test statistic for this technique is calculated much as the test statistic for the Wilcoxon rank sum test is calculated.

The first step is to rank all of the observations. As before, 1 = Smallest observation and n = Largest observation, where $n = n_1 + n_2 + n_3$. We average the ranks of any tied observations. This task is described in the following table.

Type 1 (rank)	Type 2 (rank)	Type 3 (rank)
15.5 (5)	20.5 (13)	13.3 (1.5)
17.2 (8)	18.3 (9)	18.9 (10)
13.3 (1.5)	21.2 (15)	19.5 (12)
20.6 (14)	15.7 (6)	15.2 (4)
19.2 (11)	16.3 (7)	13.8 (3)
$T_1 = 39.5$	$T_2 = 50$	$T_3 = 30.5$

If the null hypothesis is true, the ranks should be evenly distributed among the three groups. The degree to which this is true can be determined by calculating the rank sums of the three samples (labeled T_1, T_2, and T_3). In our example, $T_1 = 39.5$, $T_2 = 50$, and $T_3 = 30.5$.

The next step is to calculate the test statistic, denoted H, where

$$H = \left[\frac{12}{n(n+1)} \sum_{j=1}^{k} \frac{T_j^2}{n_j} \right] - 3(n+1).$$

(In this formula, k is the number of populations being compared.) Although it is difficult to see this from the formula, if the rank sums T_1, T_2, and T_3 are similar, then H is small. As a result, a small value of H supports the null hypothesis. On the other hand, if considerable differences exist between any two of the rank sums, then H is large. In this example, we have

$$H = \left[\frac{12}{15(16)} \left(\frac{39.5^2}{5} + \frac{50^2}{5} + \frac{30.5^2}{5} \right) \right] - 3(16)$$
$$= 1.91.$$

The key question addressed by this test is whether H is large enough to allow us to reject the null hypothesis. The question is answered by examining the sampling distribution of H, which is approximately chi-square with $k - 1$ degrees of freedom, provided that all sample sizes are greater than or equal to 5. (That is, $n_j \geq 5$ for $j = 1, 2, \ldots, k$.) Hence, the decision rule is

Reject the null hypothesis if $H > \chi^2_{\alpha, k-1}$.

Thus, in our example, we reject H_0 if

$$H > \chi^2_{.05, 2} = 5.99147.$$

We have already seen that $H = 1.91$. Therefore, since H does not exceed χ^2_α, we do not reject the null hypothesis. There is insufficient evidence to allow us to conclude that the battery lives differ. Presumably, the calculator manufacturer will equip its product with the lowest-cost battery, given that there appear to be no significant differences in longevity among the three types (see Figure 18.10).

FIGURE 18.10   SAMPLING DISTRIBUTION FOR EXAMPLE 18.5

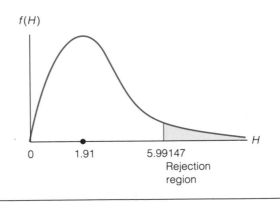

MINITAB COMPUTER OUTPUT FOR EXAMPLE 18.5*

LEVEL	NOBS	MEDIAN	AVE RANK	Z VALUE
1	5	17.20	7.9	-0.06
2	5	18.30	10.0	1.22
3	5	15.20	6.1	-1.16
OVERALL	15		8.0	

H=1.905
H (ADJ FOR TIES)=1.908

The value of the test statistic is identified by H = 1.905. The rest of the output can be ignored.

Summary of Kruskal–Wallis Test

Factors to Identify
Problem objective: Comparison of two or more populations
Data type: Ranked or quantitative

Calculation of the Test Statistic
Step 1: Rank all observations, where 1 = Smallest observation and n = Largest observation. Average the ranks of tied observations.
Step 2: Calculate the rank sums of the samples. As a check, confirm that

$$\sum T_j = n(n + 1)/2.$$

Step 3: Calculate the test statistic:

$$H = \left[\frac{12}{n(n + 1)} \sum_{j=1}^{k} \frac{T_j^2}{n_j} \right] - 3(n + 1).$$

Decision rule
Reject H_0 if $H > \chi_{\alpha, k-1}^2$.

Required Conditions
The k population distributions are identical in shape and spread; $n_j \geq 5$ for $j = 1, 2, \ldots, k$.

EXERCISES

LEARNING THE TECHNIQUES

18.13   Using the Kruskal–Wallis test, determine if there is enough evidence to enable us to conclude that at least two population locations differ. (Use $\alpha = .05$.)

---

* See Appendix 18.A for the Minitab commands that produced this printout.

Population		
1	2	3
25	19	27
15	21	25
20	23	22
22	22	29
23	28	28

18.14 Test to determine whether sufficient evidence exists to indicate that at least two population locations differ for the following Kruskal–Wallis test:

$n_1 = 7$ $n_2 = 10$ $n_3 = 8$ $n_4 = 12$

$T_1 = 133$ $T_2 = 190$ $T_3 = 152$ $T_4 = 228$.

$\alpha = .10$

18.15 Given the following data drawn from four nonnormal populations, can we conclude at the 10% significance level that at least two population locations differ?

Population			
1	2	3	4
14.5	15.3	18.3	18.8
17.3	14.6	19.5	19.3
19.8	16.8	16.6	16.5
17.4	12.1	23.3	17.0
11.9	11.6	18.8	23.5
	11.4	17.1	

18.16 In random samples of 10 from each of five nonnormal populations, the following results were generated. Can we conclude at the 5% significance level that the locations of at least two populations differ?

$T_1 = 241$ $T_2 = 281$ $T_3 = 262$

$T_4 = 233$ $T_5 = 258$.

18.17 Use the Kruskal–Wallis test to determine whether there is enough evidence, with $\alpha = .05$, to

allow us to conclude that at least two population locations differ.

$n_1 = 23$ $n_2 = 41$ $n_3 = 31$

$T_1 = 1,201$ $T_2 = 1,852$ $T_3 = 1,507$.

APPLYING THE TECHNIQUES

Self-Correcting Exercise (See Appendix 18.B for the solution.)

18.18 A consumer testing service is comparing the effectiveness of four different brands of drain cleaners. The experiment consists of using each product on 6 different clogged sinks and measuring the amount of time that elapses until each drain becomes unclogged. The resulting times, measured in minutes, are shown in the accompanying table. If a statistical analysis has shown that the times are not normally distributed, can the service conclude, with $\alpha = .10$, that differences exist among the speeds at which the four brands perform?

TIME TO UNCLOG

Brand			
1	2	3	4
17	12	19	12
25	23	29	10
19	19	31	11
12	26	26	6
14	18	29	8
16	25	33	13

18.19 Repeat Exercise 13.11, but this time assume that the data are not normally distributed.

18.20 In an effort to determine whether differences exist among three methods of teaching statistics, a professor of business taught his course differently in each of three large sections. In the first section, he taught the traditional way; in the second, he taught by the case method; and in the third, he incorporated a software computer package extensively. At the end of the semester, each student was asked to evaluate the course on a

7-point scale, where 1 = Poor and 7 = Excellent. From each section, the professor chose 5 evaluations at random. These are listed in the accompanying table.

Section 1 (traditional)	Section 2 (case method)	Section 3 (computer method)
6	4	6
4	5	7
5	5	6
4	3	7
5	3	5

At the 5% level of significance, is there evidence that differences in student satisfaction exist with respect to at least two of the three teaching methods?

18.21   A recent development in the manufacture of golf balls involves increasing the number of dimples, which manufacturers believe increases the distance the balls travel when hit. Prototype balls of three new designs were compared with a ball of the existing design, by having a machine hit each ball 7 times and measuring the yardage traveled.

The existing design has about 350 dimples, and the three experimental designs have about 370, 390, and 410 dimples, respectively. The number of yards traveled by each is shown in the accompanying table.

350 Dimples	370 Dimples	390 Dimples	410 Dimples
255	248	265	267
233	247	253	258
248	249	259	272
261	253	275	265
253	261	260	266
244	252	255	258
271	244	258	268

After analyzing the data, researchers concluded that the distances are not normally distributed. Can we conclude at the 1% significance level that there are differences in length of flight among the golf balls?

18.22   Repeat Exercise 13.12, but this time assume that the completion times are not normally distributed.

SECTION
18.5

SUMMARY

Nonparametric statistical tests are applied to problems in which the data are either ranked or quantitative and in which the preconditions for performing the relevant parametric tests are not satisfied. The Wilcoxon rank sum test is used to compare two populations, and the Kruskal–Wallis is used to compare two or more populations.

IMPORTANT TERMS

Ranked data
Ordinal data
Wilcoxon rank sum test
Distribution-free statistics

Population locations
Mann–Whitney test
Kruskal–Wallis test

FORMULAS

$$E(T) = \frac{n_1(n_1 + n_2 + 1)}{2}$$

$$\sigma_T = \sqrt{\frac{n_1 n_2 (n_1 + n_2 + 1)}{12}}$$

$$H = \left[\frac{12}{n(n+1)} \sum_{j=1}^{k} \frac{T_j^2}{n_j} \right] - 3(n+1)$$

SUPPLEMENTARY EXERCISES

18.23 Do collectors and noncollectors of supermarket trading stamps differ in their perceptions of the importance of trading stamps in their patronage of a particular supermarket? This question was addressed by Boone, Johnson, and Ferry.* Suppose that 10 collectors and 10 noncollectors were asked to rate the importance (on a 5-point scale, where 5 = Most important and 1 = Least important) of trading stamps in their choice of a supermarket. The results are shown in the accompanying table.

Collectors	Noncollectors
1	3
2	1
5	2
1	1
3	1
4	2
3	4
4	3
2	2
2	1

Can we conclude at the 5% level of significance that collectors perceive trading stamps as being more important than do noncollectors?

18.24 In a study to determine which of two teaching methods is perceived to be better, two sections of an introductory marketing course were taught in two ways.[†] At the course's completion, each student rated the course on a boring/stimulating spectrum. In this process, 1 = Boring and 7 = Stimulating. Suppose that section 1 had 8 students and section 2 had 10 students; the results are shown in the accompanying table.

---

* "Trading Stamps: Their Role in Today's Marketplace," *Journal of Marketing Science* 6 (1978): 71–76.

† R. W. Cook, "An Investigation of the Relationship Between Student Attitudes and Student Achievement," *Journal of Marketing Science* 7 (1979): 71–79.

RATINGS OF BORING/STIMULATING

Section 1	Section 2
3	5
5	3
6	4
4	3
5	4
6	6
4	2
7	2
	3
	4

Can we conclude at the 5% significance level that the ratings of the two teaching methods differ?

18.25 A rancher is trying to find which of 4 cattle feeds increases the weight of heifers the fastest. The 4 feeds are approximately equally priced. As an experiment, the rancher selects 20 heifers that are similar in age and weight, divides them into four groups of 5 heifers each, and feeds each group exclusively on feed *A*, *B*, *C*, or *D*. After several months the weight gains are measured, as reported in the accompanying table.

WEIGHT GAIN (KILOGRAMS)

Feed *A*	Feed *B*	Feed *C*	Feed *D*
100	106	88	98
105	92	95	93
112	98	106	95
98	99	99	101
102	103	98	107

If the weight gains are not normally distributed, can the rancher conclude that the weight gains from the 4 feeds differ from one another? (Use $\alpha = .05$.)

18.26 The reaction of Europeans to U.S. and Soviet nuclear weapons-limitations plans are of great interest to both sides. Of particular interest is whether differences exist among attitudes in Great Britain, France, and West Germany. Surveys were conducted in all three countries, with the results appearing in the 7 October 1985 edition of *Newsweek*. One question asked was "How confident are you that the United States would defend Western Europe, even at the risk of nuclear attack on its own territory?" The responses of 100 people in each country are summarized in Table E18.26.

In anticipation of applying a nonparametric technique, researchers ranked the data (the "Don't know" responses were omitted) and computed the rank sums. Can we conclude at the 5% significance level that differences in attitude exist among our European allies?

18.27 Another question in the survey referred to in Exercise 18.26 asked "What is the likelihood that U.S.–Soviet hostility will escalate into a third world war?" This question was posed in 1983 and again in 1985. The results are shown in Table E18.27.

For each country, the responses in 1983 and 1985 were ranked (the "Don't Know" responses

TABLE E18.26

Response	Britain	France	West Germany
Very confident (4)	16	9	9
Somewhat confident (3)	26	37	33
Not too confident (2)	33	34	34
Not at all confident (1)	24	15	18
(Don't know)	1	5	6
RANK SUMS	13,973	14,191	13,452

TABLE E18.27

Response	Britain		France		West Germany	
	1983	1985	1983	1985	1983	1985
Very likely (4)	20	10	7	5	10	4
Somewhat likely (3)	31	24	33	21	24	22
Not too likely (2)	27	36	37	48	38	48
Not at all likely (1)	17	28	17	23	28	23
(Don't know)	5	2	6	3	0	3
RANK SUMS	10,256	8,465	9,750.5	8,585.5	10,076	9,427

were omitted), and the rank sums were calculated. Is there sufficient evidence at the 5% significance level that, in each of the three countries, the perceived likelihood of a third world war decreased between 1983 and 1985?

18.28 In attempting to decide which of three brands of desk calculators to purchase for a government department, the government purchasing office buys several calculators of each make and asks one operator to solve a given set of arithmetic questions of varying complexity on each machine within a 1-hour time constraint. Each set of questions is then scored by another operator for accuracy. The percentage correct in each instance is shown in the accompanying table.

Desk Calculator		
1	2	3
85%	93%	97%
79	83	92
87	77	89
62	85	91
87	69	90

Is there sufficient evidence to indicate that differences exist among the desk calculators? (Use $\alpha = .01$, and assume that the accuracy scores are not normally distributed.)

18.29 Researchers at a large carpet manufacturer have been experimenting with a new dyeing process in hopes of reducing the streakiness that has occurred frequently with the current process. As an experiment, 8 carpets are dyed using the new process, and another 8 are dyed using the existing method. Each carpet is rated on a 10-point scale of streakiness, where 1 = Very bad and 10 = Very good. The results are shown in the accompanying table.

New Process	Current Process
7	6
6	7
8	5
6	3
6	5
5	5
6	7
7	6

Can we conclude at the 5% significance level that the new process is superior to the old?

18.30 In recent years, consumers have become more safety-conscious, particularly about children's products. A manufacturer of children's pajamas is looking for material that is as nonflammable as possible. In an experiment to compare a new fabric with the kind now being used, 10 pieces of each kind were exposed to an open flame, and the number of seconds until the fabric burst into flames was recorded. The results are shown in the accompanying table. Since the new material is so much more expensive than the current material, the manufacturer will switch only if the new material can be shown to be better. On the basis of these data, what should the manufacturer do? (Assume that the times are not normally distributed, and use $\alpha = .05$.)

IGNITING TIME (SECONDS)

New Fabric	Old Fabric
28	31
33	35
39	29
36	37
38	36
32	28
37	36
35	30
37	39

18.31 The American public's support for the space program is important for that program's continuation and for the financial health of the aerospace industry. In a poll conducted by the Gallup Organization and reported in *Newsweek* (10 February 1986), interviewees in a random sample of Americans were asked "Should the amount of money being spent on the U.S. space program be increased, kept at current levels, decreased, or ended altogether?" The survey was conducted twice, once in February 1984 and again in January 1986. The results for respondents who expressed an opinion are shown in the accompanying table. The data were ranked, and the rank sums are also shown in the table.

Preferred Funding Level	February 1984	January 1986
Increased (4)	22	27
Same (3)	49	53
Decreased (2)	24	15
Ended (1)	5	5
RANK SUMS	9,544	10,556

Can we conclude at the 10% significance level that the level of support has increased between 1984 and 1986?

18.32 The printing department of a publishing company wants to determine whether there are differences in durability among four types of book bindings. Five books with each type of binding are placed in a machine that continually opens and closes them. Shown in the accompanying table are the number of book openings that occurred before the pages separated from the binding. Assuming that the data are not normally distributed, can we conclude, with $\alpha = .05$, that there are differences in durability among the four types of bindings?

NUMBER OF OPENINGS

	Binding		
1	2	3	4
2694	2645	3271	2608
2890	2966	3056	2852
2766	2688	2985	2733
2855	2901	3061	2549
3023	2863	3100	2621

MINITAB INSTRUCTIONS

WILCOXON RANK SUM TEST

Minitab performs the Mann–Whitney test, rather than the Wilcoxon test. Nonetheless, the command

```
MANN WHITNEY C1 C2
```

will calculate a value of W, which is the rank sum of the sample stored in column 1. If we input the smaller sample size in column 1, then W will equal T_A (the value of the test statistic for the Wilcoxon test). The output includes the prob-value of a two-tail test. To perform Example 18.2, we proceed as follows:

```
SET C1
4  3  4  2  2  3  2  3  4  5
END
SET C2
6  4  5  7  3  6  4  3  5  4
END
MANN WHITNEY C1 C2
```

The resulting output is

```
C1   N=10   MEDIAN=3.0000
C2   N=10   MEDIAN=4.5000
POINT ESTIMATE FOR ETA1-ETA2 IS -0.9999
95.5 PCT C.I. FOR ETA1-ETA2 IS (-2.99, 0.00)
W=74.5
TEST OF ETA1=ETA2 VS ETA1 N.E. ETA2 IS SIGNIFICANT AT 0.0233
```

KRUSKAL–WALLIS TEST

The command

```
KRUSKAL WALLIS C1 C2
```

calculates the *H*-statistic from stacked data. The observations are stored in column 1, and the sample number from which each observation was drawn is stored in column 2. The information and command input for Example 18.5 is as follows:

```
READ    C1  C2
15.5    1
17.2    1
13.3    1
20.6    1
19.2    1
20.5    2
18.3    2
21.2    2
15.7    2
16.3    2
13.3    3
18.9    3
19.5    3
15.2    3
13.8    3
END
KRUSKAL WALLIS C1 C2
```

The resulting output is

LEVEL	NOBS	MEDIAN	AVE RANK	Z VALUE
1	5	17.20	7.9	-0.06
2	5	18.30	10.0	1.22
3	5	15.20	6.1	-1.16
OVERALL	15		8.0	

```
H=1.905
H(ADJ FOR TIES)=1.908
```

SOLUTIONS TO SELF-CORRECTING EXERCISES

18.8 H_0: The two population locations are the same.

H_A: The location of population A is to the left of the location of population B.

Decision rule: Reject H_0 if $T \leq T_L = 83$.

A: Exercise	Ranks	B: No Exercise	Ranks
403	15	229	10
38	2	99	5
0	1	385	14
55	3	526	19
121	7	415	16
354	12	367	13
183	8	504	18
106	6	298	11
95	4	601	20
210	9	422	17
	$T_A = 67$		$T_B = 143$

Value of the test statistic: $T = 67$

Conclusion: Reject H_0.

Companies that provide exercise programs should be given discounts.

18.18 H_0: The locations of all four populations are the same.

H_A: At least two population locations differ.

Decision rule: Reject H_0 if

$H > \chi^2_{\alpha, k-1} = \chi^2_{.10, 3} = 6.25139.$

Value of the test statistic: From Table E18.18, we find T_1, T_2, T_3, and T_4. Thus, we calculate

$$H = \left[\frac{12}{24(25)} \left(\frac{67.5^2}{6} + \frac{85^2}{6} + \frac{123.5^2}{6} + \frac{24^2}{6} \right) \right] - 3(25) = 17.03.$$

Conclusion: Reject H_0.

There are differences in speed of performance among the brands.

TABLE E18.18

1	Ranks	2	Ranks	3	Ranks	4	Ranks
17	11	12	6	19	14	12	6
25	17.5	23	16	29	21.5	10	3
19	14	19	14	31	23	11	4
12	6	26	19.5	26	19.5	6	1
14	9	18	12	29	21.5	8	2
16	10	25	17.5	33	24	13	8
	$T_1 = 67.5$		$T_2 = 85$		$T_3 = 123.5$		$T_4 = 24$

STATISTICAL INFERENCE: CONCLUSION

INTRODUCTION

You have now studied about 30 statistical techniques in Chapters 8 through 18. If you are like most students, you probably understand estimation and hypothesis testing and can do the actual calculations of any of the methods. You may feel, however, that the system of identifying which technique to use is still somewhat vague. In this chapter we will complete the systematic approach we began in Chapter 7 and continued in Chapter 12, adding the techniques covered in Chapters 13 through 18 to the methods summarized in Section 12.2.

In the next section, we present the complete system, which we hope will make determining which technique to use much easier. We begin by stating the problem objective, followed by the data type. Once these are specified, various specific factors that depend on particular combinations of problem objective and data type can be identified. For each method, we also present the conditions necessary for executing the technique. Use this guide in handling the exercises and cases given at the end of the chapter; these should provide you with excellent practice in the practical use of statistical techniques.

COMPLETE GUIDE TO IDENTIFYING THE CORRECT TECHNIQUE

I. Problem Objective: Description of a Single Population
   A. Data type: Quantitative
      1. σ^2 known

Parameter: μ

Test statistic: $z = \dfrac{\bar{x} - \mu}{\sigma/\sqrt{n}}$

Interval estimator: $\bar{x} \pm z_{\alpha/2}\dfrac{\sigma}{\sqrt{n}}$

Required condition: x is normally distributed, or n is large enough.

2. σ^2 unknown

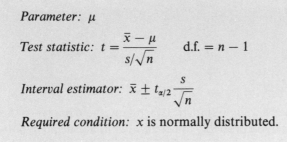

Parameter: μ

Test statistic: $t = \dfrac{\bar{x} - \mu}{s/\sqrt{n}}$ d.f. $= n - 1$

Interval estimator: $\bar{x} \pm t_{\alpha/2} \dfrac{s}{\sqrt{n}}$

Required condition: x is normally distributed.

B. Data type: Qualitative
  1. Binomial experiment

Parameter: p

Test statistic: $z = \dfrac{\hat{p} - p}{\sqrt{\dfrac{pq}{n}}}$

Interval estimator: $\hat{p} \pm z_{\alpha/2} \sqrt{\dfrac{\hat{p}\hat{q}}{n}}$

Required conditions: $np \geq 5$ and $nq \geq 5$ (for test statistic)

$n\hat{p} \geq 5$ and $n\hat{q} \geq 5$ (for estimation)

2. Multinomial experiment

Parameters: $p_1, p_2, \ldots, p_k$

Test statistic: $\chi^2 = \displaystyle\sum_{i=1}^{k} \dfrac{(O_i - E_i)^2}{E_i}$ d.f. $= k - 1$

Required condition: $E_i \geq 5$

C. Data type: Ranked—not covered in this textbook.

II. Problem Objective: Comparison of Two Populations

  A. Data type: Quantitative
    1. σ_1^2 and σ_2^2 known

Parameter: $\mu_1 - \mu_2$

Test statistic: $z = \dfrac{(\bar{x}_1 - \bar{x}_2) - (\mu_1 - \mu_2)}{\sqrt{\sigma_1^2/n_1 + \sigma_2^2/n_2}}$

Interval estimator: $(\bar{x}_1 - \bar{x}_2) \pm z_{\alpha/2}\sqrt{\sigma_1^2/n_1 + \sigma_2^2/n_2}$

Required conditions: x_1 and x_2 are normally distributed, or n_1 and n_2 are large enough. If x_1 and x_2 are nonnormal, apply the Wilcoxon rank sum test.

2. σ_1^2 and σ_2^2 unknown: $n_1 > 30$ and $n_2 > 30$

Parameter: $\mu_1 - \mu_2$

Test statistic: $z = \dfrac{(\bar{x}_1 - \bar{x}_2) - (\mu_1 - \mu_2)}{\sqrt{s_1^2/n_1 + s_2^2/n_2}}$

Interval estimator: $(\bar{x}_1 - \bar{x}_2) \pm z_{\alpha/2}\sqrt{s_1^2/n_1 + s_2^2/n_2}$

Required conditions: x_1 and x_2 are normally distributed, or n_1 and n_2 are large enough. If x_1 and x_2 are nonnormal, apply the Wilcoxon rank sum test.

3. σ_1^2 and σ_2^2 unknown: $n_1 \le 30$ or $n_2 \le 30$

Parameter: $\mu_1 - \mu_2$

Test statistic: $z = \dfrac{(\bar{x}_1 - \bar{x}_2) - (\mu_1 - \mu_2)}{\sqrt{s_p^2(1/n_1 + 1/n_2)}}$ d.f. $= n_1 + n_2 - 2$

Interval estimator: $(\bar{x}_1 - \bar{x}_2) \pm t_{\alpha/2}\sqrt{s_p^2(1/n_1 + 1/n_2)}$

Required conditions: x_1 and x_2 are normally distributed; $\sigma_1^2 = \sigma_2^2$. If x_1 and x_2 are nonnormal, apply the Wilcoxon rank sum test.

B. Data type: Qualitative

Parameter: $p_1 - p_2$

(continued)

Test statistic: Case 1: $H_0: (p_1 - p_2) = 0$.

$$z = \frac{(\hat{p}_1 - \hat{p}_2) - (p_1 - p_2)}{\sqrt{\hat{p}\hat{q}(1/n_1 + 1/n_2)}}$$

Case 2: $H_0: (p_1 - p_2) = D \qquad (D \neq 0)$.

$$z = \frac{(\hat{p}_1 - \hat{p}_2) - (p_1 - p_2)}{\sqrt{\dfrac{\hat{p}_1\hat{q}_1}{n_1} + \dfrac{\hat{p}_2\hat{q}_2}{n_2}}}$$

Interval estimator: $(\hat{p}_1 - \hat{p}_2) \pm z_{\alpha/2}\sqrt{\dfrac{\hat{p}_1\hat{q}_1}{n_1} + \dfrac{\hat{p}_2\hat{q}_2}{n_2}}$

Required conditions: $n_1\hat{p}_1, n_1\hat{q}_1, n_2\hat{p}_2,$ and $n_2\hat{q}_2 \geq 5$

C. Data type: Ranked

Nonparametric technique: Wilcoxon rank sum test

Test statistic: $T = T_A$

Required conditions: $n_1 \geq 3$ and $n_2 \geq 3$; population distributions are identical in shape and spread.

III. Problem Objective: Comparison of Two or More Populations
   A. Data type: Quantitative

Parameter: $\mu_1, \mu_2, \ldots, \mu_k$

Test statistic: $F = \dfrac{MST}{MSE}$ \qquad d.f. $\begin{aligned} v_1 &= k - 1 \\ v_2 &= n - k \end{aligned}$

Required conditions: $x_1, x_2, \ldots, x_k$ are normally distributed; $\sigma_1^2 = \sigma_2^2 = \ldots = \sigma_k^2$. If $x_1, x_2, \ldots, x_k$ are nonnormal, apply the Kruskal–Wallis test.

B. Data scale: Qualitative

Statistical technique: Contingency table

Test statistic: $\chi^2 = \sum \dfrac{(O_i - E_i)^2}{E_i}$ d.f. $= (r-1)(c-1)$

Required condition: $E_i \geq 5$

C. Data type: Ranked

Nonparametric technique: Kruskal–Wallis test

Test statistic: $H = \left[\dfrac{12}{n(n+1)} \displaystyle\sum_{j=1}^{k} \left(\dfrac{T_j^2}{n_j} \right) \right] - 3(n+1)$

chi-square distributed, d.f. $= k - 1$

Required conditions: $n_j \geq 5$; population distributions are identical in shape and spread.

IV. Problem Objective: Analysis of the Relationship Between Two Variables
A. Data type: Quantitative

Parameter: β_0, β_1, ρ (simple linear regression and correlation)

Test statistics: $t = \dfrac{\hat{\beta}_0 - \beta_0}{s_{\hat{\beta}_0}}$ d.f. $= n - 2$

$\qquad\qquad\quad t = \dfrac{\hat{\beta}_1 - \beta_1}{s_{\hat{\beta}_1}}$ d.f. $= n - 2$

Confidence intervals: $\hat{y} \pm t_{\alpha/2} s_{\varepsilon} \sqrt{\dfrac{1}{n} + \dfrac{(x_g - \bar{x})^2}{SS_x}}$

$\qquad\qquad\qquad\quad \hat{y} \pm t_{\alpha/2} s_{\varepsilon} \sqrt{1 + \dfrac{1}{n} + \dfrac{(x_g - \bar{x})^2}{SS_x}}$

Required conditions: ε is normally distributed, with mean zero and variance $= \sigma_{\varepsilon}^2$; ε terms are independent.

B. Data type: Qualitative

Statistical technique: Contingency table

(continued)

Test statistic: $\chi^2 = \sum \dfrac{(O_i - E_i)^2}{E_i}$ d.f. $= (r - 1)(c - 1)$

Required condition: $E_i \geq 5$

    C. Data type: Ranked—not covered in this textbook.

  V. Problem Objective: Analysis of the Relationship Among Two or More Variables

    A. Data type: Quantitative

Parameter: $\beta_0, \beta_1, \ldots, \beta_k$ (multiple regression)

Test statistic: $t = \dfrac{\hat{\beta}_i - \beta_i}{s_{\hat{\beta}_i}}$ d.f. $= n - k - 1$

$\qquad\qquad F = \dfrac{MST}{MSE}$ d.f. $\begin{array}{l} v_1 = k \\ v_2 = n - k - 1 \end{array}$

Required conditions: ε is normally distributed with mean zero and variance $= \sigma_\varepsilon^2$; ε terms are independent.

    B. Data type: Qualitative—not covered in this textbook.

    C. Data type: Ranked—not covered in this textbook.

To help you choose the appropriate method, a flowchart of the complete system is presented in Figure 19.1.

EXAMPLE 19.1*

Many university instructors continually seek better ways to teach their courses. That is, they try to develop a teaching style that will result in a more positive attitude toward both the professor and the course, which in turn will elicit greater student achievement. In an experiment to compare teaching methods, two sections of an introductory marketing course were taught in two distinctly different ways. Section 1 was taught primarily with lectures: a minimum of discussion was allowed, several unannounced quizzes were given, and there was no bell-curving of grades. Section 2 was a combination of lectures and discussions, no quizzes were given, and the students were graded on the curve.

At the completion of the course, each student rated the fairness of the professor and the relevance of the course on 5-point scales. The ratings were 5 = Fair and

---

* Adapted from Robert W. Cook, "An Investigation of the Relationship Between Student Attitudes and Student Achievement," *Journal of the Academy of Marketing Science* 7 (2, 2) (1979): 71–79.

FIGURE 19.1   FLOWCHART FOR IDENTIFYING STATISTICAL TECHNIQUES

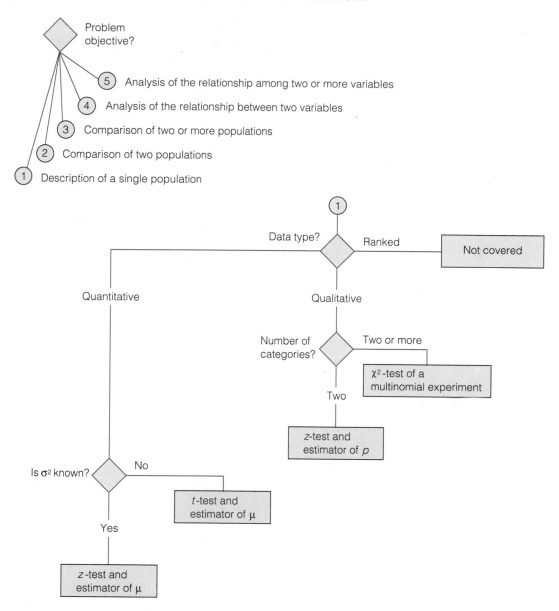

FIGURE 19.1 (*continued*)

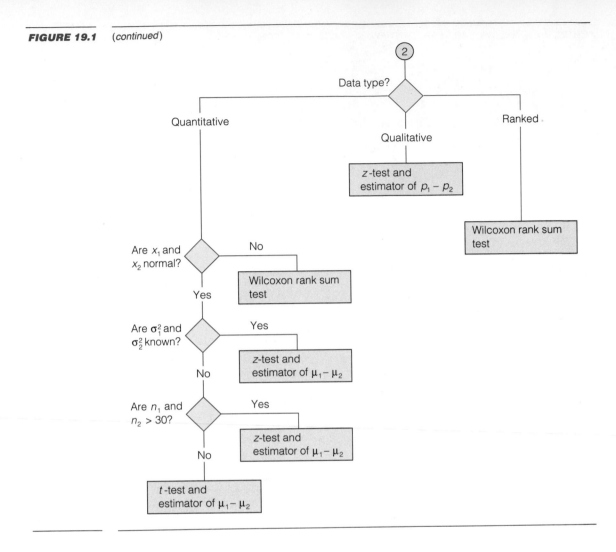

FIGURE 19.1 (*continued*)

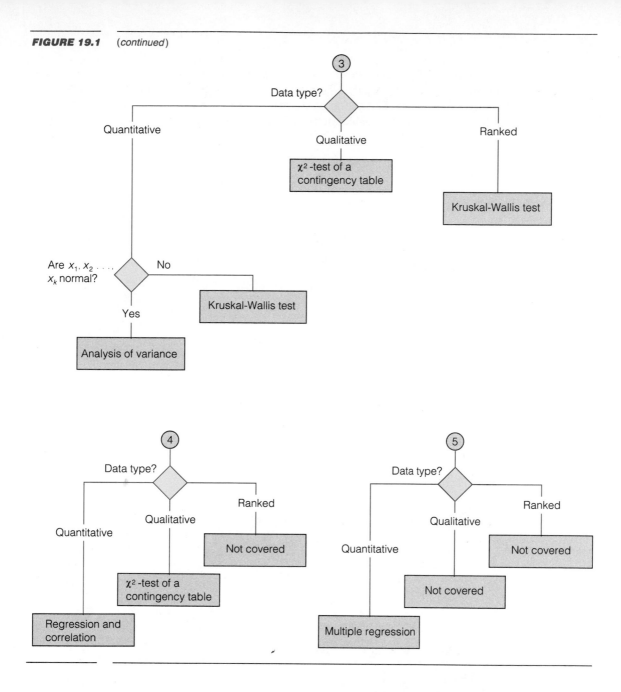

1 = Unfair and 5 = Very relevant and 1 = Irrelevant, respectively. All students also were assigned marks on a 100-point scale. The results are summarized in the two accompanying tables. The actual data (not shown) were stored in computer memory, and Minitab was used to calculate the required statistics.

DISTRIBUTION OF RATINGS

Type of Rating	Frequency	
Fairness Rating	Section 1	Section 2
1	8	4
2	18	9
3	23	22
4	16	19
5	7	10
SAMPLE SIZE	$n_1 = 72$	$n_2 = 64$
Relevance Rating	Section 1	Section 2
1	4	2
2	19	11
3	25	20
4	20	23
5	4	8
SAMPLE SIZE	$n_1 = 72$	$n_2 = 64$

DISTRIBUTION OF FINAL MARKS

Class Mark	Frequency	
	Section 1	Section 2
0–9.9	0	0
10–19.9	0	0
20–29.9	0	0
30–39.9	0	0
40–49.9	1	3
50–59.9	6	10

DISTRIBUTION OF FINAL MARKS

Class Mark	Frequency	
	Section 1	Section 2
60–69.9	14	9
70–79.9	33	28
80–89.9	14	11
90–100	4	3

a. Can we conclude that the fairness ratings received by the professor in the two sections differ?

b. Can we conclude that the relevance ratings received by the course in the two sections differ?

c. Can we conclude that the marks received by students in the two sections differ?

The significance level will be set at $\alpha = .05$.

Solution, Part (a).   The first question we encounter on the flowchart asks us to identify the problem objective. Here the objective is to compare two populations. Next, the flowchart asks us to recognize the type of data. Since the data are ranked, we identify the appropriate method as the Wilcoxon rank sum test. Because we want to know whether the two populations differ, the alternative hypothesis is

H_A: The location of population A is different from the location of population B.

Recall from Section 18.3 that the test statistic is the rank sum of sample A, where A is the smaller sample (that is, Section 2 of the class). The complete test is as follows:

H_0: The two population locations are the same.

H_A: The location of population A is different from the location of population B.

Test statistic: Since the sample sizes are large, the test statistic is

$$z = \frac{T - E(T)}{\sigma_T}.$$

Significance level: $\alpha = .05$

Decision rule: Reject H_0 if $|z| > z_{\alpha/2} = z_{.025} = 1.96$.

Value of the test statistic: From the Minitab output that follows, we have $T = W = 4,842$. The test statistic is

$$z = \frac{T - E(T)}{\sigma_T},$$

where

$$E(T) = \frac{n_1(n_1 + n_2 + 1)}{2} = \frac{64(64 + 72 + 1)}{2} = 4,384$$

and

$$\sigma_T = \sqrt{\frac{n_1 n_2(n_1 + n_2 + 1)}{12}} = \sqrt{\frac{(64)(72)(137)}{12}} = 229.$$

Hence,

$$z = \frac{4,842 - 4,384}{229} = 2.0.$$

Conclusion: Reject H_0.

There is sufficient evidence to allow us to conclude that a difference exists in the fairness ratings assigned in the two sections.

MINITAB COMPUTER OUTPUT

```
C1   N=64   MEDIAN=3.0000
C2   N=72   MEDIAN=3.0000

POINT ESTIMATE FOR ETA1-ETA2 IS    -0.0001
95.0 PCT C.I  FOR ETA1-ETA2 IS (-0.00, 1.00)
W=4842.0
TEST OF ETA1=ETA2 VS  ETA1 N.E. ETA2 IS SIGNIFICANT AT 0.0461
```

Notice that we stored the ratings for Section 2 of the class in column 1 because Section 2 is labeled Population *A* (smaller sample size).

Solution, Part (b).   The problem objective is to compare two populations, and the data are ranked. We complete the test as follows (without showing the calculations):

H_0: The two population locations are the same.

H_A: The location of population *A* is different from the location of population *B*.

Test statistic: $z = \dfrac{T - E(T)}{\sigma_T}$

Significance level: $\alpha = .05$

Decision rule: Reject H_0 if $|z| > 1.96$.

Value of the test statistic: From the printout that follows, we find

$$T = W = 4,836.5.$$

Thus,

$$z = \frac{4,836.5 - 4,384}{229} = 1.98.$$

Conclusion: Reject H_0.

There is sufficient evidence to allow us to conclude that a difference exists in the relevance ratings assigned in the two sections.

MINITAB COMPUTER OUTPUT

```
C1    N=64    MEDIAN = 3.0000
C2    N=72    MEDIAN = 3.0000

POINT ESTIMATE FOR ETA1-ETA2 IS    -0.0001
95.0 PCT C.I FOR ETA1-ETA2 IS (-0.00, 1.00)
W=4836.5
TEST OF ETA1=ETA2 VS   ETA1 N.E. ETA2 IS SIGNIFICANT AT 0.0488
```

Solution, Part (c). The problem objective is the same as it was for parts (a) and (b): to compare two populations. The data, however, are not the same. To answer part (c), we use the assigned marks out of 100; hence the data type is quantitative. Next, we recognize that the marks appear to be normally distributed, that σ_1^2 and σ_2^2 are unknown, and that $n_1 > 30$ and $n_2 > 30$. Hence, we apply the z-test of $\mu_1 - \mu_2$.

$H_0: (\mu_1 - \mu_2) = 0.$

$H_A: (\mu_1 - \mu_2) \neq 0.$

Test statistic: $z = \dfrac{(\bar{x}_1 - \bar{x}_2) - (\mu_1 - \mu_2)}{\sqrt{\dfrac{s_1^2}{n_1} + \dfrac{s_2^2}{n_2}}}$

Significance level: $\alpha = .05$

Decision rule: Reject H_0 if $|z| > 1.96$.

Value of the test statistic: From the computer output that follows, we have $z = 1.42$.

Conclusion: Do not reject H_0.

There is not enough evidence to allow us to conclude that the marks received by the two sections differ.

MINITAB COMPUTER OUTPUT

```
        N     MEAN    STDEV    SE MEAN
C1     72     73.7    10.4      1.2
C2     64     70.9    12.2      1.5

95.0 PCT C.I FOR MU C1-MU C2: (-1.1, 6.7)
T TEST MU C1 = MU C2 (VS NE): T=1.42 P=0.16 DF = 124.7
```

Our overall conclusion is that, although the students do not perceive the fairness of the professor and the relevance of the course equally, they do not appear to perform significantly differently in the two sections.

SUMMARY

At this point we think (and hope) you're ready to tackle real-life statistical problems. Some of the exercises and all of the cases deal with real problems or real data. By using the guide presented in this chapter, you should be able to produce accurate solutions within a reasonable amount of time. Have fun!

EXERCISES

19.1   Sales of a product can depend on its placement in a store. Cigarette manufacturers often offer cost discounts to retailers who display their products more prominently than competing brands. In order to examine this phenomenon more carefully, a cigarette manufacturer (with the help of a national chain of restaurants) planned the following experiment. In 5 restaurants, the manufacturer's brand was displayed behind the cashier's counter with all the other brands. (This was called *position 1*.) In another 5 restaurants, the brand was placed separately but close to the other brands (*position 2*). In a third group of 5 restaurants, the cigarettes were placed in a special display next to the cash register (*position 3*). The weekly sales were recorded, and the results appear in the accompanying table.

NUMBER OF CARTONS SOLD

Position		
1	**2**	**3**
22	24	28
17	29	24
25	21	35
32	32	39
26	33	42

a. Is there sufficient evidence to allow you to conclude that sales of this brand of cigarettes differ depending on placement? (Use $\alpha = .10$.)

b. What assumption must you make in order to answer part (a)?

c. Redo the test, assuming that the assumption in part (b) is not satisfied.

d. Comment on the policy of offering discounts to the retailer for displaying the product more prominently.

19.2   One of the ways advertisers measure the value of television commercials is through telephone surveys conducted shortly after the commercial is aired. Respondents are asked if they watched a certain television station at a given time period, during which the commercial appeared. People who answer affirmatively are then asked if they can recall the name of the product in the commercial. Suppose that an advertiser wishes to compare the recall proportions of two commercials. The first commercial is relatively inexpensive. A survey of 500 television viewers finds that 138 can recall the product name. A second commercial shown a week later features a well-known rock star and (as a result) is quite expensive to produce. The advertiser decides that the second commercial is viable only if its recall proportion is at least 15% higher than the recall proportion of the first commercial. If a survey of 800 viewers finds that 389 people recall the product name from the second commercial, can we conclude at the 5% significance level that the second commercial is viable?

19.3   A large textile firm has been accused by the federal government of discrimination in hiring. In compliance with a court order, the firm produces the results of the last 1,000 job applications; these results are summarized in Table E19.3.

TABLE E19.3

	Caucasian		Black		Hispanic	
	Males	Females	Males	Females	Males	Females
Number hired	193	75	47	15	14	9
Number rejected	199	111	114	51	96	76
Number of applications	392	186	161	66	110	85

a. On the basis of these data, can we conclude at the 5% significance level that the firm is guilty of discriminatory practices?

b. If yes, can we conclude that the discrimination is on the basis of race, sex, or both?

19.4 The widespread use of salt on Canadian roads during the winter and acid precipitation throughout the year combine to cause rust on cars. Car manufacturers and other companies offer rust-proofing services to help purchasers preserve the value of their cars. A consumer protection agency decided to determine whether there are any differences between the rust protection provided by automobile manufacturers and that provided by two competing types of rust-proofing. As an experiment, 21 identical new cars are selected. Of these, 7 are rust-proofed by the manufacturer. Another 7 are rust-proofed by a method that applies a liquid to critical areas of the car. The liquid hardens, forming a (supposedly) lifetime bond with the metal. The last 7 are treated with oil and are re-treated every 12 months. The cars are driven under similar conditions in a Canadian city. The number of months until the first rust appears is recorded. These data appear in the accompanying table.

a. If we assume that the time until rusting is normally distributed, is there sufficient evidence to allow you to conclude that at least one rust-proofing method is different from the others? (Use $\alpha = .05$.)

b. Repeat part (a), but in this case assume that the time until rusting is not normally distributed.

NUMBER OF MONTHS UNTIL RUST

	Rust-Proofing Method	
Manufacturer	**Permanent Bond**	**Oil Treatment**
33	42	47
38	36	39
27	25	43
35	38	42
29	32	46
39	29	47
32	37	38

19.5 In response to the energy crisis of 1973, the U.S. government instituted the 55 mph speed limit on all highways. If states failed to enforce this limit, they risked losing millions of dollars in highway funds (*Newsweek,* 15 July 1985). Suppose that a state were judged to be in violation of the law if at least 50% of all motorists exceeded the posted speed limit or if the average speed exceeded 55 mph. In order to determine whether a state was properly enforcing the law, 500 cars selected at random were clocked on radar; the cars' speeds were as summarized in the accompanying table.

Car Speed	Frequency
Less than 43	0
43 up to but not including 47	17

(continued)

Car Speed	Frequency
47 up to but not including 51	63
51 up to but not including 55	154
55 up to but not including 59	182
59 up to but not including 63	47
63 up to but not including 67	24
67 up to but not including 71	13
More than 71	0

Can we conclude at the 5% significance level that this state was violating the law?

19.6 In the door-to-door selling of vacuum cleaners, various factors influence sales. The Birk Vacuum Cleaner Company considers its sales pitch and overall package to be extremely important. As a result, it often thinks of new ways to sell its product. Because the company's management dreams up so many new sales pitches each year, there is a two-stage testing process. In stage 1, a new plan is tested with a relatively small sample. If there is sufficient evidence that the plan increases sales, a second, considerably larger test is undertaken. The statistical test is performed so that there is only a 5% chance of concluding that the new pitch is successful in increasing sales when it actually does not increase sales. In a stage 1 test to determine whether the inclusion of a "free" 10-year service contract increases sales, 20 sales representatives were selected at random from the company's list of several thousand. The monthly sales of 10 of these representatives were recorded for 1 month prior to use of the new sales pitch, and the monthly sales of the remaining 10 representatives were recorded for 1 month after its introduction. The results are shown in the accompanying table.

Sales Before New Sales Pitch	Sales After New Sales Pitch
15	20
27	29
22	24
19	22

Sales Before New Sales Pitch	Sales After New Sales Pitch
28	15
11	27
32	19
25	21
15	31
17	25

a. If the sales are normally distributed, should the company proceed to stage 2?

b. If the sales are not normally distributed, should the company proceed to stage 2?

19.7 An investor who correctly forecasts the direction and size of shifts in foreign currency exchange rates can reap huge profits in the international currency markets. A knowledgeable reader of the *Wall Street Journal* (and in particular, of the currency futures market quotations) can determine the direction of change in various exchange rates that is predicted by all investors, viewed collectively. These predictions, together with the subsequent actual directions of change, are summarized in the accompanying table for a sample of 216 observations.

a. Test the hypothesis that a relationship exists between the predicted and actual directions of change, at the 5% level of significance.

b. To what extent would you make use of these predictions in formulating your forecasts of future exchange rate shifts?

EXCHANGE RATE CHANGES

Predicted Change	Actual Change	
	Positive	Negative
Positive	65	64
Negative	39	48

SOURCE: Lee R. Thomas, III, "A Winning Strategy for Currency Futures Speculation," *Journal of Portfolio Management* 11 (1985): 65–69.

19.8 In the spring of 1985, the Coca-Cola Company changed the recipe of its product, first introduced in 1886. As might be expected, this change is being carefully monitored by market surveys. Prior to the recipe change, A. C. Nielsen Company of Canada surveyed soft-drink consumers and found the following percentages:

Coca-Cola   20.6%   Pepsi-Cola   18.1%

In April/May 1985 (after the recipe change), another survey produced the following results:

Coca-Cola   21.4%   Pepsi-Cola   17.5%

(All of these statistics were reported in the *Toronto Star,* 10 July 1985.) Assuming that both surveys were based on samples of 1,000 consumers, can we conclude at the 5% significance level that the popularity of Coca-Cola has increased?

19.9 A small but important part of a university library's budget is the amount collected in fines on overdue books. Last year the library collected $25,652.75 in fine payments; however, the head librarian suspects that some employees are not bothering to collect the fines on overdue books. In an effort to learn more about the situation, she asked a sample of 400 students (out of a total student population of 50,000) how many books they returned late to the library in the previous 12 months. They were also asked how many days overdue books were. The results indicated that the total number of days overdue ranged from 0 (either no books borrowed or all books returned on time) to 58 days (one student borrowed 10 books, returned 6 on time, but kept the remaining 4 books a total of 58 days too long). The average per student was 4.1 days, with a standard deviation of 2.8 days.

a. Estimate with 95% confidence the average number of days overdue for all 50,000 students at the university.

b. If the fine is 25 cents per day, estimate the amount that should be collected annually. Should the librarian conclude that not all the fines were collected?

19.10 Companies that send us bills naturally seek prompt action and are always seeking methods to induce us to pay quickly. Advertisers and marketing managers who perform mail surveys are interested in eliciting responses from the people selected to be sampled. An experiment was performed to determine whether enclosing a mild threat would increase the response rate.* A sample of 600 residents of Cincinnati was randomly selected, and each person selected received a questionnaire. Half of the residents were sent questionnaires that included a casual cover letter requesting action. The other half were sent a questionnaire that included a cover letter implying that, if the questionnaire was not returned by a certain date, the respondent would be called on the telephone and asked to answer the questionnaire. A total of 105 people (out of 300) responded to the threat, while 90 people (out of 300) responded to the casual cover letter. Do these data allow us to conclude that the two approaches have different response rates? (Use $\alpha = .05$.)

19.11 The image of the post office has suffered in recent years. One reason may be the perception that postal workers are rude in their dealings with the public. In an effort to improve its image, the post office is contemplating the introduction of public relations seminars for all of its inside workers. Because of the substantial costs involved, it has decided to institute the seminars only if there is at least a 25% reduction in the number of written complaints received by the postmaster about personnel who took the seminars. As a trial, the employees of 10 large postal centers attended the seminar. The monthly average number of complaints per center (for all centers) was 640 before the trial. The numbers of written complaints one month after the trial for the 10 sample centers are shown in the accompanying table.

Postal Center	Number of Written Complaints
1	525
2	386
3	128
4	615
5	319

(continued)

---

* C. J. Dommeyer, "How Does a Threat in the Initial Cover Letter Affect Mail Survey Response," *Developments in Marketing Science* 6 (1983): 578.

Postal Center	Number of Written Complaints
6	256
7	428
8	388
9	456
10	299

Can we conclude at the 5% significance level that the seminars should be instituted?

19.12 Some psychologists believe that there are at least three different personality types: type A is the aggressive workaholic; type B is the relaxed under-achiever; type C displays various characteristics of types A and B. The personnel manager of a large insurance company believes that, among life-insurance salespersons, there are equal numbers of all three personality types and that their degree of satisfaction and sales ability are not influenced by personality type. In a survey of 30 randomly selected salespersons, he determined their person-ality type, measured their job satisfaction on a 7-point scale (where 1 = Very dissatisfied, and 7 = Very satisfied), and determined the total value of life insurance each sold during the previous year. The results are listed in Table E19.12.

a. Test all three of the personnel manager's beliefs at the 5% level of significance. That is, test to determine whether enough evidence exists to justify concluding that:
   (i) The proportions of each personality type are different.
   (ii) The job satisfaction measures for each personality type are different.
   (iii) The life insurance sales for each personality type are different.

b. State all of the assumptions you made in order to answer each subsection of part (a).

c. How would you perform the test(s) if the assumptions you made turned out not to be satisfied?

19.13 Because of the large number of appli-cations to its graduate school of business, a university's admissions officer wants to determine the factors that influence success or failure in the MBA program. The two factors under investiga-tion are the score on the entrance exam (which can range from 200 to 800) and the undergraduate degree. A random sample of 600 students was selected, and from their records the following data were determined: the entrance score result, the undergraduate degree, and whether the student graduated from the MBA program or not. These results are summarized in the two following tables. On the basis of these results, what can you conclude about the value of the entrance exam score and the type of undergraduate degree as factors in deter-mining success or failure in the MBA program? (Use $\alpha = .01$.)

ENTRANCE EXAM SCORES AND SUCCESS IN THE PROGRAM

Program Status	Mean	Standard Deviation
Graduated	579.2	98.2
Did not graduate	537.6	80.9

UNDERGRADUATE DEGREE AND SUCCESS IN THE PROGRAM

Program Status	B.A.	B.Sc.	B.Eng.	B.B.A.
Graduated	211	151	68	81
Did not graduate	49	28	8	4

19.14 It is generally believed that salespeople who are paid on a commission basis outperform sales-people who are paid a fixed salary. Some manage-ment consultants argue, however, that in certain industries the fixed-salary salesperson may well sell more because the consumer will feel less sales pressure and will respond to the salesperson less as an antagonist. In an experiment to study this, a random sample of 15 salespeople from a retail clothing store was selected. Of these, 9 salespeople

TABLE E19.12

Salesperson	Personality Type	Job Satisfaction	Total Amount of Life Insurance Sold ($100,000s)
1	B	4	7.5
2	C	5	10.7
3	A	2	9.3
4	B	5	2.3
5	B	5	5.3
6	B	4	2.4
7	C	5	8.1
8	B	4	7.0
9	C	6	18.7
10	B	3	5.6
11	A	3	8.4
12	C	6	6.2
13	B	4	7.2
14	C	5	17.6
15	A	3	9.3
16	C	5	8.1
17	B	2	9.2
18	C	4	4.4
19	A	4	9.8
20	B	3	2.9
21	C	5	13.6
22	B	2	10.4
23	B	3	2.6
24	B	3	2.8
25	C	6	16.1
26	A	1	15.3
27	A	2	14.7
28	C	6	8.1
29	B	4	6.1
30	B	5	6.3

were paid a fixed salary, and the remaining 6 were paid a commission on each sale. The total dollar amount of one month's sales for each was recorded; these results are shown in the accompanying table.

a. Can we conclude that the commission salesperson outperforms the fixed-salary salesperson? (Use $\alpha = .05$ and assume that the sales figures are normally distributed.)

b. Estimate the difference in average monthly sales between the two types of salespeople, with 95% confidence.

c. Redo part (a), assuming that the sales are not normally distributed.

MONTHLY SALES ($1,000s)

Fixed Salary	Commission
40.1	37.3
29.6	43.8
33.7	49.6
37.2	25.3
36.0	51.0
43.5	46.1
39.8	
38.6	
36.3	

19.15   Every summer the most recent graduates of Wilfrid Laurier University are surveyed to determine their employment status. The 1984 survey is shown in Table E19.15.

a. Can we conclude at the 5% significance level that the unemployment rate differs among holders of the four types of degrees?

b. Can we conclude at the 5% significance level that the unemployment rate for business graduates is lower than that for the graduates of all other groups combined?

19.16   An insurance company that offers dental plans to large companies is seriously reconsidering its premium structure. Currently, the premium paid by each individual is the same throughout the country. The insurance company's executives believe that the incidence of cavities differs from one part of the country to another. If that is the case, the premiums should also vary according to locale. As part of a preliminary study, the company chooses the records of ten 8-year-old children who are covered by the dental plan in each of four different parts of the country. The number of cavities each child had filled during the previous year was recorded and is shown in Table E19.16.

a. Assuming that the number of cavities is normally distributed, do these data provide sufficient evidence at the 5% level of significance to indicate that children in different geographical locations differ in the number of cavities they have?

b. Repeat part (a), this time assuming that the number of cavities is not normally distributed.

TABLE E19.15

Employment Status	Bachelor Degrees			Masters Degrees	Total
	Business	Science	Arts/Music		
Employed	298	11	416	131	856
Unemployed	9	2	37	9	57
TOTAL	307	13	453	140	913

TABLE E19.16

CAVITIES IN CHILDREN GROUPED
GEOGRAPHICALLY

East	Central	Midwest	West
0	5	0	3
2	1	1	2
3	3	2	2
6	1	2	0
4	4	1	4
3	4	1	3
2	1	0	2
3	1	1	2
1	2	3	1
2	0	1	3

19.17   The executives of a large supermarket chain are considering introducing new electronic machines for checkout counters. These machines read the code of a product and automatically add the price on the cash register. Because the machines are still not perfected, they may occasionally miss an item, forcing the cashier to punch in the price manually. For this reason, the executives are uncertain about adopting the new technology. They decide to try the machines in one store and adopt them for all stores in the chain if it can be shown that checkouts are faster with the machines than without.

As an experiment, the new device is installed at one of the counters, and the service times for 100 customers are recorded at the counter with the new device. Concurrently the service times of 100 customers are recorded at one of the conventional counters. The means and standard deviations (in seconds) are as follows:

Conventional Counter	New Counter
$\bar{x}_1 = 127.2$	$\bar{x}_2 = 121.8$
$s_1 = 22.1$	$s_2 = 19.3$

Is there sufficient evidence at the 5% significance level to establish that the new device should be installed in all stores?

19.18   Second-hand smoke can be detrimental to one's health. As a result, an insurance company that sells life insurance at group rates to large companies is considering offering discounts to companies that have no-smoking policies. In order to help make the decision, the records of two companies are examined. Company 1 has had a no-smoking policy for the past five years, while company 2 does not have such a policy. A total of 1,000 men between the ages of 50 and 60 are randomly selected from each company. The number who suffer from lung disease, heart disease, both heart and lung disease, and neither heart nor lung disease are recorded. These data are shown in the accompanying table.

Health Status	Company 1	Company 2
Lung disease	9	17
Heart disease	18	33
Both diseases	4	6
Neither disease	969	944
TOTAL	1,000	1,000

Do the data provide sufficient evidence to indicate that the no-smoking policy reduces the incidence of heart and lung disease? (Use $\alpha = .01$.)

19.19   There are three distinct types of hardware wholesalers: independents (independently owned), wholesaler voluntaries (groups of independents acting together), and retailer cooperatives (retailer-owned). In a random sample of 137 retailers, the retailers were categorized according to the type of wholesaler they primarily used and according to

TABLE E19.19

Store Location	Retailer Cooperatives	Wholesaler Voluntaries	Independents
Multiple locations	14	10	5
Free-standing	29	26	13
Other (mall, strip)	20	14	6

SOURCE: Adapted from F. Robert Dwyer and Sejo Oh, "A Transaction Cost Perspective on Vertical Contractual Structure and Interchannel Competitive Strategies," *Journal of Marketing* 52 (1988): 21–34.

their store location, as shown in Table E19.19. Is there sufficient evidence to allow you to conclude that the type of wholesaler primarily used by a retailer is related to the retailer's location? (Test using $\alpha = .05$.)

19.20 In a letter to *National Geographic* (February 1986), a reader accused the publication of bias in its published letters. He pointed out that of the 773 letters published between September 1981 and May 1985, 642 came from the United States, 51 from Canada, 11 from England, and 69 from the rest of the world. The Society responded by noting that 82% of its members live in the United States, 7.3% in Canada, 1.8% in England and 8.9% in the rest of the world. At the 5% level of significance, can we conclude that the number of letters published from each country does not reflect the fraction of members from each country?

CASE 19.1*   COMPARING MBAs AND UNDERGRADUATE ACCOUNTING MAJORS

In recent years many accounting firms have hired MBAs instead of BAs in accounting. It is generally believed that MBAs are more mature and ambitious, have broader business knowledge and problem solving skills, and possess superior communication and leadership abilities. On the other hand, MBAs usually have less knowledge of accounting and typically demand higher salaries. Moreover, they sometimes have unrealistic expectations with regard to promotions and a reluctance to perform routine, uninteresting tasks.

A research project was organized to examine this issue. The study traced the performance of 56 BAs and 54 MBAs who were hired as entry-level accountants in 1973. Over the next 9 years, the performance of these 110 individuals was measured in terms of advancement, turnover, and salary increases.

Advancement was measured in three different ways:

1. The number of years it took to advance to four possible staff levels (semi-senior, senior, supervisor, and manager)

2. Advancement compared to the office mean, expressed as the ratio

---

* Based on A. Wright, "The Comparative Performance of MBAs vs. Undergraduate Accounting Majors in Public Accounting," *Accounting Review* 63(1) (1988): 123–36.

$$\frac{\text{Time to attain a staff level position}}{\text{Office mean time to attain a staff level position}}$$

3. The percentage of individuals who have attained each of the four staff levels

Table A presents summaries of the advancement performance measures. Turnover was measured in two ways:

1. The amount of time with the company that originally hired the individual
2. The percentage of individuals still with the same company at the end of the 9-year study

Table B summarizes these results. Table C presents salary data for the years 1973–1981.

Based on these results, what conclusions can you draw?

TABLE A   ADVANCEMENT WITH THE FIRM

	BAs		MBAs	
	Mean	Standard Deviation	Mean	Standard Deviation
Years to achieve staff level				
	(n = 51)		(n = 45)	
Semi-senior	1.06	.28	.97	.27
	(n = 36)		(n = 40)	
Senior	2.29	.58	2.17	.72
	(n = 19)		(n = 21)	
Supervisor	3.89	.70	3.48	.58
	(n = 12)		(n = 14)	
Manager	5.67	.87	4.54	.72
Advancement as compared to firm norm*				
To semi-senior	.93	.24	.90	.28
To senior	1.03	.35	.93	.32
To supervisor	1.14	.29	.97	.20
To manager	.96	.13	.96	.15
Percentage of hires achieving staff levels[†]				
Semi-senior	91%		83%	
Senior	64		74	
Supervisor	34		39	
Manager	21		26	

* Mean values represent a ratio of actual time/firm average time. Thus, values over 1.0 indicate that greater time than the firm norm was necessary to reach a certain position.

[†] Percentages relate to the original number of individuals hired in each group.

TABLE B   STAFF TURNOVER

	BAs (n = 56)		MBAs (n = 54)	
	Mean	Standard Deviation	Mean	Standard Deviation
Years with the firm	3.56	2.29	3.76	2.54
Percentage of hires still with the firm in 1981	16%		22%	

TABLE C   BASE PAY DATA

	BAs			MBAs		
Year	n	Mean	Standard Deviation	n	Mean	Standard Deviation
1973	56	$11,000	$1,194	54	$12,753	$1,016
1974	46	11,886	1,096	51	13,367	1,259
1975	45	13,650	1,402	46	15,241	1,580
1976	40	15,608	1,725	39	17,174	1,892
1977	29	17,300	2,069	25	19,910	1,966
1978	18	20,283	2,082	17	22,839	2,354
1979	16	23,369	2,871	13	26,762	2,481
1980	11	29,141	2,866	13	31,354	3,098
1981	9	33,556	2,465	12	36,183	2,690

CASE 19.2*   THE CUSTOMER AND THE SALESMAN

In many retail purchases, the customers' decisions depend to a large extent on the customer–salesman interaction. In a project to examine the effect of customer characteristics on the sales approach employed by salesmen, salesmen at 19 automobile dealers were studied. Male and female researchers posing as potential customers visited the dealerships a number of times, under four different conditions:

---

* Adapted from M. Etgar, A. K. Jain, and M. K. Agarwal, "Salesman-Customer Interaction: An Experimental Approach," *Journal of the Academy of Marketing Science* 6(1, 2) (1978): 1–11.

Male or female shopper

Casual or formal dress

Morning or evening visit

Shopping for a compact or subcompact car

The following five variables of the sales routine were observed:

1. Salesman introduced himself
2. Salesman inquired about name and address of shopper
3. Salesman inquired about type of car desired
4. Salesman gave his card
5. Salesman gave brochure

The frequencies of each combination of one condition and one sales routine are shown in the accompanying table.

Specify the circumstances under which the sales routines varied.

EFFECT OF CUSTOMER CHARACTERISTICS ON SALES ROUTINE

	Sex		**Dress**		**Time**		**Size**	
	Male	Female	Casual	Formal	Morning	Evening	Compact	Subcompact
Salesman Introduced Himself								
Yes	49	31	41	39	36	44	41	39
No	51	69	59	61	64	56	59	61
Salesman Inquired Name and Address								
Yes	42	23	31	34	21	44	35	30
No	58	77	69	66	79	56	65	70
Salesman Inquired Type of Car								
Yes	93	83	90	86	86	90	84	92
No	7	17	10	14	14	10	16	8
Salesman Gave Card								
Yes	62	41	51	52	45	58	57	46
No	38	59	49	48	55	42	43	54
Salesman Gave Brochure								
Yes	48	28	38	38	31	45	38	38
No	52	72	62	62	69	55	62	62

███████   **CASE 19.3***   *DO BANKS DISCRIMINATE AGAINST*
                          WOMEN BUSINESS OWNERS?

More and more women are becoming owners of small businesses. However, questions concerning how they are treated by banks and other financial institutions have been raised by women's groups. Banks are particularly important to small businesses, since studies show that bank financing represents about one-quarter of their total debt; for medium businesses, the proportion rises to approximately one-half. If women's requests for loans are rejected more frequently than are men's requests or if women must pay higher interest charges than men do, women have cause for complaint. Banks may then be subject to criminal as well as civil suits. To examine this issue, a research project was launched.

The researchers surveyed a total of 3,217 business owners, of whom 153 were women. The percentage of women in the sample, 4.8%, compares favorably with other sources that indicate that women own about 5% of established small businesses.

The survey asked several questions to determine the nature of the business, its size, and its age. Additionally, the owners were asked about their experience in dealing with banks. The questions asked in the survey are as follows:

1. Did you ever apply for a loan or a line of credit?

2. If so, was it approved?

3. If it was approved, what interest rate did you get? (How much above the prime rate was your rate?)

4. Did you require a cosignature by your spouse? (This question was only asked if the owner was married.)

The responses to these questions are summarized in Tables A through C. What do these data disclose about possible gender bias by the banks?

TABLE A   APPLICATIONS AND APPROVALS OF LOANS AND LINES OF CREDIT

	Applied for Loan or Line of Credit	**Loan or Line of Credit Approved**	**Proportion Requiring Cosignature of Spouse**
Women	123	15	39/83
Men	2,208	210	557/1,804

---

* Adapted from A. L. Riding and C. S. Swift, "Giving Credit Where It's Due: Women Business Owners and Canadian Financial Institutions," Carleton University Working Paper Series WPS 89-07, 1989.

TABLE B   *INTEREST RATES OF LOANS*

	Number of Owners with Loans	Interest Rates (points above prime)	
		Mean	Standard Deviation
Women	65	1.48%	.60%
Men	1,499	1.28	.61

TABLE C   *INTEREST RATES OF LINES OF CREDIT*

	Number of Owners with Lines of Credit	Interest Rates (points above prime)	
		Mean	Standard Deviation
Women	84	1.61%	.73%
Men	1,808	1.23	.62

ANSWERS TO SELECTED EVEN-NUMBERED EXERCISES

CHAPTER 2

2.2 a. quantitative
        b. qualitative
        c. qualitative
        d. qualitative
        e. quantitative
2.10 d. .2
2.12 b. 3/20

CHAPTER 3

3.2 Shift 1: 22; shift 2: 17.4
3.4 mode
3.8 1.4; 1; 1
3.10 a. 293,400
        b. 1974: 16.28; 1984: 19.63
        c. 1–3: 15.17; 4–6: 22.89
3.12 19; 35.56; 5.96
3.14 a. 9; 12.5; 3.54
        b. 0; 4.67; 2.16
        c. 6; 5.33; 2.31
        d. 5; 0; 0

3.16 lower quartile: median;
        upper quartile
3.18 mean; standard deviation
        (or variance)
3.20 a. 5.67%;   277.16(%)^2;
        16.65%
        b. 70%; 5%; −7.5%: 8%
3.22 a. 10.2; −4.5; 13.65; 4.75;
        30.7; 34.1; 21.3; 7.95; .9;
        20.95
        b. 14%   c. 12.63%
        d. Fund *A*, Portfolio, Fund
        B (lowest return and risk)
3.24 a. Mattel: 1263.57;
        Tonka: 1085.91;
        industry: 668.15;
        statement supported
        b. Mattel: 4.21;
        Tonka: 6.31;
        industry: 1.59;
        statement supported
3.26 approx. 680; approx. 950;
        almost all 1,000
3.28 a. approx. 68%;
        approx. 100%

        b. approx. 5%
        c. approx. 2.5%
3.30 a. 16.98; 11.08
        b. 17.75; 16.24
3.32 a. 32.8; 230.34   b. 256
3.34 a. 21.33; 163.77   b. 100
3.36 35.56; 4.68
3.38 48.08; 47; 5.93
3.40 17; 38.5; 6.20
3.42 a. 1987; 1979
3.44 a. 47.6   b. 115.42
        c. 10.74
3.46 b. 47.8; 121
3.48 b. 12.76; 1.84   c. 12.5
        d. approx. 12.81;
        approx. 2.01
3.50 b. 2.12%; 1.23%
        c. 2.6%
        d. bank yields are more
        concentrated
        e. bank yields are more
        concentrated
3.C.2 15

CHAPTER 4

4.4 a. $s = \{www, \bar{w}ww, w\bar{w}w,$
            $ww\bar{w}, \bar{w}\bar{w}w, \bar{w}w\bar{w},$
            $\bar{w}\bar{w}\bar{w}\}$
      b. $\{www, \bar{w}\bar{w}\bar{w}\}$

4.6 a. $A \cup B = \{2, 3, 6\}$
      b. $A \cap B = \{3, 5\}$
      c. $A = \{1, 6\}$
      d. $A = \{3\}$ is a simple event
      e. yes

4.8 b. $A \cup B = \{O1, O2, O3, C2\}$
      c. $A \cap B = \{O2\}$
      d. $B = \{O1, O3, C1, C3\}$
      e. no

4.10 a. .65   b. .60   c. .85
      d. 0

4.12 a. $S = \{HH, HT, TH, TT\}$
      b. $P\{HH\} = P\{HT\} =$
         $P\{TH\} = P\{TT\} = 1/4$
      c. 1/2   d. 3/4

4.14 b. $S = \{0, 1, 2, 3, 4\}$
      c. $P\{0\} = 36/80; P\{1\} =$
         $28/80; P\{2\} = 12/80;$
         $P\{3\} = P\{4\} = 2/80$
      d. relative frequency
      e. .05

4.16 a. .90   b. .595   c. .09
      d. .495

4.18 a. 49/75   b. 17/25
      c. 3/25   d. 32/75

4.20 a. 1   b. 6/7   c. 2/5
      d. 2/7   e. 1/5   f. 1/6

4.22 a. independent
      b. independent
      c. dependent

4.24 a. 1/13   b. 1/13   c. yes

4.26 .20

4.28 a. 67/125   b. 41/125
      c. no   d. no

4.30 12/44

4.32 a. .88543; .58259   b. .658
      c. .745

4.34 $P(A \cap B) = .1; P(B \mid A) = .5$

4.36 a. .32   b. .58   c. .64

4.38 a. .25   b. .60   c. .15
      d. .70

4.40 a. .15   b. .4   c. .06
      d. .49

4.42 b. $P(A \cap B) = .06;$
         $P(\bar{B}) = .66$

4.44 b. .84; .24

4.46 a. .2   b. .7

4.48 a. .08   b. .73

4.50 a. .25   b. .33   c. 1
      d. .42   e. .63   f. .56

4.52 a. approx. .615
      b. approx. .28
      c. approx. .23

4.54 a. $(.75)^3$ b. $(.25)^3$
      c. $3(.75)(.25)^2$

4.56 .999

4.58 .8

4.60 .97

4.62 a. $S = \{HHH, HHT, HTH,$
         $HTT, THH, THT, TTH,$
         $TTT\}$
      b. 1/8 to each   c. 4/8
      d. 5/8   e. 0   f. 3/8
      g. 3/4   h. no
      i. A and C; B and C

4.64 yes

4.66 a. .04   b. .31

4.68 .88

4.70 a. .000027   b. .084681
      c. .087327

4.72 a. .8   b. .6   c. .375

4.74 a. 5/15; 4/15; 3/15
      b. 3/15

4.76 2/3

CHAPTER 5

5.2 a. 1   b. .9   c. .5
      d. .4   e. 0

5.4 a.

x	1	2	3	4	5	6
$p(x)$	1/6	1/6	1/6	1/6	1/6	1/6

5.6 a. 2.0; 1.0   b. yes

5.8 a. 15.75; 33.1875
      b. 63; 531

5.10 a. 8.5; 6.73   b. 117.5

5.12 b. positively skewed
      c. 0   d. .10

5.14 a.

x	0	1	2	3
$p(x)$	.512	.384	.096	.008

      c. .104

5.16 a. up to $18   b. $55.46

5.18 $500 in cash

5.20 a. 10   b. 15   c. 15
      d. 1   e. 1

5.22 a. .1488   b. .2461
      c. .3151

5.24 a. .0512   b. .3241
      c. .3115

5.26 a. .127   b. .131   c. .147
      d. .688   e. 0   f. .046

5.28 a. .250   b. .078; .014

5.30 a. .018   b. 3

5.32 a. 0   b. .434   c. .319

5.34 a. .015   b. .558   c. .594

5.36 a. .758   b. .028   c. .713
      d. .456

5.38 .036

5.40 a. .050   b. .577   c. .146

5.42 a. .968   b. .027   c. .006

5.44 .393

5.46 c. .8   d. 0

5.48 b. .25   c. .40

5.50 a. .0446   b. .8289
      c. .025   d. .9925
      e. .0823   f. .8037

5.52 a. 2.575   b. 2.33
      c. 1.645

5.54 a. .25   b. -1.25
      c. -1.875 d. 1.75
      e. -2.25 f. -1.625

5.56 a. .0918   b. .9962
      c. .9082   d. .0918
      e. .8854

5.58 a. .0475   b. .3830
      c. .9901   d. $2,902,000

5.60 a. .9544   b. .1587

5.62 a. 10   b. 7,796

5.64 a. .0465   b. 1.0
      c. 36

5.66 a. 20; 3.46   b. .0968
c. .9429

5.68 a.

x	0	1	2
$p(x)$	2/12	8/12	2/12

5.70 b. 5
c. $V(Y) < V(X) < V(W)$
5.72 a. .016   b. .012   c. .874
d. .245   e. .545   f. .505
5.74 a. .677   b. .165   c. .323
d. .866
5.76 a. .096   b. .994
5.78 $89.20
5.80 a. .303   b. .184   c. .09
5.82 a. .538   b. .001
5.84 a. .0668   b. .1747
c. .6915   d. .3345
5.86 18.56 oz
5.88 73.11 inches
5.90 .0066

CHAPTER 6

6.2 a. .0062   b. .0228   c. 0
6.4 .6687
6.6 a. .0038   b. 0.
The manufacturer is
probably wrong.
6.8 .1056

CHAPTER 7

7.4 a. qualitative
b. quantitative
c. qualitative
d. quantitative

CHAPTER 8

8.2 a. widens   b. widens
c. widens
8.4 1500 ± 7.40
8.6 22.5 ± 5.82
8.8 1386 ± 80.59
8.10 $110,000 \pm 2575$

8.12 27.3 ± 2.32
8.14 156.3 ± 9.47
8.16 9.6 ± 7.78
8.18 22.5 ± 10.22
8.20 $236,500 \pm 8892$
8.22 $32 \pm .97$
8.24 $.84 \pm .025$
8.26 $.245 \pm .080$
8.28 $.2 \pm .078$
8.30 $.2 \pm .025$
8.32 $.08 \pm .017$
8.34 $.44 \pm .028$
8.36 385
8.38 55
8.40 385
8.42 1849
8.44 a. $27,500 \pm 832$
b. (i) widens
(ii) narrows
(iii) no change in interval
width
8.46 $.30 \pm .031$
8.48 a. 33.06 ± 2.81
b. No, just second-year business students.
8.50 a. 1041   b. 150 ± 10
8.52 $.33 \pm .11$
8.54 $.125 \pm .035$
8.56 $4.9 \pm .067$
8.58 a. $.41 \pm .053$
b. $.42 \pm .053$. The two polls
do not contradict each
other.

CHAPTER 9

9.2 -35 ± 5.37
9.4 25 ± 17.75
9.6 1.2 ± 2.57
9.8 $-.40 \pm .75$
9.10 -17.4 ± 13.50
9.12 188 ± 22.79
9.14 -10.31 ± 7.46
9.16 $.25 \pm .10$
9.18 $1.19 \pm .33$
9.20 222 ± 121.09
9.22 -10.2 ± 13.67
9.24 $-5.2 \pm .51$

9.26 $.05 \pm .052$
9.28 $.13 \pm .09$
9.30 $-.043 \pm .059$
9.32 $.11 \pm .13$
9.34 $.05 \pm .027$
9.36 $-.09 \pm .051$
9.38 20 ± 16.72
9.40 $.03 \pm .038$
9.42 $.02 \pm .035$
9.44 $.10 \pm .056$

CHAPTER 10

10.2 a. $|z| > 1.96$ b. $z > 2.33$
c. $z < -1.28$
10.4 $z = -1.41$; do not reject H_0.
10.6 a. $\bar{x} > 505.13$
b. $\bar{x} < 19.77$ or $\bar{x} > 20.23$
c. $\bar{x} < 977.08$ or
$\bar{x} > 1022.92$
10.8 $z = 2.5$; reject H_0.
10.10 $z = 1.34$; no
10.12 $z = 1.99$; yes
10.14 .0901
10.16 0
10.18 .0446
10.20 .9599
10.22 prob-value = .1056; no
10.24 a. $t = 1.58$; do not reject
H_0.
b. $t = 10.77$; reject H_0.
c. $t = -2.5$; reject H_0.
10.26 $t = 1.82$; yes
10.28 $t = 4.82$; yes
10.30 a. $t = 1.64$; yes
b. We assume that the
speeds are normally
distributed.
10.32 $t = -.97$; no
10.34 a. $z = -1.01$; do not reject
H_0.
b. $z = 3.45$; reject H_0.
c. $z = -2.07$; reject H_0.
10.36 $z = 3.13$; yes
10.38 $z = -1.84$; reject H_0.
10.40 $z = 2.36$; yes
10.42 $z = 1.67$; yes
10.44 .1056

10.46 .0694
10.48 $z = -1.18$; no
10.50 $z = 2.24$; yes
10.52 $z = -1.68$; yes
10.54 $t = 1.46$; no
10.56 $z = -2.14$; yes
10.58 $t = 1.67$; no
10.60 $t = -5.45$; yes

CHAPTER 11

11.2 $z = -1.85$; do not reject H_0.
11.4 .0274
11.6 $t = -3.16$; yes
11.8 .1660
11.12 $t = 2.21$; yes
11.14 $z = 3.79$; yes
11.16 $z = -1.75$; no
11.18 $z = 2.33$; yes
11.20 $z = -3.90$; yes
11.22 a. $z = -1.56$; do not reject H_0.
  b. $z = 3.25$; reject H_0.
11.24 $z = -.73$; no
11.26 $z = 3.51$; yes
11.28 $z = -1.81$; yes
11.30 $z = .93$; no
11.32 $z = 3.56$; yes
11.34 $z = 1.30$; no
11.36 a. $z = -5.02$; yes
  b. $z = -2.39$; no
11.38 a. $t = -3.64$; yes
  b. $t = -2.43$; yes
11.40 $t = 1.11$; no
11.42 $z = 1.01$; no
11.44 a. $z = 1.83$; yes
  b. $z = .93$; no
11.46 $t = 1.64$; no difference in cholesterol reduction
11.48 $t = -2.59$; yes

CHAPTER 12

12.2 a. 5.25 ± 1.96
  b. $z = 2.88$; yes
  c. $z = .96$; no
  d. $.48 \pm .14$

12.4 $t = 2.26$; yes
12.6 $z = 2.99$; yes
12.8 $.117 \pm .054$
12.10 a. -16.8 ± 3.43
  b. 23.1 ± 2.40
12.12 $.68 \pm .062$
  $.48 \pm .067$
12.14 $t = -2.41$; yes
12.16 $z = 2.93$; yes
12.18 385
12.20 $.44 \pm .17$
12.22 6.2 ± 3.62
12.24 $z = 1.90$; yes

CHAPTER 13

13.2 $F = 5.04$; do not reject H_0.
13.4 $F = 9.50$; reject H_0.
13.6 $F = 3.49$
13.8 $F = 1.08$; no
13.10 $F = 3.47$; management should tailor its advertising toward the industry that uses the computer most frequently.
13.12 $F = 6.06$; yes
13.14 $F = 1.04$; no
13.16 $t = 1.16$; forms C and D do not differ.
13.18 a. 17.6 ± 3.658
  b. 8.80 ± 3.658
  c. 8.80 ± 5.173
  d. -1.0 ± 5.173
13.20 a. 3.21 ± 5.449
  b. 6.01 ± 6.093
  c. 1.59 ± 6.306
  d. $-.23 \pm 7.462$
13.22 a. 8.75 ± 6.399
  b. -7.45 ± 6.650
13.24 a. $14.018 \pm .755$
  b. $.855 \pm 1.068$
13.26 a. 8.36 ± 1.578
  b. $.14 \pm 2.232$
13.28 a. 20.4 ± 1.93
  b. -5.2 ± 2.73
13.30 $F = .20$; Henry should go to U. of A.
13.32 $F = 58.08$; yes

13.34 $F = .80$; no
13.36 $F = 2.49$; no differences among the cities

CHAPTER 14

14.4 $\chi^2 = 3.88$; do not reject H_0.
14.6 $\chi^2 = 9.96$; reject H_0.
14.8 $\chi^2 = 5.70$; no
14.10 $\chi^2 = 14.07$; yes
14.12 $\chi^2 = 19.22$; current year differs.
14.14 a. $\chi^2 > 13.2767$
  b. $\chi^2 > 24.9958$
14.16 $\chi^2 = 16.57$; reject H_0.
14.18 $\chi^2 = 2.27$; no
14.20 United States: $\chi^2 = 16.51$; yes
  Mexico: $\chi^2 = 3.57$; (we combined rows 3 and 4) no
  Australia: $\chi^2 = 7.24$; (we combined rows 2, 3, and 4) no
14.22 $\chi^2 = 3.34$; no
14.24 $\chi^2 = 7.6$; do not reject H_0.
14.26 $\chi^2 = 19.68$; inducement is important.
14.28 $\chi^2 = 5.40$; no
14.30 a. $\chi^2 = 1.73$; no difference
14.32 $\chi^2 = 20.69$; no relationship
14.34 $\chi^2 = 8.20$; (we combined rows 1 and 3) relationship exists.

CHAPTER 15

15.4 $\hat{y} = 8.24 - 1.07x$
15.6 $\hat{y} = 21.53 - 5.75x$
15.8 a. $\hat{y} = 14.77 + 2.13x$
15.10 a. $\hat{y} = 6.86 + .54x$
15.12 a. $\hat{y} = -644.95 + 195.07x$
15.14 6.429
15.16 $s_\varepsilon = 157.09$
15.20 $s_\varepsilon = 2.05$
15.22 $s_\varepsilon = 1.50$
15.24 $s_\varepsilon = 73.52$
15.26 $t = 1.14$; there is not enough evidence to indicate a linear relationship.
15.28 $t = 2.30$; no

15.30 $t = 3.42$; more hours of study result in higher exam scores.

15.32 $t = 16.91$; advertising and sales are positively linearly related.

15.34 $t = 2.55$; yes

15.36 $r = .964$

15.38 $r = -.611$, $r^2 = .374$

15.42 $r = .770$, $r^2 = .593$

15.44 a. $\hat{y} = 102.94 + 44.71x$
c. $s_\varepsilon = 73.52$
d. $t = 4.82$; yes
e. $r^2 = .745$

15.46 $r^2 = .908$

15.48 a. -37.5 ± 9.11
b. -47.5 ± 3.97

15.50 Both intervals disappear.

15.52 330.4 ± 136.3

15.54 83.92 ± 26.09

15.58 43.86 ± 5.19

15.60 a. $\hat{y} = .378 + 5.76x$
b. $t = 15.67$; yes
c. $r^2 = .947$
d. 29.18 ± 11.35

15.62 a. $\hat{y} = -2.06 + .345x$
c. $t = 13.62$; yes
d. $r^2 = .912$
e. $15.19 \pm .63$
f. 8.29 ± 4.64

15.64 a. $\hat{y} = -542.07 + 11.61x$
c. $t = 3.09$; there is evidence of a linear relationship.
d. 479.61 ± 274.02
e. $r = .759$, $r^2 = .576$

15.66 b. $\hat{y} = .574 + .167x$
c. $t = 13.57$; there is evidence of a linear relationship.
d. $r^2 = .939$
e. 84.074 ± 14.11

15.68 a. $\hat{y} = 2084.03 - 86.61x$
c. $t = -11.07$; there is evidence of a linear relationship.
d. $r^2 = .925$
e. 698.27 ± 120.39

CHAPTER 16

16.2 $x_1: t = -1.79$; no
$x_2: t = 1.78$; no
$x_3: t = -2.5$; yes

16.4 a. $t = 3.80$; reject H_0.
b. $t = 1.35$; do not reject H_0.
c. $t = -4.02$; reject H_0.

16.6 b. (i) $t = 2.067$; yes
(ii) $t = -1.839$; no
(iii) $t = 4.400$; yes

16.8 b. $t = 2.125$; yes
c. $t = -3.161$; yes

16.10 $F = 2.70$; do not reject H_0.

16.12 $F = 3.12$; yes

16.14 a. 2   b. 97   c. 99
d. 352.3   e. 286.8
f. 3.63

16.16 a. $r^2 = 12.7\%$
b. $F = 4.28$; the model is useful.

16.18 a. $s_\varepsilon = 1.480$
b. $r^2 = 95.9\%$; the proportion of unexplained variability is 4.1%.
c. $F = 69.50$; yes

16.20 a. $r^2 = 7.6\%$; 92.4% of the variability in the mathematics scores is not explained by the model.
b. 8.16   c. $F = .71$; no

16.22 a. $r^2 = 92.3\%$
b. $F = 88.3$; the model is useful.
c. 2251.15

16.24 a. $F = 34.433$; the model is useful.
b. $t = 5.51$; yes
c. $t = -.80$; no

16.26 a. $F = 37.556$; yes

16.28 a. $t = 4.18$; yes
b. $t = 3.89$; yes
c. $F = 8.49$; the model is useful.
d. $r^2 = 60.7\%$

CHAPTER 17

17.2

Period	Five-period Moving Average
1	—
2	—
3	38.8
4	35.4
5	35.8
6	38.8
7	44.4
8	46.8
9	48.8
10	46.2
11	—
12	—

17.4

Period	Four-period Centered Moving Average
1	—
2	—
3	50.500
4	55.750
5	60.000
6	60.875
7	—
8	—

17.6

Period	S_t
1	12
2	16.80
3	16.16
4	22.43
5	18.09
6	16.42
7	23.28
8	21.46
9	22.69
10	15.74

17.8 b.

Period	Three-day Moving Average
1	—
2	36.7
3	30.7
4	26.0
5	35.7
6	41.0
7	43.0
8	33.3
9	28.0
10	29.0
11	40.7
12	42.3
13	40.0
14	33.3
15	44.7
16	53.0
17	51.7
18	43.0
19	32.0
20	—

17.10

Period	Four-quarter Centered Moving Average
1	—
2	—
3	29.750
4	28.625
5	28.375
6	28.750
7	28.375
8	31.250
9	34.500
10	37.875
11	40.750
12	39.750
13	36.375
14	33.625
15	—
16	—

17.22 a.

Period	Percentage of Trend
1	106.7
2	95.0
3	83.5
4	72.3
5	78.4
6	91.0
7	110.1
8	125.5
9	134.0
10	122.9
11	137.7
12	114.2
13	91.1
14	74.6
15	61.6

17.24 b.

Period	Percentage of Trend
1	115.7
2	105.6
3	95.9
4	92.1
5	87.7
6	94.0
7	95.0
8	100.7
9	108.5
10	117.9
11	103.2
12	96.1
13	94.9
14	104.8
15	103.6
16	95.1
17	87.2
18	91.5
19	97.5
20	116.8

17.30

Quarter	Seasonal Index
1	.839
2	1.057
3	1.275
4	.829

17.32

Quarter	Seasonal Index
1	1.055
2	.959
3	.927
4	1.059

17.34

Quarter	Seasonal Index
1	1.092
2	.963
3	.694
4	1.251

17.36 14.2

17.38 40.1

17.40 16,567.6

17.42

Quarter	Forecast
1	1118.75
2	934.50
3	708.00
4	792.00

17.44

Day	Forecast
Monday	16.430
Tuesday	21.497
Wednesday	21.561
Thursday	32.236
Friday	35.007

17.46

Quarter	Forecast
1	68.597
2	87.668
3	107.253
4	70.714

17.48

Day	Forecast
Sunday	258.035
Monday	99.543
Tuesday	98.034
Wednesday	122.042
Thursday	139.446
Friday	236.692
Saturday	439.710

17.50 b.

Period	Percentage of Trend
1	197.7
2	140.7
3	115.9
4	100.3
5	92.7
6	89.6
7	88.1
8	87.3
9	86.7
10	88.2
11	92.4
12	97.6
13	101.1
14	103.0
15	104.6
16	105.4
17	106.9

17.52 13.92

17.56

Quarter	Forecast
1	22.624
2	37.792
3	51.776
4	34.935

CHAPTER 18

18.2 $T = 19$; yes
18.4 $T = 64.5$; yes
18.6 $z = 1.15$; no
18.8 $T = 67$; yes
18.10 $T = 35.5$; no
18.12 $T = 81$; no
18.14 $H = 0$; no
18.16 $H = .67$; no
18.18 $H = 17.03$; yes
18.20 $H = 7.46$; yes
18.22 $H = 9.98$; yes
18.24 $T = 98.5$; yes
18.26 $H = .51$; no
18.28 $H = 6.64$; no
18.30 $T = 95.5$; do not switch.
18.32 $H = 13.10$; yes

CHAPTER 19

19.2 $z = -2.24$; yes
19.4 a. $F = 9.32$; yes
    b. $H = 10.82$; yes
19.6 a. $t = -.83$; no
    b. $T = 95$; no
19.8 $z = -.44$; no
19.10 $z = 1.31$; no
19.12 a. (i) $\chi^2 = 3.2$; we can't
        conclude that the
        proportions differ.
     (ii) $H = 16.73$; the job
        satisfaction measures
        are different.
     (iii) $F = 8.72$; the sales
        are different.
19.14 a. $t = -1.40$; no
    b. -4.98 ± 7.66
    c. $T = 62$; no
19.16 a. $F = 1.86$; no
    b. $H = 5.31$; no
19.18 $z = -2.73$; yes
19.20 $\chi^2 = 1.24$; no

TABLES

TABLE 1 *BINOMIAL PROBABILITIES*

Tabulated values are $P(X = k) = p(k)$. (Values are rounded to three decimal places.)

$n = 5$

k	.01	.05	.10	.20	.25	.30	.40	.50	.60	.70	.75	.80	.90	.95	.99
								p							
0	.951	.774	.591	.328	.237	.168	.078	.031	.010	.002	.001	.000	.000	.000	.000
1	.048	.204	.328	.410	.396	.360	.259	.156	.077	.028	.015	.006	.000	.000	.000
2	.001	.021	.073	.205	.264	.309	.346	.312	.230	.132	.088	.051	.008	.001	.000
3	.000	.001	.008	.051	.088	.132	.230	.312	.346	.309	.264	.205	.073	.021	.001
4	.000	.000	.000	.006	.015	.028	.077	.156	.259	.360	.396	.410	.328	.204	.048
5	.000	.000	.000	.000	.001	.002	.010	.031	.078	.168	.237	.328	.591	.774	.951

$n = 6$

k	.01	.05	.10	.20	.25	.30	.40	.50	.60	.70	.75	.80	.90	.95	.99
								p							
0	.941	.735	.531	.262	.178	.118	.047	.016	.004	.001	.000	.000	.000	.000	.000
1	.057	.232	.354	.393	.356	.303	.187	.094	.037	.010	.004	.002	.000	.000	.000
2	.001	.031	.098	.246	.297	.324	.311	.234	.138	.060	.033	.015	.001	.000	.000
3	.000	.002	.015	.082	.132	.185	.277	.313	.277	.185	.132	.082	.015	.002	.000
4	.000	.000	.001	.015	.033	.060	.138	.234	.311	.324	.297	.246	.098	.031	.001
5	.000	.000	.000	.002	.004	.010	.037	.094	.187	.303	.356	.393	.354	.232	.057
6	.000	.000	.000	.000	.000	.001	.004	.016	.047	.118	.178	.262	.531	.735	.941

TABLE 1 BINOMIAL PROBABILITIES (continued)

$n = 7$

k	.01	.05	.10	.20	.25	.30	.40	.50	.60	.70	.75	.80	.90	.95	.99
								p							
0	.932	.698	.478	.210	.134	.082	.028	.008	.002	.000	.000	.000	.000	.000	.000
1	.066	.257	.372	.367	.312	.247	.131	.055	.017	.004	.001	.000	.000	.000	.000
2	.002	.041	.124	.275	.312	.318	.261	.164	.077	.025	.012	.004	.000	.000	.000
3	.000	.004	.023	.115	.173	.227	.290	.273	.194	.097	.058	.029	.003	.000	.000
4	.000	.000	.003	.029	.058	.097	.194	.273	.290	.227	.173	.115	.023	.004	.000
5	.000	.000	.000	.004	.012	.025	.077	.164	.261	.318	.312	.275	.124	.041	.002
6	.000	.000	.000	.000	.001	.004	.017	.055	.131	.247	.312	.367	.372	.257	.066
7	.000	.000	.000	.000	.000	.000	.002	.008	.028	.082	.134	.210	.478	.698	.932

$n = 8$

k	.01	.05	.10	.20	.25	.30	.40	.50	.60	.70	.75	.80	.90	.95	.99
								p							
0	.923	.663	.431	.168	.100	.058	.017	.004	.001	.000	.000	.000	.000	.000	.000
1	.075	.279	.383	.336	.267	.198	.090	.031	.008	.001	.000	.000	.000	.000	.000
2	.003	.052	.149	.294	.312	.297	.209	.109	.041	.010	.004	.001	.000	.000	.000
3	.000	.005	.033	.147	.208	.254	.279	.219	.124	.047	.023	.009	.000	.000	.000
4	.000	.000	.005	.046	.087	.136	.232	.273	.232	.136	.087	.046	.005	.000	.000
5	.000	.000	.000	.009	.023	.047	.124	.219	.279	.254	.208	.147	.033	.005	.000
6	.000	.000	.000	.001	.004	.010	.041	.109	.209	.297	.312	.294	.149	.052	.003
7	.000	.000	.000	.000	.000	.001	.008	.031	.090	.198	.267	.336	.383	.279	.075
8	.000	.000	.000	.000	.000	.000	.001	.004	.017	.058	.100	.168	.431	.663	.923

n = 9

k	.01	.05	.10	.20	.25	.30	.40	p .50	.60	.70	.75	.80	.90	.95	.99
0	.914	.630	.387	.134	.075	.040	.010	.002	.000	.000	.000	.000	.000	.000	.000
1	.083	.299	.387	.302	.225	.156	.061	.018	.004	.000	.000	.000	.000	.000	.000
2	.003	.063	.172	.302	.300	.267	.161	.070	.021	.004	.001	.000	.000	.000	.000
3	.000	.008	.045	.176	.234	.267	.251	.164	.074	.021	.009	.003	.000	.000	.000
4	.000	.001	.007	.066	.117	.172	.251	.246	.167	.074	.039	.017	.001	.000	.000
5	.000	.000	.001	.017	.039	.074	.167	.246	.251	.172	.117	.066	.007	.001	.000
6	.000	.000	.000	.003	.009	.021	.074	.164	.251	.267	.234	.176	.045	.008	.000
7	.000	.000	.000	.000	.001	.004	.021	.070	.161	.267	.300	.302	.172	.063	.003
8	.000	.000	.000	.000	.000	.000	.004	.018	.061	.156	.225	.302	.387	.299	.083
9	.000	.000	.000	.000	.000	.000	.000	.002	.010	.040	.075	.134	.387	.630	.914

n = 10

k	.01	.05	.10	.20	.25	.30	.40	p .50	.60	.70	.75	.80	.90	.95	.99
0	.904	.599	.349	.107	.056	.028	.006	.001	.000	.000	.000	.000	.000	.000	.000
1	.091	.315	.387	.268	.188	.121	.040	.010	.002	.000	.000	.000	.000	.000	.000
2	.004	.075	.194	.302	.282	.234	.121	.044	.011	.001	.000	.000	.000	.000	.000
3	.000	.011	.057	.201	.250	.267	.215	.117	.043	.009	.003	.001	.000	.000	.000
4	.000	.001	.011	.088	.146	.200	.251	.205	.112	.037	.016	.006	.000	.000	.000
5	.000	.000	.002	.026	.058	.103	.201	.246	.201	.103	.058	.026	.002	.000	.000
6	.000	.000	.000	.006	.016	.037	.112	.205	.251	.200	.146	.088	.011	.001	.000
7	.000	.000	.000	.001	.003	.009	.043	.117	.215	.267	.250	.201	.057	.011	.000
8	.000	.000	.000	.000	.000	.001	.011	.044	.121	.234	.282	.302	.194	.075	.004
9	.000	.000	.000	.000	.000	.000	.002	.010	.040	.121	.188	.268	.387	.315	.091
10	.000	.000	.000	.000	.000	.000	.000	.001	.006	.028	.056	.107	.349	.599	.904

TABLE 1 BINOMIAL PROBABILITIES (continued)

$n = 15$

k	.01	.05	.10	.20	.25	.30	.40	.50	.60	.70	.75	.80	.90	.95	.99
0	.860	.463	.206	.035	.013	.005	.001	.000	.000	.000	.000	.000	.000	.000	.000
1	.130	.366	.343	.132	.067	.031	.005	.001	.000	.000	.000	.000	.000	.000	.000
2	.009	.135	.267	.231	.156	.092	.022	.003	.000	.000	.000	.000	.000	.000	.000
3	.000	.031	.129	.250	.225	.170	.063	.014	.002	.000	.000	.000	.000	.000	.000
4	.000	.005	.043	.188	.225	.219	.127	.042	.007	.001	.000	.000	.000	.000	.000
5	.000	.001	.011	.103	.165	.206	.186	.092	.025	.003	.001	.000	.000	.000	.000
6	.000	.000	.002	.043	.092	.147	.207	.153	.061	.012	.003	.001	.000	.000	.000
7	.000	.000	.000	.014	.039	.081	.177	.196	.118	.035	.013	.004	.000	.000	.000
8	.000	.000	.000	.004	.013	.035	.118	.196	.177	.081	.039	.014	.002	.000	.000
9	.000	.000	.000	.001	.003	.012	.061	.153	.207	.147	.092	.043	.011	.001	.000
10	.000	.000	.000	.000	.001	.003	.025	.092	.186	.206	.165	.103	.043	.005	.000
11	.000	.000	.000	.000	.000	.001	.007	.042	.127	.219	.225	.188	.129	.031	.000
12	.000	.000	.000	.000	.000	.000	.002	.014	.063	.170	.225	.250	.267	.135	.009
13	.000	.000	.000	.000	.000	.000	.000	.003	.022	.092	.156	.231	.343	.366	.130
14	.000	.000	.000	.000	.000	.000	.000	.001	.005	.031	.067	.132	.343	.366	.130
15	.000	.000	.000	.000	.000	.000	.000	.000	.001	.005	.013	.035	.206	.463	.860

n = 20

k	.01	.05	.10	.20	.25	.30	.40	.50	.60	.70	.75	.80	.90	.95	.99
								p							
0	.818	.359	.122	.012	.003	.001	.000	.000	.000	.000	.000	.000	.000	.000	.000
1	.165	.377	.270	.058	.021	.007	.001	.000	.000	.000	.000	.000	.000	.000	.000
2	.016	.189	.285	.137	.067	.028	.003	.000	.000	.000	.000	.000	.000	.000	.000
3	.001	.060	.190	.205	.134	.072	.012	.001	.000	.000	.000	.000	.000	.000	.000
4	.000	.013	.090	.218	.190	.130	.035	.005	.000	.000	.000	.000	.000	.000	.000
5	.000	.002	.032	.175	.202	.179	.075	.015	.001	.000	.000	.000	.000	.000	.000
6	.000	.000	.009	.109	.169	.192	.124	.037	.005	.000	.000	.000	.000	.000	.000
7	.000	.000	.002	.055	.112	.164	.166	.074	.015	.001	.000	.000	.000	.000	.000
8	.000	.000	.000	.022	.061	.114	.180	.120	.036	.004	.001	.000	.000	.000	.000
9	.000	.000	.000	.007	.027	.065	.160	.160	.071	.012	.003	.001	.000	.000	.000
10	.000	.000	.000	.002	.010	.031	.117	.176	.117	.031	.010	.002	.000	.000	.000
11	.000	.000	.000	.001	.003	.012	.071	.160	.160	.065	.027	.007	.000	.000	.000
12	.000	.000	.000	.000	.001	.004	.036	.120	.180	.114	.061	.022	.000	.000	.000
13	.000	.000	.000	.000	.000	.001	.015	.074	.166	.164	.112	.055	.002	.000	.000
14	.000	.000	.000	.000	.000	.000	.005	.037	.124	.192	.169	.109	.009	.000	.000
15	.000	.000	.000	.000	.000	.000	.001	.015	.075	.179	.202	.175	.032	.002	.000
16	.000	.000	.000	.000	.000	.000	.000	.005	.035	.130	.190	.218	.090	.013	.000
17	.000	.000	.000	.000	.000	.000	.000	.001	.012	.072	.134	.205	.190	.060	.001
18	.000	.000	.000	.000	.000	.000	.000	.000	.003	.028	.067	.137	.285	.189	.016
19	.000	.000	.000	.000	.000	.000	.000	.000	.001	.007	.021	.058	.270	.377	.165
20	.000	.000	.000	.000	.000	.000	.000	.000	.000	.001	.003	.012	.122	.359	.818

TABLE 1 *BINOMIAL PROBABILITIES (continued)*

n = 25

k	.01	.05	.10	.20	.25	.30	.40	.50	.60	.70	.75	.80	.90	.95	.99
0	.778	.277	.072	.004	.001	.000	.000	.000	.000	.000	.000	.000	.000	.000	.000
1	.196	.365	.199	.024	.006	.001	.000	.000	.000	.000	.000	.000	.000	.000	.000
2	.024	.231	.266	.071	.025	.007	.000	.000	.000	.000	.000	.000	.000	.000	.000
3	.002	.093	.227	.136	.064	.024	.002	.000	.000	.000	.000	.000	.000	.000	.000
4	.000	.027	.138	.187	.118	.057	.007	.000	.000	.000	.000	.000	.000	.000	.000
5	.000	.006	.065	.196	.165	.103	.020	.002	.000	.000	.000	.000	.000	.000	.000
6	.000	.001	.024	.163	.183	.147	.044	.005	.001	.000	.000	.000	.000	.000	.000
7	.000	.000	.007	.111	.165	.171	.080	.014	.003	.000	.000	.000	.000	.000	.000
8	.000	.000	.002	.062	.124	.165	.120	.032	.009	.000	.000	.000	.000	.000	.000
9	.000	.000	.000	.029	.078	.134	.151	.061	.021	.001	.000	.000	.000	.000	.000
10	.000	.000	.000	.012	.042	.092	.161	.097	.043	.004	.001	.000	.000	.000	.000
11	.000	.000	.000	.004	.019	.054	.147	.133	.076	.012	.003	.000	.000	.000	.000
12	.000	.000	.000	.001	.007	.027	.114	.155	.114	.027	.007	.001	.000	.000	.000
13	.000	.000	.000	.000	.003	.012	.076	.155	.147	.054	.019	.004	.000	.000	.000
14	.000	.000	.000	.000	.001	.004	.043	.133	.161	.092	.042	.012	.000	.000	.000
15	.000	.000	.000	.000	.000	.001	.021	.097	.161	.134	.078	.029	.000	.000	.000
16	.000	.000	.000	.000	.000	.000	.009	.061	.151	.165	.124	.062	.002	.000	.000
17	.000	.000	.000	.000	.000	.000	.003	.032	.120	.171	.165	.111	.007	.000	.000
18	.000	.000	.000	.000	.000	.000	.001	.014	.080	.147	.183	.163	.024	.000	.000
19	.000	.000	.000	.000	.000	.000	.000	.005	.044	.103	.165	.196	.065	.001	.000
20	.000	.000	.000	.000	.000	.000	.000	.002	.020	.057	.118	.187	.138	.006	.000
21	.000	.000	.000	.000	.000	.000	.000	.000	.007	.024	.064	.136	.227	.027	.002
22	.000	.000	.000	.000	.000	.000	.000	.000	.002	.007	.025	.071	.266	.093	.024
23	.000	.000	.000	.000	.000	.000	.000	.000	.000	.001	.006	.024	.199	.231	.196
24	.000	.000	.000	.000	.000	.000	.000	.000	.000	.000	.001	.004	.072	.365	.277
25	.000	.000	.000	.000	.000	.000	.000	.000	.000	.000	.000	.000	.000	.277	.778

(column headings .01 – .99 are values of *p*)

TABLE 2 *CUMULATIVE BINOMIAL PROBABILITIES*

Tabulated values are $P(x \leq k) = \sum_{x=0}^{k} p(x)$. (Values are rounded to three decimal places.)

$n = 5$

k										p									
	.01	.05	.10	.20	.25	.30	.40	.50	.60	.70	.75	.80	.90	.95	.99
0	.951	.774	.590	.328	.237	.168	.078	.031	.010	.002	.001	.000	.000	.000	.000
1	.999	.977	.919	.737	.633	.528	.337	.187	.087	.031	.016	.007	.000	.000	.000
2	1.000	.999	.991	.942	.896	.837	.683	.500	.317	.163	.104	.058	.009	.001	.000
3	1.000	1.000	1.000	.993	.984	.969	.913	.812	.663	.472	.367	.263	.081	.023	.001
4	1.000	1.000	1.000	1.000	.999	.998	.990	.969	.922	.832	.763	.672	.410	.226	.049

$n = 6$

k										p									
	.01	.05	.10	.20	.25	.30	.40	.50	.60	.70	.75	.80	.90	.95	.99
0	.941	.735	.531	.262	.178	.118	.047	.016	.004	.001	.000	.000	.000	.000	.000
1	.999	.967	.886	.655	.534	.420	.233	.109	.041	.011	.005	.002	.000	.000	.000
2	1.000	.998	.984	.901	.831	.744	.544	.344	.179	.070	.038	.017	.001	.000	.000
3	1.000	1.000	.999	.983	.962	.930	.821	.656	.456	.256	.169	.099	.016	.002	.000
4	1.000	1.000	1.000	.998	.995	.989	.959	.891	.767	.580	.466	.345	.114	.033	.001
5	1.000	1.000	1.000	1.000	1.000	.999	.996	.984	.953	.882	.822	.738	.469	.265	.059

TABLE 2 *CUMULATIVE BINOMIAL PROBABILITIES (continued)*

n = 7

								p							
k	.01	.05	.10	.20	.25	.30	.40	.50	.60	.70	.75	.80	.90	.95	.99
0	.932	.698	.478	.210	.133	.082	.028	.008	.002	.000	.000	.000	.000	.000	.000
1	.998	.956	.850	.577	.445	.329	.159	.063	.019	.004	.001	.000	.000	.000	.000
2	1.000	.996	.974	.852	.756	.647	.420	.227	.096	.029	.013	.005	.000	.000	.000
3	1.000	1.000	.997	.967	.929	.874	.710	.500	.290	.126	.071	.033	.003	.000	.000
4	1.000	1.000	1.000	.995	.987	.971	.904	.773	.580	.353	.244	.148	.026	.004	.000
5	1.000	1.000	1.000	1.000	.999	.996	.981	.937	.841	.671	.555	.423	.150	.044	.002
6	1.000	1.000	1.000	1.000	1.000	1.000	.998	.992	.972	.918	.867	.790	.522	.302	.068

n = 8

								p							
k	.01	.05	.10	.20	.25	.30	.40	.50	.60	.70	.75	.80	.90	.95	.99
0	.923	.663	.430	.168	.100	.058	.017	.004	.001	.000	.000	.000	.000	.000	.000
1	.997	.943	.813	.503	.367	.255	.106	.035	.009	.001	.000	.000	.000	.000	.000
2	1.000	.994	.962	.797	.679	.552	.315	.145	.050	.011	.004	.001	.000	.000	.000
3	1.000	1.000	.995	.944	.886	.806	.594	.363	.174	.058	.027	.010	.000	.000	.000
4	1.000	1.000	1.000	.990	.973	.942	.826	.637	.406	.194	.114	.056	.005	.000	.000
5	1.000	1.000	1.000	.999	.996	.989	.950	.855	.685	.448	.321	.203	.038	.006	.000
6	1.000	1.000	1.000	1.000	1.000	.999	.991	.965	.894	.745	.633	.497	.187	.057	.003
7	1.000	1.000	1.000	1.000	1.000	1.000	.999	.996	.983	.942	.900	.832	.570	.337	.077

$n = 9$

								p							
k	.01	.05	.10	.20	.25	.30	.40	.50	.60	.70	.75	.80	.90	.95	.99
0	.914	.630	.387	.134	.075	.040	.010	.002	.000	.000	.000	.000	.000	.000	.000
1	.997	.929	.775	.436	.300	.196	.071	.020	.004	.000	.000	.000	.000	.000	.000
2	1.000	.992	.947	.738	.601	.463	.232	.090	.025	.004	.001	.000	.000	.000	.000
3	1.000	.999	.992	.914	.834	.730	.483	.254	.099	.025	.010	.003	.000	.000	.000
4	1.000	1.000	.999	.980	.951	.901	.733	.500	.267	.099	.049	.020	.001	.000	.000
5	1.000	1.000	1.000	.997	.990	.975	.901	.746	.517	.270	.166	.086	.008	.001	.000
6	1.000	1.000	1.000	1.000	.999	.996	.975	.910	.768	.537	.399	.262	.053	.008	.000
7	1.000	1.000	1.000	1.000	1.000	1.000	.996	.980	.929	.804	.700	.564	.225	.071	.003
8	1.000	1.000	1.000	1.000	1.000	1.000	1.000	.998	.990	.960	.925	.866	.613	.370	.086

$n = 10$

								p							
k	.01	.05	.10	.20	.25	.30	.40	.50	.60	.70	.75	.80	.90	.95	.99
0	.904	.599	.349	.107	.056	.028	.006	.001	.000	.000	.000	.000	.000	.000	.000
1	.996	.914	.736	.376	.244	.149	.046	.011	.002	.000	.000	.000	.000	.000	.000
2	1.000	.988	.930	.678	.526	.383	.167	.055	.012	.002	.000	.000	.000	.000	.000
3	1.000	.999	.987	.879	.776	.650	.382	.172	.055	.011	.004	.001	.000	.000	.000
4	1.000	1.000	.998	.967	.922	.850	.633	.377	.166	.047	.020	.006	.000	.000	.000
5	1.000	1.000	1.000	.994	.980	.953	.834	.623	.367	.150	.078	.033	.002	.000	.000
6	1.000	1.000	1.000	.999	.996	.989	.945	.828	.618	.350	.224	.121	.013	.000	.000
7	1.000	1.000	1.000	1.000	1.000	.998	.988	.945	.833	.617	.474	.322	.070	.001	.000
8	1.000	1.000	1.000	1.000	1.000	1.000	.998	.989	.954	.851	.756	.624	.264	.012	.004
9	1.000	1.000	1.000	1.000	1.000	1.000	1.000	.999	.994	.972	.944	.893	.651	.401	.096

TABLE 2 CUMULATIVE BINOMIAL PROBABILITIES (continued)

$n = 15$

k								p								
	.01	.05	.10	.20	.25	.30	.40	.50	.60	.70	.75	.80	.90	.95	.99
0	.860	.463	.206	.035	.013	.005	.000	.000	.000	.000	.000	.000	.000	.000	.000
1	.990	.829	.549	.167	.080	.035	.005	.000	.000	.000	.000	.000	.000	.000	.000
2	1.000	.964	.816	.398	.236	.127	.027	.004	.000	.000	.000	.000	.000	.000	.000
3	1.000	.995	.944	.648	.461	.297	.091	.018	.002	.000	.000	.000	.000	.000	.000
4	1.000	.999	.987	.836	.686	.515	.217	.059	.009	.001	.000	.000	.000	.000	.000
5	1.000	1.000	.998	.939	.852	.722	.403	.151	.034	.004	.001	.000	.000	.000	.000
6	1.000	1.000	1.000	.982	.943	.869	.610	.304	.095	.015	.004	.001	.000	.000	.000
7	1.000	1.000	1.000	.996	.983	.950	.787	.500	.213	.050	.017	.004	.000	.000	.000
8	1.000	1.000	1.000	.999	.996	.985	.905	.696	.390	.131	.057	.018	.002	.000	.000
9	1.000	1.000	1.000	1.000	.999	.996	.966	.849	.597	.278	.148	.061	.013	.001	.000
10	1.000	1.000	1.000	1.000	1.000	.999	.991	.941	.783	.485	.314	.164	.056	.005	.000
11	1.000	1.000	1.000	1.000	1.000	1.000	.998	.982	.909	.703	.539	.352	.184	.036	.000
12	1.000	1.000	1.000	1.000	1.000	1.000	1.000	.996	.973	.873	.764	.602	.451	.171	.010
13	1.000	1.000	1.000	1.000	1.000	1.000	1.000	1.000	.995	.965	.920	.833	.794	.537	.140
14	1.000	1.000	1.000	1.000	1.000	1.000	1.000	1.000	1.000	.995	.987	.965			

$n = 20$

k								p							
	.01	.05	.10	.20	.25	.30	.40	.50	.60	.70	.75	.80	.90	.95	.99
0	.818	.358	.122	.012	.003	.001	.000	.000	.000	.000	.000	.000	.000	.000	.000
1	.983	.736	.392	.069	.024	.008	.001	.000	.000	.000	.000	.000	.000	.000	.000
2	.999	.925	.677	.206	.091	.035	.004	.000	.000	.000	.000	.000	.000	.000	.000
3	1.000	.984	.867	.411	.225	.107	.016	.001	.000	.000	.000	.000	.000	.000	.000
4	1.000	.997	.957	.630	.415	.238	.051	.006	.000	.000	.000	.000	.000	.000	.000
5	1.000	1.000	.989	.804	.617	.416	.126	.021	.002	.000	.000	.000	.000	.000	.000
6	1.000	1.000	.998	.913	.786	.608	.250	.058	.006	.000	.000	.000	.000	.000	.000
7	1.000	1.000	1.000	.968	.898	.772	.416	.132	.021	.001	.000	.000	.000	.000	.000
8	1.000	1.000	1.000	.990	.959	.887	.596	.252	.057	.005	.001	.000	.000	.000	.000
9	1.000	1.000	1.000	.997	.986	.952	.755	.412	.128	.017	.004	.001	.000	.000	.000
10	1.000	1.000	1.000	.999	.996	.983	.872	.588	.245	.048	.014	.003	.000	.000	.000
11	1.000	1.000	1.000	1.000	.999	.995	.943	.748	.404	.113	.041	.010	.000	.000	.000
12	1.000	1.000	1.000	1.000	1.000	.999	.979	.868	.584	.228	.102	.032	.000	.000	.000
13	1.000	1.000	1.000	1.000	1.000	1.000	.994	.942	.750	.392	.214	.087	.002	.000	.000
14	1.000	1.000	1.000	1.000	1.000	1.000	.998	.979	.874	.584	.383	.196	.011	.000	.000
15	1.000	1.000	1.000	1.000	1.000	1.000	1.000	.994	.949	.762	.585	.370	.043	.003	.000
16	1.000	1.000	1.000	1.000	1.000	1.000	1.000	.999	.984	.893	.775	.589	.133	.016	.000
17	1.000	1.000	1.000	1.000	1.000	1.000	1.000	1.000	.996	.965	.909	.794	.323	.075	.001
18	1.000	1.000	1.000	1.000	1.000	1.000	1.000	1.000	.999	.992	.976	.931	.608	.264	.017
19	1.000	1.000	1.000	1.000	1.000	1.000	1.000	1.000	1.000	.999	.997	.988	.878	.642	.182

TABLE 2 *CUMULATIVE BINOMIAL PROBABILITIES (continued)*

n = 25

k	.01	.05	.10	.20	.25	.30	.40	p .50	.60	.70	.75	.80	.90	.95	.99
0	.778	.277	.072	.004	.001	.000	.000	.000	.000	.000	.000	.000	.000	.000	.000
1	.974	.642	.271	.027	.007	.002	.000	.000	.000	.000	.000	.000	.000	.000	.000
2	.998	.873	.537	.098	.032	.009	.000	.000	.000	.000	.000	.000	.000	.000	.000
3	1.000	.966	.764	.234	.096	.033	.002	.000	.000	.000	.000	.000	.000	.000	.000
4	1.000	.993	.902	.421	.214	.090	.009	.000	.000	.000	.000	.000	.000	.000	.000
5	1.000	.999	.967	.617	.378	.193	.029	.002	.000	.000	.000	.000	.000	.000	.000
6	1.000	1.000	.991	.780	.561	.341	.074	.007	.000	.000	.000	.000	.000	.000	.000
7	1.000	1.000	.998	.891	.727	.512	.154	.022	.001	.000	.000	.000	.000	.000	.000
8	1.000	1.000	1.000	.953	.851	.677	.274	.054	.004	.000	.000	.000	.000	.000	.000
9	1.000	1.000	1.000	.983	.929	.811	.425	.115	.013	.000	.000	.000	.000	.000	.000
10	1.000	1.000	1.000	.994	.970	.902	.586	.212	.034	.002	.000	.000	.000	.000	.000
11	1.000	1.000	1.000	.998	.989	.956	.732	.345	.078	.006	.001	.000	.000	.000	.000
12	1.000	1.000	1.000	1.000	.997	.983	.846	.500	.154	.017	.003	.000	.000	.000	.000
13	1.000	1.000	1.000	1.000	.999	.994	.922	.655	.268	.044	.011	.002	.000	.000	.000
14	1.000	1.000	1.000	1.000	1.000	.998	.966	.788	.414	.098	.030	.006	.000	.000	.000
15	1.000	1.000	1.000	1.000	1.000	1.000	.987	.885	.575	.189	.071	.017	.000	.000	.000
16	1.000	1.000	1.000	1.000	1.000	1.000	.996	.946	.726	.323	.149	.047	.000	.000	.000
17	1.000	1.000	1.000	1.000	1.000	1.000	.999	.978	.846	.488	.273	.109	.002	.000	.000
18	1.000	1.000	1.000	1.000	1.000	1.000	1.000	.993	.926	.659	.439	.220	.009	.000	.000
19	1.000	1.000	1.000	1.000	1.000	1.000	1.000	.998	.971	.807	.622	.383	.033	.001	.000
20	1.000	1.000	1.000	1.000	1.000	1.000	1.000	1.000	.991	.910	.786	.579	.098	.007	.000
21	1.000	1.000	1.000	1.000	1.000	1.000	1.000	1.000	.998	.967	.904	.766	.236	.034	.000
22	1.000	1.000	1.000	1.000	1.000	1.000	1.000	1.000	1.000	.991	.968	.902	.463	.127	.002
23	1.000	1.000	1.000	1.000	1.000	1.000	1.000	1.000	1.000	.998	.993	.973	.729	.358	.026
24	1.000	1.000	1.000	1.000	1.000	1.000	1.000	1.000	1.000	1.000	.999	.996	.928	.723	.222

TABLE 3 POISSON PROBABILITIES

Tabulated values are $P(X = k) = p(k)$. (Values are rounded to three decimal places.)

k	.10	.20	.30	.40	.50	1.0	1.5	2.0	2.5	3.0	3.5	4.0	4.5	5.0	5.5	6.0
0	.905	.819	.741	.670	.607	.368	.223	.135	.082	.050	.030	.018	.011	.007	.004	.003
1	.091	.164	.222	.268	.303	.368	.335	.271	.205	.149	.106	.073	.050	.034	.023	.015
2	.005	.016	.033	.054	.076	.184	.251	.271	.257	.224	.185	.147	.113	.084	.062	.045
3	.000	.001	.003	.007	.013	.061	.126	.180	.214	.224	.216	.195	.169	.140	.113	.089
4	.000	.000	.000	.001	.002	.015	.047	.090	.134	.168	.189	.195	.190	.176	.156	.134
5	.000	.000	.000	.000	.000	.003	.014	.036	.067	.101	.132	.156	.171	.176	.171	.161
6	.000	.000	.000	.000	.000	.001	.004	.012	.028	.050	.077	.104	.128	.146	.157	.161
7	.000	.000	.000	.000	.000	.000	.001	.003	.010	.022	.039	.060	.082	.104	.123	.138
8	.000	.000	.000	.000	.000	.000	.000	.001	.003	.008	.017	.030	.046	.065	.085	.103
9	.000	.000	.000	.000	.000	.000	.000	.000	.001	.003	.007	.013	.023	.036	.052	.069
10	.000	.000	.000	.000	.000	.000	.000	.000	.000	.001	.002	.005	.010	.018	.029	.041
11	.000	.000	.000	.000	.000	.000	.000	.000	.000	.000	.001	.002	.004	.008	.014	.023
12	.000	.000	.000	.000	.000	.000	.000	.000	.000	.000	.000	.001	.002	.003	.007	.011
13	.000	.000	.000	.000	.000	.000	.000	.000	.000	.000	.000	.000	.001	.001	.003	.005
14	.000	.000	.000	.000	.000	.000	.000	.000	.000	.000	.000	.000	.000	.001	.001	.002
15	.000	.000	.000	.000	.000	.000	.000	.000	.000	.000	.000	.000	.000	.000	.000	.001
16	.000	.000	.000	.000	.000	.000	.000	.000	.000	.000	.000	.000	.000	.000	.000	.000
17	.000	.000	.000	.000	.000	.000	.000	.000	.000	.000	.000	.000	.000	.000	.000	.000
18	.000	.000	.000	.000	.000	.000	.000	.000	.000	.000	.000	.000	.000	.000	.000	.000
19	.000	.000	.000	.000	.000	.000	.000	.000	.000	.000	.000	.000	.000	.000	.000	.000
20	.000	.000	.000	.000	.000	.000	.000	.000	.000	.000	.000	.000	.000	.000	.000	.000

TABLE 3 POISSON PROBABILITIES (continued)

k	6.5	7.0	7.5	8.0	8.5	9.0	9.5	10	11	12	13	14	15
0	.002	.001	.001	.000	.000	.000	.000	.000	.000	.000	.000	.000	.000
1	.010	.006	.004	.003	.002	.001	.001	.001	.000	.000	.000	.000	.000
2	.032	.022	.016	.011	.007	.005	.003	.002	.001	.000	.000	.000	.000
3	.069	.052	.039	.029	.021	.015	.011	.008	.004	.002	.001	.001	.000
4	.112	.091	.073	.057	.044	.034	.025	.019	.010	.005	.003	.001	.001
5	.145	.128	.109	.092	.075	.061	.048	.038	.022	.013	.007	.004	.002
6	.158	.149	.137	.122	.107	.091	.076	.063	.041	.026	.015	.009	.005
7	.146	.149	.147	.140	.129	.117	.104	.090	.065	.044	.028	.017	.010
8	.119	.130	.137	.140	.138	.132	.123	.113	.089	.066	.046	.030	.019
9	.086	.101	.114	.124	.130	.132	.130	.125	.109	.087	.066	.047	.032
10	.056	.071	.086	.099	.110	.119	.124	.125	.119	.105	.086	.066	.049
11	.033	.045	.059	.072	.085	.097	.107	.114	.119	.114	.102	.084	.066
12	.018	.026	.037	.048	.060	.073	.084	.095	.109	.114	.110	.098	.083
13	.009	.014	.021	.030	.040	.050	.062	.073	.093	.106	.110	.106	.096
14	.004	.007	.011	.017	.024	.032	.042	.052	.073	.091	.102	.106	.102
15	.002	.003	.006	.009	.014	.019	.027	.035	.053	.072	.089	.099	.102
16	.001	.001	.003	.005	.007	.011	.016	.022	.037	.054	.072	.087	.096
17	.000	.001	.001	.002	.004	.006	.009	.013	.024	.038	.055	.071	.085
18	.000	.000	.001	.001	.002	.003	.005	.007	.015	.026	.040	.055	.071
19	.000	.000	.000	.000	.001	.001	.002	.004	.008	.016	.027	.041	.056
20	.000	.000	.000	.000	.000	.001	.001	.002	.005	.010	.018	.029	.042
21	.000	.000	.000	.000	.000	.000	.001	.001	.002	.006	.011	.019	.030
22	.000	.000	.000	.000	.000	.000	.000	.001	.001	.003	.007	.012	.020
23	.000	.000	.000	.000	.000	.000	.000	.000	.001	.002	.004	.007	.013
24	.000	.000	.000	.000	.000	.000	.000	.000	.000	.001	.002	.004	.008
25	.000	.000	.000	.000	.000	.000	.000	.000	.000	.000	.001	.002	.005
26	.000	.000	.000	.000	.000	.000	.000	.000	.000	.000	.001	.001	.003
27	.000	.000	.000	.000	.000	.000	.000	.000	.000	.000	.000	.001	.002
28	.000	.000	.000	.000	.000	.000	.000	.000	.000	.000	.000	.000	.001
29	.000	.000	.000	.000	.000	.000	.000	.000	.000	.000	.000	.000	.000

μ

TABLE 4 CUMULATIVE POISSON PROBABILITIES

Tabulated values are $P(x \leq k) = \sum_{x=0}^{k} p(k)$. (Values are rounded to three decimal places.)

k									μ							
	.10	.20	.30	.40	.50	1.0	1.5	2.0	2.5	3.0	3.5	4.0	4.5	5.0	5.5	6.0
0	.905	.819	.741	.670	.607	.368	.223	.135	.082	.050	.030	.018	.011	.007	.004	.002
1	.995	.982	.963	.938	.910	.736	.558	.406	.287	.199	.136	.092	.061	.040	.027	.017
2	1.000	.999	.996	.992	.986	.920	.809	.677	.544	.423	.321	.238	.174	.125	.088	.062
3	1.000	1.000	1.000	.999	.998	.981	.934	.857	.758	.647	.537	.433	.342	.265	.202	.151
4	1.000	1.000	1.000	1.000	1.000	.996	.981	.947	.891	.815	.725	.629	.532	.440	.358	.285
5	1.000	1.000	1.000	1.000	1.000	.999	.996	.983	.958	.916	.858	.785	.703	.616	.529	.446
6	1.000	1.000	1.000	1.000	1.000	1.000	.999	.995	.986	.966	.935	.889	.831	.762	.686	.606
7	1.000	1.000	1.000	1.000	1.000	1.000	1.000	.999	.996	.988	.973	.949	.913	.867	.809	.744
8	1.000	1.000	1.000	1.000	1.000	1.000	1.000	1.000	.999	.996	.990	.979	.960	.932	.894	.847
9	1.000	1.000	1.000	1.000	1.000	1.000	1.000	1.000	1.000	.999	.997	.992	.983	.968	.946	.916
10	1.000	1.000	1.000	1.000	1.000	1.000	1.000	1.000	1.000	1.000	.999	.997	.993	.986	.975	.957
11	1.000	1.000	1.000	1.000	1.000	1.000	1.000	1.000	1.000	1.000	1.000	.999	.998	.995	.989	.980
12	1.000	1.000	1.000	1.000	1.000	1.000	1.000	1.000	1.000	1.000	1.000	1.000	.999	.998	.996	.991
13	1.000	1.000	1.000	1.000	1.000	1.000	1.000	1.000	1.000	1.000	1.000	1.000	1.000	.999	.998	.996
14	1.000	1.000	1.000	1.000	1.000	1.000	1.000	1.000	1.000	1.000	1.000	1.000	1.000	1.000	.999	.999
15	1.000	1.000	1.000	1.000	1.000	1.000	1.000	1.000	1.000	1.000	1.000	1.000	1.000	1.000	1.000	.999
16	1.000	1.000	1.000	1.000	1.000	1.000	1.000	1.000	1.000	1.000	1.000	1.000	1.000	1.000	1.000	1.000
17	1.000	1.000	1.000	1.000	1.000	1.000	1.000	1.000	1.000	1.000	1.000	1.000	1.000	1.000	1.000	1.000
18	1.000	1.000	1.000	1.000	1.000	1.000	1.000	1.000	1.000	1.000	1.000	1.000	1.000	1.000	1.000	1.000
19	1.000	1.000	1.000	1.000	1.000	1.000	1.000	1.000	1.000	1.000	1.000	1.000	1.000	1.000	1.000	1.000
20	1.000	1.000	1.000	1.000	1.000	1.000	1.000	1.000	1.000	1.000	1.000	1.000	1.000	1.000	1.000	1.000

TABLE 4 CUMULATIVE POISSON PROBABILITIES (continued)

k	μ												
	6.5	7.0	7.5	8.0	8.5	9.0	9.5	10	11	12	13	14	15
0	.002	.001	.001	.000	.000	.000	.000	.000	.000	.000	.000	.000	.000
1	.011	.007	.005	.003	.002	.001	.001	.000	.000	.000	.000	.000	.000
2	.043	.030	.020	.014	.009	.006	.004	.003	.001	.001	.000	.000	.000
3	.112	.082	.059	.042	.030	.021	.015	.010	.005	.002	.001	.000	.000
4	.224	.173	.132	.100	.074	.055	.040	.029	.015	.008	.004	.002	.001
5	.369	.301	.241	.191	.150	.116	.089	.067	.038	.020	.011	.006	.003
6	.527	.450	.378	.313	.256	.207	.165	.130	.079	.046	.026	.014	.008
7	.673	.599	.525	.453	.386	.324	.269	.220	.143	.090	.054	.032	.018
8	.792	.729	.662	.593	.523	.456	.392	.333	.232	.155	.100	.062	.037
9	.877	.830	.776	.717	.653	.587	.522	.458	.341	.242	.166	.109	.070
10	.933	.901	.862	.816	.763	.706	.645	.583	.460	.347	.252	.176	.118
11	.966	.947	.921	.888	.849	.803	.752	.697	.579	.462	.353	.260	.185
12	.984	.973	.957	.936	.909	.876	.836	.792	.689	.576	.463	.358	.268
13	.993	.987	.978	.966	.949	.926	.898	.864	.781	.682	.573	.464	.363
14	.997	.994	.990	.983	.973	.959	.940	.917	.854	.772	.675	.570	.466
15	.999	.998	.995	.992	.986	.978	.967	.951	.907	.844	.764	.669	.568
16	1.000	.999	.998	.996	.993	.989	.982	.973	.944	.899	.835	.756	.664
17	1.000	1.000	.999	.998	.997	.995	.991	.986	.968	.937	.890	.827	.749
18	1.000	1.000	1.000	.999	.999	.998	.996	.993	.982	.963	.930	.883	.819
19	1.000	1.000	1.000	1.000	.999	.999	.998	.997	.991	.979	.957	.923	.875
20	1.000	1.000	1.000	1.000	1.000	1.000	.999	.998	.995	.988	.975	.952	.917
21	1.000	1.000	1.000	1.000	1.000	1.000	1.000	.999	.998	.994	.986	.971	.947
22	1.000	1.000	1.000	1.000	1.000	1.000	1.000	1.000	.999	.997	.992	.983	.967
23	1.000	1.000	1.000	1.000	1.000	1.000	1.000	1.000	1.000	.999	.996	.991	.981
24	1.000	1.000	1.000	1.000	1.000	1.000	1.000	1.000	1.000	.999	.998	.995	.989
25	1.000	1.000	1.000	1.000	1.000	1.000	1.000	1.000	1.000	1.000	.999	.997	.994
26	1.000	1.000	1.000	1.000	1.000	1.000	1.000	1.000	1.000	1.000	1.000	.999	.997
27	1.000	1.000	1.000	1.000	1.000	1.000	1.000	1.000	1.000	1.000	1.000	.999	.998
28	1.000	1.000	1.000	1.000	1.000	1.000	1.000	1.000	1.000	1.000	1.000	1.000	.999
29	1.000	1.000	1.000	1.000	1.000	1.000	1.000	1.000	1.000	1.000	1.000	1.000	1.000

TABLE 5   NORMAL CURVE AREAS

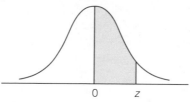

z	.00	.01	.02	.03	.04	.05	.06	.07	.08	.09
0.0	.0000	.0040	.0080	.0120	.0160	.0199	.0239	.0279	.0319	.0359
0.1	.0398	.0438	.0478	.0517	.0557	.0596	.0636	.0675	.0714	.0753
0.2	.0793	.0832	.0871	.0910	.0948	.0987	.1026	.1064	.1103	.1141
0.3	.1179	.1217	.1255	.1293	.1331	.1368	.1406	.1443	.1480	.1517
0.4	.1554	.1591	.1628	.1664	.1700	.1736	.1772	.1808	.1844	.1879
0.5	.1915	.1950	.1985	.2019	.2054	.2088	.2123	.2157	.2190	.2224
0.6	.2257	.2291	.2324	.2357	.2389	.2422	.2454	.2486	.2517	.2549
0.7	.2580	.2611	.2642	.2673	.2704	.2734	.2764	.2794	.2823	.2852
0.8	.2881	.2910	.2939	.2967	.2995	.3023	.3051	.3078	.3106	.3133
0.9	.3159	.3186	.3212	.3238	.3264	.3289	.3315	.3340	.3365	.3389
1.0	.3413	.3438	.3461	.3485	.3508	.3531	.3554	.3577	.3599	.3621
1.1	.3643	.3665	.3686	.3708	.3729	.3749	.3770	.3790	.3810	.3830
1.2	.3849	.3869	.3888	.3907	.3925	.3944	.3962	.3980	.3997	.4015
1.3	.4032	.4049	.4066	.4082	.4099	.4115	.4131	.4147	.4162	.4177
1.4	.4192	.4207	.4222	.4236	.4251	.4265	.4279	.4292	.4306	.4319
1.5	.4332	.4345	.4357	.4370	.4382	.4394	.4406	.4418	.4429	.4441
1.6	.4452	.4463	.4474	.4484	.4495	.4505	.4515	.4525	.4535	.4545
1.7	.4554	.4564	.4573	.4582	.4591	.4599	.4608	.4616	.4625	.4633
1.8	.4641	.4649	.4656	.4664	.4671	.4678	.4686	.4693	.4699	.4706
1.9	.4713	.4719	.4726	.4732	.4738	.4744	.4750	.4756	.4761	.4767
2.0	.4772	.4778	.4783	.4788	.4793	.4798	.4803	.4808	.4812	.4817
2.1	.4821	.4826	.4830	.4834	.4838	.4842	.4846	.4850	.4854	.4857
2.2	.4861	.4864	.4868	.4871	.4875	.4878	.4881	.4884	.4887	.4890
2.3	.4893	.4896	.4898	.4901	.4904	.4906	.4909	.4911	.4913	.4916
2.4	.4918	.4920	.4922	.4925	.4927	.4929	.4931	.4932	.4934	.4936
2.5	.4938	.4940	.4941	.4943	.4945	.4946	.4948	.4949	.4951	.4952
2.6	.4953	.4955	.4956	.4957	.4959	.4960	.4961	.4962	.4963	.4964
2.7	.4965	.4966	.4967	.4968	.4969	.4970	.4971	.4972	.4973	.4974
2.8	.4974	.4975	.4976	.4977	.4977	.4978	.4979	.4979	.4980	.4981
2.9	.4981	.4982	.4982	.4983	.4984	.4984	.4985	.4985	.4986	.4986
3.0	.4987	.4987	.4987	.4988	.4988	.4989	.4989	.4989	.4990	.4990

SOURCE: Abridged from Table I of A. Hald, *Statistical Tables and Formulas* (New York: John Wiley & Sons, Inc.), 1952. Reproduced by permission of A. Hald and the publisher, John Wiley & Sons, Inc.

TABLE 6 *CRITICAL VALUES OF THE STUDENT t DISTRIBUTION*

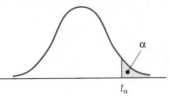

Degrees of Freedom	$t_{.100}$	$t_{.050}$	$t_{.025}$	$t_{.010}$	$t_{.005}$
1	3.078	6.314	12.706	31.821	63.657
2	1.886	2.920	4.303	6.965	9.925
3	1.638	2.353	3.182	4.541	5.841
4	1.533	2.132	2.776	3.747	4.604
5	1.476	2.015	2.571	3.365	4.032
6	1.440	1.943	2.447	3.143	3.707
7	1.415	1.895	2.365	2.998	3.499
8	1.397	1.860	2.306	2.896	3.355
9	1.383	1.833	2.262	2.821	3.250
10	1.372	1.812	2.228	2.764	3.169
11	1.363	1.796	2.201	2.718	3.106
12	1.356	1.782	2.179	2.681	3.055
13	1.350	1.771	2.160	2.650	3.012
14	1.345	1.761	2.145	2.624	2.977
15	1.341	1.753	2.131	2.602	2.947
16	1.337	1.746	2.120	2.583	2.921
17	1.333	1.740	2.110	2.567	2.898
18	1.330	1.734	2.101	2.552	2.878
19	1.328	1.729	2.093	2.539	2.861
20	1.325	1.725	2.086	2.528	2.845
21	1.323	1.721	2.080	2.518	2.831
22	1.321	1.717	2.074	2.508	2.819
23	1.319	1.714	2.069	2.500	2.807
24	1.318	1.711	2.064	2.492	2.797
25	1.316	1.708	2.060	2.485	2.787
26	1.315	1.706	2.056	2.479	2.779
27	1.314	1.703	2.052	2.473	2.771
28	1.313	1.701	2.048	2.467	2.763
29	1.311	1.699	2.045	2.462	2.756
∞	1.282	1.645	1.960	2.326	2.576

SOURCE: From M. Merrington, "Table of Percentage Points of the *t*-Distribution," *Biometrika* 32 (1941): 300. Reproduced by permission of the *Biometrika* Trustees.

TABLE 7(a) CRITICAL VALUES OF THE F DISTRIBUTION, $\alpha = .10$

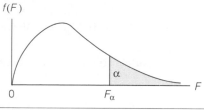

v_2 \ v_1	Numerator Degrees of Freedom								
	1	2	3	4	5	6	7	8	9
1	39.86	49.50	53.59	55.83	57.24	58.20	58.91	59.44	59.86
2	8.53	9.00	9.16	9.24	9.29	9.33	9.35	9.37	9.38
3	5.54	5.46	5.39	5.34	5.31	5.28	5.27	5.25	5.24
4	4.54	4.32	4.19	4.11	4.05	4.01	3.98	3.95	3.94
5	4.06	3.78	3.62	3.52	3.45	3.40	3.37	3.34	3.32
6	3.78	3.46	3.29	3.18	3.11	3.05	3.01	2.98	2.96
7	3.59	3.26	3.07	2.96	2.88	2.83	2.78	2.75	2.72
8	3.46	3.11	2.92	2.81	2.73	2.67	2.62	2.59	2.56
9	3.36	3.01	2.81	2.69	2.61	2.55	2.51	2.47	2.44
10	3.29	2.92	2.73	2.61	2.52	2.46	2.41	2.38	2.35
11	3.23	2.86	2.66	2.54	2.45	2.39	2.34	2.30	2.27
12	3.18	2.81	2.61	2.48	2.39	2.33	2.28	2.24	2.21
13	3.14	2.76	2.56	2.43	2.35	2.28	2.23	2.20	2.16
14	3.10	2.73	2.52	2.39	2.31	2.24	2.19	2.15	2.12
15	3.07	2.70	2.49	2.36	2.27	2.21	2.16	2.12	2.09
16	3.05	2.67	2.46	2.33	2.24	2.18	2.13	2.09	2.06
17	3.03	2.64	2.44	2.31	2.22	2.15	2.10	2.06	2.03
18	3.01	2.62	2.42	2.29	2.20	2.13	2.08	2.04	2.00
19	2.99	2.61	2.40	2.27	2.18	2.11	2.06	2.02	1.98
20	2.97	2.59	2.38	2.25	2.16	2.09	2.04	2.00	1.96
21	2.96	2.57	2.36	2.23	2.14	2.08	2.02	1.98	1.95
22	2.95	2.56	2.35	2.22	2.13	2.06	2.01	1.97	1.93
23	2.94	2.55	2.34	2.21	2.11	2.05	1.99	1.95	1.92
24	2.93	2.54	2.33	2.19	2.10	2.04	1.98	1.94	1.91
25	2.92	2.53	2.32	2.18	2.09	2.02	1.97	1.93	1.89
26	2.91	2.52	2.31	2.17	2.08	2.01	1.96	1.92	1.88
27	2.90	2.51	2.30	2.17	2.07	2.00	1.95	1.91	1.87
28	2.89	2.50	2.29	2.16	2.06	2.00	1.94	1.90	1.87
29	2.89	2.50	2.28	2.15	2.06	1.99	1.93	1.89	1.86
30	2.88	2.49	2.28	2.14	2.05	1.98	1.93	1.88	1.85
40	2.84	2.44	2.23	2.09	2.00	1.93	1.87	1.83	1.79
60	2.79	2.39	2.18	2.04	1.95	1.87	1.82	1.77	1.74
120	2.75	2.35	2.13	1.99	1.90	1.82	1.77	1.72	1.68
∞	2.71	2.30	2.08	1.94	1.85	1.77	1.72	1.67	1.63

SOURCE: From M. Merrington and C. M. Thompson, "Tables of Percentage Points of the Inverted Beta(F)-Distribution," *Biometrika* 33 (1943): 73–88. Reproduced by permission of the *Biometrika* Trustees.

TABLE 7(a) CRITICAL VALUES OF THE F DISTRIBUTION, $\alpha = .10$ (continued)

v_2 \ v_1	**Numerator Degrees of Freedom**									
	10	12	15	20	24	30	40	60	120	∞
1	60.19	60.71	61.22	61.74	62.00	62.26	62.53	62.79	63.06	63.33
2	9.39	9.41	9.42	9.44	9.45	9.46	9.47	9.47	9.48	9.49
3	5.23	5.22	5.20	5.18	5.18	5.17	5.16	5.15	5.14	5.13
4	3.92	3.90	3.87	3.84	3.83	3.82	3.80	3.79	3.78	3.76
5	3.30	3.27	3.24	3.21	3.19	3.17	3.16	3.14	3.12	3.10
6	2.94	2.90	2.87	2.84	2.82	2.80	2.78	2.76	2.74	2.72
7	2.70	2.67	2.63	2.59	2.58	2.56	2.54	2.51	2.49	2.47
8	2.54	2.50	2.46	2.42	2.40	2.38	2.36	2.34	2.32	2.29
9	2.42	2.38	2.34	2.30	2.28	2.25	2.23	2.21	2.18	2.16
10	2.32	2.28	2.24	2.20	2.18	2.16	2.13	2.11	2.08	2.06
11	2.25	2.21	2.17	2.12	2.10	2.08	2.05	2.03	2.00	1.97
12	2.19	2.15	2.10	2.06	2.04	2.01	1.99	1.96	1.93	1.90
13	2.14	2.10	2.05	2.01	1.98	1.96	1.93	1.90	1.88	1.85
14	2.10	2.05	2.01	1.96	1.94	1.91	1.89	1.86	1.83	1.80
15	2.06	2.02	1.97	1.92	1.90	1.87	1.85	1.82	1.79	1.76
16	2.03	1.99	1.94	1.89	1.87	1.84	1.81	1.78	1.75	1.72
17	2.00	1.96	1.91	1.86	1.84	1.81	1.78	1.75	1.72	1.69
18	1.98	1.93	1.89	1.84	1.81	1.78	1.75	1.72	1.69	1.66
19	1.96	1.91	1.86	1.81	1.79	1.76	1.73	1.70	1.67	1.63
20	1.94	1.89	1.84	1.79	1.77	1.74	1.71	1.68	1.64	1.61
21	1.92	1.87	1.83	1.78	1.75	1.72	1.69	1.66	1.62	1.59
22	1.90	1.86	1.81	1.76	1.73	1.70	1.67	1.64	1.60	1.57
23	1.89	1.84	1.80	1.74	1.72	1.69	1.66	1.62	1.59	1.55
24	1.88	1.83	1.78	1.73	1.70	1.67	1.64	1.61	1.57	1.53
25	1.87	1.82	1.77	1.72	1.69	1.66	1.63	1.59	1.56	1.52
26	1.86	1.81	1.76	1.71	1.68	1.65	1.61	1.58	1.54	1.50
27	1.85	1.80	1.75	1.70	1.67	1.64	1.60	1.57	1.53	1.49
28	1.84	1.79	1.74	1.69	1.66	1.63	1.59	1.56	1.52	1.48
29	1.83	1.78	1.73	1.68	1.65	1.62	1.58	1.55	1.51	1.47
30	1.82	1.77	1.72	1.67	1.64	1.61	1.57	1.54	1.50	1.46
40	1.76	1.71	1.66	1.61	1.57	1.54	1.51	1.47	1.42	1.38
60	1.71	1.66	1.60	1.54	1.51	1.48	1.44	1.40	1.35	1.29
120	1.65	1.60	1.55	1.48	1.45	1.41	1.37	1.32	1.26	1.19
∞	1.60	1.55	1.49	1.42	1.38	1.34	1.30	1.24	1.17	1.00

Denominator Degrees of Freedom

TABLE 7(b) CRITICAL VALUES OF THE F DISTRIBUTION, $\alpha = .05$

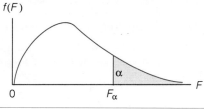

v_2	v_1	Numerator Degrees of Freedom							
	1	2	3	4	5	6	7	8	9
1	161.4	199.5	215.7	224.6	230.2	234.0	236.8	238.9	240.5
2	18.51	19.00	19.16	19.25	19.30	19.33	19.35	19.37	19.38
3	10.13	9.55	9.28	9.12	9.01	8.94	8.89	8.85	8.81
4	7.71	6.94	6.59	6.39	6.26	6.16	6.09	6.04	6.00
5	6.61	5.79	5.41	5.19	5.05	4.95	4.88	4.82	4.77
6	5.99	5.14	4.76	4.53	4.39	4.28	4.21	4.15	4.10
7	5.59	4.74	4.35	4.12	3.97	3.87	3.79	3.73	3.68
8	5.32	4.46	4.07	3.84	3.69	3.58	3.50	3.44	3.39
9	5.12	4.26	3.86	3.63	3.48	3.37	3.29	3.23	3.18
10	4.96	4.10	3.71	3.48	3.33	3.22	3.14	3.07	3.02
11	4.84	3.98	3.59	3.36	3.20	3.09	3.01	2.95	2.90
12	4.75	3.89	3.49	3.26	3.11	3.00	2.91	2.85	2.80
13	4.67	3.81	3.41	3.18	3.03	2.92	2.83	2.77	2.71
14	4.60	3.74	3.34	3.11	2.96	2.85	2.76	2.70	2.65
15	4.54	3.68	3.29	3.06	2.90	2.79	2.71	2.64	2.59
16	4.49	3.63	3.24	3.01	2.85	2.74	2.66	2.59	2.54
17	4.45	3.59	3.20	2.96	2.81	2.70	2.61	2.55	2.49
18	4.41	3.55	3.16	2.93	2.77	2.66	2.58	2.51	2.46
19	4.38	3.52	3.13	2.90	2.74	2.63	2.54	2.48	2.42
20	4.35	3.49	3.10	2.87	2.71	2.60	2.51	2.45	2.39
21	4.32	3.47	3.07	2.84	2.68	2.57	2.49	2.42	2.37
22	4.30	3.44	3.05	2.82	2.66	2.55	2.46	2.40	2.34
23	4.28	3.42	3.03	2.80	2.64	2.53	2.44	2.37	2.32
24	4.26	3.40	3.01	2.78	2.62	2.51	2.42	2.36	2.30
25	4.24	3.39	2.99	2.76	2.60	2.49	2.40	2.34	2.28
26	4.23	3.37	2.98	2.74	2.59	2.47	2.39	2.32	2.27
27	4.21	3.35	2.96	2.73	2.57	2.46	2.37	2.31	2.25
28	4.20	3.34	2.95	2.71	2.56	2.45	2.36	2.29	2.24
29	4.18	3.33	2.93	2.70	2.55	2.43	2.35	2.28	2.22
30	4.17	3.32	2.92	2.69	2.53	2.42	2.33	2.27	2.21
40	4.08	3.23	2.84	2.61	2.45	2.34	2.25	2.18	2.12
60	4.00	3.15	2.76	2.53	2.37	2.25	2.17	2.10	2.04
120	3.92	3.07	2.68	2.45	2.29	2.17	2.09	2.02	1.96
∞	3.84	3.00	2.60	2.37	2.21	2.10	2.01	1.94	1.88

SOURCE: From M. Merrington and C. M. Thompson, "Tables of Percentage Points of the Inverted Beta(F)-Distribution," *Biometrika* 33 (1943): 73–88. Reproduced by permission of the *Biometrika* Trustees.

TABLE 7(b)   *CRITICAL VALUES OF THE F DISTRIBUTION, α = .05 (continued)*

v_2 \ v_1	10	12	15	20	24	30	40	60	120	∞
1	241.9	243.9	245.9	248.0	249.1	250.1	251.1	252.2	253.3	254.3
2	19.40	19.41	19.43	19.45	19.45	19.46	19.47	19.48	19.49	19.50
3	8.79	8.74	8.70	8.66	8.64	8.62	8.59	8.57	8.55	8.53
4	5.96	5.91	5.86	5.80	5.77	5.75	5.72	5.69	5.66	5.63
5	4.74	4.68	4.62	4.56	4.53	4.50	4.46	4.43	4.40	4.36
6	4.06	4.00	3.94	3.87	3.84	3.81	3.77	3.74	3.70	3.67
7	3.64	3.57	3.51	3.44	3.41	3.38	3.34	3.30	3.27	3.23
8	3.35	3.28	3.22	3.15	3.12	3.08	3.04	3.01	2.97	2.93
9	3.14	3.07	3.01	2.94	2.90	2.86	2.83	2.79	2.75	2.71
10	2.98	2.91	2.85	2.77	2.74	2.70	2.66	2.62	2.58	2.54
11	2.85	2.79	2.72	2.65	2.61	2.57	2.53	2.49	2.45	2.40
12	2.75	2.69	2.62	2.54	2.51	2.47	2.43	2.38	2.34	2.30
13	2.67	2.60	2.53	2.46	2.42	2.38	2.34	2.30	2.25	2.21
14	2.60	2.53	2.46	2.39	2.35	2.31	2.27	2.22	2.18	2.13
15	2.54	2.48	2.40	2.33	2.29	2.25	2.20	2.16	2.11	2.07
16	2.49	2.42	2.35	2.28	2.24	2.19	2.15	2.11	2.06	2.01
17	2.45	2.38	2.31	2.23	2.19	2.15	2.10	2.06	2.01	1.96
18	2.41	2.34	2.27	2.19	2.15	2.11	2.06	2.02	1.97	1.92
19	2.38	2.31	2.23	2.16	2.11	2.07	2.03	1.98	1.93	1.88
20	2.35	2.28	2.20	2.12	2.08	2.04	1.99	1.95	1.90	1.84
21	2.32	2.25	2.18	2.10	2.05	2.01	1.96	1.92	1.87	1.81
22	2.30	2.23	2.15	2.07	2.03	1.98	1.94	1.89	1.84	1.78
23	2.27	2.20	2.13	2.05	2.01	1.96	1.91	1.86	1.81	1.76
24	2.25	2.18	2.11	2.03	1.98	1.94	1.89	1.84	1.79	1.73
25	2.24	2.16	2.09	2.01	1.96	1.92	1.87	1.82	1.77	1.71
26	2.22	2.15	2.07	1.99	1.95	1.90	1.85	1.80	1.75	1.69
27	2.20	2.13	2.06	1.97	1.93	1.88	1.84	1.79	1.73	1.67
28	2.19	2.12	2.04	1.96	1.91	1.87	1.82	1.77	1.71	1.65
29	2.18	2.10	2.03	1.94	1.90	1.85	1.81	1.75	1.70	1.64
30	2.16	2.09	2.01	1.93	1.89	1.84	1.79	1.74	1.68	1.62
40	2.08	2.00	1.92	1.84	1.79	1.74	1.69	1.64	1.58	1.51
60	1.99	1.92	1.84	1.75	1.70	1.65	1.59	1.53	1.47	1.39
120	1.91	1.83	1.75	1.66	1.61	1.55	1.50	1.43	1.35	1.25
∞	1.83	1.75	1.67	1.57	1.52	1.46	1.39	1.32	1.22	1.00

Numerator Degrees of Freedom

Denominator Degrees of Freedom

TABLE 7(c) *CRITICAL VALUES OF THE F DISTRIBUTION,* $\alpha = .025$

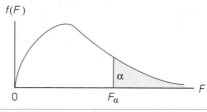

v_2	v_1 Numerator Degrees of Freedom								
	1	2	3	4	5	6	7	8	9
1	647.8	799.5	864.2	899.6	921.8	937.1	948.2	956.7	963.3
2	38.51	39.00	39.17	39.25	39.30	39.33	39.36	39.37	39.39
3	17.44	16.04	15.44	15.10	14.88	14.73	14.62	14.54	14.47
4	12.22	10.65	9.98	9.60	9.36	9.20	9.07	8.98	8.90
5	10.01	8.43	7.76	7.39	7.15	6.98	6.85	6.76	6.68
6	8.81	7.26	6.60	6.23	5.99	5.82	5.70	5.60	5.52
7	8.07	6.54	5.89	5.52	5.29	5.12	4.99	4.90	4.82
8	7.57	6.06	5.42	5.05	4.82	4.65	4.53	4.43	4.36
9	7.21	5.71	5.08	4.72	4.48	4.32	4.20	4.10	4.03
10	6.94	5.46	4.83	4.47	4.24	4.07	3.95	3.85	3.78
11	6.72	5.26	4.63	4.28	4.04	3.88	3.76	3.66	3.59
12	6.55	5.10	4.47	4.12	3.89	3.73	3.61	3.51	3.44
13	6.41	4.97	4.35	4.00	3.77	3.60	3.48	3.39	3.31
14	6.30	4.86	4.24	3.89	3.66	3.50	3.38	3.29	3.21
15	6.20	4.77	4.15	3.80	3.58	3.41	3.29	3.20	3.12
16	6.12	4.69	4.08	3.73	3.50	3.34	3.22	3.12	3.05
17	6.04	4.62	4.01	3.66	3.44	3.28	3.16	3.06	2.98
18	5.98	4.56	3.95	3.61	3.38	3.22	3.10	3.01	2.93
19	5.92	4.51	3.90	3.56	3.33	3.17	3.05	2.96	2.88
20	5.87	4.46	3.86	3.51	3.29	3.13	3.01	2.91	2.84
21	5.83	4.42	3.82	3.48	3.25	3.09	2.97	2.87	2.80
22	5.79	4.38	3.78	3.44	3.22	3.05	2.93	2.84	2.76
23	5.75	4.35	3.75	3.41	3.18	3.02	2.90	2.81	2.73
24	5.72	4.32	3.72	3.38	3.15	2.99	2.87	2.78	2.70
25	5.69	4.29	3.69	3.35	3.13	2.97	2.85	2.75	2.68
26	5.66	4.27	3.67	3.33	3.10	2.94	2.82	2.73	2.65
27	5.63	4.24	3.65	3.31	3.08	2.92	2.80	2.71	2.63
28	5.61	4.22	3.63	3.29	3.06	2.90	2.78	2.69	2.61
29	5.59	4.20	3.61	3.27	3.04	2.88	2.76	2.67	2.59
30	5.57	4.18	3.59	3.25	3.03	2.87	2.75	2.65	2.57
40	5.42	4.05	3.46	3.13	2.90	2.74	2.62	2.53	2.45
60	5.29	3.93	3.34	3.01	2.79	2.63	2.51	2.41	2.33
120	5.15	3.80	3.23	2.89	2.67	2.52	2.39	2.30	2.22
∞	5.02	3.69	3.12	2.79	2.57	2.41	2.29	2.19	2.11

Denominator Degrees of Freedom

SOURCE: From M. Merrington and C. M. Thompson, "Tables of Percentage Points of the Inverted Beta (*F*)-Distribution," *Biometrika* 33 (1943): 73–88. Reproduced by permission of the *Biometrika* Trustees.

TABLE 7(c)   *CRITICAL VALUES OF THE F DISTRIBUTION, α = .025 (continued)*

v_2	\ v_1 10	12	15	20	24	30	40	60	120	∞
1	968.6	976.7	984.9	993.1	997.2	1001	1006	1010	1014	1018
2	39.40	39.41	39.43	39.45	39.46	39.46	39.47	39.48	39.49	39.50
3	14.42	14.34	14.25	14.17	14.12	14.08	14.04	13.99	13.95	13.90
4	8.84	8.75	8.66	8.56	8.51	8.46	8.41	8.36	8.31	8.26
5	6.62	6.52	6.43	6.33	6.28	6.23	6.18	6.12	6.07	6.02
6	5.46	5.37	5.27	5.17	5.12	5.07	5.01	4.96	4.90	4.85
7	4.76	4.67	4.57	4.47	4.42	4.36	4.31	4.25	4.20	4.14
8	4.30	4.20	4.10	4.00	3.95	3.89	3.84	3.78	3.73	3.67
9	3.96	3.87	3.77	3.67	3.61	3.56	3.51	3.45	3.39	3.33
10	3.72	3.62	3.52	3.42	3.37	3.31	3.26	3.20	3.14	3.08
11	3.53	3.43	3.33	3.23	3.17	3.12	3.06	3.00	2.94	2.88
12	3.37	3.28	3.18	3.07	3.02	2.96	2.91	2.85	2.79	2.72
13	3.25	3.15	3.05	2.95	2.89	2.84	2.78	2.72	2.66	2.60
14	3.15	3.05	2.95	2.84	2.79	2.73	2.67	2.61	2.55	2.49
15	3.06	2.96	2.86	2.76	2.70	2.64	2.59	2.52	2.46	2.40
16	2.99	2.89	2.79	2.68	2.63	2.57	2.51	2.45	2.38	2.32
17	2.92	2.82	2.72	2.62	2.56	2.50	2.44	2.38	2.32	2.25
18	2.87	2.77	2.67	2.56	2.50	2.44	2.38	2.32	2.26	2.19
19	2.82	2.72	2.62	2.51	2.45	2.39	2.33	2.27	2.20	2.13
20	2.77	2.68	2.57	2.46	2.41	2.35	2.29	2.22	2.16	2.09
21	2.73	2.64	2.53	2.42	2.37	2.31	2.25	2.18	2.11	2.04
22	2.70	2.60	2.50	2.39	2.33	2.27	2.21	2.14	2.08	2.00
23	2.67	2.57	2.47	2.36	2.30	2.24	2.18	2.11	2.04	1.97
24	2.64	2.54	2.44	2.33	2.27	2.21	2.15	2.08	2.01	1.94
25	2.61	2.51	2.41	2.30	2.24	2.18	2.12	2.05	1.98	1.91
26	2.59	2.49	2.39	2.28	2.22	2.16	2.09	2.03	1.95	1.88
27	2.57	2.47	2.36	2.25	2.19	2.13	2.07	2.00	1.93	1.85
28	2.55	2.45	2.34	2.23	2.17	2.11	2.05	1.98	1.91	1.83
29	2.53	2.43	2.32	2.21	2.15	2.09	2.03	1.96	1.89	1.81
30	2.51	2.41	2.31	2.20	2.14	2.07	2.01	1.94	1.87	1.79
40	2.39	2.29	2.18	2.07	2.01	1.94	1.88	1.80	1.72	1.64
60	2.27	2.17	2.06	1.94	1.88	1.82	1.74	1.67	1.58	1.48
120	2.16	2.05	1.94	1.82	1.76	1.69	1.61	1.53	1.43	1.31
∞	2.05	1.94	1.83	1.71	1.64	1.57	1.48	1.39	1.27	1.00

Numerator Degrees of Freedom

Denominator Degrees of Freedom

TABLE 7(d)   *CRITICAL VALUES OF THE F DISTRIBUTION, $\alpha = .01$*

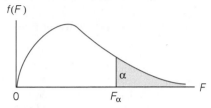

v_2	v_1 Numerator Degrees of Freedom								
	1	2	3	4	5	6	7	8	9
1	4,052	4,999.5	5,403	5,625	5,764	5,859	5,928	5,982	6,022
2	98.50	99.00	99.17	99.25	99.30	99.33	99.36	99.37	99.39
3	34.12	30.82	29.46	28.71	28.24	27.91	27.67	27.49	27.35
4	21.20	18.00	16.69	15.98	15.52	15.21	14.98	14.80	14.66
5	16.26	13.27	12.06	11.39	10.97	10.67	10.46	10.29	10.16
6	13.75	10.92	9.78	9.15	8.75	8.47	8.26	8.10	7.98
7	12.25	9.55	8.45	7.85	7.46	7.19	6.99	6.84	6.72
8	11.26	8.65	7.59	7.01	6.63	6.37	6.18	6.03	5.91
9	10.56	8.02	6.99	6.42	6.06	5.80	5.61	5.47	5.35
10	10.04	7.56	6.55	5.99	5.64	5.39	5.20	5.06	4.94
11	9.65	7.21	6.22	5.67	5.32	5.07	4.89	4.74	4.63
12	9.33	6.93	5.95	5.41	5.06	4.82	4.64	4.50	4.39
13	9.07	6.70	5.74	5.21	4.86	4.62	4.44	4.30	4.19
14	8.86	6.51	5.56	5.04	4.69	4.46	4.28	4.14	4.03
15	8.68	6.36	5.42	4.89	4.56	4.32	4.14	4.00	3.89
16	8.53	6.23	5.29	4.77	4.44	4.20	4.03	3.89	3.78
17	8.40	6.11	5.18	4.67	4.34	4.10	3.93	3.79	3.68
18	8.29	6.01	5.09	4.58	4.25	4.01	3.84	3.71	3.60
19	8.18	5.93	5.01	4.50	4.17	3.94	3.77	3.63	3.52
20	8.10	5.85	4.94	4.43	4.10	3.87	3.70	3.56	3.46
21	8.02	5.78	4.87	4.37	4.04	3.81	3.64	3.51	3.40
22	7.95	5.72	4.82	4.31	3.99	3.76	3.59	3.45	3.35
23	7.88	5.66	4.76	4.26	3.94	3.71	3.54	3.41	3.30
24	7.82	5.61	4.72	4.22	3.90	3.67	3.50	3.36	3.26
25	7.77	5.57	4.68	4.18	3.85	3.63	3.46	3.32	3.22
26	7.72	5.53	4.64	4.14	3.82	3.59	3.42	3.29	3.18
27	7.68	5.49	4.60	4.11	3.78	3.56	3.39	3.26	3.15
28	7.64	5.45	4.57	4.07	3.75	3.53	3.36	3.23	3.12
29	7.60	5.42	4.54	4.04	3.73	3.50	3.33	3.20	3.09
30	7.56	5.39	4.51	4.02	3.70	3.47	3.30	3.17	3.07
40	7.31	5.18	4.31	3.83	3.51	3.29	3.12	2.99	2.89
60	7.08	4.98	4.13	3.65	3.34	3.12	2.95	2.82	2.72
120	6.85	4.79	3.95	3.48	3.17	2.96	2.79	2.66	2.56
∞	6.63	4.61	3.78	3.32	3.02	2.80	2.64	2.51	2.41

Denominator Degrees of Freedom

SOURCE: From M. Merrington and C. M. Thompson, "Tables of Percentage Points of the Inverted Beta (*F*)-Distribution," *Biometrika* 33 (1943): 73–88. Reproduced by permission of the *Biometrika* Trustees.

TABLE 7(d) *CRITICAL VALUES OF THE F DISTRIBUTION, $\alpha = .01$ (continued)*

v_2 \ v_1	Numerator Degrees of Freedom									
	10	12	15	20	24	30	40	60	120	∞
1	6,056	6,106	6,157	6,209	6,235	6,261	6,287	6,313	6,339	6,366
2	99.40	99.42	99.43	99.45	99.46	99.47	99.47	99.48	99.49	99.50
3	27.23	27.05	26.87	26.69	26.60	26.50	26.41	26.32	26.22	26.13
4	14.55	14.37	14.20	14.02	13.93	13.84	13.75	13.65	13.56	13.46
5	10.05	9.89	9.72	9.55	9.47	9.38	9.29	9.20	9.11	9.02
6	7.87	7.72	7.56	7.40	7.31	7.23	7.14	7.06	6.97	6.88
7	6.62	6.47	6.31	6.16	6.07	5.99	5.91	5.82	5.74	5.65
8	5.81	5.67	5.52	5.36	5.28	5.20	5.12	5.03	4.95	4.86
9	5.26	5.11	4.96	4.81	4.73	4.65	4.57	4.48	4.40	4.31
10	4.85	4.71	4.56	4.41	4.33	4.25	4.17	4.08	4.00	3.91
11	4.54	4.40	4.25	4.10	4.02	3.94	3.86	3.78	3.69	3.60
12	4.30	4.16	4.01	3.86	3.78	3.70	3.62	3.54	3.45	3.36
13	4.10	3.96	3.82	3.66	3.59	3.51	3.43	3.34	3.25	3.17
14	3.94	3.80	3.66	3.51	3.43	3.35	3.27	3.18	3.09	3.00
15	3.80	3.67	3.52	3.37	3.29	3.21	3.13	3.05	2.96	2.87
16	3.69	3.55	3.41	3.26	3.18	3.10	3.02	2.93	2.84	2.75
17	3.59	3.46	3.31	3.16	3.08	3.00	2.92	2.83	2.75	2.65
18	3.51	3.37	3.23	3.08	3.00	2.92	2.84	2.75	2.66	2.57
19	3.43	3.30	3.15	3.00	2.92	2.84	2.76	2.67	2.58	2.49
20	3.37	3.23	3.09	2.94	2.86	2.78	2.69	2.61	2.52	2.42
21	3.31	3.17	3.03	2.88	2.80	2.72	2.64	2.55	2.46	2.36
22	3.26	3.12	2.98	2.83	2.75	2.67	2.58	2.50	2.40	2.31
23	3.21	3.07	2.93	2.78	2.70	2.62	2.54	2.45	2.35	2.26
24	3.17	3.03	2.89	2.74	2.66	2.58	2.49	2.40	2.31	2.21
25	3.13	2.99	2.85	2.70	2.62	2.54	2.45	2.36	2.27	2.17
26	3.09	2.96	2.81	2.66	2.58	2.50	2.42	2.33	2.23	2.13
27	3.06	2.93	2.78	2.63	2.55	2.47	2.38	2.29	2.20	2.10
28	3.03	2.90	2.75	2.60	2.52	2.44	2.35	2.26	2.17	2.06
29	3.00	2.87	2.73	2.57	2.49	2.41	2.33	2.23	2.14	2.03
30	2.98	2.84	2.70	2.55	2.47	2.39	2.30	2.21	2.11	2.01
40	2.80	2.66	2.52	2.37	2.29	2.20	2.11	2.02	1.92	1.80
60	2.63	2.50	2.35	2.20	2.12	2.03	1.94	1.84	1.73	1.60
120	2.47	2.34	2.19	2.03	1.95	1.86	1.76	1.66	1.53	1.38
∞	2.32	2.18	2.04	1.88	1.79	1.70	1.59	1.47	1.32	1.00

Denominator Degrees of Freedom

TABLE 8 *CRITICAL VALUES OF THE χ^2 DISTRIBUTION*

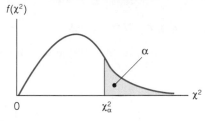

Degrees of Freedom	$\chi^2_{.100}$	$\chi^2_{.050}$	$\chi^2_{.025}$	$\chi^2_{.010}$	$\chi^2_{.005}$
1	2.70554	3.84146	5.02389	6.63490	7.87944
2	4.60517	5.99147	7.37776	9.21034	10.5966
3	6.25139	7.81473	9.34840	11.3449	12.8381
4	7.77944	9.48773	11.1433	13.2767	14.8602
5	9.23635	11.0705	12.8325	15.0863	16.7496
6	10.6446	12.5916	14.4494	16.8119	18.5476
7	12.0170	14.0671	16.0128	18.4753	20.2777
8	13.3616	15.5073	17.5346	20.0902	21.9550
9	14.6837	16.9190	19.0228	21.6660	23.5893
10	15.9871	18.3070	20.4831	23.2093	25.1882
11	17.2750	19.6751	21.9200	24.7250	26.7569
12	18.5494	21.0261	23.3367	26.2170	28.2995
13	19.8119	22.3621	24.7356	27.6883	29.8194
14	21.0642	23.6848	26.1190	29.1413	31.3193
15	22.3072	24.9958	27.4884	30.5779	32.8013
16	23.5418	26.2962	28.8454	31.9999	34.2672
17	24.7690	27.5871	30.1910	33.4087	35.7185
18	25.9894	28.8693	31.5264	34.8053	37.1564
19	27.2036	30.1435	32.8523	36.1908	38.5822
20	28.4120	31.4104	34.1696	37.5662	39.9968
21	29.6151	32.6705	35.4789	38.9321	41.4010
22	30.8133	33.9244	36.7807	40.2894	42.7956
23	32.0069	35.1725	38.0757	41.6384	44.1813
24	33.1963	36.4151	39.3641	42.9798	45.5585
25	34.3816	37.6525	40.6465	44.3141	46.9278
26	35.5631	38.8852	41.9232	45.6417	48.2899
27	36.7412	40.1133	43.1944	46.9630	49.6449
28	37.9159	41.3372	44.4607	48.2782	50.9933
29	39.0875	42.5569	45.7222	49.5879	52.3356
30	40.2560	43.7729	46.9792	50.8922	53.6720
40	51.8050	55.7585	59.3417	63.6907	66.7659
50	63.1671	67.5048	71.4202	76.1539	79.4900
60	74.3970	79.0819	83.2976	88.3794	91.9517
70	85.5271	90.5312	95.0231	100.425	104.215
80	96.5782	101.879	106.629	112.329	116.321
90	107.565	113.145	118.136	124.116	128.299
100	118.498	124.342	129.561	135.807	140.169

SOURCE: From C. M. Thompson, "Tables of the Percentage Points of the χ^2-Distribution," *Biometrika* 32 (1941): 188–89. Reproduced by permission of the *Biometrika* Trustees.

TABLE 9   *CRITICAL VALUES OF THE WILCOXON RANK SUM TEST*

Test statistic is $T = T_A$, where T_A is the rank sum of the sample with the smaller sample size.
(a) $\alpha = .025$ one-tailed; $\alpha = .05$ two-tailed

n_2 \ n_1	3		4		5		6		7		8		9		10	
	T_L	T_U	T_L	T_U	T_L	T_U	T_L	T_U	T_L	T_U	T_L	T_U	T_L	T_U	T_L	L_U
3	5	16														
4	6	18	11	25												
5	6	21	12	28	18	37										
6	7	23	12	32	19	41	26	52								
7	7	26	13	35	20	45	28	56	37	68						
8	8	28	14	38	21	49	29	61	39	73	49	87				
9	8	31	15	41	22	53	31	65	41	78	51	93	63	108		
10	9	33	16	44	24	56	32	70	43	83	54	98	66	114	79	131

(b) $\alpha = .05$ one-tailed; $\alpha = .10$ two-tailed

n_2 \ n_1	3		4		5		6		7		8		9		10	
	T_L	T_U	T_L	T_U	T_L	T_U	T_L	T_U	T_L	T_U	T_L	T_U	T_L	T_U	T_L	T_U
3	6	15														
4	7	17	12	24												
5	7	20	13	27	19	36										
6	8	22	14	30	20	40	28	50								
7	9	24	15	33	22	43	30	54	39	66						
8	9	27	16	36	24	46	32	58	41	71	52	84				
9	10	29	17	39	25	50	33	63	43	76	54	90	66	105		
10	11	31	18	42	26	54	35	67	46	80	57	95	69	111	83	127

SOURCE: From F. Wilcoxon and R. A. Wilcox, "Some Rapid Approximate Statistical Procedures" (1964), p. 28. Reproduced with the permission of American Cyanamid Company.

TABLE 10 *RANDOM NUMBERS*

Row								Column						
	1	2	3	4	5	6	7	8	9	10	11	12	13	14
1	13284	16834	74151	92027	24670	36665	00770	22878	02179	51602	07270	76517	97275	45960
2	21224	00370	30420	03883	96648	89428	41583	17564	27395	63904	41548	49197	82277	24120
3	99052	47887	81085	64933	66279	80432	65793	83287	34142	13241	30590	97760	35848	91983
4	00199	50993	98603	38452	87890	94624	69721	57484	67501	77638	44331	11257	71131	11059
5	60578	06483	28733	37867	07936	98710	98539	27186	31237	80612	44488	97819	70401	95419
6	91240	18312	17441	01929	18163	69201	31211	54288	39296	37318	65724	90401	79017	62077
7	97458	14229	12063	59611	32249	90466	33216	19358	02591	54263	88449	01912	07436	50813
8	35249	38646	34475	72417	60514	69257	12489	51924	86871	92446	36607	11458	30440	52639
9	38980	46600	11759	11900	46743	27860	77940	39298	97838	95145	32378	68038	89351	37005
10	10750	52745	38749	87365	58959	53731	89295	59062	39404	13198	59960	70408	29812	83126
11	36247	27850	73958	20673	37800	63835	71051	84724	52492	22342	78071	17456	96104	18327
12	70994	66986	99744	72438	01174	42159	11392	20724	54322	36923	70009	23233	65438	59685
13	99638	94702	11463	18148	81386	80431	90628	52506	02016	85151	88598	47821	00265	82525
14	72055	15774	43857	99805	10419	76939	25993	03544	21560	83471	43989	90770	22965	44247
15	24038	65541	85788	55835	38835	59399	13790	35112	01324	39520	76210	22467	83275	32286
16	74976	14631	35908	28221	39470	91548	12854	30166	09073	75887	36782	00268	97121	57676
17	35553	71628	70189	26436	63407	91178	90348	55359	80392	41012	36270	77786	89578	21059
18	35676	12797	51434	82976	42010	26344	92920	92155	58807	54644	58581	95331	78629	73344
19	74815	67523	72985	23183	02446	63594	98924	20633	58842	85961	07648	70164	34994	67662
20	45246	88048	65173	50989	91060	89894	36063	32819	68559	99221	49475	50558	34698	71800
21	76509	47069	86378	41797	11910	49672	88575	97966	32466	10083	54728	81972	58975	30761
22	19689	90332	04315	21358	97248	11188	39062	63312	52496	07349	79178	33692	57352	72862
23	42751	35318	97513	61537	54955	08159	00337	80778	27507	95478	21252	12746	37554	97775
24	11946	22681	45045	13964	57517	59419	58045	44067	58716	58840	45557	96345	33271	53464
25	96518	48688	20996	11090	48396	57177	83867	86464	14342	21545	46717	72364	86954	55580

TABLE 10 RANDOM NUMBERS (continued)

Row	1	2	3	4	5	6	7	8	9	10	11	12	13	14
26	35726	58643	76869	84622	39098	36083	72505	92265	23107	60278	05822	46760	44294	07672
27	39737	42750	48968	70536	84864	64952	38404	94317	65402	13589	01055	79044	19308	83623
28	97025	66492	56177	04049	80312	48028	26408	43591	75528	65341	49044	95495	81256	53214
29	62814	08075	09788	56350	76787	51591	54509	49295	85830	59860	30883	89660	96142	18354
30	25578	22950	15227	83291	41737	79599	96191	71845	86899	70694	24290	01551	80092	82118
31	68763	69576	88991	49662	46704	63362	56625	00481	73323	91427	15264	06969	57048	54149
32	17900	00813	64361	60725	88974	61005	99709	30666	26451	11528	44323	34778	60342	60388
33	71944	60227	63551	71109	05624	43836	58254	26160	32116	63403	35404	57146	10909	07346
34	54684	93691	85132	64399	29182	44324	14491	55226	78793	34107	30374	48429	51376	09559
35	25946	27623	11258	65204	52832	50880	22273	05554	99521	73791	85744	29276	70326	60251
36	01353	39318	44961	44972	91766	90262	56073	06606	51826	18893	83448	31915	97764	75091
37	99083	88191	27662	99113	57174	35571	99884	13951	71057	53961	61448	74909	07322	80960
38	52021	45406	37945	75234	24327	86978	22644	87779	23753	99926	63898	54886	18051	96314
39	78755	47744	43776	83098	03225	14281	83637	55984	13300	52212	58781	14905	46502	04472
40	25282	69106	59180	16257	22810	43609	12224	25643	89884	31149	85423	32581	34374	70873
41	11959	94202	02743	86847	79725	51811	12998	76844	05320	54236	53891	70226	38632	84776
42	11644	13792	98190	01424	30078	28197	55583	05197	47714	68440	22016	79204	06862	94451
43	06307	97912	68110	59812	95448	43244	31262	88880	13040	16458	43813	89416	42482	33939
44	76285	75714	89585	99296	52640	46518	55486	90754	88932	19937	57119	23251	55619	23679
45	55322	07589	39600	60866	63007	20007	66819	84164	61131	81429	60676	42807	78286	29015
46	78017	90928	90220	92503	83375	26986	74399	30885	88567	29169	72816	53357	15428	86932
47	44768	43342	20696	26331	43140	69744	82928	24988	94237	46138	77426	39039	55596	12655
48	25100	19336	14605	86603	51680	97678	24261	02464	86563	74812	60069	71674	15478	47642
49	83612	46623	62876	85197	07824	91392	58317	37726	84628	42221	10268	20692	15699	29167
50	41347	81666	82961	60413	71020	83658	02415	33322	66036	98712	46795	16308	28413	05417

Column

SOURCE: Abridged from W. H. Beyer, ed., *CRC Standard Management Tables*, 26th ed. (Boca Raton: CRC Press, 1981). Reproduced by permission of the publisher. Copyright CRC Press, Inc., Boca Raton, Florida.

Symbol	Read	Definition
$\bar{x}$		sample mean
μ	*mu*	population mean
Q_1		first (lower) quartile
Q_2		second (middle) quartile
Q_3		third (upper) quartile
σ^2	*sigma* squared	population variance
σ	*sigma*	population standard deviation
s^2		sample variance
s		sample standard deviation
CV		coefficient of variation
N		population size
n		sample size
Σ	upper-case sigma	summation
f_i		frequency of class i
m_i		midpoint of class i
E		simple event
$P(A)$		probability that event A will occur
$\cup$		union
$\cap$		intersection
S		sample space
$\bar{A}$		complement of event A
$P(A\mid B)$		conditional probability
$P(X = x)$ $p(x)$		probability that random variable X will assume value x
$E(X)$		expected value of X
p		probability of success in a binomial experiment
q		probability of failure in a binomial experiment
$n!$	n factorial	$n! = n(n-1)(n-2)\cdots(2)(1)$
C_x^n	n choose x	binomial coefficient $\dfrac{n!}{x!\,(n-x)!}$
Z		standard normal random variable

Symbol	Read	Definition
z_α	z (sub *alpha*)	value of z such that the area to its right under the standard normal curve is alpha
$\mu_{\bar{x}}$	*mu* (sub *x*-bar)	mean of the sampling distribution of the sample mean
$\sigma_{\bar{x}}^2$	*sigma* (sub *x*-bar) squared	variance of the sampling distribution of the sample mean
$\sigma_{\bar{x}}$	*sigma* (sub *x*-bar)	standard deviation of the sampling distribution of the sample mean
v		degrees of freedom
t		t-statistic
t_α	t (sub *alpha*)	value of t such that the area to its right under the Student t curve is alpha
B		bound on the error of estimation
$\hat{p}$	*p*-hat	sample proportion of successes
$\hat{q}$	*q*-hat	sample proportion of failures
s_p^2		pooled variance estimator
O_i		observed frequency of cell i
E_i		Expected value for cell i
χ^2	*chi* squared	chi-square statistic
χ_α^2	*chi* squared (sub *alpha*)	value of chi-square such that the area to its right under the chi-square curve is alpha
F		F-statistic
F_α	F (sub *alpha*)	value of F such that the area to its right under the F curve is alpha
β_0	*beta* (sub zero)	y-intercept
β_1	*beta* (sub one)	slope
ϵ	*epsilon*	error variable
$\hat{\beta}_0$	*beta* (sub zero) hat	estimator of the y-intercept
$\hat{\beta}_1$	*beta* (sub one) hat	estimator of the slope

Symbol	Read	Definition
e_i		residual
σ_ϵ	*sigma* (sub *epsilon*)	standard deviation of error variable
s_ϵ	s (sub *epsilon*)	standard error of estimate
ρ	rho	coefficient of correlation
r		sample coefficient of correlation
r^2		sample coefficient of determination
β_i	*beta* (sub i)	coefficient of x_i
$\hat{\beta}_i$	*beta* (sub i) hat	estimator of coefficient of x_i

Symbol	Read	Definition
$s_{\hat{\beta}_i}$	s (sub *beta* (sub i) hat)	standard error of beta (sub i) hat
y_t		time series
S_t		exponentially smoothed time series
w		smoothing constant
T_A		rank sum for sample A
T_B		rank sum for sample B
T		Wilcoxon rank sum test statistic
H		Kruskal–Wallis test statistic

INDEX

NORMAL CURVE AREAS

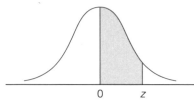

z	.00	.01	.02	.03	.04	.05	.06	.07	.08	.09
0.0	.0000	.0040	.0080	.0120	.0160	.0199	.0239	.0279	.0319	.0359
0.1	.0398	.0438	.0478	.0517	.0557	.0596	.0636	.0675	.0714	.0753
0.2	.0793	.0832	.0871	.0910	.0948	.0987	.1026	.1064	.1103	.1141
0.3	.1179	.1217	.1255	.1293	.1331	.1368	.1406	.1443	.1480	.1517
0.4	.1554	.1591	.1628	.1664	.1700	.1736	.1772	.1808	.1844	.1879
0.5	.1915	.1950	.1985	.2019	.2054	.2088	.2123	.2157	.2190	.2224
0.6	.2257	.2291	.2324	.2357	.2389	.2422	.2454	.2486	.2517	.2549
0.7	.2580	.2611	.2642	.2673	.2704	.2734	.2764	.2794	.2823	.2852
0.8	.2881	.2910	.2939	.2967	.2995	.3023	.3051	.3078	.3106	.3133
0.9	.3159	.3186	.3212	.3238	.3264	.3289	.3315	.3340	.3365	.3389
1.0	.3413	.3438	.3461	.3485	.3508	.3531	.3554	.3577	.3599	.3621
1.1	.3643	.3665	.3686	.3708	.3729	.3749	.3770	.3790	.3810	.3830
1.2	.3849	.3869	.3888	.3907	.3925	.3944	.3962	.3980	.3997	.4015
1.3	.4032	.4049	.4066	.4082	.4099	.4115	.4131	.4147	.4162	.4177
1.4	.4192	.4207	.4222	.4236	.4251	.4265	.4279	.4292	.4306	.4319
1.5	.4332	.4345	.4357	.4370	.4382	.4394	.4406	.4418	.4429	.4441
1.6	.4452	.4463	.4474	.4484	.4495	.4505	.4515	.4525	.4535	.4545
1.7	.4554	.4564	.4573	.4582	.4591	.4599	.4608	.4616	.4625	.4633
1.8	.4641	.4649	.4656	.4664	.4671	.4678	.4686	.4693	.4699	.4706
1.9	.4713	.4719	.4726	.4732	.4738	.4744	.4750	.4756	.4761	.4767
2.0	.4772	.4778	.4783	.4788	.4793	.4798	.4803	.4808	.4812	.4817
2.1	.4821	.4826	.4830	.4834	.4838	.4842	.4846	.4850	.4854	.4857
2.2	.4861	.4864	.4868	.4871	.4875	.4878	.4881	.4884	.4887	.4890
2.3	.4893	.4896	.4898	.4901	.4904	.4906	.4909	.4911	.4913	.4916
2.4	.4918	.4920	.4922	.4925	.4927	.4929	.4931	.4932	.4934	.4936
2.5	.4938	.4940	.4941	.4943	.4945	.4946	.4948	.4949	.4951	.4952
2.6	.4953	.4955	.4956	.4957	.4959	.4960	.4961	.4962	.4963	.4964
2.7	.4965	.4966	.4967	.4968	.4969	.4970	.4971	.4972	.4973	.4974
2.8	.4974	.4975	.4976	.4977	.4977	.4978	.4979	.4979	.4980	.4981
2.9	.4981	.4982	.4982	.4983	.4984	.4984	.4985	.4985	.4986	.4986
3.0	.4987	.4987	.4987	.4988	.4988	.4989	.4989	.4989	.4990	.4990

Source: Abridged from Table I of A. Hald, *Statistical Tables and Formulas* (New York: John Wiley & Sons, Inc.), 1952.
Reproduced by permission of A. Hald and the publisher, John Wiley & Sons, Inc.